P9-BTM-387

v.1

MARGARET FULLER

An American Romantic Life

BY CHARLES CAPPER

Margaret Fuller: An American Romantic Life

VOLUME I
The Private Years

VOLUME II
The Public Years

MARGARET FULLER

AN AMERICAN

ROMANTIC LIFE

The Private Years

CHARLES CAPPER

New York   Oxford
OXFORD UNIVERSITY PRESS
1992

Oxford University Press

Oxford   New York   Toronto
Delhi   Bombay   Calcutta   Madras   Karachi
Kuala Lumpur   Singapore   Hong Kong   Tokyo
Nairobi   Dar es Salaam   Cape Town
Melbourne   Auckland

and associated companies in
Berlin   Ibadan

Published by Oxford University Press, Inc.,
200 Madison Avenue, New York, New York 10016

Oxford is a registered trademark of Oxford University Press

Library of Congress Cataloging-in-Publication Data
Capper, Charles.
Margaret Fuller : an American romantic life / Charles Capper.
p.   cm.   Includes bibliographical references and index.
Contents: [1] The private years
ISBN 0-19-504579-3 (v. 1)
1. Fuller, Margaret, 1810–1850—Biography.
2. Authors,   American—19th century—Biography.
3. Feminists—United States—Biography.
I. Title.   PS2506.C36   1992   818'.309   dc20   91-32599

For Carole

Contents

Preface   ix
Acknowledgments   xiii

1. *A New England Inheritance   3*
2. *Childhood Enlightenment   24*
3. *Rustication   57*
4. *Cambridge Renaissance   84*
5. *A Tangled Pastoral   121*
6. *Apprenticeship   160*
7. *The Schoolmistress   206*
8. *Conversations   252*
9. *The Transcendentalist   307*

Abbreviations   351
Notes   357
Index   407
Illustrations follow page 208.

Preface

In 1970, as a fledgling teaching assistant at the University of California, Berkeley, I taught a course on what I portentously called "The American Avant-Garde between the World Wars." This course underscored an interest that led me in a strange way eventually to Margaret Fuller. During the previous few years I had become fascinated with a seemingly ubiquitous, modern American intellectual figure—the conflicted, alienated, avant-garde thinker who, despite or because of his (and sometimes her) alienation, looked hopefully to popular, world-historical transformations. A few years later, searching for that type's archetype, I found myself turning to the antebellum Romantic era, specifically its Transcendentalist intellectuals. Meanwhile, I became interested in the flowering of women's history, which was then pushing to the center of the historical stage whole battalions of heretofore marginalized outsiders. But how and when, if ever, these two outsider-insider currents were linked remained a mystery to me. This mystery increased with the deepening post-1960s disillusionment with transcendent ideals and the simultaneous preoccupation of women's historians with social-behaviorist paradigms over high-cultural ones. At this ambiguous moment at the end of the decade, I found Margaret Fuller and experienced a shock of recognition.[1]

Before I quite knew what to do with this fact, I also began to discover other things about Margaret Fuller. One was that she was the most written-about woman in early American history. This did not surprise me. Fuller was not only the best-known American intellectual woman of her day, she was one of antebellum America's leading Transcendentalist theoreticians, its most important literary critic, its most sophisticated women's cultural leader, and one of its most widely read international journalists. But it soon became clear to me that Fuller's importance as a historical figure went deeper than these achievements: she was nothing less than the first woman in America to establish herself as a dominant figure in highbrow culture at large. In short, if there was one man or woman whose life might shed light on the early American connections among gender, intellectual culture, and the avant-garde, it was Margaret Fuller. Yet, when I turned to the dozen or so published biographies of her, I found very little of this illuminated. Except for the century-old life by her younger contemporary and family friend Thomas Wentworth Higginson, none is factually very reliable. And, apart from Higginson's book and the untrustworthy but fascinating *Memoirs of Margaret Fuller Ossoli* by her friends Ralph Waldo Emerson, James Freeman Clarke, and William Henry Channing, none is intellectually very interesting. Despite the often provocative discussions of aspects of Fuller, as a biographical subject, Fuller has remained elusive and enigmatic. Equally frustrating, her historical significance—how and why she achieved what she did *when* she did—has seemed a great puzzle.[2]

I have written this biography of Fuller, then, on one level as an act of historical recovery. To accomplish this I have gone back to the sources. These include not only her letters and journals, which have never been used before in any extensive or accurate way, but also the voluminous papers of her family, friends, and colleagues. My purpose has been three-fold. First, I have simply wanted to get the facts straight. This is no small matter. Most biographers of Fuller have freely reproduced "facts" based on legends, claims of previous biographers, and, in several cases, sentimentally imagined scenes. By contrast, all my factual assertions, unless otherwise indicated in a note, are derived from critically examined, first-hand sources. Second, I have tried to do justice to Fuller's complex personality. "What a Sphynx is that girl!" burst out one day in his journal James Freeman Clarke, who had known Fuller intimately and often encountered her daily for a decade, "who shall solve her?" I do not pretend to have solved her, but I have tried to understand her, especially the practical and hyperemotional sides to her character, which in virtually all Fuller biographies are selectively privileged. Third, I have used my sources to create a social biography. My text is filled, as Fuller's life was, with people, many famous, many obscure, but almost all interesting and all revealing of Fuller as she was—shifting, responsive, and ultimately comprehensible only in relation to the people with whom she interacted. The "real Margaret Fuller" is a phantom. What makes her live—and what my biography tries to provide—is Fuller thinking and acting with others. Yet, I should add, acting not just with other individuals. For Fuller's interactions were also with movements—from American Unitarianism to German Romanticism, from women's education to Italian republicanism. "Such a predetermination to *eat* this big universe as her oyster or her egg, and to be absolute empress of all height and glory in it that her heart could conceive, I have not before seen in any human soul," wrote Thomas Carlyle, who was not exactly an abstemious soul himself. When properly read, her life presents an illuminating window on these oysters and eggs of her time.[3]

At its deepest level, though, my biography is about Fuller's life as an intellectual. This approach has been shaped by my interest in the American intellectual as a cultural type, of course. But it also seems to me to be dictated by her life itself. Fuller spent most of her waking hours reading, thinking, and writing. Without knowing what she believed, what she argued for, what she conceptualized, what she made into symbols, we cannot possibly know Margaret Fuller. More important, ideas and fantasies of intellectual identity, both of herself and of her culture, were the ruling preoccupations of her life. This truth was no better revealed than in the great moral drama of her life, which the titles of my two volumes are meant to highlight. That was her sudden movement at the beginning of her thirties from a "private" life of family, study, Boston-Cambridge socializing, and anonymous magazine-writing, to the life of a "public" personage, speaking in a commanding, if often complex and ambiguous voice, defining for America the intellectual character of womanhood and, a little later, from the vantage point of New York and Europe, pronouncing on its literary works and on the international political movements of her age. In the space of a few short years, she became America's female intellectual prophet in the mode of her difficult mentors Carlyle and Emerson.[4]

This first of two volumes narrates (to borrow Emerson's admiring but somewhat puzzled characterization of Walt Whitman's early life) the "long foreground" of this transformation. From one point of view, Fuller's early years were part of a sea change in middle-class women's culture. Many educated yet restricted antebellum women were in these years redefining what their culture liked to think of as women's "private" activities—whether mothering, school teaching, or writing—in ways that allowed for their expansion into the public sphere. In that sense Fuller's life was paradigmatic. Yet in eventually defining for herself a role as cultural arbiter and prophet and, partly as a consequence, challenging the whole "masculine"–"feminine" dichotomy on which the official gender culture was based, she went considerably beyond the positions of most female teachers, reformers, and writers of her era. What made for this difference? Readers may find in her early life many possibilities, but three psychologically resonant intellectual influences were certainly critical. One was her father's encouragement of a grandiose yet domestic republican intellectuality. A second was her early embrace of a Romantic world view. Her Romanticism would vary throughout her life, but it would always include at least something of her early magical notion of it: that through self-consciousness one could expand that most private of all spheres—the subjective self—into the limitless possibilities of intellectual and spiritual endeavor. Yet a third influence was the New England Transcendentalists. This circle of American Romantics looms large in my biography, as it should. For at the heart of their movement was a paradox very much like the one that defined Fuller's life—the ironic and surprising conversion of a subjectivist, alienated, elitist, and self-consciously "private" faith into an instrument of radically democratic cultural and (for some at least) social change. The Transcendentalists were also important because they benefited Fuller in two very practical ways: they provided her with her first flesh-and-blood constituency and, even more critically, her first opportunities for public action. This volume thus closes with Fuller's emergence as a leader of "Conversations" for a circle of Transcendentally inclined women in Boston and as an organizer of the movement's journal, the *Dial*.[5]

To state things this way, though, makes Fuller's story sound a good deal more triumphant than it was. All her early "resolutions" were highly problematical— republicanism without politics, Romanticism without personal romance, Transcendentalism without religious transcendence, and (as she herself put it many times) "masculine" intellectual styles with "feminine" proclivities and circumstances. She would wrestle with these troubling paradoxes for most of her life. In these early years they encouraged her to think about intellectual womanhood as well as to exert herself in the broader intellectual discourse of her time. This dual engagement would be her lasting legacy. Also lasting would be the mental attitude that undergirded it in these years—"extraordinary generous seeking," to quote from a motto of her revered Goethe that she inscribed on the first page of a fancy bound blank book she gave to James Freeman Clarke at the end of their adolescence. In this minimalist era of diminished expectations, such Romantic extravagance is a bracing reminder of an America that once was and in some form may still be.[6]

Chapel Hill, N.C.   C.C.
August 1991

Acknowledgments

A work as long in gestation as this one has accumulated many debts, and I am very pleased to be able to acknowledge them here. The research and writing of my book have been materially aided by several generous grants and fellowships. Two of them allowed me to take leaves from my teaching to work on this volume: a Fellowship for University Teachers from the National Endowment for the Humanities in 1987–1988 and a Faculty Fellowship from the Institute for the Arts and Humanities at the University of North Carolina at Chapel Hill, in the spring of 1990. Additionally I received from Carolina an IBM Junior Faculty Development Award and grants from the University Research Council and the College of Arts and Sciences.

This volume of my biography would not have been possible but for many curators and librarians. For their numerous attentions and their liberal permission to quote from their unpublished manuscripts, I am indebted to the staffs of the American Antiquarian Society, the Department of Rare Books and Manuscripts of the Boston Public Library, the John Hay Library of Brown University Library, the Fruitlands Museums, the Houghton Library of Harvard University, the Andover-Harvard Theological Library of Harvard Divinity School, the Massachusetts Historical Society, the Maine Historical Society, the Schlesinger Library of Radcliffe College, the Beinecke Library of Yale University, the Thomas Cooper Library of the University of South Carolina, and the Department of Special Collections at the University of California, Santa Barbara. For their ready responses to my many requests for help or information, I especially want to thank Rodney G. Dennis, Elizabeth A. Falsey, and James L. Lewis of the Houghton Library; Alan Seaburg of the Andover-Harvard Theological Library; Peter Drummey and Conrad E. Wright of the Massachusetts Historical Society; Sidney E. Berger (formerly) and Thomas Knoles (currently) of the American Antiquarian Society; Giuseppe Bisaccia of the Department of Rare

Books and Manuscripts at the Boston Public Library; M. N. Brown of the John Hay Library; Charles M. Sullivan of the Cambridge Historical Commission; and Elizabeth Witherell of the Department of Special Collections at the University of California, Santa Barbara. The institutions and individuals that supplied me with copies of photographs and paintings are noted in the captions to the illustrations. I thank them both for their help with collecting these copies and for their permission to reproduce them in my book.

Closer to home, the interlibrary loan department at Carolina's Davis Library expedited my numerous requisitions for rare books and journals. My research assistant, Stuart Leibiger, retrieved materials and skillfully ferreted out countless arcane facts from their antiquarian holes. I am obliged to Gary Kulik of the *American Quarterly* for permission to use in the last two sections of Chapter 8 portions of an article of mine that appeared in that journal.

Over the years I have been blessed with more than my share of faithful critics. My teacher at Berkeley, Henry May, has offered me invaluable advice on my writing and interpretations as well as provided me with a model of an erudite, aesthetic, and morally engaged historian. My friend and anthology-partner, David Hollinger, discerning as always in the discipline of intellectual history, has also given me vital support and counsel. Robert Hudspeth, the editor of Margaret Fuller's letters, has been unfailingly generous in responding to my endless queries about this or that piece of obscure evidence that seemed to always need to be cleared up immediately. I also want to thank Ruth Bloch, Eileen Boris, Richard Bridgman, Lawrence Buell, Peter Filene, Philip Gura, Samuel Haber, Jacquelyn Hall, Daniel Walker Howe, John Kasson, Joy Kasson, Linda Kerber, Donald Mathews, Joel Myerson, and Charles Sellers. These friends and colleagues read and criticized various chapters or, in many cases, versions of the entire manuscript. Their many valuable suggestions and corrections have strengthened my book immeasurably.

The staff at Oxford University Press has borne out its well-earned reputation in the making of this volume. I particularly want to thank my editor, Sheldon Meyer, whose steady enthusiasm for my biography and astute shepherding of it through the process of production have served as continual bolsterers of my confidence. My line editor, Gail Cooper, has given my manuscript careful and expert editing, for which I am grateful.

Lastly, I want to express my appreciation to my family and friends, who have provided me with a host of material and spiritual supports while researching and writing my book. Of my friends, I especially wish to thank Carol and Michael Kort, who gave me loving comfort, old-time ideological conversations, and a room of my own at their Brookline house during my frequent trips to the Boston area. My father and mother made clear their belief in my project, and I appreciate their trust. Although after a long illness my remarkably stoic father died just when I was completing the final editing, I like to think he would have been pleased with my account of a nineteenth-century woman's life so sturdily lived. My parents-in-law, Mildred and Paul Broner, have given me the benefit of their familial warmth and cultural sophistication. I am also grateful that my joyful and imaginative daughter, Emily, was born at the inception of this biography, thus affording me rich sources for imaginings of my young subject. Finally, I wish to mention my wife, Carole Broner Capper, whose large fund of knowledge of the craft of writing has been my constant resource and whose faith and love have sustained me in everything I write. For all of this and for things I cannot hope to say, my dedication is slight repayment.

MARGARET FULLER

An American Romantic Life

CHAPTER ONE

$\mathcal{A}$ New England Inheritance

I

Although many of her contemporaries would have been slow to admit it, Margaret Fuller was in her habitat and ancestry a thorough new Englander. Her lineage was long, beginning with the first Puritans of the Massachusetts Bay Colony. It was compact, confining its offspring exclusively to eastern Massachusetts and mostly to small towns on or near the eastern outskirts of Middlesex and Norfolk counties surrounding the Boston county of Suffolk. And it was determining: Fuller herself lived for almost all but the last half-dozen years of her life in Boston or Cambridge under the roof of her immediate family. Yet Fuller would never have said, in answer to the question, "What are my advantages?"—as did her fellow cultural rebel Ralph Waldo Emerson—"The total New England." Fuller's inheritance was a very partial New England—more ethical than religious, more worldly than ethical, more idiosyncratic than either, and, above all, late-blooming. Yet perhaps *because* of its very partialness it cut deep. On the eve of publishing the first issue of the most self-consciously non–New England periodical in American literature, Fuller wrote to a close friend, "It is for dear New England that I wanted this review." Coming from someone who wrote more scornfully of New England culture than any New England intellectual of her generation, it was a remarkable tribute. For the primeval sources of both the scorn and the love—and therefore her identity itself—her ancestry suggests some clues.[1]

"You cannot make poetry out of the Puritans," Margaret Fuller would write in her journal during her last years in New England; "there is too much daylight and reality about them." For such a harsh Romantic view, she had ample support in the records of her own Puritan ancestors. The first was a doughty English immigrant named Thomas Fuller, who at the age of twenty arrived in Cam-

3

bridge, Massachusetts, in 1638 for a one-year "tour of observation," but soon decided to settle permanently. Although he attributed his change of plans to his conversion to Puritan doctrine, provoked by the "soul-ravishing" preaching of Anne Hutchinson's eloquent censor, the Reverend Thomas Shepard, several of his descendants have insisted that a young woman who refused to return with him to England also influenced his decision. Similarly, family chronicles tell us, after soon marrying another New England woman, Elizabeth Tidd of Woburn, and living for twenty-five years in this new settlement north of Cambridge, he moved his family to New Salem (afterwards Middleton), where he remained untouched by the nearby witchcraft hysteria. This is plausible. Certainly the autobiographical doggerel that he left suggest he was more a man of plain good sense than enthusiastic religious habits. After the usual hackneyed account of the tremors of conversion, he ended with this stoutly confident un-Calvinist conclusion:

> But surely God will save my soul!
> And, though you trouble have,
> My children dear, who fear the Lord,
> Your soul at death, He'll save.[2]

Thomas and Elizabeth had nine children, and the families that sprang from these children were for the most part equally large, in which sturdy biblical names like Ruth, Hannah, Jacob, and Joseph were well represented. Their characters also seem to have been sturdy; most lived into their seventies, and none, as far as one can tell, died a pauper. Yet none became very wealthy or prominent, either. "Lieut. Fuller," as he signed his name on several records, was a farmer and blacksmith like his father, and virtually all of his male descendants continued throughout the seventeenth and eighteenth centuries on about the same social level—as artisans, small farmers, and minor officials in various positions of trust in local churches, governments, and militias. It was not until the fourth generation—when economic prospects, historians tell us, began to dim for many New England farming young men—that a Fuller appeared who was to reach, though somewhat awkwardly, beyond this heritage of Puritan yeomanry.[3]

Born in Middleton in 1739, Timothy Fuller, Margaret Fuller's grandfather, was descended from a line of favored younger sons who, according to one family chronicle, had been noted for their intellectual strength. Confirming this inheritance, Timothy became the first Fuller of any branch and the only one of his family of ten children to graduate from college and assume a learned profession. Rising up the social and intellectual ladder, he married Sarah Williams, who connected him with her mother Anna Buckminster Williams's prominent family of well-to-do, scholarly ministers; including, most notably, Anna's grand-nephew and Sarah's younger cousin, the celebrated Boston Unitarian minister Joseph Stevens Buckminster. The Williams connection also injected a healthy dose of post-Puritan righteousness into the Fuller blood. "I know I needed the rod or I should not had it," Sarah's mother wrote to her after the death of one of her grandchildren. Sarah's father, Abraham Williams, the minister at Sandwich, on Cape Cod, and a Fellow of the American Academy of Arts and Sciences, was rigorous even in death in imposing on his family the moral rod. In his will he directed the emancipation of his two slaves and required his ten children to contribute to their support, adding the caveat that should any refuse, they were to be deprived of their share of the estate and given instead "a new bible of the cheapest sort, hoping that by the blessing of God it may lead them to do justice & love mercy." Margaret Fuller's Grandmother Sarah was also given to robust assertions of her ethical claims. She appears affectionate in her letters to her children and grandchildren, but she was also said by one of her grandsons to have possessed "a vigorous understanding and an honorable ambition, which she strove to infuse into her children." Perhaps most telling of her liberal *and* Puritan sides was her "keen relish" for the satirical and somewhat bawdy novels of Henry Fielding, which she liked, she told one of her sons, because they "treated the world much as it deserves."[4]

Sarah's husband, Timothy, felt similarly about the world, but unfortunately the world sometimes felt the same way about him. His first fall occurred at Harvard, where he was demoted to the bottom of his class for throwing bricks and sticks into a classroom during a Hebrew recitation. After humbly confessing, he returned to his original rank, graduated in 1760, and even came back for a second degree, which he earned for a *Quaestio* defending the cagey proposition that "not all dissimulation is untruthfulness." A rather more major fall occurred in his ninth year as minister in his first permanent pulpit in the frontier town of Princeton, Massachusetts. The precipitating cause was the widely broadcast charge that he was a Tory sympathizer. On the face of it, the complaint seems incredible. Certainly it appeared so to Fuller, who in pamphlets and at meetings repeatedly protested his complete sympathy with the colonists' grievances, his scrupulous adherence to their various boycotts, his total rejection of British parliamentary domestic authority, and even his support for the recent armed resistance of the colonial army. Yet, other statements of his suggest that, if hardly disloyal, he was rather lukewarm in his patriotism. Even before the Revolution, he had publicly worried that taking militant action would lead to precipitous armed conflict, and once the war began, wondered aloud whether the Revolution, which he seems to have reluctantly supported, was worth all the bloodshed. In one sermon, only two years into the war, he spoke darkly about the future dangers from maneuvering and corrupt party men taking over the reins of government and becoming rich through "Slaughter and Blood." His brusque personality clearly exacerbated his difficulties. Generally undevotional in his habits as well as somewhat coarse and (in the words of one parishioner) contemptuously "Jockeying & Bantering" in the pulpit, Fuller in addition seems to have had a knack for making his points in perversely provocative ways. At the very peak of heated feelings engendered by the first bloody encounter with British troops at Lexington and Concord, he preached to a group of Minutemen from the text I Kings xx:11, "Let not him that girdeth on the harness boast himself as he that putteth it off." Not surprisingly, the sermon and other similar provocations caused great offence, and in the spring of 1776, the town dismissed him and sent a delegation of burly men to his church to bar him from entering.[5]

Following his dismissal, Fuller moved his family to the somewhat antiwar town of Chilmark, on Martha's Vineyard, where he preached to the Congregational church until the end of the war. Meanwhile he studied law and obtained admission to the bar solely to pursue his suit against the town for the payment of his salary on the ground that a minister (as he claimed) "holds his office for life determinable upon misbehavior." Unfortunately for Fuller, the Supreme Court jury, unimpressed by Fuller's anachronistic idea of ministerial prerogative and apparently also prejudiced by the charges of Toryism, found for the town. Rather, though, than "crushing" him, as many townsmen had vindictively hoped, the verdict elicited the prudent and independent qualities that marked his whole life: he paid the large court costs in money he had carefully saved for the outcome and returned to re-establish his family in the town that had rejected him. For their part, the democratic-minded citizens of Princeton soon showed they liked Fuller better as a politician than they had as a minister by electing him over their leading townsman, the Federalist lieutenant governor Moses Gill, to represent them at the state convention called to ratify the federal Constitution. He repaid their confidence by casting a firm vote against ratification. Part of his objection, as he stated it in his "Reflections on the Constitution," was to the clauses that implicitly sanctioned the "indelible Stigma" of slavery. But his memorandum shows he also opposed the Constitution on a host of agrarian and democratic grounds, ranging from its insufficient representation to the absence of a freehold requirement for suffrage. Yet, whether antislavery or Antifederalist, that vote, as did his dissent from revolution in the first place, well illustrates the essential point—that Protestant rectitude and provincial caution were more important than great achievement to Margaret Fuller's first publicly notable Fuller ancestor.[6]

After the adverse verdict and the convention, Timothy Fuller, still in his forties, withdrew from public life entirely and returned to his ancestral vocation. In the coming years he successfully cultivated a large farm of 700 acres encompassing Mount Wachusett, that had been mostly given to him by the General Court to supplement his small salary. He also cultivated a healthy crop of ten children who seem to have proved infinitely more responsive to his patriarchal leadership than his parishioners had been. ("I am sixteen years old," the lively Elizabeth, Margaret Fuller's future aunt, wrote in her diary on her birthday, in the midst of accounts of occasional family hymn-singing and quilt-making and daily reports of planting, cropping, spinning, weaving, and sewing. "How many years have been past by me in thoughtlessness & vanity.") But the most important accomplishment of this little commonwealth was Timothy Fuller's education of his children, all ten of whom attended his family school exclusively. There was one palpable inequity in this academy, however, that certainly his granddaughter Margaret would not have appreciated. While he provided his five daughters with the usual elementary instruction given to country New England girls, he made all his sons know from early childhood that (as one of his grandsons put it) "the great object of his ambition" was to send them to Harvard College. Frustrated in his own post-Harvard career, their father until he died served as their sole college preparatory tutor.[7]

For his efforts Timothy Fuller was handsomely rewarded by his sons' achievements. Four graduated near the top of their class at Harvard. Also, all five—carefully avoiding their father's unhappy choice of profession—became lawyers, most with thriving practices. Ambitious, hardworking, combative, buoyant, and politically active, the brothers were among the most prominent members of the Boston bar of their day. Henry was four times elected to the Massachusetts House of Representatives. Yet, despite their enviable successes and (except for Timothy and Abraham) impeccably conservative Whig politics, some Bostonians found them barely tolerable. Horace Mann, who knew them well when he was practicing law, told Higginson that if Margaret Fuller was unpopular, "it was not from any prejudice against her as a woman, but because she probably combined 'the disagreeableness of forty Fullers.'" Higginson, who also knew them, described them more judiciously as "men of great energy, pushing, successful, of immense and varied information, of great self-esteem, and without a particle of tact." Perhaps (as the well-established Higginson's portrait slightly betrays) their status as upstarts worked against them. In Henry's case, several of his colleagues thought his "reckless . . . shafts of raillery and sarcasm," although popular among jurors, caused some of his opponents to harbor lifelong grudges against him. But the personal trait that seems to have most often rankled—in spite of their properly busy Bostonian literary and antiquarian interests (Henry lectured for the Lyceum circuit on Egyptian and Assyrian antiquities)—was their crassness. "He lived wholly in the world," one friendly colleague admitted about even the scholarly Henry, "as one in which everything worth attaining or knowing must be found . . . in its capability of present or future application to the business of life."[8]

Margaret's family also sometimes found, for all their "volubility" and family attentiveness, the brothers' crass and overbearing sides difficult to take. From family letters, Henry, "a slippery customer" (as Margaret once called him), seems to have bothered them the most. Ungrateful and "selfish" was how Margaret's ordinarily benevolent mother bitterly described him to her husband Timothy after Henry had bragged to her about the superiority of the furniture at the competing law office for which he had "unpropitious[ly]" abandoned his older brother's practice. But gruff Abraham, the second-oldest brother, was a close second. After years of trying to get him to marry one or another delicate, accomplished, and impecunious young lady, Margaret's father finally gave him up as "too much attached to *the world* . . . to be attracted by such virtues." Margaret's mother was more pointed. Reporting once on his manner toward her at a reception, she told her husband, "I thought he manifested something of the disposition of a wealthy Cit receiving the unavoidable greetings of country relations in the Douglass Hall." On the other hand—these genteel Bostonian judgments notwithstanding—it should be noted that all these Fuller brothers had to make their way in a world that had foiled their quirky and stubbornly idealistic father, and by their own lights they did it well. Even Margaret's crusty Uncle Abraham turned his (as she saw them) "vulgar" or (as he saw them) "prudent" traits to some account. The only Fuller brother not to graduate from college, the only lifelong bachelor, he was also the only Fuller to become very rich—most of his money having come from careful investments made during the Jefferson Embargo, which ruined many well-to-do Federalist merchants, including, among others, Higginson's father. His fortune made, he finally died of a heart attack, precipitated, his family thought, by "the excitement" brought on by three postdinner games of chess. He was, in a word, a living testimony, as much as his father had been, to the difficulty of matching Fuller idealism with Fuller success. It was a Puritan combination their famous niece and granddaughter would also find elusive.[9]

II

The one Fuller brother who came closest to achieving this combination was Margaret Fuller's father, Timothy Fuller, Jr. He was born on July 11, 1778, in Chilmark. Although puny and sickly as a child, he eventually rallied to average strength, one of his sons tells us, by a regimen of spare diet, outdoor exercises, and other spartan routines that he kept up all his life. (His son recalled that he regularly each morning took an ice-water bath and at night slept with the window open, even in the dead of winter.) As the first son and his father's namesake, he was also the first to attend Harvard, which he entered (probably because of all the family disruptions caused by the Revolution) at the then comparatively late age of nineteen. While there he supported himself, like other Harvard boys from struggling families, by teaching at various nearby schools between terms. Such early experience of difficult circumstances well met undoubtedly helps explain, not only his intense industriousness ("your father often regretted that so much time was necessary to refresh the body," his wife would later tell one of his sons), but also his large self-confidence, which distinguished him even among his energetic brothers. In the only surviving portrait of him (Illus. 1)—with his florid complexion; golden-brown hair curled in small tendrils over his broad, fair forehead; blue, watching eyes; pursed lips; and slightly disdainful expression— one can detect something of these bright and hard qualities. But the clearest picture of them is contained in his diary, which he began at the age of seven and continued for most his life. From beginning to end it shows him to be unwearyingly earnest, ordered, conscientious, ambitious, and, above all, extraordinarily self-assured. To be sure, occasionally in college and afterward he privately worried, usually about failure in competition or some minor habit he indulged in at the expense of his work. Yet in his diary he rarely dwelt on these things. Instead, where they did not lead him to fault for prejudice or stupidity his teachers or colleagues or (as he called one insufficiently appreciative commencement audience) "the rabble," they merely spurred him to self-reform and greater efforts.[10]

Fuller's studies at Harvard (which he assured his father were "very easy") evidently did little to ruffle this self-confidence. His college themes of these years— which invariably received the highest marks—reflected well the post-Calvinist, Arminian outlook and Common Sense curriculum then predominant at Harvard. Most of these essays eagerly and easily associate virtue and practical effort, reason and good taste. They are written in the highly stilted, Latinate style that

marred his public and, to a large extent, private, writing throughout his life.
Slightly more challenging are a few themes that suggest a faint tendency toward
religious skepticism and a zeal for science and intellectual progress that show the
influence of Joseph Priestley, William Godwin, Claude-Adrien Helvétius, and
other radical Enlightenment thinkers whom the young Fuller, like other undergraduates at the time, revered. But these influences were offset by his beloved
Augustan Roman authors, whom he learned to admire for their balance, moderation, and literary ornamentalism. These were also qualities he found mirrored in his favorite Augustan English poetry and—despite their sometimes (as
he thought) "blamably indelicate" cast—eighteenth-century English novels he
also avidly read in college.[11]

Bolder—or at any rate more revealing of Fuller's passionate side at Harvard—
were several of his student orations in which he adapted traditional republican
ideology to very special purposes. Whereas for classical republicans ambition
was the mother's milk of tyrants, one to be resisted by virtue, in Fuller's speeches
it was also the nourishment of young patriots. Typically he opened with an invo-
cation to the Revolutionary fathers, whom he associated with the students' bio-
logical fathers. Then at some point he conjured up, as in one Hasty Pudding
Club oration, a future scene of horror in which these fathers, "who have spent
their fortunes and their lives in the service of their country," were thrust aside
by a selfish, slothful, tyranny-loving "race of monsters." Finally, dissolving this
nightmare, Fuller appealed to his student listeners to arise and imitate the ambitions and enthusiasm of the fathers and "by their talents & their love of glory &
their country, cast a lustre over their own laurel." Less melodramatically, but
even more pointedly, in the one college theme on a comparable subject, Fuller
began by rejecting the loathsome ambition of a Caesar or a Robespierre. Yet,
very quickly, aspiration overshadowed virtue. Warming to his argument, he
sharply condemned any "contemptible mortal" who checked his rising ambition and blasted his future glories. He considered it mortifying that no illustrious
geniuses had arisen when there existed such innumerable opportunities throughout the world, but especially in America, where the gloom and despondency over
the recent death of Washington required a new hero. He concluded by imagining
a band of young heroes, patriots, and sages advancing "with emulous trepida-
tion," while posterity contemplated their future careers and they exclaimed,
"'Aut Washington, aut nullus!'"[12]

Fuller was not the only college student in these postwar years to have felt the
anxious excitement of wanting to emulate the glories of one's Revolutionary
fathers, but he seems to have voiced the idea especially well. Perhaps his own
nonrevolutionary father's rejection added a personal dimension to the ambivalent appeals in his orations to ambition and fears about patricide. In any case,
his student audiences seemed to have liked his speeches, for in his senior year he
was catapulted to the leadership of a college-wide student rebellion against a new
series of college government regulations. Wary as a freshmen of any sign of student disorderliness, by his senior year he "boil[ed] with indignation" at the
administration's "oppressive laws." If not quite tyranny, the faculty did attempt

to enforce what seemed to the students petty and tyrannical regulations. (One ordinance, prohibiting students from sitting forward in their seats, drew from Fuller a sarcastic retort: "Admirable legislators. Such laws call for prompt opposition.") Unfortunately for the students, though, their petition—which a committee headed by Fuller wrote up and presented to the president—was (as he dryly noted in his diary) "very ungraciously, and ungracefully received," and the rules remained in effect. Worse yet, for his reward he was demoted from first to second honors at graduation. Even this defeat left him outwardly unshaken. "This is precisely my wish," he boasted to his Harvard-delinquent father after learning he might not get even a commencement part because of his role in the rebellion. "My fellow students all very well know the cause; this was a salvo necessary to my character."[13]

Fuller's rebelliousness continued after college. He practiced law and worked hard at it, but he found it a bit humdrum, even vulgar. ("The petty arts of obtaining petty clients & petty business & petty lucre," he sniffed a week after he opened his law office.) Also, Fuller defied his elders more fundamentally than in just the matter of a few college rules: soon after he graduated in 1801, he declared his allegiance to the Republican party and solidly Federalist Boston-Cambridge's nemesis, Thomas Jefferson ("the *greatest* man-brute in America," one partisan Harvard student visiting Washington blustered to his father). Fuller even publicly defended President Jefferson's policies of neutrality and embargo at a time when these were anathema throughout mercantile, pro-English New England. Yet this second rebellion should not be put in too radical a light. Although Timothy bragged of the "boldness" of his politics to his father, they were in fact considerably less quixotic than his father's had been. At Harvard he had been a John Adams man, and—like many rural Adams men after their leader's defeat in 1800—found his own antispeculation, anti-British views comported better with Jefferson's agrarian, old republican ideology than they did with the "visionary" pro-British, protariff politics of the Hamiltonian Federalists. Also, Republican politicians in Massachusetts were mostly ambitious, middle-class men outside the Federalist network of wealth and family connections— circumstances that fitted exactly Fuller's status and interests as a self-made lawyer and rising young politician. And rise he did. Using as his primary base of support the large numbers of Middlesex County farmers who surrounded Cambridge, Fuller ascended through various minor political posts, got elected to the Massachusetts Senate in 1813, and served four terms in Congress during the administration of James Monroe. With the eclipse of strong party organizations and the partial adoption of much of the Federalist program by Republican administrations, a moderate, independent-minded politician like Fuller was able to cut a fairly formidable figure in these years of Republican-dominated national politics. As chairman of the House Naval Committee, he successfully fended off radical Republican efforts to slash the defense budget; he helped lead the fiery and nearly successful House floor fight against the Missouri Compromise because it admitted a slave state; and, at countless caucuses, dinner parties, and "cozy & *frank* conversations," he found himself frequently consulted and courted by President Monroe, Andrew Jackson, John C. Calhoun, Henry Clay, Daniel Webster, and numerous other Washington luminaries.[14]

Still, there were obvious limits to Fuller's career as a politician. Of course, given the lingering Federalist hold on New England, any Massachusetts Republican would have had difficulty rising much beyond Congress in these years. But Fuller was further handicapped—despite his acknowledged erudition, especially on international questions—by a political ideology that was increasingly archaic in the new world of American democratic politics. Although personally benevolent ("In all cases with laborers I rather incline to favor their pretensions," he once advised his wife when she was hiring a handyman), politically he was antiseptic on social issues. Neither a government favor–seeking Whig, a class-conscious Jacksonian democrat, nor an evangelical humantarian, he rested his democratic beliefs on a cosmopolitan, ideal faith in economic and intellectual progress and the solid virtues of the rational and autonomous but public-spirited citizen. (In a typical pronouncement, after sympathetically describing all the ragged children begging in the streets of Washington one winter, he told his wife, "The want of education in rational religion & industry is the greatest source of vice, want, & misery.") These eighteenth-century enlightened republican maxims still had power in American life. But Fuller seemed only able to express these beliefs in his speeches and writings in stock, antiquated rhetoric unconnected with any concrete, contemporary national experience. For example, though he was a fervent supporter and sometimes shrewd presidential campaign advisor for John Quincy Adams (with whom he had much in common both psychologically and intellectually), Fuller never really understood Adams's enlightened nationalism. Instead, he seemed most genuine when he was most New England, as in his campaign attack on Adams's opponent Henry Clay for spending "*his nights at the gaming table, or in the* revels of a *brothel,*" or, more impressively, in his closely reasoned and widely noticed House speech in favor of the censure of General Jackson's "sanguinary" and unconstitutional invasion of Spanish Florida. Eventually political realities caught up with him. His speech against Jackson and his efforts against the Missouri Compromise, although praised by many of his New England Federalist colleagues, were extremely unpopular with some of his Republican constituents, and in 1824 he declined to stand for re-election. During the next few years, he served once as Speaker of the Massachusetts House and one "stupifying" term (as he put it) as a member of the governor's executive council. Finally, in 1832, he ran for lieutenant governor as the candidate of that antiparty graveyard of old republicans, the Anti-Masonic party. Like the party, he was soundly defeated. With the continued rise of Jackson—and, with him, of a new generation of just those kinds of "disciplined" and "younger and more active classes" of ambitious demagogues, subversive of virtue, he had warned against in his last campaign—Fuller's political career was finished.[15]

Politics, though, was not the only preoccupation of Fuller after college. He also pursued almost as vigorously various intellectual interests that had been stimulated at Harvard. In religion he sloughed off the lingering moderate Calvinism of his father and adopted his alma mater's scholastic Unitarian faith. On

Sundays he loved to cultivate religious feeling, sometimes by singing the old hymns of his childhood. He also studied after college the standard texts of liberal Christian apologetics popular at Harvard. But it was clearly—as it was for most Harvard Unitarians—the judicious and practical aspects of Unitarianism that most attracted him. Abhorring equally the Calvinist belief in divine determination and the evangelical faith in sudden religious conversions, he liked to argue, as he did in one diary entry refuting an orthodox tract he had read, "God will not reward the slothful with the harvest of eternal glory; for he has promised it only to those 'who work, while the day lasts.'" And in his "Washington Bible" that he always carried with him when Congress was in session, he singled out for marking the last verse in the Forty-ninth Psalm, "'He that is in honor and understandeth not is like the beasts that perish.'" In fact, it was this rationalistic aspect of religion that most raised his ardor—and his spleen. He scoffed at the "vogue" of "falling together on their knees on the carpet," emitting "almost a groan," and other displays of religious piety he sometimes observed in private religious meetings in Washington in the 1820s, even "among some of the first & most fashionable classes of society, especially the ladies." Even more vexing to him were the evangelical "camppreachers & whining ignorant pretenders to religion" who, he grumbled in his diary, only produced in his Southern and Western colleagues who knew no other kind of religion, infidelity and impiety. Likewise, reporting in 1820 on "the most common place exhortation" by the Methodist chaplain of the Senate, he wrote, "He appears to me to be one of those self taught mendicants, who abound in these regions, & who will soon be the spiritual guides of our own Massachusetts, if the Convention should abolish the excellent provision in the Constitution to support religious instruction." Needless to say, like most Massachusetts Unitarians at the time, he heartily favored—without giving much thought to how it would advance rational Christianity—a pluralistic version of the old Puritan idea of "supporting publick worship by law."[16]

Consistent with his Unitarian intellectualism, Fuller spent much of his spare time from law and politics in what he called his "scientific reading." His Washington diary is filled with references to a host of ancient and modern authors whom he studied for purposes that ranged from understanding history and keeping up on the contemporary European political scene to practicing his Greek and improving his diary style. The literary lawyer-politician was a familiar figure in the early Republic. Still, Fuller's intellectual pursuits had a distinctive edge to them. First, there was his difficulty simply in finding time for them in his busy schedule. In his diary he confessed he often had to lock himself in his office or rooms so he could "shut out" clients and colleagues and keep them from "encroach[ing] on my evening studies." Also, if his diary accounts are any guide, he pursued these studies in virtual isolation. Here we come to the central tragedy in Timothy Fuller's life. On one hand, in his later years most of his Federalist, Enlightenment-minded college friends drifted away from him. ("The negligence of friends or their indifference is quite provoking," he complained bitterly to his wife. "I sometimes determine to take no thought about any of them except when chance brings us together.") At the same time he knew, despite his polite social-

izing with many of them, that his well-connected Washington Federalist colleagues and their wives never really considered him one of them. (In a telling
admission to his wife, he apologized for being delayed returning from Washington because he had to make a call on Mrs. Daniel Webster and her friends, since
they obviously did "not . . . care a fig for me.") On the other hand, Fuller often
bemoaned the "intellectual laziness" and *"sneer*[*ing*]*"* philistinism of his
Republican colleagues. "I verily believe that of our whole mess, seven in number," he complained to his wife, "three or four have hardly read a duodecimo *in
all* during the session except newspapers, or possibly novels." And in his diary,
after lamenting the cultural indifference of his "indolent & consequently unin-
formed" colleagues, he grumbled: "The disinclination to exertion & to *reading*
appears to me as most general. They affect to think me unsociable & recluse—I
know them to be unpardonably idle, & . . . doomed to a feeble state of intellectual acquirement." Like his mentor Adams, Fuller nurtured a cultural sensibility
that had more in common with the Boston-Cambridge Federalism that rejected
him than it did with the Massachusetts Republicanism that he reluctantly
embraced. The emerging American split between democratic politics and intellectual cultivation Timothy Fuller felt in a very personal way.[17]

These mixed or modest results ought not detract from the fact that Fuller's
public and private life was centered in a core of ideals that gave his personality
(as he might have said) exactly what he wished for—decided strengths of character. These included a vigorous self-reliance, an enormous passion and capacity
for work, a disinterested love of knowledge in a variety of departments, and a
confident association of all these qualities with individual and social advancement, moral enthusiasm, and public service. These values represented an eighteenth-century secularization of the New England Puritanism of his forefathers—or an Americanization of the Roman republican virtues so admired by
the men and women of Timothy Fuller's youth. They were values his daughter
Margaret—despite their conflicts over his implementation of them in her life—
honored and, in her own way, tried to reproduce. They were also ideals Timothy
Fuller attempted to realize in his social and marital life. If here, again, he did not
entirely succeed, it was not for want of effort.

For Fuller the greatest obstacle to social success was undoubtedly his own difficult personality. Proud and competitive, he could also sound painfully moralistic about his friendships. "The most respectable characters in the class," he
described his college "Coffee Club" circle of friends, "not *fishers* for popularity,
but such as will act on liberal principles, uninfluenced by a love of temporary
applause or disapprobation." Some of this, of course, was stock republican rhetoric. Yet one finds set pieces like this so often in his diary and correspondence
that it is hard to avoid the conclusion that the priggishness it suggests he often
displayed. Still, his papers suggest he evinced little of the gratuitous rudeness of
his fathers and brothers. At least whenever he saw these traits in them or in others, he quickly condemned them. In virtually his only criticism of John Quincy
Adams he ever recorded, he cuttingly contrasted the "polished & conciliatory
manners" of European diplomats with (as he put it in another letter) the "coarse

& harsh" ones of the Secretary of State. Indeed, unlike Adams, he tried hard throughout his life to acquire at least the appearance of these gallant manners himself. One youthful incident is characteristic. A few weeks after his graduation, he took a stagecoach trip, during which he paid, according to his diary account, numerous attention to a young women and her little girl, who had become sick from traveling. "This behavior," he noted with pleasure, "turned favorable & partial eyes upon me; & as far as I could judge, I have reason to think, I appeared, what I have, so long wished, *amiable.*" It was clearly never easy.[18]

Besides his social awkwardness, this stagecoach incident suggests something else—that Fuller liked to think of himself as a lady's man. In one of his college orations, he had warned against his youthful audience's attraction to the "ornaments of our species" and the rewards for "our unwearied pursuit of science & virtue," degenerating into "that base passion for the sex," which is inspired, he had noted darkly, only by "the most sordid appetite." His flurry of flirtations at Leicester Academy, where he taught for a year while gathering funds for his law studies, showed he had a pretty ample appetite himself. In his diary he recorded his numerous "*delicious* hour[s]" and "repeated contact of souls *through our lips!*" with a half-dozen adolescent female students he pursued during the term, quieting his conscience with the observation that "I have . . . long since perceived myself capable of *plurality* of loves." His students, however, disproved this easily enough. One day in class just before the end of the term, after he sympathetically suggested his most recent favorite, who had been coughing, go outside, several girls "expressed their malignant feelings by coughing in mimicry & loud giggling." Exasperated, Fuller reprimanded them, "& I believe they read my anger in my looks, for they seemed to shrink with shame & some have since exculpated themselves." The following day, on dismissing the class, he added some remarks "on the line of behavior a lady should adopt, to obtain the character of being judicious, well informed, delicate, & amiable. I cautioned them," he assured his diary, "with all the feeling in my constitution against envy, advising them instead of envying to imitate those ladies, who attracted esteem and affection." Even in defeat Fuller kept his righteous banner waving.[19]

His escapades at Leicester, his diary shows, were the last time he let his social passions run away with him. As a congressman in Washington, like most prominent politicians, he regularly attended each month a large assortment of balls, levees, and dinner parties. Although he complained about their pressing on his business and study time ("I [am] almost always . . . among the first to separate," he claimed to his wife), he seems to have appreciated them both for their political and occasional intellectual conversation as well as for the opportunity they afforded for tête-à-têtes with "the ladies." When home he also amicably socialized with his Cambridge friends and neighbors. But in a lifetime of correspondence and diary-keeping, one finds few hints that he enjoyed much casual intimacy in any of these affairs and none at all that they tapped in him any deep feeling. His collegiate opinion (as he stated it to one friend) that such infatuations are "quite improper between men" he seems to have acted out with both men and women. Indeed, even when circumstances would seem to have required some expression of feelings, he preferred reticence, as in his rather frigid diary account of a distant relative whose wife had recently died. The husband, he approvingly noted, was "a man of sense & moderation" who knew his loss but "spent little time in useless or ostentatious grief." This stoical grimace would remain one of Fuller's favored masks throughout his life.[20]

In sharp contrast to his restrained relationships with colleagues and friends, Fuller's relations with his immediate family after college remained warm, constant, and demonstrative. "Though I have at the moment of writing this been absent from them several days," he wrote typically in his diary after a visit home, "I am melted in tenderness and affection at the recollection." But after his father died in 1805, Fuller became the legal guardian for his younger brothers, and this seems to have strained relations for a while. After several clashes he wrote to his mother to complain of his brothers' and sisters' "censures, & coldness, & distrust." The love between siblings ought to be at least somewhat like, he plaintively suggested, "the mutual affection between virtuous Parents & virtuous Children," which, he declared, "is nearest of any thing conceivable, to the pure love which unites God to his saints & his saints to each other." This was no small requirement, and certainly not one likely to be realized by a family that was on the verge of breaking up. Fortunately an alternative soon presented itself. One day in church in Cambridge, Timothy Fuller saw a pretty young woman, who he learned was from Canton, Massachusetts. After a few months of "*accidental* walks" on the West Boston Bridge and other acts of courtship, Timothy Fuller, when he was nearly thirty-one and she barely twenty, took as his wife Margarett Crane of Canton. They were married May 28, 1809, and the opportunity to try out Timothy Fuller's version of the saintly family was soon at hand.[21]

III

In biographies of Margaret Fuller, Margarett Crane Fuller (as she spelled her name) is usually almost a nonentity. Where she appears, it is generally as an alien, saccharine figure, dutifully hoving around the distant horizons of her strong-willed husband and daughter. Like most caricatures, this one has some semblance of truth. But—also like most caricatures—what it leaves out makes all the difference. Certainly her hundreds of surviving letters show her to be a woman of significant character. And this record shows that character etched clearly, if subtly, into the life of young Margaret and her family. If in the end Margaret Fuller took a different path than that of her mother, the road not taken is also revealing. Like many rejected historical roads, it had a way of reappearing in surprising places.

Margaret Fuller's mother's different way began with her ancestry. Born on February 15, 1789, Margarett Crane, like her husband, descended from a family of first-generation Puritan immigrants. If anything, her mostly farmer-and-artisan ancestors had planted themselves even more firmly in New England soil than had her husband's. The first Cranes migrated from Dorchester, England, to

Dorchester, New England, and most of their descendants, including all of Margarett Crane's direct ancestors, remained in the same area, later called Canton, for the next four generations. On the other hand, Puritan blood ran a bit thinner in the Cranes than in the Fullers. Margarett Crane's paternal grandfather, Henry, was a warden of the town's Anglican Church, while his son, Peter, Margarett's father, although a nominal member of the First Unitarian parish, belonged to no church and, according to one of his grandsons, entertained "rather crude views of his own in religious things." The Cranes' status was also humbler than that of the Fuller family. Peter Crane was a gunsmith. Family chronicles suggest that he was independent-minded and intellectually curious but untutored. Judging by the few books his daugher Margarett once reported finding in their house, one suspects he also was not much of a reader. Still, the Cranes were an offshoot of the largest clan in Canton. Also, Peter Crane—a Republican in this mostly Unitarian, Republican town—had his share of local influence. He served as a major and a temporary chaplain in the Massachusetts Twenty-fourth Regiment during the Revolution, a prover of firearms for the county of Norfolk, and a member of several town committees. His wife, Elizabeth, Margarett's mother, was of a similar cast. Pipe-smoking, affectionate, and, according to her grandson, "very pious," she was an ardent hymn singer and a faithful follower of Richard Baxter and his school of devotional, moderate Calvinism. Baxter's *Saint's Everlasting Rest* and similar works by Isaac Watts and Philip Doddridge, he attested—along with her "ever-diligently conned and well-worn Bible"—constituted virtually all her literary reading. Margaret Fuller, her grandaughter—who was a grateful recipient of her attentions as a child—affectionately described her, after she died at the age of ninety, as "bright to the last, . . . with her bowed, trembling figure, and her emphatic nods, and her sweet blue eyes, . . . a picture of primitive piety."[22]

Growing up, Margarett Crane seems to have been happy and well adjusted. One of her sons reported that both as a child and a young girl she was noted for her "almost irrepressible gayety and buoyancy of temper." In addition, she had been very attached to both her parents as well as to her two sisters, Elizabeth and Abigail. The one family cloud was Margarett's beloved older and only brother, Peter Jr., who had left home when they were adolescents and, ashamed of his failures, cut himself off from the family and died alone and poor in middle age. This was a serious blow to the Cranes, and naturally they saw in the marriage of their Margarett, according to their granddaughter Margaret, an immense "piece of good fortune." (They were apparently right: "During his life-time," Margaret noted, "my father upheld the house and supplied the place of the wandering son.") Margarett Crane's only major experience outside of her family before her marriage was teaching while still a teen-ager in the local district school. There she showed, not only her buoyancy, but also something of her mettle by (in the words of her son) "ferrul[ing] . . . soundly"—as her mother had occasionally done to her—a large boy who had taken advantage of her playfulness by misbehaving in class.[23]

It is not difficult to see why Timothy Fuller was attracted to this lively country girl. To begin with, Fuller was, as he so often said in his diary, an "admirer of pretty Girls," and by all accounts she was strikingly pretty: slender, tall, even statuesque—at five feet ten she was a head taller than her husband, who, like his brothers, was rather small. Her attractive features most remarked on by family and friends were her clear blue eyes, smooth, milky white skin, high, peach-blooming cheeks, and, above all, a perennially youthful appearance. ("I could hardly believe it possible, she appeared so young," a student of her daughter Margaret's would write in her diary after meeting her when she was fifty.) Then there was what Higginson, who knew her well in later years, called her "'timid-friendly'" demeanor. One Cambridge tradeswomen thought, a friend told her, she was too "*dignified* . . . to 'talk & *carry on*' before." But her friends and neighbors, by all accounts, found her sweet, awkward manner charming.[24]

Timothy Fuller's letters and diary show him highly pleased with these outward characteristics of his wife. He repeatedly urged his "*too* frugal" wife (who herself liked pretty clothes, but was also careful about money) to "equip" herself with "elegant" bonnets, shawls, dresses, and other fancy furnishings. "The improvement of your *beauty* and *shape* are always pleasing to an amateur like me." He was also pleased with her enjoyment of parties, balls, the theater, and other "polite and rational" events, which (as he once confessed in his diary) he only really enjoyed when "my Margarett is by my side." Above all, he was proud of her "easy talent" for letter writing during what he liked to call his "long & tedious banishment" in Washington. (After showing several of her letters to two colleagues, he beamed to her, "They both commended them very much, & *discerned* that they felt how much *inferior* their own dear spouses sent them.") For these and other qualities, Timothy Fuller loved his wife passionately and single-mindedly, and he told her so in courtly and sentimental letters he continued to write until the end of his life. "I played more foolish capers in kissing [your] letter, &—almost—shedding tears, than I am willing any body—but you,—should know," he wrote in their ninth year of marriage, and, six years later, when she was six months' pregnant with their sixth child: "I will now make a lover's appointment with you—On Saturday 14th. inst. the moon full, & at 9 O'clock I will meet your eye upon the center of her bright dish for an hour's confidence—you at your parlor window nearest the entry door & I at my window at Mrs. Arguelles'. Do you accept my invitation. I know your heart says yes." Indeed, these letters, which he wrote almost daily when he was in Washington—by turns tender, protective, demanding, scolding, teasing, sarcastic, flirtatious, even occasionally confessional of weaknesses like "egregious vanity" and fears of failing, and, as always, piously self-righteous—are more revealing of his whole personality than anything he ever wrote.[25]

On her side, Margarett Crane was also captivated. Her letters show her charmed by her husband's sentimental effusions and, of course, grateful for his economic support and guidance. "I never forget to bless God," she wrote typically in one letter, "for your dear presence, and protection." She was also very proud of his political achievements. Although she sometimes chafed and occasionally broke down over his long absences in Washington, she still felt (as she confessed in one letter) "throbs of ambition" every time she read or heard of his legislative speeches and exploits. In return she gave him in her letters sober "exhortations" to achieve *"Fame,"* tender concern about his health and diet, and, what he liked best of all, after her *"family picture[s]"* and "little *dialogue[s]*," abundant displays of heartfelt sentiment. "How can I express the joy the delight the thankfulness I felt when I received your letters to day," she wrote immediately after receiving his first package of letters from the Capitol. "I have hardly recovered sufficient composure to write. I have seldom felt such an overflowing of joy. . . . I was obliged to run up stairs to hide my tears as I thought my Father would expect a Matron of 28 would have more command of her feelings." And at the start of the second session the following year: "Dear Timothy I dreamed of seeing you reposing in our chamber last night and sitting down by your bed and listening to you in a kind of extacy that I cannot describe." It is hard to imagine a couple who better exemplified the era's companionate marital ideal than Timothy and Margarett Fuller.[26]

In addition to a love of sentimental expressions, Margarett Fuller also shared with her husband, on the other hand, many traditional, tough-minded, middle-class, Enlightenment-republican New England values. Hired servants she liked to think of (as she once told her daughter Margaret) as "beings placed under us" who should be treated "with consideration & kindness," but never with excessive friendliness. ("It is injurious to them & degrading to you.") The South, which she saw a little of years later when she visited one of her sons who was a businessman in New Orleans, she looked on with a jaundiced eye. While praising its *"picturesque"* people and plantings, she decried its lower-class "disorganizers," its upper-class nabobs who shamelessly flouted the Sabbath, and, above all, although her son employed several slaves, its peculiar institution. "I never look upon them without sorrow for the injustice that is heaped upon them," she would write to Margaret with enlightened Puritanical indignation, "by those who ought to lead them to the fountains of knowledge, and virtue, and not to the bitter waters of sin and death." But the shared New England Enlightenment sentiment she most honored was learning. "The *first* wish of my heart is to make you happy," she wrote to her husband in an early letter, "and the second to cultivate my mind." Some of this intellectual homage, of course, may have simply reflected her sense of what was required, as she once jokingly intimated, as "Lady F. at the head of the Right Hon T Fuller's establishment." Still, there remains something singular—not to mention poignant—about a young woman with only an elementary schooling, without a husband for half the year and preoccupied with the sundry chores of a large, still partly preindustrial household, assiduously studying a Harvard logic text or, out of embarrassment, "retreat[ing] to a private corner" away from the view of the children to review the elements of arithmetic.[27]

In fact, her letters show that her everyday reading was rather ample for a New England woman of her class and background. The books she mentions in her letters include a fair amount of eighteenth-century English literature as well as a good many of the popular, moderately highbrow novels and histories that her husband enjoyed reading. Her literary opinions, as she expressed them in her letters, also did justice to both the style and point of view of "the Right Hon T Fuller." Her critique of Madame de Staël's recently published pro-English *Considerations on the French Revolution* was indicative: "She indulges herself in the grossest invective against Napoleon, and records every little silly anecdote that she overheard to his prejudice; and dwells upon the sapient Louis 18th with as much delight, as she does upon the excellences of the great Alexander of Russia, which convince me that [she] has not the discrimination, or magnanimity that I have given her credit for." Her later letter appraising James Fenimore Cooper's recent American Revolutionary romance, *The Pilot*—a critique that so impressed Timothy that he showed it off to several of his colleagues—shows that Margarett Fuller could also on occasion match her husband's lofty but measured cultural patriotism. Taking issue with one of his fellow boarder's effusive praise of the novel, which Cooper had written in imitation of Sir Walter Scott's *The Pirate,* she opined: "I think there is more distinctness of character, more of *nature* in the colouring & interest *sustained* thro' the whole than any other of the author's productions. *I* do not think it can *compare* with many of [Scott's] 'Waverly novels.' . . . No *these* will survive the frosts of *many* winters, but I am *predisposed* to think favorably of *American* geniuses, and I should mark the 'Pilot' among the first of *American novels.*"[28]

Margarett Fuller's intellectual efforts were like her husband's in another sense: they were driven by the same rationalistic Unitarian faith. Like many Unitarians, she shied away from difficult theological questions, which seemed to her (as she told her more theologically interested husband) "unprofitable . . . to write or meditate upon." At the same time, just like her husband, as well as all Unitarians, she loved to invoke her faith in "the *first Cause*" (as she often referred to God) as productive of learning and morality. "I never lay my head on my pillow," she would later tell one of her sons, "without praying fervently that God would preserve my dear children from all sin, quicken them in their diligence to acquire knowledge, and to enable them to improve in every good word and work." She was even sufficiently enamored of religious reasonableness to see the merits of infidelity. "Perhaps we can get at the ecclesiastical history of England better from an infidel like Hume than a sectarian historian," she once wrote to her son after reading David Hume's *History of Great Britain.* "It is often amusing to me how he treats the collisions among christians. He can see very clearly where the worldly motive assumes the sanction of *christian duty.*" On the other hand, like her husband and other Puritan-minded Unitarians, her religious rationalism made her detest not only orthodox "sectarian[s]," but also "ignorant enthusiasts" and radical freethinkers. She could sometimes even sound as pompously judicious about her Unitarian dislikes as her husband. In a letter to him she recounted overhearing on a stage ride a freethinking member of the General Court discourse "very learnedly of the extreme wickedness of connecting civil with ecclesiastical institutions." He declared brazenly, she said, "if every one was left to worship God in his own way we should be as free & happy as the savages who are accepted by their Maker without subscribing to any of the doctrines of men. I was disgusted with the fool."[29]

Still, despite their common liberal dogmas, there were sides of each of the Fullers that did not touch. One was the style and tone of their Christian faith.
Although both delighted in sacred music and family prayers to Christ the mediator, one has to search hard to find expressions of contribution or dependency
on Providence in Timothy's diary and letters, whereas in Margarett's letters they
are abundant. "I am sensible that pride is my easily besetting sin," she wrote in
one letter to her husband—who was not exactly unbeset by this sin himself—"&
I have often implored the Divine assistance with tears to overcome this enemy
to peace & holiness." And in another, but very typical, sigh so different from
anything one finds in her husband's papers, she wrote in later years to one of her
sons, "What unutterable happiness to lie passive in our weakness in the arms of
Almighty love." She also knew these feelings marked a difference between them.
"Let us be carefull dearest," she implored, after admonishing him to retire sometimes to his chambers to pray, "while we attend less to the *forms* of religion than
some sects, not to lose the spirit of habitual devotion. I say this to *you* because *I*
feel the danger of being too much confirmed to this world, and one would think
your temptations much greater than mine."[30]

As she obliquely hinted to him here, Margarett Fuller was different from her
husband, not only in her spiritual, but also in her social, good will. "I am very
much grieved for" is almost a refrain in her letters. Nor was this just rhetoric.
Letters about her from family friends are filled with praises of her "sweet & gentle
spirit" and "tender understanding sympathy," as well as rhapsodies about her
"nursing talents"—which, by all accounts, she freely lavished on in-laws, neighbors, servants, children of friends, and even strangers she encountered when she
was traveling. (Her unmarried younger sister, Abigail, half-enviously reported
that whenever Margarett went on trips, "she always finds agreeable companions.") It is true her letters show she could sometimes be pretty sharp-tongued
about lazy servants and even, occasionally, some of her insensitive brothers-in-
law. But this was a side she never displayed in her letters to her children—nor,
apparently, in person. "We sometimes made up the faults of others merely to
notice the ingenuity with which she would seek for excuse, or strive to throw the
veil of charity over them," her son Richard affectionately remembered. Of
course, except for her parish charity work when she went to live with her son
Arthur after he became a Unitarian minister, most of her benignity she directed
at her children. "Our sisters complain of my recluse behavior," this gay, sociable
young matron once wrote indignantly to her husband. "*You* and my children
are *my* work and I need not go from home for amusement." After her husband
died, for twenty-five years she shuttled among her seven children's homes, orga-
nizing their households, nursing their children, encouraging their careers, and
indulging their foibles. The one object of her nurturing talents other than family
and friends was her large flower gardens, which, family letters show, she not only
toiled over with religious zeal, but managed to transplant largely intact to each
of the nine homes she occupied over the course of her adult life. Explaining her
zeal for this second extended family to her daughter Margaret, she would later
write: "One must have grown up with flowers, and found joy and sweetness in

them, amidst disagreeable occupations, to take delight in their whole existence as I do. They have long had power," she added (echoing countless antebellum writers on the garden's maternally spiritual character) "to bring me into harmony with the Creator, and to soothe almost any irritation." If Timothy Fuller represented Puritanism republicanized, Margarett Crane Fuller embodied the same ethos (to borrow Margaret's favorite adjective for her mother) "domesticated."[31]

Was Margaret Fuller's mother, though—modern readers want to know—also "domesticated" in the less honorific sense of the term? Certainly she was not unaware of the intellectual compromises her domestic role entailed. "I have long thought," she wrote to her husband after her fifth child was born, "that the constant care of children narrowed the mind, or disqualifies me for a brilliant display of my faculties." Nor was she unaware of the intellectual disabilities forced on her sex by its exclusion from politics, as she showed in her clever defense to her husband of Louisa Adams for complimenting their husbands' foe, Andrew Jackson. "Ladies are not allowed by the lordly sex to express so nice discrimination as *the men* so *you* may allow them to admire the brave in war—without *discerning* the defects of judgment in the *Politician* in times of peace." But there is nothing in her writings that suggests she deeply resented this exclusion. Apart from keeping informed about Washington party maneuvers and her husband's career, and occasionally echoing her husband's views, she showed little interest in political questions. As to the related question of whether Margaret Fuller's mother's sense of herself as a woman in her own sphere gave her, as historians tell us it gave many middle-class New England women in these years, a sense of female solidarity that carried over into woman-conscious public views apart from politics, the answer seems to have been generally no. Until her husband died and her children grew up, she was not active in organized women's benevolent work. Only once in a lifetime of correspondence did she register a gender-based dissent from her husband—on the gossip about the sudden second marriage of their Unitarian minister and friend, Thomas Brattle Gannett. Timothy saw the attacks on Gannett, in liberal and paternalistic terms, as an "intolerable" attempt by a zealous evangelical Cambridgeport neighbor and "a very few females who follow [him] & lead their husbands" to "dictate the doctrines of our parlor." She, on the other hand, like many of her female Unitarian friends, saw Gannett's quick marriage as an insult to the memory of their dead friend Mrs. Gannett and an "example of the instability of affection given to the world." But she soon became a good friend of the Gannetts, and, in any case, the rarity of the incident only underlines the point—that her public world view deviated very little from her husband's.[32]

On the more personal question of power in the Fuller marriage, the answer is a bit more complicated. *"Margarett always speak out,"* Timothy urged her in one letter, and she often did. One subject about which she certainly did was her husband's ostentatious fondness while in Washington for the company of "the ladies." But it was not Timothy's sexual gallantry—which Margarett rather seems to have liked—but his penchant for (in her words) *"enlarg[ing]"* in his

letters on all the "handsome ladies" he encountered at Washington parties that
clearly annoyed her. Occasionally she wrote indignant letters about it, but usually she preferred the weapon of satire. In one typical letter she elaborately par-
odied his detailed accounts of the characteristics of certain Washington "fashionable Belles" by minutely describing the physical attributes of "a very polite
young man" she had recently met at a Cambridge party, ending with the domestic news that their three-year-old son "wishes me to tell you that he can spell
buxomness & jeopardy & Fuller."[33]

A more serious issue was the subject of her letters. Timothy loved his wife's
chatty and witty letters about family and neighbors, which she dutifully wrote
while he was in Washington—as he implored her to do—every other day. At the
same time he could not forbear trying to get them to conform to his idea of a
proper epistolary exchange. For months he even tried to get her to attend with
her children a handwriting school, a suggestion that—much to his bewilder-
ment—she pointedly ignored. But what clearly most irritated her—even more
than his lists of her "orthographical inadvertances"—were his criticisms of the
contents of her letters. "You say I acknowledge letters that I *have not* received &
omit those that have been," she wrote with some exasperation in one letter.
"That you wish I would sometime 'allude to some topicks of your letters;' that
you advise me when no treason is intended to write the names of the persons just
hinted about in full or at *least intelligibly'* &c &c &c. My first resolution on reading this *encouraging* epistle was to write no more until you would for the children's sake say that you would excuse my deficiencies, overlook faults & accept
just such letters as I could write in the midst of a noisy group of little ones that
are enough half the time to distract the intellect of wiser & stronger Mothers than
I am." But mostly in the face of Timothy's obsessive criticisms, she showed, as
in her letters about the Washington ladies, humor rather than resentment, as in
one sprightly letter where she turned the tables on his "high Mightiness" by
lightly satirizing one of *his* letters as sounding as if it had been written "by a
literary member of Congress to his wife and the very seat of Science, and
intended as a sort of Circular for the edification of the whole family!!" Adding a
bit of unsolicited advice, she requested he "write only what your affection and
your sense suggest to you—introducing Mr Adams, gossip, the ladies &c only
when you are interested in bringing them forward—making your own dear self
the theme."[34]

Still—Margarett's spunkiness notwithstanding—Timothy Fuller *was* the
authoritative figure in the family. And if he was not tyrannical in exercising his
authority, he was certainly intrusive enough. "We are *debating* the subject [of
the name for a new baby] a little," she once wrote to Margaret when she was an
adolescent, "so you see your father allows me a voice in the matter as he is the
fourth son." Yet her laughter here—like her toughly humorous defenses of her
sexual dignity and her letters—showed a woman looking, when necessary, for a
way around her dominating husband. In her attempts she sometimes had to
admit that her own sentimental personality often got in the way. In one letter
after lamenting some recent "harsh expressions that wounded my feelings," she

suddenly burst out, "Dear Timothy my heart overflows with tenderness and gratitude toward you who have been the *instrument* in the hand of God of much happiness to me." She then confessed—in a flash of Puritan self-consciousness—"I love to look up to God as the Author of all our happiness but I am too apt to look upon you as the dearest object that engrosses my affections without those sentiments of devout thankfulness to the giver of every good & perfect gift that aught to rise spontaneous in the heart." Although Margaret Fuller's language would be very different, she would also find the task of establishing spiritual independence from paternal divinities a difficult project. In that project her mother's identity would never be far from her mind.[35]

Of course, however rationalistic or sentimental their marriage, from the beginning neither of Margaret's parents intended to create a marriage without children. In ringing New England tribal phrases ("a glimpse of the promised land" and children "to support [our] hopes . . . & bind [us] to [our] country & to posterity"), Margarett and Timothy Fuller fondly described to each other their idea of their future progeny. And in this holy civic enterprise, both could expect to assume major responsibilities. Happily then, on May 23, 1810, less than a year after moving into their new house in Cambridgeport, Margarett gave birth to a baby girl, whom they decided to name Sarah Margarett, after the two most important women in Timothy's life.[36]

CHAPTER TWO

Childhood Enlightenment
(1810–1821)

I

"Old Cambridge," as Victorian Cantabrigians liked to call it, still bore a striking resemblance to the compact English-style hamlets the Puritans had carved out of the wilderness two centuries before. The town's hundred or so clapboard wood-frame houses and the few dark, dingy seventeenth-century dwellings that had been made into stores were still mostly confined to the original circle of set-tlement—an area of unpaved roads about a mile around the village center at Harvard College. The college itself was in 1810 essentially four sturdy, unadorned Georgian brick buildings, dating mostly from the early and mid–eighteenth century. The dozen professors' houses, soon to be clustered mostly around "Professors' Row" (later Kirkland Street)—each with its well-kept lawn and garden, gravel walk, white picket fence, and stately elm trees—added a touch of elegance, as did the several spacious mansions along Brattle Street, then called "Tory Row" after the wealthy royalist families from whom the houses had been confiscated. But otherwise the greater part of the town remained the same pristine, uninhabited woods, marshes, and open fields seen by the first settlers. One could still see women washing clothes in the town spring, or cows pasturing in the Common, or a light scattering of pigs, chickens, and other domestic ani-mals grazing among many of the houses. It is true, of course, that Boston, with its rich history and culture, was only about three miles to the east across the Charles River. Yet Boston was still a preindustrial, unincorporated city of fewer than forty thousand inhabitants, and for a child not always easily accessible. The only public transportation was the town's single stagecoach that departed twice daily and lumbered along for nearly an hour before arriving in Boston. For those who wished to attend meetings or lectures at night, there was only the densely dark, lonely walk on dirt roads through the town and across the recently opened West Boston Bridge. The world beyond Boston was still more remote. Before the

24

beginnings of railroad construction in the 1830s, a visit to a nearby state was a rare occasion.[1]

Old Cambridge society was almost as simple and cohesive as its physiography. To be sure, the town had its elite, which mimicked and overlapped with Boston's. Overwhelmingly Harvard-educated and Federalist in politics; professional or mercantile in status; refined and dignified in manner; clannish and interconnected through frequent intermarriage; and with a strong, post-Puritan commitment to public service and a healthy respect for the good sense and republican rights of their New England country inferiors—both Bostonians and Cantabrigians unquestionably believed in the value of class distinctions. Yet compared to the circumstances of Boston's elite, those of the Cambridge branch were fairly modest. The most prominent Cantabrigians, the college's professors, earned salaries significantly lower than those paid to Boston ministers. Even those who came from well-to-do families, like the Lowells, Danas, and Higginsons, found their family fortunes in these years dwindling. Nor were any of them as inclined toward the lavish balls and dinner parties that, since the late eighteenth century, had become customary among many of their Boston cousins. Nor, finally, except for house servants, some artisans who worked mainly in Boston, and a few laborers, was there much of a lower class in Cambridge. What there was, Higginson recalled, academic families liked to think of (patronizingly but appreciatively) as "a rather picked class."[2]

Even more than by relative economic homogeneity, though, Cambridge was drawn together by its close culture. Partly this closeness was a function of the town's small size. Numbering in 1810 just over two thousand, townspeople not only knew nearly everyone personally, but they also knew, as one professor's son later said, "much of everybody's tradition, connections, and mode of life." If what they knew they also generally approved of, it was no doubt because they were so much alike. First of all, in the 1810s nearly all Cantabrigians were Congregationalists and, like their Boston brethren, mostly inclined toward Unitarianism. Even the orthodox minority who followed the Reverend Abiel Holmes were temperate about asserting their moderate Calvinism; when they finally seceded from the parish church the following decade, they did so with contention but with a minimum of rancor. Also, as the large Irish immigration to the Northeast was still several decades away, the town was ethnically almost completely homogeneous. Nearly everyone was a native New Englander, usually descended from the first English Puritans, and more than half were native Cantabrigians. Not surprisingly in such a town, the range of popular ethical values was fairly narrow. Everyone, except for a few tolerated, colorful cranks and loafers, contemporaries recalled, accepted some version of the classic middle-class Puritan ethic of sobriety, thriftiness, and hard work.[3]

Besides comparatively plain living, Margaret Fuller's Cambridge also embodied, if not the high thinking that the Puritans also enjoined, at least a good deal of bookishness. Nearby Boston to some extent facilitated this, as did the town's highly cultured Unitarianism. But nothing helped as much as its own Harvard College. Cantabrigians were immensely proud of having in their midst America's first and foremost college. Also "Cambridge" (as Harvard was usually called) overwhelmingly dominated the tiny town's social and cultural life. Academic exhibitions, which were held several times a year, were great community festivals, drawing as observers and revelers a sizeable portion of the general population. In such an atmosphere intellectual matters naturally had an appeal that went far beyond the classroom. Virtually every Old Cambridge memoirist fondly recorded recollections like those of the town's lone Irish laborer leaning on his spade and quizzing schoolboys on their Horace and Virgil; or of a contingent of farmers earnestly leading the applause for the first Latin quotation at a commencement; or of a group of children playing in the churchyard cemetery, continually fascinated by the long-winded Latin inscriptions on the tombstones, which always seemed to them to testify as much to the dignity of knowledge as to that of virtue, and almost never to that of wealth. The result of this inheritance has often been disputed. On one hand, later avant-garde critics would charge that it was precisely the provincial bookishness of popular Cambridge authors like Oliver Wendell Holmes, James Russell Lowell, and others, that made them worthless as standard-bearers of a vibrant American literature. They, on the other hand, thought their inherited Old Cambridge traditions of popular intellectuality were just what America needed. But however one evaluates the contribution of the Cambridge literati, one thing is certain: early nineteenth-century Cambridge had its benefits for a literary child. "No child is old enough to be a citizen of the world," Higginson argued plausibly in his autobiography. "You do not call a nest provincial." And Holmes, who wore his provinciality as a badge of superiority, never tired of asking,

> Know old Cambridge? Hope you do.—
> Born there? Don't say so! I was too. . . .
> A kind of harbor it seems to be,
> Facing the flow of a boundless sea.[4]

If Margaret Fuller—who all her life carried with her a good deal of Cambridge culture—nonetheless later came to see more "narrowness" than coziness in Cambridge, one subliminal reason might have been that for her the town's harbor was no mere metaphor. For she was born and lived most of her youth in a house, not in Old Cambridge proper—or "the Village" surrounding the college—but in the town's new development, "Cambridge Port," about a mile to the southeast along the shore of the Charles River. Her father had originally chosen to live in "New Cambridge"—as Cambridgeport and the even newer East Cambridge were called—largely because he thought its new commercial activity, made possible by the opening of the West Boston Bridge and the recent declaration of Cambridge as a port of entry, "might introduce business to me." Others had had the same idea. In the decade before Margaret's parents moved into their new house, wharves had been built, canals dug, and rows of brick houses erected to absorb the expected rush of settlers—all financed by speculators who had confidently planned to make out of what had been for over a century and a half little more than tangled woodlands, a great emporium of trade that would one day rival the Boston port. But sadly this "American Venice" (as its promoters unhappily styled it) never came about. First came Jefferson's Embargo, and then the War of 1812, and within a decade most of the original investors lost their investments or were ruined. And while—dotted among some stores and taverns—the several dozen original houses of mostly tradesmen's and artisan's families remained, property values plummeted and development ground to a resounding halt, reviving only with the building of local railroads a half-century later. Meanwhile, with its decaying wharves, blocks of unsold, empty houses, and vast stretches of undrained marshes and overgrown huckleberry patches, Cambridgeport looked altogether, James Russell Lowell recalled, as if it "had been struck by *malaria*."[5]

Margaret Fuller's house in Cambridgeport, although not exactly malaria-struck, did share the utilitarian cast of the neighborhood. It was a big, square, three-story, Federal-style wood-frame building with a two-story ell on its left, standing on a deep but narrow lot on the newly laid out Cherry Street. Its placement was not fortunate. Barely twenty feet back from the road, its primary view was of an "unsavory" soap factory. Other unappealing aspects of the place included the nearby saltwater channels in which her younger brothers sometimes drenched themselves and, still more inconvenient, the floods of two-foot-deep marsh water that occasionally poured into the kitchen, forcing family members to scurry to their "strong hold" in adjoining rooms. Margaret Fuller's recollections of the house were fairly scathing. "Though comfortable," she recalled glumly, it "was very ugly." The only aspects of its she remembered liking were the three tall, graceful elm trees in front that her father planted on the day she was born, and her mother's extensive garden of flowers and fruit trees in the back—"much injured in my ambitious eyes," she recalled feeling, "by the presence of the pump and the tool-house." She was even more scathing about Cambridgeport itself, which she remembered only as "a vulgar neighborhood which I detested." Years later she would claim to one of her brothers that her experience growing up in the pinched environment of Cambridgeport was one source of her later feeling that "merely gentle and winning scenes are not enough for me." As a child, she recalled, "I used to long and pine for beautiful places such as I read of. There was not one walk for me, except over the bridge. I liked that very much, the river, and the city glittering in sunset, and the undulating line all round, and the light smokes, seen in some weathers."[6]

As an infant, of course, Margaret's chief interest was not aesthetic, but physical and emotional. Most of her comforts naturally came from her mother. Like most middle-class women in the early Republic, Margarett breastfed her children well into their third year. She also, her letters show, constantly hugged Margaret, kissed her, slept with her, and played with her. The fact also that for most of her first five years Margaret was her only child meant, as she later noted, Margaret "occupied more of my thoughts, and observations than among subsequent years." But Margaret's father was evidently also important for the infant Margaret. His letters show him often enraptured by his children when they were very young. He often dreamed about them, begged letters from his wife about them, and wrote sentimental letters about them that occasionally rivaled some he wrote about her. His young children even brought out a rarely disclosed playful side in him. "If you bring Mama to Washington," he chuckled in a letter to his two-and-a-half-year-old son, "take care not to let her fall out of your waggon." Predictably, he also worried a good deal about their welfare. Even if this advice in his letters from Washington about clothing, airing, feeding sometimes sounded more anxious than useful, most of it was sensibly aimed, as he told his wife, at protecting them from "dangers" while giving them all "a *fair chance* to excel." In any case, myriad such attentions from both of her parents obviously served Margaret well enough, for her mother thought (and other family letters confirm) she was "remarkably good natured in infancy" and displayed (as her mother had in childhood) "buoyant spirits, and extreme activity."[7]

The first event to disturb this apparent lightheartedness was the death of her one-year-old sister Julia Adelaide on October 5, 1813. She had been thought by many, her father wrote sadly in his diary, to have been an "unusually forward, pretty, & engaging" child, and her death for months cast a pall over the Fuller family. It was also Margaret's earliest memory, which she vividly recorded in her fictionalized autobiographical sketch.

> I remember coming home and meeting our nursery-maid, her face streaming with tears. That strange sight of tears made an indelible impression. . . .
>
> She took me by the hand and let me into a still and dark chamber—then drew aside the curtain and showed me my sister. I see yet that beauty of death! The highest achievements of sculpture are only the reminder of its severe sweetness.

In the rest of her account, she grimly described in dreamlike detail the family mourning: her "still and dark" house, the "dreary faces," "the newly-made coffin" scent, and the slow procession to the grave. As the Fullers were Unitarians, one can be sure there was no mention—as there was at Calvinist children's funerals—of the possible eternal damnation of the deceased. Still, she added, "I have no remembrance of what I have since been told I did,—insisting, with loud cries, that they should not put the body in the ground." She did not mention what her feelings were at the time. Yet the circumstances of the event—its occurrence at a period when sibling rivalries over the mother are often intense—her curious association of the beauty of her sister and her death, and, in this context, her wild, almost remorseful grief at the end, all suggest an experience that was more than ordinarily sad, even if one takes into account (as one always must with her sketch) a good deal of retrojection and literary embellishment. "Thus my first experience of life was one of death," she wrote, touching on a paradox that would fascinate and trouble her all her life. Julia Adelaide's death was ill-timed for another reason: within a little over a year, Timothy began his tutoring of Margaret. Although Julia Adelaide would probably not have made the "vast difference" in "temper[ing]" her later character that she claimed in her sketch, her presence might at least have tempered the father-daughter bond that for some crucial years enveloped it.[8]

II

Many have wondered about Timothy Fuller's motives in educating Margaret at home rather than at school. But the primary reason was quite simple: he thought she would attain (as he told his wife) "much greater proficiency." In this thinking he was not alone. Since John Locke, numerous Enlightenment intellectuals had strongly argued that only home instruction instilled young minds with "Vertue." Nor were ethics the only consideration. Even in schools-conscious Boston and Cambridge, a fair number of professional families preferred instructing their children at home, at least in the beginning. This was better than handing them over to the men and women "of a very low type" (as one partly home-educated Boston newspaper editor's son recalled) who often taught in the lower-grade schools. As to the fact that it was Margaret's father who did most of the instructing, this, too, was an old tradition in New England that lingered on, in both rural and even some urban professional families, despite the growing preference in middle-class child-rearing literature for the mother as the family's moral and intellectual pedagogue. But more than traditions and pedagogy, Timothy Fuller's own experiences probably spurred him to want to tutor his daughter. One experience was teaching. He had, after all, been taught by *his* father; he had tutored several of his younger brothers; and, his wife claimed, he had "great[ly]" enjoyed his teaching at Leicester. Yet another likely stimulus was his frustration over his cherished "literary pursuits." Indeed, as Margaret Fuller would later perceive, this last factor—his need for an intellectual "companion" or "heir" that neither his colleagues nor, for that matter, his wife, could provide him—was probably the crucial one in making him want, even crave, to teach Margaret. "Sometimes I try the memory & judgment of my daughter by questions in chronology, history, Latin &c," he once wrote wistfully to his wife from Washington. "It is rather an effeminate & idle life I lead when in my room alone in the evening."[9]

Timothy Fuller's desire for an intellectual companion probably in part explains an even more controverted question about his tutoring in biographies of Margaret Fuller—why, when he instructed her, he made no reservation on account of her sex. Of course her birth order may have been a factor; she was (as he himself had been) the eldest and for some years only educable child in the family. Yet if this was all that guided him, it is highly unlikely that he would have been quite as free as he was in disregarding the conventions of his day. For although, inspired by post-Revolutionary reformers like Benjamin Rush, private school opportunities for girls had been growing since the Revolution, the prodomestic evangelical reaction of recent years had dampened some of the ideological enthusiasm for them. Many Americans continued to regard the whole concept of providing instruction for young women beyond the bare rudiments or (for the well-to-do) polite graces as inimical to their daughters' feminine nature and future domestic role. Several influences probably stimulated Timothy Fuller's very different views. In intellectual-minded Unitarian Boston and Cambridge, a fair number of learned professional men saw to it that their young daughters received advanced instruction at home or, when they were older, at one or two of the city's select schools for girls. Possibly, too, his enjoyment of the company of women (as his "effeminate" reverie about tutoring Margaret suggests) encouraged him to be extra attentive to his daughter's studies. Teaching girls at one of the few boys' academies to admit them also probably helped. (While he was teaching at Leicester, he censured in his diary both his father and uncle for giving to their daughters a "disgusting" education in mere elements or, in the case of his uncle, finishing-school accomplishments.) But above all, Timothy Fuller's diary and letters show, his commitment to giving Margaret advanced intellectual training was sparked by his two favorite Enlightenment cultural values—his faith in the universality of reason and his neoclassical delight in exercising the rational faculties of the mind. In fact, in these stances, he went further than most post-Revolutionary republican reformers had: like Mary Wollstonecraft, whose feminist educational ideas in her *Vindication of the Rights of Woman* he praised to his wife as "very sensible & just" and a valuable guide in their instruction of Margaret, he placed no limits on the subjects he thought appropriate for the female mind. Not only did he espouse classical training for girls, which most republican reformers thought inappropriate for young women who were not going to enter the professions, but he saw no conflict at all between domesticity and classical learning. Indeed, he even found—in an enlightened pastoral way—an intellectual advantage in the woman's limited sphere of the home. Writing to an old female friend—herself touted for both her domestic training and her "accomplishments"—he opined:

> Perhaps you would not agree with me in the opinion that such acquirements are often, perhaps generally, purchased at too great a sacrifice; My notions were always somewhat ["beyond the" crossed out] *behind the age* & are becoming quite obsolete; I would like to see a lady even a Miss in her teens an *early riser,* a complete adept in all the affairs of the family including the arrangements of the kitchen & even the mysteries of making bread, puddings & pies.— Next let her know history and geography, not like a school boy by rote, but intelligently & familiarly as subjects not for exhibition but for daily use. So literature & science— O that she would step far enough into Euclid & into Algebra to long for a nearer acquaintance with them.[10]

Theories, of course, are one thing, but a child's responses are quite another. Fortunately for her father, though, Margaret was naturally bright. "We always remarked her superior intelligence, and ready invention," her mother recalled, attributing the latter to the absence of another child "to tempt to childish amusements" and the great pleasure she took instead in intercourse with her parents. This last was not lost on her rationalistic father. "My love to the little Sarah Margarett," he wrote to his wife a month before she turned four. "I love her if she is a good girl & learns to read." And learn she quickly did. Eight months later, on New Year's Day—a few months after he began tutoring her—he happily reported in his diary that "our little Sarah Margarett . . . reads & understands . . . in a very great degree" the stories in Maria Edgeworth's popular (and prudently enlightened) *Parent's Assistant* he had purchased for her. (Many of the stories feature sensible boys *and* girls who—without recourse to religion—learn the virtues of rational self-reliance.) He also reported that she "reads tolerably in any common book." Nor were hers exactly common books, for on this subject Timothy Fuller had very definite ideas. "Never give your children a surfeit of *children's books* & stories," he advised his female friend, "or even of history in children's language, the *language* of the *nursery*." Instead of these "childish" books—which kept the reader of them "forever feeble, frivolous & childish"— he favored such universal books as *Aesop's Fables* and *Mother Goose's Melodies.* These he saw as good transitions to the best reading: classical literature and what he called, without a trace of irony, speaking of "the sage writings" of authors like Hume and Adam Ferguson, "*true history* & in a *manly style*." Probably to give her a head start on these classics, when she turned six, he gave her, along with her first lessons in English grammar, comparable ones in Latin. By nine, she was reading standard political histories and biographies and many of the major texts of Latin literature.[11]

Precocity, however, was only one side to Margaret's childhood mental life. She also experienced, she later claimed, hallucinations, nightmares, fits of somnambulism, and "attacks of delirium" off and on up until the age of about twelve. In one vivid dream, which she recounted several times as an adult in her journals, she remembered "wading in a sea of blood" and grasping at twigs and rocks that "all streamed blood on me." She also remembered reading of "trees that dripped with blood" in her Virgil, and her family, she recalled, attributed it to that. She thought, and most biographers have agreed, that these nightmares and other emotional disturbances were fundamentally *caused* by her father's precocious teaching. The historical record suggests otherwise, however. Although a sharp reaction would ensue in a couple of decades against it, much evidence indicates that the encouragement of children's "intellectual precocity" was in these post-Revolutionary years very much (as a friend of Margaret Fuller's put it) "the habit of the time." These were years, after all, when college-bound boys usually entered classical "grammar schools" at ten or eleven before going on to college at the historically low age of about fifteen. And in Enlightenment-minded Unitarian Boston and Cambridge, many young children were encouraged to go further. James Russell Lowell, for example, was an avid reader of French literature at the age of seven, while Higginson himself read Latin by eight and entered Harvard at thirteen. Harvard professors' sons were on a faster track yet. President Quincy's Josiah was reading Virgil by six, and Professor Hedge's Frederic Henry—who later speculated that all the sons of college-bred men in Cambridge were brought up in "much the same way"—was fitted for college by eleven and had by then read, he said, "half the body of Latin Literature." None of these boys, Higginson pointed out in his reminiscence of them in *Old Cambridge,* exhibited any behavioral eccentricities like those that Margaret Fuller reported having suffered.[12]

If, then, her father's tutoring did trigger her childhood torments, as she later thought, the cause was probably less the lessons themselves than the peculiar circumstances and temperaments surrounding them. In the first place, Margaret's instructor was her own father. It is certainly not farfetched to imagine that her tender feelings for him, nurtured over her infant years, carried over more than a little into the time now spent on intellectual subjects. The fact, too, that at the time her lessons began Margaret was at an age when, psychoanalysts tell us, a girl's libidinal attachments to her father are ordinarily at their peak, may well have given to these lessons a certain erotic content. It seems reasonable that her sentimental, gallantly woman-conscious father may have stimulated this kind of attachment. At least she seems to have thought so. In her fictionalized autobiographical sketch, she claimed that after Julia Adelaide's death he concentrated "all [his] feelings . . . on me." And in another place she wrote, "In the more delicate and individual relations," he approached, apart from her mother, only her. Finally, as opposed to all these affectional pressures, he was, she remembered ("both from his habits of mind and his ambition for me"), a severe teacher. She was able to recite her lessons only in the evening after he had returned from his office. These sessions, because he often had to interrupt them to attend to his legal briefs, usually did not end until several hours past her bedtime. From all this it seems highly probable that Margaret's problem was not that her father's tutoring overstimulated her intellect, but that it stimulated very contradictory, and therefore anxiety-producing, pleasurable and punishing fixations about both her studies, and by extention her father who gave them to her, that as a child she was unable to find sufficient ego strength to resolve.[13]

Regardless of how much her anxiety about her studies was connected to a fixation on her father, there is little question that she was right about its lasting effect. Throughout much of her later life, she suffered from continual severe headaches and "nervous affections," especially whenever she wrote or studied intensively. "I am a worse self-tormentor than Rousseau," she would later write, "and all my riches are fuel to the fire." Yet she would also later frequently claim that pain sharpened her intellectual abilities. "I can always understand anything better when I am ill," she would later write in her journal, explaining why she chose to read an intellectually difficult book when she was very ill. Moreover, these remembered fears and fantasies were also very probably a major source of at least one literary benefit: her later acute sensitivity in her writing—unusual among her idealistic New England friends—to the darkly irrational side of human consciousness. She herself, on the other hand, saw this "morbid sensibility" as at best a mixed blessing, and in more than one childhood reminiscence expressed her bitterness over her father's intellectual "forcing" that she thought brought it out. Writing in the third person—as if to underline her point—she concluded in her fictionalized autobiographical sketch that "these glooms and terrors" of her childhood bequeathed to her *too* great an attraction to the irrational: "These dreams softened her heart too much, and cast a deep shadow over her young days; for then, and later, the life of dreams,—probably because there was in it less to distract the mind from its own earnestness,—has often seemed to her more real, and been remembered with more interest, than that of waking hours."[14]

III

At noon on December 24, 1817, Timothy Fuller boarded the Boston stage bound for New York, and a week later he took his seat at the first session of the

Fifteenth Congress. Thus began the first of eight such half-year absences of her father in Washington. If there was any question in seven-year-old Margaret's mind about how her father's leaves would affect her studies, it was soon dispelled. In his very first letter to her, on January 4, he told her that he hoped she would attend to her studies "with diligence" and that he expected regular reports on her "considerable progress." Before he had left he had recruited family members to substitute for him when he was in Washington. For the first couple of years, her mother or her visiting unmarried aunts Elizabeth Fuller and Abigail ("Abba") Crane irregularly oversaw her arithmetic, writing, and singing. History and chronology, which, along with her Latin, he usually taught her when he was at home, she studied more or less on her own. With occasional assists from her Uncle Henry, her Uncle Elisha, then a Harvard Divinity student, heard her recite her Greek grammar and Latin. Despite these substitutes, her father, both in his pedagogical instructions to his wife and in his regular stream of assignments, corrections, criticism, and advice on her studies to Margaret, demonstrated his intention to continue to function as his daughter's chief tutor and mentor. Nor did he let what his diary shows was an often crushing weight of political business stem the flow of his instructive letters. He frequently wrote to her, as he did to her mother—hat on head and writing elbow inches away from a speaking colleague—while listening to a contentious debate on the House floor. Finally, in these letters he made it clear to Margaret that he would continue to press her to reject conventional privileges of age and gender. "Do you remember," he pointedly asked her in his second letter on January 20, a certain "very much . . . humored" little girl whom he had recently seen with her parents in Washington? "As she had been a little indisposed she was kept from school & for want of amusement or an inclination to read, she had a large doll as big as William Henry [Margaret's infant brother], & was busy in making caps & ruffles for her. I thought this quite trifling employment for a girl of her age."[15]

Apart from revealing Margaret's father's continuing efforts to guide and stimulate her precocity, his letters to her are also important for another reason: they give a direct and rounded picture of just what Timothy Fuller was trying to achieve, besides mere brain-stuffing, in his rearing of Margaret. In particular these letters, largely ignored by her biographers, thoroughly explode the usual view of Margaret's father as a tyrant in paternal clothing. On the contrary, his letters show that he was consistently liberal-minded in his intellectual treatment of Margaret, at least as that phrase was understood by most Americans of the early Republic. Absolute obedience was of course assumed, but those physically coercive, verbally repressive, and sometimes lax practices of many rural Calvinist families were clearly shunned by both of Margaret's parents in favor of occasional rewards, but mainly rational manipulations: frequent praise and blame, setting good examples, and entreaties to her *"good sense."* As for the will—that hobgoblin of the Puritans and their evangelical descendants—Margaret's father was plainly interested, consistent with the best Enlightenment child-rearing advice, not in breaking it, but in hardening it. His letters to Margaret throughout her childhood are filled with constant exhortations to diligence, achievement, and, undergirding both, emotional control. "I should not be proud of you for my daughter," he wrote to her that first winter about a badly broken tooth of hers that needed to be extracted (and about which both parents had exchanged several very anxious letters), "if you could not bear pain with courage, when it is necessary." Above all, he urged on her intellectual rigor. To ensure that she fully absorbed this last trait, he sent her periodically, in the first couple of years of his absence, a series of increasingly challenging assignments: a specimen of her writing, a composition, a Latin translation of her composition, a translation from some "plain & easy" passage in English (he suggested ten or twelve verses of the first chapter of St. John as "very easy"), a translation of Oliver Goldsmith's classically agrarian lament, *The Deserted Village.* He also—exactly as Locke had advised fathers to do—tried to inculcate rational and competitive talents by exploiting the filial correspondence itself. He described his trips to Washington so that she could "trace my route" on her maps; he characterized various regional dialects he encountered in Washington so that she could correct her own and check any budding prejudices against "other parts of the country"; he wrote to her in Latin and asked her to reply in the same language. "You may easily excel me," he encouraged her, "as I had no dictionary."[16]

Along with her father's liberal pedagogy, though, went other, less attractive, tutoring traits. One was his insistence not only on clarity, but also on rhetorical definitiveness. "You must not speak," she remembered he often told her, "unless you can make your meaning perfectly intelligible to the person addressed; must not express a thought, unless sure of all particulars—such were his rules. 'But,' 'if,' 'unless,' 'I am mistaken,' and 'it may be so,' were words and phrases excluded from the province where he held sway." Even more taxing, she recalled, was his passionate "love" (as his wife put it, although obsessiveness might be a better word) of *"order"* and "extreme accuracy." ("I have often said & I repeat," he once told her, "that I will give a *double portion* to that son or daughter who most conforms to my wishes in neatness & exactness.") Certainly his letters to Margaret are often enough filled with blunt accounts of dating, spelling, penmanship, and other minor errors, intended to demonstrate (as he put it in his letter criticizing her Latin translation of the Lord's Prayer) her "one *fault,* which you will remember I have often mentioned, as the source, the very fountain of others—carelessness."[17]

Such stringent criticism had its benefits and, indeed, might even have been acceptable, but for two facts. First, whereas his critiques were often forceful and specific ("Your short letter *without any date* . . . is open before me"), his praises, although sometimes encouraging, were in general meager and few. "It contained several very correct & proper sentiments" (or some such dry phrase) was usually about the most he could muster. Curiously, his letters to his wife and friends show that he was very proud of his *"promising & precocious* daughter" and was often highly pleased with her "well written," "very apt," and "quite entertaining" letters (to quote a few of his encomiums). But he rarely communicated this to Margaret herself. This is related to the second peculiarity of her father's epistolary teaching: he saw his many corrections of her as not only beneficial, but a way—perhaps his main way—of expressing his love for her. Sometimes he told her as much. "Perhaps you will be tired of so many corrections," he wrote after a detailed critique of one of her Latin letters to him, "but you must never be weary of the efforts of those who love you, to make you a good scholar & a good girl." To be sure, when she was very young, he often expressed (although, again, more through his wife than to her directly) warm physical endearments. ("Did my dear Sarah Margarett inquire if I sent a kiss to her—I sent two for her this time—This (kiss) & this (kiss)—both these places I kissed this moment on purpose for my girl.") But as his preoccupation with her studies and manners intensified as she grew older, even these secondhand embraces disappeared from his correspondence. To his wife he was absolutely clear about what he was doing in substituting rational criticism for affection. "I have the utmost confidence in her good understanding; otherwise I should not so often remonstrate with her," he explained. "My remonstrances are applications to her reason, & are the best evidence I can give of any good opinion of her as well as of my affection."[18]

Margaret's reaction to this tough-minded cultivation was not simple. Like everyone in the family, she was extremely proud of her father's position in Congress. After reading his account of his maiden speech in the House, her mother reported to him, she glowed so "complacently" that she ran to the looking glass "to see if the consequence that she felt at her heart, was apparent in her looks." Certainly, too, her father's absence did not diminish her desire for his approval and attention. "S.M. was in the full expectation of receiving a letter from you in answer to her one," her mother informed him after his second month in Washington. "She shed tears when she saw me open the letter and saw nothing but the Intelligencer enclosed." It also did not take her very long to comprehend where her father put his praises of her. "Sarah Margarett looked at the last page of your letter to see what you said about her before reading it, and her eye brightened to find you had spoken of her so particularly." And again: "SM . . . wished me to tell *all* you write of her." Nor did it take her long to discover that the way to her father's heart was through her studies. In her very first letter to him after he left for Washington, she wrote: "I have been reviewing Valpy's Chronology. We have not been able to procure any books [on] either Charles 12th of Sweden or Philip IId of Spain but Mama intends to send to Uncle Henry. I hope to make greater proficuncy in my Studies. I have learned all the rules of Musick but one." A month later: "Why do you not write to me. I want to read letters if I cannot books. Uncle Henry has not sent us any books. I wish you to buy me the play you saw performed at the Theatre." And again, the following week: "I was very much disappointed not to receive a letter from you. I cannot think my letters go. It is three mails since I wrote to you. I think I have improved a good deal in writing and I can sing one part whil Aunt Abigail sings another. I geuss you will buy my pianno forte. . . . The time is almost expired when you will get home. O how glad I shall be to see you."[19]

Despite her father's steadfast use of their correspondence to teach and exhort—and Margaret's to show how much she was learning—these early letters also exhibit something of her own enthusiastic, affection-craving voice. A give-and-take that nicely illustrates this occurs in several letters she wrote at age eight to her father shortly after he returned to Washington for his second session in Congress. In her opening letter, before outlining, as usual, her various studies and accomplishments since his departure ("If you have spies they will certainly inform you that we are not very dissipated"), she immediately turned to a more personal subject—the overturning of her father's stagecoach during his trip to Washington, which had kept him laid up for nearly two weeks. Pressing him for details, she told him she dreamt the night her mother received his letter about his accident that he was on the verge of death when he suddenly recovered; closing with: "You say a relation of your pain would be uninteresting to any but an affectionate wife. Do not forget that I am Your affectionate Daughter/ Sarah M. Fuller." In his reply the following week, her father duly supplied her with the information about his accident, cautioned her against putting any stock in dreams, and advised her on the importance of promptness in replying to letters. This was a fairly typical Timothy Fuller letter. But also typical was Margaret's response—at once self-critical, self-assertive, and exuberant, even as she strained to adapt herself to her father's rational expectations. "Dear Papa," she began,

> I think your maxim with regard to letter writing is good, but it is not easy for me to use it. For anybody whose ideas flow it is easy but as mine do not it is not to me. Like you Papa I have no faith in dreams. I want to ask you a question. Whether my manners ought to increase with my growth or with my years. Mamma says people will judge of me according to my growth. I do not think this is just for surely our knowledge does not increase because we are tall.

From there she plunged into a discussion of his theater-going and bits of gossip about some recent local engagements, concluding with the upright maxim, "Weddings Balls parties all are nothing to me, for I am not invited to them."[20]

In later years, looking back, Margaret Fuller would express deep ambivalence about these tensions in her relationship with her father. She was particularly severe on what she felt were the alienating effects of his intrusively rationalistic methods:

> Trained to great dexterity in artificial methods, accurate, ready, with entire command of his resources, he had no belief in minds that listen, wait, and receive. He had no conception of the subtle and indirect motions of imagination and feeling. His influence on me was great, and opposed to the natural unfolding of my character, which was fervent, of strong grasp, and disposed to infatuation, and self-forgetfulness.

The psychological result of this kind of influence, she thought, was a tragic splitting of her personality: "My own world sank deep within, away from the surface of my life; in what I did and said I learned to have reference to other minds." In sum, she accused him of making her intellectual by forcing her to internalize an alien or (as some post-Freudian psychoanalysts might say) false self. If this was true—that she experienced her childhood intellectual life as too much connected to fantasies about "other minds"—it was undoubtedly one source of her later frequently lamented feeling that her intellectual life, while seeming magical in some moments, felt hollow in others and, in still others, alien or (as she would often say) "masculine."[21]

Notwithstanding these sharp criticisms of her father, principally in her fictionalized autobiographical sketch—which she wrote at the age of thirty when she was undergoing the most severe psychological crisis of her life—in later middle age she came to look back on her outwardly sharp "Martinet" father (as she called him) less resentfully: as "kind" and even, perhaps, understanding of her prideful "heart ache" that his contradictory ways engendered in her. After recalling that once in her adolescence, seeing her walking proudly with her younger sister, he called out to her the line about Jupiter's proud and jealous sister-wife Juno from Virgil, "Ast ego quae divum incedo regina" ("I who am divine walk a queen"), she added, "Poor Juno! Father admired me, and, though he caused me so much suffering, had a true sense at times of what is tragic for me." She also came to see him tenderly as himself a sadly frustrated figure who had, despite his frustrations, great personal strengths. Praising their father's "quickness," she said to one of her brothers: "Your father had beside very great power of attention. I have never seen any person who excelled him in that." And speaking in another letter to her brother of their father's firm welding of his private and public characters, she wrote, "Your father [was] a man all whose virtues had stood the test; he was no 'Word-Hero.'" Finally, in these later years, she came to see these strengths of her father's as critical to her own development as a female intellectual. Tellingly, she liked to style herself, not after Jupiter's haughty, jealous wife Juno, but after Minerva, the virgin warrior-daughter who sprang from his brain. Less fancifully, in a thinly veiled panegyric to her father in her *Woman in the Nineteenth Century,* she made him the ultimate source of her autobiographical heroine Miranda's intellectual powers and charisma. Calling on her as a child "for clear judgment, for courage, for honor and fidelity," she claimed, he had bequeathed to her "a dignified sense of self-dependence" that later made it possible—in contrast with most women whose fathers had "indulge[d]" but not "respected" them—to take her place "easily . . . in the world of mind."[22]

This last filial boast was, of course, hyperbolic: there was nothing at all easy about the way she took her intellectual place. Nor had there evidently been anything easy about having had a father who had traded love for never-quite-adequate intellectual accomplishment. "The ideal Father, the profoundly wise, provident, divinely tender and benign, he is indeed the God of the human heart," she wrote to a close friend upon learning that a mutual friend had just become a father. "When I recollect how deep the anguish, how deeper still the want, with which I walked alone in hours of childish passion, and called for a Father often saying the Word a hundred times till it was stifled by sobs, how great seems the duty that name imposes." Given such hyperemotional childhood reactions to an exalted image of "the Father," it is hardly surprising that in later life she would continually be looking for him—sometimes (as she confessed to a lover) "childishly" and sometimes, more successfully, within herself.[23]

How much Margaret's mother filled this affectional void is difficult to say. When Margaret was a child, her mother fed her, clothed her, tutored her in singing, relied on her for minding infants, and introduced her to various cooking, sewing, and other household arts. She also tried hard to be—in contrast with her husband—a comparatively lenient parent. "I wish above all things," she told him, "to preserve [Margaret's] confidence & affection, & not appear to be a severe judge, but a judicious *tender* mother to her and to each of our children." To Margaret herself, a few years later, she explained her philosophy: "Almost all children are affectionate by nature and capable of appreciating the unwearied kindness shown them in infancy, childhood and riper years."[24]

Still, it is evident from her letters that she saw Margaret even when she was very young as her husband's child. Tracing resemblances between Margaret and her husband when Margaret was but a few months old, she wrote to him wishfully, "May heaven grant a mind like yours my love." And when it came to instructing Margaret, she deferred entirely to him. He encouraged her to assist him ("considering I am doomed to be absent so much," he added equivocally in one letter), but his halfhearted encouragements were obviously not enough. "I feel some times," she once told him, speaking of her efforts to instruct the children while he was away, "as if 'these things were too hard for me.'" This exclusion—or self-exclusion—from Margaret's education weighed on her conscience. "I told S. Margarett that in looking back upon the last year," she wrote to her husband on her birthday and at the end of his second session in Washington, "I could not recollect any sin of omission so great as my neglect of her disposition & the cultivation of her mind." She did her best, but from her perplexed and sometimes frustrated letters to her husband about Margaret's reading and studies, it would seem she found the task difficult. Even in her own province of singing, success did not come easily. After reporting in another letter that same month that Margaret had told her she should be happy if she were to die "as she did not know of any sin she had ever committed," she said she had answered her that "disobedience was a sin and I could recollect several instances of her neglecting to follow my advise if no more." To this Margaret had replied, her mother said, that she "could do any thing we wished her to cheerfully but learn to sing and she could not *love* to sing to please any body." (As usual when difficulties arose with Margaret, her father quickly intervened. "Do not urge SM. to learn to sing so much against her inclination," he advised her the following week; "when I get home I hope to give her quite a new view of things.") Despite her intellectual awkwardness with Margaret, her mother, her letters show, clearly loved and admired Margaret. "She is certainly a very uncommon *child,*" she wrote to her husband after describing ten-year-old Margaret's French tutoring of an attentive and very impressed husband of a cousin of his. "Whenever I find any little scraps of her writing, I find something *original* & worth preserving in them." Yet her wonderment only underlined the distance. This distance, family correspondence shows, increased as she became increasingly preoccupied with her growing brood of infants. "Sarah Margarett seems quite a stranger, so little is said of her," her husband complained more than once to his wife, and for some years it seems to have been true.[25]

Margaret's mother's minimal involvement in her education seems to have been matched by a certain detachment on Margaret's part. It is true her early childhood letters show her busily engaged in various family tasks and affairs with her mother. But her letters to her have a certain blandness and even formality about them that stand in marked contrast with her alternately awed and bantering letters to her father. "As I promised to write to you concerning the behaviour and health of the children I take the opportunity to fulfil my promise," she wrote in one communiqué to her mother. When she did say something revealing, what she sometimes revealed was her tendency to disregard her, at least intellectually. In one letter—which Margaret would write to her mother a few years later when she was eleven and going to school in Boston and her mother was visiting Margaret's father in Washington—after giving a detailed account of her studies, she stopped abruptly, as if she suddenly remembered whom she was speaking to: "But dear mother I forget, this is probably not as interesting to you as it is to me." Still more dismissive was the caveat she issued the following week after learning from her father that he was considering giving her mother some secretarial work to do (which, much to her mother's regret, he eventually decided against). In her very first lines she poured cold water on the idea: "I do not think his plan of making you his secretary a very feasible plan," she told her frankly. "I fancy you will be too much engaged besides you do not write half so fast as he can, and are not sufficiently fond of letter writing; do tell my father that I expect some letters from him."[26]

Margaret's intellectual dismissal of her mother, of course, hardly meant that as a child she felt no love for her. Her letters show that when she was away from home, she often missed her mother and sometimes cried for her. She also seems to have admired her mother's beauty and sympathetic sensibility. Yet what she admired she appears to have admired (as her mother did her) somewhat from afar. In her fictionalized autobiographical sketch, for example—which includes detailed, if often critical, accounts of her father's dealings with her—she had almost nothing to say about her interactions with her mother. On the other hand, she later *did* have a great deal to say, both in her sketch and in other more straightforward childhood recollections, about her interactions with her mother's flowers: her mother's avocation and (by extension) symbolic embodiment. Furthermore, she remembered the ideals they symbolized, not as influences on her character, but as coveted objects of her adoration. In one recollection, which she wrote in her journal when she was twenty-eight, after asserting "my haughty ambitious spirit might have ruined me, but for the teachings of the little garden," she wrote:

I loved to gaze on the roses, the violets, the lilies and the pinks which my dear Mother reared so carefully. I culled the most beautiful. I looked at them on every side, I kissed them, I pressed them to my bosom with passionate emotions I have never dared to express to any human being. An ambition swelled my heart to be as beautiful, as perfect as they.

A little further on she wrote of the clematis creeper—"my protecting vine" that embowered the gate to the garden and that she most associated with her mother's love—that she "never would pluck one of its flowers at that time I was so jealous of its beauty."[27]

Finally, not only does this reminiscence indicate that her mother appeared to her in her childhood as less a rational ego ideal and more an enviable, even erotic (if untouchable) object, but other evidence suggests her mother's very existence, on some level, threatened her. "Many times from earliest childhood I have dreamt of my mother's death and interment," she would write in her journal in her early twenties; "never, that I can recollect of any other person's; I never passed from such a dream to the particoloured scenes of any other but always woke in tears." On one level, of course, she was obviously terrified of the thought of her mother's death, which possibly symbolized for her her mother's perceived withdrawal from her during her childhood. But in several recounted dreams, she describes her mother's death neutrally, even lightheartedly, suggesting, on another level, she unconsciously wished it. What did her mother so threaten of hers that she unconsciously wished her dead? Perhaps—as the hints of jealousy and rivalry in her correspondence and later recollections suggest—it was her relationship with her father. Or perhaps it was even more her sense of her own masterful and, by association with him, "masculine" self that her father's tutoring did so much to inculcate in her. Several of her adult fantasies about her childhood support this interpretation. In two unpublished, autobiographically allusive fragments, she made her protagonist into a boy whose "beautiful . . . girlish" mother actually dies, and in one of them the boy speculates that he would have made for her, had she lived, a more sympathetic lover than his father. Surely, too, it is significant that as an adult she would most frequently dream of her mother's death, her journals show, just around the times she was engaged in some difficult literary undertaking. Both private pleasure and public success, it would seem, sadly required her mother's absence.[28]

In later years, her mother often expressed deep regret, as she told Margaret in one letter, that she had "not been more to you" during her childhood years. She particularly regretted not having encouraged her as a child to "constant exercise" to balance her mental activity. For her part, Margaret, in the privacy of her journal, sometimes sharply criticized her mother both for this "fault" and, generally, for not having provided more of a counterweight to her father's intellectual forcing. But these private regrets and resentments need to be set beside many later journal and letter entries that show that, after her father's death, Margaret and her mother became toward each other exceedingly tender, affectionate, and, in their mutual practical helpfulness, almost spousal. No one before her marriage, she later told a close friend, "loved me as genuinely" as her mother did, and she was probably right. She also came to appreciate traits in her mother she had earlier disregarded. "We cannot be sufficiently grateful for our mother," she would later write to a younger brother. "Indeed, when I compare my lot with others, it seems to have had a more than usual likeness to home." And in a letter to a newly acquired brother-in-law, she boastfully described her mother as a "saintly . . . lay nun." Finally, she also came to see, as her own interests in these later years became more benevolent and semimystical, that her mother had been an important influence on her. "Margaret used to say," one of her younger brothers wrote after she died, "that we derived our ideal sentiment mainly from our mother."[29]

Still, her journals show that during most of her life she cried many remorseful tears over her recurrent mother-death dreams. "I used to fancy," she wrote in her journal, "these dreams sent by divine direction to make me treat her with peculiar tenderness." Nor was she ever able to surmount until almost the end of her life her sense that her mother's principal virtues—her beauty, "gentleness," and "disinterested . . . genero[sity]"—were qualities she coveted but could never emotionally or physically embody. After saying in her flower garden remembrance that she never kept her vow to be as beautiful and perfect as her mother's flowers, she wrote: "I cannot get over this feeling of being unworthy to be a part of nature. It is not enough to have the types of these beauteous forms within me. I long adequately to embody them— But my influence, such as it is, is that of the viewless air." She would be many years exorcising this feeling that both her parents presented her with alluring, but impossible-to-internalize ego ideals.[30]

IV

Despite—or because of—her intense entanglements with her parents' psyches, Margaret Fuller for much of her life would seek out alternative, especially maternal, attachments. The first was Ellen Kilshaw. She was the eldest daughter of a wealthy but financially troubled Liverpool manufacturer, who was on a fourteen-month visit to America in the company of her sister and her sister's husband, a Boston merchant. She met the Fullers in the summer of 1817 and shortly thereafter was a frequent visitor at their house. By the time she left to return to England in November—the month before Timothy Fuller left for Washington—the young woman had become one of the family's most intimate friends. The three adults had many things in common: they were all Unitarians (a religion, Ellen said, "which inculcates all the mild virtues" and has a "cheerful invigorating effect"); they were from liberal, upwardly mobile families; and the two women were about the same age, pretty, and sociable. In addition, Ellen was very taken with the Fuller marriage, as well as, undoubtedly (although she did not mention it in her letters), Timothy's political prominence. The Fullers in turn were equally taken by Ellen's freedom from "national prejudices," by her "beauty & accomplishments," and, most of all, by her social charms. These, to judge by her letters, leaned heavily on talents for girlish confidences (with Margarett) and coquettish flattery (with Timothy). Ellen also cultivated a friendship with Margaret, with whom she was as much impressed as with her parents. Soon after returning to Liverpool, she wrote to her former hosts:

I can give [family and friends] no idea of what my dear Margaret is[;] she is so surprising for her years, and expresses herself in such appropriate language upon subjects that most of twice her age do not comprehend. I was really astonished when she first conversed with me; for her manners are quite childish: I remember when I first called upon you, after the pleasant evening I had passed at your house, she was at the window, she flushed (as I have reason to flatter myself with pleasure) at my approach; and opened the door; but after opening, ran and concealed herself behind your chair; the simplicity of the child, triumphing over her matured understanding.[31]

For their part, Margaret's parents encouraged Ellen to think of herself (in Timothy's phrase) as a model "in forming her little friend Sarah Margaret." She did her conventional best. In her letters she waxed eloquent over the inferiority of "men . . . to ladies" and "boys . . . to girls," but she also made it clear that females' superiority consisted in steering clear of any of their inferiors' provinces. "I never interfered in politics," she assured Margaret's mother. "I fear I should become too fond of them; and that will never do, for the lords of the creation, do not admire ladies who meddle with public affairs; and you know it is our duty to please them, and endeavor to obtain their approving smiles." With Margaret herself, Ellen was equally direct. Writing three years after she returned to England, she told her she was "greatly please[d]" by " a serious vein of sentiment" she detected in her recent letter.

> Shall I confess to you that I feared you would not take delight in the soft feelings, if I may express myself, but would be more pleased with grand heroic descriptions, but your favor has quite removed all my fears on that head. There is nothing more delightful than learning in either sex, a well educated female, with soft feminine manners is quite an object to be admired and loved; but as learning is most seducing, it is apt to make ladies dislike domestic avocations, and that is one reason why 'learned ladies' are frequently satirized.

She went on to compliment Margaret for her "talent" and "taste for literature," while reminding her that "the acquirements of a female are not for the world" but "for the private domestic circle." ("Let the men publicly harangue, discuss and dispute.") She concluded with a lengthy dissertation discounting the "advantage" of "extreme beauty," but warning her about the importance of maintaining good teeth.[32]

Margaret's answer to this cautionary letter has not survived. But from her letters to her parents, it is clear she was (as she later put it) "intoxicat[ed]" with Ellen. It is not difficult to understand why. Besides being Margaret's parents' admired friend, she was attractive, "accomplished," exotic, and, for the moment, husband-hunting. (For a while Margaret's parents tried unsuccessfully to marry her off to Margaret's Uncle Henry.) As her letter shows, she also appreciated and encouraged Margaret's sentimental side. She was the first adult to call her by her preferred second name alone. She was, in short, a fashionable object of romantic attention. She does not, however, seem to have been very successful in getting Margaret to combine learning's seductions (to borrow her term) with her own conventional view of feminine identity. In one place in her fictionalized autobiographical sketch, Margaret Fuller remembers daydreaming about Ellen as a lost love and herself as the little Harry Bertram in Scott's novel *Guy Mannering,* desperately seeking Ellen on the seacoast among the threatening crags and splashing waves. Leaving aside the obvious homoerotic and no doubt partly retrojected overtone of this passage, at the very least it suggests that Ellen inspired in Margaret something more than "soft feminine manners." On a more realistic level, Ellen probably fascinated Margaret because she provided her with an ego ideal that was superficially more "cultured" than that of her country-bred mother, yet more feminine than that of her father. In later years she would find other mother substitutes, also English, cultivated, and in their twenties or thirties, who would play something of this role. Meanwhile, for several years after Ellen returned to England, the Fullers kept up an active correspondence, which ironically centered on the "misfortunes" of "poor Ellen" in failing to find a suitable husband and her "mortification" of having to hire herself out for several years as a governess before finally marrying. If Ellen was supposed to be for Margaret a model of the single, accomplished, and socially adept young lady, she was also a lesson in how precarious *that* role could be.[33]

Besides relations with parents—or parent substitutes—Margaret in her childhood had extensive dealings with a wide circle of adults and children. Indeed—in contrast to the image presented in her fictionalized sketch of her youth and in most biographies as a virtual recluse in her childhood—her family papers show her constantly surrounded by people. Her house was abuzz with two or three family servants plus aunts, uncles, cousins, and grandparents coming and going. Margarett's mother and her sister Abigail and Timothy's older unmarried sisters Sarah ("Sally") and Elizabeth often lived at the Cherry Street house for months to a year at a time, helping out with various household, nursing, and tutoring tasks. On their side, Margaret, her mother, and her siblings frequently spent months and—as that first winter—sometimes whole winters, while Timothy Fuller was in Washington, either with her aunts and uncles in Boston or with her grandparents in Canton. Also, because when he went away Timothy left Elisha in charge of Margaret's classical tutoring and Abraham and Henry partly in charge of family finances, few days passed without Margaret's uncles' checking on Fuller family doings. Relations were not always smooth. Abraham and Henry overbore, Elisha threw temper tantrums, aunts meddled, and servants rebelled. But Margaret's parents generally "wink[ed] at" their foibles, appreciated their relatives' help and affection, and often repaid both in kind. True, Margaret's mother was sometimes annoyed with their two or three servants' "saucy" "ultra Republican principles." (She "does not intend to *slave & drudge* all her days," one of them, she reported, constantly told their neighbors.) This did not, however, keep her from devoting to them—as her Republican husband frequently prodded her to do—some of her best hours in tutoring them and occasionally nursing them when they were ill. At least it is clear that Margaret did not suffer from household dullness.[34]

But the main source of domestic liveliness for Margaret was her younger siblings, now coming every few years: Eugene in 1815, William Henry in 1817, and Ellen Kilshaw, named after the family's revered English friend, in 1820, followed by Arthur in 1823, Richard in 1824, and James Lloyd in 1826. (A last sibling, Edward, was born on Margaret's birthday in 1828, but died in his fourth month.) They were diverting, her letters about them show, but they also added another dimension to her studious life. With baby Ellen the addition seems to have been easy enough to handle. "Sarah M. is fond of Ellen K. & never complains at getting up in the morning to take her," her mother reported to her husband, "but she is so fond of reading that she sometimes forgets the cradle when she has the charge to *rock steadily.*" Margaret's occasional task of playing elder sister *in loco parentis* was harder going. "William Henry has been a very good boy I wish I could say the same of Eugene," she sadly recounted to her mother, who was visiting her parents in Canton during her husband's third year in Washington and had left nine-year-old Margaret in charge. "To punish him I did not let him go to meeting in the afternoon and ever since he has behaved as bad as he possibly can. He says he will spoil this letter if I write how he has behaved." She seems to have been only barely more successful in the tutoring that her father asked her to do. "W H is not at the head of his class," she testily wrote to him after one review session two years later. "I am glad I have not little children to teach, tis in my opinion a disagreeable occupation to repeat twenty times to a stupid child A B C and at last not have to have him remember it in all probability."[35]

Margaret's tutoring difficulties did not just reflect her sisterly impatience. Her two brothers *were* (as their father dryly noted in his diary) "reluctant" scholars. Perhaps this indifference was inborn. But if it was—whether because of his intellectual bias toward girls or because of, as he claimed, his lack of "leisure" to tutor his sons as he had Margaret—their father unwittingly reinforced it. To be sure, he worried a good deal about the "unsatisfactory" accounts of them he received from their teachers. Yet at the same time he told his wife to tolerate their "noise, roguery, & sport" and "by no means" make them anxious about their studies. If Eugene did not like to study Latin "& other useful subjects," he told his wife, he could train him to be "a farmer or a carpenter, or a shopkeeper or some such business." He also told *them.* Be diligent in school, he advised Eugene, but do "not cry or feel vexed when any other scholar happens to go above you." In the short run this difference between her father's treatment of Margaret and that of her brothers confirmed her constant worry about her parents' affection for her. She more than once, according to her mother, accused her of favoring especially the "pretty" and "waggish" Eugene. And, ever watchful of her father's feelings, she was not thrilled, as she sometimes told her mother, to read in letters to her mother her father's copiously affectionate effusions to her mother, abundant physical endearments for the boys, and pointed instructions for her. Nor was she probably pleased when her father tried to enlist *her* in his little indulgences. "Sarah M. should *commend* him freely, & correct him with gentleness," he once urged his wife, concerning Eugene's studies, "remembering how painful it has always been to *her* to be corrected."[36]

On the other hand, this "more indulgent nurture" (as Margaret later characterized it) eventually demanded a price. In their later youth their lack of attention to school bitterly disappointed their father. William Henry, who never attended college and never showed any interest in intellectual matters, grew to be a likable, ebullient, but constantly harried merchant. Eugene, by contrast, did graduate from Harvard, although just barely and only with the assiduous help of his older sister. A tall, handsome, sweetly humorous, easygoing young man, addicted to theater-going and other amusements, he drifted from practicing law to one lowly clerkship or tutoring job after another in the South, much to his own anguish and that of his family, and especially Margaret, whom he had become attached to in their later adolescence. Eventually he married a kind but minimally educated New Orleans Creole widow with a son and worked for a while in that city as a newspaperman until "a softening of the brain," caused apparently by a sunstroke, required him to travel at the age of forty-four to New York for medical treatment. Left alone on board the ship by his attendant, he wandered off and was never seen again, presumably lost overboard. "He has no ambition," Margaret would tell a friend in exasperation, after trying hard to tutor him in languages so he could raise his rank at Harvard. "My poor brother," she would write more gently in her journal a few years later, "I shall ever love thee most dearly. It is not thy fault that thou came into this world with less energy and more loveliness than thy life wanted." This would certainly not be her fate. Now would it be that of most of her younger siblings, who would also receive from their father something of the more "self denying . . . nurture" she would later curse and bless.[37]

Beyond family, most of Margaret's socializing naturally revolved around other children. Of course this was restricted for a while by her home tutoring. But in the fall of 1819, she began attending the newly opened Cambridge Port Private Grammar School. The C.P.P.G.S.—or (as it was called more simply) the "Port School"—was started at the initiative of Harvard's President Kirkland, the Reverend Abiel Holmes, and other local notables to provide a school that would prepare for Harvard, Cambridge boys whose parents preferred them not to have to go into the city to attend the college's traditional preparatory school, Boston Latin. Because of its prestigious sponsors (Timothy Fuller himself would later serve as the chairman of its trustees), the school attracted some of the best students in Cambridge, including a contingent of well-dressed young boys from around the college who daily trudged down to Mr. Dickinson's rented upper room on Main Street near Inman, braving the taunts of young Port ruffians, affectionately known as "Port-chucks" by the more genteel Village intruders. Indeed, in one sense—and to Margaret an obviously important one—the Port School was superior to Boston Latin: it admitted girls. Moreover, unlike students in the few other New England academies that also admitted girls (for instance, Timothy Fuller's Leicester) the twenty-five or so Port School boys and girls attended classes together. And so, over the next three quarters, along with a handful of other girls seated on the girls' benches and in the company of such later Boston-Cambridge luminaries as Oliver Wendell Holmes, Samuel Kirkland Lothrop, and William Stearns, Margaret recited her Virgil and Cicero and wrote out her English compositions.[38]

Margaret appears to have done well at the Port School. Edwards Dickinson, a recent Harvard graduate then studying medicine, had a reputation for being a popular teacher. At least he seems to have eschewed the hair-raising physical punishments used by most classical school teachers in the period. Margaret's letters show her deeply interested in the school's examinations, proud of her successes, and, in general, happy to distinguish herself among her classmates. "I assure you," she wrote to her father, enclosing her last theme of the fall quarter, "I . . . made *almost* as many corrections as your critical self would were you at home." How she fared socially among those classmates, especially the male ones, is another question. "She came with the reputation of being 'smart,'" Oliver Wendell Holmes would somewhat sneeringly later recall. "Her air to her schoolmates was marked by a certain stateliness and distance, as if she had other thoughts than theirs and was not of them. She was a great student and a great reader of what she used to call 'náw-véls.'" Sixty years afterward the feeling still rankled. Some of the students' themes, he recalled, were brought to his house for examination by his father, and among them was one of Margaret's. "I took it up with a certain emulous interest (for I fancied at that day that I too had drawn a prize, say a five-dollar one, at least, in the great intellectual life-lottery) and read the first words. 'It is a trite remark,' she began. I stopped. Alas! I did not know what *trite* meant." To this later "crushing discovery," he wrote, only half-humorously, he traced his lifelong prejudice against his former schoolmate.[39]

If Margaret's relations with some young boys were not easy, she seems to have made up for it to some extent with her female friends. It is true her remarks on some of these make them sound more like competitors than intimates. "Miss Kimball informs me that Miss Mary Elliot went through Virgil in thirty days," she wrote to her father after starting her second quarter at the Port School, "and I have studied with renewed vigor ever since." Yet several of her companions were close friends for life. The closest were a trio of Boston-area girls: Elizabeth Randall, the daughter of a prosperous Boston physician, Dr. John Randall; Almira Penniman of Brookline; and Amelia Greenwood, the daughter of the prominent dentist William Pitt Greenwood and sister of the later Unitarian King's Chapel minister, Francis William Pitt Greenwood. Her closest Cambridge friend was her Port School classmate Harriet Fay, the beautiful curly-haired blonde daughter of her father's colleague Judge Samuel Fay, whose family were the Fullers' next-door neighbors and most intimate friends. ("The day of her appearance in the school," Holmes remembered, was "a revelation to us boys.") Margaret's letters show that her intercourse with these girls was both playful and bookish. "Two evenings I have been out with my *aunts*," she wrote breezily when she was ten to Amelia, "and passed eight long long hours, in duress vile, a damsel all forlorn, sad victim to politeness." But perhaps the best indication of Margaret's ordinary manner with Boston and Cambridge girls was a letter she wrote on August 7—after her third quarter at the Port School—to Mary Vose, the twenty-two-year-old daughter of a Cambridgeport rum and real estate dealer, who had lost out in a rivalry over a beau, Thomas Redman of Natchez, Mississippi. "Ah my poor Mary," she affected to sigh, "I fear that the die is cast and that you have lost the generous independent noble highminded and spirited Redmond." From more about the "pity" of "a man of such elegant manners" not seeing his true match "in beauty and genius," she turned to her own problems of misidentification:

> If you ever write to me leave out that name Sarah. Out upon it. I will not be content to be called by it till I am sixty years old. Then I will take it for it is a proper, good, old maidish name. I will be willing to sit down and knit stockings look cross and be called Miss Sarah Fuller for the rest of my life. But for the present time I will be

addressed by the name of Margarette or as Ellen calls it Marguerite since I cant change it.

Mrs. Olney [of Canton] asked me to recommend a name for her little girl. Helen Angelica I said. You will laugh but I selected it as her name that I might amuse myself with the mistakes of the good country folk who I'll warrant would call the poor little thing Hellun Arnchelika or perhaps to improve it might say Arnchela or Anshellicka. I have a cousin named Eleanor and they call her Hellin. And another whose name was Juliet. A good woman wishing to speak to her called. I remember the time very well. I was talking with poor Juliet. She said to me and Miss Sally Woont you tell your cousin Shulet to step this way. I ran away feigning not to have heard her and ran away to where I could laugh unrestrained by the fear of her seeing me.[40]

Margaret's letter is an interesting childhood document. Apart from its obvious presumptuousness, it portrays well three features of her personality that would be constant throughout her youth—a fascination with exotic identities, a heavily ironic (and defensive) hauteur, and a love of social satire. The first her mentor Ellen Kilshaw might have appreciated, but the last two she would decidedly have not. Yet both show Margaret attempting, however awkwardly, to mediate between her affective and intellectual selves. And that had been, after all, what Ellen had wanted Margaret to do all along.

V

Margaret also tried to accomplish this mediation through books. One meaty source was her Latin readings. By ten she had read through most of the standard Virgil, Caesar, and Cicero, and, within another couple of years, a good deal of Horace, Livy, Tacitus, and, in translation, the Greek and Roman character portraits in Plutarch's *Parallel Lives.* Collectively these authors gave her, she later recalled, a powerful, almost Promethean reverence for fact and action. Her autobiographical remembrances of these childhood authors bristle with aggressive, thrusting, warlike metaphors of Roman figures "standing like the rock amid the sea," "moving like the fire over the land," or "piercing to the centre." She steadily loved these Roman ideals of "an earnest purpose, an indomitable will," "hardihood" and "self-command" in her childhood, she claimed, and speculated that this was probably the source of her adulthood belief that "man must know how to stand firm on the gound, before he can fly." Even the ironic Horace she recalled loving for his racy, bloodletting satires of life's "stern realities." In sum, she recollected:

I thought with rapture of the all-accomplished man, him of the many talents, wide resources, clear sight, and omnipotent will. A Caesar seemed great enough. I did not then know that such men impoverish the treasury to build the palaces. I kept their statues as belonging to the hall of my ancestors, and loved to conquer obstacles and fed my youth and strength for their sake.[41]

She was right about her ancestors: these moralists, historians, and poets of the late Roman Republic and early Principate *were* the writers most admired by her father and his generation. Indeed, her recollection sounds strikingly like a

romanticized version of one of her father's college themes on the glories of ambition. On the other hand, her father and his generation's anxious concern for
communal virtue does not seem to have caught her eye as a child, although (as
her recollection shows) it would later. The same may be said of that other major
tradition of her parents—Christianity. Family habits may have played a role in
this. Although the Fullers assiduously kept up the usual New England family
devotions of prayers and hymn singing and faithfully attended the Sunday meetings at the Reverand Thomas Brattle Gannett's Cambridgeport Parish Unitarian
Church, as an intellectual subject the Fuller's Unitarianism does not seem to
have figured largely in Margaret's childhood education. Her father never mentioned it in his advice-filled letters to Margaret, and her mother, who often
alluded to God and the Bible, if not specifically Christ, still, in one letter conceded—and regretted—her and her husband's "neglect in instructing our children in the principles & practice of our blessed religion." But the main source,
Margaret Fuller later thought, of her childhood lack of interest in Christianity—
as well as, she speculated, her adult "skeptical suffering[s]"—was her readings in
the Greco-Roman myths in her Virgil and Ovid. (She would never learn enough
Greek beyond the grammar to read Greek literature in the original.) "I well
remember what reflections arose in my childish mind," she would later recount
to a friend, "from a comparison of the Hebrew history where every moral oli-
quity is shown out with such naïveté and the Greek history full of sparkling deeds
and brilliant sayings and their gods and goddesses, the types of beauty and power
with the dazzling veil of flowery language and poetical imagery cast over their
vices and failings." As an adult she would look on Christianity very differently,
but the feeling that it was "naked" compared to Greek and Roman mythology
would never entirely leave her.[42]

Margaret's recollections of her delight in Greek and Roman mythology show
that her childhood literary taste—despite her stern Romans—had a fanciful
side. This is revealed even more luminously in a debate she carried out with her
father over the value of popular novels during the winter of her ninth year—or
just when she was first intensely studying her Latin authors. On Christmas day
she raised the issue by informing him in her letter that *Zeluco* (the English physician and author Dr. John Moore's clinical thriller about an unrelievedly lust-
ful, sadistic, and violent Sicilian nobleman) was "a very intelligent sensible
book," and she asked that he send her "'carte blanche'" to read it. She also told
him that she had just been reading Mrs. Ross's recent novel, *Hesitation; or, To
Marry, or Not to Marry?* "Do not let the name novel," she assured him, "make
you think it is either trifling or silly. A great deal of sentiment a great deal of
reasoning is contained in it. In other words it is a moral-novel." Not content with
generalities, she then proceeded with a paragraph of character descriptions
designed to show that this heavily didactic novel was not only moral and rational, but also actually realistic and complex! Thus, the principal heroine, her
father learned, "has not such superhuman wit beauty and sense as to make her
an improbable character," and likewise the Earl of Montague "is a sensible well
informed man possessing a superior genius and deeply versed in the human

character but improbably delicate in his ideas of love," while Lord Percival Lorn is "a person of very shallow judgement and very malignant feelings two things apparently incompatible."[43]

While appealing to her father's higher sensibilities, Margaret was fairly restrained, something that cannot be said of her insistently florid letter to him three weeks later. It began with the usual account of her studies, followed by an extravagant expression of feeling for the now-impoverished Ellen Kilshaw. ("I am not romantic, I am not making professions when I say I love Ellen better than my life. I love her better and reverence her more for her misfortunes. . . . She will be exposed to many a trial [and] temptation. . . . I shall feel all her sorrows.") Eventually Margaret got to what was clearly behind her lavish protestations; namely, her desire to have validated her newly found literary and emotional self-consciousness. She began by reminding her father of her earlier request to read *Zeluco,* and this time she added, with less French and more force, "and no conditions." She then sought—in almost every way, it would seem, that she could—to engage him in artistic discussions. Had he been to the theater this winter? Did they have any oratorios in Washington? She herself, she said, was writing a new tale called "The young satirist." Had he read *Hesitation* yet? "I knew you would (though you are no novel reader) to see if [the characters] were rightly delineated for I am possessed of the greatest blessing of life a good and kind father. Oh I can never repay you for all the love you have shown me[.] But I will do all I can[.]" From here it was but a short jump, without a period to spare, to her next series of novel-like subjects: the dreadful snowstorm that day, "those *wretched* creatures who are wandering in all the snow without food or shelter," and a poor woman in Boston to whom she wished to give "that handsome dollar that I know your generosity would have bestowed on [me] when I had finished my Deserted Village. I shall finish it well," she assured him; but meanwhile, she said, "my dear father send it to me immediately I am going into town this week." After closing, she added a "P S": "I do not like Sarah, call me Margaret alone, pray do!"[44]

Whatever else Margaret's father thought about these letters, this last request—that she drop his mother's sturdy New England name in favor of his wife's—clearly irritated him, although he contented himself with a heavy quip to his wife. "What whim," he asked her, had made Margaret leave off her first name in writing to him? "That," he scoffed, "cannot be done without an act of the General Court—is she willing to petition for the alteration? She has too much good sense I am persuaded." (Needless to say, she did not petition, and he continued to call her, with rare exceptions, Sarah Margaret until the end of his life; his wife eventually switched to Margaret some years later.) Regardless of his private thoughts, though, in his actual reply to Margaret the following week, her father was either noncommittal or fairly positive. He pointedly ignored her request for a shortened name, but he gave permission to give the poor woman a dollar "& *charge* it to me." On the question of her reading, however, his primary concern, he was cautionary. He informed her that he had consented to her reading *Zeluco,* but urged her to limit herself to a moderate portion (he suggested eighty or a hundred pages a day), and warned her against the danger of excessive indulgence in pleasure. *"Moderate* indulgence," he intoned, "is a law of nature; if we disregard it, our actual satisfaction is much less, & *often* we are betrayed into vice & crime." Having at this point presumably gained her attention, he continued. "It is now time, my dear Margarett, for you to acquire a taste for books of *higher* order, than tales & novels." History, travels, and biography ranked next to fiction, but superior still, he emphasized, were "well chosen works of *taste* and imagination." Of these, besides (what New England list would be without it?) *Paradise Lost,* he listed *The Spectator,* Samuel Johnson's *Rambler,* James Thomson's *Seasons,* and a number of other pastoral or wholesome eighteenth-century English works. He also urged her to read slowly and frequently review important passages and, in passing, added yet another (by now well-worn) plea for his beloved Oliver Goldsmith: "If you read the Deserted Village & the traveller with *real pleasure,* I shall think it a good symptom."[45]

The first thing one might say about her father's canon is that it is just the kind that the adult Margaret Fuller would have regarded as hopelessly provincial. Yet, as far as it went, it was a good list. If not, apart from *Paradise Lost,* among the world's greatest literature, the books were at least, as her father thought, tasteful and thoughtful. As far as his prejudices against novels were concerned, most of the novels then pouring from the British and American presses and being eagerly consumed by middle-class American girls and their mothers *were* (as her mother said to her father) "ridiculous" and "enough to make the 'judicious grieve.'" Even his warnings about "vice and crime," however startling to modern ears, were not heavily moralistic or prohibitionist, as were most contemporary conservative denunciations of novel-reading, especially for young girls. They were rather typical Augustan injunctions to moderation in the pursuit of pleasure of any sort. (He did not, after all, forbid her to read *Zeluco.*) Mainly her father's concern over her novel-reading was intellectual. In a letter he wrote to her on the subject a few months later, he expanded on his worry that her novel-reading would dull her critical faculties:

> When you have true taste you will read more for the *fine sentiments* & imagery than for the *story* or narrative of any work of fiction. In all such books the narrative being false, is not worth reading for its *own sake;* but when it is full of just thoughts & poetical figure expressed in elegant style, then it is worth the time of the reader. But unfortunately unthinking girls read with precisely the *contrary* view—the story is all they regard & all they remember—perhaps many of them even skip over all such passages as interrupt the story a moment.[46]

Despite, though, their comparatively liberal character, her father's literary injunctions still created difficulties for Margaret. For one thing, as in other controversial matters, he could sound rather abrasive. "It is rather too high a word to speak of *stile* as if you really had acquired *any stile,* which in fact you have not," he gratuitously informed his budding literary daughter in a follow-up a few weeks after sending her his reading list. More important, his disparagement of narrative fiction to Margaret was sometimes quite sweeping. He was even extremely reluctant to grant, although he finally did, Margaret's fervent request to read William Sotheby's version of Christoph Martin Wieland's lightly ironic romantic verse tale *Oberon* ("I never read any thing that delighted me so much") because he feared its interesting narrative would distract her from "the stile and imagery." Like many American Enlightenment intellectuals who were more Augustan than enlightened (a thoroughgoing "Queen Anne's man," Margaret Fuller would later categorize him), Margaret's father had a great deal of difficulty assigning a positive spiritual value to works whose epistemologies or moralities were not fairly obvious or whose aesthetic value was not essentially imitative or ornamental. Finally, there was the question, if not of sexuality, then of gender interests. Like his brother Abraham, Margaret's father admired the picaresque novels of Fielding and other male English writers because of their "wit sarcasm and satyre, and knowledge of human nature," but seems to have dismissed "modern novels" that were (as Abraham disparagingly put it) all about "love & matrimony." Yet it was precisely subjects like love and matrimony, increasingly told in England and soon in America from a female point of view, that were highly interesting to Margaret as she began to define her own partly sentimental, feminine literary sensibility. Contrariwise, the very qualities that attracted her father to the works he urged on her—their moralistic, decorative, or paternalistic aspects (Goldsmith's novel of pastoral domesticity, *The Vicar of Wakefield,* was one favorite he particularly urged on Margaret)—were properties that were clearly not so interesting to her. She would always revere Milton, of course. She also read *some* of Timothy Fuller's favorite books; she remembered particularly liking the "flashing fancies" and "lively sallies" she found in *The Spectator.* But in general her father's eighteenth-century English favorites had little impact on her inner life, and she soon put them far down in *her* canon.[47]

Fortunately, though, for Margaret's future avant-garde sensibility, not all of Margaret's extracurricular books were her father's Augustan classics or her sentimental or picaresque potboilers. She also had at her disposal the large collection of works in her father's library. His rules were liberal enough: except on the Sabbath, when she was not allowed to read a novel or a play, any book she found there, she seems to have been allowed to read. (In her fictionalized autobiographical sketch she recalled in melodramatic detail the one time she persisted in reading on Sunday *Romeo and Juliet,* which, she claimed, angered her father immensely.) This liberalism even extended to her father's somewhat lascivious English novels that most American schools and families were beginning to proscribe or bowdlerize for children. She recalled not liking them much, however. "Smollett, Fielding, and the like, deal too broadly with the coarse actualities of life," she later wrote, explaining her lack of interest. Her father's favorite Scott novels, on the other hand, she enjoyed, and she seems to have read a fair number. His book room also contained a good many prorepublican American history books, like Mercy Warren's *History of the Rise, Progress, and Termination of the American Revolution* and David Ramsay's *Life of Washington,* and she read a few of these. Her father also owned a large number of books by eighteenth-century French authors, and by age ten, when she began reading French, she started to dip into these, too. But the European writers, whom she later claimed discovering at this time, who impressed her the most were three she reverently called in her autobiographical sketch her "demi-gods": Shakespeare, Cervantes, and Molière. Like her Roman authors, these great Renaissance writers appealed to her, she thought, because they, too, were realists. "Not what [man] should be, but what he is, was the favorite subject of their thought." But they were also attractive to her, she speculated, because they were deeper and wider than her Romans. "They loved a thorough penetration of the murkiest dens, and most tangled paths of nature; they did not spin from the desires of their own special natures, but reconstructed the world from materials which they collected on every side."[48]

Clearly, then (even if we discount some of her recollected thoughts as retrojections from her adulthood), Margaret acquired, just as her father had hoped, a taste for books of a higher order than popular novels. In her autobiographical sketch, though, she anguished about the long-term effects these mature books had on her intellectual identity. On one hand, she thought, they gave her important lifetime strengths. For one, "they taught me to distrust all invention which is not based on a wide experience." They also gave her, she felt—just as in his own way her father had done—a high "standard . . . of sight and thought." On the other hand, she feared they also had damaged her. She thought, for one thing, they encouraged her to be for many years too severe on lesser authors. (Of course her childhood idealization of her teacher-father probably added to this, as she subtextually conceded in explaining her dismissal of the novels of Fielding and Smollett: "Early youth is prince-like: it will bend only to 'the king, my father.'") More significant, she worried that "they taught me to overvalue an outward experience at the expense of inward growth," with the result that (as she said about her advanced reading generally) "the force of feeling, which, under other circumstances, might have ripened thought, was turned to learn the thought of others." But the most pernicious effect she thought such early reading in great works had on her was to give her a lifelong feeling of intellectual inferiority. In a cogent Romantic critique of her early "rapid acquisition"—and, by extension, of her father's pet theories about children's reading—she wrote:

> Expectations and desires were thus early raised, after which I must long toil before they can be realized. How poor the scene around, how tame one's own existence, how meagre and faint every power, with these beings in my mind! Often I must cast them quite aside in order to grow in my small way, and not to sink in despair. Certainly I do not wish that instead of these masters I had read baby books, written down to children, and with such ignorant dulness that they blunt the senses and corrupt the tastes of the still plastic human being. But I do wish that I had read no books at all till later,—that I had lived with toys, and played in the open air. Children should not cull the fruits of reflection and observation early, but expand in the sun, and let thoughts come to them. They should not through books antedate their actual experiences, but should take them gradually, as sympathy and interpretation are needed. With me, much of life was devoured in the bud.[49]

VI

Such were Margaret Fuller's thoughts on her childhood reading from the perspective of an engaged Romantic intellectual. It would not do, however, to attribute any of these kinds of insights to Margaret as a child, and certainly not to her father, who continued to pursue, in Margaret's tenth year, the generally tough-minded policies he had introduced some five years earlier. To be sure, he was pleased, now that Margaret was older, as he told his wife, "that she improves in her needle work; for that & other domestick acquisitions may be very necessary to her. How thankful our Ellen must be," he added half-forebodingly, "that her education has been so useful & domestick." Also, admirer of "pretty girls" that he was, he was beginning to become concerned about certain peculiarities of Margaret's physical development; her discernible slouch and nearsighted "habit of shutting her eyes when she first enters a room & when you first speak to her" especially bothered him. Yet these domestic and physical warnings were more than balanced by continued proddings to his wife about Margaret's studies. "Does Sarah Margarett read Greek or learn the Greek Grammar as I requested?" And ten days later: "Sarah Margarett['s] . . . habits of reading *solid books* & acquiring a knowledge of household affairs, sewing &c, should be continually attended to." Similarly, on the subject of Margaret's burgeoning aesthetic interests, her father kept before her, as he had with her studies, not only his own high standards of excellence, but also—and this was even more unusual, certainly for a girl—ambition for fame and public recognition. Thus, in the same letter that contained his critique of narrative fiction, written the month before her tenth birthday, he extolled some busts he had recently seen at a studio of an Italian artist in Washington—a laudatory account that led him to lament the poverty of American music, painting, and sculpture and, from there, to inquire about Margaret's own potential interest in the arts. In particular, he wanted to know, "Apropos of Musick," if he purchased a piano and obtained instruction, would she endeavor to excel? And by this he obviously meant something more than a merely polite feminine grace: "To excel in all things," he exhorted her, "should be your constant aim; mediocrity is obscurity." Then again, on the same theme several months later, he reminded her how much all her various efforts during the coming winter—her studies, her lessons, and now, he hoped, her artistic accomplishments—belonged to the very same charmed circle of great achievement. "*All* accomplishments, & the whole circle of the virtues & graces should be your constant aim, my dear child."[50]

As for Margaret that year, it would similarly be a mistake to assume that her bookish fantasies of Roman gods and European ladies, however estranging from her more mundane life on Cherry Street, ever passed over into any openly expressed dissatisfaction with her situation. (In an unsent half–tongue-in-cheek letter to Ellen Kilshaw she described herself as "a queen [and] the duchess of Marlborough.") Once that winter she wrote a literary-sounding *"desponding"* note (as her mother, who found it, described it to her husband) about having some unspecified "feeling which few have and which is the source of SORROW to every one who posesses it." But her one literary effort that survives from these months shows her struggling valiantly—and neoclassically—with her inner demons:

> Love your enemies
> Love your enemies
> Love your enemies
> Come bright improvement, on the car of time,
> And rule the spacious world from clime to clime
> Errors like straws upon the surface flow
> He who would search for truth must dive below.[51]

In the meantime, Margaret's life outwardly remained pretty much unchanged. For part of the winter, her mother, at her father's request, hired the Reverend Gannett's promising younger brother and divinity student, Ezra Stiles Gannett, the future American Unitarian Association president, to come to the house two evenings a week in place of her Uncle Elisha, who was starting his law studies, to hear her recite in Caesar's *Commentaries* and Greek grammar. She also pluckily plunged on through a dizzying round of classes in the polite arts: painting, singing, handwriting, and, most determinedly, piano playing. This last particularly concerned her father. "I lately dreamed of hearing her play one of her first lessons," he wrote wishfully to his wife, "*that* one which she could never play in true time." He need not have worried. His wife's reports to him about Margaret that winter show that she was about as indefatigably diligent and earnest as he could have wished. "She practiced her last lesson continually for two days until I was weary of it," her mother sighed in one letter, and in another she reported Margaret's complaint to her teacher that she was not getting advanced-enough lessons. "She said my father will think I have made no progress at all." Meanwhile, she displayed, as this last report shows, an ever-spiraling concern with pleasing her father. Informing him that Margaret had recently made a box to contain her work and writing implements, her mother reported she had told her: "Don't you think Pa will feel *proud* when I show him my beautiful box & tell him I painted it? She thinks *'some'* of sending it to England to convince the people there that Americans are not entirely destitute of genius." Indeed, her letters show, Margaret's desire to please her father was fast becoming almost an obsession. She worried whether he would like her painting she sent him, whether she was "witty" or "entertaining" enough in her family reports; and, most of all, she worried about the quality of her letters. "I have a very bad pen," she wrote soon after his departure in November, "and hope you will not criticise my writing very severely." Two months later, after reporting on her most recent accomplishments, she wrote: "I am sorry my dear sir you write to me so seldom. Has your affection decreased? I fear it has; I have often pained you but I hope you still love me. . . . I will endeavor to gratify all your wishes."[52]

Her father did, of course, write to her that winter, and, if not quite as frequently or as unqualifiedly as she might have liked ("Dear Sarah Margarett, I am always pleased to have your letters—the better you write, the better I am pleased"), the replies did not at all deter her from asking for more. She did try to show her father one new side to her character that winter—her growing penchant for social sarcasm. She repeatedly begged her father to send her all of the brilliantly brutal, slashing speeches of the (in her father's words) "whip in hand, cloak on shoulders, & dogs by his side" radical Republican, Virginia congressman, John Randolph. Her father, alternately fascinated and repelled by Randolph, described them to his family as the "harangue[s]" of a brilliant "maniack," but she thought them, she told her father, "very keen, witty (tho' satirical), and eloquent." She also tried to show a bit of this eloquence herself; in her case, at the expense not of Yankees, but of hapless local Cambridge folk she encountered at various balls and church meetings, while, of course, always being careful to proclaim—indeed to shout—her complete identification with her father's superiority. In one letter requesting Randolph's speeches that winter, Margaret assured him, "I never troubled my head much about any of the speeches except yours unless to laugh at the endless repetition observable in some." She wished he would send her, on the other hand, his own speeches. "I assure you notwithstanding the very mean opinion you have of my understanding, I should value one of my dear fathers speeches more than a thousand lighter works." Having thus begun, she returned to the attack two weeks later, though this time at the expense of a couple of local Calvinists. "Mr. Stanisbury is as active and mischivous as ever," she informed her father. "He walks to meeting in a plaid cloak hooked so closely across his throat that I should think it would strangle him. He very condescendingly makes me a bow and grants me a smile (and so indeed does the doctor.) He has a great idea of his own genius and wishes extremely to preach here thinking he can illumine our minds." Finally, as with the politicians, Margaret was careful to place her father by her side, even, as in this case, on an issue they had been arguing about for most of the year. Thus she wrote in her letter that the Connecticut Congregational orthodox minister Daniel Waldo had been in town the other evening "and protested as vehemently against novels and *such trash* as you do papa and he is not even so moderate as you for he will not even except historical novels." As for herself, she said, garbling her syntax but perhaps not her meaning, she assumed that he would be as wise "as silly *I* when arrived at the same age. . . . At present though you tell me I am foolish, you are angry at me for being so. I wish I could be wiser, but that person is illiberal who condemns Scotts and Edgeworths novels."[53]

As usual at this time, when Margaret was being slightly provocative, she also exaggerated her father's anger. He specifically denied to his wife "her remark 'that I think her silly'" and insisted "that I am very far from any such thought, & never expressed myself in that manner seriously." Indeed, except for the argument about novels, there is little evidence in these closing years of Margaret's childhood of any overt father–daughter conflict. Certainly he does not seem to have been concerned much about his daughter's sarcastic tongue—as suggested not only by his silence on the subject, but also by the fact that he actually copied and saved her heavily satirical note to her friend Mary Vose. Perhaps he even recognized in her new voice something of the family style of aiming (as he described one of his brother Henry's newspaper pieces to Margaret) "red hot shot between wind & water." It is true in a few letters to his wife he expressed annoyance over what seemed to him Margaret's recent novel-inspired withdrawals. "Sarah Margarett forgot to send her love," he complained to his wife; "I suppose she was *bending* over some tale of woe or mystery, & so forgot it." But this was a minor note. Margaret's mother continued to send him glowing accounts of Margaret's "thousand castles & . . . frolick[s] of imagination" around the house and the "flattering" "commendations" she was hearing from family and friends of her talents in languages. Also, both Margaret and her parents were beginning to be buoyed up by a new prospect on the horizon for her—a new school.[54]

The idea of sending Margaret to a school other than the Port School had been talked about on and off among Margaret and her parents ever since her last quarter there the previous spring. Like all the girls who went there, Margaret had been attending the school only part-time, mainly to recite her Latin. Also because the Port School's primary function was to teach boys Latin and Greek to prepare them for college, its narrow curriculum was obviously less than ideal for a girl for whom secondary education was meant to be final. Then there were other considerations. Mr. Dickinson left the school after the spring quarter. In addition, her father wanted her to continue her music lessons, which made a school in Boston, where most of the teachers were, preferable to one in Cambridge. But what was that school? Margaret and her parents had various answers, each of which revealed a good deal about the dilemmas that were already beginning to shape her young intellectual life. Margaret's mother inclined to sending her to the boarding school in Jamaica Plain run by the fastidiously manners-conscious Elizabeth McKeige and her widowed, French-born daughter, Mrs. Colman. "She appears perfectly *well bred* in all polite forms of etiquette in social life," she told her husband, "& I think myself SM in her deportment & manners would derive much advantage in her school & under her influence." Margaret, however—although she did concede that Mrs. McKeige was conscientious about her French ("If any one speaks English," she informed her father, "they are fined two cents")—did not like the idea at all. "She *wisely* observed," her mother reported to her father, "that Mrs. McKeig's was not so much a school for improvement in Literature, as in 'elegant accomplishments' which is the case." The school Margaret favored—indeed had been asking to be sent to for over a year—was the very different Boston school of Dr. John Park. Margaret's father supported her. Dr. Park's school, he told his wife, was "much preferable," and, if she went there, she could keep up her "musick instrumental & vocal." Margaret's mother, who was also impressed with the school, and perhaps mollified too by the thought that Margaret would be attending a school exclusively for girls, in the end agreed. Margaret's father's wish that she acquire "all accomplishments" seemed on the verge of realization. And so, her father having arranged to secure her a place, on April 2, 1821, Margaret stepped off her front stoop and headed toward the West Boston Bridge on the way to Dr. Park's Boston Lyceum for Young Ladies.[55]

CHAPTER THREE

Rustication

$\left(1821-1825\right)$

I

Margaret and her father's confidence in Dr. Park's school was well founded. Of course these were exciting years for American private school secondary education. Not only were multicurriculum academies and seminaries for both boys and girls proliferating throughout the Northeast, but in education-minded Massachusetts, progressive schools like George B. Emerson's English Classical and George Bancroft and Joseph Cogswell's Round Hill were offering instruction that, in downgrading emulation and rote recitations, was more innovative than any before offered in America. Still, even in this field, Dr. Park's school ranked near the top. Scholarly and enterprising, Dr. Park, who was a Dartmouth graduate, had led a varied career as a successful hospital surgeon in the West Indies and an arch-Federalist newspaper editor in Boston. In 1811 he sold his paper, which two years later became the *Boston Daily Advertiser,* and opened his school for girls, a decade before most female seminaries were founded. Then at the height of its reputation, the school, which Park kept at his exclusive 5 Mount Vernon house, attracted students from many of the city's most prominent and well-to-do Unitarian families. Because of this, but also because of Park's own interests, the school's curriculum was rigorously academic: Latin, French, Italian, rhetoric, trigonometry, and several natural sciences. (He had earlier dropped Greek only because he thought it crowded the other studies too much). Furthermore, as Park was something of a literary scholar himself, most of the texts he used were high literary ones, including Cicero, Caesar, Sallust, Virgil, Horace, Molière, Fénelon, Voltaire, Torquato Tasso, and Vittorio Alfieri, plus, for rhetorical guidance, the standard college Scottish Common Sense critical works of Hugh Blair and Archibald Alison. Pedagogically, Park was moderately liberal. In class he de-emphasized memorization, stressed weekly compositions, and utilized a variety of maps and scientific instruments, which he imported from Europe. Yet, unlike English Classical and the Round Hill school (but very

57

much like virtually all boys' college-preparatory classical schools) he encouraged strenuous competition. ("Yes," he once reportedly answered Boston's leading liberal Unitarian minister William Ellery Channing, whose niece went to his school and who had told him he feared his use of medals fostered jealousies among the students; "I do use medals, and I find, also, that my finest scholars are most intimate with each other.") His literary cosmopolitanism also had its limits: he refused to teach German literature, because it dealt, as he put it, in "rhapsodical intimations rather than distinct sentiments." In short, the Fullers could hardly have found a school in America more likely to continue the basic thrust of Margaret's childhood education than Dr. Park's.[1]

Certainly Margaret was happy enough with the popular Dr. Park. "Very kind and sweet" she would soon describe him to her father, and her mother would report to her husband, "She . . . *discovers* traits in the good Dr to expatiate upon daily." The only drawback was the three-mile walk each way to the school, but she does not seem to have minded it. "It will be rather fatiguing walking in and out again every day to be sure," she had written her father before enrolling, "but then I shall have a pleasant walk to pay for it." The doctor, she had added, began at nine and ended at two, and therefore "I shall have to study all the time out of school." The problem of the walk was solved in the fall when her parents made new living arrangements. Her father had been intending to bring her mother with him to Washington to spend a winter ever since he had first left for Congress, and now that Margaret was attending a school in the city there was an additional reason to carry out the plan. So in late November, baby Ellen, Eugene, and William Henry were sent off to their grandparents and Aunt Abigail in Canton, and Margaret went to live with her father's youngest sister, Martha Whittier, and her merchant husband, Simeon, in Boston. At first, of course, there was the slight shock of separation to get over. "Tell my dear father," she wrote to her mother on December 2, "that I have not cried once since he went away. I am as happy here as I can be separated from you." But three days later these brave fronts gave way to her usual concern in writing (in this case through her mother) to her father. "Tell [papa] I am writing a long composition but it will be three weeks before it is given up," she somewhat anxiously informed her. "He will not have it till I know what the Dr. says to it." She also showed her rather grim determination to succeed. At the end of a long and convoluted comparison of the medals she had won so far and the many medals won by William Ellery Channing's niece, Susan Channing, who had enrolled in the school three months before her, she explained to her mother that Susan had gotten "the eye of Intelligence" only because she was at the head of her English parsing class, from which position she hoped soon to dislodge her. "If I can get up to the head I shall keep there for I have not made one mistake in that class; indeed I have taken great pain not to, perhaps I may have the eye, before you return which is the highest medal in school."[2]

Happily, she soon got her "eye" and much more as well. Meanwhile, she enjoyed several social benefits from living in the city. One was the company of her father's moderately well-off Boston relatives. The Whittiers lived at Central

Court No. 3, in what was then a fashionable neighborhood and just around the corner from where her Uncle Henry would soon be building his large house. In the Whittiers' house, besides their two young daughters and baby boy, there were also living her Aunt Sally and her affectionately solicitous Grandmother Fuller. In addition, nearby were several families on her grandmother's side, including her father's fifteen-year-old cousin, Susan Ann Buckminster Williams, who also attended Dr. Park's and whom Margaret much admired for both her studiousness and her "extensive acquaintance"—as well as, no doubt, her friendliness to *her*. (She had originally encouraged Margaret to come and live with her "that we might study together.") Another related benefit of city living was that, thanks to her culturally inquisitive uncles, she could sample some of the city's entertainments, high and low. On Thanksgiving she went to hear, at the Reverend Nathaniel Frothingham's prestigious First Church, Unitarian Boston's favorite young man eloquent, Edward Everett, then professor of Greek at Harvard. "I liked his sermon or rather lecture much," she reported to her mother on December 9, "except two or three expressions which I could not understand such as 'the active centres of fermentation' and in my opinion his pronunciation was not very good." Evidently more satisfying was the performance of *Blue Beard* to which her Uncle Abraham took her and her Aunt Sally and the two Whittier sisters, "in which we had the pleasure of seeing fire, smoke, battles, death, blood, skeletons and all the ghostly preparations." As her mother and father had acceded to her request to attend dancing school ("you know mother that I am not a very good dancer," she had noted), she also began attending balls put on by her dancing teacher, Dana Parks. These were the first Boston balls Margaret attended, and the reports, not surprisingly, were less than glorious. Writing to her mother on December 23 about one such affair, she testily reported: "I danced thirteen times. Twelve of my partners were grown up gentlemen and of course very bad dancers but I had one good partner who knew what he was about and he was one of the scholars." Nor did it seem to Margaret that the female adults knew much better what they were about. Most of them, she primly informed her mother, were so "indecently dressed" that they "could not be content without shewing their bosoms and shoulders completely." One lady in particularly, she said, had "her sash brought up so as to come over a part of her bosom and nothing more. Mr. Whittier said he hoped she would dance her gown completely off and that he expected nothing more than that she would jump out of her clothes. I am sure I was ashamed for her, for she was not a young girl neither but rather in the decline of life and her neck none of the whitest."[3]

Margaret's most important social experience, though, was with her schoolmates, and about them her reports were anything but crabby. Reporting to her mother in this same letter on a recent, tearful farewell party for some of Dr. Park's older pupils, she wrote:

> I think that we are all sisters, it is hard for me to stand unconnected; and all girls who have no intimate friends are not so much beloved. Tell papa that I do not believe I shall be happy if I leave school soon. Ask him mamma whether I shall not stay more

than a year. Ah I hope I shall for I love the Dr so much, and my companions seem
so amiable that I long to stay. I talk about this too much perhaps but it is the upper-
most in my thoughts.[4]

Or so she wrote to her mother in December. In fact, Margaret's life in Boston
was not as roseate as this hopeful report would imply. For one thing, the physical
arrangements for Margaret in the Whittier house left something to be desired.
She frequently had to study in the parlor because her room was often without a
fire (which probably also contributed to the cough she had for most of the winter). According to her mother, who visited her in February, she generally slept
"on a little trundle bed about two thirds her length." The Whittiers' domestic
situation—at least from the Fullers' point of view—was also awkward. Margaret
complained bitterly to her mother that Aunt Sally was an unbearable scold.
("SM says that she has made her shed more tears by her 'unmerited severity' than
she had shed before since her birth.") Margaret's mother, on the other hand,
found Martha's "domestick regulations" to have been unbearably lax. Her children constantly played cards, they neglected their studies, and—worst of all—
Martha herself, she reported to her husband, constantly read "trash[y]" popular
novels. Although not quite perhaps the "evils" Margaret's mother feared, they
must have been somewhat disconcerting to a bookish child used to more intellectual domestic habits.[5]

But the most disconcerting disappointment that Margaret had to face was not
at home but in school. To begin with, her cousin Susan became ill in December
and had to withdraw from school for the entire winter quarter. Whether, though,
the presence of her popular cousin would have made much of a difference for
Margaret seems unlikely. For the fact was that, however "beloved" Margaret
claimed to have found her companions, they seem to have found her considerably less so. Perhaps part of her difficulty was the grim eagerness with which she
had immediately started competing with her more established classmates. But
in addition she seems to have arrived at Dr. Park's already trailing clouds of—
by Boston standards anyway—a somewhat questionable reputation. Elizabeth
Peabody, who had just begun to teach in Boston, remembered hearing of her at
this time "as a wonderful child at Dr Park's school," who talked "pure mathematics with her father, at 12 years" and " 'had not religion.' " Similarly, Susan
Channing's brother William Henry later recalled that although she was generally
thought of in Boston Unitarian circles as "a prodigy of talent and accomplishment," nonetheless, "a sad feeling prevailed, that she had been overtasked by her
father, who wished to train her like a boy, and that she was paying the penalty
for undue application, in nearsightedness, awkward manners, extravagant tendencies of thought, and a pedantic style of talk, that made her a butt for the ridicule of frivolous companions." Finally, along with these negative perceptions
seem to have gone social snobberies of a meaner sort. Frederic Henry Hedge,
who would meet Margaret the following year, later recalled what he had heard
of these:

Here the inexperienced country girl was exposed to petty persecutions from the dashing misses of the city, who pleased themselves with giggling criticisms not inaudible, nor meant to be inaudible to their subject, on whatsoever in dress and manner fell short of the city mark. Then it was first revealed to her young heart, and laid up for future reflection, how large a place in woman's world is given to fashion and frivolity. Her mind reacted on these attacks with indiscriminate sarcasms. She made herself formidable by her wit, and, of course, unpopular. A root of bitterness sprung up in her which years of moral culture were needed to eradicate.[6]

Margaret's letters at the time give indirect support for these later recollections. After her initial enthusiasm all mention of her schoolmates ceased, and she concentrated instead, in her letters to her father, on her relentless intellectual labors and triumphs. On March 13 she wrote to him that in two days Dr. Park was to give an examination, "which will I think go off with great splendour." At the moment, she said, she was surrounded by books and maps and was glad that he could not be there to witness her first public examination. "I know what your feelings would be, mine are sufficient." Her Uncle Abraham, though, she said, would be there, and "he will acquaint you with my success, perhaps it may be a failure, but I hope not, be assured that I will do my utmost to acquit myself well." Geography, she conceded, she was a little worried about ("the numberless questions on the map quite disconcert me"), but otherwise she felt confident. "History unless I am frightened quite out of my wits I am sure of and 'tis very improbable that I shall miss in parsing or Latin (by the bye I have learned to scan and parse) or French and I think my Italian will be right. I wonder if this is as interesting to any body else as it is to me, I think of nothing else." The examination went as she had hoped. A week afterwards she wrote to her father that despite being "extremely hoarse" from a bad cold, "I made out much better than I had expected I should." Even her rather grumpy Uncle Abraham had been impressed. He had "no thought," her mother reported he had proudly told Margaret when it was over, "of there being a class of females so highly endowed with literature in America."[7]

The days after her examination were crowded ones. On March 19 she left Boston to spend her intersession with her mother in Canton. Her mother had been living there since January when she had had to leave Washington suddenly to go to Eugene and William Henry, who had come down with a bad case of measles. On the thirtieth, Margaret returned to Boston to begin the spring quarter at Dr. Park's. Two weeks later her Grandmother Fuller died. The strain of her Boston stay was obviously beginning to take a toll. "Sarah M. was *not* well yesterday," her mother wrote to her father on the morning of April 16. "She was very faint while Mr Frothingham was making the funeral prayer—& I was obliged to go out into the air with her." So, later that afternoon—to "restore her health," her mother told her father (she "looks very thin in flesh"), as well as to get her out of what she regarded as a "vexatious" environment at the Whittiers', and one that Margaret herself was by this time weary of—her mother brought her with her when she returned to Cambridgeport.[8]

Consequently, for the rest of the spring of 1822 through the following fall, Margaret continued where she had left off the previous winter—walking (and in bad weather riding in a chaise) to and from Dr. Park's. If there was any change at all, it was in her scholastic status. For it was now absolutely clear what many of her classmates probably suspected at the beginning: she was Dr. Park's star pupil, and after the fall quarter ended on December 20, he "made an address" to her that confirmed it. After saying (according to Margaret) "that he never *flattered*" and praising her father for his precocious tutoring of Margaret "'more than she could remember,'" he bluntly told her that (according to her mother) "he had never had a pupil with half her attainments at her age." Coming from Boston's premier schoolmaster, it was high praise indeed, and so it must have seemed even to Margaret's exacting father.[9]

Margaret's letters to her father that December showed that her year and a half at Dr. Park's had helped ingrain two intellectual traits that Margaret had begun to evince in her childhood and that would remain permanent parts of her make-up all her life: a critical feeling for literature combined with a heated literary voraciousness. On the twenty-second, she reported to her father that she lately had read Washington Irving's new book of romantic sketches, *Bracebridge Hall,* and was "much disappointed" in it. "It seems to me to possess very little incident or originality of idea; I think that although it has considerable wit, yet that is often farfetched. The style is good, but I think this work is much inferior to any of Irving's preceding works, which I have seen." And the following week, on December 30, twelve-year-old Margaret wrote to her father this slightly worrisome but no doubt also welcome account of her latest reading in some of his favorite—and impeccably enlightened—moral philosophy texts:

> My eyes are . . . extremely weak. I hoped to have been able to have studied this week eight hours each day, but I have determined not only not to study, but not to look into a book for seven days. I am very sorry to be obliged to do this for I had begun "Smith's Wealth of Nations" and I wished to finish it. I wished for two books "Bacon's Essays" and "Paleys Internal Evidences" but mother can not find them in either of the bookcases. I thought that, when I asked you whether we had them, you said yes. Did I misunderstand you? The Dr. told me that he thought me sufficiently advanced in my studies to begin some works upon ethics, and that I had better begin as soon as possible. I shall expect on Wednesday, the first of January, an answer to my letter of the 22d. A letter from you will be as good as a New year's present.[10]

II

Margaret received her New Year's letter, although it was not exactly a present. To his wife Timothy suggested that perhaps Margaret should spare her eyes a bit, while rejoicing that his two-year campaign in favor of *"useful books"* and against "frivolous" novels was having such a good effect. But to his daughter he addressed a more immediate issue—the aftermath of his decision, which she had carried out the week before "with much regret," to withdraw her from Dr. Park's school. He was not very clear about the reasons for this sudden turnabout. In his initial letter he primarily dwelt on the importance of Margaret's being discreet about it all. After suggesting she consult with her uncles Henry and Elisha about buying farewell presents for some of her schoolmates, he told her: "As you will soon part from some, to whom you may perhaps feel considerable attachment, and who may continue at the school, I advise you not to say that you never expect to return to the school; still less to suggest any dissatisfaction on *my part* with Dr. P.'s arrangements." It was only a little later on, when he discussed his plans for her to enroll again in the Port School, now taught by Mr. John Frost and attended by her brother Eugene, that he betrayed a hint of the concern that was on his mind. In this next school, he warned, "it will be prudent in you to be a little reserved . . . & by no means," he stressed, "display your attainments too soon, lest you should excite observation and incur dislike." To underline the word and the point—but without revealing anything he knew about her conduct at Dr. Park's—he added, "You are now at an age, especially of a *size,* when *great prudence* is indispensable, & I hope will by no means be found wanting."[11]

So, having been duly, if a little mysteriously, forewarned, Margaret returned for the next year and a half to mostly old patterns—off and on attending Latin classes at the Port School, studying by herself her French, Italian, and Greek, submitting to her father an occasional Latin translation for correction, sending him frequent letters (and receiving more corrections), hearing the recalcitrant Eugene recite in his "Liber Primus," dutifully practicing her piano, and helping her mother with sundry sewing and baby-tending tasks. She did begin one thing new that winter: she began to "go into society." It has sometimes been suggested that her father's Republican politics made this difficult for Margaret in Federalist Cambridge. There is no evidence for this at all. The heated partisan divisions that in earlier years, as her father once complacently remarked to her, had "kept assunder many agreeable & well bred families," had all but disappeared by then. Their family correspondence confirms this. Year after year it shows the Fullers constantly and easily socializing at "genteel" "galas and parties" with the Lowells, the Danas, the Higginsons, the Holmeses, the Gannetts, the Kirklands, the Storys, the Nortons, the Everetts, the Wares, the Farrars, the Frisbies, the Hedges, and others of the town's academic and professional (as Margaret's mother called them) *"patrician"* families. If the Fullers' ties with Boston's patricians were considerably more tenuous, they were at least somewhat sociable, as is shown by the occasional invitations they received to attend affairs of the Otises, the Websters, the Saltonstalls, and other leading Boston Federalist families. Then, too, Margaret's bustling uncles saw to it that they had their share of invitations to the city's major social and cultural fêtes. Whatever were the personal prejudices against the pushy Fuller brothers in Boston, they did not seem to have interfered appreciably with Margaret's social opportunities.[12]

Actually, her first real experience in these higher reaches was of her own making. At the suggestion of her uncles Elisha and Henry, she had asked her father two days after she withdrew from Dr. Park's for permission to invite about forty of her schoolmates to a dance and party to be held at their Cambridgeport house. ("The expense of it would not be great," she quoted her uncles as saying, "since suppers are not fashionable now.") After her father agreed, Elisha and Henry hired a violinist and a clarinetist, her frugal mother nervously doled out the fifty dollars needed to cover expenses, and Elisha and Margaret made up a long list of Cambridge adults and children to be invited. Unfortunately, though, like her social life in general at Dr. Park's, the party turned out be something between an awkward misfire and a disaster (depending on the account one chooses to believe). One indication of impending trouble was her touchiness over the guest list. "I think it is very rude," she wrote to her father, that of the ninety invitations sent out, she had thus far only "received nine answers," and the party was two days off. As it turned out, when the hour arrived, many of the Boston girls did not show up. Worst yet, according to Frederic Henry Hedge, who attended the affair, she gave "great offence" to her Cambridge girlfriends by paying "marked attention" to the Boston girls who did come. For three weeks, and through a dozen increasingly anxious letters, Margaret's father pestered her mother to give him her "promised account of SM.'s party," but he finally had to content himself with Henry's bland remark that it was "pleasant," Margaret's that it was "agreeable," her reported real feeling (as told to him by her mother) that she was "disappointed," and her mother's cryptic confession that she was "relieved" it was *"well over."*[13]

Margaret's party was on January 15. By then Cambridge's social life was in full swing, and Margaret, obviously undaunted, plunged in. Indeed there hardly seems to have been a party, ball, or cotillion that winter that she did *not* attend. Another difference from her childhood socializing—and perhaps partly another belated consequence of her experience at Dr. Park's school—was that, although she continued her intimacy with close girlfriends like Harriet Fay, she more and more associated, Hedge recalled, "with [a] much older set." Most of these were Harvard undergraduates and their female friends, but she also hobnobbed—at least at parties—with faculty members. Nor did she exactly try to conceal this from her parents. In her first letter to her father following her party, after a brusque one-sentence account of it, she switched immediately to this enthusiastic description of an obviously to her more congenial kind of social event:

> I went to a cotillon party in Cambridge last night. Your Lady would not consent to go and it was lucky she would not. I staid till after two and if she had staid as long, I do not know what would have become of the poor child. I had a delightful evening. Professor Hedge [Frederic Henry's father, Levi Hedge, College Professor of Logic and Metaphysics] told me "that you had obliged him exceedingly by sending him a packet of *Congressional Dockments.*" Elliot, Hilliard and Stearns were the Managers. Your three brothers attended. The gentlemen were almost all Southerners.

And on she chatted about "the gentlemen," their appearances, and their conversation.[14]

This sort of forwardness was not unique in antebellum America. These were years, as both contemporary memoirists and later historians have pointed out, when a great deal of age-mixing in schools, homes, and private and public entertainments was still quite common. These were also years when—according to

European travelers who claimed to be horrified by them—American children were encouraged by their parents to show the kind of outspokenness that befitted ambitious future republicans. This said, however (and one should not take the observations of European travelers completely at face value), it should also be said that even in this supposedly bumptious culture, Margaret's social forwardness stood out. To begin with, there was her appearance. At ten she had been (as she had boasted to her Grandmother Fuller) "a tall girl five feet two inches high," and now, "robust" at thirteen, Hedge recalled, she "passed for eighteen or twenty." She also suffered several adolescent blemishes—some permanent, like squinting at people to compensate for her nearsightedness, and others temporary, like the rash or possibly acne that her father called the "eruption on her face." These minor disfigurements bothered her parents (as their many references to the subject show), as they did her. But they also gave her a personal motive to shine socially. "Both [my parents]," she would later write (speaking of her "ugly and very painful flush" on her forehead), "were much mortified to see the fineness of my complexion destroyed— My own vanity was for a time severely wounded but I recovered and made up my mind to be bright and ugly." Even if she had not tried so hard, though, her reading and verbal facility would have made her a conspicuous figure in Cambridge society. And conspicuous she was. Hedge first saw her that winter when she was not yet thirteen, after he had just returned from studying in Germany and had started his junior year at Harvard. He was "amazed" at her intellectual sophistication and fluency. Adults also took notice. Dr. Abiel Holmes, her mother happily reported to her husband, spoke with her about Margaret "a great deal the other evening. . . . 'I see your daughter almost a lady in size.' He spoke of her talents, & acquirements in literature in very flattering terms."[15]

Not everyone who saw Margaret at these functions was quite as impressed with her as Hedge and Dr. Holmes. Her main difficulty seems to have been that same penchant for sarcasm and ridicule that had alienated some of her Boston schoolmates. "It frightened shy young people from her presence," Hedge recalled, "and made her, for a while, notoriously unpopular with the ladies of her circle." And not only young ladies, but a number of the Fullers' adult friends, too. At this, her parents began to sit up and take notice. "She certainly begins to think herself a Lady among the Beaux," her mother wrote to her father around the time she was finishing at Dr. Park's. She then proceeded to describe a recent scene at their house during which Margaret had summarily dismissed the recently graduated young schoolmaster Mr. Frost, who for a long time had been begging her to show him some of her themes. "He looked surprised & I was amazed at the girl's daring. What do you think of such a beginning from this hopeful of ours." Her husband's reaction was sharp but flippant: "She should not take too great liberty with Mr. F. as he may make reprisal with the ferule, when she is his scholar." He was not so flippant three weeks later when he received a letter from Margaret ridiculing his "modish and fashionable" sisters Martha and Sally for criticizing her for dressing wrongly on the way to a wedding reception and then, once they got there, appearing foolishly dressed themselves.

"Your account," he coughed dryly, "is entertaining, but I think you should not exult in happening to be dressed suitably, when it seems to imply ridicule of your seniors, & especially when those seniors are near relatives." It was not a ferrule blow, but a sharp tap, nonetheless.[16]

Meanwhile, her parents had other worries on their minds. First, they were beginning to hear bitter complaints from Sally as well as several of Margaret's other aunts that Margaret (as her mother reported in a worried letter to her husband) was "too independent" of their authority. More ominously, not only Sally but also Abraham and a number of his brothers—who were often quite free in dispensing advice concerning Margaret's schools, entertainments, and even her clothing—were starting to raise questions about Margaret's entire "*habits* & education . . . freely, & frequently,*" Margaret's mother anxiously reported, both among themselves and with other relatives. And—most ominously—family and friends were even beginning to cast a cold eye on Margaret's active socializing. This last particularly worried Margaret's father. In the previous two seasons, he had been all for Margaret's coming out. ("Did SM. take her share of the dancing? I hope she did & that she will have as much relish for that innocent occupation as her Mother.") But now, when Margaret was thirteen, he was having serious second thoughts. "Abraham," he reported to his wife at the beginning of the second winter after Margaret's return, "says S. Margarett is no *small* child, and Mr. Fay in his letter recv'd yesterday, says he hears much of her being in company, &c. Perhaps we may think it best for her to keep more at the domestic hearth a few years yet." And, a few weeks later, he asked, "How did you send S. Margarett to Boston & bring her home? I hope the good girl danced moderately & returned early; that is the way to preserve health & obtain the approbation of the wise. She has too much sense I trust to wish to cheapen her value by too frequent appearance in company." Finally, by the season's end, he dispensed with argument altogether and simply said that he hoped the cotillions were at last over, but even if they were not, he was sure that "S Margarett must be too discreet to wish to attend."[17]

Obviously Timothy Fuller was concerned for Margaret's social life. And Margaret's mother? After all, even those New England fathers who took it as their special role to oversee the intellectual development of their daughters, usually turned over to the mother the main responsibility for their social and moral training. Not so, however, Higginson adamantly insisted (and many others have echoed him ever since) with Margaret. "It is the testimony of those who then knew the family well," he flatly asserted, that Margaret's father's exclusive domination of his daughter "did not stop with the world of books," but extended to, indeed enveloped, her manners and morals as well. "Had Margaret an invitation, her father decided whether it should be accepted, and suggested what she should wear; did she receive company at home, he made out the lists; and when the evening came, he and his daughter received them: the mother only casually appearing, a shy and dignified figure in the background."[18]

Higginson was generally a shrewd commentator on Margaret Fuller's social world, and there is little question that this in fact was probably pretty much how

Margaret and her parents appeared to friends and observers. Family letters, however, tell a more complicated story. To begin with, they show that her mother was quite concerned—for better or worse—about Margaret's social standing. It was her mother, for example, and not her father, who fretted about the *"respectability"* of her Boston dancing school and whether she would find there the right "sort of people." Again, it was her mother who, while her father was away, had to make, however timidly, the day-to-day decisions about whether or not Margaret should go to this or that party or dance. And her letters show she was greatly—even more than her husband—worried about Margaret's morals and "deportment."[19]

Still, when it came to actually intervening with Margaret on these last matters in this critical year, her mother, as her letters show, checked herself. These were unusually demanding times for her. Her father had died the year before; in the winter she developed a tumor in her breast; and, although it eventually healed after being opened, her health for the next couple of years was not good. Also, the previous August, while Margaret was at Dr. Park's, Margaret's mother gave birth to a third son, Arthur, and two years later to a fourth son, Richard. Her letters around this time show her often *"mournful"* (as Margaret described her) over the constant rounds of nursing, wet-nursing, child-care, and other household responsibilities without, for much of the year, support from her husband. In addition, her husband was authoritative and even overbearing when he *was* home, and this, too, probably made her less interventionist with Margaret. But what influenced her the most in her treatment of Margaret at this time, her letters show, was Margaret's treatment—as she saw it—of *her*. "She is so opinionative that it is extremely difficult to direct her studies," she complained to her husband in one letter the second winter after Margaret's departure from Dr. Park's. And, in another letter written around the same time, even more revealingly, she described for the benefit of her husband a recent evening spent with a neighbor and friend of the family. "He wished SM to sing, & nothing could be more repulsive than her manner of refusing. Her *manner* is often such to pain me excessively and all my arguments *seem* lost upon her." Then, after complaining some more about her "affectionate" but "extremely opinionative and unyielding . . . disposition now," she finally added, "She is ambitious of *your* praise and often says she wishes she knew what *you* would advise." Faced with Margaret's rebelliousness, her mother used two ploys. Rather than directly advising Margaret in social matters—which she did only occasionally—she urged her to follow her father's advice. "You well know my dear child your father's *views & wishes* on this subject" was, in one form or another (even, as in this instance about novel reading and card playing, when she had strong opinions about an issue herself) a leitmotif in her advice to Margaret at this time. When this failed, she appealed to her husband to intervene—as she did repeatedly that year. She was hardly a passive onlooker, but her influence was severely limited.[20]

If, then, it was left to Margaret's father to mediate between society's demands and his daughter's burgeoning social aggressiveness, the obvious question is: what precisely were those demands that were beginning to worry Margaret's parents seriously? Certainly one of her father's biggest worries, his letters show, was that Margaret's haughty, critical attitude toward other young people was fast alienating her peers. Both parents were obviously also concerned about negative adult judgments of Margaret. Clearly not all early nineteenth-century American adults were quite as indulgent toward youthful presumptuousness as many European travelers thought they were. Even liberal Unitarian parents like the Fullers mixed with their rationalism and encouragement to autonomy and aggression a sufficient amount of intrusive moralism to have made growing up a fairly complicated affair. Also, it should not be forgotten that Margaret was a girl and, as such, potentially subject to myriad special constraints. These included the constantly reiterated opinions in magazines and advice books that a woman's only legitimate place was in the home and that her only true personality consisted of the womanly virtues of piety, passivity, submissiveness, and sexual purity. In America these burdens were made all the more difficult for many middle-class young women to bear because of the stark contrast—astutely noted by Alexis de Tocqueville—between these womanly ideals and the relative freedom they had often enjoyed in their girlhood. Nor did young women always have to wait until marriage to experience this contrast. In the early nineteenth century, the popular tendency seems to have been to grant middle-class young men a prolonged period of youth before settling down and channeling their aggression into an appropriate career. But precisely because no such opportunities were available to girls, the crisis years for them, when they were thought to be most subject to threats to the successful internalization of their proper feminine role, were pushed back to puberty and were defined often in quasi-sexual terms. As a recent historian of American youth in this period has written, "A society which failed to provide a significant social role for women outside of marriage had difficulty envisioning girls passing through a protracted period of adjustment to responsibility, but no trouble recognizing the threat to female virtue posed by the onset of sexual maturity."[21]

Of course gender conventions were not always Margaret's father's strongest suit. He had, after all, practically since her infancy, been generally heedless of prevailing gender ideas about what was proper in her education. This is not to say, however, that Margaret's father was altogether unmindful of the ways of the world in these matters. In a letter to his wife about this time, he sympathized with a poor colleague of his, who had "four *daughters* of whom only one is handsome," and, worse yet, who had been so indiscreet as to send them all into society at the same time, thus producing "his whole *stock in trade* at once" and spoiling "the chance of them all." Nor were potential threats to Margaret's sexual reputation exactly foreign to his consciousness. Three years earlier, he had told his wife to read in the newspaper a story about a local woman's "elopement & return, with her husband's unrelenting cruelty. It is an affecting instance of the infatuation of some of our hapless species." He added that the story and the prefatory lines "'Home, sweet home'" deserve to be "learned by heart. I think Sarah Margaret will think so too & will commit the lines to memory." Considering Margaret was all of nine-and-a-half at the time, one cannot accuse her father of being excessively relaxed about the subject.[22]

Still, the fact remains that when Timothy Fuller decided to alter somewhat the character of preadolescent Margaret's education, the reason was not only that he feared society's wrath, but also that he, too, held, along with his liberal ideas about female education, some fairly traditional attitudes about a woman's proper social role. His notion, for example, of exactly what a woman ought to be for a man seems to have been pretty much the conventional schoolboy one he had articulated in his college orations. "Agreeable," "amiable," "delicate," "handsome," "always smiling"—these and few others are the adjectives of praise that appear over and over again in his diary. Probably his most nuanced statement of his feminine social ideal was his early description in his diary of what he liked about his favorite sister, Debby (and clearly, later, also his wife): "docility without surrendering her judgment too far." Sometimes he showed a spark of self-consciousness. In one diary entry, for example, around this time, he mentioned recently meeting at Mrs. John Quincy Adams's a woman famed for her accomplishments and European travels, but having, it seemed to him, "a little too much confidence for *nice* delicacy," adding that "perhaps I am *too* nice however in my notions." Still, the qualification underlined his prejudice. Furthermore, even the most radical side of Timothy Fuller's view of women—his belief in their potential intellectuality—had its conservative aspect. In particular, like virtually all supporters of advanced female education before the mid–nineteenth century, Margaret's father could not even conceive of, let alone consider legitimate, any kind of female education that was irrelevant to or destructive of a girl's future domestic role. Indeed, it was precisely Timothy Fuller's enlightened pastoral, republican devotion to the family as *the* institutional source of individual virtue that is the key to understanding his whole outlook for Margaret. On one hand, this was what had led him to assume in the first place much of Margaret's education himself, in the Lockean belief that home education was superior to the kind of education for display that he thought was too much encouraged in both schools for boys *and* schools for girls. On the other hand, it now led him to recoil at the prospect of Margaret's turning that domestic enlightenment into a means of social display and power far beyond the sphere of the pristine, paternalistic household that had originally nourished it.[23]

And so, in the months after Margaret returned from Boston and began going into society, her father's admonitions began to show a very definite shift of emphasis. Not only, that is, did he try to discourage her excessive socializing, but along with her studies, still not forgotten ("Does Sarah Margt. study Greek?—does she teach Eugene Latin?"), more and more he began to place equal weight on the importance of docile manners and domestic pursuits. "Nothing can be nearer my heart," he had written to her as a sort of forewarning the previous year, "than to see you fast improving in your manners & disposition—in your habits of neatness & regularity, no less than in your acquirements of literature. . . . I hope," he added rather menacingly, "you will *be pleased* to have me touch the same subject very frequently." So he did, and not just to Margaret; but also, by the following year, in almost weekly letters to her mother. "I hope S Margt. applies herself to her musick & her sewing as well as to her Greek," he urged in one letter. In another he pointedly asked, "What are Sarah M.'s *employments* &

studies? The needle & the arrangements of her chamber are not forgotten I hope." And in yet another he approved buying her a new bonnet "if her improvements in *neatness* and in all other respects merit it, as I hope they do."[24]

Both sides of Timothy Fuller's thoughts on these matters—both, that is, what he thought proper in the education of a girl and what he deemed necessary in the making of a woman—must have seemed to him perfectly reasonable and thoroughly consistent. Perhaps they might have even seemed so to Margaret, had it not been for certain stubborn psychological facts. In the first place, since early childhood, Margaret had been identified—both by herself and by everyone else in the family—as her father's special child. And this fact—along with the gradual withdrawal of her articulate but self-effacing mother as a figure of authority over her—had bred in her a pride and assertiveness that mere ideology or social pressure could not simply wipe away overnight. Finally, however clear the difference between intellect and social role was in her father's mind, the fact remains that her father's most important exhortations to her had never been, strictly speaking, purely intellectual. They had also included a core of tough-minded personal goals, particularly ambition and great achievement—hardly the sorts of goals that could be easily reconciled with the kind of docility and domesticity her father was now coming to insist on. Indeed, even as he now demanded social discretion, he continued to press on her not just learning—which by itself might have supported a more conservative posture—but also, according to those who knew him well, verbal brilliance and even the very social display that at other times he tried so hard to discourage. Caroline Healey Dall, a younger follower of Margaret Fuller's, many years later reported an anecdote of William C. Todd's, a colleague of Margaret's father, about Margaret at this time that nicely illustrates this. Margaret was about fourteen, Todd recalled, and he had stopped by the Fuller house to discuss some important political matter with her father and observed the following little scene: "Margaret sat apart apparently occupied with a book open upon her knee. At some moment Mr Fuller said 'Margaret what have you to say about this?' She lifted her eyes for a moment and gave him an answer, good, full of common sense, but such as many people might have given. 'Is this the best that you can say?' returned her father. She started, laid down her book, and instantly recast her thought, giving the same idea but a most eloquent statement!" Todd went away, he remembered, "much impressed" and wondering "at the marvellous training which had made the re-cast of thought possible."[25]

III

Perhaps none of these contradictions would have developed into a really major conflict, however, or at least not so quickly, had it not been for one very practical question that soon needed to be answered: what was to be done about Margaret's schooling? By the beginning of 1824, she would have been without a regular, full-time school for over a year, a prospect that neither Margaret nor her parents seem to have envisioned for her when she abruptly withdrew from Dr. Park's. If anything, Margaret seems to have been even more concerned about the situation than her parents. In her letter to her father on December 18, she sent, along with an account of her readings in Cicero and Tacitus, the same message she would repeat throughout the winter: she studied Greek but needed instruction; she wanted a companion in study; she needed, above all, "to facilitate my progress ... in the languages," to be sent to school. The school she wished to be sent to was that of Boston's leading progressive schoolmaster, George B. Emerson. Having resigned from his principalship at the English Classical School, he had just recently opened his school for girls on Beacon Street. Innovative and prestigious, Emerson's school would have been both socially familiar and intellectually helpful.[26]

Margaret's parents, however, had a very different idea of the best kind of school for her—Miss Susan Prescott's Young Ladies' Seminary at Groton. Although short-lived, Miss Prescott's school was in its day a fairly famous institution in Massachusetts. The twenty-seven-year-old eldest daughter of Judge James Prescott, she had opened the school in 1820 and continued it until 1829, when she married John Wright, a Harvard graduate and a lawyer. From an advertisement in Boston's *Columbian Centinel* for April 10, 1824, we learn that the subjects taught at the school included "Orthography, Reading, Poetry and Prose, Writing, English grammar; Geography, ancient and modern, Arithmetic, Projection of Maps, History, Composition, Rhetoric, Logic, Natural and Intellectual Philosophy, Geometry, Astronomy, Chemistry, Botany, French Language." Considering the fact that all these were taught entirely by Susan Prescott herself or her younger sister and assistant Mary Oliver, this is a rather breathtaking list. It was, however, standard fare for female seminaries, which, like the male academies they were modeled on, often sacrificed depth for coverage for their non–college-bound students. Also standard was the absence of Latin and Greek, a lack widely defended on the grounds either that they were too hard for girls or that they were irrelevant to a sex excluded from the learned professions. Finally, most of these seminaries shared with Miss Prescott's several conservative, non-academic features. Like most of the male academies, they were often located in remote rural areas where the surrounding countryside was thought to provide the most suitable setting for the protection of innocence and the inculcation of virtue. Likewise comforting to traditional yet modern parents, their elaborate rules and regulations for their student boarders were supposed to guarantee a uniquely efficient kind of "family" (and the analogy was often emphasized) to do the inculcating. In addition, female seminaries were generally thought to have had certain special responsibilities in molding their female charges into model young women. Consequently, along with their academic offerings, almost all included courses on the domestic and ornamental arts designed to prepare their scholars for their future roles as wives and mothers.[27]

To be sure, Miss Prescott's seminary had a few unusual characteristics. Since both Susan Prescott and most of her clientele were upper-middle-class Unitarians, Miss Prescott's had none of the revivalistic religious excitements that were encouraged at many of the evangelical female seminaries. Instead, Miss Prescott organized plays, gymnastics, and other extracurricular activities rarely found in the more conservative seminaries. Otherwise, though, Miss Prescott's seems to have been fairly typical. Social life, by all accounts, was just as carefully regulated as at the more orthodox schools. Presumably Miss Prescott herself faithfully executed her pledge to devote a major part of her attention "to the manners, morals and habits of all the pupils who are confided to her care." Nor in the matter of true womanhood did Miss Prescott evidently deviate much from the norm. Besides an instructor in music and dancing, the Prescott seminary boasted as its fourth teacher a woman whose whole duty it was to teach "plain and various kinds of ornamental Needle Work, Drawing and Painting."[28]

If the idea of sending Margaret to Miss Prescott's did not exactly threaten to reverse her educational progress entirely, it certainly threatened to alter its content, especially in the area that had been, up to this time, its center—her classical studies. In particular, were she actually to go to Miss Prescott's, she would have to discontinue her Latin readings, abandon her Italian, and give up any hope of learning more Greek—the very studies, she implicitly reminded her father in several letters, that made her want to be sent to school in the first place. These were persuasive arguments, and for a long time he wavered. On December 24, he wrote to Margaret that "I rather incline to Miss Prescott's," but to his wife, as late as March 2, after getting another plea from Margaret on behalf of Mr. Emerson's school, he sounded unsure. "It would indeed be a painful thing to have my eldest daughter *far away* all the summer." Meanwhile, his brothers and sisters, particularly the unmarried Sally and Abraham, pressed the case to him in favor of Margaret's going to Miss Prescott's. But the person who was most adamant about her going was Margaret's heretofore nonassertive mother, who was suddenly beginning to panic about the kind of daughter her husband's tutelage had produced. "Do not give her the least encouragement of attending school in Boston again at present," she wrote almost furiously on March 16 in answer to her husband's recent tentative talk. "Her thoughts are sufficiently engrossed with company, beaux &c for a lady of 25, & I think now she should learn something of *real* and *varied* life or she will never have any liberal enlarged *practical* views of any thing useful in this world." But her concern was not just with Margaret's sexual forwardness and lack of domesticity. Harvard undergraduate culture was remarkably rambunctious. Nearly two-thirds of the entire last class had been expelled the previous year in the worst rebellion the college had ever experienced. Her mother feared such events would somehow feed Margaret's general iconoclasm and irreverence, and she wanted her farther away from the place. Taking her cue from the educationally reform-minded, but theologically conservative and socially priggish young George Bancroft, she wrote: "George Bancroft told SM. that a young man must possess 'salamander qualities' to pass thro' *our* University & be *at all* religious. This is too true almost[;] serious subjects are treated with contempt by the sons of Harvard & it is no advantage in a *moral point of view* to SM. to have much intercourse with students at her age." She concluded this reactionary *cri de coeur* with a ringing resolution: "I am so well convinced that we have *erred* in our system of educating SM. that I intend with your excellent advice [to] reform our method as much as possible." Finally, the following week, she made one last plea: "Do not listen to feelings dearest Timothy but to your judgment & knowledge of her *deficiencies*."[29]

He did. Although not quite as confident as his wife that Miss Prescott's was "our best course & hers" ("I *persevere* in fortitude thro' this conviction, or I could not *appear* so *cruel* to her," she told him), he certainly shared his wife's view of their daughter's deficiencies. And so, in his first full letter to her on the subject on December 24, he betrayed nothing of the uncertainty he had indicated to his wife, but instead supported her mother's preference in no uncertain terms. The arguments he marshaled were decidedly not academic. "I am certain," he bluntly informed her, "that you are in need of some of the instruction & feminine discipline which Miss P. is sure to excel in." Warming to the subject, though no more specifically, he went on to say that there were many things which Miss Prescott could inculcate "in regards to manners, female *propriety,* & disposition." He even threw into the argument the question of her complexion, saying that if she were to attend Mr. Emerson's school, she would frequently have to ride into Boston, "for I should grieve to have your complexion ruined past remedy by exposure to the heat & violent exercise." Reminding her of some prescribed lotion for her skin, he then went on to criticize her spelling and handwriting; some errors, he wrote, were "intolerable." He concluded with a plea: "You can never know how near my heart it is that you should become a young lady of *prepossessing manners* & *estimable character*. At the bottom of such a character I have often assured you must be *virtue* & *religion*." At this point he alluded to a story, which he said was unworthy of repeating, about the profaneness of a colleague of his in attending prayer, and so closed the letter.[30]

If by this rather crabbed and rambling, though obviously heartfelt, communiqué Timothy Fuller hoped to lay to rest the issue of his daughter's schooling, he could not have been more disappointed. In her answer on January 25, she began immediately: "I should very much prefer going to Mr Emerson's on every account." One account that clearly concerned her was the very thing her parents hoped Miss Prescott's School would facilitate—the curtailment of her bumptious socializing. "I was very happy," she informed her father about a recent Boston party directly after stating her preference for Emerson's school; "I am passionately fond of dancing and there is none at all in Cambridge except at the Cotillon parties." From there—as if to advertise the very social traits her parents feared—she ridiculed an unfortunate miss for her bad singing and "silly and affected" manner; chatted on about dancing with young George Ripley, who had just graduated first in his class, Edward Emerson, Ralph Waldo Emerson's brilliant younger brother, and other notable young Harvard men; and concluded by listing all the young Cambridge ladies who were going to an upcoming cotillion party, adding—in case he missed the point—"Indeed all the young ladies of my age in Cambridge except Harriette Alston, H Fay and poor Sarah M. Fuller are going, and Sarah M. is going to Groton next summer and in all human probability will not go to a dance this two years." She made one concession: "If you wish it, I am willing to go, only, I hope you will not keep me there very long."[31]

Even this reluctant resignation did not last. For in her very next letter, on February 22, she asked again for instruction and a companion in studying Greek, again asked to be sent to school, and stated again her wish to be sent to Mr. Emerson's. She closed by reminding her father that if she was forced to go to Miss Prescott's, she would "not see you the whole year round." Her impending rustication—as well as, no doubt, its connection with her father's apparent new critical views of her social manners—seems to have raised in Margaret's mind, as she brooded about these things that winter, a recurrent and devastating concern: whether her father loved her any more. "I wrote her immediately," he noted in his diary, "assuring her that I loved as I shall ever love a dutiful child. She has fine talents & has made great progress in her studies considering her age." In fact, as he actually wrote it, his letter on April 3 was in essence a more tactful and coherent version of his initial letter of December 24. After expressing his pride in her and giving her the ultimate praise of her letter ("It was so fairly written, that at the first glance I thought it was from Miss Kilshaw"), he put the case for Miss Prescott's School on the highest classical republican, agrarian grounds. "A few months with a judicious country lady, who will be *free* & *faithful* in watching & correcting your faults, & in imparting a relish for *rural scenes,* & rural *habits,* & rural *society,* may & must contribute immensely to your immediate *worth,* & to your permanent happiness." He also stressed, more clearly than before, the value of Miss Prescott's school in helping her acquire "a discreet, modest, unassuming deportment. These qualities," he reminded her, "are indispensable to endear any one, especially a young lady to her friends, & to obtain the 'world's good word'—than which few things are more desirable, this side of Heaven. I would not willingly suppose you inferior to Harriet Fay or Elizabeth Ware [a daughter of Henry Ware, Sr., the Hollis Professor of Divinity at Harvard and a social friend of Margaret's] in good sense, discretion, and *observation;* but I should be VERY much gratified to find your *deportment* exhibit as much true tact, as theirs. . . . Depend upon my undiminished affection," he assured her in closing, "as long as you continue dutiful."[32]

However (as usual) conditionally affectionate, her father's instructive letter does seem to have at least calmed Margaret down some. "Sarah M. . . . yesterday . . . brought your most affectionate letter to herself," his wife wrote to him on April 10. "She was as much gratified as I ever saw her with any mark of your favor, & I found she had braced up her mind to follow your advice even to 'banishment' from home & 'civilized society.'" To this she added a little less hopefully, "*Your* consent to her going to Groton I found was not expected by her but I much discern a resolution to acquiesce cheerfully even thro' her silence, & tears." Actually, her still-simmering pique and displeasure was not far from the surface, and it soon set off, with the term only weeks away, one final exchange of blasts from father and daughter. First Margaret, on the nineteenth:

> I thank you most sincerely for the assurances of your continued affection, which
> have set my heart at ease. I shall willingly go to Groton for the summer, at your
> pleasure, though nothing else could in the least reconcile me to it. I shall entirely

depend upon an immediate visit from you according to your promise.... How much I regret to leave this charming place, where I am beloved and go to one where I am an entire stranger and where I must behave entirely by rule. I hope you have no intention of keeping me there four years. My very affectionate Aunt Fuller and my excellent uncles wish me to stay four years. But I hope *you* are not quite so anxious to get rid of your *little* daughter.

To which her father quickly responded on the twenty-fourth:

Your reluctance to go "among strangers" cannot too soon be overcome; & the way to overcome it, is not to remain *at home,* but to go among them and resolve to *deserve* & obtain the love & esteem of those, who have never before known you. With them you have a fair opportunity to *begin the world anew,* to avoid the mistakes & faults, which have deprived you of *some esteem,* among your present acquaintances.

And so it was, with her father's sharply worded revolutionary admonition and farewell no doubt reverberating in her mind, that Margaret prepared to set off for the six-hour stagecoach ride to Groton.[33]

IV

As Miss Prescott's was formally to open on May 12, 1824, Margaret's arrival with her Uncle Elisha the day before gave her just enough time to settle into her room and take in her new surroundings. It is true, she conceded, when she wrote to her father on May 21, that "this part of the country is exceedingly beautiful." But otherwise her tone in this first letter was a bit downcast and obviously still a little resentful. Addressing him the only time in her correspondence as "Dear Sir," she wrote, "I am contented here, which I think is as much as could be expected." Although she was generally neutral-to-positive about most of her fellow boarders, she did mention (though she canceled the line) that one of her roommates was "a very disagreeable girl, whom I would not tolerate except to please Miss Prescott." But it was for her studies that she saved her sharpest barbs. Even many years later, she would still write acerbically about her teachers, who foolishly "believed that exercise of memory was study." In her letter to her father she put it less philosophically, but no more charitably: "I feel myself rather degraded from Cicero's oratory to One and two are how many? It *is* rather a change is it not?" Actually Margaret's studies included one of Warren Colburn's acclaimed "inductive" arithmetic textbooks and two widely assigned college texts, Professor Hedge's *Elements of Logick* and Hugh Blair's *Lectures on Rhetoric and Belles Lettres.* Of the last two she only said, "I do not believe [they] will do any good except as exercise of the memory, but Miss Prescott knows best, of course." Finally, she was obviously not too sure about Miss Prescott, for she immediately added, "I wish you would write to Miss Prescott, for I do not know myself exactly what were your wishes with regard to the course of my studies." She closed by asking him to send her copy of *Paradise Lost* and her Bible.[34]

Margaret's father's first response to this no doubt not entirely welcome letter was as sanguine as he could make it. He and her mother were very pleased to perceive, he wrote on May 25, "by the cheerful tone of your remarks that your situation is in a good degree agreeable." He ignored (if he was able to read it) her canceled comment on her roommate, and simply said hopefully, "I know you will cultivate *benevolence* towards all even the disagreeable, if any should unexpectedly cross your path." He then gave a presumably exemplary account of his congressional mess, which, as he went along, became increasingly critical until it ended with the unbenevolent observation, "This last sketch by a cynick would be far more harshly drawn." About Margaret's study complaints, he was also a bit shaky. She should be happy to go back to "the first rudiments" of mathematics, he told her, because they would train her to fix her attention and to advance "by regular graduations" in that "noble science. That 'one & one makes two,' & that 'a part is less than the whole,'" he added sententiously, "are truths not unworthy of the notice even of a Newton, & were by him duly noted in his journey to the 'Principia.'" Dropping Newton, he added that he did want her to find six hours a week to devote privately to her Latin and Italian studies. His next letter, written a few days later—probably after giving these matters some thought—was both more ebullient and more critical. "Now tell me, Sarah M.," he gamely began, "if you are not nearly reconciled to this agreeable country life—surrounded by so many agreeable objects, & in the very center of innocent cheerfulness, frank & graceful manners, & at the same time so amply provided with means of improvement." From this fanciful pastoral sketch he quickly got down to cases: "I assure you, that I expect not only a vast addition to your present stock of knowledge, commonly so called; but more especially to the *little* you now possess of *self knowledge*—that is an acquaintance with those peculiarities & defects, which are so difficult to learn, & the knowledge of which is so indispensable in giving a value, a *real* value, to your character." And from cases to anticlimax: he wished that she would always mention the dates of his letters as received, and after she read them, "fold & label them as I have shown you, & tie them carefully up in a file."[35]

Margaret's initial reaction to her father's pronouncements was, perhaps predictably, not exactly "agreeable." She wrote wondering where all the news in his letters had gone, and to her mother she complained that her father no longer bothered to send his love. Meanwhile her mother added her voice to the father–daughter duet. What this revealed was pretty much what the family argument about Miss Prescott's school had suggested: that despite her strong feelings and opinions about Margaret, the role she usually assumed or was left with was secondary and rather awkward. Much of her time was spent simply reassuring Margaret about her father's affection. "You *cannot* think my dear child," she typically wrote, "because your father omitted to 'send my love' to you that you are less remembered and loved than you *could wish*." Occasionally she took a more authoritative stance, but usually, as before, she did so in such a way as to orient Margaret toward her father—or now Miss Prescott. "Cherish a recollection of your father's excellent advice, and conform to Miss Prescott's excellent good sense" was a frequent plea of hers. And even when her advice was more specific, she preferred, whether out of timidity or sensitivity, to veil her points in subterfuge. "Cherish in your mind the love of your fellow creatures, & above all perfect integrity," she wrote to her that fall. "I do not *exhort* you to this because I think you in the least deficient . . . , but my thoughts are on a certain individual who would be altogether lovely with this single deficiency supplied." Finally, she usually abandoned even these circumlocutions in favor of endearments, local gossip, anxious concern for Margaret's health or clothing, or—perhaps most frequently—vaguely worded injunctions to turn her thoughts to the "Divine truths of the Gospel" for the elevation of her spirits. "Cultivate religious principles my dear child," she characteristically wrote, "and all good things will be added."[36]

Compared with her mother's social advice during her stay at Miss Prescott's, Margaret's father's admonitions were blunt, didactic, and, as always, obsessively critical. They were also sometimes highly provocative. Margaret's initial complaint about the lack of news in his letters, for example, elicited this extended sarcasm about her lack of interest in the very unbenevolent world of politics:

> It is difficult to recollect, when in the very act of writing, any thing which *you* would consider news. For instance you have no inclination to hear, that Mr. Crawford [William H. Crawford, President Monroe's Secretary of the Treasury and a contender against Adams in the ongoing presidential campaign] has had a shock of the palsy—& a still severer attack from Mr. Ninian Edwards—that the electoral law of Massachusetts was deserted by the Speaker, Mr. Jarvis, at a critical moment, by which many thought its passage was endangered. These things are unimportant to you;—you would prefer hearing of some negotiation or treaty of marriage, to those between nations; & the rivalry of beaux or beauties would more affect you than the defeat of Mr. Chas McCarty [Sir Charles MacCarthy, British governor of the Gold Coast] by the Ashantees in Africa.[37]

Of course Margaret's father was not just a somewhat contradictory advice machine (although he sometimes seemed that way to Margaret). He also kept her supplied with abundant clothes, books, newspapers, sheet music, "entertaining" literary magazines, and—at least after her initial complaints—family and society news. Also some of his proddings—for example, toward self-examination and social benevolence—were probably useful, perhaps even necessary. But there was still one difficulty with all this advice. Although he stressed over and over again in his letters "the *very great* value of benevolent & charitable feelings toward all your sex & especially those of your own age," he said virtually nothing (apart from urging her to keep a diary) about how or, more important, why she should acquire them. All he could suggest was that she feel differently for the sake of behavior, so that "*such* feelings . . . will prevent you from putting on an unfavorable construction upon anything *said* or *done* by them—from speaking of them with ridicule or contempt, or even with an *innuendo*." In other words, he urged on Margaret not real introspection or benevolence, but a kind of Franklinesque social wariness—or just the sort of enlightened artificial check he had learned to inflict upon himself in his own youth. Indeed, the only really transcendent ideal he seems to have put forth was (despite his occasional claims to Margaret that religion was at the bottom of all moral virtues) less Christian than

Augustan—and a rather attenuated Augustan ideal at that. "Let your approbation & *affection,*" he intoned—warning her against her (as he thought) equally
deplorable proneness "to speedy & strong predilections & attachments to your
female acquaintances"—"be so measured & adjusted as to have its proper
value."[38]

In sum, if there was one approach least likely to succeed with the kind of ambitious and passionate young girl that Margaret was fast growing up to be, it was
this latest one of her father's. Margaret's letters were by no means overtly rebellious. On the contrary, after the first month or so, she ceased all complaints and
grumblings about her situation and seemed—at least on the basis of everything
she said—well contented with both her school and her schoolmates. But what
did soon appear was something that was in the long run perhaps more subversive
than rebellion—a newly independent, even irreverent, tone as she adapted and
reshaped her father's values to meet her own personality. Did he criticize, for
example, her tendency toward exaggerated attachments? She wrote him of her
changed opinion of Miss Prescott and that she now adored her. Did he ridicule
her fondness for local gossip? She asked him several letters later to write what
was interesting to him and what he thought would please him and, by the way,
to send her a newspaper whenever he could, as they gave her "more pleasure to
read them, than you, who live where they make the news, can easily imagine,"
adding, for good measure: "The good people of C. [which she had recently vis-
ited] were wonderfully pleased when pretty Sarah McKean married that stupid,
awkward man; I was told that no event had enlivened them so much for a year."
Did he chide her for her lack of interest in affairs of state? She wrote him several
months later, when the presidential campaign was approaching its climax, that
she suspected by "the Stoical tone of indifference and calmness which you would
assume that the hopes of Mr Adams's friends are not so high as formerly," and
went on to ask if "the General" ever reminded him of his fiercely anti-Jackson
Seminole speech; she reread it the other day, she said. Finally, did he continue
to prod her about her studies at Miss Prescott's? She informed him in January
that this term she studied "Geo Enfields Philosophy, Chemistry and Lord
Kames's Criticisms," but would be glad when she was finished and could go back
to "my beloved study, the languages. Not that this is disagreeable to me but I
love them best"—a position she stuck to despite her father's rejoinder that the
study of languages was useful, "but rather as an *instrument* of knowledge than
knowledge itself."[39]

It is true that her continuing inability to impress her father with the value of
her interests obviously continued to irritate her—as also did his still fairly frequent criticisms of some of her personal habits. But by the middle of the second
term, even about these subjects she began to strike up a new note of critical
detachment. On February 6, for example, or a month and a half after Margaret
returned from her winter vacation in Cambridge (and two days before he wrote
his wife describing Margaret's letter as "playful and animated"), her father sent
her a heavily admonitory letter about her letter and her writing. He reminded
her to acknowledge all his letters by date, to record her health in each, to remem-

ber his lessons in "chirography," and, above all, to avoid both *"stiffness"* (*"this is not your fault,"* he inserted) and "extravagant panegyrick." ("A just taste in writing letters, as well as conversation, does not come by chance, but is the fruit of cultivation.") He then added, pointedly, "In looking at some of my letters written when in College & since, I was lately very much mortified to find them studied & quaint, not however in general liable to the charge of *slovenliness.*" In her reply on the fourteenth, Margaret fired off the following message—half-teasing, half-satirical, and, all in all, a good indication of the direction in which she was tending as she approached her fifteenth year. She began by explaining that she could not have acknowledged the receipt of a recent letter of his because it did not arrive until after she wrote hers, and continued:

> I believe, papa, if you will take the trouble to overlook my letters, that you will find (though, I confess, my general want of that exactitude necessary to please *men* of *business* may have given you just reason to suspect me) that I *have endeavored* to comply with your wishes in this respect, as far as I know them; the receipt is always mentioned, I fancy though perhaps the dates may not be. I will try to remember in future. . . . I should always, as you have desired send you word how I do, but when I reperuse the letter, these formal notices of my health and well being look *so* egotistical, they remind me so forcibly of the invariable beginning of the little girl's letters with whom I used to go to school "I take this opportunity to inform you that we are all well and hoping that you enjoy the same blessing." Besides, mon cher pere, you do not conform to your own rule; not once this winter have you told me whether you are well, ill, or indifferent. However, if you wish it 'tis enough, here it comes without any more prosing. "J' ai un rhume avec une tous qui me génent beaucoup, d' ailleurs, je me trouve asser bien."
>
> By the emphasis laid on the word slovenliness I see what you think of my letters. I confess that I do not bestow on you that attention that I do on other correspondents, who will I think be more critical and less kind. I have abused your indulgence I own. I must request that you will burn my letters, all that you have, let this affair of confessions, extenuations and palliations share the common lot: and I will in future assume a *fairer outer* guise at least in my epistles though this matter may not recommend them more highly to your eye, mind's eye I mean. Indeed, I cannot make myself interesting to you; to your strictures on my conduct manners &c however valuable to me I can return nothing but thanks; my delineations of such scenes and characters as I meet with in my retired situation, however much matter of reflection they may afford to me, would not probably interest you, who can contemplate human nature on so much more extensive a scale and under so many diversified forms.

After saying that she had "numberless things to say to you, that I hope will interest you who I know . . . makes all the views and affairs of his *little daughter* his own," she ended her witty brief with a gloss on John Howard Payne's recent popular musical paean to innocent domesticity. "When we all meet again," she assured her father, "(and I trust that time is not far distant) we shall have a delightful time by our own fireside then, we will all sing.

> 'Through pleasures and palaces though we may roam
> Be it ever so humble there's no place like home.'"

It was an ironic conclusion to a warm, but not entirely innocent, domestic correspondence.[40]

V

The time for another reunion was, indeed, not far distant. But in the meantime one would like perhaps a more day-to-day picture of her life at Miss Prescott's than Margaret and her parents' cautionary letters usually allowed. There are some useful details in her letters. Her father had thought it "indispensable" that Margaret board with Miss Prescott, which she did in the same large house that served as the school. Her father had also urged Margaret to look to Miss Prescott as an "advisor . . . *friend* [and] parent." ("Miss P.," he encouraged her, "no doubt sees all your deficiencies.") She did not disappoint him. "Miss Prescott is I think proved to be gold without alloy," she wrote to her Uncle Abraham in late September; "how people change their ideas." And to her father she wrote cheerfully at the beginning of the second term: "Miss Prescott has honored me by allowing me to call myself her adopted daughter." Her father's other hope—that Margaret would make a more "favorable impression" on Miss Prescott's students than she did on Dr. Park's—seems to have been fulfilled. The fact that it was an all-girls boarding school probably made camaraderie easier. Perhaps the slightly broader class character of the student body also helped. Looking through the names of students who were among the twenty boarders and thirty or so day scholars at the school, one finds a sprinkling of daughters of artisans, small merchants, sea captains, and even a few Calvinist professionals. Still, most of the girls came, if not from eminent families (although the wealthy merchant-turned-textile-industrialist Amos Lawrence sent his ward Elizabeth Hale there), then at least from small-town eastern Massachusetts professional or mercantile Unitarian families; and it was from among these that Margaret made up her circle of friends. Some of these—like Martha Dana, the daughter of her father's state senate colleague, Judge Samuel Dana of Groton; and Mary Soley, the daughter of his Massachusetts House colleague, John Soley of Charlestown—remained friends for life. Her relations with the general run of the students seem to have also been good. After her first month or so, her references to her schoolmates in her letters home were uniformly favorable, and family letters frequently mentioned her participation in plays, debates, dances, hill-climbing, horseback rides, and other school activities. As for direct evidence of Margaret's schoolmates' feelings towards her, we have a few bits and pieces. Her father mentioned several times that he had heard "very flattering" things about her from several of her friends visiting in Cambridge. Once he even received (and gallantly, if a little uncertainly, agreed to) a petition signed by a large number of her schoolmates, asking him to grant permission for Margaret to appear in a school play. We also have the testimony of one friend of Margaret's that in the school's various activities, she "inspired all her mates."[41]

These glimpses are rather skimpy. But there is one sketch Margaret Fuller wrote many years later about a girl named Mariana who attended a boarding school like Miss Prescott's, which many of her biographers have relied on for a literal rendering of her experience at Groton. This is clearly a mistake. Much about Mariana is fictional, and even psychologically, like Margaret Fuller's fictionalized sketch of her youth, the tale is probably more revealing of her adulthood fantasies than of her childhood realities. On the other hand, Margaret Fuller herself later claimed the Mariana sketch was partly autobiographical, and numerous details would tend to support this (such as Mariana's "too early stimulated" childhood and her nighttime sleepwalking). Even if only as an embellished, fictionalized self-portrait, the tale is too biographically suggestive to ignore.[42]

In her story, Mariana appears as an affectionate but haughty, histrionic, and pensive girl, addicted to freaks of passion and wit, wild dances and sudden song, with a semihysterical habit of spinning around and around until her brain becomes so excited that she stops and declaims verses or acts out the parts of various characters drawn from her childhood, her companions, local dignitaries, or her fancy. Eventually, we are told, these quirks and humors—including her fondness for slight affectations of hair or dress that would allow her to break the narrow routine of the school—found natural vent in school plays, in which for a time, as the principal parts and arrangments fell to her, "she ruled masterly and shone triumphant." Unfortunately, though, theater was not enough for Mariana, for she continued to put on her artificial blush every morning even after the plays were over—an action that so irritated the other girls that they determined to hatch a plot to punish her for it and all her other eccentricities, once and for all, the next day at dinner.

> When she took her seat in the dining-hall, and was asked if she would be helped, raising her eyes, she saw the person who asked her was deeply rouged, with a bright glaring spot, perfectly round, in either cheek. She looked at the next, same apparition! She then slowly passed her eyes down the whole line, and saw the same, with a suppressed smile distorting every countenance. Catching the design at once, she deliberately looked along her own side of the table, at every schoolmate in turn; every one had joined in the trick. The teachers strove to be grave, but she saw they enjoyed the joke. The servants could not suppress a titter.

The rest can be quickly told. She returns to her room and throws herself on the floor in convulsions. When she recovers, horrified that not one took her part, she becomes an unconscious troublemaker, sowing, by innuendo and half-truth, discord and suspicion throughout the school. Eventually she is formally confronted with charges, tries to defend herself, but then throws herself down again, this time dashing herself against the iron hearth of a fireplace and losing consciousness. She is revived but only finally brought back to active life as a result of entreaties from her teacher—a proud and reserved woman who tearfully tells her a story "of pain, of shame" taken out of her own life, with the result that Mariana arises from her sickbed and soon afterwards returns home "a wonderfully instructed being." "A wild fire was tamed in that hour of penitence at the boarding school," Margaret Fuller concludes, "such as has oftentimes wrapped court and camp in its destructive glow."[43]

What are we to make of all this? Clearly *something* happened at Miss Prescott's school, something that she remembered for many years and out of which she spun her tale. Her mother reported that as early as ten Margaret constantly acted out the characters she read about in her books. We know from her letters that she was active in dramatics and appeared in several productions, including, in late November, Richard Sheridan's *The Rivals*. Also, the incidents are strikingly consistent with Margaret's tendency throughout her youth to try to combine her tastes for self-dramatizing fantasy and (as she later put it) "absolute sway" over her companions. Even the Mariana pattern of self-assertion and social manipulation followed by social crisis, unconscious self-reproach, and falling ill was one Margaret would repeat again in later years. And then, of course, there is hardly any question about her late-blooming adoration of Miss Prescott, a phenomenon strongly echoing her relationship with Ellen Kilshaw as well as foreshadowing a number of other apparent mother-figure attachments in later years. Finally, there is this letter, written by Margaret to Susan Prescott some five years later. It clearly shows that whatever it was exactly that occurred at her school (Prescott many years later told Caroline Dall it was a "childish error"), it was not something likely to be soon forgotten:

> You need not fear to revive painful recollections. I often think of those sad experiences. True, they agitate me deeply. But it was best so. They have had a most powerful effect on my character. I tremble at whatever looks like dissimulation. The remembrance of that evening subdues every proud, passionate impulse. My beloved supporter in those sorrowful hours, your image shines as fair in my mind's eye as it did in 1825, when I left you with my heart overflowing with gratitude for your singular and judicious tenderness. Can I ever forget that to your treatment in that crisis of youth I owe the true life,—the love of Truth and Honor?[44]

Despite, then, Margaret's adjustment to Miss Prescott's school, her life there was evidently not without its problematical side. Even if her parents were unaware of *how* problematical, from her letters alone it must have been clear that while they may have sent her to Miss Prescott's to acquire (in her father's words) a "modest & unassuming deportment," it did not exactly work out that way. Likewise, if their concern had been to socialize Margaret among her peers, her letters again must have shown them that what socialization took place only increased her independence from some of their family ways. Clearly, if Margaret were to become in her father's eyes truly "feminized," it would not be in the enlightened republican-domestic way he had originally hoped. Then, too, there had obviously not been much real intellectual growth at Miss Prescott's. Even if her father disagreed, he could not have been deaf to his daughter's entreaties to return to the classical studies that had been his own first intellectual love and his early prescription for Margaret. Also, by the spring, Margaret's mother was now pregnant and looking after not only Eugene, William Henry, and Ellen, but also two-year-old Arthur and one-year-old Richard. Her father had already indicated before Margaret went to Miss Prescott's that he counted on her *"utmost aid"* in the future to help him instruct her younger siblings. Her mother had begun that winter to complain to her husband of feeling "lonely" without her eldest daughter's company and help. Certainly these were two good motives for her parents to conclude that it might be (as her father had told her in the winter he was beginning to feel) "best for you to remain at home." Whatever the reasons, after the term ended on April 1, Margaret, not quite fifteen, returned to Cambridgeport and did not go again to Miss Prescott's. Instead, gathering the strengths and weaknesses learned at Groton, she plunged back into the Cambridge society from which she had been so summarily removed a year before.[45]

CHAPTER FOUR

Cambridge Renaissance

(1825–1833)

I

If Margaret was (as family letters suggest) happy to be back in Cambridge, she had some good reasons for being so. Under Harvard's suave and genial president, Dr. John Kirkland—and with generous support from Boston's wealthy men—the college was undergoing the first major renovation in its history. The law and divinity schools were established, the number of buildings doubled, and, most important culturally, a large number of new teachers were recruited who gave the town an invigorating air of cosmopolitanism. Some of these were already established national figures like Joseph Story, the Supreme Court justice and new Dane Professor of Law, and Edward T. Channing, the former *North American Review* editor and new Boylston Professor of Rhetoric and Oratory, soon to be acclaimed for all the future famous American writers he would train. But they also included a group of young scholars who brought to Cambridge a little bit of Europe as well. For four years after the end of the War of 1812 with England, George Ticknor, Edward Everett, Joseph Cogswell, and George Bancroft lived in Europe, dining and conversing with most of Europe's leading literary lions, studying at the University of Göttingen, Germany's leading university, and, with Bancroft and Everett, earning the first German Ph.D.'s awarded to foreigners. Fired up by the unheard-of erudition and critical brilliance that they had encountered in Germany, Europe's cultural giant, once back they strove earnestly to emulate it in Cambridge. Cogswell reorganized the college library on the same plan as that at Göttingen; Ticknor taught the first courses on modern literature ever given in an American college; and Everett, in his Greek classes, electrified his young listeners, not so much with his ideas (which would never be Everett's forte), but with his new learning and rhetorical panache. Political reaction after the war brought to Cambridge also a sizable number of erudite émigré scholars: men like Charles Follen, who became Harvard's first instructor in German; Charles Beck, who taught Latin; and Pietro Bachi, who taught Italian. They, in turn, were joined by other recent arrivals like the celebrated painter Washington Allston, a long-time resident of England and the Continent and an intimate of Europe's leading writers; and, along with his brother-in-law and fellow Cantabrigian, Richard Henry Dana, Sr., among the first of American intellectuals to espouse and propagate European Romantic literary ideas. All these new men Margaret knew socially, borrowed books from, and discussed ideas with. She was also, her journals show, stimulated by them, as was also true of many other young people in Margaret's circles. Indeed, when one considers that the entire town still numbered barely five thousand residents, it is not surprising that during these years Harvard graduated a larger proportion of students who achieved future renown than in any other period in the college's history. There were also a number as well who suffered breakdowns in their pursuit of great cultural laurels.[1]

Cambridge's cultural awakening, of course, was not merely a local academic phenomenon. Throughout the Western world in the decade following the overthrow of Napoleon, internationally circulating books, translations, travel memoirs, literary correspondence, and critical exchanges burst forth from the pens and presses of nations that had been fiercely fighting for nearly a generation. Romanticism—whose root cultural principle was human creativity—flourishing now, not just in one or two, but in all the major European nations, gave further stimulus and unity to this worldwide awakening. Naturally, Americans in this international exchange were mostly consumers. Still, literary nationalists could point out two happy portents—the astoundingly successful English edition of Washington Irving's *Sketch Book* and the beginnings of James Fenimore Cooper's enormous European vogue. America's future literary greatness appeared set. How could it be otherwise (so the argument ran) now that the United States, after its second successful war against England, was finally militarily secure, facing a boundless continent in the West, and ready to turn its attention to achieving the same kind of greatness for its economy and culture that it had won for its polity?[2]

Meanwhile, New Englanders, including even those Federalists who harbored grave doubts about where the country was headed politically, had little doubt about what region would lead the nation in this cultural leap forward. Two different social developments animated their hopes. On a popular level, the 1820s saw not only the taking off of private (and in another decade public) education in New England, but also the region's launching of the American Lyceum—a sprawling, private, nonprofit system of popular lectures that brought together, in towns and villages, speakers, audiences, and subjects from the crude or pedantic to the scholarly and original, helping to nourish a popular middle-class thirst for knowledge and culture, unparalleled anywhere in the world. On an elite level, Boston's civic-minded capitalists, buoyed by the high profits gained from their new investments in manufacturing, and desirous of seeing, in Puritan fashion, their influence extended to new cultural institutions, generously funded private libraries like the recently founded Boston Athenaeum, new university professorships like those of Everett's and Follen's, and, most important, new literary publications like the *North American Review*. Although stodgy in format, conservative in politics, and critical rather than creative in content, the *North American* was the first American journal that could be compared to the British quarterlies. It was also the first major American journal to champion fully, if judiciously, American nationalist literary pretensions and to lend a friendly, if selective, ear to European Romantic authors. Needless to say, academic literati like Everett and Ticknor welcomed such beneficence—of course because they benefitted from it—but also because it supported so well the traditional Boston-Cambridge Federalist notion of intellectuals as the patronized civic clerisy and conscience of culture. At the same time, these cultural institutions, like the changes at the college, were the first steps in securing Boston-Cambridge's status as the country's leading literary center, a position it would hold until well past the Civil War.[3]

Above all, Cambridge's cultural awakening was undergirded by its Unitarian religion. The 1820s, as Samuel Eliot Morison has written, were "the palmy days of Unitarianism." The liberals (as Unitarians initially liked to call themselves) had easily captured Harvard two decades earlier, and since then had won over a majority of the Congregational churches in eastern Massachusetts, arousing even greater expectations. It was in these years that Harvard missionaries preached in Southern legislative halls and that none other than that most un–New England personage, Thomas Jefferson, predicted that the rational faith would become the religion of America. Even more critically, leaders emerged, in both Boston and Cambridge, Unitarianism's intellectual centers, who seized the moral and philosophical initiative, no longer content merely to affirm, as their eighteenth-century Arminian predecessors had, the reasonableness of their faith while palely protesting against "dogmatism" and "enthusiasm" in the pulpit. The formidable Andrews Norton, Dexter Professor of Sacred Literature, argued that one could, by applying the laws of logic and evidence, absolutely separate biblical truth from opinion and base one's faith solely on the former. The Reverend William Ellery Channing eloquently denounced the "gloomy," "servile" Calvinist view as a moral perversion, degrading both to God and to man, and proclaimed instead a positive faith in divine benevolence and man's "likeness to God." Countless Boston ministers and Cambridge professors assured their congregations and students that not just the Bible but all good literature helped cultivate a person's moral and benevolent character—a position that goes a long way toward explaining why for a good part of the century to come nearly half of all the major authors in America would be Unitarians.[4]

Of course Boston-Cambridge Unitarian ministers and professors hardly unleashed a Romantic democratic revolt in American Protestantism. Their devotion to Christ's divinity and the New Testament's revelations were too great; their confidence in "judiciousness," "common duties," and "a reasonable frame of mind" (to quote even the quasi-Romantic Channing) was too firm; their belief in conservative Federalist or Whig politics was too basic; their ties to the Boston textile and railroad capitalists were too strong. With but a few exceptions, their Romantic poets were Scott and Felicia Hemans, not Byron or Shelley; their causes schools and asylums, not antislavery and labor; their political heroes Daniel Webster and Nicholas Biddle, not Jackson and Orestes Brownson. These loyalties, together with the overwhelming preference of antebellum Americans for the more fervid religion of evangelical Protestantism, would keep established Unitarian intellectuals, like the sect itself, at the periphery of American culture. But these revelations still lay mainly in the future. In the meantime, Boston-Cambridge's Unitarian faith contributed its mild seasoning to the cultural stew of Margaret Fuller's later youth.[5]

II

That Margaret was more than ready to take it all in is poignantly shown in the very first letters she wrote after returning to Cambridge. On the evening of June 16, 1825, she attended with her parents in Boston a lavish reception given at the home of Mayor Josiah Quincy for the Marquis de Lafayette, just then concluding his sixteen-month triumphal tour of America. Lafayette's constantly fêted journey had given politicians, journalists, and ordinary Americans the opportunity to express their gratitude for the French hero's Revolutionary sacrifices for America—and, in so doing, to betray their most grandiose fantasies about themselves and their country—and Margaret was no exception. "Sir," she had written to him earlier that day, "the contemplation of a character such as yours fills the soul with a noble ambition. Should we both live, and it is possible to a female, to whom the avenues of glory are seldom accessible, I will recal my name to your recollection." Presumably she did. In a letter she wrote to Susan Prescott on July 11, she revealed something of her own efforts to find, despite her femaleness, avenues of glory. By this time she was back at the Port School, now taught by Yale graduate George Perkins and attended by Oliver Wendell Holmes's genial younger brother John and the headstrong ten-year-old future author and politician Richard Henry Dana, Jr. In her report to her former teacher, though, her attention was fixed squarely on her noble ambition, which she now defined in terms rather different from any she had so far suggested in her letters to her parents from her previous schools. After describing her typical day ("I rise a little before five") and her twelve-hour schedule of Greek, French, Italian, philosophy, and piano practicing, she announced:

> I feel the power of industry growing every day. . . . I have learned to believe that nothing, no! not perfection, is unattainable. I am determined on distinction, which formerly I thought to win at an easy rate; but now I see that long years of labor must be given to secure even the "*succès de société*,"—which, however, shall never content me. I see multitudes of examples of persons of genius, utterly deficient in grace and the power of pleasurable excitement. I wish to combine both. I know the obstacles in my way. I am wanting in that intuitive tact and polish, which nature has bestowed upon some, but which I must acquire. And, on the other hand, my powers of intellect, though sufficient, I suppose, are not well disciplined. Yet all such hindrances may be overcome by an ardent spirit. If I fail, my consolation shall be found in active employment.[6]

Such was the point to which Margaret's "all-powerful motive of ambition" had brought her by the beginning of her fifteenth year. That such high hopes also reflected a high degree of self-esteem is fairly obvious—or so it apparently seemed to Margaret's father. "My father would often try to check my pride," she years later painfully recalled, "or as he deemed it my *arrogance* of youthful hope and pride by a picture of the ills that might come on me, . . . sickness, poverty, the failure of ties and all my cherished plans." Did he also worry (as his reference to her poverty might suggest) that Margaret would never marry? Perhaps. She later claimed that he wanted her to marry the unmarried thirty-two-year-old Republican congressman for Buffalo, Albert Tracy, whom he invited to stay with the family for a visit that summer. Although (as she later told Tracy) "with a head full of Hamlet, and Rousseau, and the ballads of chivalry," she was not at the time "inclined to idealize lawyers and members of Congress and *father's friends,*" she obviously found him chivalrous enough. Even when she saw him years later when she was an adult, she breathlessly described to a friend his "powerful eye" and "imposing manier d'être." But whatever this (as she later described herself to Tracy) "ardent and onward-looking" girl inspired in this classically educated congressman, it was not marriage. By the end of the year he married, and he did not see his "dear child" (as he liked to call Margaret even as an adult) for another fifteen years.[7]

Yet—however he saw her marriage prospects—her father clearly did, as she later testified, "admire" her, and, if he had seen them, would probably have also admired the goals she outlined to Susan Prescott. Grace, intellectual distinction, and the power of pleasurable excitement were, after all, his fondest hopes for her. As for her somewhat labored self-consciousness about it all, had he not himself long cultivated and likewise recommended to her just such a strategy for moderating an otherwise dangerous self-assertion? Of course her penchant for making her "series of characteristics" (as she called the self-criticisms she was now recording in her journal) quite so public was something else again, though even here Margaret's behavior would seem to have fitted the family mold. Speaking of the Fuller family, one woman told Higginson, "Their only peculiarity was that they said openly about themselves the good and bad things which we commonly suppress about ourselves and express only about other people." A friend of Margaret's from these years was more blunt. "Margaret's egotism," she would write to a mutual friend, "is the consequence of her father's early injudicious culture, never *allowed* to forget *herself.*"[8]

Despite her perfectionist ambitions, Margaret does not seem to have been a domestic rebel. Family letters in her later adolescent years show her amicably socializing with the Fullers' Cambridge friends, at least dutifully helping out with the household sewing, complacently overseeing children and servants, and from time to time tutoring Eugene and William Henry. "I have . . . finished nearly all my own sewing which weighed so heavily on my mind," she wrote in one letter to her parents when they were visiting relatives in Maine. "Arthur reads 'Sandford and Merton' [the rationalistic, didactic *History of Sandford and Merton* by the Edgeworths' friend Thomas Day] to me evegs while I work; he seems to like it very much and I think we form quite a nice little domestick groupe. Lloyd says often that I am 'a nice good girl as ever was.'" Margaret may not have become entirely the young intellectual domestic her father had hoped to make her, but she does seem to have learned how to behave like one.[9]

After her first term ended, Margaret stopped going to the Port School to recite her Greek and Latin. This left her for the first time in her life with an uncertain future. Had she been a boy, college would have been the next natural step. But this was not a possibility. So, instead, with the help of books borrowed from the Athenaeum and from her college friends, she fashioned around herself her own Harvard and Yale. It was a somewhat eclectic school, a fact she humorously admitted to Susan Prescott. "I am studying Madame de Stael, Epictetus, Milton, Racine, and Castilian ballads, with great delight. There's an assemblage for you." But it was also an extensive school. She earnestly read Locke, Helvétius, Thomas Brown, and other Harvard and non-Harvard texts of Enlightenment and Common Sense philosophy. She also read, with clearly more interest and with her father's encouragement, a large number of books on modern political history. What the character of that interest was, though, is hard to gauge. Frederic Henry Hedge told Higginson that when he first became acquainted with her after he returned from Europe, he was "amazed at her interest in the national gov't defending it strongly agst those who had some European ideas." Undoubtedly this was true. Yet her letters show that while her politics may have been Republican, her interests—like, to a certain extent, her father's—were very European. "Duke Nicholas is to succeed the Emperor Alexander," she wrote portentously to Susan Prescott that spring, "thus relieving Europe from the sad apprehension of evil to be inflicted by the brutal Constantine, and yet depriving the Holy alliance of its very soul. We may now hope more strongly for the liberties of unchained Europe; we look in anxious suspense for the issue of the struggle of Greece, the result of which seems to depend on the new autocrat." Furthermore, the bulk of the history books she read were memoirs like those of Cardinal de Retz, Frederick the Great, the Prince de Ligne, and other great European statesmen of the previous two centuries. Finally, her letters show, she scanned the lives of these cosmopolitan and enlightened figures, not for their politics, but for their exemplary intellectual qualities—particularly their wit, learning, and above all, rugged worldliness. "I am reading Sir William Temple's works, with great pleasure," she wrote to Susan Prescott the following year in a typical gloss on one of these great men.

> Such enlarged views are rarely to be found combined with such acuteness and discrimination. His style, though diffuse, is never verbose or overloaded, but beautifully expressive; 't is English, too, though he was an accomplished linguist, and wrote much and well in French, Spanish, and Latin. The latter he used, as he says of the Bishop of Munster, (with whom he corresponded in that tongue,) "more like a man of the court and of business than a scholar." He affected not Augustan niceties, but his expressions are free and appropriate.[10]

Her fascination with political-literary heroics was also fed, of course, by her Latin readings, which her father continued to direct. This is shown well enough by a college-type theme (one of a number she wrote for her father around this

time) on the apposite motto "'Possunt quia posse videntur.'" The position she
took was cautiously balanced: although men can and should, up to a point, do
what they imagine themselves able to do, their wills must be counterbalanced by
reason, or an understanding of the force of circumstances, which teach us that
"each man can[not] be his own Destiny." This she demonstrated by examples:
"Leonidas saved his country by a strong exertion of will inspired by the most
generous sentiment. Brutus nerved his soul to break those ties most sacred to
one like him and failed. Resolved, united hearts, freed America— The strongest
exertion, the most generous concentration of will for a similar purpose left
Poland in blood and chains at the feet of a tyrant." Still, she added, defeat in the
pursuit of great deeds is good if a man learns in their pursuit "the genuine happiness and glory"—the sustained exertion of his powers, fitting him for his suited
station and teaching him the nature of his talents and character. For even though
the most brave and ambitious may never become a Napoleon or a Demosthenes,
she concluded, "it is not in the power of circumstance to prevent the earnest will
from shaping round itself the character of a great, a wise, or a good man."
Although her father made his usual corrections for clarity, such an impeccably
Stoic conclusion presumably earned her a high mark.[11]

But Margaret's greatest reading in her later teen-age years was in an area furthest removed from her father's interests and quite independent of his direction—her favorite subject, modern literature. In English she read a fair number
of Reformation authors, while skipping lightly (except for the sentimentalist
Samuel Richardson) over most of the eighteenth century. She also devoured a
large quantity of contemporary English fiction. She thought Jane Austen's novels "beautiful." She was captivated by the tales of youthful aristrocratic intrigue
of the "fashionable" novelists Benjamin Disraeli and Edward Bulwer-Lytton.
But probably her greatest favorites were the politically liberal, Gothic intellectual
romances of crime and passion by Charles Brockden Brown (the only American
writer who seems to have impressed her) and, most of all, Brown's master, William Godwin. ("He has fully lived the double existence of man," she solemnly
urged to a friend in recommending Godwin, "and he casts the reflexes on his
magic mirror from a height where no object in life's panorama can cause one
throb of delirious hope or grasping ambition.") She also read a good deal of
Renaissance Spanish literature, but even more in Renaissance and eighteenth-
century French literature. (Acknowledging the predominance, she later labeled
these years her "French period.") She was particularly drawn to French elegance
and skepticism (Voltaire she called "my pleasure") and—with the proper regrets
about its "odious" character—French passion. "I am swallowing by gasps that
cauldrony beverage of selfish passion and morbid taste the letters of Mlle Lespinasse," she wrote to a friend. "It is good for me." In Italian, her letters show,
she read virtually all the major poets and dramatists from Dante and Petrarch,
through Ludovico Ariosto and Tasso, down to Alfieri. ("I am engrossed in reading the elder Italian poets," she wrote to Susan Prescott her second year, "beginning with Berni, from whom I shall proceed to Pulci and Politian. I read very
critically.") Her later close Cambridge friend James Freeman Clarke testified
that when he first became acquainted with her when she was nineteen, she

"already . . . had become familiar with the masterpieces of French, Italian and Spanish literature." Considering that at this time very few in Cambridge outside of Professor Ticknor and his staff's small classes read Italian or Spanish literature—and the college consigned even his courses to an entirely noncredit, "voluntary" status—Margaret's self-designed and self-taught curriculum was by itself something of an avant-garde achievement.[12]

In one were to ask, though, what authors most shaped Margaret's intellectual outlook at this time, the answer would clearly be Romantic ones—some more than others. The enormously popular Sir Walter Scott she had learned to put near the bottom of her canon. By contrast, as with highbrow American Romantic critics like Allston, Dana, and William Cullen Bryant, she placed William Wordsworth and Samuel Taylor Coleridge near the top. At the same time, it is clear from her letters that more personally moving to her than the contemplative works of the Lake Poets at this time were (as she characterized them in her letters) the "haunt[ingly] . . . sad" poetry of Percy Bysshe Shelley and the iconoclastically "tragick" poems of Scott's popular rival, Lord Byron. But the Romantic writer who moved her the most was Jean-Jacques Rousseau. His "prophet[ic]" and deeply burning inner "fire" was so impressive to her, she would later recall, that in these years she "sat at [his] feet." She also read the French Rousseauist novelist and critic Germaine de Staël, whose sentimental novels about extraordinary women of feeling and intellect in tragic conflict with narrow gender conventions also touched a sympathetic spark in her. "Now tell me," she asked her Unitarian intellectual confidante Susan Prescott, "had you rather be the brilliant De Stael or the useful Edgeworth?—though De Stael is useful too," she quickly added, "but it is on the grand scale, on liberalizing, regenerating principles, and has not the immediate practical success Edgeworth has."[13]

Like the preferences themselves, the outlook Margaret concocted from them was Romantic, but in special ways. Her letters show that by the end of her adolescent years she had come very vaguely to accept the two key Romantic concepts—that the universe was ideally an organic whole, and that an individual's sense of that wholeness depended on her nonrational perceptions. The Wordsworthian Romantic exaltation of nature proper, on the other hand, left her cold. "The 'beauties of nature' never could console me for any ill," she wrote in her twentieth year to a friend. "I do not believe any one finds peace from their contemplation. . . . If bright, Nature jars, if clouded, she sadly analogizes with the troubled soul." She was even more dismissive of the "imbecile . . . horror . . . of the startling and paradoxical" that she claimed (without naming names) "admirers of the great poet whom I have known in these parts" derived from Wordsworth's religion of nature. *Her* adolescent Romanticism, by contrast, like that of her revered Rousseau, and, to a lesser extent, that of Byron, was startlingly heroic and paradoxically fatalistic. Characteristic was a letter she wrote to a friend in her nineteenth year, citing a passage in Rousseau's *Confessions,* in which he had claimed that Tasso had involuntarily written a certain line in one of his epics that predicted Rousseau's misfortunes. This "instance of beautiful credulity," she commented, "has taken my mind greatly. This remote seeking for the decrees of fate, this feeling of a destiny, casting its shadows from the very morning of thought, is the most beautiful species of idealism in our day. 'T is finely manifiested in [Friedrich Schiller's] Wallenstein, where the common men sum up their superficial observations on the life and doings of Wallenstein, and show that, not until this agitating crisis, have they caught any idea of the deep thoughts which shaped that hero, who has, without their feeling it moulded *their* existence." Finally, with her Romanticism, and also fully in line with Rousseau and with much of late eighteenth-century continental Romanticism generally, went a broad streak of nostalgic primitivism. "How delighted am I," she wrote to Susan Prescott at the end of her first year back in Cambridge, in a letter defending her taste for intellectual-minded Gothic novels and picaresque tales,

> to read a book which can absorb me to tears and shuddering,—not by individual traits of beauty, but by the spirit of adventure,—happiness which one seldom enjoys after childhood in this blest age, so philosophic, free, and enlightened to a miracle, but far removed from the ardent dreams and soft credulity of the world's youth. Sometimes I think I would give all our gains for those times when young and old gathered in the feudal hall, listening with soul-absorbing transport to the romance of the minstrel, unrestrained and regardless of criticism, and when they worshipped nature, not as high-dressed and pampered, but as just risen from the bath.[14]

It is important, of course, not to overestimate the coherence of Margaret's later adolescent thinking. Like her reading, much of it was eclectic. But even at its most random, it was often discriminating and sophisticated. It was also, even more than her ideas, methodologically Romantic: individual, diverse, restless, and full of its own kind of heroic pathos. That she carried on her reading without the prods to systematizing—much less academic rewards or hopes for future professional success—that a college education was designed to provide goes without saying. But perhaps the most poignant illustration of both the strengths and weaknesses of Margaret's self-education was a long letter she wrote to her probably somewhat bewildered sounding-board, Susan Prescott, in her seventeenth year before her reading had quite acquired its Romantic definition. After an even longer and more discursive account than usual of her recent reading ("I have passed a luxurious afternoon, having been in bed from dinner till tea, reading Rammohun Roy's book [the liberal Hindu reformer's recently published pro-Christian *Precepts of Jesus*], and framing dialogues aloud on every argument beneath the sun"), she uttered this baffled war cry: "Really, I have not had my mind so exercised for months; and I have felt a gladiatorial disposition lately, and don't enjoy mere light conversation. The love of knowledge is prodigiously kindled within my soul of late; I study much and reflect more, and feel an aching wish for some person with whom I might talk fully and openly." Both the disposition and the yearning showed that her childhood inclinations remained firmly intact.[15]

III

In the summer of 1826, shortly after Margaret's father completed his term as Speaker of the Massachusetts House, the Fullers moved from their Cambridgeport house into the Dana Hill mansion about a quarter of a mile from the college, off of the main road to Boston. "Oh, I shall not see the Soap Works any more!" four-year-old Arthur reportedly cried out on the day of the move. This was a decidedly minority point of view. In later years Margaret and her siblings would look back on their years in the Dana mansion as their most "prosperous." Certainly their *"home-house"* (as little Richard called it) looked prosperous enough. Built in 1785 by the late Chief Justice Francis Dana, atop the crest of a small hill two hundred feet from the road, this large, wooden, two-story Georgian house rivaled even Cambridge's premiere residence, Andrew Craigie's Vassall mansion, which it generally resembled. The family particularly admired the estate's ample stables, flower-lined connecting avenue, and wide lawns dotted with fruit and ornamental trees surrounded by acres of undeveloped land. But Margaret took greatest pleasure in its magnificent prospect, the best in the town, with a clear view of the Brighton and Brookline hills twelve miles away. "I love to look on it," she told a friend, "the river so slow and mild, the gentle hills, the sunset over Mt. Auburn."[16]

While elegantly ensconced, the Fullers found their fortunes in these years waxing and waning. Margaret's father, bored with the "skirmishes" in Congress and sick of his regular half-year "exile" from his family, had refused to stand for a fifth term. His replacement was Boston-Cambridge's rising young political star, the cultivated Professor Edward Everett, with whom he and his wife had pleasantly socialized and whose literary attainments he respected, but whom he nonetheless firmly, if unsuccessfully, opposed. (*"The candidate of the Federalists"* and an upstart "deficient . . . in the discipline of the forum," he snorted, classical republican style, in letters to his constituents and privately to Margaret.) Meanwhile, several of his colleagues had assured him that he could expect that newly elected President John Quincy Adams would offer him a diplomatic appointment as a reward for his efforts on behalf of his candidacy. But as Adams did not do so right away, Fuller bided his time: he revived his Boston law practice, he served a couple more terms in the state legislature, and he kept up his close association with Adams. He even arranged, in late September, a large dinner and ball in the President's honor. Higginson called it (presumably on the basis of talking to someone who had attended) "one of the most elaborate affairs of the kind that had occurred in Cambridge since the ante-revolutionary days of the Lechmeres and Vassalls." Certainly it was an important affair for Margaret, and she evidently did her best to appear as she thought she was expected to on such a momentous occasion. But her best was apparently not good enough for one young Cambridge lady, who later recalled for Higginson this unflattering picture of Margaret that night—"a young girl of sixteen with a very plain face, half-shut eyes, and hair curled all over her head; she was laced so tightly, . . . by reason of stoutness, that she had to hold her arms back as if they were pinioned; she was dressed in a badly cut, low-necked pink silk, with white muslin over it; and she danced quadrilles very awkwardly, being withal so near-sighted that she could hardly see her partner."[17]

These do seem to have been physically awkward years for Margaret. Plump, nearsighted, and still plagued by her facial rash, she was definitely not one of Cambridge's belles. She was also, Frederic Henry Hedge recalled, "painfully conscious" of her looks, a consciousness no doubt increased, as several of her friends thought, by the "*uncommon* beauty" of her mother, her "waxen doll" sister, and her handsome brother Eugene. (Nor, probably, did her ever-critical father help much. "I hope you will not be impatient to see the youth," he had written to her on the day her brother Richard was born, "as it cannot be pretended that he has any extraordinary beauty to recommend him, tho by no means deficient in that respect, as you will very readily believe when I tell you, that he is said to resemble his eldest sister.") On the other hand, Hedge reported—with only a slightly patronizing touch—"She escaped the reproach of positive plainness, by her blond and abundant hair, by her excellent teeth, by her sparkling, dancing, busy eyes, which, though usually half closed from near-sightedness, shot piercing glances at those with whom she conversed, and, most of all, by the very peculiar and graceful carriage of her head and neck." If not a beautiful girl, she was at least an athletic one. She rose early, practiced gymnastics, climbed hills, took long walks—preferring usually to walk rather than take the omnibus into Boston—and, most energetically of all, took long "delightful" horseback rides into the countryside.[18]

Then, too, Cambridge was a town where physical blemishes were not the only thing people saw when they looked on bright adolescent girls. Many Cambridge girls, after all, had attended, as Margaret had, academic private schools or studied under their fathers, older brothers, or some of the college's instructors. It is not surprising, then, that when years later Higginson interviewed a number of these women, they remembered not ridiculing, but actually envying some of Margaret's physical quirks. One woman—recalling Margaret's much-commented-on long, waving neck and half-shut eyelids—told Higginson that she and her friends thought "that if we could only come into school that way, we could know as much Greek as she did." This same woman also remembered Margaret's habit of wearing a hooded cloak when she went to a social library at one of the village shops, which she would take off, fill with books, swing over her shoulders, and so carry home. "We all wished," she told Higginson, "that our mothers would let us have hooded cloaks, that we might carry our books in the same way." Another woman, Anna Parsons—three years Margaret's junior and later a cordial but not intimate friend—remembered first meeting her that year at a party at Parson's house, where "the tall stranger, handkerchief in hand," a little overawing her at first, but soon taking them in hand, "like a born leader," spiritedly directed them in plays and games. "My mother and sister [were] relieved . . . of all responsibility of entertaining us. They were much amused by her manner of directing us—as she held her handkerchief—large as was the fashion that far away time—by one corner & waved it about like a baton as she instructed & guided us— There was a peculiar swaying grace in her motion. . . . I was greatly drawn to her."[19]

As this last reference to Anna's mother and sister suggest, some of Margaret's seniors were also beginning to pay her some favorable attention. The most notable was the twenty-four-year-old Lydia Maria Francis (later, as Lydia Maria Child, the prominent abolitionist writer and editor) with whom Margaret struck up a friendship soon after moving into the Dana mansion. Having published two well-received sentimental historical novels and founded the first American magazine for children, Maria Francis was already on her way to being touted in American journals (before her abolitionist views earned her their censure) as one of the leading woman writers in America. But neither their difference in ages or in literary status interfered with their mutual studies in de Staël and Locke and their friendly exchanges of opinions on the latest American books and reviews. In a letter to Susan Prescott in January, Margaret described her new friend in high Romantic terms, as "a natural person,—a most rare thing in this age of cant and pretension." And Maria, characterizing a teasing letter of Margaret's a few months later, told her, "Like you, it was full of thought, raciness, originality, and queerness; and like you it excited the pleasantest emotions in my heart."[20]

Meanwhile, Margaret had available other older women. Mostly they were the wives or relatives of Harvard professors and officials. Although by no means scholars or prominent literary celebrities, they were nonetheless well read, knowledgeable, dignified, and highly respected in their community. These included, Higginson recalled, his own mother, Louisa Storrow Higginson, and her sister in-law Susan Higginson Channing, the widowed mother of Margaret's later Transcendentalist friend William Henry Channing, and sister Ann Storrow, the intellectual confidante of William Ellery Channing and Harvard historian Jared Sparks and, from her letters, a woman of much learning and wit. Family letters show Margaret also cheerfully and often affectionately writing and visiting Mrs. Hedge, Mrs. Peck, Mrs. Webster (the wife of the later-infamous Harvard chemistry professor, John White Webster, who would murder his colleague George Parkman), and sundry other Harvard faculty wives. Margaret, on the lookout since Ellen Kilshaw for cultivated mother-figures, evidently took whatever opportunities were available. Mrs. Higginson's daughter Susan later remembered vividly "this studious, self-conscious, overgrown girl . . . sitting at my mother's feet, covering her hands with kisses and treasuring her every word." Most of these women, Higginson reported, responded solicitously to Margaret. Yet some of them sometimes seem to have shrunk back a bit. Mrs. Hedge, after observing an animated philosophical discussion between Margaret and her son, remarked (as Margaret reported it to a friend) "'that Henry and Margaret thought themselves such high geniuses that nobody could get up to or comprehend them.'" Mainly, though, with large families of their own, they were, as Higginson recalled, too busy to give more than passing attention to the intellectual, but needy Margaret. Fortunately, though, there was one who was able and willing to do much more.[21]

She was Eliza Farrar, the wife of John Farrar, Harvard's popular Hollis Professor of Mathematics and Natural Philosophy. Born in Dunkirk during the French Revolution into a wealthy Quaker whaling family and raised there and in England and Wales in an atmosphere of Quaker rectitude, bourgeois opulence, and much socializing with many of England's literary notables, Eliza Ware Rotch, by her mid-twenties, had lived a comfortably cosmopolitan life.

Her father, however, had soon lost his fortune, and she was forced to come to America to live with relatives in New Bedford. After shedding, along with others in her family, her none-too-rigorous "New Light" Hicksite Quakerism for Unitarianism, she moved to Cambridge, where, in 1828, she married the widowed fifty-two-year-old Farrar and also first became acquainted with Margaret. In Cambridge the Farrars soon made their home on Professors' Row, the center of college society. Having no children of their own, they also made it into a youthful social center—and frequently boardinghouse—for the children of many of their friends.[22]

For Margaret, though, Eliza Farrar went considerably further. Perceiving, as one of their mutual friends would later recollect, both Margaret's "extraordinary promise" and "false social position," she set herself to put her on the best footing in Boston-Cambridge society. Or, as Higginson, who was himself for a time one of her boarders, put it more pointedly: "She undertook to mould her externally, to make her less abrupt, less self-asserting, more *comme il faut* in ideas, manners, and even costume. She had her constantly at her own house, reformed her hairdresser, and instructed her dressmaker; took her to make calls, took her on journeys." As for what she specifically advised Margaret, we can get a fair inkling from her book of a few years later, *The Young Lady's Friend.* Compared with the mass of sentimental ladies' manners books then spewing from the presses, Farrar's book might seem to a modern reader, if prudish in its sexual advice, in other respects almost worldly. In its pages one finds little heavy or obsessive religious moralizing. It also displays a firsthand familiarity with European manners, which she realistically urges be adapted to egalitarian American social conditions. On the question of woman's sphere, her position was, as one might expect from a Unitarian woman, socially conservative, but culturally liberal. While making it absolutely clear that housekeeping was a woman's "express vocation," for girls she mainly stressed, besides mastering their domestic tasks, acquiring the virtues of self-possession, social consideration, and, above all, academic learning, which was valuable itself and not something that ended with school or marriage. At one point the late-marrying Farrar even bemoaned the fact that matrimony was with women the great business of life, whereas with men it was only an incident. "Now this difference," she wrote, "gives the other sex a greater advantage over you; and the best way to equalize your lot, and become as wise as they are, is to think as little about it as they do." The most profitable and agreeable relationships with men may be attained, she urged, by regarding them as "intellectual beings" rather than constantly thinking of them as "candidates for matrimony [or] possible future admirers and lovers." There was one area, though, besides housework, where she was emphatically sex-conscious—dress. Her models, not surprisingly, were the ladies of Philadelphia who, she said, followed Quaker moderation and French taste. She was especially emphatic, almost to the point of fastidiousness, about girls spending a minimum of one to two hours on their morning toilet. For studious girls she had a special word. Urging "that they should not bring . . . literary pursuits into disrepute by neglecting their personal appearances," she reminded them of the very close connection in many minds between *"blue stockings* and *dirty stockings."*[23]

How much Margaret took of this advice Eliza Farrar presumably gave her in some fashion is hard to say. Years later she warmly recalled to her "the lessons" Farrar had given her "on the niceties of a Lady's dress," and it is very possible Margaret owed her later appreciation of fine dressing partly to these lessons. Judging from one letter in which she apologized for appearing to Farrar's husband "harsh and arrogant in my strictures," Farrar also seems to have had some effect on Margaret's social conscience. To the mother-starved Margaret, though, obviously more important than dress and manners was the maternal encouragement that this tall, smartly dressed, meticulous woman ("I never go to bed without arranging my room & preparing myself as I w^d wish to be if I were to die that night") clearly supplied to her in great abundance. "At 17 I elected a Mother," she would later write in a fictionalized autobiographical fragment, and her many later appreciative references to her older friend's sympathy, gifts, and kindnesses, show she thought she elected well. Finally, and perhaps most important, both by precept and (unlike Margaret's parents) by example, Eliza Farrar showed her that it was perfectly possible to carry on intellectual and literary pursuits while pursuing the role of "Lady." This liberally religious-minded, kind-hearted, generous woman, who devoted two decades of her life to nursing her chronically ill husband and always called herself on the title pages of her books "Mrs. John Farrar," could hardly have provided much help for Margaret in her deeper, more complicated search for great achievement and emotional self-expression. But for the time she seems to have sufficed for Margaret quite well.[24]

IV

Margaret's friendship with Eliza Farrar coincided with a general quickening of her social life. To be sure, one can find plenty of evidence of Boston-area young people put off or repelled by Margaret's "dogmati[c]" and "sneering" ways (to quote the most common complaints). Likewise, it is easy to find in Margaret's journals telltale sneers sputtering out, as in one entry where she lashed out at the "haughty, rigid, prudish girls" ("I hardly dare breathe in their presence") that she encountered at one Cambridge party. Yet she had an abundance of friends. Among the girls, the core continued to be her childhood chums Almira Penniman, Elizabeth Randall, and Amelia Greenwood. Each was as individual as Margaret herself. Soon to marry (in 1830) the young Unitarian minister David Hatch Barlow, Almira had (in her friends' descriptions) a "half-voluptuous" beauty, a witty, "laughter-loving" manner, and the reputation of being both attractive to men and fond of their company. (After her divorce from Barlow, she joined the Transcendentalist socialist community Brook Farm, where she probably served—along with her very different friend Margaret—as one source for the figure of the ill-fated feminist heroine Zenobia in Hawthorne's *Blithedale Romance.*) Elizabeth, who had been forced by her physician father through something of the same precocious regimen as Margaret, was by contrast (according to Margaret) "in-dwelling" and "morbid" in her sensibility. Amelia was different still: lively, sympathetic, and (as Margaret and another friend thought) almost "Wordsworthian" in her "harmonious" self-complacency. In contrast with the unhappily married Almira and Elizabeth, she would soon become a contented wife (in Margaret's phrase) "as her 'Mother was before her.'" The girls were in their own way a definite group: all three were high-spirited, droll, multilingual, enamored of English Romantic literature, and, if not intellectually profound, certainly carefree. "It is perfectly idle to talk of a young woman's being injured by reading anything," Amelia told Margaret in one repartee over the moral dangers of reading certain authors. "When you have read it, you are the same person you were before."[25]

Of a similar cast, although more sedate and well-to-do, were two more recent friends of Margaret's—Ellen Sturgis, the daughter of a rich Boston merchant, well educated, witty, and already considered something of a prodigy as a poet, and Anna Barker, a younger cousin of Eliza Farrar's and the daughter of an even wealthier merchant. Residing in New York, but often visiting Cambridge, the beautiful and charming Anna for years would exercise a powerful sway over both Margaret and many of her friends. Not every Cambridge girlfriend of Margaret's was (as she called Almira) a "blue-stocking." Purely social friends included her Prescott classmate Mary Soley of Charlestown, as well as Helen Davis, in Higginson's words, the "musical queen of our Cambridge world," whose highly dramatic, sentimental songs thrilled an entire generation of Boston-Cambridge young people. Even though Helen was not a close friend of Margaret's, she and her sister Margaret were indefatigable party-givers, and through them Margaret was connected with a large number of Boston-Cambridge girls.[26]

Although less numerous, Margaret's young male friends were also an impressive lot. Of these the most intellectually impressive was Frederic Henry Hedge. Hedge had been fitted for college by age twelve by his ambitious philosophy professor father, Levi Hedge. He spent four years under the care of the Göttingen pioneer George Bancroft while studying at Germany's best gymnasia, and was soon to be graduating from the Divinity School. By the time they renewed their friendship after her return from Groton, Hedge was fast establishing himself as Cambridge's most learned young man. With his "cold and haughty" intellectual demeanor (which Margaret later confessed she had "prize[d]" then) and his unaffected enthusiasm for German philosophy and literature, young "Germanicus" (as Margaret called him) for many years exerted a strong influence on Margaret and her Cambridge friends. Unlike Hedge, who was nearly five years older than Margaret, most of Margaret's male friends were around her age, many of them belonging to Harvard's famous Class of 1829, which counted, among other later notables, Oliver Wendell Holmes and the mathematician Benjamin Peirce. Margaret's friends in the class included the future liberal Whig editor and congressman George T. Davis, the later Unitarian leader and editor James Freeman Clarke, and Dr. William Ellery Channing's nephew, the future Transcedentalist socialist minister William Henry Channing. Two other promising young Harvard men in her circle were the talented star pupil of Justice Story, George S. Hillard, later the law partner and advisor of the antislavery senator Charles Sumner, and William Greenleaf Eliot, future Western Unitarian organizer and founder of Washington University in St. Louis. All these young men and women were in turn friends with each other. They talked, corresponded, and socialized constantly—at each other's houses, at music and riding parties organized by the Davis sisters, at excursions to Fresh Pond and Mount Auburn, and at gatherings in the homes of socially active Harvard faculty like the Farrars and the elder Henry Wares. Altogether they made up one of the brightest and liveliest circles of young people in Unitarian Boston-Cambridge.[27]

Of course, not all of these friends were always fond of Margaret. The temperamental Helen Davis grumbled about Margaret's lack of "gracious[ness]" toward her. Elizabeth Randall's songstress sister Belinda complained that Margaret "put herself on [her] & allowed [her] no chance." The ambitious William Eliot muttered to friends that Margaret treated him "like a plaything." And the courtly William Channing kept his distance from what he remembered as her "saucy sprightliness." Still, it is clear from both later recollections and contemporary letters that Margaret was an attractive figure in her circles. One woman later testified that as early as 1829 "all the girls raved about Margaret Fuller." Cultural circumstances might have had something to do with this. Social historians tell us that the loosening of parental controls in the early Republic facilitated a tightening of bonds for many American middle-class adolescents, and this, if true, probably helped. Then, all the heroic Romantic literature that she and her friends read perhaps also predisposed them, as some of their rhetoric in their letters suggest, to find in her Romantic overtures something exciting and admirable. Yet in explaining Margaret's transformation in these years from an awkward young girl to an object of some fascination, one cannot leave out of the equation Margaret herself. First of all she was funny. Some of her friends may have found her satire "scathing," but most found it, as many of them confessed, also vastly entertaining. Even the earnest young teacher Elizabeth Peabody, about as humorless a soul as Boston Unitarianism ever produced, perfectly captured this aspect of Margaret in her remembrance of her first meeting with her in 1828. "Margaret said almost nothing, but I thought she was laughing at me, for which there seemed good cause. I was impressed strongly with her perfect good nature. It seemed to me her eyes overflowed with fun, & this fun was a pure sense of the comic,—inevitable to an intellect sharp as a diamond; the conviction was irresistible that she had no malice in her heart." Another appealing trait was her conversation. Even in these early years, her friends testified, knots of listeners would gather around her at parties to hear her brilliant sallies. Of the general manner of this talk, Hedge—a sharp observer of Margaret from these years—has left a persuasive account:

Her conversation, as it was then, I have seldom heard equalled. It was not so much attractive as commanding. Though remarkably fluent and select, it was neither fluency, nor choice diction, nor wit, nor sentiment, that gave it its peculiar power, but accuracy of statement, keen discrimination, and a certain weight of judgment, which contrasted strongly and charmingly with the youth and sex of the speaker.[28]

Finally, there were two other personal qualities of Margaret's that especially appealed to her male friends. One is implied in Hedge's reminiscence—her formidable intellect. Hedge recalled being immediately struck by "what in woman is generally called a masculine mind; that is, its action was determined by ideas rather than sentiments"; and James Freeman Clarke's journals at the time are filled with encomiums to her analytical powers and, above all, her fierce independence. Hedge agreed. "The question with her was not what should be believed, or what ought to be true, but what is true. Her yes and no were never conventional; and she often amazed people by a cool and unexpected dissent from the commonplaces of popular acceptation." The other trait that her Cambridge friends claimed bound them to her—both male and female—was her uncanny knack for making them believe (in Clarke's words) in their "secret interior capability." "All her friends will unite in the testimony, that . . . they have never seen one who, like her, by the conversation of an hour or two, could not merely entertain and inform, but make an epoch in one's life. We all dated back to this or that conversation with Margaret, in which we took a complete survey of great subjects, came to some clear view of a difficult question, saw our way open before us to a higher plane of life, and were led to some definite resolution or purpose which has had a bearing on all our subsequent career." How did she do this? Mainly, it would seem from her friends' accounts of their conversations with her in these years, by (as she herself admitted) "poetiz[ing]" their lives. As Clarke wrote, "Margaret saw all her friends . . . idealized. She was a balloon of sufficient power to take us all up with her into the serene depth of heaven, where she loved to float, far above the low details of earthly life." So it was that her friends came to feel in her company "truer, wiser, better, and yet more free and happy, than elsewhere." It is not surprising that although, according to Clarke, she constantly prodded her friends in stern language to "aspire to something higher," they came back so many times for the balloon ride. For "self-satisfied mediocrity . . . she felt and expressed something very like contempt."[29]

Margaret's youthful letters to her friends confirm many of these recollections. This is particularly true of those to her girlfriends. Hedge later recalled, "She loved to draw these fair girls ["the belles of their day"] to herself, and to make them her guests, and was never so happy as when surrounded, in company, with such a bevy," and her letters show this well enough. Historians have suggested that these were years when the heightened awareness of the gender differences in roles and sensibilities often threw young women back on themselves, encouraging them to see in their female friends superior objects of intellectual and romantic fascination. One can see something of this in Margaret's letters: by turns erudite, witty, coquettish, and—in a Gothic sort of way—sentimental. In one letter to Amelia Greenwood, she recommended a poem of Shelley's to support Amelia's opinions on "those faint and shadowed reminiscences of a former state of being which haunt the troubled soul in this." And in a very different mood, in a letter to Amelia at the end of her nineteenth year, she described sitting and listening for three hours "in boarding-school attitude hemming a ruffle and saying never a word" to the jokes of Nathan Weston, a justice of the Maine Supreme Court ("Pa—always thinks my presence gives a finish to the scene"). Cutting short the domestic news, she turned abruptly to Amelia, jauntily demanding to know,

> How do you live or *do* you live? I hope so!. . . . You know, Amelia, I've long wished that the customs of society would permit to be intoxicate *only once* as I've read them to be in the [*illegible word*] et cetera— Well! I was so yesterday; I'm sure of it— In the morng I went into the fields and passed the morng reading Moore's Byron and inspiring delight in every breath. *Then* I was a *happy*. . . . I was in kind of delireum I read senselessly and dreamed consciously at the same time. . . . My whole being is Byronized at this moment c'est à dire my whole mind is possessed with one desire—to comprehend Byron once for all.

Indeed, the whole of young Cambridge seemed at this moment fairly well Byronized: "What a splended quantity of tragick talk is going on in society; every body hoping to have life diversified and self complacency flattened by somebody taking the trouble to knock down or shoot." In a yet racier letter a few months later—this one to one of her wittiest confidantes, Amelia Barlow, then living in Lynn, where her new husband was the Unitarian minister—she wrote this flippant, flirtatious, and defiantly self-satirical bit of nonsense: "My dear Simplicetta, why don't you get well? Really this additional pain in your fascinating ankles is too heart-breaking. The Trevetts, Coffins, Breeds [prominent parishioners of her husband's] &c, are too exciting for you I know. Never before have your *ankles* been excited, even by my overwhelming power." She devoted the remainder of her letter to a lengthy, droll account of her recent gender-bending "adventures." Conceding she had neither cried, fainted, nor played the harp, still, she pleaded, "in my own soft feminine style," she had done much: from sewing for her siblings "several garments fitted for the wear of American youth" and shedding "tears for others' woes," to devouring newspaper accounts of a recent, lurid murder trial.

> In short, to climax this journal of many-colored deeds and chances, so well have I played my part, that in the self-same night I was styled by two several persons, "a sprightly young lady", and "a Syren!!" Oh rapturous sound! I have reached the goal of my ambition; Earth has nothing fairer or brighter to offer. "Intelligency" was nothing to it. A "Supercilious", "satirical", "affected", "pedantic" "Syren"!!!! Can the olla-podrida of human nature present a compound of more varied ingredients, or higher gusto?[30]

About the only appealing things one *cannot* find in Margaret's letters to her young female friends in these years were unaffected passion or tenderness. This fact, however, did not stop Margaret from demanding that her female friends' letters be "sentimental." "Sentiment," she told Almira—calling her (with side allusions to Goethe's androgynous Mignon and her girlfriend Leila) "my beloved!" and "loveliest of created minister's wives!"—"now bears unbounded sway in the palace of my heart." Yet when even the witty Almira once complained in a letter that Margaret had (as she quoted her) "'never before told you I loved you,'" Margaret answered, dismissively, "The tender and weakly souls have need to be fed on *words,* and to such I use them."[31]

These were high-minded, heroic words—quite different from the passionately sublimated and cloyingly sentimental ones historians have discovered in the friendship letters of middle-class antebellum women. There was another difference, too: Margaret was not especially gender-conscious in these adolescent years, but practiced her intensive arts equally on her close female *and* male friends. To be sure, one finds more exuberantly playful, flirtatious flourishes in letters to her female friends and likewise more high-minded allusions to great deeds in those to her male ones. But otherwise her letters to and from the two sexes are very similar. One can find in them all the same touting of the same English semi-Gothic novels and Romantic poetry, the same literarily allusive analyses of the personalities of their mutual friends, and the same playful trumpeting of Margaret's non-"ladylike" manners. One finds also the same incongruous mix of humorous, incestuously cozy expressions, frequent affirmations of contempt for "sentimentalities" and of "pride" in their sincerity and "Realism," and constant encouragement to "noble sentiment." Yet there was one gender difference: the incongruity of these impulses led to no evident difficulties with her female friends. But they certainly did with her two closest male friends.[32]

V

The oldest of these male friends was Margaret's distant cousin George Davis. An acquaintance since her childhood, Davis had a special allure for many of his friends, but none more than for Margaret. In a thinly disguised fictionalized sketch written some years later, Margaret described him as an analytical voluptuary: "He was as premature as myself; at thirteen a man in the range of his thoughts, analyzing motives, and explaining principles, ... while mentally accompanying Gil Blas [his "favorite reading"] through his course of intrigue and adventure, and visiting with him the impure atmosphere of courtiers, picaroons, and actresses." His most obvious appeal for Margaret and her friends, though, was as an intellectual talker. "The greatest conversationalist" he met in America, Thackeray would later call him, and they would have readily agreed. Clarke recalled, "His memory was prodigious, and he quoted in conversation innumerable passages from all authors—grave and gay, lively or severe." His friends were especially impressed, he added, by Davis's "intellectual abandon" or, as he put it, his "habit of *letting himself go* in conversation." Beyond this, Clarke speculated that Margaret was taken with Davis "on account of his quick, active intellect, and his contempt for shows and pretenses; for his inexhaustible wit, his exquisite taste, his infinitely varied stores of information, and the poetic view which he took of life, painting it with Rembrandt depths of shadow and bursts of light." In other words, she liked him because he was a sort of young, male Margaret Fuller. Certainly James Clarke's sister Sarah—at this time a highly skeptical observer of Margaret—thought the two were quite compatible. Speaking a few years later of James's "college frolics" with them, which she heartily disliked, she recalled to her brother: "I could not conceive what you were all *at*. It seemed to be something. If I had judged only from George and Margaret, I should thought the plan was to pull people to pieces to see what they were made of, and then divert themselves with the fragments. I felt all the time I was with either of them that there was some such design concealed under a manner which was intended to mystify from its very recklessness." Yet it was precisely, of course, such mutual recklessness that nourished their intimacy. Even after their friendship later soured, she told Clarke "we can still communicate more closely with one another than either could with the herd."[33]

Their iconoclasm also relected certain common intellectual outlooks. Aphorisms of Davis's to his young friends strongly echoed Margaret's own defiantly naturalistic, youthful Romanticism: a letter "fit to eat," "surrender the whole mind to a new impression till one had tried its influence," "outwardly ugly but . . . natural therefore right." It is hardly surprising, therefore, to find in Margaret's letters to Davis her most pointed critiques of Romantic poetry, her most Rousseauistic discussions of heroic fatalism, her most militant defenses of Byron against the poet's moralistic English and local Unitarian detractors. But the most intellectually revealing letter of Margaret's to Davis along these lines was one she wrote at the beginning of 1830, in which, in response to a question of his about them in a previous letter, she sketched her religious views. After asserting at the outset that she had "determined not to form settled opinions at present," she went on to explain:

Loving or feeble natures need a positive religion, a visible refuge, a protection, as much in the passionate season of youth as in those stages nearer the grave. But mine is not such. My pride is superior to any feelings I have yet experienced: my affection is strong admiration, not the necessity of giving or receiving assistance or sympathy. When disappointed, I do not ask or wish consolation,—I wish to know and feel my pain, to investigate its nature and its source; I will not have my thoughts diverted, or my feelings soothed; 't is therefore that my young life is so singularly barren of illusions. I know, I feel the time must come when this proud and impatient heart shall be stilled, and turn from the ardors of Search and Action, to lean on something above. But—shall I say it?—the thought of that calmer era is to me a thought of deepest sadness; so remote from my present being is that future existence, which still the mind may conceive. I believe in Eternal Progression. I believe in a God, a Beauty and Perfection to which I am to strive all my life for assimilation. From these two articles of belief, I draw the rules by which I strive to regulate my life. But, though I reverence all religions as necessary to the happiness of man, I am yet ignorant of the religion of Revelation. Tangible promises! well defined hopes! are things of which I do not now feel the need. At present, my soul is intent on this life, and I think of religion as its rule; and, in my opinion, this is the natural and proper course from youth to age.

To this Davis responded by expressing his satisfaction with her opinions, but strongly deprecating believing even "temporarily" in deism. She answered, "I do not consider them in this light, because I do not *dis*believe or even *carelessly set aside* Revelation; I merely remain in ignorance of the Christian Revelation because I do not feel it suited to me at present." As for Davis's standard liberal Christian argument that "the philosophers . . . appealed to the intellect,— Christ to the sympathies," she replied, "These sympathies I do not wish to foster— shall I quicken the heart to a sense of its wants when I can so ill supply those of the mind?" If not militantly deistic, this was certainly at least a boldly skeptical and Romantically Stoic answer, and indicative of both Margaret's youthful religious radicalism and her free-wheeling intellectual relationship with Davis.[34]

But on a purely personal level, it was also a somewhat disingenuous pronouncement. Even if she was not exactly "loving or feeble," she did need love. Only a year or so before, she had written in her journal a poem that—after her usual paeans to a "true Friendship" that stimulates "the noblest deeds and thoughts" for "souls of high mould"—finally sighed out at the end for "Some *equal bosom* open to the flood / Which at the electric touch will make its way / Borne on by faith that *once in life* the heart is understood." The evidence is also clear that the one she wished love from was Davis. One can see something of his appeal in this department. Several surviving letters to their female friends show him broadly hinting, Byronic-fashion, that beneath his gay façade there lies hidden a tender heart of melancholy and sorrow. Margaret herself described him to Clarke as a "hero" and, in another letter, as a young man whose talk could make a girl feel "giddy"; she told him admiringly (while professing to *"detest"* and *"pardon"* his prototype's acts) that he resembled the charming, violent, love-crazed, rapist-antihero Lovelace in Richardson's *Clarissa* ("the resemblance to you . . . is in his levity, nay! brilliant vivacity and airy self-possession under circumstances of the greatest apparent difficulty, doubt and mortification"); she wrote to him still other letters that in their gentle, come-hither tenderness were almost unique for her in these years ("I shall always be glad to have you come to me when saddened. The Melancholick does not misbecome you"). Indeed even years after their friendship had become embittered, she still looked back on their early intimacy, she told him, as "conjugal" and containing ("Possibly!") a "tinge of love." Did Davis feel any of this tinge? She at least thought he did. "I found that during [our] yrs of youth," she later told him, "when I had treated you with the most unshrinking sincerity—when you had known *all* that lay in my mind with regard to you, you on yr side had cherished sweet thoughts of me wh you had never announced. I thought at the time that was what I never shld forgive." If this were true, it would not have been out of character for this witty, intellectual, and sensitive, but also calculating young man. ("Designs are not like plants," his friend Clarke quoted one of his favorite sayings; "they thrive best in the dark.") In any case, he did not tell her any "sweet thoughts," and as the implications of that fact began to dawn on Margaret during her twentieth year, their friendship rapidly cooled.[35]

In the same year that Margaret was beginning to see George Davis in a less flattering light, she found a new companion in his best friend, James Freeman Clarke. The son of an energetic but unsuccessful inventor-druggist and an enterprising, garrulous mother who for many years kept a popular boardinghouse in Boston, Clarke had spent most of his childhood as the cherished only child in the home of his grandfather, Dr. James Freeman, Boston's King's Chapel minister and America's first avowed Unitarian preacher, who had prevailed on his parents to let James live with him. Unfortunately, the experience of being tutored alone at home by this kindly, scholarly, elderly liberal minister, while it was enjoyable and instructive, also made him, he later thought, highly sensitive and, despite his outward humor and gregariousness, almost pathologically self-questioning. The contrast between his liberal childhood education under the direction of his Rousseau-influenced grandfather and the very different one he encountered at Harvard was another disappointment. By the late 1820s the new day at Harvard presaged earlier in the decade by the young Göttingen scholars was fast receding. Everett, Bancroft, Cogswell, and Ticknor had all quit, frustrated in their attempts to broaden the curriculum and reform instruction, and anxious to strike out in more rewarding careers in education, literature, or politics. Consequently, the Harvard that Clarke and many of his friends encountered seemed to them almost moribund—narrowly classical in subject offerings, rigidly neoclassical in aesthetic taste, and still committed to the time-honored nonteaching methods of recitation and correction. In reaction, Clarke, Davis, Channing, and others of their classmates pursued their own extracurricular course of readings in English Renaissance and Romantic authors. But it was the American edition of Coleridge's *Aids to Reflection* that Clarke and his friends came across their senior year that, he would later claim, transformed his life. "Coleridge showed me from Kant," he wrote, "that though knowledge begins *with* experience it does not come *from* experience." With this insight it suddenly seemed to him that his own inward, purely subjective thoughts and feelings that had been so crippling to him could now be related to the loftiest disciplines of religion and philosophy. Soon after this discovery he definitely decided on the ministry as his future profession and that fall entered Harvard Divinity School.[36]

What James Clarke, then, brought into Margaret's life was an earnest, if inchoate, philosophical aspiration that, apart from Hedge's similar but more secure one, she had not known before. In the meantime, though, there was the more immediate issue of the making of a suitably Romantic friendship. In this matter Clarke was the initiating one. To get the process going that spring, he wrote several cozily titillating notes to his "Cousin Mine." ("I believe I am as much your cousin as George is"; actually, his Fuller ancestor was no relation of Margaret's.) He also wrote more serious letters, imploring her to give him a history of her mind and "views of life." But she resisted, sometimes flippantly, sometimes frankly. "A sad process of feeling" over the last two years, she said in one note, in an obvious allusion to George Davis, had led her to suppress her desire for "gentler and more sympathetick" affections. Finally, after one particularly earnest plea by Clarke, she gave in. She could not promise him limitless confidence, she said, but "I *can* promise that no timid caution, no haughty dread shall prevent my telling you the truth of my thoughts on any subject we may have in common. Will this satisfy you? Oh let it; suffer me to know you." In a post-script she added: "No other cousin or friend of any style is to see this note." To this Clarke responded in kind: "You cannot think how full of gratitude my heart was when I read your last note. . . . I said, there has come an aera, a wonderful epoch in my life; I shall now begin to live out of my own soul, and I went, every-where ruminating on my approaching happiness."[37]

Was Clarke in love with Margaret? Not at all, though this fact did not always seem obvious to those unfamiliar with the conventions of Romantic friendship. Rebecca Clarke, James's mother, later recalled one day having tea with Mar-garet, James, and James's Grandfather Freeman. "They were very polite and all that. Father Freeman sat looking at them & when they were off, he said, *'Poor James!'* 'What's the matter Father Freeman?' said I. 'Poor James!' said he, 'he'll go and marry that woman, and be miserable all the days of his life. Don't you see what a cross mouth she's got? she won't make him happy!" But the plain fact is—however it might have sounded to uninitiated father-figures—Clarke wanted and very much needed a friend, not a lover. For one thing, he already had a lover, or rather a would-be lover—Margaret's friend Elizabeth Randall. For another, besides being constantly perplexed about what he called "the Eliz-abeth affair," he was also in his first year of theology school, full of enthusiasm for Coleridge and the "lofty metaphysics of the day," and deeply worried about how he was going to make them relevant to the rationalistic theological studies he was forced to endure in Divinity School. But most of all he worried that his ingrained self-consciousness and lack of confidence would keep him from being able to act on the world at all. In a word, he sought psychological support and a practical guide to life, and in Margaret—so different from his skeptical male friends Davis and Channing—he thought he found both.[38]

On her side, Margaret's primary need (as her letters clearly show) perfectly coincided with Clarke's: in the wake of Davis's increasing distance from her, she needed a "confiding and earnest" young male intellectual friend (as Clarke tried hard to be) with whom she could exchange ideas and confidences. But she also needed something else: she needed a new male friend with whom she could share—as she seems to have been unable to do with her exuberant but private young female friends—her most lavish Romantic fantasies of heroic public achievement. This is shown—indeed trumpeted—in a letter Margaret wrote on May 7, 1830, in response to Clarke's continuing entreaties to tell him her "fan-cies"—or something, he had told her, that would "electrify my stupor with your generosity," "thrill me," and, not the least, of course, "show your confidence in me." She gave him her best shot. In this fervidly alienated and ego-centered yet messianic statement, Fuller spelled out for Clarke's benefit her early Rousseauis-tic-Byronic, perfectionist faith. "I have greatly wished to see among us," she told him,

> such a person of Genius as the nineteenth century can afford—ie. one who has tasted
> in the morning of existence the extremes of good and ill both imaginative and
> real— I had imagined a person endowed by nature with that acute sense to Beauty,
> (ie Harmony or Truth) and that vast capacity of desire which give soul to love and

ambition.— I had wished this person might grow up to manhood *alone* (but not *alone in crowds*); I would have placed him in a situation so retired, so obscure, that he would quietly but without bitter sense of isolation stand apart from all surrounding him; I would have had him go on steadily feeding his mind with congenial love, hopefully confident that if he only nourished his existence into perfect life, Fate would at fitting season furnish an atmosphere and orbit meet for his breathing and exercise; I wished he might adore not fear the bright phantoms of his mind's creation and believe them but the shadows of external things to be met hereafter. After this steady intellectual growth had brought his powers to manhood so far as the ideal can do it, I wished this being might be launched into the world of realities, his heart glowing with the ardor of an immortal towards perfection; his eyes searching every-where to behold it; I wish he might collect into one burning point those withering palsying convictions which in the ordinary routine of things so gradually pervade the soul; That he might suffer in brief space agonies of disappointment commensurate with his unpreparedness and confidence. And I thought thus thrown back on the representing, pictorial resources I supposed him originally to possess; With such material— And the need he must feel of using it, Such a man would suddenly dilate into a form of Pride, Power, and Glory— A centre round which asking, aimless hearts might rally— A man fitted to act as interpreter to the one tale of many-languaged ages!

What words are these! Perhaps you will feel as if I sought but for "the longest and strongest"— Yet to my ear they do but faintly describe the imagined powers of such a being.[39]

VI

There is no record of how Margaret's begging auditor responded to her Romantic messianic sketch. On a personal level he might have found it a *little* puzzling. It could not have been entirely clear to him, for example, whether he was expected to buckle on his sword and armor or watch as she buckled on hers. But in either case he was certainly (as he had wished) "*roused* to thought." Meanwhile, the two new friends roused each other about their mutual intellectual enthusiasms. In some of these the naturalistic Margaret and the sentimentalist James flatly disagreed. He ranked Scott high; she ranked him low. He loved pathetic fallacies; she abhorred them. ("Expliquez moi 'The soul of Each,'" she demanded in answer to a sentimental sonnet Clarke sent her. "Does my Cousin believe that stately trees, pensive flowery &c have their souls. Is that your philosophy?"—adding for good measure: "'Pensive flowers,' have flowers characteristicks in your eyes? When people talk so about them I always think if they are conscious how they must detest us! no wonder they wither near us.") On other favorite subjects, like Disraeli's *Vivian Grey* and Godwin's *Mandeville* (in whose "unsocial, proud and sensitive" character, Clarke told Margaret, he found many resemblances to himself), the two alienated Romantics entirely agreed.[40]

About one esoteric Romantic topic—and one about which she had had some experience and that would all her life fascinate her—they wrestled around a bit: the subject of dreams. In a long letter on "the life-like phantoms of Dreamland," Clarke detailed several of his and observed how he often perceived on awakening "a regular plot to my dreams which I was entirely ignorant of while the action was proceeding," concluding, with Coleridge as his source ("a high authority in matters of psychology"), that the voice of dreams "was no foreign voice, but that of our soul," yielding to us the kind of knowledge akin to that which we receive from our *"Imagination"* in our everyday waking life. He also added— good Unitarian divinity student that he was— that we cannot know "whether or not it is . . . by this point that the human soul is connected with the divine," but we can be sure that "its influences on the character are all heavenly as they direct and urge its strivings toward that *truth* which is immortal." On the other hand, Margaret— whose youthful Romanticism was more Promethean than pious— balked at such an uplifting philosophy of dreams. She too, she said, believed dreams revealed "strange secrets." But she also thought they revealed things that were both truthful and terrible.

> The realization of hope which you describe *I* have never known except in *day-dreams*— All that I can recollect of the night presents detached scenes, sometimes ludicrous, sometimes distorted and terrible— Sometimes sanctified by ineffable tenderness. And I never felt this in a dream save to persons with whom I have a genuine magnetick affinity. Waking I walk in delusion; I seek and fancy qualities in those I meet which they cannot possess. I force myself to esteem many, to appreciate good-qualities which never roused one *answering* thrill amid my sensibilities. But in sleep Time and circumstance being unheeded, the interested blindness which springs from them vanishes and the liberated soul feels its nature and distinguishes its allies.

As an example of her more naturalistic view that dreams revealed, not transcendent goodness, but strange and sometimes terrible truths, she provided a sample of "a horrid dream" she had had the previous night.

> Last night I suffered from mean jealousies and ceaseless suspicions of I know not what ill— At last I was in a room with a person whom I felt that I loved very much but whose face I could not see. I believed I urged or tempted this person to look up a chimney. I heard two loud reports quick one after the other; this person exclaimed 'God Almighty' in a voice of the utmost anguish and horror, and seemed about to fall back into my arms when I awoke. . . . Now what do you think of this dream?— Oh Jean Jacques the second.

As Clarke's reply is lost, one can only guess what he had to say. But one can be sure that he found such a strangely impassioned, paranoid, and (to a modern Freudian reader) sexually tempting dream rather difficult to fit into his Coleridgian schema.[41]

Of course, not all of their talk was intellectual. Mostly they tried to jostle each other into the intimacy they both claimed they wanted. It was not easy. The combination of his own insecurities and Margaret's simultaneous critical pronouncements and demands for "generous confidence[s]" frequently made the young Clarke, as he sometimes readily confessed to Margaret, highly nervous. Still, he was powerfully drawn to Margaret and, as his letters show, looked to her as a bolsterer of his confidence, inspirer of his studies, and advisor in his love life:

in sum, a sort of sisterly sybil. And Margaret readily obliged him. "I do not think you are now capable of feeling or inspiring a constant and ardent attachment," she bluntly told him in answer to a long letter declaring he had decided "I must give up Love" (read "Elizabeth Randall"). "But," she added— mixing frankness, common sense, and a heavy dose of prophetic incense— he should not worry. "Your character will poise itself." In the meantime, "accomplish yourself my dear James, for the world here and beyond and in due time the taste for tete a tete dinners &c &c will steal upon your well warmed and lighted heart." The test of this sort of advice should be: did it work? did he feel better about himself? The answer is clearly a resounding yes. In one entry, after recording praises George Davis had told him she had made to him about some of Clarke's letters that she had shown to him, he wrote in his journal: "If I have been able to affect so forcibly such a mind as M.F.'s, I am sure that I have powers which may one day be brought to bear upon men & make them thrill whilst I speak. . . . I think I may now say without being an idle boast, that M. herself shall see a crowd hanging on my tones— & when that happens I shall come to her & say— 'you encouraged me to the labour, to you I owe it.'"[42]

These hopeful words Clarke wrote in the spring. By the winter his friendship with Margaret took, for a while, a dip. He finally determined that his "fair Elschen"—whom he had been pursuing with decreasing success over the previous year—did not love him as he loved her, and in late December these feelings exploded in a nasty quarrel. Within a few days he wrote Elizabeth an apologetic note asking for forgiveness. But she never received it because, somehow or other, Margaret had managed to intercept it. She also for some time failed to tell him what she had done, causing further pain and embarrassment. Why she took it upon herself to intervene in such a seemingly cruel way is not clear. Jealousy, if not specifically over Clarke, then over a flirtation she had not yet experienced, may have been a factor. (She would years later insist that their "sober suited friendship" had always been "strictly fraternal.") Her own explanation to Clarke, though, was thoroughly high-minded: certain that Elizabeth's "morbid" and "premature" character and James's sentimental and insecure one made them "altogether unsuited to each other," she simply took it upon herself to deliver the coup de grâce to a hopeless affair. As for her reason for keeping Elizabeth's letter, she said, "I looked upon you at that time as a man infatuated, and thought your fever must work itself off and that your pains would not be lessened by such sympathy as she could offer." But whether high- or low-minded, her method was certainly high-handed. Yet—and this is a good indication of how much deference she could command from her friends—Clarke fully accepted it. In fact, two years later, although still smarting over his wounded pride, he looked back on Margaret's rude intervention as a turning point in his life. Margaret's shattering his illusions about Elizabeth, he wrote in his journal, gave him a "Faith in the wealth of happiness which lives in the world of eternal truth & reality."[43]

Ironically, just at the time that Margaret was rudely seeing Clarke through his crisis of romantic rejection, she was passing through one of her own. Indeed, the fact that the two events overlapped leads one strongly to suspect that if there *was* any malice in her interception of Elizabeth's letter, it might well have reflected displacement of anger she really felt toward her own rejecter, George Davis. For in these very weeks of her contretemps with Clarke, her "conjugal" friendship with George Davis reached a crisis point: he made it clear to her that he wanted to end or at least cool their intimacy. Why he did this is unclear. Since his graduation he had been studying law in Greenfield in western Massachusetts and, most recently, courting there (at least as she appears in letters of Margaret and her friends) a pretty, witty, coquettish, but somewhat immature young woman named Harriet Russell, whom he would eventually marry. Margaret was hurt and confused, and she confronted him with her feelings that winter while he was in town. After one particularly upsetting meeting on February 1, 1831, she wrote him the next day an agitated, if somewhat obscure, letter.

> My cousin and (at this moment) dearest friend. . . . I did now know what I said; I was so troubled and surprized that you cd. still excite a new sensation.
> I feel that but for you I should be free at least in the common [*illegible*] sense of the world. You are the only person who can appreciate my true self. This thought has been most grievous to me.
> You alone can now see me as I truly am.
> O would my cousin that I could act out my present feelings and show gratitude to the person who has embellished my life with one sweet emotion. Alas! I dare not hope it.
> . . . . Long ere that my cousin may you be happy and untroubled by me. My heart does not wish this but my reason does.

What exactly Davis made of this presumable attempt at acceptance of his withdrawal or perhaps Harriet (Margaret's letter only survives in a fragment) is not clear, but he did not answer it. So she wrote again, this time feverishly: "You have not answered my note; you have not given me what I asked. You do not come here. Do not you act so,—it is the drop too much." Finally, she did receive his answer and, whatever it was (the letter has not been recovered), it at least seems to have calmed her, for she answered righteously, if a little tremulously: "You need not have delayed your answer so long; why not at once answer the question I asked? Faith is not natural to me; for the love I feel to others is not in the idleness of poverty, nor can I persist in believing the best, merely to save myself pain, or keep a leaning place for the weary heart. But I should believe you, because I have seen that your feelings are strong and constant; they have never disappointed me, when closely scanned."[44]

And scan them she certainly did. "He had confided in me & I in him, he had shown me his whole character & become acquainted with mine," she complained to Clarke in one of many bitter conversations she had with him about Davis over the following year. And now, she said, instead of allowing "the decay of affection" that different experiences would naturally have dictated, he suddenly wanted to end their intimacy. For his part, Clarke, who had never been as enraptured with Davis as had Margaret, assured her that Davis' standoffishness "seems only a phase of his essential temper. Circumstances have led him to put his trust in different objects, but he will always be the same speculating, man-nerless dog—absorbed in the present excitement." She agreed up to a point. "She supposed," Clarke recorded in his journal she told him, "the amount of the whole was that he had treated her only as he had done every one else & her vanity had always made her suppose that she would be different to him from every one else." But she also felt that his avoidance of her showed a deep and fundamental flaw in his character. "G. wanted something more than the confidence that sub-sisted between us," Clarke reported her telling him. "He wanted to be interesting to me. He wanted me to respect him." And this, she said, bespoke his "vanity," nurtured his "proud reserve," and proved, in sum, that he was "not a great man after all."[45]

This is a perfectly plausible analysis of her self-deception and Davis's likely vanity. What is missing from it, though—as from all her righteous comments on her quarrel with Davis that have survived—were several rather important ele-ments. One was the fact that she was in love with Davis, perhaps more than she realized. Another was Davis's courtship of Harriet Russell, which was the obvi-ous trigger of her panic over him as well as very probably his new resistance to Margaret's demands for confidences (or what he told Clarke were her *"suspi-cious"* scrutinizing of "the smallest things"). Nor, finally—and this is the most important point for her—can one find in her ruminations on the affair any rec-ognition that there was at the center of her friendship with Davis a fundamental flaw: namely, that her demand for severe "realism" in her "confessional[s]" with friends was not the sort of quality that easily combined with either the "sweet thoughts" she wanted Davis to feel for her or the disdainful heroism she had always encouraged in her male friends. Clarke—even through the fog of Coler-idgian jargon—grasped something of her difficulty with Davis and, by extension, young men in general, when he told her in one letter, "To give yourself up entire, you need to have before you a whole being, but your imagination could create none while your understanding was busy in dissecting the person *en question*." In a word, denied—or denying herself—the role of an unironic Byronic hero, she sought it in male friends like Davis, while she busily made sure they had no illusions they were cut out for such a figure.[46]

She sometimes had an inkling of the problem. "I shall not have a friendship I fear," she said to Clarke in one of their conversations. "The natural friendship for me would have been with some other girl— We should tell each other all our love affairs, talk it all out, & then go on buying shawls & consulting each other about crockery to the end of our days. But I wanted something more." What that "more" was she did not say. But in a postscript to a long letter she wrote to Clarke about Davis a year after their breakup, she acknowledged that one thing it was—vicarious heroism—Davis's aloofness and vanity had now soured her on. Urgently asking Clarke to return a letter she had written to him on some heroic theme connected with Davis, she wrote, "I *must* burn it— George's resolve to 'come as a hero or come not at all'— has disgusted me with all *that*." But these were exceptions. For the most part, to Margaret, Davis's separation from her was a betrayal of their friendship and a fall from the "nobleness" of heroic intimacy and little more. In her letter to Clarke (who had included in his letter one of Davis's, which explained—as Clarke characterized his position—his need to be now "independent of your influence"), she wrote in grief and anger:

It is painful to lose the friend whose knowledge and converse mingled so intimately with the growth of my mind, the only friend to whom I was all truth and frankness, seeking nothing but equal truth and frankness in return— But this evil may be borne— the hard, lasting evil was to learn to distrust my own heart and lose all faith in my power of knowing others—

   In this letter I see again that peculiar pride, that contempt of the forms and shews of goodness— that fixed resolve to be any-thing but "like unto these Pharisees" which were to my eye such happy omens— Yet how strangely distorted are all his views! The daily influence of his intercourse with me was like the breath he drew, it has become a part of him— can he escape from himself?— Would he be unlike all other mortals? his feelings are as false as those of Alcibiades— and of his also vanity is the spring— He influenced me and helped form me to what I am? others shall succeed him?— shall I be ashamed to owe any-thing to friendship? But why do I talk?— for nothing can be more false than such ideas of independence— a child could confute them by defining the term *human being*.[47]

Eventually, over the next several years, her righteousness and anger gave way to sadness and longing. "I feel dreadfully lonely," she confessed in her journal the year following her letter to Clarke, whenever she read in Ludwig Tieck's novel about the depraved, hedonistic seducer William Lovell (whose eloquence made her "sympathize with" even while "loathing" him) and then took a walk by herself. "I would not go alone, but there is no person whose companionship would be endurable to me— except one— and reason forbids me even to wish for that person's society— reason alas! pride too— In a profound but not a cold reserve I must shroud my heart, if I would escape the most deadly wounds." With Clarke a year later she was more pointed yet: "George is to me a walking memento mori— haunting [my] day-dreams."[48]

That Margaret's break with Davis was a significant event in her life is suggested by the fact that it was very soon followed by her near mental and physical collapse. In the summer of 1831 she was bled and administered medicines by a physician. "Thanks to his medicines," she recalled, "my nerves became calmed, flushes and headaches gradually disappeared— I craved sleep, so long almost impossible to me. . . . I would now lie down in the middle of the day and sleep for hours." But the real confirmation of the importance of the Davis quarrel for Margaret is the fact that it precipitated or, at any rate, was again closely followed by, a major religious experience, the first one in her life.[49]

   Her parents and most of her friends, of course, held to the standard Unitarian faith, which in New England was still firmly grounded in a belief, if not in Jesus Christ's divinity, at least in his divine attributes and mission as teacher and savior as revealed in the Four Gospels. Margaret, as her letters to Davis showed, believed none of this. There is some evidence that she had recently become concerned about her unbelief. The previous winter she had had a long conversation with Eliza Farrar about how Farrar had come to know (as she described it for

Margaret) "that inner life which brought the soul into communion with God." But Unitarians generally distrusted sudden, emotion-laden changes of heart, and preferred to think of the process as a gradual coming (in Farrar's words) "to the knowledge of it." Margaret's religious change of heart was neither so slow nor so rational. As she described the circumstances to a friend seven years later: "For bitter months a treble weight had been pressing on me; the weight of deceived friendship, domestic discontent, and bootless love. I could not be much alone; a great burden of family cares pressed upon me; I was in the midst of society, and obliged to act my part there as well as I could." And in her journal, two years after this letter, she recollected precisely the day in question: "It was Thanksgiving day, . . . and I was obliged to go to church, or exceedingly displease my father. I almost always suffered much in church from a feeling of disunion with the hearers and dissent from the preacher; but to-day, more than ever before, the services jarred upon me from their grateful and joyful tone. I was wearied out with mental conflicts, and in a mood of most childish, child-like sadness. I felt within myself great power, and generosity, and tenderness; but it seemed to me as if they were all unrecognized, and as if it was impossible that they should be used in life." As she would again at such moments, she thought of herself as a child, and she thought of her father: "I looked around the church, and envied all the little children; for I supposed they had parents who protected them, so that they could never know this strange anguish, this dread uncertainty. I knew not, then, that none could have any father but God. I knew not, that I was not the only lonely one, that I was not the selected Oedipus, the special victim of an iron law." After this, she remembered, she left the church and walked fast through the fields, and she continued this way for several hours until she came to a little stream— "shrunken, voiceless, choked with withered leaves"—and then to a pool, dark and silent, and there she sat down. The rest she described as follows:

> I did not think; all was dark, and cold, and still. Suddenly the sun shone out with that transparent sweetness, like the last smile of a dying lover, which it will use when it has been unkind all a cold autumn day. And, even then, passed into my thought a beam from its true sun, from its native sphere, which has never since departed from me. I remembered how, a little child, I had stopped myself one day on the stairs, and asked, how came I here? How is it that I seem to be this Margaret Fuller? What does it mean? What shall I do about it? I remembered all the times and ways in which the same thought had returned. I saw how long it must be before the soul can learn to act under these limitations of time and space, and human nature; but I saw, also, that it MUST do it,—that it must make all this false true,—and sow new and immortal plants in the garden of God, before it could return again. I saw there was no self; that selfishness was all folly, and the result of circumstance; that it was only because I thought self real that I suffered; that I had only to live in the idea of the ALL, and all was mine. This truth came to me, and I received it unhesitatingly; so that I was for that hour taken up into God. In that true ray most of the relations of earth seemed mere films, phenomena.[50]

How should one interpret this incident? That it signified a genuine and deeply felt experience is not to be doubted. Whether it also meant, as she claimed later on, that her "earthly pain at not being recognized never went deep after this hour" is another question. Certainly it did not immediately erase the pain at not being recognized by George Davis, for two months later she wrote her bitter lament to Clarke over Davis's betrayal of their friendship. On a more psychological level, though, the experience probably allowed her, at least for a time, to distance herself from a whole complex of fears and fantasies of dependency developed since her childhood—some, as her references to the incestuous, patricidal Oedipus and her father suggest, filial ones connected with her father; some, as the trope of "the last smile of a dying lover" hints at, conventional feminine ones associated with George Davis; and some more recent ones connected to her desire, announced after her return from Groton, to make herself into a *"succès de société."* Intellectually, of course, her experience was also significant. This was not because it caused her to alter noticeably her religious opinions, or at least not in any doctrinal sense. Rather, what Margaret's "conversion experience," if one were to call it that, does seem to have added to her life were two things at once subtler and, in the long run, much more important. One was a certain intuitive religiosity she had never known before. The other was a new degree of philosophical seriousness and urgency—a desire, as she suggests in her reminiscence, not for self-renunciation but for some sort of self-transcendence. She was on her way to transforming herself from a bookish adolescent to an intellectual with a mission.

VII

The first signs of this transformation appeared that winter. In place of the joking and buoyant artifices, her letters to friends showed a new pensiveness. "It seems to me that I have reached the 'parting of the ways' in my life," she wrote to a friend that winter, "and all the knowledge which I have toiled to gain only serves to show me the disadvantages of each. None of those who think themselves my friends can aid me; each, careless, takes the path to which present convenience impels; and all would smile or stare, could they know the aching and measureless wishes, the sad apprehensiveness, which makes me pause and strain my almost hopeless gaze to the distance." Her new soberness, to be sure, took none of the sting from the naturalistic Romantic cultural opinions she continued to dispense to her friends. Indeed, if anything, it seems to have added another critical edge to them. "Father lectured me for looking satirical when the man of Words spake," she told Clarke after attending church one day, "and so attentive to the Man of Truth,—that is, of God." More philosophically, after describing her defense of the virtues of selfishness in a conversation they had with another friend that year, Clarke, Margaret's Boswell, wrote in his journal: "These are the two great points of Margaret's philosophy 1*st* That every thing natural in man is right. 2*nd* That consistency in thought and action is the object of all exertion. She protests against and opposes every thing unnatural & every thing inconsistent, whether hap-hazard or deliberate. Want of principle is naturally odious to her"; adding the qualifier, "By natural she understands the inner, constantly operating powers which are ever urging us onward." If nothing else, these comments show an intellectual sobriety missing from the avatar-of-genius fantasies with which Margaret had beguiled Clarke two years before.[51]

But above confessions and pronouncements, the most important sign of her new seriousness was her decision that winter to begin the study of German. This was not an easy undertaking. German books were extremely hard to obtain in Boston and Cambridge; instruction, outside of Charles Follen's classes, was almost nil; and familiarity with the basic texts, even among Boston-Cambridge's erudite intellectuals, was minimal. On the other hand, German was not exactly esoteric, either. Twenty years before, Madame de Staël had sung the praises of German culture in her *De l'Allemagne* (which Margaret first read that October), and since that time others closer to home had been adding their voices of approval: the Göttingen scholars most enthusiastically, of course, but also influential Unitarians like William Ellery Channing (at least in private), and, most important, Follen himself, who that September delivered his "Inaugural Discourse" as the college's first Professor of German Literature. But the consideration that really provoked Margaret and her friends' interest in German was neither academic nor literary but ideological: German thought had become in the last few years in Unitarian circles a hotly controversial subject. On one side, conservative Unitarians like Andrews Norton—echoing almost verbatim their orthodox opponents—excoriated modern German writers for promoting licentiousness in literature, skepticism or even atheism in theology, and an obscure and dangerous kind of mystical subjectivism in philosophy. On the other side, Coleridge had openly drawn on German philosophers for defining in his recent books his entire self-reflective philosophy. Younger Unitarian ministers like George Ripley, interested in breathing some Romantic life into their rationalistic faith, were beginning to defend in print German writers from their conservative Unitarian detractors. And, in Margaret's circle, young Henry Hedge— whose knowledge of German literature and philosophy was probably greater than that of anyone in Boston and Cambridge except Follen—hammered away on the theme in conversations with Margaret and her friends that modern German thought provided the only intellectually satisfying basis for a Christian faith. Margaret listened to all these voices, but to Hedge's especially. According to Clarke, though, the figure who finally induced Margaret and him actually to study the language was the most ideological of all the promoters of German literature—Thomas Carlyle. For the previous year or so, Clarke recalled, he, Margaret, and Davis had been reading in the Boston Athenaeum Carlyle's articles in the *Edinburgh* and *Foreign* reviews, which mocked and denounced the meaningless mechanism of modern civilization and called for its replacement by a new sense of wonder, duty, purposefulness, and revelations—and they had been deeply impressed. "It was like being introduced into another world; a world of new thoughts, hopes and opportunities." So, later that year, when Margaret and Clarke came across Carlyle's earlier essays on German Romantic authors, trumpeting them as modern antidotes to the evils of modernity, they took this, Clarke wrote, as their "wild bugle-call," and early in 1832 (Clarke having started a little earlier), Margaret began her study of German.[52]

Actually, "study" is hardly accurate. Within three months, Clarke recalled,

Margaret was "reading with ease" German masterpieces. By the end of the year, he reported, she had read many of the major works of Goethe, Ludwig Tieck, Novalis, Jean Paul, and Theodor Körner, plus all the principal dramas and lyric poetry of Friedrich Schiller. Margaret and Clarke undertook this breakneck course together. "Almost every evening," Clarke recalled, "I saw her, and heard an account of her studies." They also carried it on privately, and not only in the sense that, apart from some help from Hedge on pronunciation, they taught themselves the language. Both their classic Romantic choice of authors and their remarks in their journals show their critical spirit was quite independent—if not of Carlyle, whose preferences they generally followed—then certainly of their more classically moral-minded, pro-German Cambridge elders. ("J. I think Dr Follen did not catch the true interior character of Göthe. M. Could you expect he would? He has not a philosophic, only a tasteful mind.") Week after week the two committed Germanicos exchanged opinions, critiques, "German journal[s]," translations, and earnest testimony about what their readings meant for their characters and lives.[53]

Their studies also deepened their personal relationship. Some of the old problems remained, of course. Margaret still found herself having to deliver stern lectures to Clarke on his "proud reserve" and resistance to confessionals (à la George Davis, she told him darkly). She also continued to puzzle him with provocative statements like (in obvious reference to him and Davis, as Clarke paraphrased her remark in his journal), "She needs something that is hard to push against, every thing yields & feels soft to her hand, or else it cuts her." And *he* continued to worry about Margaret's intellectual superiority. In fact, if anything, their German studies seem to have exacerbated this last problem. After quoting in his journal at length some incisive remarks Margaret had recently made to him about the "war of opinions in Germany for the last hundred years," he wrote: "Now when Margaret said this, I had a very decided feeling of mental inferiority. I felt how she traced ideas through minds & works, how questions rose before her, how she carried the initiative idea everywhere. In other words how comprehensive & understanding is her intellect. I felt as if my opinions (could I be said to have any?) were heterogeneous & disconnected—that my knowledge amounted to nothing—that my mind at least was a sheet of white paper on which any one might write." Still, their studies, their constant companionship—and no doubt also the fading-away of both their would-be loves—clearly raised their friendship that year to a new level of intimacy. They also increased Clarke's enthrallment with Margaret's "powers." "I went to see M. full of self dissatisfaction," he wrote in a typical journal entry in the spring, "and came away excited & ready to exert myself"; and from there he launched into a panegyric on her lofty eloquence, her "high, spiritual doctrines," and her intellectual realism. "Her head has not chilled her heart—her heart shall never lead her where her mind will not suffer her to go. Enthusiasm, & sincere ardent feelings she admires & reverences most of all, yet if unreasonable & thoughtless she turns resolutely away from it."[54]

Despite his captivation with Margaret, Clarke was not entirely uncritical of her. In his journal he conceded she had some faults, and he listed them: her "pride . . . of knowledge" and her occasional attendant "contempt of others"; the "tinge of over refinement" in her sentiments; and—despite the fact that she was "perfectly open, ardent, & selfsacrificing to her friends"—her lack of a "general tenderness of feeling." But all these faults, he thought were rooted in a fundamental tragedy in her life. In a slightly earlier journal entry, he described it in poignent terms. He started with one of his hymns to her intellectual powers: "Never at a loss to explain what to others is inscrutable, never blinded by appearances, with sentiments most noble and general, with sympathies most wide, with reasoning powers most active and unshackled, standing free from all prejudice, with an understanding that revels in the widest prospects." Then suddenly he stopped and abruptly wrote: "Yet what is the effect of these powers. She is not happy—it all ends in nothing—it produces no commensurate effects—she has no sphere of action. Why was she a woman? She has studied her own heart till she understands those of others, but she cannot bring this knowledge into action."[55]

This was a shrewd observation. Certainly Margaret's exclusion from an opportunity for public action marked a difference between their two worlds that was becoming increasingly evident to both of them that year. Although Clarke continued to ruminate darkly on his abilities, his journals show he was also gaining self-confidence. He would later attribute this to his discovery of "the Carlyle philosophy," with its stress on intuitions and actions as opposed to mere outward acquisitions of the "Understanding." But his confidence was materially nourished, as his journals also clearly show, by the fact that he was beginning to look with "longing and hope" on his impending career as a minister and his chance to give to his new ideas "a more practical character." No such possibilities were open to Margaret—a fact *she* began to lament to the somewhat startled Clarke. "She has nothing to do—no place in the world & fears she never shall have," he recorded in his journal that she one day in the spring told him in a rambling unburdening of herself. "At least as she cannot do any thing, she might have some one to reverence"; but now that Goethe had just died, there was no one. Formerly, she went on, he reported, mixing his pronouns as chaotically as she mixed her gender roles,

> she should admire to spend part of the day in working with her hands, part in visiting poor people (that always enters into her scheme of happiness), part by myself—& the evening with Shelley. But now I feel as if I should pick to pieces much that he said. Yet I want something to lean on. I don't see why I should not have it like other women. I sometimes doubt too whether I really have any talents. Persons who have real talents make for themselves a place. I know that I have not original powers—I cannot create. But if I have been deceived all along, & this is only an unnatural & unreal show, produced by an early persuasion that I was something remarkable & I have wasted so much time in this belief, it will be too bad.[56]

By the fall her laments became, as Clarke reported them in his journal, increasingly pathetic. "With infinite pathos & natural overflow of heart," he wrote in his journal after one difficult conversation in the fall, "with tears glistening in her eyes—but with few words & those elicited by chance[—]she expressed the often before expressed feelings of infinite capacities unsatisfied, powers unemployed & wasting, wants & burning desires unmet." "It is plain," he noted, "she has as yet not found a free sphere of activity—and it seems to me to be too long deferred." Her fervor, he wrote, "moved me excessively." But what could he say? "I said nothing to console her, but recollecting her kind pressure of my hand when I was in as miserable a mood, and how it rejoiced me, I pressed hers at parting." Back in his study he reflected: "What can I do for her? this was my question to myself— Can I not show her that her present course is truly the noble one—that the powers can find full employment in a better sphere, because the sphere of duty. It seems to me that a full Religious feeling alone can help her."[57]

If by "religious feeling," he meant that she should look beyond this world, perhaps this was true. In the meantime, though, what *was* she to do? Marriage and motherhood prospects were nil. The emerging popular alternative profession for educated, unmarried young women was teaching. But except for a few enterprising women like Elizabeth Peabody and Dorothea Dix, who with mixed success and low income intermittently kept schools in the Boston area, and the small number of dedicated and poorly paid women who taught in the better female seminaries, women's teaching invariably meant rudimentary, lower-grade instruction. In any case, there is nothing in Margaret's papers that suggests she *wanted* to enter what her once longed-for teacher George B. Emerson called women's "special vocation." This left one other possibility natural to an intellectually minded young woman—writing. During the previous decade, Bryant, Irving, and Cooper had all shown that it was possible for an American author to be not merely, as in the past, a learned gentleman who wrote for similar gentlemen, but a full-time, popular professional writer. Successful female authors like Catharine Sedgwick and Margaret's friend Lydia Maria Child were beginning to enter the literary marketplace, and in the coming decades, women authors, especially of sentimental domestic fiction, would have highly successful careers. Indeed, Clarke thought this was the answer to Margaret's vocational quandary. "Margaret," he wrote in the fall,

> you are destined to be an author. I shall yet see you wholly against your will and drawn by circumstances, become the founder of an American literature! For my own part, I have long since determined to form myself secretly to enter into your *school* when it is founded. The North Americans and American Quarterlies shall fly before our Maga. like chaff before the angry wind. We shall live through a stormy scene, but Art shall soften and gild our later days.[58]

Margaret, however, in her response, rejected these Margaret-like words of prophecy with a wave of disdain and self-doubt. "I know not whether to grieve that you too should think me fit for nothing but to write books or to feel flattered at the high opinion you seem to entertain of my powers." Elaborating on the self-doubt, she added, "I have supposed that people who spoke of me thus were dazzled by a superficial brilliancy of expression which I am some times excited into." But both she and he knew, she said, "the ceaseless fluctuation of my mind" and its "want of depth and accuracy." As for her disdain for professional authorship, she wrote, "My bias towards the living and practical dates from my first consciousness and all I have known of women authors' mental history has but deepened the impression." In a word, she had lived too long under the shadow of the very living and practical Timothy Fuller—not to mention the differently living Byron and Shelley—not to cast a cold eye on anything that smacked (as she seemed to imply) of mere bookishness or sentimentality. It would be several years more before she would see the possibility of a different kind of literary career. Meanwhile, she said—speaking of the competing poles of "action" and writing—she had "two souls and they seem to roll over one another in the most incomprehensible way— All my tastes and wishes point one way and I seem forced the other." Still, she knew that it would be best "if I could resign myself to the stream of events and take the day at its due worth. It is at such times that I can learn— But I fear, *I fear* that I shall see my vocation too darkly to accomplish any-thing of consequence here below."[59]

Whether Margaret found such sorting out helpful or not, like all aspects of her Cambridge life, it was about to come to an end. For Margaret's fate as an unmarried young woman was ultimately dependent on that of her family, or, more particularly, her father—and his life was just then taking a fairly radical turn. For one thing, the diplomatic assignment he had hoped for—and, with it, Margaret's hopes for a European tour that she had been privately nurturing—never materialized. His son Richard later claimed that this failure "somewhat disgusted him with public life," but his letters show that long before this and his defeat for the lieutenant governorship that November, he had seriously contemplated quitting his law practice and politics so he could (as he told his wife) "engage in literary pursuits, to which I always had a strong attachment." In particular he wanted to write a history of the United States for which he had long been collecting materials, but his political and professional duties, he complained to his wife, had never allowed him to "strike the *first blow*." And so, with the support of his wife—who had always wanted him (as she told him in one letter) to "give . . . utterances to many of the excellent thoughts that lie concealed in your literary cabinet"—Timothy Fuller, at the age of fifty-three, determined to realize his longstanding desire by removing himself and his family out of Cambridge and retiring to a farm in the country.[60]

If Margaret's parents gave much thought to what such a move might do to Margaret's prospects for marriage or her literary studies, they left no record of it. But presumably they considered that she had none of the first, at least not for now, and that in the meantime she could pursue the second in the country as well as in Cambridge. In August of the previous year, as a preliminary to their move and while looking about for a suitable residence, Margaret's father had sold the Dana house. In late September the family had moved into the Brattle mansion on Tory Row, then owned by Margaret's Uncle Abraham. There for her last year and a half in Cambridge, she lived in this large, century-old, gambrel-roofed house on sprawling, picturesque grounds of formal gardens, fish ponds, bridges, a marble grotto gurgling with spring water, springhouses, and a long, meandering mall that ran down to the river, alongside a magnificent row of great linden trees. But even these elegant grounds hardly compensated Margaret for her anticipated losses, of companionship, of books, of intellectual stimulation—in a word, of all the things that had made her last Cambridge years, however checkered, also exciting and full. Nor could it have been very inspiriting for her to contemplate, as she undoubtedly did, the fact that virtually all of her close female friends were either just married or were engaged to be married, and all her male friends were about to launch their careers, while she retired with her family to an uncertain future in the country. "Very sad," she told Clarke, her new life seemed to her. Yet she also tried to be philosophical about it. In another letter to him, after saying she had been seeing "so many acquaintances" and saying "so many words" yet never feeling *"called out"* and therefore feeling "strangely *vague* and *moveable*," she wrote:

> 'Tis true the time is probably near when I must live alone to all intents and purposes— separate entirely my acting from my thinking world, take care of my ideas without aid (c'est à dire except from the "illustrious dead") answer my own questions, correct my own feelings and do all that "hard work" for myself— How tiresome 'tis to find out all one's self-delusion— I thought myself so very independent because I could conceal *some* feelings at will and did not need the *same* excitement as other young characters did— And I am not independent nor never shall be while I can get any-body to minister to me. But I shall go where there is never a spirit to come if I call ever so loudly.[61]

Such, then, was Margaret's apprehensive state of mind on the eve of her departure from Cambridge. By early April of 1833, she said her last farewells and prepared to join her family in their new home in Groton.

CHAPTER FIVE

A Tangled Pastoral
(1833–1835)

I

If, while waiting for her father to return to get the last of the Brattle house furniture, Margaret Fuller had expected a glowing report about their new home, she was sadly disappointed. Instead she learned that her favorite brother, ten-year-old Arthur, had met with a terrible accident and that she should go to Groton immediately. When she arrived, she found the boy—who had been struck in the face by a large piece of wood carelessly thrown by their hired man—with bandaged eyes, swollen head, and burning fever, crying out for his "Margaret." "I confess," she would write to Eliza Farrar on April 29, "I greeted our new home with a flood of bitter tears." Frightened he would be blind, she spent most of her days for the rest of the month in his room, helping her mother nurse him. Eventually, by June, he recovered, although not without losing the sight of his right eye. It was not a good omen.[1]

Of course, Groton also had its potential charms. Her father had purchased their estate from Judge Samuel Dana, his former state senate colleague and the father of Margaret's Prescott schoolmate Martha Dana. Situated at a major bend of Farmers' Row, about three-quarters of a mile from the Parish Unitarian Church and the Groton Academy (soon to be renamed the Lawrence Academy, after its wealthy former Groton and now Boston textile capitalist benefactors), the property comprised about forty acres of mowing and tillage and some ten acres of pasturage surrounded at the outskirts by a thick forest of towering pine trees. The house, which Judge Dana had built in 1815, although not as elegant as the family's Cambridge mansions, was nonetheless one of the largest and most attractive buildings in Groton. Among its appealing features were its ten high and spacious rooms, its peaked roof and tall, shuttered windows, and its wraparound, colonnaded veranda that overlooked imposingly, on all sides, downward-sloping lands and a large orchard of apple, pear, and cherry trees. Also quaintly imposing—as Margaret might have remembered from her Prescott schooldays—was the town itself. Lying thirty-five miles northwest of Boston, along the banks of the Nashua River, in the heart of Massachusetts's agricultural district, Groton was (and still is) among the state's most picturesque settlements. Even then its dozens of shimmering ponds and brooks, its floral meadows, grassy, dome-like hills, and handsome colonial architecture were beginning to attract a trickle of well-to-do families, some from as far away as Connecticut and New York. Otherwise, though, Groton resembled nothing so much as a small, sleepy, New England country town. The village was at the center, along Groton's only real street, the old Great Road, where the town's few stores and mechanics' shops were located. Culturally, Groton could be described as a kind of Cambridge without its Boston or Harvard: the majority of its two thousand inhabitants were small farmers, moderate Whigs, and Unitarians, the orthodox minority of the Congregational society having seceded, like their Cambridge brethren, several years earlier. Otherwise, apart from Lawrence Academy, Groton's only claim to institutional culture was a modest athenaeum organized soon after Margaret Fuller moved there.[2]

The Fuller family's first reactions to this rustic scene varied widely. Margaret's father, whose idea the move had originally been, was the most enthusiastic. The reasons are not hard to imagine. Besides the reduction of living expenses and the obvious appeal of writing his Jeffersonian history on a farm in the country, there were also personal considerations. Not only since his boyhood had he always loved the country, his old Princeton homestead was only a few miles away. (His family's Wachusett Mountain was even visible from his Groton house.) Undoubtedly, too, he remembered his father, who also late in life had traded a failing professional career for a successful life as family farmer and paterfamilias. Finally, like Jefferson and Timothy Fuller's beloved Dr. Goldsmith, Margaret's father had long ago learned to find, not just personal pleasure, but high moral benefits in country living. In particular he was convinced, his son Richard later wrote, that his own success had been largely due to habits of industry and endurance that he had gotten from his boyhood farm labor, so he looked forward to Groton as an opportunity to subject his own children to the same "hardening process." In moving to Groton, Timothy Fuller was returning to the fount.[3]

Although Margaret's mother brought with her no such heavy ideological baggage, she, too, had been born and bred in the country. From time to time she had even wistfully expressed the idea to her husband that (as she once told him) he "renounce all your towering hopes" and "retire to a farm with me." Of course, once she got there, Margaret reported, she had "many fatiguing and sordid tasks to perform." But she always went through them, it seemed to Margaret anyway, "with a cheerful spirit." As for the children, their feelings varied according to age and circumstances. The youngest boys—Richard, Arthur, and Lloyd—adjusted to their new utopia the best. This was particularly true of Richard and Arthur, who, despite Arthur's bad beginning, grew quickly excited that first summer over the abundance of wild forest animals and tame farm pets, sunbaths on the piazza, and early morning walks with their father, whose gently spoken "maxims"—on reason and prudence, on the superiority of writers to war-makers, on the evils of speculation and the low "temporal" aims of most men, as Richard remembered them—mingled pleasantly with the soft, radiant skies, sparkling air, and glittering dew. The older children, on the other hand, were considerably less impressed with their rural abode. Ellen, already beginning to become (as her mother said) *"engaged"* in society, repeatedly complained to her about the move. Eugene and William Henry, anxious to establish their own lives, openly revolted. Eugene, the oldest boy, after graduating from college the following year, immediately headed for a tutoring job in Virginia, while William Henry, who clashed repeatedly with his father over his various schemes to move South or, as he managed to do once, ship out to the West Indies, absented himself as much as possible on various trips to Boston in search of employment.[4]

The one older Fuller child who had no such escapes and who, from the very first, deeply resented the move to Groton was, of course, Margaret. Cut off from her friends and the intellectual excitement of Cambridge and Boston, she felt (as her mother reported to her father that April) *"excessively* homesick." Nor, in her self-pitying mood, did her father's agrarian enthusiasms do anything to win her over. On the contrary, she later confessed, "I . . . secretly wondered how a mind which had for thirty years been so widely engaged in the affairs of men could care so much for trees and crops." Her father, attempting in some part to appease her resentfulness, named the little wood adjoining the pasturage "Margaret's Grove." Here he selected a spot to place a seat where she might go to read alone and urged her to visit it. But she contented herself, she later wrote in her journal, with only a "where you please, Father," and never went. Still, all her journals and letters show that after the first month or so, she learned to keep her resentments either at a distance or at least unexpressed.[5]

One thing that probably helped was the sheer numbing effect of all the labor required, for her father intended the Groton farm to be, not merely a place of retirement and study, but a fully working, self-sustaining enterprise as well. The full significance of this fact was apparently, though, a little slow in dawning on the family. Richard and Arthur, for example, the rural enthusiasts, conceived the bright idea that farm work was preferable to schoolwork and begged their father to release them from study and let them work full-time outdoors. But, alas, within a week or so, they wept and pleaded to their father to let them quit. Once, even, Richard recalled, "we threw ourselves on the floor" before their sympathetic mother, begging her to get their father to dissolve the contract, which she tried to do, but he "mildly but firmly" told them that they had made a bargain and it would be "unmanly" of them to break it, and he would not allow it. Submitting to their fate, they worked the remainder of the summer in the fields and eagerly awaited the beginning of school in the fall. One reason the work was so hard was the great difficulty—typical of so many small country farms in labor-poor America—of hiring outside help. For housework the Fullers felt fortunate if they could secure even one full-time servant, while for field work they had to rely on a shifting medley of drunks, eccentrics, and other assorted local ne'er-do-wells. ("A dog" and "more like an idiot, or knave than a rational crea-

ture" were two of Margaret's mother's kinder descriptions of one of these men.)
Mostly, though, they relied on themselves: Margaret's father superintended the
clearing, tilling, haying, and cropping; her mother was in charge of the vegetable
farming and animal tending along with the usual cooking, cleaning, and washing; and Arthur and Richard helped with the plowing and planting. Margaret's
main farm task was sewing family clothing, sometimes as much as eight hours'
worth a day. "I have been sewing," she wrote to Clarke that summer, "till my
spirit is faint from inanition."[6]

When not farming, the younger Fullers often found themselves learning about
farming or country living from their more experienced father, who expounded
to them his various rural notions—like the importance of making their feet
strike the floor "at once" when he called them in the early morning, or, on
another day, the medicinal value of running barefoot through the snow in the
winter, as he liked to do. Usually these little talks were instructive and attentively
listened to, undoubtedly none more so than the time he lectured them about the
dangers of pistols, a brace of which he had brought with him to Groton. "Now
children," Richard later remembered him beginning, "I know well that these
pistols are not loaded; yet, in showing you the operation of the lock, I shall not
point the pistol at the head of some one, as a boy might do, for bravado. For
instance, I shall not point it at your sister Margaret." With this remark, according to Richard, he pointed the weapon at the wall near the floor, drew the trigger,
and discharged a bullet through the wall into the cellar. Someone, apparently,
had been practicing with the pistols and had inadvertently left them loaded.[7]

Margaret's life in Groton, though, was more than hard work and misfired lectures. For one thing, she was not entirely isolated in Groton. There was always
the stagecoach that rumbled out daily for its six-hour trip between Boston and
Groton, bringing with it letters that kept her abreast of her friends' doings and
local gossip and, not the least improtant, reassurance that she was not forgotten.
("My former intimates *sigh* at least, if they do not pine, for my society," she
happily told Hedge after reading the first batch.) The stagecoach sometimes
brought the friends themselves. That summer, Clarke, the Randall sisters, the
Barlows, and numerous other friends paid her lengthy visits. She also visited
them; for as long as she lived in Groton she made at least one major visit to Boston and Cambridge or her friends' various vacation spots every summer and fall.
And she packed a lot into her visits. In the first ten days of her month-long stay
beginning at the end of September, she attended four "soirées" organized in her
honor by Eliza Farrar, with whom she stayed, and by several others of her female
friends; dined with George Bancroft and chatted with him about Goethe; talked
with professors Henry Ware, Jr., John Gorham Palfrey, Cornelius Felton, and
Andrews Norton about Unitarian affairs and a hodgepodge of literary questions;
and caucused with Hedge, Eliot, and others of her former Divinity School
friends about their professional plans. After more talks, lectures, sermons, book
borrowing, and parties—including an enormous one at the Edward Everetts'—
she finished off the trip with an additional two weeks of visiting Anna Barker

and concert-going and art gallery–visiting in New York with Elizabeth Randall and Clarke's mother and sister Sarah. She even managed finally to make friends with the reticent Sarah. "We began, as usual," Sarah informed her brother, "by expressing our certainty that we should never get along together; and, that being conceded, we did get along most swimmingly." After several more of these Boston get-togethers, Margaret would write exultingly to James: "*Dear* Sarah. I not only *like* but *love* her now. All the little obstacles to our intercourse have vanished. I am no longer too much for her and she, I think is quite frank with me."[8]

Nor was she exactly a recluse in Groton. True, her letters sometimes drip a bit with condescension toward some of the town's "learned" folk. But she was friendly with the First Parish's Reverend Charles Robinson, and she amicably socialized with the Danas, the Lawrences, and others of her parents' friends among the town's Unitarian elite. She also found the general run of people (as she told Hedge on July 4), if not greatly pleasurable, still "very kind" and "much more agreeable than in most country-towns—there is no vulgarity of manner, but little of feeling and I hear no gossip." Finally, despite her claim some years later that she had found the scenery there "too tamely smiling and sleepy," her letters at the time show her for the first time appreciating the natural scenes that would be a lifelong pleasure to her. "Such gorgeous light, such rich deep shadows—such sweet, *sweet* wind!" she exclaimed about that day's walk to and from church in one letter to Clarke late in June. "And this evening I have been sitting in the piazza hearing it rustle the vines against the Moon's benignant face. . . . I send you this leaf of geranium which I have been wearing in a nosegay." As for her intellectual isolation, even here she sounded outwardly stoical, even sanguine. "I am alone," she wrote to Clarke in July. "I shall not have profound intellectual sympathy with anyone— I feel my situation now profoundly but calmly— Two years ago when I began to realize all I must do for myself or be lost, I could not think of it a moment without anguish— I thought I never never could see this day with composure." But now she had, she assured Clarke, and she went on to describe a recent "imaginary conversation" she had held with him about some books she had brought to the woods with her. "At last a bird flew past me and I laughed to perceive that I am still myself. . . . Sometimes I feel so wild and free— I mourn that I was not brought up in this solitude."[9]

In fact, her private feelings about her situation were not all so cheerful—nor so benignly rational. As often at critical times in Fuller's life, she dreamt her darkest thoughts. Her second month in Groton she had a dream of her mother's death and her father's ruination. On one level, of course, her dream probably reflected her extreme fears about what her father's retirement portended for her and the family. Yet most of the action of the dream, as she recounted it, takes place before these terrible events "in a large stately unfurnished house something like Sir Harry Franklands. I have the impression that 'twas the residence of our family though not one member of it figured in the dream." Morever, what actually happens in this stately mansion without parents and siblings is wildly bizarre and vaguely licentious cavorting by Margaret, the Davis sisters, and Elizabeth

Randall. At one point, she wrote, "we seemed to make the walls ring again with bursts of wild laughter." At another point, just before she learns of her parents' destruction, "I seemed to read as in a book or letter from H. D. to myself reproaching me for my levity, foretelling the death of my mother and the ruin of my father's fortunes; saying, I remember 'Your mother has seen all her lustres.'" All of this would seem to suggest that her family's removal triggered in her not only an irrational fear of her parents' ruination, but also, an unconscious wish, if not precisely for that, then at least for their disappearance so that she might become truly "wild and free" and, of course, rich. As she had the many times since childhood when she had dreamt of her mother's death, when she awoke, she wrote, "My cheeks were yet wet with the tears I had shed."[10]

If such angry or fearful demons did torment her that summer, her journals show she tried mightily to stifle them. A major aid in her struggle was her newly found religious aspiration. "Heaven's discipline has been invariable to me," she wrote in one meditation in her journal that same month. "The seemingly most pure and noble hopes have been blighted; the seemingly most promising connections have been broken. The lesson has been endlessly repeated: 'Be humble, patient, self-sustaining; hope only for occasional aids; love others but not engrossingly, for by being much alone your appointed task can best be done.'" But her most considered assessment of her prospects was this journal entry, written the very Independence Day she composed her considerably more cheerful letter to Hedge. After listing her family duties and dismissing "all hopes of travelling," she wrote:

> All youthful hopes of every kind I have pushed from my thoughts— I will not, if I can help it, lose an hour in castle-building and repining— Too much of that already! I have now a pursuit of immediate importance[—] to the German language and literature I will give my undivided attention— I have made rapid progress for one quite unassisted— I have always hitherto been too constantly distracted by childish feelings to acquire any thing properly but have snatched a little here and there to feed my restless Fancy therewith— Please God now to keep my mind composed, that I may store it with all that may be conducive hereafter to the best good of others—
>
> Oh! keep me steady in an honorable ambition. Favored by this calm, this obscurity of life I might learn every-thing, did not these feelings lavish away my strength— Let it be no longer thus— Teach me to think justly and act firmly— Stifle in my breast those feelings which pouring forth so aimlessly did indeed water the desert and offend the sun's clear eye by producing weeds of rank luxuriance— Thou art my only Friend, thou hast not seen fit to interpose one feeling, understanding breast between me and a rude, woful world. Vouchsafe then they protection that I may "hold on in courage of soul."

It was a conclusion more stoically Romantic than Christian. But like her Thanksgiving epiphany, it was also one that mingled vocational commitment, religious transcendence, and emotional failure. The combination would preoccupy her for the rest of her early life.[11]

II

When Fuller came to Groton, she was determined, as she pledged to God and Shelley on the Fourth, to make of her isolated farmhouse a place of study and reflection. Furthermore, her letters show that she was acutely conscious that her studies at Groton needed to be a turning point in her self-education. They also show that the prospect was deeply humbling. On October 25, she wrote to Clarke from Boston: "I wish to study ten-thousand, thousand things this winter— Every day I become more sensible to the defects in my education— I feel so ignorant and superficial." And again: "I am tired of these general ideas. They did well enough for conversation but cannot satisfy me when I am alone." Her letter to Clarke three months later about her mental character was even more self-lacerating: "such absence of the power of concentration, such want of mental discipline, and just enough smattering of every-thing to show me my apparent wants and palsy all my plans." Indeed, she added sorrowfully, "I am inclined to agree with the seemingly ill-natured assertion of the Edinburgh review that a well taught schoolboy of 16 possessed more thorough knowledge of [*illegible*] than the most accomplished woman—I am not an accomplished woman; yet I cannot but feel with Me Roland that comparing myself with the herd je vaux rien."[12]

As usual with Fuller, once she was under conviction, she strove strenuously for salvation. Although she often complained of her difficulty in getting books, one would not know it from the long lists of those she read. She got some of the books she needed from the Reverend Mr. Robinson and, once it opened, the Athenaeum. But mostly she borrowed them from friends when she was in the Boston area or got them from them by mail. (Her "Recd payment" notes read like memos from a private interlibrary loan network.) Ralph Waldo Emerson later wrote that her reading at Groton was "at a rate like Gibbon's." Considering her limited time, one might think it even faster. European history and architecture, contemporary French and English novels, modern Italian fiction and drama, travel books, treatises on mental illness—and, as always, all the British quarterlies (as she told Clarke) to "keep up with the gallop of the age"—these and hundreds of other miscellaneous works she consumed voraciously while she was at Groton.[13]

This was her familiar Cambridge pattern, of course. But if Cambridge had been her college, Groton was her graduate school: her letters and journals show her reading not only with a new critical intensity and purpose, but also with new focus. One new focus that had been sharpening since her religious experience was her appreciation of the less high-heroic and more introspectively contemplative aspects of English Romanticism. Shelley she continued to admire as much as ever, but now, as she said, more for his intellectual stimulation than for his haunting atmosphere. "Pour moi," she wrote to Clarke in the summer, "a Shelley *stirs* my mind more than a Milton and I'd rather be excited to think than have my tastes gratified." Similarly, her fascination with Byron faded and her appreciation of Wordsworth grew. She wrote in her journal, in answer to her former heroic-Romantic comrade Clarke, who had disparaged Wordsworth, that she herself was not quite ready to embrace his philosophy. Still, she said, she, too, like old men and young women (who "feed their souls on *affections* not designs"), sometimes found great delight in Wordsworth's beautiful poetry of "subdued affections and bounded wishes." She also read in a similarly sympathetic spirit for the first time that summer four dialogues in French of the English Romantics' ancient ancestor, Plato. She found unconvincing his specific idealistic arguments about pre-existence, but she praised his "noble tone of sentiment and beautiful calmness." Indeed, she told Clarke, his dialogues inspired her to believe a Romantic idea that she never used to think true: namely, that "the mouth sometimes talketh virtue from the overflowing of the heart as well as love, anger &c."[14]

But above all, she devoted her intellectual energies, Romantic and otherwise—as she had said she would in her Independence Day journal entry—to her German books. Apart from some she owned, most of these she borrowed (as she had when she had been in Cambridge) from Hedge and Clarke. In return, she sent them some of her many translations. The most ambitious of these that she completed that summer was of Goethe's verse drama *Torquato Tasso*. Both in her journal and in her letters to Hedge and Clarke, she also wrote out critiques of her German authors, following a point of view that could best be described (as could that of her English poets) as moderately Romantic. The vehement but classical Schiller, whose complete works Eliza Farrar had given her, she admired enormously but not unconditionally. "Schiller does not thrill but he exalts us," she wrote in her journal. "Moral force is commensurate with his intellectual gifts, & nothing more." Likewise she wrote to Clarke, returning the plays of the rigorously balanced "Aufklärer" Gotthold Ephraim Lessing: "Well-conceived and sustained characters, interesting situations but never that profound knowledge of human nature, those minute beauties and delicate, verifying traits, which lead on in the writings of some authors who may be nameless. I think him easily fathomed, strong, but not deep." And, more ambivalently, of the authoritative classicist Johann Joachim Winckelmann, she wrote, using the German Romantic jargon of the day, "Happy man!— fashioned his being in delightful unconsciousness— It is useless to think of this— I am a modern." On the other hand, she was equally critical of the popular sentimental and discursive Jean Paul—a great favorite of both Hedge's and Clarke's. "Too rambling and melting," she wrote to Clarke; and to Hedge she added, "Besides his philosophy and religion seem to be of the sighing sort, and having some tendency that way myself I want opposing force in a favorite author."[15]

Who were her "nameless" favorites? One core was the Jena-Berlin circle of psycho-philosophical Romantics: the "Kunstmärchen" master Ludwig Tieck, whose complete works she read at Groton; the literary aesthetic theoreticians August Wilhelm and Friedrich Schlegel (she even appreciated Friedrich's ecstatically erotic feminist novel *Lucinde,* which the moral-minded Schiller detested); and, above all, the author she correctly recognized as the group's literary center—Novalis. She knew his limitations. His poetry, she thought, was poetically inferior to his prose. ("He loved to expand and dwell upon rather than paint a thought.") But she praised his highly symbolistic novels *Die Lehrlinge zu Sais* and *Heinrich von Ofterdingen*—in part *because* of their lack of sure formal artistry, which she thought made them psychologically illuminating as well as illustrative of the central principle of the writers of "the Romantic School." This precept had little to do with their later Catholic medievalism, which she noted in her journals, but otherwise quietly ignored. It was rather their intellectual inwardness: "They loved to study the secret principles of the individual mind and to study the inward workings of love and grief rather than criticize or dramatize the words or acts which were their outward results." And she left no doubt of her own sympathy for this "metaphysical turn." "Let no one," she wrote at the end of her "Novalis journal," "be deterred by the word mysticism or refuse to read Novalis because he is called a mystic. For mysticism is by no means fanaticism nor is it necessarily Swedenborgianism or any ism unless it be spiritualism. In its pure signification it implies merely a steadfast listening to the still small voice of the soul within in preference to the trumpet calls of the outward world." The intuitionist aspect of Fuller's thought would take various forms in later years, but it would never deviate greatly from this early statement of it. At the same time the dark uncanniness that was an essential ingredient in German Romantic literature would also for many years be an important ingredient in Fuller's Romantic thought.[16]

But the German she preferred at Groton (as she told Hedge) "to anybody"—most of whose works she read there—was the classically Romantic Johann Wolfgang von Goethe. In this she showed the avant-garde character of her German enthusiasm. For if there was one German author who was almost universally excoriated in all the American journals, it was Goethe. Political liberals disliked him because of his political conservatism; religious conservatives, both Unitarian and orthodox, abhorred him because of his supposed pantheism; and virtually all denounced him for the supposed libertinism of his personal life and the unashamed sensuality of some of his writing. Indeed, even some younger, Romantic-minded Unitarians who were attracted to the more spiritual aspects of German thought rejected Goethe (in the words of Elizabeth Peabody, who had argued with Clarke about him the previous fall) as a shallow "Epicurean" who "had no ideal—no moral standard of perfection." On the other side of the Atlantic, though, Thomas Carlyle regarded Goethe as virtually his moral mentor, and in this respect Fuller, like her fellow Germanist Clarke, could be said to be simply following the Scotsman's lead. Yet Goethe was clearly a natural complement to traits that had long been a part of Fuller's intellectual makeup. His idea of the progressive evolution of personal character through the natural unfolding of one's inner self, his quasi-paganistic religious views, his ideal of "extraordinary generous seeking"—and even his sensualism—were all ideas that found echoes in the kind of naturalistic Romanticism that Fuller had been cultivating since her adolescence. In fact, if anything, her naturalism and aestheticism made her sympathetic to dimensions of Goethe that the more moral-minded Goethe enthusiast Clarke, influenced by Carlyle, could not fully appreciate. In one letter that fall, he complained to her that he could not understand

Goethe's lyric poetry. ("Those little *Lieder,* proverbs, etc., are darkness visible to me.") "What fault do you find with Goethe's lyricks," she answered. "Each one gives a mood of the mind with marked expression and intense and beautiful language— Does not the perusal of them rouse your imagination and make you think or in some cases rouse you to unexpected passion— What would you have? If you want sympathy read Schiller." Likewise in her journal she rejected Novalis's severe attack on Goethe's *Bildungsroman, Wilhelm Meisters Lehrjahre,* as a "prosaic and modern" evasion. "The Romantic is completely levelled in it," she quoted him in her journal. On the contrary, she wrote, the novel was "an attempt at a reconcilement with life as a whole," which, to be sure, combined "visions" with "tragical" and sometimes "uncontrollable bursts of irony."[17]

Nevertheless, Goethe presented difficulties for Fuller. One was his very "genius." Although rejecting Novalis's ideas, she conceded in one early letter to Clarke written the previous year that "the one-sidedness, imperfection and glow of a mind like Novalis's seem refreshingly human" and "a relief after feeling the immense superiority of Goethe. It seems to me as if the mind of Goethe had embraced the universe. . . . I am enchanted while I read; he comprehends every feeling I ever had so perfectly, expresses it so beautifully, but when I shut the book, it seems as if I had lost my personal identity— All my feelings linked with such an immense variety that belong to beings I had thought so different. What can I bring? There is no answer in my mind except 'It is so' or 'It will be so' or 'No doubt such and such feel so.'" Also contributing to her "attracting and repelling . . . feelings" toward Goethe was the fact that so much of his philosophy, as in his *Lehrjahre,* depended on wide experience and activity—two things she obviously found it difficult to come by in her little Groton enclave. In one letter to Clarke in August, she wrote: "Three or four afternoons I have passed very happily at my beloved haunt in the wood reading Goethe's 'second residence in Rome'— your pencilmarks show that you have been before me. I shut the book each time with an earnest desire to live as he did— always to have some engrossing object of pursuit— I do sympathize deeply with a mind in that state. While mine is being used up by ounces I wish pailfulls might be poured into it." Finally, there was clearly (as Clarke once said to her) a "volcanic" side to Fuller that a soul as poised as Goethe could obviously not entirely speak to. She knew this. In another letter to Clarke that same month, she wrote: "How often I have thought if I could see Goethe and tell him my state of mind he would support and guide me— he would be able to understand— he would show me how to rule circumstances instead of being ruled by them and above all he would not have been so sure that all would be for the best without our making an effort to act out the oracles." Yet she also realized, she said, that all such "Wertherian" cries for help would have been met by Goethe with a cold rebuff. Despite her doubts about the "great sage" as her ultimate "Master," her devotion to him and to his world view, beginning at Groton, remained firm. "I constantly think of Goethe," she wrote in her journal after translating a fragment of his autobiography. "He is the light of the age, verily, I learn all the other men from him, him from them. I learn to [*illegible*] him, myself, all, yet we must not rest where he did."[18]

While Fuller was studying German Romantic writers, her fellow Germanists Hedge and Clarke from time to time encouraged her to study the related post-Kantian philosophers they were excited about. She had for some time admired Hedge's enthusiasm for the "new metaphysics," and she also knew of Clarke's less sure fascination with it. ("That position which Plato took for granted," Clarke wrote glibly in his journal in February, "the Germans demonstrate.") Still, evidently feeling no need of systematizing *her* Romantic subjectivism, she declined to read them. Indeed, like her mentor Goethe, she sometimes expressed a certain repugnance toward the post-Kantian project of trying to convert subjective insights into an all-embracing system of objective truths. This she showed clearly enough in her tartly phrased, point-by-point critique, which she dispatched to Clarke that summer, of a long, literary-philosophical "Letter-journal" he had sent her. The journal had included an account of another recent argument he had had with Elizabeth Peabody about the absence of an "all-comprehending idea" in Goethe's *Lehrjahre*. Aroused, Fuller lashed out, not only at Peabody's suggestion, but at the whole idea of a "metaphysical philosophy" propounded by Novalis and his German Romantic philosopher friends. Conceding "I do not know the Kantites," she nonetheless polemically asked Clarke:

> Do you really believe there is any-thing "all comprehending" but religion?— Are not these distinctions imaginary? Must not the philosophy of every mind or set of minds be a system to guide them and give a home where they can bring materials among which to accept, reject, and shape at pleasure. Novalis calls those who harbour these ideas "unbelievers"— but hard names make no difference— He says with disdain "to *such,* philosophy is only a system which will spare them the trouble of reflecting"— Now this is just my case— I *do* want a system which shall suffice to my character and in whose applications I shall have faith— I do not wish to *reflect* always, if reflecting must always be about one's identity, whether *"ich"* am the true ich &c— I wish to arrive at that point where I can trust myself and leave off saying "it seems to me" and boldly feel it *is* so *to me,* my character has got its natural regulator, my heart beats, my lips speak truth. I can walk alone, or offer my arm to a friend, or if I lean on another, it is not the debility of sickness but only wayside weariness— This is the philosophy *I* want— This much would satisfy me.

She added, as her final, militantly pragmatic, Goethean flourish,

> Then Novalis says
>   "Philosophy is the art of discovering the place of
> truth in every encountered event and circumstance; to attune
> all relations to truth.—
>   Philosophy is peculiarly homesickness— an
> overmastering desire to be at home"—
>   I think so— but what is there *all-comprehending,*
> eternally conscious about that?[19]

That Fuller was skeptical about the philosophical project of her young minister friends did not mean that she felt the same way about its motivation—their desire to find a satisfying intellectual basis for their Christian faith. On the contrary, even in her deistic days she had told George Davis that she admired enormously Hedge's quest to find in his religion "a home for theories" and not just "sympathies." Meanwhile, since her religious experience, she had become increasingly interested in the quest herself. At Groton she decided to do something about it. On the first Sunday in March she began (she wrote in her journal) "a regular course of religious study." In a letter to Hedge later in the fall, she described her object: "to examine thoroughly as far as my time and abilities permit the evidences of the Christian religion." Enlarging on her motives, she wrote, a little fastidiously but earnestly: "I have endeavored to get rid of this task as much and as long as possible [and] to content myself with superficial notions and knowledge— and, if I may so express it, to adopt the religion as a matter of taste— But I meet with Infidels very often, two or three of my particular friends are Deists—their arguments and several distressing skeptical notions of my own are haunting me for ever— I *must* satisfy myself and having once begun I shall go as far as I can." And she did. She read and reread the Bible, both in English and German ("thinking it would seem more fresh in a foreign tongue"). She asked Clarke for the texts of some of his sermons and wrote out some of her own. She assiduously studied the Kantian or (in Hedge's phrase) "critical i.e.. . . . *antidogmatical*" works of Johann Gottfried Eichhorn and Johann Jahn and "a closet full" of other biblical commentaries that he recommended and lent to her or that she borrowed from the Reverend Mr. Robinson. And she solicited Hedge's biblical views on (as he put it) "the internal spirit & deeper meaning of the sacred writings," which he freely dispensed in their most post-Kantian, "spiritualist" form. "To those who have not themselves & within themselves experienced the truth of the Xn religion it is a fable though the *outward* evidence of its origins be made never so clear to them," he lectured her—in the context of discussing how much the possible human "fabrication" of biblical texts weakens the authority of Christianity— "& to those who *have,* the outward evidence signifies but little."[20]

Despite Hedge's cheering intuitionist conclusion, Fuller had great difficulties reaching similar ones herself. One obstacle in shoring up her faith, she thought, was her "rapid" but "shallow" and "undisciplined" habits of mind. ("I wish to think before I have proper materials to think upon and at all the picturesque places I have a restless desire to write stories or rather fragments of stories which have nothing to do with my present purpose.") But her biggest problem, she recognized, was emotional. In one "Sunday meditation," after quoting an intuitionist lecture in favor of Christianity very similar to the one Hedge had delivered to her—touting "that greater blessing pronounced to those [moderns] who believe and saw not"—she wrote: "I cannot speak thus proudly and heartily against the intellectual and celestial world. It is easy to believe in our passionless moments or in those when earth would seem *too* dark without the guiding star of faith— But to *live* in faith, not sometimes to feel but always to have it is difficult." And this lack of a living faith, she told Hedge two months later, was exactly her difficulty: "I have felt myself a Christian but it was at times of excitement, skepticism returns." Finally, she knew her returning skepticism rested on a bedrock doubt, not about the immortality of souls—she had none on that score, she assured Hedge—but the more worldly one she had lamented during her Thanksgiving religious experience: a pessimistic fatalism that made her doubt the providence of God. "It so often seems to me that we are ruled by an iron destiny," she bluntly told Hedge. "I have no confidence in God as a Father." She also seems sometimes to have hardly felt a desire for him either. Writing in her journal of pagan heroes devoid of Christian morality like Caesar, Pompey, and, in modern times, she thought, Bonaparte, she wrote, "I feel much sympathy with that misdirected longing after immortality which dictated their being."[21]

Still, as she had not during either her pagan childhood or her Romantic Promethean adolescence, as a self-proclaimed Romantic "modern," she now desperately wanted to believe. She longed, as she wrote over and over in her journal, for a faith upon which she thought depended her present and future happiness. "The prayer of most of us must be," she wrote in one of her journal meditations, "Lord we believe— help thou our unbelief— These are to me the most significant words of Holy writ— I *will* to believe— O guide support strengthen and soothe me to do so." Even if she made little progress in establishing the inward spiritual bases of her faith, she did make some in her outer understanding of it. Speaking of the satisfaction she was taking in her Bible studies, she wrote to Hedge the following month, "I am gradually creating a new world out of the chaos of old, confused and inaccurate impressions." Meanwhile, her friend Clarke, to whom she had been, as usual, jauntily reporting on her studies, was at least suitably impressed. "Let me assure you that in my opinion," he wrote to his skeptical Divinity School friend William Henry Channing around the time she began them, "she has become regenerate."[22]

Along with her theological studies, Fuller also took up a rather more worldly subject that second spring—American history. From this, too, Fuller took some idealistic notions. For one thing, since most of the books she read were those her father was using for his history, the American past she studied was not the typical New England Federalist–Whig intellectual's one of Pilgrims and Puritans, but of the Revolution, and specifically, its radical Jeffersonian wing. Furthermore, her Thomas Jefferson—whose collected works she read almost in their entirety—was not Jefferson the radical democrat, but Jefferson the intellectual republican. ("Education first, political freedom after," she summed up his cultural and political creed; in happy agreement, she noted, with Goethe's.) Most intriguing to her of all was Jefferson the religious radical, whom she encountered especially from the speculative and erudite letters he wrote late in life to John Adams ("particy interesting on every account"). She did not *only* see in Jefferson what she wanted to see. In her journal she noted his frequent "abuse" of Plato, and a number of his other materialist chestnuts. But clearly, in reading especially his post-Christian religious opinions, she experienced a shock of recognition. "So reflecting, though so bold was all he said on the subject of Christianity that I really thought him a Christian till I came to the letter in which he quarrels with grief &c," she wrote in her journal. "Those sentiments are pagan. I have had them myself, indeed they are my characteristicks and only very powerful considerations have worked a partial conversion in me." She finally concluded sadly, "I was obliged to set down Mr Jefferson as one of those who (according to Mr Adams's classification) *honor* God only," musing, "Can self-respect without the love of God keep man so upright in these modern times?"[23]

But if Jefferson gave Fuller a powerful figure both to identify with and to worry about in terms of religion, he still more importantly provided her with a model of an engaged American intellectual. "I was charmed," she wrote in her journal,

> with his mental activity, his philosophical spirit of enquiry, his freedom and firmness in thought or action. He has given me a higher idea of what a genuine citizen of this republic might become— He may become a *genuine man*— He need not stoop to be a demagogue— He need not swagger his Demosthenian thunder on every petty local question, he need not be a narrow-minded braggart,—he need not despise— nay he ought not to disregard general literature, nor elegant pursuits.

And more personally, in a letter probably to either Hedge or Clarke, she exulted in her feeling that Jefferson and his comrades had reconnected her both to her father and to her culture and, in so doing, had given her a new, practical sense of herself.

> American History! Seriously, my mind is regenerating as to my country, for I am beginning to appreciate the United States and its great men. The violent antipathies,—the result of an exaggerated love for, shall I call it by so big a name as the "poetry of being?"—and the natural distrust arising from being forced to hear the conversation of half-bred men, all whose petty feelings were roused to awkward life by the paltry game of local politics,—are yielding to reason and calmer knowledge. Had I but been educated in the knowledge of such men as Jefferson, Franklin, Rush! I have learned now to know them partially. And I rejoice, if only because my father and I can have so much in common on this topic. All my other pursuits have led me away from him; here he has much information and ripe judgment. But, better still, I hope to feel no more that sometimes despairing, sometimes insolently contemptuous, feeling of incongeniality with my time and place. Who knows but some proper and attainable object of pursuit may present itself to the cleared eye. At any rate, wisdom is good, if it brings neither bliss nor glory.[24]

Groton may have taken Fuller out of her little Cambridge world, but it also brought her home. In this sense, her father's Jeffersonian hopes for the place were not entirely chimerical.

III

While Goethe and Jefferson were suggesting to Fuller visions of rooted but expansive intellectual vocations, her own actual new work, which she began that first fall, offered her a somewhat narrower field of vision. The work in question was teaching her younger brothers and sister. Her father, who had from time to time since her childhood prodded her to tutor her siblings, had decided that it would be an excellent plan to place her as head, as he and his father had been, of a full-fledged family school; promising her, in return for her services, money that she could use for her long-wished-for European tour. And so, for her entire morning and several hours in the afternoon, through most of every fall, winter, and spring for the three years she lived in Groton, she gave daily lessons in three languages—French and Italian to thirteen-year-old Ellen, and Latin to eleven-year-old Arthur and nine-year-old Richard. She also taught history, geography, grammar, and composition to all three and sometimes to seven-year-old Lloyd. After her first five months, she wrote to Amelia Greenwood on March 20, 1834—in one of her more understated pronouncements—that she found the job "a serious and fatiguing charge for one of my some what ardent and impatient disposition." Her charges, no doubt, would have agreed with the last part. Indeed, ironically, in these very months when Margaret was privately in her journal, with some help from her Romantic texts, venting her anger at her father for "forcing" the "premature development" of her mental powers, her letters show her doing pretty much the same thing with her younger brothers. "Only eleven years old," she exclaimed to Richard from Boston a few weeks before she opened her school, reporting on a nephew of Eliza Farrar's who "has made such progress in Mathematicks that his Master sent him back to his parents saying that he had no boys who could keep up with little Frank. When," she asked pointedly, "shall we have any thing so pleasant said of Richard!—Two years hence?" In a like pedagogical vein she went on to report sadly that she did not think they could afford the good set of building blocks ("those which have little books with them showing how to build the foreign churches &c"), adding "The cheaper-sets are mere baby's toys and would give no knowledge of architecture."[25]

Her siblings' later recollections confirm this impression. Richard later recalled that whenever in their studies they would come across Roman, Greek, or modern patriotic figures, "she would expatiate upon them with glowing eloquence" and "try to incite us to emulation." Sometimes these methods seem to have worked and sometimes not. For one thing, like all the Fuller children, both Arthur and Richard could be obstinate. (While at Groton they preferred to attend, much to the amusement and dismay of their family, the Reverend Mr. Kittredge's Calvinist church.) "I remember discouraging her," Richard later recalled, "after one of her historical talks in which she urged us to be ambitious of what was really valuable in life by remarking that I would never be ambitious. Caesar was ambitious, and I knew it was not right." Also, from her side, Margaret seems to have had an equally low tolerance for recalcitrance or dullness. Once, Richard later wrote, "she openly reproached me with mediocrity of understanding," a pronouncement that "always troubled me." At other times, just their habit of incessantly moving their hands, "as if catching at succor, in our recitations when we were drowning in the deep places of Virgil," he recalled, was enough to annoy her "inexpressibly."[26]

In general, though, Richard remembered, she preferred to laugh rather than snap, and their "bright responses" she inscribed at the end of their geography textbook would seem to bear this out. (One read: "Richard, being asked where Turkey in Asia was, replied that it was in Europe!") Her loss of time, on the other hand, was clearly no laughing matter. On March 1, entitling her new notebook "Reading journal," she grumbled that "literary journal or study journal are terms too grand for me now-a-days that I pass the best two thirds of my time in drilling little recusants and in needle work." Still, she seems to have kept her Stoic humor. On March 9 she wrote to her friend Almira Barlow: "I will tell you how I pass my time, without society or exercise. Even till two o'clock, sometimes later, I pour ideas into the heads of the little Fullers; much runs out;—indeed I am often reminded of the chapter on home-education in the New-Monthly. But the few drops which remain mightily gladden the sight of my Father." And two weeks later, after describing to Amelia Greenwood her teaching as well as all the extra sewing and nursing she had to do that winter on account of the frequent illnesses of both her mother and her Grandmother Crane, who was living with them, she nonetheless assured her: "Do not suppose me either alienated or sad— I have done some good. . . . My parents are *both* perfectly satisfied with me"; and besides, she added—borrowing a favorite phrase from Goethe—"I had adopted the idea that the edn of my little brothers and sister was my dearest duty." Privately, she translated a fable of Goethe's that month that ended with the apropos moral, "He who disdains small things shall finally be obliged to toil to accomplish those still smaller."[27]

Besides ministering to the little Fullers that first year, Fuller also ministered to some of her male friends, whose clerical careers were then beginning to sputter forward. Many of them faced a similar difficulty—finding some avenue in their rationalistic and decorous denomination for the rather undecorous spiritualistic ideas they had been absorbing from European Romantic authors since their college years. The first to try to find such an avenue was Henry Hedge, then preaching to a divided and somewhat disaffected small West Cambridge congregation while faintly hoping that Harvard might ask him to succeed his father as the college's professor of philosophy. The month before Fuller left for Groton, he started publishing articles in the leading Unitarian journal, the *Christian Examiner,* beginning most notably with an essay on Coleridge, containing the first defense in print by an American of German intuitive or "transcendental" post-Kantian philosophy. ("More than metaphysics ever before accomplished, these men have done for the advancement of the human intellect.") In her journal, Fuller ignored Hedge's metaphysics and expressed skepticism about his social idealism. ("I do not think he allows quite enough for the *re*action of institutions on the public mind.") Still, she praised his "elegance," "eloquence," and "precision," and wrote to him of all the good things she was hearing about him in the circles of her Unitarian friends. But mainly she urged him to step forward in the public arena and start battling. "Could you once be brought into unison with your day and country without sacrificing your individuality all would be well," she told him in her Independence Day letter. "Let me once again intreat you to *write,* to bring your opinions into collision with those generally received. Nobody can be more sensible than myself that the pen is a much less agreeable instrument for communication than the voice, but all our wishes will not bring back the dear talking times of Greece and Rome. And believe me, you cannot live, you cannot be content without acting on other minds 'it's no possible.'"[28]

Meanwhile, eight hundred miles away, another Romantic-minded clerical friend of Margaret's was floundering. Three months after Fuller had moved to Groton, James Clarke, having graduated from Divinity School, had left Cambridge to assume a pulpit in Louisville, Kentucky, joining a half-dozen other recent graduates who had accepted or would soon accept similar assignments in the Ohio Valley. In part they were responding to the Unitarian church's call for missionary work to win at least part of that supposedly barbarous region, then being zealously worked by orthodox and evangelical sects, for (as one Unitarian report glowingly put it) "rational preaching." But, as these young Divinity graduates saw it, their mission also gave them the chance to promote, in the supposedly freer, less settled West, a more vibrant and spiritualistic Unitarianism than they thought the tradition-minded and *too* rationalistic Unitarians of the East were then willing to accept. Eventually all but William Eliot in St. Louis would return, chastened to discover how little receptive the mostly evangelical-minded Westerners were to liberal Christianity, rational *or* Romantic. But for several years they worked hard to proselytize, and none harder than Clarke. Unfortunately, from the start, the contrast between his hopes and his realities plunged the self-doubting Clarke into despair, which he carefully hid from his family and friends, but which, just as typically, he exposed to his confessor-friend, Margaret. "I am fully realizing at this moment, and have for the last week," he wrote to her in his very first letter after arriving in Louisville, "all that the blackest raven foreboded to me of heartsickness and mental languor. . . . I thought that here I could be myself, not being perverted by the demands (praise and blame) of conventional opinions. I find that I can be myself in nothing—that I must make myself over, body and soul, to the requisitions of Kentucky taste." And so, month after month, he poured out his grief over his indifferent or hostile audiences and his desperate homesickness for "minds of *culture* and *polish* and *refinement*—(Alas, Margaret, I miss them)," while begging her: "Margaret, do not say a word of this to any one. My letters to every one else are as placid as cucumber parings."[29]

From her side, Fuller did what she had always done with Clarke—and what she would later do for others of her young male Unitarian friends who would have difficulty adjusting their Romantic sensibilities to the requirements of Jacksonian America: she exhorted him to greater efforts. After receiving one particularly self-pitying letter from him in December, she sent him a letter reminding him of his speeches to *her* during her last year in Cambridge about "the power of human will" over circumstances. She concluded with this clarion call:

> You say you are become a machine, if so I shall expect to find you a grand, high-pressure, wave-compelling one. . . . None of your *pendulum* machines for me! I should to be sure turn away my head if I should hear you *tick* and mark the quarters of hours— but the bang and whizz of a good life-Endangerer would be musick to mine ears!. . . . But we must all be machines— you shall be a steam engine— George shall be a mill— with extensive water privileges— and I will be a spinning Jenny— no upon second thoughts I will not be a machine— I will be an instrument not to be confided to vulgar hands, for instance a chisel to polish marble— or— a whetstone to sharpen steel!![30]

Her homely metaphors were apt. Certainly she would soon prove herself a better whetstone than spinning jenny. Meanwhile, that winter, she, too, began to look for a chance for some wider vistas. One was her old hope of European travel. For this she knew she needed more money than she could expect to get teaching her brothers and sister. For a while she hoped to gain some by publishing her *Torquato Tasso* translation. She even concocted, with the help of Eliza Farrar, an elaborate plan to have Farrar offer the manuscript to a publisher and (as Sarah Clarke related the conspiracy to her brother James) "to make as if it came from England. This is an excellent plan," Sarah thought, "only that any one who has ever heard Margaret talk and who reads the preface will recognize her in an allusion to the 'meditative few and the tasteful many.' No one else could have so expressed it. That is not the only place, either, where she betrays herself. She, however, maintains that no one will observe it." Whether because of this supposed notoriety or, as seems more likely, the opposite—her obscurity—nothing came of the plan, and Fuller gave up the idea of trying to get her translation published.[31]

She then thought of another idea: she would go to the West; not to preach, as her male friends were doing, but to teach. In these years, scores of young, unmarried New England women were beginning to think of such an idea, lured on by the chance to earn an income, however paltry, and, for the evangelical among them, to lend their voices to the crusade to diffuse Eastern culture and Protestant piety in what Eastern ministers and educators thundered was the dangerously backward West. Fuller's goals, however, were strictly personal and utilitarian. On her first day back in Groton after her fall trip to Cambridge and New York, she had written to Clarke: "What should you think of my coming to the West and teaching a school— I wish to earn money to go to Italy— Not quite yet— My children want me at present— But by and by would this be a feasible plan?" If she wanted a positive answer, she could hardly have asked—as she ought to have known from his woeful letters—a worse person. For nearly three months and several more letters from Clarke, she heard nothing from him on the subject. Finally, after a gentle reminder in her letter of February 7 that he had not yet replied to her query about "the schoolmistress plan" (she was not even sure, she said, that her father would consent, but "I cannot yet give up my beloved plans of travel and I can think of no other way of fulfilling them"), she got her answer from her Western pioneer. "This Western country," he told her flatly in his February 24 letter, "is a wild country and I would advise no female friend of mine to come to it in any capacity which would bring her into such collision with the natives as you would be as a teacher." To be sure, he conceded, Cincinnati might do, but only if she were willing to teach only four- and five-year-olds so that she might have nothing left to unteach! And as far as teaching anywhere else in the West went, she should forget it: the children were disrespectful and lawless, the citizens for the most part savage and rude, having "no higher thoughts than how to raise hogs and timber," and throughout there was an indifference to human life that a New Englander would find absolutely shocking. "Duels, dirkings, shootings, beatings to death, etc., happen here every day, and no one troubles themselves about them." Nevertheless, he added in a postscript, if, after all this, she still wished to come to Cincinnati, he ought to be able, he thought, to make the arrangements.[32]

She did not come. In her reply on April 17, she blandly thanked Clarke for his "information about the school" and said that it was doubtful she would be able to act on the plan anyway, because her mother had been recently ill and needed her at home. Besides, she added, "I have spoken to her (though not to my Father) of the plan and observe she regards it with great aversion." (She was, after all, as she had reminded Amelia Greenwood the previous month, "the *only* grown-up daughter.") Still, this double discouragement did not make her entirely shelve the plan. "Money— Money— root of all evil," she hated to talk about it, she airily said. ("It is hardly proper for a lady to talk to a gentleman on such topics even between you and me, who have always been more bluntly Citoyen and Citoyenne to one another than two young persons brought up in *tolerably* polished society ever were.") Yet she knew she needed money, and so—without saying a word about all his dark warnings—asked him, in case her situation changed, to keep a lookout for information about a possible position, including "what compensation for such an undertaking (horrible I confess to my imagination)." She also made it clear to Clarke that the popping of her schoolkeeping balloon did nothing to dampen her new zeal for making contact with her national culture. "I am at present engaged," she cheerfully informed him,

> in surveying the level on which the public mind is poised— I no longer lie in wait for the tragedy and comedy of life— the rules of its *prose* engage my attention— I talk incessantly with common-place people, full of intense curiosity to ascertain the process by which materials apparently so jarring and incapable of classification get united into that strange whole the American publick. (Observe I have read all Jefferson's letters— North Americans, daily papers &c without end) H. Hedge seems to be weaving his Kantisms into the American system in a tolerably happy manner.[33]

By this time, Clarke—perhaps feeling a little nervous that his earlier harsh letter had annoyed her ("I have not heard of or from you since you wrote me Feb. 7th," he wrote anxiously on April 7. "Two months! What can be the matter?")— in his reply on May 6, went out of his way to sympathize with Fuller's money complaints. And, as a kind of consolation, he closed by leaving her with this fitting, if hyperbolic, picture of their respective plights at the end of their first year away from Cambridge:

> Your mind has been acquiring ideas; you, in your worst estate, can think, and learn, and do more things than I in my best. You envy me my situation without which your powers are useless. I envy you your abilities without which I cannot fulfill the demands of my situation. You are the Bengal tiger confined in a cage to leap over a broomstick for the amusement of staring clowns. I am a broken-winged hawk, seeking to fly at the sun, but fluttering in the dust.[34]

IV

At the end of May, her first year of family teaching over, Fuller visited Boston and Cambridge, where she remained for most of the summer. Of course "her children" (as she liked to call them) were not entirely forgotten. From Boston she opened her letter to Arthur—in a vein uncannily reminiscent of her father's letters to her at that age: "I could not but regret, my dear Arthur that your letter, which would otherwise have given me so much pleasure to receive should require to be prefaced and concluded with so many apologies for bad writing, brevity &c— you are old enough to write a neat and a long letter and I hope your next will be both." After a pleasant account of the prodigious studies of his former playmates Wentworth Higginson and the Norton children back in Cambridge, she concluded with, "My dear, I hope you are doing *nothing* for which I shall be sorry and *something* for which I shall be glad. Say the same to Richard with my love. Do not let weeds grow in my garden. I trust to have radishes from it when I return."[35]

But mainly summer in Boston and Cambridge was a time to renew friendships with "the circle of my ci-devant intimates" (as she somewhat ironically called them to Clarke). One she particularly concentrated on was the elegant Cambridge visitor Anna Barker, with whom she stayed at the Farrars. ("It is a real grief to me that I must live so far from the light of those sweet eyes," she sighed to Clarke.) In August she traveled with Anna to Newport, where the two spent the month with Anna's family at their summer farmhouse six miles outside the town, taking in the mornings long horseback rides across the beaches, and at night quiet moonlit walks among the rocks overlooking the water in "the beautiful glen" near their house. As Newport was (as she noted to Clarke) "a very fashionable resort," she also saw many fashionable people. These included, of course, the Barkers' large extended family, but also William Ellery Channing, who had a second house nearby. ("I was charmed by the clearness of his expressions and the kind simplicity of his manner.") Every afternoon and evening at the Barkers' house, large parties of their many wealthy friends from New York, Philadelphia, and New Orleans assembled. Although Fuller later told Clarke that these non–New Englanders had "amused me," she hastened to add, middle-class New England style, "They were not of a description with whom I could form any permanent acquaintance having all the outwardness and heartlessness which should only belong to a society of an old country without its graces and accomplishments." Still, despite all the "crude" and "foolish talk" of "coxcombs" and "dressed dolls," she afterward exulted to Almira Barlow, "I was so happy! Had you seen me then I could have flashed and sparkled, and afforded you some amusement."[36]

There was nothing amusing, however, about one social occurrence that summer; namely, Fuller's long-awaited reunion with James Clarke. Back in late June, when Clarke had first arrived in Boston for a six-week vacation, Fuller, naturally enough, had expected them to return to their past confessionals. But Clarke, embarrassed over his failings—and evidently unable to say face-to-face what he had been complaining about in his letters—resisted. Worse yet, at a party on the last evening they saw each other, he committed the rather large faux pas of ignoring Margaret and spending most of the evening talking with, of all people, Harriet Russell. It was the whole George Davis problem all over again, with even one of the same dramatis personae! Deeply hurt and convinced that (as his sister later told him) he "had given her up," she insisted that he not come to Newport to visit her. But James Clarke was not George Davis. Immediately after getting back to Louisville, on September 8 he wrote her a frantic letter, begging her to take him back. In it he basically admitted the charges, but pleaded "outward" habits he had picked up in the West and his social befuddlement. But most of all he defended his own character as a Romantic friend. "I am the same being essentially that I was. . . . I have not become worldly. . . . I revere Truth. I love Excellence. I despise Appearance. I hate mere, outside, temporary Effect. I thirst for deeper draughts of spiritual life, for closer communion with noble minds, for more far reaching, deep penetrating thoughts. I wish also to do something among men—not to pine away unheard, unknown, but to act out myself, and die struggling on the arena." And, more to the point, despite his struggles on the arena, he had no intention at all of acting out with her any (as he called them in another letter) "ugly George Davis thoughts." "Toward you I am essentially the same," he assured her. "There is nothing I would conceal from you. I would communicate to you sooner than to any one else. There are many things you alone can appreciate and understand. I do not wish, like George, to be independent of your influence. I do not wish to separate what is yours from what is mine in the web of my character. I feel grateful for the high intellectual culture and excitement of which you have been to me the source." Finally—and most fervently of all—he pleaded for transcendental mercy: "I beg you not to determine rashly, from a pride of Understanding, that our friendship is over—and so make it over. Do not determine that if we are not all to each other we shall be nothing. I can never find such another as you. . . . Out of my own family you are about the only friend left me."[37]

Clarke's heartfelt and noble-sounding plea had the desired effect. (It probably also helped that James's sister Sarah showed her one of his Cambridge journals testifying to how much knowing her had changed his life.) In her reply on the twenty-eighth, she heartily agreed to resume their friendship, loftily adding her "good hope that we may begin a new era and that we may alter the nature of our friendship without annihilating its soul." Meanwhile, she said, "Time will decide whether we can resist the changes in one another." And time did. For the next half-dozen years of Clarke's stay in Louisville, they continued to write long, lively, monthly letters full of literary talk, social gossip, personal news, and sometimes moral support and advice. But their sublimated confessionals ("so intellectual, so unimaginative," as Fuller bluntly described them in one Groton letter to Clarke) waned. Furthermore, although Fuller sometimes lightly tweaked Clarke for marking her "as the 'friend of your *mind*' only," her letters show she did pretty much the same with him. Apart from the obvious one of distance, however, their reasons for withdrawal—as their letters also show—were very different. Whereas with him one big reason was (as he half-admitted in his letter of defense) his "commencing the active business of life," with her it was just the opposite—her increasing struggles with the baffling trials of a private existence. She sometimes acknowledged this to Clarke. "If I am not frank towards you the cause will be the old one," she wrote in one letter that year, "want of self-complacency." And in another, she confessed, "I think I am less happy in many respects than you but particularly in this. You can speak freely to me of all your circumstances and feelings can you not?— It is not possible for me to be so profoundly frank with any earthly friend. Thus my heart has no proper home only can prefer some of its visiting-places to others and with deep regret I realize that I have at length entered upon the concentrating stage of life." In later years, when they both resided again in the Boston area, they would regain something of their earlier intimacy. But for now the waning of their friendship marked the closing of a final door on her former innocent Cambridge life.[38]

By the time Fuller sent off her peace letter, she was back in Boston, having spent September after Newport partly with Anna Barker at the Farrars and partly "wandering about" among various friends' houses. On October 11 she returned to Groton, still obviously not quite able to shake off the aftereffects of her quarrel with Clarke. Writing a few days earlier to Almira Barlow, a correspondent with whom she was ordinarily sparkling, she confessed: "Surely the intercourse I used to have with you and other friends of my youth, was penetrating, was satisfying, compared with that I have with people now. I am more and more dissatisfied with this world, and *cannot* find a home in it."[39]

Meanwhile, once back in Groton, she returned to her work at the home she did have. She resumed, she informed Clarke on November 13, her "fascinating . . . employment of needlework." With more alacrity, she reopened her school, now swollen to six with the addition of three neighboring Groton youths. True, she could sound rather cynical even about this. Speaking to Clarke of "stranger damsels who crave to learn foreign languages" under her, she said they "wish to know the Latin for E pluribus unum and to be able to translate French and Italian quotations in the novels they may have occasion to peruse." Still, as usual, once she got going, so did her spirits. Indeed, if anything, she seemed pleased with the progress of her charges. Boasting to Clarke later in the winter about how much good she was doing "my children," she wrote, "I do not believe you will ever get three human beings at a time into better order than I have them." But mainly she was pleased by what her teaching was doing for *her*. "Yes James, I am beginning to serve my apprenticeship to the world in good earnest," she exulted. "Earning *money*— think of that.— Tis but a little but 'tis a beginning. I shall be a professional character yet."[40]

Actually, her ambition ran a bit higher than that. While she said nothing directly about it to friends, her journal shows that by this time she wanted desperately to become, not just a "professional character," but a professional author. Despite her dismissal of the idea to Clarke two years before, it had clearly been simmering in her mind. In one of her first letters from Groton, she had boasted to Clarke that Amelia Greenwood had earlier shown a couple of her fictionalized "letters" to the *bon viveur* and worldly editor of Boston's *American Monthly Magazine,* Nathaniel P. Willis, "who only thought they were 'capital.'" And in her journal later that winter, she wrote, speaking of Victor Hugo's *Hunchback of Notre Dame,* which she had just read: "This brilliant work has impressed my imagination strongly. Hugo is only eight years older than I. O that I might hope to produce a similar one in the course of eight years." So, beginning that spring, she started to write in earnest: poetry, criticism, fiction, even drama, she tried her hand at. She also planned—sometimes largely. Inspired by the plays of Schiller and Alfieri, she wrote up plans for two dramas based on the life of Gustavus II Adolphus of Sweden, the martyred Reformation Protestant conqueror. Intending to illustrate (appropriately enough) the theme, "The mind accustomed to large thoughts and vast plans cannot easily contract and he who finds his toils for others vain must begin to labour on his own account," her idea eventually ballooned into a plan for six historical tragedies. But worrying that she lacked "minute information" and "dramatick power," she let them lie as a few bare outlines. Inspired once again, this time by her Old Testament studies, she wrote the following spring a draft of a story for a projected series of tales of Hebrew biblical history. She also wrote a number of fictional dialogues, including an ethereally sentimental one of the pietistic German poet and dramatist Friedrich Gottlob Klopstock and his dead wife, Meta. Meanwhile, as she wrote, she anguished. Indeed—now that she was actually trying to write—her anguishing doubts about her literary abilities became, if anything, stronger than ever. In one journal entry, after reporting that she had just read a book about Egypt "that filled my head completely" and had attempted to write something about it, she wrote in staccato phrases:

> Enjoyed it the first time the second grew cold— invention flagging— style tame— oh! I am very wretched— I cannot finish it— there it must lie in my desk with my other plans! tragedies forsooth! What fiend has put into my head and heart this purpose of writing— I cannot write— yet something I was born for— O Lord, Lord show me what it was— It cannot be to educate these children— or *that* would make me happy when I do my best— Once I thought I knew what I wanted— I had two wishes [probably George Davis and her European tour] both of them were thwarted, my heart bled—O God thou knowest that I have striven to be reconciled to thy will but I fear— I fear that when the fount of hope dried up energy invention all the bright intellectual gifts vanished too— Must it be so O God must I descend into the grave without fame as without happiness[—] Shall I never have an hour of self-complacency[—] Shall all these bitter tears, this heart-burning and silent pain end in nothing— Chance people admire me and call me good and bright— This is mockery— cutting irony to my consciousness— I receive letters telling me that I am laying up treasures in heaven or that I must "revel in intellectual pride" &c— No matter what they say— In my own eyes I am imbecile, abased.[41]

In addition to pouring out, in literary Puritan fashion, her "lamentations" over her creative failings, she also tried to figure them out. One problem about her writing that she especially worried about was that it was bookish and unsensual, traits she blamed on her precocious youth. ("My mind too early filled the outward sense," she wrote in one Wordsworthian poem.) She also worried that her love of conversation vitiated her imagination. "Conversation is my natural element," she told Clarke in one letter explaining why she thought her mind was perceptive rather than creative. "I need to be called out and never think alone without imagining some companion.— Whether this be nature or the force of circumstances I know not; it is my habit and bespeaks a second-rate mind."[42]

Finally, she continued to fret, as she had in Cambridge, about the lack of contemporary female models. After moving to Groton she started to read for the first time an assortment of popular female English authors, and the experience left her, to say the least, unimpressed. One or two, like the Romantic critic Anna Jameson, she faintly praised, but most she ridiculed. "Now there's a woman most comfortably conceited," she wrote of the educator Emma Willard's *Journal and Letters from France and Great Britain* after one of her laments about herself. "[She] *stared* at Coleridge and *laughed* at Combe— He was so original she could not for her life help laughing." And again, this time after reading a novel of the chronicler of the fashionable, Catherine Gore: "This woman is shallow with all her *lightness* and brightness." In other references to contemporary women writers in her letters, she liberally sprinkled "cloyed," "spiced," "sweetened," and other similar phrases. Indeed, in her journal in the spring, she wrote darkly, "Reason why all women do not become poetical," and then went on to cite Jameson's Wordsworthian opinions about the impediment to literary creation of imaginatively unmediated passion and feelings. Many antebellum American female authors were originally attracted to authorship, as several historians have suggested, because they thought, compared with other vocations, it comported so well with what they took to be women's private and sentimental feminine character. If they worried at all, they worried that writing was not feminine *enough*. Fuller worried about just the opposite—that writing, as practiced by most women writers, was not *sufficiently* tough-minded and publicly intellectual, or (in the words of her original letter to Clarke) "living and practical."[43]

In the fall, she got her first opportunity to test her own literary powers before the public, and her subject was very much the dead. The occasion was a long article on slavery in ancient Rome by George Bancroft that appeared in the October 1834 issue of the *North American Review*. That month, Bancroft had won the endorsement of the Anti-Masonic party for his ultimately unsuccessful candidacy for the Massachusetts General Court from Northampton. More generally, he was trying to parlay the acclaim he was receiving for his recently published first volume of his *History of the United States* into a career as a literatus-turned-politician, a sort of Jacksonian Edward Everett. For the moment his article was his chief scholarly weapon in his campaign. In it he argued that Rome's slavery, the principal cause of its decline, had been nurtured solely by the Roman artistocracy—an argument clearly intended both to appeal to anti-Whig voters and to illustrate the theme of his *History:* that popular democracy was the spring of enlightenment and reform. But what caught Margaret's father's Anti-Masonic eye was one strand in his argument—his vituperative attack on the character of Brutus. No doubt Timothy Fuller detected in the incipient young Jacksonian's denigration of Brutus and concomitant glorification of Caesar as a friend of the people something of the populist statism that classical republicans like Fuller had always detested as much as they did the aristocracy.[44]

In any case, sufficiently aroused, her father asked Margaret to write a reply, which he published in the November 27 issue of the *Boston Daily Advertiser.* Signed "J." (after "Justice"), Fuller's "Brutus" was certainly vigorous enough. One by one she examined the charges—that Brutus was merely an assassin, a timeserver, a dupe, that he was unusually cruel and avaricious—exposing contradictions, analyzing instances mentioned, and marshaling contrary evidence mainly drawn from Plutarch, whom she cited in English, but also from Caesar's friend Velleius Paterculus, whom she quoted in Latin, adding modestly, "I doubt not an infinity of similar authorities might be quoted by one of more extensive reading and accurate memory." What was most remarkable about her piece was its unabashed filiopietism. In phrases that strongly echoed some of her father's youthful republican perorations, she heaped scorn on what she saw as a newly arisen class of American iconoclasts or (as she put it) "band of irreverent levellers," who sought to win notoriety in a crowded field "by broaching new opinions on topics and characters apparently long since . . . settled." Standing firmly by the fathers and against the patricidal sons, she delivered this grandiloquent warning:

> The hearts of the illustrious departed are now tranquillized. . . . They can no longer answer the forgotten or refuted calumnies of obscure foes. But the faith of the living bleeds, and young ambition droops, when the shades of the just are summoned back from Elysium to which their appropriate judges had consigned them, to repass the consecrating river, and appear before some revolutionary tribunal of modern date.

"Let us not," she concluded, "be too hasty in questioning what is established, and tearing to pieces the archives of the past. There are other sorts of scepticism, not less desolating in their tendency, than that of religion." Noting that America's "greatest danger lay in *want of reverence,*" she pointedly added, "Those most distinguished among us for talent and culture should rather check than encourage this tendency." If she worried, as she had confessed in the spring, that her Romantic intellectual pursuits had led her away from her father, she made up for it here with a vengeance.[45]

Naturally, such a spirited attack on so prominent a figure as Bancroft (she even twitted him a bit by quoting a youthful effusion of his in praise of Brutus) was not likely to go unnoticed. And, sure enough, in the same newspaper there appeared the following Thursday the inevitable rejoinder by a correspondent signing himself "H." from Salem. H.'s letter, however, was hardly a broadside defense. After praising his opponent for writing "with ability and candor," he brought forth but a single letter of Cicero's, which he took from Gibbon, purporting to show an instance of apparent cruelty and avarice on Brutus's part. Otherwise, on most other issues raised by Bancroft, he either equivocated or backed away. In sum, then, if not a clear win, it was at least a draw and, as she saw it, a triumph, too, to be answered so gravely in print by (she guessed) "some big-wig." Writing happily to Bancroft's former pupil Henry Hedge three months later, she gave this assessment of the contest: "He detected some ignorance in me nevertheless as he remarked that I wrote with 'ability' and seemed to *consider me* as an eldery gentleman *I considered* the affair as highly flattering and beg you will keep it in mind and furnish it for my memoirs as such after I am dead."[46]

V

Despite her injunction to Hedge to start thinking about her memoirs, Fuller was not exactly overwhelmed by her first success. "I think they had best take the following as Motto to my memoirs," she wrote in her journal soon afterwards. "'Though an indefatigable writer, Mr Townley never printed anything but a "Dissertation on an ancient Helmet found at R.—in the 'Vetusta Monumenta' of the Society of Antiquaries.""' Still, she was clearly buoyed by it. At the same time she was growing increasingly frustrated with her Groton exile. A letter arrived from Hedge that winter, in which he anguished over whether to agree to edit the *Christian Examiner* for a starvation salary or to accept a much more lucrative offer to take a permanent pulpit in the isolated boom town of Bangor, Maine. Fuller answered, after sympathizing with his money needs, with a warning that "this going into mental solitude is desperately trying. . . . To me the expression of thought and feeling is to the mind what respiration is to the lungs and much suffering and probable injury will ensue from living in a thick or harsh atmosphere." Naturally, her rising discontent with Groton led her to think, even more poignantly than she had the previous winter, of healthier atmospheres elsewhere. After reading that November her old friend Lydia Maria Child's description of South American scenery in her antislavery collection, *The Oasis,* she wrote in her journal: "How would it be to go there. I might establish a school, maintain myself and get so many new thoughts and emotions." And farther down the page—speaking of the militant band of Cincinnati theological students who were in the news for resisting their school trustees' demand to cease their antislavery agitation—she wrote: "What is said of Lane Seminary makes me wish to visit Cincinnati. In fact where do I *not* wish to go and try life for a time." (The antislavery issue in little Groton, on the other hand, only inspired a yawn. "There is the greatest fuss about slavery in *this* little nook," she told Clarke. "An idle gentleman weary of his ease has taken to philanthropy as a profession and here are incessant lectures. I rarely go.") She also ached, more than ever, to make her cultural mark. In an enormous thirteen-page letter to Clarke on February 1—which included envious glances at his labors in Louisville ("I think your progress is vast compared to mine") and a lengthy dissertation on the relative merits of all the famous orators she had recently heard—she made this clear enough. "I felt," she wrote (referring to hearing the English abolitionist George Thompson, who had spoken in Groton two weeks before), "as I have so often done before if I were a man decidedly the gift I would choose would be that of eloquence— That power of forcing the vital currents of thousands of human hearts into *one* current by the constraining power of that delicate instrument the voice is *so* intense— Yes I would prefer it to a more extensive fame, a more permanent influence."[47]

Three weeks after revealing this wish, Fuller learned of her first chance, if neither for fame nor for the "living and practical" platform eloquence that was denied her as a woman, at least for a small bit of influence. On February 1, Hedge wrote to her, saying that he had decided not to edit the *Christian Examiner* because, as it was an official Unitarian publication, he could not make it what he wished. So instead he and the Purchase Street Unitarian congregation's minister George Ripley were intending to establish "a journal of spiritual philosophy in which we are to enlist all the Germano-philosophico-literary talent in the country." He listed an impressive roster of contributors, including not only prominent young Unitarian ministers like Ralph Waldo Emerson, but also Harvard's Charles Follen, President James Marsh of the University of Vermont, and even Thomas Carlyle. "It is our desired & strong hope to introduce new elements of thought & to give a new impulse to the mental action of our country," he told her. On March 6, Fuller answered encouragingly, "Your periodical plan charms me: I think you will do good and what is next best gain fame." As for herself, she said, "I feel myself honoured if I am deemed worthy of lending a hand albeit I fear," she warned, "I am merely 'Germanico' and not 'transcendental.'" The warning about her indifference to German idealist metaphysics proved needless. In April, Hedge, who was to have been the magazine's chief editor, left to settle in Bangor, and, after an unsuccessful attempt by him and Emerson to get Carlyle to come to Boston to edit it, the project collapsed.[48]

No sooner, though, did this one transcendental air castle disappear, than another rose up to take its place. The prime mover this time was James Clarke. For the past two years Clarke had been meditating on his predicament in the West, and he had finally concluded, as he explained to Fuller in a letter in December, that he had indeed found the freedom of opinion he had come west for. "I say things constantly with effect," he had written her a little earlier, "that if lisped in New England would be overborne at once by the dominant opinions." But on the other hand, as he told Fuller in December, he also was beginning to realize how much he really needed "a basis of received opinion," if for no other reason than to have something to react against. "We want some place to start from, something to argue from, but there are no axioms in mental or moral philosophy given us here. We can address nothing but tastes and feelings." The solution, then? By that winter he thought he had found it: he would become a popularizer of "Transcendental Philosophy" and start a magazine, to be edited by himself and his Western Unitarian colleagues, that would exploit at once the freedom of the West and the Transcendentalist axioms (or, in this case, counteraxioms) of the East. Indeed, the *Western Messenger,* as they called their magazine, would come to rely so heavily on Transcendentalist sympathizers and Unitarian writers, either Bostonians or transplants, that one early historian suggested a more accurate name for it would have been the "eastern messenger." Sure enough, one of the first prospective messengers to whom Clarke sent his prospectus and letter soliciting contributions (which he wrote fortuitously on the very day the hapless Hedge wrote his) was his fellow "Germanico" Margaret Fuller. "We mean to make this a first rate affair," he confidently wrote, "and to combine literature and other miscellaneous matters with religious discussions. I mean it to have a Western air and spirit, a free, and unshackled spirit and form, as far as may be. I wish you to help me by writing on topics of religion, morals, literature, art, or anything *you* feel to be worth writing about." Again, a couple months later, urging her on: "Don't be afraid, there is no public opinion here. You are throwing your ideas to help form one. Be as transcendental as you please; if you express transcendentalism distinctly there is no objection to it drawn from its logical inconsistence with a domineering philosophy. Even thorough going, ripened, Priestleyan Unitarians have their minds open enough to receive all sorts of religious supernaturalism—only not under that name."[49]

As with Hedge's similar pronouncements, Clarke's knowing reassurances— as he ought to have known by then—were largely wasted. When he had origi- nally told her of his intention to become a popularizer of Transcendentalist met- aphysics, she had mildly tweaked him in much the same spirit that she had attacked Novalis the year before. ("Not see the use of Metaphysicks— Moderate portion taken at stated intervals I hold to be of much use as discipline of the faculties— I only object to them as having an absorbing and antiproductive ten- dency.") Even more blunt was her answer to his encouragement now to "be as transcendental as you please": "Why you call me 'transcendental' I don't know. I am sure if I am one it is after the fashion of le Bourgeois Gentilhomme. As far as I know myself I am at present 'all no how' except on matters of taste." Yet Clarke was hardly very technical about his "Transcendentalism." Nor did Fuller have much reason to be inhibited by mere technicalities. Like Clarke and his Romantic ministerial friends, she felt alienated from her staid New England lit- erary culture. ("I cannot well judge what effect any-thing is like to produce on a New-England public with which I have nothing in common," she had told Clarke frankly two years before, when he had asked her about whether or not to withdraw from publication an answer he had written to an attack on Goethe by Harvard's Professor Andrews Norton, which, contrary to her advice, he even- tually did take back.) And, of course, she wanted to write. So she did. On April 6, less than a month after getting Clarke's prospectus, she sent him the last of three long review-articles—the only ones, in fact, Clarke initially got from the many Eastern friends to whom he had sent his plea.[50]

Perhaps the most striking thing about these articles was their high-toned Uni- tarian liberalism. Their subjects were all English books that had generated con- troversial notices in the British reviews; their tone was an aggressive version of the same judicious, imperious one generally favored by these reviews; and their arguments, at least in the first two articles, were permeated by some very classic Unitarian and republican concepts. This was particularly true of her first article, published in the *Messenger*'s first issue in June 1835, on the memoirs of two recently deceased writers from a decidedly non-Romantic earlier era—the poet George Crabbe and the "Bluestocking Circle" religious writer Hannah More. Toward the sober, moderate-minded Crabbe she was highly complimentary, sin- gling out his "stern pictorial" style and such old republican virtues as his love of nature, his independence, and his "resolute cheerfulness" in the midst of poverty and repeated disappointments. Toward the Anglican evangelical, moralistic

More, on the other hand, she was prickly. While lauding her work among the poor and sympathizing with the special difficulties she had to face as a woman, Fuller nonetheless attacked her for being, however unconsciously, "a great flatterer" of her social and literary superiors and something of a hypocrite to boot. "We could not but wonder," she wrote quizzically, "that Miss More, so philanthropic and generally so discriminating, should not feel something wanting in that religious establishment, of which she was the stanch partizan, when she found twelve parishes of her vicinity in the state she describes, while her friends, the right reverend bishops and archbishops were residing in palaces, and had the income of princes."[51]

Something of this morally Whiggish point of view she also worked into her second *Messenger* article, published in the August issue, on the novels of the young English writer Edward Bulwer (later Bulwer-Lytton). Ever since her Cambridge years she, like her friends Davis and Clarke, had been captivated by Disraeli, Bulwer-Lytton, and others of the "silver-fork school" of satirical novelists who portrayed aristocratic circles. In her article, she staked out a firm centrist position between, on one hand, conservative critics who, she thought, "shamefully abused" Bulwer-Lytton's novels as "immoral," and, on the other hand, his many young readers who avidly read them. Essentially she argued, in good Unitarian style, that Bulwer-Lytton's novels showed a "gradual renovation and healing of the diseased soul." She traced the origin of his transformation back to his early popular novel *Pelham,* whose surface liveliness she half-appreciated, but whose studied irony (much like the sort George Davis had cultivated) she roundly condemned. ("The philosophy which teaches that it is possible to *seem* the thorough worldling, and to *be* the man of delicate feelings, independent and honorable mind, is false.") From there she argued that his socially defiant Godwinian novels, although threatening us with "libertinism" and "anarchy," showed him, she said, "on the right track." Finally, she happily pointed to his most recent, bookish historical novel *The Last Days of Pompeii,* the principal work under review, which she praised unstintingly for its "Beauty of form" and "tendency to the ideal." Only two years later she would confess to a friend she had *"overestimate[d]"* Bulwer-Lytton. But for the moment she was glad to see him—much as she would have liked to have seen herself at this time—morally progressing.[52]

Except, perhaps, for her residual sympathy for the dandy Bulwer-Lytton, Fuller's first two articles might not have seemed out of place even in the conservatively liberal *North American Review.* Her third essay, however, published in the December issue, definitely would have. Ostensibly a review of the verse drama *Philip Van Artevelde* by the newly published Colonial Office official Henry Taylor, in actuality the article was a chaotic assemblage of Romantic pronouncements on the character of modern drama, centering on the standard (though in America largely unfamiliar) German Romantic division between the "Classical" and the "Romantic." She made no apologies for her approach. "Long dissertations" on a cluster of plays forced the reader "to take a broader or more careful view of the subject than his indolence or his business would have permitted." Likewise her critical borrowings from Europe: they were necessary in a nation that for now possessed, along with its "higher degree" of happiness, its, alas, "lower one" of cultivation.[53]

Despite her aggressively theoretical stance, her actual argument, as in her Bulwer-Lytton article, was almost ostentatiously balanced. Her preference, she said, was for the drama of the "classical school," which she defined broadly as "such a simplicity of plan, selection of actors and events, such judicious limitations on time and range of subject as may concentrate the interest, perfect the illusion, and make the impression most distinct and forcible." Yet, expanding on her definition, she proceeded to give it a distinctly Romantic twist: "Art is Nature, but nature, new modelled, condensed, and harmonized. We are not merely like mirrors to reflect our own times to those more distant. The mind has a light of its own, and by it illumines what it recreates." Furthermore, after discussing several works by Alfieri and the later Goethe and Schiller that she thought best exemplified classical drama, she then tried to do justice to the "Romantic style" and (which she placed under this rubric) Taylor's *Van Artevelde.* What she liked about this admired closet drama of the soul-destroying rise to power of a revolutionary intellectual in fourteenth-century Flanders was its combination of high seriousness *and* realism. Speaking of Taylor's attack in his preface on the sentimental effusions of two English writers then enormously popular in America, she wrote: "We too rejoice to see a leader coming forward who is likely to unHemanize and unCornwallize literature. We too have been sick—we too have been intoxicated with words, till we could hardly appreciate thoughts." Indeed, she argued, it was precisely this quality of lively pathos and realism—in which, she claimed, without a great deal of evidence, Taylor surpassed the contemporary Romantic Italian dramatist Alessandro Manzoni—that was, more generally (mixing her categories a bit), the sine qua non of all successful drama. Yet this was not a quality, she concluded, that many of even the greatest writers could achieve. "Coleridge and Byron," she stated, invoking the names of one newer and one older Romantic hero of hers,

> are signal instances how peculiar is the kind of talent required for the drama. One a philosopher, both men of great genius and uncommon mastery over language, both conversant with both sides of human nature, both considering the drama in its true light as one of the highest departments of literature, both utterly wanting in simplicity, pathos, truth of passion and liveliness of action—in that thrilling utterance of heart to heart, whose absence *here,* no other excellence can atone for.

In sum, she might not have been able to write a drama, but she seemed to be dedicated to showing, Romantic theory or not, she at least knew what went into the production of one.[54]

So ended her first venture in published criticism. Not that she had any particular reason to feel too triumphant. The *Messenger,* while gaining attention in the West and soon to be perused in liberal Unitarian circles in the East, then boasted a subscription list of fewer than four hundred readers. Then there was the typical young author's chagrin at printer's errors. "Do, my dear James, have some attention paid to correcting the press," she complained in exasperation to her novice editor after receiving the second number. "My . . . pieces were full of blunders from beginning to end. . . . 'The love of *Earth* [instead of Truth] is a healing and renovating principle' (what a beautiful sentiment!)." Her reviews were also not particularly encouraging. True, Sarah Clarke wrote excitedly to her brother, "Margaret's [*Van Artedvelde*] article is beautiful, and just fit for the *Foreign Quarterly*." But this was not a view shared by Fuller's editors. The *Messenger*'s Cincinnati publishers told Ephraim Peabody, then the magazine's editor, that Fuller's first review was "undignified" and ought not to be printed, and even Peabody, who thought Fuller's pieces "good articles," worried that they were unsuitable for a Western magazine. Clarke himself, although he initially told Fuller he liked her articles, after she wrote him several letters begging him to "give me any criticisms, no matter how severe," finally sent her, on May 12, a small boatload. She had too many allusions for Western readers. ("They know nothing of books. You must not suppose any *Vorkenntnisse*.") Her train of thought was too hazy. ("We feel like an explorer in a Kentucky cavern; there are so many side-passages, opening to the right and left, leading upward and downward. . . . [The Bulwer-Lytton article] is a perfect labyrinth of thoughts to a western reader.") Finally, he thought—quite the opposite of his Western publishers—her language was "too elevated." Even in conversation," he added, "it has been your fault to speak in too lofty and sustained a style sometimes."[55]

She seems to have taken all this in stride. She knew, after all, as she told Clarke, that his Unitarian magazine's "*main* object is not literary," and, for that matter, that Clarke himself was more a literary clergyman than a religious literatus. Furthermore, she, too, was critical of her writing, although her worries were rather different from Clarke's apt ones about her diffusiveness; she worried about its lack of "fulness, precision, detail," and, above all, forcefulness. "In reading over what I have written my taste is grated by the repetition of epithets and phrases such as beauty, simplicity, distinguished excellence &c," she confessed to Clarke. But she also thought, she told him, her fault of over-generalization was due to the fact that she had "talked so much and written so little. I am sure I *can* correct it." Finally, just the experience of contemplating her works in print was obviously encouragement enough. For no sooner had she promised her articles to Clarke than she began to speak to him for the first time of her various plans for tragedies and tales. Later, on April 28, after she had written her reviews, she asked him, more mundanely, whether he thought a Cincinnati publisher might be interested in a series of translations from modern French novels she was thinking of doing. "My aim is *money*," she told him, once again. "I want an independent income very much, but I could not venture any thing in which my own pride and feelings are engaged for lucre. But to translating in four modern languages I know myself equal and if I could set some scheme of this kind going it would suit me very well." But, she feared, "with all my aspirations after independence I do not possess sufficient at present to walk into the Boston establishments and ask them to buy my work and I have no friend at once efficient and sympathizing." Meanwhile, her efficient and sympathizing friend Clarke, though discouraging as usual about the West ("I assure you that there is not a reading public on this side of the mountains"), nonetheless suggested in his letter two weeks later that she look into Eastern publishers like Harper's, who, he told her, "are rivaling each other in snapping at the last new novel." At the same time, he urged her to continue writing for the *Messenger,* particularly on religious subjects, he emphasized, "in a conversational kind of style." For her part, Fuller begged off on this last suggestion and did not write another article again for the magazine for over two years.[56]

VI

On her birthday, having digested Clarke's friendly criticism and advice, Fuller started out on the first leg of her annual extended excursion away from Groton. Her first stop was Cambridge, where she spent ten days with the Farrars, mingled with old friends, and took daily "divine" horseback excursions into the countryside. There, too, as in the last summer, she saw the vacationing Anna Barker, whose beauty, as always, dazzled her. From Cambridge she left for Boston, where on June 2 she wrote to her father of the Farrars' proposal to take her and several friends of theirs on a trip to Trenton Falls, New York, then a popular scenic vacation spot. "Oh I cannot describe," she wrote breathlessly, "the positive extacy with which I think of this journey— To see the North River at last and in such society!" After asking for the fifty-seven dollars for the approximate expenses ("you will not think of the money—will you? I would rather you take two hundred dollars from my portion than feel even the least unwilling"), she closed with: "Will you not write to me immediately and say you love me and are very glad I am to be so happy???"[57]

Her father, indulgent in practice if not always in words, naturally consented. And so, Fuller having returned to Groton on July 11, on the twenty-seventh the party set out. They traveled by boat to New York, took the Erie steamboat up the North River to the Falls, and then embarked on the meandering journey homeward. This began with a "very hot" stagecoach ride over to Little Falls and back through "the enchanting valley of the Mohawk" to Albany; continued on, via the Erie again, down to Catskill (where she told her parents to tell "our boys" she saw "an elephant with a real howdah on his back and a man dressed like a Hindoo upon him parading the streets"); and peaked with a "tedious scramble up the mountain" reclaimed by a "gorgeous prospect" at the top. From there they "drove down the mountain at a Jehu pace," and continued on down to New York, where they were met and dined "sumptuously" by Jacob Barker; on to Newport, where she saw Anna Barker and the Reverend William Ellery Channing; and finally back to Cambridge. Besides showing Fuller's early plucky enthusiasm for travel, her trip was also memorable because it introduced her for the first time to Samuel Gray Ward, a Harvard senior who had been boarding with the Farrars while he attended college and whom they took along with them. Precocious, handsome, and (like many of Eliza Farrar's friends and relations) rich, Ward did not, however, immediately impress Fuller. On the first day on board the boat to New York, she wrote in her journal: "About six, came out, & had a walk & a talk with Mr Ward: did not like him much." In this case, though, first impressions meant little, for by the end of the trip she praised him to her parents as "all kindness throughout"—a sentiment that would soon flower into a lasting and, for a while, feverish friendship.[58]

Back at the Farrars' in Cambridge on August 12—after having enjoyed, Fuller exclaimed to her parents, "three weeks of such unalloyed pleasure as are seldom allotted to mortals"—Fuller soon found herself acquiring another friend: the young English author Harriet Martineau. A materialist, a necessarian, and a radical utilitarian, Martineau would seem to have been, at first glance, one of the last sorts of intellectual figures to have appealed to Fuller. Yet she did, and for some understandable reasons. To begin with, like most English utilitarians, she was in her own way a philanthropist and social idealist. Then, too, she was, like Fuller and her friends, a Unitarian, although, like most English Unitarians, without a particle of faith in Christ's divinity. But, most of all, she was England's most famous female writer—an advisor of cabinet ministers, a confidante of some of its most distinguished writers, and the author of, among other works, *Illustrations of Political Economy*, a series of enormously popular didactic tales demonstrating the principles of free-trade economics. She was also just then at the midway point of a highly publicized two-year tour of the United States. Over the course of her first year she had traveled all over the country, dining with President Andrew Jackson, interviewing senators and Supreme Court justices, and winning the praises of hundreds of prominent Americans fully aware that she was writing a book about them and anxious that it be, after the anti-American tirades of earlier English travelers, a favorable one.[59]

She had also been a great success in personal ways. Although tall and rather plain looking and cursed with a deafness that forced her to use a cumbersome ear trumpet whenever she conversed, Martineau had so far made a highly favorable impression on most Americans she had met. This was especially true of Massachusetts's Unitarians, who fêted her that summer and fall and practically fell over themselves in praising, among themselves, her lively humor and guileless charm, excellent manners, immense curiosity and energy, and, as she seemed so well to appreciate them, of course her good sense. Naturally, some of these good impressions (the storm over her abolitionist sympathies would come three months later) found their way to Fuller. Eliza Farrar, who had known her in England, praised her to Fuller, while James Clarke, who had traveled to Lexington to see her in June, wrote Fuller a glowing report on her "fascinating" manner ("the most feminine dependence, and receptiveness, joined to a ready, self-possessed judgment, and an understanding stored with fact and argument on all topics of human interest"). Indeed, he went further. In his usual enthusiasm on these topics (though perhaps also reflecting something of Martineau's own easy garrulity during her trip), he excitedly informed her that under the influence of the Reverend William Henry Furness, the Transcendental-minded Unitarian minister in Philadelphia, Miss Martineau was now a convert to Transcendentalism! "She says it is a great mistake to suppose her a mere utilitarian; she is preparing the people for Carlylism, for they must be fed and clothed before they can be spiritualized." In case Fuller missed the point, he ended on this personal note: "She is 33—do you remember Byron's 33rd year—what will be ours? How much she has done!"[60]

Needless to say, by the time Fuller actually met Harriet Martineau at the Farrars, she was well prepared to fall within her orbit. Yet, as usual, she was not quite as entirely wide-eyed as Clarke. ("I doubt whether it is a fact that people must *be fed and clothed before they can be spiritualized,*" she answered Clarke crisply, if a little complacently; "on the contrary I am inclined to think that a degree of starvation, well managed, is favorable to this desired result.") Still, in a journal entry written afterwards, she described how her "heart beat as the carriage drove up with Miss Martineau." This was on the Monday morning of August 24. On Wednesday was the college's commencement, and during the whole of the week Martineau was there, the Farrar household was abuzz with local dignitaries paying their respects. In her letter to Clarke, Fuller had expressed to him her fear that though she and Martineau would be living in the same house, she would be unable to strike up an acquaintance with her. "Many will be seeking her and as I have no name nor fame I shall not have much chance." But in fact she did get to see quite a bit of Martineau. In her journal Fuller later left brief accounts of these meetings, which show her determination to like and appreciate her famous acquaintance despite her qualms about her spiritual character. After her first encounter, she wrote: "Miss Martineau . . . received me so kindly as to banish all embarrassment at once. We had some talk about 'Carlyleism,' and I was not quite satisfied with the ground she took, but there was no opportunity for full discussion. I wished to give myself wholly up to receive an impression of her. What shrewdness in detecting various shades of character! Yet, what she said of Hannah More and Miss Edgeworth grated upon my feelings." It was in more personal conversation, however, that Fuller—on the lookout, as always, for older female guides—most fully revealed herself. As Martineau later wrote in her autobiography:

> She told me what danger she had been in from the training her father had given her, and the encouragement to pedantry and rudeness which she derived from the circumstances of her youth. She told me that she was at nineteen the most intolerable girl that ever took a seat in a drawing room. Her admirable candour, the philosophical way in which she took herself in hand, her genuine heart, her practical insight, and, no doubt, the natural influence of her attachment to myself, endeared her to me, while her powers, and her confidence in the use of them, led me to expect great things from her.[61]

For her part, Fuller was obviously also deeply impressed. In a journal entry written shortly afterwards, she described the thrill she felt sitting with her new friend at the Phi Beta Kappa Society celebration at the church the day after commencement ("together close to the pulpit") and the prayer she silently offered up to her after the minister "deeply moved" her by opening the meeting with a prayer for "our friends." She continued:

I sigh for an intellectual guide. Nothing but the sense of what God has done for me in bringing me nearer to himself saves me from despair. With what envy I looked at Flaxman's picture of Hesiod sitting at the feet of the muse! How blest would it be to be thus instructed in one's vocation! Any thing would I do and suffer to be sure that when leaving earth I should not be haunted with recollections of "aims unreached, occasions lost." I have hoped some friend would do—what none has ever done yet, comprehend me wholly, mentally and morally, and enable me better to comprehend myself. I have had some hopes that Miss Martineau might be this friend, but cannot yet tell. She has what I want, vigorous reasoning powers, invention, clear views of her objects, and she has trained to the best means of execution. Add to that there are no strong intellectual sympathies between us, such as would blind her to my defects.

After many more such "happy hours with Miss Martineau," Fuller would soon decide (as she would tell Clarke), "we will be dear friends forever." She had found her first famous female patron.[62]

By the middle of September, Fuller returned to Groton and Miss Martineau continued on her travels. But before they separated, a whole new prospect opened before Fuller. The Farrars, who were planning to take a year-and-a-half tour of Europe beginning the coming summer, proposed to take her with them. They also made the same proposal to Sam Ward and Anna Barker, suggesting at the same time that Miss Martineau, who was planning to sail for England in August, accompany the entourage on their way to London. To see at last the source of her youthful readings, to finally find her long-deferred European trip realized, and in such company, and to know that while in London she would be with Miss Martineau and would therefore, as she later wrote her brother Eugene, "see the best literary society"—it all seemed like a plan made in heaven. But unfortunately, before it could be carried out, three events intervened that threw this and all the rest of Fuller's life plans into extreme disarray.[63]

Actually, the first was not so much an event as a consequence of a series of events, half-embarrassing, half-ludicrous, but for Fuller also extremely trying. The precipitating cause was a story entitled "Lost and Won: A Tale of Modern Days and Good Society," which Fuller had published in the August 8 issue of the *New England Galaxy,* a relatively (by American magazine standards) long-running and somewhat sensationalist literary magazine (its editorials had pro-voked several libel actions). The *Galaxy* had published writers like Susanna Rowson, the author of the popular didactic seduction novel *Charlotte Temple,* as well as fashionable authors like Bulwer-Lytton and N. P. Willis, and it was currently being edited by the flamboyant Maine writer John Neal. Fuller's tale fitted in quite well. The principal characters are Emily Williamson, an ardent, lightly literary-minded, rebellious, and, above all, nobility-craving young woman; Davenant (he has no first name), a sneering and calculating womanizer and her faithless lover; Frederick Gower, Davenant's ambitious but priggishly noble rival; and Edward Drayton, Emily's doting but ineffectual, foreign book-loving cousin. The story's climax comes when Davenant, having broken Emily's heart by coldly rejecting her in favor of fresher conquests, is humiliated when he returns again to press his suit after being rejected himself and he encounters a contemptuous and righteous Emily, now finally awakened to the virtues of self-awareness, compassion, and Gower, whose wife she has become. In sum, the losers have won, while the perennial winner has lost to become, as we learn at the end, a despised and ridiculed old bachelor.[64]

There are clearly many elements out of which Fuller spun her melodramatic moral tale. She had wanted to write fiction; she had been an interested reader of that staple of European Romantic and sentimental writings, the morally signif-icant seduction story, since her childhood; and, more recently, she had become mildly fascinated with the English fashionable novelists who made the theme of deception their stock in trade. Indeed, "Lost and Won" could be viewed as a woman-centered version of the loftily moral Bulwer-Lytton story she had trum-peted in her *Western Messenger* review—a sort of bourgeois, feminine *Pelham* without the irony. But there was also one other source for her tale. Off and on during the two years prior to George Davis and Harriet Russell's marriage the previous fall, Harriet had indulged her propensity (in Clarke's words) to "coquette a little." Another friend in their circle, Joseph Angier—a recent Divinity School graduate and reputed lady's man—did the same, apparently for a while with Harriet. This hardly, of course, made "Lost and Won" an exact roman à clef. Although, for example, the kindly but bumbling, literary-minded Drayton bears a certain resemblance to Clarke and Angier is an obvious stand-in for Davenant, the central character—the noble stuffed shirt, Fred Gower—is only very remotely suggestive of the ironical Davis. Much more important than any precise correspondence to actual characters is the fact that Fuller clearly aimed in a general way to write something from life—perhaps a bit of the "liv-ing" word she claimed she missed in the writings of female fiction writers.[65]

Unfortunately, however, as it turned out, her story was just a little *too* living. On September 15, Clarke, who had gotten a copy from Angier's sometime sing-ing partner Helen Davis, excitedly wrote her from Newton, where he was visiting his family, that her sketch, despite its "obscure" style, was absolutely admirable. And it was admirable, he thought, because, though admittedly somewhat height-ened above reality, it was so true to life. He particularly thought it "tremendous" on "poor Joseph": "If he is regenerate it will be severe but wholesome medi-cine—if not, it will make him terribly angry." Finally, after several more of these praises and cross-references (including one to himself as "Edward Drayton"), he dropped his bombshell. He had, he casually informed her, since getting Helen Davis's copy, managed to procure several more copies of her story, and these, he blithely went on, he had shown "to many individuals—for instance, Mrs. Wen-dell Davis, Miss Sturgis. I also wrote to Geo. and Harriet telling them of it. What they will think I cannot tell. But soon shall know."[66]

Why Clarke should have knowingly aired such a potentially embarrassing document is difficult to say. Probably it was simply his characteristic naïveté and enthusiasm. Nor is it possible to know what the Davises thought of this invasion of their privacy, but one can imagine. Fuller evidently thought that either the anonymous story would not be read by the principal parties involved, or, somewhat naïvely, if it ever was, they would never guess at its real-life basis, but simply take it—as she no doubt largely meant it—as her fictionalized moral statement on the subject of youthful pride and nobility that had preoccupied them all since their Cambridge years. She apparently exploded when she read Clarke's letter. If one were to judge by Clarke's response (Fuller's original is now lost), her letter must have been somewhat hysterical—indeed, so much so that Clarke, by now obviously fairly distraught himself, did not even answer it but instead ducked and let his sister Sarah, the peacemaker, make his excuses for him. What Sarah said in their letter of September 29, which they sent out the same morning they got her letter, was essentially this: First, "it was not as you suppose through his means that the meaning of the tale was made public" (Mrs. Fay and Helen Davis had figured it out for themselves and had told *them* about it); and second, insofar as it *was* made public, it was all to the good. Indeed, just to make sure there was no misunderstanding, "James was writing to George this morning and told him how far it was from being public and what you said about it in your letter and how much honor it did to Harriet and how none need be ashamed or distressed about it but Mr. Davenant. It was a letter well calculated to compose his mind supposing it was troubled. And now don't worry yourself about it, dear Margaret, for it is a good thing to have done such poetic justice to a character so genuine and primitive as Harriet's and one so likely to be misinterpreted." Finally, just in case all this honor and justice were not quite reassuring enough, she quickly added (with some slight stretching of the truth): "James begs me to say that he was exaggerating when he proposed to tell the world about it and that among us all, Helen included, we have not told more than three people." James added several paragraphs at the end, carefully avoiding any mention of "Lost and Won" and pledging his undying friendship.[67]

Whether the Clarkes' letter allayed Fuller's anxiety or not is hard to tell. For whatever reason, she would not try her hand at fiction again for several years. In any case, by the time she received Clarke's letter, the worst phase of her reaction was already over. Immediately after she returned to Groton, she fell terribly ill. "For nine long days and nights," she afterwards wrote in her journal, she had "without intermission—fever and dreadful pain in my head. Mother tended me like an angel all that time, scarce ever leaving me, night or day." Certainly Fuller's illness was a serious one. Her brother Richard later said she had "typhus [probably typhoid] fever," and if so, it could very well have killed her, given the state of medical treatment at the time. On the other hand, the circumstances of her illness strongly suggest a psychological element in Fuller's suffering. First of all, there is the rather suspicious sequence of events. She arrived in Groton sometime in mid-September, received Clarke's letter either on the sixteenth or seventeenth, read it, and on the eighteenth fell ill. A second suggestion arises from her possible motives in story writing itself. One might guess that at least one inducement to writing her tale (apart, that is, from her obvious literary interests) was a lingering resentment over her old George Davis disappointment. Another, perhaps, was a conscious or unconscious desire to set herself up as the righteous moral judge of the flirtations of her Cambridge friends—flirtations from which she had always been excluded. If either or both of these revengeful motives were at work, they might explain, certainly not the illness itself, but (reminiscent of the self-punishing responses of Fuller's fictional boarding-school heroine, Mariana, to the exposure of *her* theatrical troublemaking) something of her guilt-tinged and vaguely suicidal reaction to it. "For myself," she wrote afterwards in her journal, "I thought I should surely die; but I was calm and looked to God without fear. When I remembered how much struggle awaited me, if I remained and how improbable it was that any of my cherished plans would bear fruit, I felt willing to go." To Almira Barlow, a few months later, she wrote: "You know that I looked upon Death very near, nor at the time should I have grieved to go. I thought there never could come a time when my departure would be easier to myself, or less painful to others." Finally, such an interpretation is consistent with the account she afterwards gave in her journal of her recovery and the crucial role of her father—or so at least the logic of the narrative would seem to imply—in helping bring it about:

> My father habitually so sparing in tokens of affection was led by his anxiety to express what he felt towards me, in stronger terms, than he had ever used in the whole course of my life. He thought I might not recover, and one morning coming into my room, after a few moments conversation he said: "My dear, I have been thinking of you in the night, and I cannot remember that you have any faults. You have defects of course, as all mortals have, but I do not know that you have a single fault." These words so strange from him, who had scarce ever in my presence praised me and who, as I knew, abstained from praise as hurtful to his children—affected me to tears at the time, although I could not know how dear a consolation this extravagant expression of regard would soon become. The family were deeply moved by the fervency of his prayer of thanksgiving on the Sunday morning, when I was somewhat recovered and to Mother he said "I have no room for a painful thought now that our daughter is restored."[68]

If, then, her father's words truly were, as she seems to have felt, guilt-relieving as well as restorative, his sudden death three days later could not have been more dreadfully incongruous. Some family members thought the cause was his coming into contact with some contaminated water or vegetation while he was overseeing the draining of some low meadows that summer and early fall. (Richard later speculated that this contamination was also the cause of much of the severe family illness that season.) Margaret later implied that at least a contributing factor was his "embittered . . . over anxious" mental state produced by worries over his narrowed income and clashes with his elder sons over their careers. Still others thought his stamina had been fatally weakened by the exhausting physical labors that he habitually undertook despite his age and delicate health. "In the violent heat of summer," Richard later wrote, "I have seen him loading grain with the perspiration flowing over his heated brow. After such efforts he was obliged to lie down for hours." Whatever the cause, the event was swift. While he was in the house in the afternoon of September 30—exactly a day after finishing his newly built study at the end of the garden, in which he intended, having finally settled the last of his law cases, to write—Margaret's father began suddenly to vomit uncontrollably and within seconds sank to the floor. The children carried him upstairs and laid him on his bed. A physician was called for, who pronounced his disease "Asiatic cholera" (subsequently confirmed by a post-mortem examination), but could do nothing to stop the chills and spasms, which continued through the night and into the morning. Finally, in the afternoon, at his request, Margaret, her mother, her sister, and her brothers gathered in his room to receive, each in turn and amidst much crying and weeping, an affectionately whispered leave-taking and a kiss. Later that night he died. Margaret, by his side at the end, closed his eyes.[69]

CHAPTER SIX

Apprenticeship
(1835–1837)

I

The sudden death of her father marked a dark turning point in Fuller's life. "Returned into life," she sadly told Almira Barlow, "I . . . felt myself fatherless." This sense of being suddenly "fatherless"—echoing, as it did, anguished complaints about her father's emotional abandonment of her that she had expressed since her childhood—would haunt her for many years. It may have even contributed to the dramatic change in her physical health. Robust boasts like the one she made four months before his death that she rode "twenty two miles on horseback without any fatigue" abruptly disappear from her correspondence, replaced by constant complaints of illnesses and chronic head and back pains that would continue for most of the rest of her life. She herself thought it had been the typhoid fever that had "destroyed" her health, and it is certainly possible it injured it. But even if her illnesses were entirely physical, the recurrent states of depression into which she invariably plunged for many years after her father's death whenever she fell ill suggest something more than just a bodily problem. For nearly the entire decade, from then until just before she moved from New England—when she was ill, but sometimes even when she was not— she would casually pepper her letters and conversations with "if I live," "I [am] dying," or other, similar depressive phrases. "I constantly looked forward to death," she would later write to a friend of those years. She herself suspected there was *some* connection between her father's death and her bad health and recurrent depressions. "I suppose I shall never entirely recover from the shock my constitution received at the time of my Father's death," she told Clarke the following year after one prolonged bout of sickness. And to Clarke again, on a similar occasion the next year: "I looked forward when my father died to various pains." Of course, if her father's death did, indeed, convert her long-standing resentment of him into depressive anger at herself, it was precisely because of the

160

deep love she felt for him, and this, too, his death seems to have reinforced. Either way—through resentment or love—the pain triggered by his death would not soon disappear.[1]

Besides pain, her father's death also triggered something else—great anxiety about her ability (as she put it in a letter to Clarke on December 6) to "fill the place" of her father. "Can I make good to my fellow creatures the loss of my pious, upright and industrious Father," she plaintively asked Clarke. "Once I was more presumptuous but now I have attained more accurate ideas of the obstacles in life." (The somewhat chastened Romantic-turned-Unitarian missionary Clarke—whose own kindly, rationalist Grandfather Freeman had also recently died—readily agreed and suggested this was true of his and Fuller's entire post-Revolutionary generation: "How much impulse, how much direction, proceeded forth from them. And all this we, in our ignorance, scorned and passed by unheeded.") This feeling would never be quite effaced. Writing to a friend on the tenth anniversary of her father's death—when she was a well-established, nationally known author—she solemnly recalled, "My hand closed his eyes. Never has that hand since been employed in an act so holy yet it has done so much, it seems as I look on it, almost a separate mind." With her touch, she seemed to be saying, her father's mind had passed into her writing hand, but she could never be sure the hand was really hers.[2]

This was far in the future. In the meantime she felt desperately sad. And not only sad. Her recovery followed so quickly by her father's sudden death also clearly filled her with a good deal of guilt. Higginson later wrote that Margaret's mother used to tell the story, "to the end of her days," of how, after her father died, Margaret gathered the younger children around their father's corpse and, kneeling, "pledged to God" that if she had ever been ungrateful or unfilial to her father, she would make up for it by fidelity to her brothers and sister. Her letters and journals at the time tell a similar story. "My father's image follows me constantly," she wrote in her journal the week after his death. "Whenever I am in my room he seems to open the door and to look on me with a complacent tender smile." The remainder of this entry she filled with a remorseful account of her refusal to visit the spot he had picked out for her in her "Grove." "It was very sad: May this sorrow give me a higher sense of duty in the relationships which remain." Again, the following month: "I shall be obliged to give up selfishness in the end. May God enable me to see the way clear, and not let down the intellectual, in raising the moral tone of my mind." Finally, even four months later she was writing to her brother Eugene: "Nothing sustains me now but the thought that my God who saw fit to restore me to life when I was so very, *very* willing to leave it, more so, perhaps, than I shall ever be again, must have some good work for me to do."[3]

Fuller's first chance to put these tearful pledges to work was not long in coming. Her father, who was only fifty-seven when he died, had not left a will, and as a consequence his estate took months to put in order. Worse yet, when the family finally began to get a picture of his financial state, they were not very happy. His retirement from both politics and law had cut his income appreciably. Also, as a politician, Timothy Fuller had always professed hostility to speculative investment, and, true to his word, he left property that was neither very substantial nor very lucrative. Most of it was in notes and bank stocks that paid little or no interest and a few badly depreciated houses that barely paid for the cost of their repairs. (When they finally managed nine years later to sell their Cambridgeport house and a couple of small farms Timothy had bought, they got less than half of what he had paid for them.) Counting all the property, the total cash value of the estate would come to a little over twenty thousand dollars. Eventually this was enough to provide each child with a modest inheritance of about two thousand dollars. But because the money was so tied up in notes and real estate, it took nearly a decade for it to get distributed. In the meantime the annual net income the estate yielded for several years was less than four hundred dollars: an amount that at best allowed—and then only by encroaching on the principal—a minimal maintenance for Margaret's mother on the Groton farm and, with much scrimping, some schooling for the younger children.[4]

In addition to the general shock and disappointment that these facts elicited, they also raised the obvious question: who was going to replace Timothy Fuller as family head? Certainly this could not be Margaret's mother. "I used to feel so secure in sickness and health," she confessed to Margaret, "that I leaned too much on him and the necessity of acting alone weighs more than it might." Her son Richard was later more blunt. "The arithmetic of the business appalled my mother," he recalled. "She was as naturally inapt for it as the lilies that neither toil nor spin." Of the oldest boys, William Henry was only eighteen and trying to establish himself as a clerk in Boston. Twenty-year-old Eugene was the best candidate, and Margaret tried desperately to get him to rise to the occasion. "God grant that you, Eugene, may return to us with the spirit of a *man*," she wrote to him, "able and disposed to do for your mother what a daughter cannot." But she appealed in vain. Although he soon returned from teaching in Virginia to start law school at Cambridge—and even studied for a short while at a law office in Groton—except for occasional advice about property, he never provided anything more than moral support for his mother and siblings.[5]

This, of course, left only Margaret. But Margaret, at twenty-five, was in some ways even less up to taking charge than her mother. As she told a friend in a letter of November 3, not only was she "very ignorant of the management and value of property," she had "always hated the din of such affairs, and hoped to find a life-long refuge from them in the serene world of literature and the arts." Even if she had not been so fastidious, there were legal difficulties. As an unmarried woman, she could neither legally control family property nor exercise legal authority over her younger siblings. (This was in theory true even for Margaret's mother, although judges often used judicial discretion to grant wide, if sometimes restricted, powers to widowed and divorced mothers.) "I have often had reason to regret being of the softer sex, and never more than now," she wrote resentfully in her letter to her friend. "If I were an eldest son, I could be guardian to my brothers and sister, administer the estate, and really become head of my family."[6]

In the end, though, what finally settled the matter was neither law nor taste, but character. Margaret had inherited from her father both a fortitude and a zeal for action that evidently gave her the self-confidence to conceive of doing what her mother could not. "I am now full of desire to learn," she earnestly concluded in her November 3 letter to her friend, "that I may be able to advise and act." And she did. Over the following weeks she organized her father's financial records; she compiled a chronicle of "the dates in Father's history"; and, most important, she opened a correspondence with her Uncle Abraham, who, as her father's oldest brother and the family's only businessman, was made administrator of his estate. It was a humbling task, but she reconciled herself to it. Over and over she apologized to her uncle for being "so ignorant" of her father's concerns, but she pledged she would find the "means of becoming less so." Meanwhile, she urged, "Pray, my dear Uncle, make things as easy to Mother as you can."[7]

There remained, however, one quandary in all this that she could not reconcile herself to: what to do about her forthcoming trip to Europe? On one hand, as she would years later recall to her proposed traveling companion Sam Ward, this trip was no mere "scheme of pleasure but the means of needed development"—and no one knew this better than Fuller herself. Since her adolescence she had been hoping, and most recently working assiduously, to cap her European literary studies with a European trip. She also knew that, if she ever hoped to write extensively on European literature, not going to Europe would be, as she later told another friend, "an insuperable defect." Finally, and perhaps most critically, she knew the proposed trip was potentially critical to her whole future literary career. She was certainly right about *this*. The Göttingen scholars were only the most recent examples to prove that in nationalist-minded but still very Europe-conscious America a European tour was an extremely valuable, if not essential, launching pad for a young literary intellectual's career. And what could be a better or (as she said to George Davis) more "profitable" launch than to travel in the company of "the best literary society," shepherded by the female English writer most famous in America? "All that I could do and see," she told Davis, "would seem to open up many prospects to me." In sum, as she later told Ward, the trip was "what I was ready to use and be nourished by" as it would never be again. Yet, on the other hand, as she was painfully aware, leaving her family for an extended period was fraught with danger. Who would work with her overbearing Uncle Abraham to settle the estate? Who would oversee the education of her younger siblings? Where would the extra money come from to help pay for the advanced schooling they would later need? For that matter, where would the money come from to support Margaret herself? "The moment I return I must maintain myself," she wrote sardonically to Davis, discussing the pros and cons of going, "and you know we women have no profession except marriage, mantua-making and school-keeping."[8]

There the problem lay. Her mother urged her to take her share of the estate and simply go. But, however generous the offer, Margaret undoubtedly knew that was hardly realistic. So, for five months she wrestled with her conscience. In her journal entry of January 1, 1836, she wrote: "The New-year opens upon me under circumstances inexpressibly sad. I must make the last great sacrifice, and, apparently, for evil to me and mine. Life, as I look forward, presents a scene of struggle and privation only." And, four weeks later, to her brother: "Oh, dear Eugene, you know not how I fear and tremble to come to a decision. My temporal all seems hanging upon it, and the prospect is most alluring. A few thousand dollars would make all so easy, so safe." In trying to come to a decision, she wrote anguished letters to her friends about this "crisis of my temporal existence" (as she described it to Clarke). She even wrote to George Davis a letter that was outwardly jaunty (as she usually tried to be with him), but particularly bitter. "I rather think I shall not go; staying behind will be such a pretty trial to my fortitude and quite finish my moral education— Indeed at the expense of my intellectual but this last is quite a secondary affair— tis said." Finally, when she visited Boston and Cambridge for five weeks, beginning at the end of December ("to put an interval between herself and the images of death and sickness and *misery* of Groton," Sarah Clarke reported to her brother James), she talked for hours with her literary advisor Harriet Martineau about her dilemma, at one point reading with her passages in the New Testament that she found relevant. One of these, from John (beginning "I will not leave you comfortless"), formed the basis of a poem that she wrote out in her journal in March, which, if nothing else, shows how much the trauma of her father's death—not to mention three years of family labor and Christian study—affected her decision. In her poem she reviewed her failed literary ambitions, her years of skepticism and fallen pride (presumably the George Davis affair), and her ignorant and haughty dismissal of her father's life, as she put it, "of ceaseless toil and sacrifice," and then wrote:

> What can I do? And how atone
> For all I've done and left undone?
> Tearful I search the parting words
> Which the beloved John records.
>
> "Not comfortless!" I dry my eyes,
> My duties clear before me rise,
> "Before thou think'st of taste or pride,
> See home-affections satisfied."
>
> Do not with glorious *thoughts* content,
> But on well-doing constant bent,
> When self seems dear, self-seeking fair,
> Remember this said hour in prayer.
>
> Though all thou wishest fly thy touch,
> Much can one do who loveth much;
> More of thy spirit, Jesus, give,
> Not comfortless, though sad, to live.
>
> And yet not sad if I can know
> To copy Him, who here below
> Sought but to do his Father's will. . . .[9]

After a few more weeks of searching for her "Father's will," she began to come to a decision. On April 17, she wrote, still tentatively, to Eliza Farrar: "If I am not to go with you I shall be obliged to tear my heart, by a violent effort, from its present objects and natural desires. But I shall feel the necessity, and will do it if the life-blood flows through the rent." If she had any doubt about whether it did, her Uncle Abraham dispelled it for her the following month. In a starkly precise letter about her "means," he showed her that her share of the estate—when it was finally settled—would provide her with less than half the cost of her expenses for the projected year and a half that the Farrars planned to be in Europe. She could have still made an abbreviated trip, as did Anna Barker, who wound up joining the Farrars for their second summer in Europe. But the stark figures in her uncle's letter obviously shocked her. This—on top of her continuing, painful awareness that, as she later told her brother Richard, *"some one"* needed to oversee her family's affairs "and none else was ready"—made her finally throw in the towel. A month later, on her birthday, she wrote to a friend: "Circumstances have decided that I must not go to Europe, and shut upon me the door, as I think, forever, to the scenes I could have loved. Let me now try to forget myself, and act for others' sake."[10]

II

Some of these "others" were her Groton neighbors. She would later claim to Sam Ward that after she gave up her European trip, she began her "liberal communion with the woful struggling crowd of fellow men." Her papers in these months suggest this was not just rhetoric. That winter she nursed an impoverished, "wretched girl," dying of consumption and a botched abortion; anxiously begged information from Clarke about manual labor schools on behalf of another "poor youth"; and, in another letter—after worrying aloud how *she* was going to earn a living—earnestly entreated Clarke to find a position for "a protégée" of hers who desperately wanted to teach in the West. "She is a farmer's daughter, far from elegant or pretty but with a sterling heart and mind and really good education," adding, "I know enough of the misery of being baffled and hemmed in on every side by seemingly insignificant barriers to feel an interest in giving her a chance to try her experiment." Still, her newfound communion with Groton folk continued to have its bourgeois family limits. In a later letter to her brother Arthur, she described the opium overdose suicide of Noah Kelly, a laborer hired by the family. "He killed himself, too selfish to stay and sustain his wife and children through anticipated want, which they need not have met if he would have kept sober." She noted indignantly, "Mother caught a bald cold at the time, as she made every exertion during the aftn and night to restore him to a life, of which he was unworthy."[11]

The prime objects of her altruism, of course, were her mother and siblings on the Groton farm. As she saw it, her first task was to restore some semblance of family morale. This was not an easy task. Almost immediately after their father's death, Arthur, Richard, and their mother had all fallen ill; in Richard's case with such a high fever that for several days they thought he might die, and Margaret had to be with him constantly. Since then Margaret had had her own demons to contend with. She remained for a long time, as she admitted to a friend, "heart-broken" over not going to Europe. ("Probably, I shall not even think it best to correspond with you at all while you are in Europe," she bitterly told Eliza Farrar.) Also, she worried about her mother, whose pale, anxious, and grief-worn face frightened her. "I am appalled," she told Eugene, "by the thought that she may not continue with us long." And she worried about her future. Here she was, an orphan, without beauty, without money, and living in a society in which vocational opportunities for a single young woman were extremely limited. An inkling of the sort of fears that gnawed at the back of her mind may be gathered from a long account she gave, in a letter she wrote to a friend later that spring, about an aged woman and her spinster daughter who lived nearby in an old, run-down, one-room house. "There they sit,—mother and daughter!" she told her friend. "In the mother, ninety years have quenched every thought and every feeling, except an imbecile interest about her daughter." Of the daughter she wrote—"that bloodless effigy of humanity, whose care is to eke out this miserable existence by means of the occasional doles of those who know how faithful and good a child she has been to that decrepit creature." Not surprisingly, it was also about this time that the severe headaches, backaches, and constant "tension of nerves" that would plague her for most of her life began for the first time to set in.[12]

She seems to have communicated none of this to her family in Groton, however. As she told Almira Barlow, she was determined to preserve a "fortitude" and a "serenity which might seem heartlessness to a common observer." In these months, according to her brother Richard, she also exerted a fairly grim form of family leadership. Years later he vividly described her practice—which she would continue for many years—of presiding over frequent "family councils, like those around the Indian's fire," where she would lay out for her mother and the children the worst facts of their situation and propose various alternatives. Richard remembered them as horribly gloomy affairs. "Helplessness and fear sat there with us," he recalled. "I felt my soul harrowed up at these meetings. I acquired a fear of poverty, and I for years saw starvation or the poorhouse in the dim perspective of distance—inevitable, and the only question as to their approach being one of time." Eventually, though, time—and, according to Richard, Margaret's steely demeanor ("Margaret was a tower of strength in this emergency")—dispelled the family's more extreme fears. As they did, and as specific difficulties got resolved, the atmosphere in the household slowly improved.[13]

The first practical matter that needed to be taken up was simply getting the farm running again. With Margaret in charge of family decision-making and her mother continuing to oversee the house, garden, and dairy, all the harvesting, milling, livestock-tending, merchandising, and other farm labor fell—as they would for most of the remainder of the family's years in Groton—to Arthur and Richard. For boys fourteen and twelve, whose only assistance that first season came from a lazy and (in her mother's words) "imperious and rough" country nephew of hers and, after that, a few of the town's barely working alcoholic laborers, this was an onerous task. Still, despite the work—and the irritation of seeing their visiting older brothers sipping lemonade on the piazza while they sweated in the fields—they seem to have retained their good humor. "How I hate Groton! How I love Jane Norton!" Richard recalled them singing, in honor of one of Professor Andrews Norton's beautiful daughters whom they used to play with in their flusher Cambridge years. Occasionally, Richard remembered, Arthur liked to provoke him by narrating a sardonic fairy tale of the wealthy professor driving up in a beautiful coach and carrying him away to marriage to his lovely ten-year-old daughter and a life of "very elegant pursuits," leaving Richard still at the brush block or grinding at the mill.[14]

Despite Richard and Arthur's yeoman labors on the farm, they still needed to be cared for. Margaret's mother, of course, continued to provide for their physical care and that of their younger brother Lloyd and older sister Ellen, and that winter Margaret resumed her family school. But the death of their intrusive father obviously left a large moral gap, which Margaret, according to Richard, was expected to fill. He later recalled one indicative incident from that spring. Provoked, he claimed, by their cousin's bullying and conceited "presumption," he and Arthur had one day tried to beat him up with cornstalks, but he easily fended them off. The three appealed to Margaret to act as judge in a makeshift "civil tribunal." After loud charges and louder countercharges (Arthur tried to justify the assault "as provoked by many grievances, and instigated by the spirit of our heroic revolutionary fathers"), Margaret finally declared it, Richard happily recalled, "a balanced case" and refused to censure the boys. The verdict may have been a little biased, but the form—a replica of the family trials their legalistic father had liked to use in settling sibling quarrels—was pure Timothy Fuller.[15]

The best revelation of Margaret as the new "paterfamilias," though, is contained in family letters over the next few years. Her mother's were couched—as they had been to her when she was their age—in general and altruistic terms: she urged the children, to be sure, to shun "indolence" and acquire "knowledge," but mainly she appealed to them to avoid "selfishness" in the family and "bear one another's burdens," to look to "the great first cause," and, above all, to look to "the standard your blessed father gave you." Margaret's letters, on the other hand—as her father's had been to her—were both highly specific and all-encompassing. Over the years they would include pointed advice about everything from dress, studies, and personal finances, to, in their young adulthood, careers, courtship, and marriage. In values, too, her letters show, Margaret largely promulgated her father's favorite New England Puritan-cum-Enlightenment virtues—neatness, punctuality, diligence, self-control, and, for the boys, a "manly" Stoic hardihood. "One of your hens has proved an unnatural mother and pecked several of her children to death," she would report to Richard in one letter a few years later. "Two turkies I understand are dead also. But I hope you will behave like a man about it; perhaps these disappointments are meant to teach you that you are too old to give so much time to trifles." If Margaret's mother's letters to her children were permeated by the memory of their father, in Margaret's he sometimes seems to have been uncannily reincarnated.[16]

Of course, like those of all good parents, Margaret's child-rearing techniques were tempered by the personalities of her "children" (as she liked to call them). The most difficult was the youngest, James Lloyd. By this time, at ten, he was beginning to display the signs of bizarrely hostile behavior that a decade later would lead Arthur, Richard, and (very reluctantly) their mother to commit him for many years to a mental institution. Elizabeth Peabody, who later boarded and employed him for a while in her bookstore and also knew of him as an angry, paranoid troublemaker at Brook Farm, once told Emerson, in slyly Transcendentalist jargon, that Lloyd was "Fullerism unbalanced, unmixed with the oversoul, which sweetens & balances the original demon." The sad, pathetic letters that he would later write to his mother, Arthur, Richard, and Margaret, alternately lamenting his "slowness of mind" and outlining grandiose schemes for great pursuits, *do* read a bit like deranged parodies of a major Fuller family theme. Yet, although later she would anguish with the rest of the family over his compulsive masturbating and his wild claims that they were poisoning his food and he was hearing "'voices in the air,'" Margaret, naturally, being a Fuller herself, in these earlier years at least, took a more relaxed—not to say Romantic— view of Lloyd's whimsical craziness. "I like to listen to the soliloquies of a bright child," she wrote in a description in her journal of one of his dramatic monologues "mourning the death of a certain Harriet." ("To-night he was truly in a state of lyrical inspiration," she wrote—as though she were speaking of Wordsworth's "Idiot Boy"—"his eyes flashing, his face glowing and his whole composition chanted out in an almost metrical form.") A few years later, still enjoying his eccentricities, she wrote in her journal, "Lloyd has been, he says, delivering a lecture on the Foundation of Religion in England. He took Mr Godwin's view, and wound up with a concert." But mainly she prodded her mother, in good Unitarian fashion, to make sure "poor, *poor* Lloyd" received his fair share of schooling—as if lack of schooling was his primary problem.[17]

After Lloyd, Margaret's other difficult child was sixteen-year-old Ellen. Unlike her more plainly hewn older sister, Ellen was blessed with golden-brown ringlets, soft, regular features, and deep blue eyes like her mother's, which gave her (in her brother Richard's words) a "Madonna-like beauty." Yet she could often be petulant, tempestuous, and—what probably lay at least partly behind these quirks—painfully conscious of her inferior status in the family intellectual order. ("My family all seem to be very superior persons excepting myself," she would sadly write some years later to Richard.) In contrast with Lloyd, though, toward whom she softened her discipline, Margaret firmly instructed Ellen, especially when it came to the family's new financial realities. "You *will not* have it in your power to make Miss Dwight a present," she bluntly wrote in one letter to Ellen, who had requested money to buy a present for one of her schoolmates at a Boston school she had begun attending in February. Again, later in the summer, in her portion of a sympathetic family reply to a mournful letter of Ellen's complaining about the poor state of her wardrobe, after harping on one of their father's favorite bugaboos, "bad orthography," and bringing up—as she did in almost every letter—Ellen's touchiness ("cultivate habits of industry and a cheerful, hopeful temper"), she summarily turned aside Ellen's tears over her faded frocks. "Now that everyone knows our circumstances it is no disgrace to us not to wear fine clothes, but a credit." The important thing was to be "neat and lady-like." She herself, she pointed out, had recently worn a "'faded calico frock'" like the one Ellen complained of, in the presence of some illustrious company at Concord (here she referred to her visit with the Emerson family in July), and it had not prevented *her* from "exciting respect and interest." "You must, my sister," she urged in conclusion, "pray to our Heavenly Father to strengthen you to rise above the opinion of this world as far as vanity is concerned and only to regard it from motives of kindness and modesty."[18]

Margaret aimed her heaviest moral guns, however, at the family's last hopes for masculine success, Richard and Arthur. With them, her letters show, her main concern was to make sure they succeeded scholastically. In the case of Richard—conscientious, hardworking, and humorous, but also hypersensitive, brusque, and a bit priggish—this was not always easy. Out of his "special disgust for Latin grammar," he recalled, he once tried to induce his mother to accept the offer of a successful farming relative, who had no children of his own, to adopt him as his heir and make him a farmer. Margaret was adamantly opposed to the idea, however, and persuaded her not to yield to his pleas, an intervention for which he would later claim to be forever grateful. Meanwhile, mercurial Arthur was fast approaching the age when practical decisions needed to be made about *his* future. Margaret and her mother decided to send him the following fall to his father's old Leicester Academy. To keep him in line at this crucial time, Margaret reached into the family arsenal of rationalistic exhortations. But she also used emotionally manipulative artifices: humor, affection, and (as her father never would have done), guilt and fear. She made this last clear enough in a letter she wrote to him at the end of the following year when he was in his last term. After frankly telling him that "the confinement and care" she had taken of him and his brothers and sister—at a time, as she put it, "when my mind was much excited by many painful feelings"—had had a permanently "very bad effect on my health," she added:

> I do not say this to pain you or make you feel grateful to me, (for, probably if I had been aware at the time what I was doing, I might not have sacrificed myself so,) but I say it that you may feel it your duty to fill my place and do what I may never be permitted to do. Three precious years at the best period of life I gave all my best hours to you children—let me not see you idle away time which I have always valued so, let me not find you unworthy of the love I felt for you. Those three years would have enabled me to make great attainments which now I never may. Do you make them in my stead that I may not remember that time with sadness.

Having presumably gotten his attention, she added a pointed warning that if he failed to show at the end of the year "a decided taste for study and ambition to make a figure in one of the professions," he would be "consigned to some other walk in life" ("there is no money to be wasted on any one of us"). She concluded by pleading with him to mend his ways. Compared with Ellen and Richard, "I feel greater anxiety about you, my dear Arthur. I know you have both heart and head, but you have always been deficient in earnestness and forethought."[19]

What was the result of all of this moral training? Apart from that of Lloyd—whose only known achievement was to survive by decades all his siblings—the other children's later lives perhaps tell something. Ellen devoted most of *her* adult life to the hopeless task of trying to domesticate her needy, irresponsible husband, the Transcendentalist poet William Ellery Channing, while skillfully raising their five children—with little money, much illness, and much of the time, no husband. Richard, after falling under the personal sway of Emerson, Thoreau, and their Concord circle of Transcendentalists, went on in college to uphold (as he put it) "the family honor" by taking the same second honors as his father and Uncle Henry, while being denied a commencement part, he was convinced, because of "distrust of the sentiments which I might utter." After college he settled down to the life of a moderately prosperous lawyer, sentimental evangelical Christian Church convert, and proud father by two wives of seven young children. Eschewing the life of "a mere lawyer," he wrote his own and his brother Arthur's memoirs and several genteel literary tracts with titles like *Shakespeare as a Lawyer* and *Visions in Verse; or, Dreams of Creation and Redemption.* Like his brother and sister, Arthur, too, learned to find ways to sublimate his childhood personality. This one-eyed "jocular" youth, who after college transformed himself into a sober, combative, crusading Unitarian preacher and bowdlerizing editor of his sister's posthumous works, ended his life in one of the more peculiar martyrdoms of the Civil War. The day after he was honorably discharged in the middle of the Battle of Fredericksburg as chaplain of the Sixteenth Massachusetts Infantry, in response to a call for volunteers in a dangerous skirmish, he accosted the captain in charge—announcing, the officer later reported, "Captain, I must do something for my country"—crossed the river with the band of soldiers, and, five minutes after taking his position, was killed as he stood to aim by two bullets shot through his chest and hip. Although none of these accomplishments compared with those of their father or famous sister, they were at least more memorable—as well as more in their father's and sister's mold—than anything achieved by their older brothers.[20]

Of course, difficult family circumstances undoubtedly also contributed to the younger siblings' (in Margaret's phrase) "more robust enterprizing and at the same time self denying" lives. Still, as the general in this little moral army, Margaret had an influence on its character that was clearly decisive. Certainly her "children" thought so. Writing a few years later in response to some praise of his independence by Margaret (who called herself his "manly friend"), Richard told her frankly: "Believe me, though I do not often say it, that to hold such a place in *your* mind, will always be a support in trial & will increase highly my self respect. I shall try to imitate your example." A couple of years after this—from the frontier town of Belvidere, Illinois, where he was teaching at a school he had bought after his graduation—Arthur wrote to his brother Richard earnestly: "I hope Margaret will prove my mentor. I shall write freely just what I do *& say &* then will thank her for setting me straight." Retrospectively—writing to one of the editors of his sister's *Memoirs* after her death—Richard had this to say about her efforts:

> When now, with the experience of a man, I look back upon her wise guardianship over our childhood, her indefatigable labors for our education, her constant super- vision in our family affairs, her minute instruction as to the management of multi- farious details, her painful conscientiousness in every duty; and then reflect on her native inaptitude and even disgust for practical affairs, on her sacrifice,—in the very flower of her genius,—of her favorite pursuits, on her incessant drudgery and waste of health, on her patient bearing of burdens, and courageous conflict with difficult circumstances, her character stands before me as heroic.

If Margaret could have heard Richard's paean to her heroism, she might not have looked back on her family sacrifices "with sadness."[21]

III

As usual by now with Fuller, family cares and disappointments, rather than sap- ping her intellectual energy, seem almost to have galvanized it. "I am having one of my 'intense' times," she wrote to Clarke that first February, "devouring book after book. I never stop a minute, except to talk with mother." And to Elizabeth Peabody around the same time: "I have so much reading to go through with this month, that I have but few hours for correspondents. I have already discussed five volumes in German, two in French, three in English, and not without thought and examination." Although her reading continued to be, as usual, wide-ranging, her journals show it centered more than ever before on English and German Romantic authors. She read that year and took detailed notes on most of Coleridge's philosophical and critical prose works. She also gave Jean Paul another try, finally completing his complex novels *Titan* and *Flegeljahre* that winter. "How thoroughly am I converted to the love of Jean Paul"—she wrote penitently in her journal, after quoting him on the power of the "childish heart"—"and wonder at the indolence or or shallowness which could resist so long, and call his profuse riches want of system! What a mistake! System, plan, there is, but on so broad a basis that I did not at first comprehend it. In every page I am forced to pencil. . . . I must have improved to love him as I do."[22]

She also tried harder than ever to play with Romantic themes in her writing. She wrote a poem for Clarke's *Western Messenger* ("On Sunday Morning When Prevented by a Snow-Storm from Going to Church"), which detailed, in a labored, Wordsworthian sort of way, the equivalent value of attending a Uni- tarian service and experiencing "a blessing in the Sabbath woods." More imag- inatively, in a letter she wrote that spring to young Sam Ward, she attempted to capture something of the uncanny spirit of her German Romantics. Her vehicle was a lengthy musing on the seductive-suicidal narcissistic psychology of water- gazing. Although this was a common motif in German Romantic literature, until Hawthorne's and Melville's dark meditations some years later, it was far from common in American writing. In her own meditation she stressed the maternal, womb- and tomblike cradling temptations of water (a lifelong fascination perhaps in part inspired, as her childhood nightmare of "wading in a sea of blood" suggested, by her ambivalent feelings about maternal love):

> Perfectly do I comprehend what I have heard of gazers on a riverside tempted to drown themselves by sight of the water, and all those tales of mermaid enchantments which embody this feeling. This morning I felt a sort of timidity about standing quite at that point to which the undulatory motions (of all earthly things most lovely) seemed to tend. I felt that, unless I have an arm of flesh and blood to cling to, I should be too much seduced from humanity.
>
> These undulations I have seen compared in poesy to the heaving of the bosom, and they do create a similar feeling,—at least, I, when I see this in the human frame, am tempted to draw near with a vague, instinctive anticipation (as far as ever I could analyze my emotion) that a heart will leap forth, and I be able to take it in my hand.[23]

While continuing to read and assimilate her Romantics, Fuller also continued to appreciate "the beauty of a stricter method" she later claimed was the chief thing she had gotten from her intellectual labors at Groton. Indeed, by the spring she was beginning to sound almost as self-flagellating as she had when she had first moved there. "I have been examining myself with severity," she wrote to Eliza Farrar on March 17, 1836, "intellectually as well as morally, and am shocked to find how vague and superficial is all my knowledge." Yet that same week, to Clarke, after giving a similarly "humiliating" litany of her intellectual "poverty," she boasted: "I believe it is a great Era— I am thinking now— really thinking, I believe; certainly it seems as if I had never done so before-— If it does not kill me, something will come of it."[24]

One thing she hoped would come of it, and what was clearly behind a good deal of her soul-searching, was her plan to write a "Life of Goethe." She had envisioned the idea of writing such a life "accompanied by criticisms on his works" the previous spring when she had been trying to come up with ideas to earn money through her writing. ("If I do it," she had told Clarke, "there shall be less eloquence perhaps but more insight than a De Stael.") But it was not until her father died that she decided actually to embark on the project. That winter she had disclosed her plan confidentially to Clarke, Hedge, and, when she saw her in Cambridge in January, her new literary advisor, Harriet Martineau. They were all enthusiastic about the idea, telling her that it was "ripe," as no biography of Goethe in English had yet appeared and the controversy over his "greatness and littleness" continued to rage. They also all told her in various ways (as Clarke put it) that she "must succeed in writing a firstrate work." She was not so confident. "Shall I," she asked Clarke rhetorically in her letter of March 14, "be fit for any-thing till I have absolutely re-educated myself— Am I— can I make myself fit to write an account of half a century of the Existence of one of the Master Spirits of this world?— It seems as if I had been very arrogant to dare to think it."[25]

One difficulty, she knew, was philosophy. Not only was it clear to her, she told Clarke in her letter of February 11, that Goethe was influenced by German philosophical opinion, but she now realized, recanting her cavalier dismissal of the subject two years before, "no mind can systematize its knowledge . . . without some fixed opinions on the subject of metaphysics." She added that, trying to overcome her "indisposition or even dread of the study," she had spent some time studying the post-Kantians Friedrich Heinrich Jacobi and Johann Gottlieb Fichte when she had been in Cambridge, but she had found them, especially Fichte, scarcely intelligible. So, humbly confessing "the full extent of my ignorance" ("perhaps I shall appear to you like another of my sex who asked to have political economy explained to her in two words"), she bombarded him with questions about Kantian philosophy. He gave her some serviceable definitions of Kant's transcendental categories, but nothing more than her journals show she already knew.[26]

An even bigger worry of Fuller's than philosophy, though, was her growing uncertainty about Goethe himself. "I do not know our Goethe yet," she wrote to Clarke early in the year. "Sometimes I am tempted to think that it is only his wonderful knowledge of human nature which has excited in me such reverence for his philosophy." This suggests she may have had some difficulty reconciling Goethe's comprehensive artistry with his poised philosophy. But also she continued to harbor doubts about that philosophy itself. In her birthday letter renouncing her European trip with the Farrars and Sam Ward, after citing an epigram of Goethe's, she wrote bitingly: "It is easy to say 'Do not trouble yourself with useless regrets for the past; enjoy the present, and leave the future to God.' But it is *not* easy for characters, which are by nature neither *calm* nor *careless,* to act upon these rules. I am rather of the opinion of Novalis, that 'Wer sich der hochsten Lieb ergeben Genest von ihren Wunden nie." ("Who yieldeth himself to love's deep madness, / From its wounds is never free.") Meanwhile, Clarke goaded her from on high. "Make it a religious book," he had urged after she had first told him of her plan. "May it have this one object," he intoned, "to create faith in those who read, not by vague declamation about it, but by showing how this man, so acute, so sharp-sighted, so wholly a faculty of observation, this realist, this majestic intellect—recognized *Truth,* pervading, supporting all appearance." This was Carlyle's didactic view. But Fuller was "sceptical," warning Clarke in one letter she might "come out far enough" from his moralistic "Carlyle view" to "distaste you which will trouble me." In her journal in March she concluded one meditation on Goethe with this bit of self-confessed "Eclectic" Goethean doggerel:

> Carlyle's fair soul could never be content
> Unless to one high aim the whole was bent;
> Does he *impart,* or *find* that high intent?
> Was Goethe for a savior really meant?[27]

Meanwhile *she* pressed on her moral-minded Goethean friend other questions that "troubled" her: about Goethe's non-Christianity, his sensualism, even—on the subject of his detractors' favorite chestnut—his sexuality. Clarke's answers were again a bit murky. After admitting he "always avoided answering" her frequent questions about Goethe's religion, he conceded that perhaps "Goethe leaned close upon Pantheism," but "I am not sure about it." On Goethe's sexual morals, he was even more evasive. "As to what you say on the subject of Goethe's license," he confessed, "I have little to communicate. There is evidence enough in his Italian letters, elegies, etc., that his moral code was not of the strictest kind." The soft-minded Clarke was clearly not the tough-minded Fuller's ideal research assistant! This fact, in turn, bore on what she knew full well was her greatest difficulty in writing her capacious life of Goethe—simply getting her sources. In a poignant letter on April 19, she wrote to Clarke about this and the other obstacles she faced in writing critically about Goethe in her isolated outpost of post-Puritan America. After recounting to him an English article she had recently read, alluding to Goethe's illegitimate son and twenty-year liaison with Christiane Vulpius ("I had no idea that the mighty 'Indifferentist' went so far with his experimentalizing in *real life*"), she asked almost desperately:

> How am I to get the information I want unless I go to Europe— To whom shall I write to choose my materials— I have thought of Mr. Carlyle but still more of Goethe's friend Von Muller. I dare say he would be pleased at the idea of a life of G. written in this hemisphere and be very willing to help me. If you have anything to tell me you will and not mince matters— Of course my impressions of Goethe's works cannot be influenced by information I get about his *life* but as to this latter I suspect I must have been hasty in my inferences— I apply to you without scruple— These are subjects on which *gentlemen* and *ladies* usually talk a great deal but apart from one another— you, however, are well aware that I am very destitute of what is commonly called modesty. With regard to this, how fine the remark of our present subject. "Courage and modesty are virtues which every sort of society reveres because they are virtues which cannot be counterfeited, also they are known by the *same hue*"— When that blush does not come naturally to my face I do not drop a veil to make people think it is there. All this may be very *"unlovely"* but it is *I*.

Still—as one might expect from such an "I"—she persisted. "I will not shrink back from what I have undertaken," she assured Clarke. "Even by failure I shall learn much." She would.[28]

In the meantime, Fuller mulled over in these months the larger problem of her literary career. She continued to wrestle with her self-doubts. In her birthday letter she wrote: "What I can do with my pen, I know not. At present, I feel no confidence or hope. The expectations so many have been led to cherish by my conversational powers, I am disposed to deem ill-founded." Yet she recognized that she was "still heart-broken by sorrow and disappointment," and might be "renewed again, and feel differently." She also for the first time began to face the other side of the literary equation—the appropriate publisher. Indeed, to some extent, this was the greater, or at any rate, more immediate, problem. Her standards were high, her interests overwhelmingly European, and—perhaps most important—her publishing attitudes not exactly welcoming. Even England's lively highbrow, Tory *Fraser's Magazine* she called in a letter to Hedge "that odious vulgar magazine" and wondered aloud how Carlyle could ever be "willing to write" in it. Likewise, at the beginning of the year, in a letter replying to Elizabeth Peabody, who was then trying to get *her* magazine career launched and had been encouraging Fuller, too, to "write for the press," she made this less precious, but no less uncompromising pronouncement: "I would gladly sell some part of my mind for lucre, to get the command of time; but I will not sell my soul: that is, I am perfectly willing to take the trouble of writing for money to pay the seamstress; but I am *not* willing to have what I write mutilated, or what I ought to say dictated to suit the public taste."[29]

Given these high-minded views, her choices were not plentiful. Even the moderately highbrow Unitarian journals—the most likely candidates for a young neophyte Unitarian intellectual—were hardly very suitable. The *North American,* now in the cautious hands of John Gorham Palfrey, hewed to a conservative cultural line; although more liberal, the Unitarian *Christian Examiner* printed proportionately little belles-lettres criticism; and her former vehicle—Clarke's *Western Messenger*—appeared to her (as she had told him the year before) more religious than literary, but also too remote. ("It seems to me I have but little to give the West," she finally frankly told Clarke in April, after he had asked her again for a contribution.) Still, her papers show that after her father's death, she yearned more than ever (as she put it to Clarke) to "make my pen avail me." In her letter to Peabody she mentioned a variety of schemes, from publishing an illustrated translation of Tieck's "Little Red Riding Hood" for children, to a lengthy series of articles on German Romantic authors. ("Perhaps some might sneer at the notion of my becoming a teacher," she wrote defensively, "but where I love so much, surely I might inspire others to love a little.") Fortunately, a friendly outlet soon presented itself. In January the sensationalistic editor Park Benjamin—who the previous year had gotten possession of Joseph T. Buckingham and his son Edwin's successful *New-England Magazine*—teamed up with the famous New York *Knickerbocker Magazine's* founding editor, Charles Fenno Hoffman, to publish simultaneously in Boston and New York a new version of Hoffman's New York *American Monthly Magazine.* The idea was to join new talent in both cities with the *New-England*'s popular contributors like Nathaniel Hawthorne and Henry Wadsworth Longfellow and so transform the *Monthly,* which Hoffman had been unsuccessfully struggling to make into a rival of the *Knickerbocker,* into a major national magazine. One new talent its Boston editor recruited—undoubtedly on the recommendation of Peabody—was Fuller. Peabody likewise had boosted the magazine to *her.* "Park . . . seems really desirous to help along Margaret Fuller & me—in making our thoughts known," she excitedly told her sister Mary.[30]

Compared with her previous year's somewhat crude *Western Messenger* pieces, Fuller's *American Monthly* articles that summer and fall marked a quantum jump in her critical writing. This is certainly true stylistically of her first piece, "The Life of Sir James Mackintosh," a pithy essay published in the magazine's June 1836 issue. Since her youth she had been fascinated with intellectual men of action. But the subject also had an obvious further interest for her: she found in this genial but frustrated Whig philosopher and historian who had recently died more than a little of herself. In her essay she posed the question, Why did this man, of such extraordinary talents, generally acknowledged by his contemporaries to be the best equipped among them for great deeds, never achieve much? First, she suggested, Mackintosh was handicapped by his excessively bookish childhood. "For precocity," she wrote, speaking from personal experience, "some great price is always demanded sooner or later in life." And the price in Mackintosh's case, she thought, was to bring out "so wonderfully his powers of acquisition at the expense of those of creation, to say nothing of the usual fine of delicate health." The other circumstance that undermined Mackintosh's creative powers, she thought, somewhat opposite to the first, was Mackintosh's lack of systematic early training. "Genius *will* live and thrive without training, but it does not the less reward the watering-pot and pruning-knife," the unschooled Fuller classically opined. Besides these early circumstances, Mackintosh was also debilitated, she argued, by two of his own intellectual inclinations. The first was his early acquired habit of passively reading large quantities of books, which made him, she suggested, excessively dependent on "the stimulus of others' thoughts . . . to an enervating degree." ("A man who means to think and write a great deal, must, after six and twenty, learn to read with his fingers.") The second and related enervating habit of Mackintosh's, she thought, was his genius for conversation, whose rapid and sparkling graces, the conversationalist Fuller declared, were "the reverse of the love of method, the earnestness of concentration, and the onward march of thought, which are required by the higher kinds of writing." In sum, she concluded sadly, Mackintosh was a man not sufficiently centered in himself; who could, therefore, never fully center himself on his work. After reviewing his uncompleted histories, she rendered this stern verdict: "Man may escape from every foe and every difficulty, except what are within—himself. Sir James, as formerly, worked with a divided heart and will; and Fame substitued a meaner coronal for the amaranthine wreath she had destined for his brow. Greatness was not thrust upon him, and he wanted earnestness of purpose to achieve it for himself." It was as if she were saying—after covertly exposing just about every sin that she thought had crippled her own genius: at least earnestness would not be *her* problem.[31]

Her second piece was in a more high-flown vein. The editors published it as the lead article in the following month's July issue. Entitled "Present State of German Literature," the article opened with a Carlylean jeremiad against America's spiritually enervating enthrallment with money-getting, technological progress, and, worst of all, what they produced—a mechanistic conception of the "mind."

> We are not merely springs and wheels, which, when put in certain places and kept oiled, will undoubtedly and undoubtingly do their work and fulfill their destination. No! In each one of us there is a separate principle of vitality, which must be fostered if we would be as trees in the public garden, rich in leaves, blossoms, and perfumed fruit, rather than as dry boards in the public ship-yard, fit only to be hewn, used, and when grown old left to return in rottenness to their native dust.

Her second argument was also Carlylean in an American nationalist way—that alone among contemporary European literatures, German literature provided a counterpoise to America's utilitarianism and therefore an effective foreign aid to its cultural vitalization. But the most original part of her essay was not her American application of Carlyle's critical organicism and pro-Germanism, but her gambit of using a recent English translation of the scathingly anti-Romantic *Die Romantische Schule* by Heinrich Heine, the bitingly ironical, liberal, Parisian-exile poet and critic, to demonstrate (as she put it) "the bridge between Germany and us." Intended as an antidote to Madame de Staël's pro-German *De l'Allemagne* and as a stern warning against the reactionary Catholicism and politics of German Romantics like the Schlegel brothers, Heine's book was much lauded, even by critics who otherwise abhorred his politics and brash style, as an effective assault not only on German Romanticism, but on Romanticism in general. Yet Fuller deftly assimilated the book to her argument. First, she took a leaf from Heine's own Herderian historicism: however much the German Romantics' hyperidealism and intellectualism might be partial vices in a German context, in an American context, she said, because they were so much the opposite of our defects, they could only be virtues. Second, she showed how much Heine owed to the very Romantics, like the Schlegels, he was bent on discrediting: their appreciation of genius, their belief in the value of "reproductive" or sympathetic criticism of great works, and, above all, their belief—which, as she noted, Heine applauded in his revered Goethe—in the autonomy of art against narrow standards of social or political utility. Finally, after alternately deploring Heine's scandal-mongering and iconoclasm and extolling his eloquent and witty writing style and Goethean love of free development, she added a final, friendly Romantic word for this exile whom Carlyle called a "literary rapscallion": "We admire thee—become reverent and pitiful of heart, and we will love and esteem thee."[32]

Fuller's most ambitious article by far was her third—a lengthy, two-part essay titled "Modern British Poets," which appeared in the *American Monthly*'s September and October issues. Elizabeth Peabody would later claim that Fuller had first submitted it to Palfrey, who rejected it because, although he thought it was "splendid," it panegyrized Wordsworth. If this was true, it would only show how conservative Palfrey had managed to make the *North American.* The fact is that nearly twenty years after Bryant and Dana had first espoused him, Wordsworth had by this time finally become, if certainly not a popular poet in America, still a highly regarded figure among a fair number of highbrow, liberal critics. What really made Fuller's article "bold and original" (as the editors announced it in their introductory flourish) was not her touting of Wordsworth, but rather two other things. First, she attributed to him, and also to Coleridge, a world-historical significance. In essence, she argued that poets like Wordsworth and Coleridge were great because they were vehicles of a high kind of cultural modernity. To demonstrate this, she presented a metahistorical schema. In earlier days the greatest poets concerned themselves with "the passions or heart-emotions of their fellow-men," but now, as in *Faust* or *Manfred,* they addressed their "thoughts or mind-emotions." Her explanation for this historic change was

social: as society had become more complex and required more combined reg-
ulation, individuals who desired to assert their natural individuality found themselves incessantly struggling against the social order. As the individual mind
struggled, it mourned, and these lamentations composed the popular poetry of
the day. At the same time, she said, there were some who had tired of all this
"apparently bootless fretting and wailing" and had come to realize "that individuality of character is not necessarily combined with individuality of possession." Coleridge and Wordsworth were two of these. For what they strove for,
she wrote, was no less than transcendence through a new poetry that would be
at once perfectly, even primitively, natural, and, at the same time, consciously
illustrative "of that which lies beyond." Of course, she admitted, this could not
make for popular poetry. "Being eminently the product of reflection and experience, it could only be appreciated by those who had thought and felt with some
depth." Indeed, because of this exclusiveness, she conceded, their poetry did not
rank with that of Shakespeare or Homer, whose works delighted "minds of every
grade as much as they are competent to receive." But, she concluded, "this fault
. . . , this want of universality is not surprising," since it was necessary that they
stand apart and disregard popular tastes so that they might gain firmness and
depth and play out their historical role as "the pilot-minds of the age." This
schema was by no means original; most of it she derived from Schiller, the Schlegel brothers, and other German Romantic theorists. Still, no American critic
before had announced it so sweepingly. Nor had any before used English
Romantic poetry as a vehicle for advancing it.[33]

The other thing that was bold about Fuller's article was her rankings. Not only
had no American critic before attempted such an inclusive ranking; none had
advanced judgments that, while theoretically inspired, would later turn out to
be so presciently "modern." Thus, although praising him for his descriptive
powers, she otherwise judged Sir Walter Scott, the most popular poet in America, harshly: his poetry was without intellectual and emotional depth, and, worse
yet, she said, he failed to make up for it with the drama and characterization that
made his novels so appealing. Vastly superior to Scott, she argued, were the
younger Romantics Byron and Shelley. (She omitted John Keats, with whom
she was familiar, but who was virtually unknown in America.) On America's
favorite "Satanic" Romantic, Byron, she dismissed almost laughingly the common conservative complaint that the egoism in his poetry threatened society;
anyone could see that his scornful skepticism was too palpably "uneasy and sor-
rowful beneath its thin mask of levity" to produce any lasting, genuine misan-
thropy on his readers. On the other hand, bucking popular opinion as well as her
own adolescent Byronism, she predicted correctly that posterity would assign his
poems a place far beneath those of Wordsworth, Coleridge, and Shelley. "There
are many beautiful pictures; infinite wit, but too local and temporary in its range
to be greatly prized beneath his own time." (In this case, Fuller's "bold" opinion
was too much for her popular-minded editors; in a footnote they added, "We
disagree almost entirely.") By contrast, Shelley—whose works had not yet been
published in America and who was frequently deprecated even in liberal Uni-

tarian journals because of his atheistic religious views and radical politics—she praised almost unstintingly. Dismissing the common charge of atheism (he was "the warmest of Philanthropists" and "full of the spirit of genuine Christianity"), she zeroed in instead on two aesthetic qualities in which, she said, Shelley surpassed any poet of the day—one, his "fertility of Fancy," and the other, his sympathy with nature, to which she attributed, in good organic fashion, his strength of melodic form.[34]

Finally, in her second installment, she discussed at length the poetry of her three "pilot-minds." She praised, but without a great deal of specificity, the respected "erudite" and "elegant" Robert Southey—a judgment that showed perhaps more intellectualist ideology than critical acumen. On the other hand, she placed the more difficult and less popular Coleridge far above Southey. Indeed, although less prolific and poetically satisfying than the other two, Coleridge was, she said, more valuable intellectually because he was "more filled with the divine magnetism of intuition." She particularly singled out for praise Coleridge's ability to depict, as in his "Dejection" ode, a single mood of mind. "Give Coleridge a canvass, and he will paint a single mood as if his colors were made of the mind's own atoms," she wrote, and then made this apt comparison: "Here he is very unlike Southey. There is nothing of the spectator about Coleridge; he is all life; not impassioned, not vehement, but searching, intellectual life, which seems 'listening through the frame' to its own pulses." But in the end it was her "venerated teacher" Wordsworth who earned her highest praise. Essentially she portrayed him—as he portrayed himself—as a Romantic dualist: not an idealist, but a powerful observer of "the real present world" upon which he brought to bear enormous feeling and enthusiasm. She also praised his doctrines of human sympathy without the need of passion, his perception of beauty "amid seeming ugliness," and, above all, his originality. Indeed, this, she thought, was what made Wordsworth's poetry, whatever its formal deficiencies compared to that of other poets in "minor excellences" like melody, fancy, or dramatic power, immensely valuable culturally:

> There is a suggestive and stimulating power in original thought which cannot be gauged by the first sensation or temporary effect it produces. The circles grow wider as the impulse is propagated through the deep waters of eternity. An exhibition of talent causes immediate delight; almost all of us can enjoy seeing a thing well done; not all of us can enjoy being roused to do and dare for ourselves. Yet when the mind *is* roused to penetrate the secret meaning of each human effort, a higher pleasure and a greater benefit may be derived from the rude but masterly sketch, than from the elaborately finished miniature. In the former case our creative powers are taxed to supply what is wanting, while in the latter our tastes are refined by admiring what another has created.

In a word, Wordsworth was not only the creation of the modern age, he also allowed for that age to perpetuate itself. The implication was clear: if Americans could manage to raise themselves to a level high enough to appreciate the likes of Wordsworth, then possibly they might accomplish something poetically themselves.[35]

Fuller's articles on British Romantic poetry were her last in the *American Monthly*. Her plans for her German authors series, which she had originally hoped to kick off with her Heine article, remained—like so many of her literary ideas in these years—just plans. One reason might have been her disappointment in the magazine; in her journal she grumbled she almost never read a writer in it who had "any depth." She was not far wrong. After her articles, literary criticism virtually disappeared from the magazine and partisan Whig pieces increasingly dominated it. Within a little over a year—having failed to attract either a Boston readership or a Boston stable of writers—the magazine folded. Still, her efforts were no loss. The skeptical-minded Davis told Clarke he was "delight[ed]" with her articles. Meanwhile, regardless of their reception, her essays were valuable to *her*. Not only did she publicly articulate in two of them her first coherent statement of her Romantic critical philosophy; in publishing them where she did, she finally stepped forth, despite her literary squeamishness, as an American magazine writer. For a future Romantic editor and journalist, these were steps in the right direction.[36]

IV

Fuller reached beyond Groton that summer and fall not only through a new magazine, but also through new friendships. Since two of these alliances were with the principal leaders of the rising new current of New England Transcendentalism, it might be useful to consider at this point what this movement— which would constitute for many years much of Fuller's social and intellectual world—was about. In popular currency, Transcendentalism would soon become almost synonymous with the vague or obscure. (*"A little beyond,"* with an upward wave of her hand, was the way Almira Barlow reportedly defined it.) Yet its philosophical etymology was quite specific. A half century earlier, Immanuel Kant had argued that, whereas the empirical Understanding gave us, through the senses and our reflection on them, a limited knowledge of objects, the transcendental Reason gave us a priori concepts that imparted meaning and value to those objects. This hardly made the Transcendentalists orthodox Kantians. Kant, despite his conceptual categories, was, epistemologically anyway, a strong dualist: we have no basis for knowing, he had said, that the concepts Reason yielded up corresponded to any real objects as they were in themselves. By contrast, the New England Transcendentalists believed—or talked as though they believed—in this correspondence. Moreover, while some, like Hedge, were well-schooled in post-Kantian idealist philosophy, most only dabbled in it while cheerfully mixing its categories with other sources for their systematic subjectivism: from Plato's semimystical "Forms" and Emanuel Swedenborg's naturespirit "correspondences," to Coleridge's poetic "Imagination" and Victor Cousin's psychological "spontaneous reason."[37]

It would be a gross misapprehension, though, to try to define New England Transcendentalism in rigorously philosophical terms. For in its heart the movement was not a philosophy but—as Perry Miller pointed out long ago—"a religious demonstration." Like Romantic writers from Rousseau onward, Transcendentalists posited that the intuitive human mind and nature mirrored each other because each contained something of the same animating, organic spiritual life. The inevitable corollary was what Carlyle aptly called (in his *Sartor Resartus,* published that year and avidly studied by the Transcendentalists) "natural supernaturalism": a quasi-religion in which nature itself became a sacred object of reverence, and man and woman—because they could see into its soul from within themselves—beings akin to God.[38]

Of course the Transcendentalists' religion did not just spring to life magically out of European Romantic texts; it also grew out of their own quasi-humanistic inherited or adopted Unitarian faith. For a generation or more the most prominent ministers of their sect had been confidently asserting the religious value of secular literary texts and, even more boldly, proclaiming the human mind to be the ultimate test of the reasonableness of supernatural claims. Yet this very commitment to the mind's reasonableness, rationality, and (in their post-Lockean terminology) "common sense" understanding of God and the world made most Unitarians deeply suspicious of the Romantics' radically intuitive ways to knowledge. In addition, Unitarians traditionally held two specific, deep-seated beliefs that kept most of them far short of becoming Transcendentalists. Not only did they cling to the notion of Christ's partial divinity, but, more important, they believed it could be proven by a scholarly and objective examination of biblical texts and—still more critical—that the validity of Christianity largely depended on these proofs. The young natural-supernaturalists in their sect were beginning to assert just the contrary: that however valid or invalid the belief in Christ's divine attributes (and Transcendentalist views on this point varied widely), any attempt to assert Christianity's claim on the basis of its supernatural truths demonstrated by empirical evidence rather than the intuitive knowledge of the living God incarnate in man and nature was, by definition, as James Freeman Clarke earnestly told his sympathizing friend William Henry Channing, "skepticism & irreligion."[39]

Why did the Transcendentalists revolt against the faith of their fathers and mothers? One factor was international circumstances. The end of the Napoleonic wars brought for the first time since the Revolution a subsiding in literate circles of republican political preoccupations and, simultaneously, a sudden new accessibility of European Romantic texts. One should also not overlook the effect of German biblical criticism in worrying young Unitarian theology students (as their journals and letters amply attest) about what, indeed, their faith *could* rest on if not the internal evidence of their own consciousnesses. Nor should one ignore personal influences that probably facilitated this familial revolt. One was the fact that Transcendentalism, especially among its followers, was almost exclusively a movement of young people under thirty. Another was that some of the leading figures came from families on the fringes of the Boston-Cambridge Unitarian elite. Still another was that a large majority of the leading Transcendentalists, apart from Fuller, grew up without fathers or with weak ones. But probably the most important circumstance feeding their revolt was both subtler and more powerful than any of these: namely, the fact that these young Transcendentalists grew up in a social and cultural world very different from that of their mothers and fathers. Increasingly individualistic, entrepreneurial, and—under the driving force of the mammoth religious revivals of the Second Great Awakening—hyperemotional, it was a world in which (as Clarke described his Western corner of it to William Channing) "the Andover tone & the Cambridge drone are banished of necessity," making way (as he put it in a later letter to Emerson) for less "effeminate, self-complacent, unheroic" faiths. If Transcendentalism, as one scholar years ago observed, was Unitarianism "'getting religion,'" the young members of (as Sarah Clarke called them) "the supernal coterie" had some good intellectual and practical reasons for giving up old ways that got in the way of their getting it.[40]

Despite their sometimes rebellious private rhetoric, though, the main public activity of the coterie in the early 1830s was publishing cautiously appreciative interpretations of some of their favored Romantic texts in sympathetic or at least tolerant Unitarian journals, like the *Christian Examiner* and the *Western Messenger.* By the fall of 1836, these mixed interchanges reached a culmination. On September 8, following the bicentennial celebration at Harvard University, the ex-Unitarian minister Ralph Waldo Emerson and his ministerial colleagues Frederic Henry Hedge and George Ripley met and decided to found a discussion club with the dual purpose, as Hedge later put it, of registering "a protest" against the reigning Lockean-cum-supernatural philosophy of official Unitarianism and introducing "deeper and broader views." "Hedge's Club" (as it was called for a while because it usually met whenever Hedge was able to leave Bangor) or the Transcendental Club (as it would eventually be called) would meet some thirty times over the next four years, usually involving a dozen or so men and women, to discuss various aspects of the new philosophy and the public controversies that from time to time swirled around it. Meanwhile, the Transcendentalists lost no time in giving their views an airing. Within weeks after the first meetings of the club, Emerson, Ripley, the Boston Unitarian preacher Orestes Brownson, and the controversial schoolmaster Bronson Alcott all published major works that for the first time aggressively and positively articulated the new views. And while each of these was markedly different from the others (Clarke later said they called themselves the club of the "Like-Minded" "probably because no two of us thought alike"), they all had one thing at least in common—the denigration of both purely supernatural *and* sensationalistic-rationalistic ways to knowledge and culture in favor of intuitions, whether intellectual or emotional, that lie deep within the human consciousness.[41]

How much of a Transcendentalist was Margaret Fuller in this year that Perry Miller has called the "Annus Mirabilis" of Transcendentalism? In any strictly formal sense, one would have to say, not much. Her letters and journals give no positive pronouncements on the two key issues defining the movement—a bold and exalted faith in the divine here-and-now character of the human spirit and a corresponding attempt to root that faith in some sort of idealistic metaphysic. (Indeed, her ruminations about humanity could sometimes sound positively *un*exalted. "I felt my very heart shrank and palsied," she wrote in her journal in the fall after reading Sir John Ross's account of Eskimo tribes in his *Narrative* of his Arctic exploration. "No doubt they love and hate, laugh and speak, but where are their thoughts? and what will be their position in the future world?— Why, it will require a million of years for them to arrive even at our miserable state of mental advancement.") Nor can one find anything militant or even very hopeful about her Transcendentalist friends' efforts to challenge or reform Unitarianism. "Tell me how goes your Unitarianism," she had written teasingly to Clarke the previous winter. "Have you decided yet how regeneration is to be accomplished[?]" And, in the fall—after giving an account of a conversation with George Ripley about the French Saint-Simonians' "New Christianity" that the reform-conscious Brownson was touting as analogous to Transcendentalism—she wrote in her journal: "Xty needs to be reproduced but how?— How?—Who can tell us—Unitarianism is not exactly the thing—nay—nor St Simonianism—nor any other yet discovered ism— But every speculation which is founded on a sighing after perfectibility and a love for humanity lets in some light."[42]

It would be a mistake, however, to conclude that there was nothing at all specifically Transcendental about Fuller at this time. She was, to begin with, thoroughly steeped in European Romantic texts, her recent critical writings had evinced a deep commitment to subjectivism in literature, and, most recently, she had expressed a yearning for some sort of Christianity that would take (as she put it) "the right ground between Rationalism and ignorant faith." Also by this time—as her "British Modern Poets" articles had amply shown—she had come to embrace the central Romantic world-historical point of view, of which Transcendentalism was, from one perspective, but an American variant: namely, the impulse to bridge the gap between the natural and spiritual realms and thereby overcome human alienation by an assertion of the shaping power of the human imagination. One can add to this the facts that Fuller by this time had come to think of herself as a spokesman for modern German culture, the main contemporary foreign source of Transcendentalist philosophy; that several of her closest young ministerial friends had already announced their sympathy with the movement; that she had recently shown at least an interest in learning more about post-Kantian metaphysics; and finally, that her perennially soul-searching personality fitted perfectly with Emerson's psychological profile of Transcendentalists as young people "born with knives in their brain." With all this borne in mind, the wonder becomes, not that she eventually identified with the movement, but rather that she was so slow in doing so.[43]

The reasons for her reticence would seem to have been personal. First, ever since her quasi-mystical conversion and its humbling psychological reverberations of five years before, her taste for high-heroic philosophies of any sort had been, if not exactly on the wane, certainly at least dormant. (This was reflected in her recent attraction to the Wordsworthian philosophy of "subdued affections and bounded wishes" that she had scorned in her youth.) Also, her circumstances at Groton—her intellectual isolation, her domestic labors, and her continuing apprehension about her literary talents and opportunities—hardly put her in a culturally heroic mood. Finally, it should not be forgotten that while closely associated with many young Transcendentalist ministers, Fuller herself was not a minister, nor was she educated like one. Although philosophically and religiously interested, she never developed the same habits and professional interests in purely religious preachments, much less in systematically defining or reflecting on their philosophical bases. Like her father, she was essentially a practical intellectual; her interests were primarily social and literary, as they had been since her youth. As these issues came increasingly to dominate the movement—and as the movement, in turn, provided her with correspondingly greater opportunities for self-expression and influence—her identification with and understanding of Transcendentalism grew.

If there was a single individual who gave that identification and understanding depth and permanence, it was the first important figure she met that summer, Ralph Waldo Emerson. By any standard Emerson was pre-eminently *the* genius of American Transcendentalism. And this was so, not only because he was its greatest writer and most original thinker, but also because of his soaring moral idealism—which in turn flowed, as all genuine idealism must, out of a personality as self-centered (in several senses) as any in American literature. Henry James would later say, speaking of a certain coldness or insensitivity which he found in some of Emerson's reactions to people and art, that there were "certain chords in Emerson that did not vibrate at all." This was true, but the other side was this: whatever his social deficiencies, Emerson was, first and last, an intellectual who knew his own mind. Furthermore, the enormous spiritual power that this self-awareness gave him, at least in his early years, was not, as some have sometimes suggested, easily won, but just the opposite. It was a power deeply rooted in personal misfortunes that, at almost every step, he managed to convert into personal strengths. The son of one of Boston's leading Unitarian ministers, who died shortly before Waldo turned eight, young Emerson, along with his four brothers, grew up in an environment of respectable poverty, family devotedness, and intense pressure to succeed. A generally mediocre student overshadowed by his brilliant younger brothers, Edward and Charles, Waldo Emerson at least saved himself, by a certain humorous fancy and dreamy bookishness, from the kinds of self-punishing intellectual labor that eventually broke both of them. After college, partly to please his mother and his brilliantly eccentric, mystically Calvinist-minded spinster aunt, Mary Moody Emerson, whom he much admired, he somewhat reluctantly became a minister like his father and grandfather, soon settling at Boston's moderately prosperous Second Unitarian Church. In the second year of his ministry, his charming and beautiful teenage wife of two years, Ellen Tucker, after several years of declining health, died of tuberculosis. He had loved Ellen deeply, and he never fully recovered from her death. But he was also now free of conventional marital responsibilities and the recipient of a modest inheritance that yielded, not a fortune, but an income sizable enough to allow him the freedom to resign a pastorate with which he had grown increasingly uncomfortable. The reason he gave was his unwillingness to administer the Lord's Supper as a sacrament. This was more than a pretext, for it symbolized, as he saw it, precisely what dissatisfied him about even a liberal ministry—that its practitioners were required to invest merely conventional forms with supernatural value.[44]

After his resignation, Emerson spent most of the following year traveling in Europe, during which time he met Wordsworth and Coleridge and began a life-long friendship with Carlyle. Once back, he felt a strong call to expound a faith (as he put it on shipboard in his journal) less "selfish and timid and cold, and . . . unpractical" than that he heard articulated by Europe's Romantic greats. He quickly went about establishing a new career for himself as an itinerant preacher and a lecturer on history, literature, and what were then loosely called the natural sciences. With a mellifluous voice and a deeply poetic, yet inspiring tone and manner, he soon found himself the focus of increasingly large and admiring audiences throughout Massachusetts. Despite the tragic intervening deaths of the brilliantly promising Edward and his favorite brother, Charles, he also completed his essay *Nature,* one of the most buoyant prose works ever written. This small book of less than one hundred pages was also the first and most radical statement of the new Transcendental philosophy. It announced, too, the major themes that would preoccupy him for the next decade—in particular the idea that nature and spirit mirrored each other and the implications of that insight for language, religion, ethics, and culture. But it was in its coolly rebellious call for spiritual independence that the book sounded, for the young illuminati who read it, its most challenging note. "Our age is retrospective. It builds the sepulchres of the fathers," the fatherless Emerson began. "It writes biographies, histories, and criticism. The foregoing generations beheld God face to face; we, through their eyes. Why should not we also enjoy an original relation to the universe?" At the end, mounting higher, he had "a certain poet" sing out for him, "'A man is a god in ruins,'" and conclude in prophecy: "'The kingdom of man over nature, which cometh not with observation,—a dominion such as now is beyond his dream of God,—he shall enter without more wonder than the blind man feels who is gradually restored to perfect sight.'"[45]

The Emerson whom Fuller met that July was not only a prophet, but also a man, and, in physical appearance, a striking one. Above average in height, with a poised head atop narrow, sloping shoulders, light brown hair combed to the side, blue eyes, a broad mouth, and a full, slightly aquiline nose, Emerson at thirty-three managed to project something of that surprising fullness amidst angularity and that serene boldness that one often finds in his writing. He was also a family man, having married, the year before, Lydia, now Lidian Jackson (Emerson added the "n" to make it elide better), a tall, slender, handsome but not beautiful woman, about Emerson's age; warmhearted, humorous, intellectually independent-minded, but also given somewhat to melancholia and, like all the women to whom the Emerson boys were attracted, spiritually serious. "I announce this fact," Emerson had told his older brother William, announcing the engagement, "in a very different feeling from that with which I entered my first connection. This is a very sober joy." Emerson's friends and followers were also impressed. "A woman of the most exalted religious principles— withal very original & a despiser of the world's opinion," Hedge had written solemnly to Fuller a month after the engagement. And Sarah Clarke, after meeting her the following week, had written excitedly to her brother James: "She is a soaring Transcendentalist. She is full of sensibility, yet as independent in her mind as— who shall I say?—Margaret F." Rounding out this already exalted household in their adopted Concord, an attractive farming village seventeen miles northwest of Boston, were Emerson's austerely self-controlled, devoted sixty-eight-year-old mother, Ruth; his frequent visitor Aunt Mary, and Mary's friend, also Waldo's aunt, the phenomenally learned Sarah Alden Ripley; and a sweetly ethereal, scholarly young Concord woman by the name of Elizabeth Hoar, who had been engaged to marry Emerson's brother Charles but who now lived, as she would for the rest of her life, as a widowed "sister" and frequent guest at the Emersons' "Bush" house.[46]

Few of these developments went unnoticed by Fuller. It would have been surprising if they had. Ever since Emerson had resigned from his Boston ministry, she had been noting in her journal his movements, singing his praises, and—for the past two years—trying, without success, to find a way to meet him. "The Rev W. Emerson, that only clergyman of all possible clergymen who eludes my acquaintance," she had sighed to Almira Barlow two years earlier after hearing him spoken of admiringly at a party at the Farrars'. Again, four months later, to Henry Hedge, after expressing a wish that she might someday get to know Emerson: "I cannot think I should be disappointed in him as I have been in others to whom I had hoped to look up, the sensation one experiences in the atmosphere of his thoughts is too decided and peculiar." (Her interest even spilled over to his renowned brothers: "many tears" she had cried, she told Hedge, after learning of Edward's death, and, after Charles's funeral that May, she published anonymously the following week some tearful verses about him on the front page of the *Boston Centinel*.) Although remarkable, all this beforehand fascination with "my favorite Mr Emerson" (as she called him in her journal when he was in Europe) was not at all inexplicable. First, his colleagues Hedge and Clarke had been profusely praising him to her for the past several years. ("I seem still to glow with his influence like Werter's messenger fresh from Charlotte," the ordinarily sober Hedge gushed to her in a letter in the fall after returning from one visit with him.) Then there were the rumors she had been picking up of his growing success as a lecturer. ("I hear he is preaching at Hingham and elsewhere *with vast applause*," she excitedly reported to Clarke in Louisville.) Also, there was her own need for such a glowing influence. She had, after all, been crying out ever since she had moved to Groton for a heroic guide, and here, from all reports, was one—neither gone like Martineau nor dead like Goethe—in their very midst. The fact, too, that his reputation as a cultural preacher mingled with his image (at least in *her* mind) as a cultural rebel against Unitarian scholasticism also clearly appealed to her. "I cannot care much for *preached* elevation of sentiment unless I have seen it borne out of some proof as in the case of Mr Emerson," she had written in her journal in the fall after reading aloud to Ellen and their mother two sermons of Eliza Farrar's friend, the refined and popular New York Unitarian minister Orville Dewey. "It is so easy for a cultivated mind to excite itself into that tone. What a wealth of words has Mr Dewey; his only difficulty is in choice." Finally, the fact that her other "no 'Word-Hero'" in her life—her father—had recently died undoubtedly also added a further emotional dimension to her drive (as she described it to Clarke) to push "R. W. Emerson—the reverend, and I" over "the verge of an acquaintance."[47]

During this time, Hedge and Clarke had kept Emerson apprised of *her* virtues. Two years earlier, on Fuller's prompting, Hedge had lent him her "beautiful" *Tasso* translation, and more recently both he and Clarke had lavishly praised to him her erudition and "deep" knowledge of German literature and had urged him to seek her out. Others of Margaret's friends had done the same. Emerson recalled that when Harriet Martineau had been a guest at his house in the winter, she had "returned again and again to the topic of Margaret's excelling genius and conversation, and enjoined it on me to seek her acquaintance." Yet, despite these urgings (and despite his assurance to Hedge to the contrary) Emerson was reluctant—on the basis, he later recalled, of widespread rumors about her arrogant manner—to take the bait. Elizabeth Peabody seems to have been the one to have held out the right lure. Writing to Emerson, she tried to dispel his skepticism by explaining that she, too, had felt at first "a strong but unjustifiable prejudice" against Fuller. Finally, after Peabody's urgings were added to those of Eliza Farrar and Lidian—who told Peabody that from what *she* had heard, Fuller was "sound at *heart*"—Fuller got her invitation to the Emersons. She arrived on July 21 and stayed for three weeks.[48]

That Emerson's initial impressions of Fuller were not exactly promising is graphically shown in the account of their first meeting that he included in his section of the *Memoirs*.

> I still remember the first half-hour of Margaret's conversation. She was then twenty-six years old. She had a face and frame that would indicate fullness and tenacity of life. She was rather under the middle height; her complexion was fair, with strong fair hair. She was then, as always, carefully and becomingly dressed, and of lady-like self-possession. [She had been right about that "faded calico frock"!] For the rest, her appearance had nothing prepossessing. Her extreme plainness,—a trick of incessantly opening and shutting her eyelids,—the nasal tone of her voice,—all repelled; and I said to myself, we shall never get far. . . . I believe I fancied her too much interested in personal history; and her talk was a comedy in which dramatic justice was done to everybody's foibles. I remember that she made me laugh more than I liked; for I was, at that time, an eager scholar of ethics, and had tasted the sweets of solitude and stoicism, and I found something profane in the hours of amusing gossip into which she drew me, and, when I returned to my library, had much to think of the crackling of thorns under a pot.

Of course Fuller, for her part, did not simply let the thorns crackle. Or certainly at least this is the impression one gets from the rest of Emerson's recollection, in which he describes, with great gusto, all the various little stratagems of flattery, frankness, and just plain drollery that his young guest practiced to try to win the eager ethical scholar over—and apparently with some success. "It was impossible," he wrote, "long to hold out against such urgent assault. She had an incredible variety of anecdotes, and the readiest wit to give an absurd turn to whatever passed; and the eyes, which were so plain at first, soon swam with fun and drolleries, and the very tides of joy and superabundant life."[49]

Emerson's journals and letters at the time generally confirm these later impressions. In his journals, particularly, one can see something of the problem Fuller had to contend with. On the morning of the twenty-first, while he and Lidian were awaiting her arrival, Emerson recorded in his journal: "The worst guest is Asmodeus who comes into the quiet house sometimes in breeches sometimes in petticoats and demands of his entertainer not shelter & food, but to find him in work, and every body is on pins until some rope of sand is found for the monster to twist." Meanwhile "the monster" seems to have insisted on something more nourishing than sand, for ten days later he wrote, obviously speaking of Fuller's "assaults" on his privacy: "The wise man has no secrets. Secrets belong to the individual, local. He strives evermore to sink the individual in the universal. The friend who can bring him into a certain mood has a right to all the privacies that belong to that mood." That his guest's idea of "rights" was evidently somewhat different from his is suggested by a further entry he made the following week, on August 6: "'I know not what you think of me,' said my friend. Are you sure? You know all I think of you by those things I say to you. You know all which can be of any use to you. If I, if all your friends should draw your portrait to you—faults & graces, it would mislead you, embarrass you; you must not ask how you please me for curiosity." Finally, putting the matter most grossly: "You must not look in the glass to see how handsome you are but to see if your face is clean." This was a lesson in Olympian self-reliance with a vengeance![50]

Yet, despite these evasions and repulsions, the visit—at least from Fuller's point of view—obviously went fairly well. Emerson read to her from his nearly finished manuscript of *Nature;* he honored her (presumably without irony) with an autograph of the utilitarian Jeremy Bentham that the deceased author's literary executor, Sir John Bowring, had given him when he had visited Bentham's house in London; and, by the end of the visit, he was writing laudatory letters praising her accomplishments. "She is quite an extraordinary person," he wrote to his brother William on August 8, "for her apprehensiveness her acquisitions & her powers of conversation. It is always a great refreshment to see a very intelligent person. It is like being set in a large place. You stretch your limbs & dilate to your utmost size." Lidian seconded the opinion. "We like her—she likes us," she confided to Elizabeth Peabody after Fuller had been there for a week. "I speak in this way—because you know we came together almost strangers—all to one another and the result of the experiment—as Miss F. herself said in her letter to you on the subject of a nearer acquaintance with us—was doubtful—

the tendencies of all three being strong & decided—and possibly not such as could harmonize." And while in his journal, the day after Fuller's departure on the twelfth, Emerson, the sublimated egoist, felt compelled to add to his praises a caveat on her too-personal "egotism of place & time & blood" ("How rarely can a female mind be impersonal . . . M. F. by no means so free with all her superiority")—nevertheless, he, too, later wrote to Peabody, Fuller's faithful booster: "I believe we all here shared your respect for Miss Fuller's gifts & character. She has the quickest apprehension & immediately learned all we knew & had us at her mercy when she pleased to make us laugh. She has noble traits & powers & cannot fail of a permanent success."[51]

In the meantime, after returning to Groton on August 11, Fuller lost little time in making these good opinions secure. In September she visited the Boston area for a month and while there tried to make contact with Emerson, who was in town for a few days to attend the first Transcendental Club meeting on the nineteenth. Because of several mishaps, they missed each other. This set off, on both sides, a small flurry of notes of disappointment, including one on the twentieth from Emerson, now back in Concord, urging that Fuller "ride up hither & spend a day in our green fens," especially, he added, as he understood she would not be back in Groton by the following Sunday when he was to be filling in for the Reverend Mr. Robinson. Fuller replied the next day in a letter which, in its agitated, half-awkward, half-gushing tones, shows off quite well this early stage of her friendship with her Concord sage. "My dear friend," she began gamely ("I may venture to begin so since you have subscribed yourself my friend"). Then— in almost the identical language of many of her childhood letters to her father— she grew quickly defensive. "While I was with you you very justly corrected me for using too strong expressions on some subjects. But there is no exaggeration in saying— I *must* be allowed to say that I *detest* Mr. Robinson at this moment." She then launched into a scolding attack on the poor minister for having the effrontery to invite Emerson to preach on a day when she had to be out of town; an earnest entreaty to Emerson to postpone his coming ("I fear it is not possible, but if it is I think you will do it for my sake, for I would do twenty times as much for yours"); and finally, once finished with the subject, a further defense of herself: "If you were to see me just now, dear Sir, you would not like me at all for I am very far from calm and have quite forfited my placid brow [another worry of her father's!] but I flatter myself that my vexation will seem nothing worse than earnestness on paper." Evidently feeling that it might, though, she added a postscript: "You must not make a joke of my anxiety about next Sunday, but take it seriously as I am feeling. It is a great gain to be able to address yourself directly, instead of intriguing as I did last year." Emerson, in his reply the following day, tried to smooth her ruffles by promising to "make myself amends" by proposing to Mr. Robinson that they make another exchange for a time when she would be at home. Meanwhile he urged her again to "come & see us as soon as you can," adding that Lidian—then an ill "prisoner to her chamber"—was convinced that Fuller's visit would cure her faster than her "poppy & oatmeal." On

her return to Groton at the beginning of October, she naturally obliged. So began
the steady stream of visits and stopovers that would eventually make the Bush
house for Fuller a second—if not always entirely tranquil—home.[52]

V

By mid-October of 1836, Fuller was back in Boston. The reason for her quick
return was this time, not pleasure, but business. She was acutely aware (as she
told a friend in the summer) that her "dear, gentle, suffering mother" and her
younger siblings were counting on her to make up the deficit in the family
income. As she had recently decided the pen would not do it for her, she knew
she needed (as she said to Clarke) to "take other means." Those means, of
course, were the only ones she had ever had available to her. As she announced
with a firm sigh that summer in another letter to a friend, "I will make up my
mind to teach." And she did. In the summer she even briefly resuscitated her old
plan of teaching in the West, but as usual Clarke discouraged her from thinking
of *that* as a "money-making" idea. So she tried something nearer to home—her
own school in Boston. After making arrangements to board with her Uncle
Henry and his family at No. 1 Avon Place and taking rooms for her school next
door at No. 2, she had printed up and distributed a circular proposing "to give
instruction to classes of Ladies in GERMAN, ITALIAN, and FRENCH LIT-
ERATURE," for the then fairly steep per-student price of fifteen dollars for one
twelve-week course of twenty-four lessons. Like her rates, her objectives were
high. "Pupils," the circular read, would read only "the best authors." They could
also be expected to receive sufficient "historical and critical" instruction
enabling them to become, "with ease and pleasure," both "familiar with the style
of the prominent writers of those nations, at different eras in their literary history" as well as cognizant of "some part of the treasures of thought" contained
in their works. In her circular Fuller frankly confessed that she herself had been
impeded in the past by not having had sufficient oral instruction, and this is the
key to what she was trying to do. Essentially she was offering college-level
instruction to adolescent girls who had been denied, as she had been, a college
education. Her descriptions of her classes' pace and content confirm this. With
her elementary German students, she sped. "At the end of three months," she
reported to Clarke, "they could read 20 pages of Gn at a lesson and very well."
Her advanced German classes she drove at an even faster clip: during their first
three-month session they read three dramas of Lessing's, two of Schiller's, and
five of Goethe's, including the first part of *Faust* ("as valuable to me as to them"),
along with a good deal of Tieck and the first volume of Jean Paul's difficult *Titan*.
In Italian her students read large parts of Tasso, Petrarch, Ariosto, and Alfieri,
as well as the entire *Divina Commedia* ("with the aid of the fine Athenaeum copy
and all the best commentaries"). She also managed to secure with Emerson's
help ("it would be their great pleasure to do it," he graciously reported), the assistance of Harvard language instructors Hermann Bokum, Francis Sales, and Pietro Bachi to provide special classes in speaking and pronunciation. With the

exception of Henry Wadsworth Longfellow's classes at Harvard just then beginning, Fuller's Boston school probably provided more comprehensive instruction in modern European literature than that offered anywhere in America.[53]

Besides teaching the twenty or so adolescent girls and young women who began her classes on November 9, Fuller that winter gave (at the hefty rate of two dollars per hour per student) private lessons to five other young women. She also once a day for ten weeks instructed in Latin orally and read English history and Shakespeare's historical plays to a little blind boy. ("Very interesting, but very fatiguing," she described this last experience to Clarke.) Her students came to her in various ways. Many were from her growing collection of protégées. "You know my magnetic power over young women," she had boasted to Clarke the year before; "well! some ten or twelve have been drawn into my sphere since you knew me— to all I have given sympathy and time (more than was agreeable)." Others were drawn by word of mouth. A November 8 letter from her young friend Sam Ward, then traveling with the Farrars in London, to his sister Mary, shows how one word got around:

You tell me that Miss Fuller is coming to Boston to give lessons in the languages, and I wish you by all means to take the opportunity of being with her. She not only has read more than any woman of my acquaintance but understands more thoroughly the spirit of the German and Italian literatures than anyone I know. But whether or not you study German or Italian with her, make her if you can your friend; talk with her and consult her on any subject from a ribband to your Bible. I am sure you will find her a delightful acquaintance and with a universality of knowledge that will surprise you.[54]

Both Fuller's boast and Ward's broadside also showed something else—that for some of her adolescent girls, her teaching was as much personal as intellectual. Certainly this was true with her inner circle of pupils. They came from wealthy and highly literate Boston families: Caroline Sturgis, the younger sister of Margaret's old friend Ellen Sturgis and the daughter of the wealthy William Sturgis, whose firm, Bryant and Sturgis, controlled over half of the American trade with the Pacific Coast and China; Jane Tuckerman, a talented songstress and the daughter of another well-to-do Boston merchant; Marianne Jackson, the daughter of the state Supreme Court justice Charles Jackson and the niece of Patrick Tracy Jackson, the cofounder with his brother-in-law Francis Cabot Lowell of the Boston Manufacturing Company and the architect of its famous Lowell town and mills; Mary Ward, the daughter of the banker and American Baring Brothers agent Thomas Wren Ward; and Mary Channing, the oldest child of Boston's illustrious Dr. William Ellery Channing. These were some of Boston's most cultivated girls, and their families were anxious—in good Boston Unitarian tradition—that they receive the best moral and intellectual training their money could buy. Fuller did her best to provide it. "My dearest, you must suffer," she wrote in answer to one note from the "sensitive, . . . overstrained" Jane about Jane's despondency over her mother's illness, "but you will always be growing stronger, and with every trial nobly met, you will feel a growing assurance that nobleness is not a mere sentiment to you." Recalling "the bootless fear and agitation I endured about my Mother, and how strangely our destinies were guided," she urged her to "take refuge in prayer when you are most troubled," adding, "I send you a paper which is very sacred to me." To sturdier souls she wrote sturdier advice. In a lengthy letter to the affable Mary Channing, she bluntly told her that if Marianne and Caroline "are too severe in their views of life and man, I think you are too little so." To counter this weakness she urged her to develop her ability to make judgments by being more analytical in her writing. ("Do not write down merely your impressions that things are beautiful or the reverse, but what they are and why they are.") In a like spirit, reminiscent of her father's advice to her at the same age, she approved her recent course of reading books that were addressed to "the judgement" rather than just to "the taste and the imagination." ("The love of beauty has rather an undue development in your mind.") Finally—except perhaps for the slight Romantic flourish, again well within the tradition of cultural domesticity she had inherited from her father—she advised Mary to take care not to let her literary study eclipse domestic work. "Now learn buying and selling, keeping the house, managing the servants, all that will bring you worlds of wisdom if you will only keep it subordinate to the one grand aim of perfecting the whole being." In closing she added, "I always feel ashamed when I write with this aid of wisdom." Her shame, however, did not keep her from playing for these girls—and for many others like them in years to come—the role (as she called herself in her letter to Mary) of "one of your preachers."[55]

While transmogrifying herself into a Boston teacher, Fuller also became something of a Bostonian herself. For a future urban cosmopolitan, this was a good time to do so. Even Harriet Martineau, whose contempt for Boston's social pretense and caste-consciousness was boundless, assured her English readers— speaking of both the city's Unitarian intellectuals and its lengthening list of reformers—"I certainly am not aware of so large a number of peculiarly interesting and valuable persons living in near neighborhood, anywhere else but in London." Likewise, a few months later the militant Transcendentalist reform ideologue Orestes Brownson assured *his* sympathetic Boston readers, "Boston is, say what you will of it, the city of 'notions,' and of new notions too; and in the progress of liberal ideas in this country, it ever has and ever will take the lead." However wish-fulfilling, Brownson's boast was accurate: Boston *was* awash with new notions, and for a good reason. Along with its galloping, eighty-thousand-plus population and its roaring commercial expansion fueled by the outlying textile factories and connecting railroads that were mushrooming around it, the city was undergoing its greatest identity crisis since its founding. Irish Catholic immigrants were pouring into increasingly segregated poor neighborhoods, the city's artisans were beginning to organize for the first time class-conscious trade unions, and expanding evangelical denominations were threatening to outpace Boston's traditionally dominant Unitarian churches. In response to these challenges, myriad middle-class reformers—from health cult-

ists and abolitionists to public-school zealots and philanthropic-minded ministers—were feverishly trying to reassert, through their variously corporatist or
hyperindividualistic movements, the old Puritan vision of a worldwide acknowledged, ideal-intoxicated city on a hill.[56]

For the moment, though, Fuller's interest in all this diverse ferment was minimal. Indeed, if anything, her Boston teaching attached her to the city's upper-
middle-class Unitarian world more firmly than she had ever been before. "Last
night I took my boldest peep into the Gigman [Carlyle's metaphor for fashionable society] world of Boston," she wrote with some satisfaction to Emerson later
in the spring. "I have not been to a large party before and only seen said world
in half-boots, so I thought as it was an occasion in which I felt real interest, to
wit, a fete given by Mrs Thorndike for my beautiful Susan [the wealthy Boston
merchant's wife Sarah Dana Thorndike and her niece Susan Dana], I would look
at it for once in satin slippers." She went on in the remainder of the letter to give
an evocative portrait of her companions, "graceful Mary" Channing and her
mother, and the "many fair maidens dressed as if they had stepped out of their
Grandmothers' picture frames, and youths, with their long locks, suitable to represent pages, if not nobles." On the other hand, despite her claim that "my fashionable fellow creatures were very civil to me and I went home glad to have
looked at this slide in the magic lantern also," it is obvious from her carefully
detached tone and her slyly irreverent remarks (for example, her sighting of the
sybaritic "Daniel [Webster] the Great, not however, when I saw him, engaged in
an operation peculiarly favorable to his style of beauty, to wit eating oysters")
that she was still more than a little the smart daughter of a Middlesex County
Jeffersonian congressman, skeptically looking in at a somewhat questionable
affair.[57]

Besides her background, there were two other reasons why Fuller, despite her
elite Unitarian connections, was not exactly on her way to becoming the proper
Bostonian. For one thing, as several of her friends later attested, the reputation
of her "unpopular" father in ex-Federalist circles made some elite Boston families suspicious of her. For another, Boston Unitarians themselves were beginning to divide up ideologically, and it is clear from her letters and a notebook of
"interviews" she kept that winter that her sympathies did not lie with the Unitarian establishment. She lavishly praised the humanitarian antislavery merchant Jonathan Phillips ("dispassionate yet tender, discriminating yet so
benign"). She likewise reported spending many "delightful hours" talking about
post-Kantian philosophy and theology and other intellectual matters with the
Purchase Street Transcendentalist Unitarian minister George Ripley, who later
predicted to her that she and his wife Sophia would be "great friends." By contrast she poured mild scorn on the complacently urbane views her old schoolmate, the newly minted physician Dr. Oliver Wendell Holmes, expressed to her
one evening. "W. H. took the ground that there was no need of settling any-thing
about God and the world, that if you went on zealously with any study, seeking
truth alone, you would be led unconsciously to the proper ground.— I was grat-

ified to perceive," she happily noted, "that I was as superior to W. H. in my training in precision of thought and clearness of utterance as I am inferior to some
with whom I talk on these subjects." This last competitive twist suggests perhaps
the most important reason for Fuller's outsider consciousness: as an intellectual
woman, she *was* an outsider—and she knew it. In one of her memoranda, after
giving an account of a friendly argument she had had with the conservative
Romantic Richard Henry Dana, Sr., over the danger for "the thinking man" of
reading newspapers and periodicals ("He railed against [them]. . . . I plead in
favor of reading them moderately"), she added with a sigh: "Women might be
of use in this society by explaining the speculative man to the practical. But
where could an Aspasia take her stand?"[58]

Nothing of this competitive concern colored her relationship with another
Boston intellectual with whom she spent a good deal of time that winter—the
Reverend William Ellery Channing. She had already gotten to know him a little
during her two brief summer vacations in Newport. Frail, eloquent, and
intensely serious, Channing was then preaching a heady mixture of social
idealism, moral uplift, and political caution to his admiring, but sometimes
uncomfortable, well-to-do Federal Street congregation. ("All social institutions
[are] so hostile to Xty," he told James Clarke that fall, Clarke reported—saving
his strongest medicine as usual for private conversation—"that I doubt whether
it can go much further till those are broken up. . . . I once shrank from com-
motions, but *I do not now dread storms.*") Fuller found Channing's sermons
inspiring. After hearing one that winter on human spirituality, she wrote in her
journal: "I came away in the most happy, hopeful, and heroic mood. . . . I felt
purged as if by fire. If some speakers feed intellect more, Dr. C. feeds the whole
spirit." (She then added, like a good Channingite parishioner: "O for a more
calm, more pervading faith in the divinity of my own nature! I am so far from
being thoroughly tempered and seasoned, and am sometimes so presumptuous,
at others so depressed.") But mainly she got to know Channing that winter by
orally translating for him, one evening a week, German literary and theological
works. As Channing was an incurable monologist, the talk not surprisingly usually overwhelmed the reading. Still, neither this nor the severe emotional
restraint of the man seems to have bothered her much. After speaking of his
manner of taking in subjects ("more deliberate than is conceivable to us feminine people, with our habits of ducking, diving, or flying for truth"), she wrote:
"I do not feel that constraint which some persons complain of, but am perfectly
free, though less called out than by other intellects of inferior power. . . . He
seems desirous to meet even one young and obscure as myself on equal terms,
and trusts to the elevation of his thoughts to keep him in his place." Nor was she
distressed by the fact that Channing's mix of idealistic rhetoric, social philanthropy, and rational supernaturalism was beginning to seem to some of her
Transcendentalist friends a little passé. "I think the younger class of clergymen
are disposed to undervalue Dr Channing," she wrote one day in her notebook,
after George Ripley had spoken disparagingly about him. They exaggerated his

faults, she thought, and "forget what he has done, because he is not doing anything new." And although she regretfully noted in her notebook Channing's moralistic objections to Goethe, she had only praise for his liberal Whiggish remarks on the recent election of Jackson's successor, Martin Van Buren. Contrasting his more hopeful "tone" (as always, her concern) with the more partisan observations of her father's nemesis, the newly elected Whig governor Edward Everett, with whom she had spoken on the same subject a few weeks before, she broke out in her notebook: "O man of expediency how poor and faded are thy once fair words beside those of the man of principle!"[59]

The person Fuller was most intellectually involved with that winter, however, made even Channing look like a time-bound worldling. If Emerson was Transcendentalism's poet-philosopher, Amos Bronson Alcott, for better or worse, was the movement's saint. With extremely fair skin; a rugged jaw and dimpled chin; friendly blue eyes; long, flowing, flaxen hair swept back; and a large, dome-like forehead and shaggy, protruding brows; he might have looked to a scrutinizing phrenologist like some kind of otherworldly, Stone Age savage. But in manner he was thoroughly gentle, courtly, and, if intellectually self-absorbed, unlike his friend Emerson, was naturally, almost disarmingly, gregarious. He was also generally regarded by the public, at this time even more than Emerson, as the principal spokesman of New England Transcendentalism. Actually, in background, as in some of his ideas, he stood out rather glaringly from most of his Transcendental colleagues. At thirty-seven he was a little older, and, unlike most of them, he was raised, not in Boston or Cambridge or at Harvard, but in an impoverished, if marginally genteel, family in the tiny rural village of Spindle Hill, near Wolcott, Connecticut. Largely self-taught, he had spent several years peddling housewares and conversation to Virginia families from whom he imbibed some of his quasi-aristocratic manners. In 1828 he settled in Boston, where he taught school, associated with the city's leading Unitarian lights, and kept a sprawling "journal of observation" on the spiritual growth of his three infant daughters, which he later called "Psyche," along with an even more sprawling, but fascinating and (considering his considerable capacity for self-deception) often remarkably insightful diary that he would continue until the end of his life.[60]

It was in 1834 that he took his first step in putting into public practice the theory of "Spiritual Culture" that underlay all his works: with the assistance of Elizabeth Peabody and the blessing of Dr. Channing, he opened his famous Temple School. There in Room 7 of the Masonic Temple—in whose large lecture hall Emerson and Brownson expounded to growing audiences of the curious and the faithful their advanced ideas on religion, reform, and culture—in the light of a tall Gothic window, with colored carpets, busts of Milton, Shakespeare, Plato, and Socrates, and a bas-relief of Jesus, Alcott implemented his avant-garde educational views. Sharply departing from the standard school practices of the day, Alcott in his school eschewed physical punishment and gave lessons not by rote, but by means of a kind of Socratic question-and-answer method designed to encourage students to strengthen their mental faculties as well as expose them to ideas, of which words (as he liked to tell his students) were "emblematic." Philosophically this whole schema rested, at least in Alcott's mind, on the Romantic notion that children—being freer than adults from pre-occupation with outward knowledge gained from the senses—were therefore more closely attuned than adults, given the proper encouragement, to the kinds of truths and values that lay within. Furthermore, Alcott believed, because these truths ultimately had their source in a pre-existent soul, children—who were, chronologically speaking, the least removed from pre-existence—were therefore that much more capable of "remembering," again with encouragement, the truths that the soul had to teach. This last idea—essentially Platonic and more mystically idealistic than any held by most of Alcott's Transcendentalist colleagues—also had profoundly radical implications for religion and society. Boston society, much to its chagrin, was beginning to realize these just about the time Fuller stepped forward to become Alcott's new assistant.[61]

Fuller had first met Alcott back on August 2 while staying at the Emersons'. Elizabeth Peabody—partly out of uneasiness over Alcott's uninhibited class-room interrogations, but mainly out of fear—had just quit, and Alcott was look-ing for a replacement. Gossip about Alcott's heterodox ideas and methods had been increasing, and Peabody—a single woman, a teacher, and a transcriber of Alcott's students' responses, which she feared (correctly) he was planning to pub-lish uncensored—was, quite literally, scared for her professional life. Fuller, on the other hand, younger and more heedless of consequences—or perhaps simply less knowing about either Alcott or Boston—seems to have felt none of this fear. Besides, she needed money, and, as she told Alcott on August 25, in a letter fol-lowing up on his suggestion to her just before he left the Bush house on the third that he would like to consider her for his new assistant, she was genuinely inter-ested in his teaching methods. She was also anxious, she said, if only as "an experiment," to try her hand at teaching in a regular school under someone's supervision. And of course, one need scarcely add, Alcott was a close friend and a fellow colleague of Waldo Emerson. On September 2, while she was in Boston, she had a further talk with Alcott about the position, and, after completing the first month of her own classes, in early December she began the work. Essentially her responsibilities were what Peabody's had been—to teach Latin and French and record Alcott's "conversations" with the children on the Gospels, which he resumed, after a six-month hiatus, on January 4, 1837. Although she found her labors "very fatiguing," she later told Clarke, the twenty-five children, who ranged from six to about ten, she absolutely "loved." As well she might have. Many were from (as Alcott happily noted in his journal) some of Boston's most cultivated and prominent Unitarian families, several of which she knew well. Also, the children's naïve and animated weekly exchanges—which Emerson and others of the faithful often attended as observers—exposed Fuller to more con-centrated doses of Boston Transcendentalist philosophy than she had ever got-ten in her life. Her transcriptions show the children discussing subjects that ranged from the "figurative" character of biblical language and (as one child put it) "see[ing] with our imagination," to the "persecution" of Boston reformers and (in the face of some strong challenges from a couple of the class's skeptics) the evil of "indulging your appetites." She appreciated the exposure. After finishing the last of her transcriptions, she would tell Clarke that the children's conversations had given her "many valuable thoughts."[62]

Meanwhile, Alcott's opinion of Fuller grew accordingly. Quite evidently the idea of having as his assistant a young woman, every bit as cultivated as Elizabeth Peabody, but both more intellectually daring and socially mannered, was immensely satisfying to him. (As Alcott, who abhorred his former assistant's personal eccentricities, happily noted in his diary, Fuller was "familiar, from childhood, with good society.") On January 21 he recorded in his journal with satisfaction:

> I passed an evening with Miss Fuller. She is given to free and bold speculation, and has more unity of mind, than most of her sex, with whom, I have become acquainted. In point of acquirement, she has the reputation of being more varied and thorough than almost any person of her years among us. Not wanting in imaginary power, she possesses rare good sense, so necessary to balance the character of a woman, ambitious of literary name, and resting in her own worth, for success in life. She adopts the spiritual philosophy, and has a truer perception of its bearings and necessity. Of those who promise to add enduring glory to female literature, she seems most conspicuous among us.

And again, after spending another evening with her two months later, on March 28, he wrote even more exultingly:

> Miss Fuller seems more inclined to take large and generous views of subjects than any woman of my acquaintance. I think her more liberal than almost any mind among us. She has more of that unspoiled integrity of being, so essential to the apprehension of truth in its unity, than any person of her sex whom I meet; and vastly more of intellectual power. Her skill in conversation is ready; few converse with greater freedom and elegance. Her range of topics seems wide; and she looks at them without narrowness or partiality.

To this he added—ever mindful from personal experience of the importance for an intellectual adventurer of civic patronage—"I am glad that some interest is felt in her behalf, by those of this metropolis, whose good word is a passport to success. . . . To her has been given, with the gift of genius, that of prudence."[63]

As for Fuller's opinion of Alcott, one thing is clear: she was not as enamored of him as he was of her. It is true she obviously harbored none of the usual conservative prejudices against him. Back in September she had written Emerson that she had been "entertained" by the remarks of the school administrator Frederick Emerson, who at the recent American Institute of Instruction at Worcester had sharply rebuked Alcott for a speech he had made. Frederick Emerson had expressed, Fuller said, paraphrasing the *Boston Daily Advertiser*'s account, "horror at the idea of this common earth being peopled by gods, 'an idea upon which he would not dilate.'" On the other hand—her little joke notwithstanding—she herself had her own serious reservations, if not about Alcott the man, at least about his philosophy. On January 19 she wrote in her journal: "Conversation at Mr Alcott's room. Regeneration. I wish I could define my distrust of Mr Alcott's mind. I think constantly he is one-sided without being able to see where the fault lies. There is something in his view of every subject, something in his philosophy which revolts either my common-sense or—my prejudices—I cannot be sure which." It did not take her too long to decide which. Later that winter she wrote out in her journal an "impression" of Alcott preaching his twin ideas of promoting radical intuitionism and redeeming society through the education of children. Although she claimed when she sent him a copy of it three years later, that she intended it to be sympathetic ("it was written one day after I had been talking with you, and trying to put myself into your state of mind"), the piece was laced throughout with obviously parodying phrases. ("O for the safe and natural way of Intuition," she began. "I cannot grope like a mole in the gloomy ways of Experience.") Furthermore, she concluded her impression with a firmly dualistic critique of Alcott's "spiritual philosophy." "But, Preacher," she quoted herself as saying,

> You made three mistakes.
> You did not understand the nature of Genius or creative power.
> You did not understand the reaction of matter on spirit.
> You were too impatient of the complex; and, not enjoying variety in unity, you became lost in abstractions, and could not illustrate your principles.[64]

Fuller's reservations did not, however, interfere with either her loyalty to Alcott or her sympathy with his educational goals and methods. She showed this well enough by her reaction to the public outcry over his *Conversations with Children on the Gospels*. Certainly this edited transcript of the discussions he had held earlier in the year with his pupils on the four New Testament Gospels—which were published in two volumes on December 22 and February 18—was a remarkable document. In it Alcott sought to demonstrate, in addition to the validity of his theory of pre-existence and his teaching methods, the way Christianity itself could be validated by the pure, unmediated influx of the spirit as it revealed itself in the souls of untutored children. Although in the charming inventiveness and ludicrously Alcottian answers that Alcott managed to elicit from some of his pupils, the book showed Alcott—probably better than anything he ever wrote—at his best and his worst, it was not as a scientific experiment or as an educational treatise that *Conversations* was greeted. Harvard's Professor Andrews Norton was quoted anonymously in the press as giving his considered opinion that Alcott's book was "one third absurd, one third blasphemous, and one third obscene." Not to be outdone, Joseph T. Buckingham, from his post as the combative editor of the *Boston Courier*, flatly declared that "the *Conversations on the Gospels* is a more indecent and obscene book . . . than any other we ever saw exposed for sale on a bookseller's counter," and recommended that the author be turned over to the Municipal Court and prosecuted for blasphemy, as the agnostic Abner Kneeland had recently been.[65]

The underlying reasons for all this hue and cry are not hard to find. The city's rising social tensions probably contributed to some of the hysteria. Mob violence against abolitionists and other reformers had been erupting in Boston with increasing frequency for the past several years. But if social tensions stoked the fires, ideology provided the kindling. To put it simply, Alcott managed, by his book, to offend virtually every important segment of Boston society. The orthodox were outraged by Alcott's radical theology; even moderate Unitarian ministers were nervous that their liberal doctrines would be associated with his; and more aggressively conservative Unitarian ministers and academics were plainly disgusted by the thought of a simple, self-made teacher claiming to teach religion while calmly dispensing with all the learning and professional scholarship that liberals had always said needed to be the basis of a rational religion. Nearly everyone, of course, was upset—and this was the basis of the charge of obscenity—over the children's occasionally startling comments about conception and birth, by which Alcott purported to show, in ways delicate to the point of obscurity, the breathing in of the spirit at the beginning of life.[66]

Alcott's little experiment in spiritual self-consciousness and social democracy had its supporters, of course, but they were almost entirely from among the faithful. Peabody, despite her horror at the *Conversations'* "physiological" passages, bravely defended in the Unitarian *Christian Register* Alcott's educational method. Clarke wrote scathingly in the *Register* of the "LYNCHING" in Boston and, in his *Western Messenger,* compared the persecution of Alcott to the trial of Socrates. Emerson fired off letters of protest to the *Courier* and the *Daily Advertiser.* Meanwhile, Emerson tried to give his friend—who was aghast that his adopted city did not recognize him as the prophet he knew he was—needed moral support in face of the "miserable" press attacks on him. Fuller added her bit to the defense. Some time in early April, when the furor against Alcott's *Conversations* was at its peak, she had heard that Henry Hedge was writing a sharply critical article on Alcott and his book for the *Christian Examiner.* Obviously such an attack from a fellow Transcendentalist—even as moderate a one as Hedge—would have been, for Alcott, the final blow. Fuller did what she could to scuttle it. On April 6, two days after the *Courier* published Emerson's protest letter, she dashed off to her old friend and mentor in Bangor a stinging note.

Why is it that I hear you are writing a piece to "cut up Mr Alcott?" I do not believe you are going to cut up Mr Alcott. There are plenty of fish in the net created solely for markets &c no need to try your knife on a dolphin like him.—I should be charmed if I thought you were writing a long, beautiful, wise like article showing the elevated aim and at the same time the practical defects of his system. You would do a great service to him as well as the public and I know no one so well qualified as yourself to act as a mediator between the two and set both sides of the question in a proper light. But the phrase "cutting up" alarms me. If you were here I am sure that you would feel as I do and that your wit would never lend its patronage to the ugly blinking owls who are now hooting from their snug tenements, overgrown rather with nettles than with ivy, at this star of purest ray serene. But you are not here, more's the pity, and perhaps do not know exactly what you are doing, do write to me and reassure me.[67]

Hedge did write to her, though not for a month and a half. When he did, he sheepishly confessed, "You are right about Alcott & my reputed design upon him." But, he assured her, after thinking about it, he had essentially come around to her view. Although, that is, he had many critical things to say about "Mr. A's system," he was unwilling, he told her, "to increase the uproar," and, since the editor, James Walker, he implied, had wanted only a severe review, he "determined to say nothing." Presumably Fuller found Hedge's answer satisfying. But whether satisfying or not, by this time it hardly mattered. The Temple School's enrollment, which had been dwindling since the beginning of the fall term, fell off precipitously after the press attacks began, as anxious parents hastily withdrew their children from the school and wealthy patrons withdrew their support. By selling his prized school library and moving into a basement room, Alcott managed to struggle on with a handful of students for another year before closing his school for good. But in the meantime, two things he knew he could not do were to bring out, as he had originally intended, Fuller's transcriptions of that winter's conversations or pay her her salary. And so, shortly after she wrote her letter to Hedge, she notified Alcott of her intention to quit and began preparing to return to Groton.[68]

VI

While winding up her teaching in Boston, Fuller wrote to friends, complaining about her lack of time for serious thought. ("I am as ill placed as regards a chance to think as a haberdasher's prentice or the President of Harvard University," she told Hedge.) But this was in a very different mood from her "forlorn" letters at the beginning of the winter about thinking that "perhaps I must die," or feeling "vulgarized" and "profaned" because she was "buying and selling" her enthusiasm "about the things I loved best." In her letter to Hedge, she even managed to make light of the illnesses that had plagued her all winter. "If May flowers and June breezes do no good I must prepare either to leave this scene or become 'that extremely common character, a confirmed invalid.' But I intend to get perfectly well, if possible, for Mr Carlyle says [in a letter Emerson had evidently shown her] 'it is wicked to be sick.'" And to Clarke, a few weeks later, after saying she was "still quite unwell"—and tracing her suffering back, as she often did, to the shock of her father's death—she added jauntily: "All my pursuits and propensities have a tendency to make my head worse. It is a bad head; as bad as if I were a great man." The reason for all this cheerful stoicism was, of course, obvious: she felt satisfied and faintly amazed at all—with or without a great man's head— she had managed to accomplish. As she explained to Clarke, detailing her labors of the past six months with her literature classes and recently at Alcott's school:

I was so new to a public position and so desirous to do all I could that I took a great deal more upon myself than I was able to bear. Yet now the twenty five weeks of incessant toil are over I rejoice in it all and would not have done an iota less. I have fulfilled my engagements faithfully. I have acquired more power of attention, self-command and fortitude. I have acted in life as I thought I would in my lonely bower. I have acquired some knowledge of means, and, blessed be the father of our spirits [and, she might have added, Emerson and Alcott!] my aims are the same as they were in the happiest flights of youthful fancy.

I have learnt too at last to rejoice in all past pain. I have now found its practical benefit. I see that my spirit has been so judiciously tempered for its work— In future I may sorrow but can I ever despair?

In reply Clarke exulted:

How glad I have been in hearing of your succeeding so well in this first plunge into active life, maugre all evil augury from without and sad foreboding from within. Your letter did not give me the first account of it, however; I heard through various birds of the air (such as Chas. Jackson, Jr., and Dr. Hooper [Robert William Hooper, Ellen Sturgis's fiancé]) of the delight and interest which you had inspired in your pupils, and that that important character "Public Opinion" (embodied in some half dozen Beacon Street and Summer Street gentlemen and ladies) had declared that confidence might be placed in you. "My daughter," now would the Abbé [in *Wilhelm Meisters Lehrjahre*] say, "your Apprenticeship is over."[69]

This apprenticeship—as Clarke implied— was also a social one. But the most valuable socializing she did that winter and spring was with the very un–Beacon Street Ralph Waldo Emerson. No letters have survived for the months between November and March, but she did attend his winter lecture series at the Masonic Temple on the philosophy of history, and scattered references (and, of course, the fact that Concord was only two hours by stage from Boston) would indicate they saw each other sometimes during this time. Letters become increasingly frequent through the spring and early summer. These letters show how far Fuller had come in nine months—both intellectually and personally—in her friendship with Emerson. On the intellectual front one finds, although nothing of the lengthy philosophical talk of later years, still, many books exchanged, eagerly proffered and eagerly grabbed up on both sides. During the spring she lent him, among other works, a half-dozen or so "very valuable" and "inestimable" (as he called them) German books she had been using in her Goethe research. This is interesting because it was during these months that Goethe's star, in Emerson's eye, was beginning to rise, despite his worry about the Weimar poet's "ghastly hard & ironical" voice, and his journals and letters show that conversations and exchanges with Fuller were helping it rise even higher. Meanwhile he lent her his volumes of Coleridge and Carlyle. He also gave her a good many English Renaissance books, thus confirming his later claim that he "had the pleasure" of filling this rare gap in her literary reading.[70]

The only discernible difference of opinion in their letters had to do with Fuller's Orphic schoolmaster. "Mr Alcott," Emerson wrote to her bluntly on May 19, "is the great man & Miss Fuller has not yet seen him. His book does him no justice and I do not like to see it." He had, he told her, "more of the godlike than any man I have ever seen and his presence rebukes & threatens & raises. He *is* a teacher. I shall dismiss for the future all anxiety about his success. If he cannot

make intelligent men feel the presence of a superior nature the worse for them—
I can never doubt him." He made only one concession: "He told me he had
never spoken happily to you. And I admit now as always a monotony even to
tedium when Homer nods." Eventually their points of view about Alcott's relative divinity and monotony would roughly coincide, but not until their mutual
tastes for the prophetic somewhat reversed themselves. In the meantime, she
made it clear she vastly preferred Emerson intellectually to his godlike colleague.
A year later, in response to Emerson's entreaty to send him "Mr Alcott's List of
thoughts; and mine: Our *Thus far no farther,*" she would tell him why. First, she
candidly said, it was absurd to think she could put "a schedule of your mental
furniture" merely "on a page," as she could Alcott's. "For though you do not
take a more elevated view of Man and his destiny than Mr A. as, indeed, who
could?— You have a thousand more organs by which to make acquaintance
with the subject." Besides (as she called it in her journal) his "salt," there was, in
the second place, the matter of their respective idealisms. After reproducing
another version of the same slightly parodying impression of Alcott that she had
written in her journal in December, she gave him a considerably more sympathetic portrait of his own kind of idealistic philosophy:

Truth the primary law.—
The Universal Mind the only legitimate existence
Love of the intellect for dualism and
Desire of the spirit to suppress it.

Whatever else she might think of Emerson's philosophy, this intellectual love of
a fluid kind of subject–object dualism *and* the desire to transcend it—so different
from Alcott's wish to put matter (as she had him say in his monologue) "out of
my way as much as possible"—would never lose its appeal for Fuller.[71]

On a personal level their friendship was growing. To see this, one has only to
compare Fuller's awkward, half-suppressed letters of the previous summer with
her witty, breezy letters that spring. A letter in May she addressed, "R. W. Emerson.—/what shocking familiarity!" And in her April 11–12 letter, she teased him
for asking to have back so soon the proof sheet of Carlyle's about-to-be-pub-
lished *French Revolution,* which he had sent her the week before and now told
her he wanted to show to his Aunt Sarah Alden Ripley:

I think it is somewhat ungracious in you to resume your gift of the proof sheet which
I was about to lay in lavender by the side of that first most appropriate token of your
regard, with which you honored me during my first visit to Concord, to wit the autograph of Jeremy Bentham. To me, as a lady of enthusiasm and taste, such twigs from
the tree of genius, however dry [she was certainly right here about the Bentham
token!], are of course inexpressibly valuable. I shall expect from you, in lieu of the
proof sheet (if you *will* give it to Mrs Ripley) an autograph of Bonaparte, or Metternich or at the very least of Grandison, Cromwell La Fayette [a nickname of Mirabeau mentioned by Carlyle].[72]

With letters went visits. Repeatedly throughout April, Emerson urged Fuller
to come to Concord, saying, in one letter, "My wife will not take No for an

answer." So, on April 26, on her return to Groton, she stopped in Concord and remained there a week. In a letter she wrote to Jane Tuckerman on the day before she left, one can trace the vicissitudes of her emotions. "I am . . . so unwell that I fear I must go home. . . . The excitement of conversation prevents my sleeping." But then, quickly reversing herself, she added, "The wisdom lies in schooling the heart not to expect too much; I did that good thing when I came here, and I am rich." In other words, for now at least, she was willing to accept things as they were, content to bask in the pride of being the Great Man's friend. "On Sunday I drove to Watertown with the Author of '*Nature*,'" she told her young friend, transcendentalizing a bit. "The trees were still bare but the little birds care not for that; they revel, and carol, and wildly tell their hopes, while the gentle, 'voluble' South wind plays with the dry leaves, and the pine-trees sign with their soul-like sounds for June. It was beauteous; and care and routine fled." Inside the house, too, the scene to Fuller seems to have been something of a Transcendental idyll. The Emersons' first child, Waldo Junior, was now six months old, and she described him thus: "The baby here is beautiful. He looks like his father, and smiles so sweetly on all hearty, good people. I play with him a good deal, and he comes so *natural*, after Dante and other poems." From Emerson's papers also, one gets a sense that this was—as far as it went—a harmonious visit. In his journal on the twenty-ninth, he recorded, "Miss Fuller read Vivian Gray & made me very merry." On subsequent days they talked a good deal about Goethe; Fuller even managing, "rather against my will," to give her budding Germanico five or six lessons in German pronunciation, "so that now spite of myself I shall always have to thank her for a great convenience—which she forsaw." If all of this sounds just a bit academic, his comments in his letters were quite a bit less so. To Henry Hedge he wrote two days after she left, "Margaret Fuller has just gone to Groton having spent a few days here—Woman wise!" And to Fuller herself he wrote two weeks later, in reply to some books and letters of friends she had sent: "You are very good to me to send me so many fine things. Certainly there is a bound to bankruptcy. You certify me of great riches and these too of many proprietors, good books, good friends, wit, beauty, art, character, certainly society still exists: the cynics, the ravens must be wrong." Sending him these private letters, of course, hinted at greater intimacy. Whether he was willing to respond in kind was still far from clear.[73]

On May 3, Fuller was back in Groton and quickly set about putting her post–school term affairs in order. Bronson Alcott had given her before she had left Boston several of his journals to read—an honor that, Fuller doubtless was aware, he bestowed on few individuals. In her letter of May 18 sending them back, she sounded, befitting the occasion, just about as solemn and honorific as even Alcott could have wanted. "I thank you for the look you have esteemed me worthy to take into your views and feelings and trust you will never have reason to repent your confidence, as I shall always rejoice in the intercourse which has been permitted me with so fair a soul." But mainly, exhausted and still feeling ill, she was content, as she told Jane Tuckerman, simply to "vegetate beneath her [mother's] sunny kindness for a while." Otherwise, she walked and rode and slept as much as she could, and, as she was (she informed Caroline Sturgis) "in a more receptive state than I have been for years," she had what she called "a grand reading time at home." She also attended to her literary plans. She had managed to do nothing on her "Life of Goethe," but she was now, she told Clarke, "beginning to work in good earnest" on it. Then there were other possibilities. George Ripley was beginning to organize a series of translations of recent French and German Romantic and post-Kantian books. On April 6 he had written to her, eagerly accepting her proposal to translate, as a later volume in the series, the recently published book of Johann Peter Eckermann's conversations with Goethe. ("Did you show Mr Ripley that the translation of Eckermann could be of no mercenary value to translator or bookseller unless done now? before a British comes," the entrepreneurial Emerson reminded her when she was negotiating the agreement.) Even more promising was Ripley's other offer that month to publish her Goethe biography in the same series on what (she later revealed to a friend) were "very advantageous terms."[74]

Both of these projects, though, had one thing in common: they would take time. Meanwhile, she needed money to support herself, not to mention extra cash for her siblings' schooling. Her Boston classes, it is true, were flourishing, but they were not yet large enough, she thought, to be sufficient. Fortunately a more immediate opportunity presented itself in the person of Hiram Fuller. Fuller, not a relative, was a young, enterprising teacher who was then in the process of completing the building of a large private school in Providence, Rhode Island. In the spring, before she had quit the Temple School, he had offered her a teaching position, undoubtedly on the recommendation of Alcott, who had several times praised her to him. Hiram Fuller, in turn, had every reason for taking Alcott's praise seriously: for the past year he had been touting himself in Providence (as Alcott put it happily in his journal) as Alcott's "disciple in the work of Education." (It had been Hiram Fuller whom Alcott had originally tried to hire to replace Peabody before he had met Fuller.) From Fuller's side, Hiram Fuller's offer was also very attractive. He proposed that Fuller teach the older girls "in my own department" of "history, *languages,* literature," she told friends; choosing her own hours and arranging her own courses. For this Fuller had offered to pay her the rather extraordinary sum of one thousand dollars a year—or roughly equal to what Harvard professors got and more than seasoned Boston male teachers and most starting ministers made. (It was also more than three times what a female teacher could usually expect to make.) To what extent this sum came as a result of Margaret Fuller's bargaining is not known. But Elizabeth Peabody, whom she consulted about the job, later claimed that when Hiram Fuller had asked her what salary she would have, she had said, "How much do you give the Governor of your State? A teacher deserves as much." Though he might have thought the governmental rank a bit low, Alcott (who noted in his diary Fuller's proposed salary as "ample beyond former precedent") would have been pleased. Certainly Fuller was pleased, if not with the idea of having to leave Boston, at least with the money and the chance (as she told a friend) for "immediate independence." And so, after a little hesitation, she notified Hiram Fuller in April before returning to Groton that she accepted the offer to teach at his school.[75]

By the end of May, family preparations for Fuller's departure were nearly complete. Richard, though troublesome, was already becoming Margaret's favorite younger child, as he had been his father's. Years later he recalled Margaret's last hours, packing to leave:

> I expressed my thanks to her for her faithful teaching. She replied pleasantly that she hoped it had done us some good in the way of learning how to study, though she did not suppose we remembered much of the textbooks. I endeavored to give her a more encouraging view on the last point by repeating a good deal of grammar to her. She expressed herself thankful that I remembered so much. This was like Father's "praise," and agreeably perpetuated that little interview in my recollection.

This was on the morning of June 1. In the afternoon she took the mail-stage to Concord to spend one last night at the Emersons'. ("Seeing the stage stop this afternoon," Emerson had written expectantly two days before, "I gladly left my corn, threw down my Admiral Vernon's hoe & hastened to receive you—and was much dissatisfied to find it was only some books.") The following morning she left for Boston, where she saw Alcott one last time. ("He looked beautiful and seems well prepared," she told Emerson, alluding to his persecution and basement demotion, "to be the Anaxagoras of the joiner's shop.") The next day, on Saturday the third, she caught the eight A.M. train for Providence.[76]

CHAPTER SEVEN

The Schoolmistress

(1837–1838)

I

Margaret Fuller's first impressions of Providence were not especially happy ones. Feeling both sick and a little homesick, she wrote wistfully to Emerson on June 6, 1837: "Every day I have mentally addressed Concord, dear Concord, haven of repose where headach—vertigo—other *sins* that flesh is heir to cannot long pursue." But she rejoiced, she said, that he was to come on Saturday. "I look forward to your presence as the weary traveller does to the Diamond of the Desert— Flowers will I trust, spring up, but at the present all is too new for my weak head." The occasion of Emerson's coming was the dedication of the new Greene Street School. Originally Hiram Fuller had invited Alcott to give the principal address, but after the furor over his book, Alcott unhappily but self-lessly (and to the relief of his more worldly disciple) bowed out from a fear that any public identification of himself with the new school would harm it. This left Emerson, somewhat reluctantly, he had confessed to Margaret, to be the one "to waft benedictions from Concord." Actually, the address Emerson delivered was neither the conventional benediction nor exactly the "good, genial preachment" Fuller had urged him to bring to cheer her up. Instead, shortly after four in the afternoon on June 10, to the overflow audience jamming the Reverend Frederick A. Farley's Westminster Unitarian Church, with the dual calamities of the persecution of Alcott and the nation's spreading financial panic as barely concealed backdrops, he preached a Transcendental jeremiad. "A desperate conservatism clings with both hands to every dead form in the schools, in the state, in the church. A timid political tithe-paying and churchgoing zeal takes the place of religion. That utter unbelief which is afraid of change, afraid of thought, super-venes." After conjuring up the current cultural paralysis that that unbelief had produced ("At times the land smells with suicide. Young men have no hope. The educated class stand idle in the streets. No man calleth them to labor"), he went on to urge an antidote: scholars and educators must learn "the capital secret of their profession"; namely, the converting of life into truth by showing "the symbolic character of life." Only by teaching this truth, he said, and its corollary "self-trust," could teachers arouse the interior activity of their students and thereby help overcome the present-day torpor that a society without an inner life inevitably bred.[1]

Nowhere is it recorded how the Greene Street School's prospective students and their parents, relatives, and friends reacted to this challenging exhortation. Fuller was certainly pleased with it. "I wish you and Cary could have been here last Saturday," she excitedly wrote to Jane Tuckerman on June 16. "Our schoolhouse was dedicated and Mr. Emerson made the address; it was a noble appeal in behalf of the best interests of culture, and seemingly here was fit occasion." The very next day, however, there appeared in the city's leading newspaper, the *Providence Daily Journal,* a notice of the opening of the school that put Emerson's sermon in a different light. Although praising what he condescendingly called "the intelligible parts of the address," the writer frankly confessed, "There was much of what he said that I could not possibly understand." He had, though, understood enough to be offended. "We cannot join the cry of vulgar *wonderment* at every taunting gibe and sarcasm covertly thrust at existing opinions and institutions. If we cannot understand what ideas a speaker or writer attaches to the simplest words in our mother tongue, we think that calling his discourse 'transcendentalism,' is speaking of it in very mild terms. . . . His friends must try to pardon it, if some persons here in Providence have not yet acquired a taste for Germano-Sartor-Resartus-ism." Undoubtedly alluding to this and perhaps other critical comments she had heard, Fuller wrote to Alcott ten days later a considerably more chastened account of the dedication ceremony. Although she herself was "much cheered and instructed" by them, "Mr Emerson's 'good words' . . . fell, if I may judge from the remarks they called forth, on stony soil."[2]

This disgruntlement over the barrenness of Providence's soil, spiritual and physical, remained a constant in her letters for many months. "I sigh for the country," she lamented to Jane; "I must walk through streets many and long, to get sight of any expanse of green." Indeed, she reported to Alcott, even compared with Boston's surrounding villages, Providence's cultural state was low, "for here is the hostile element of money getting with but little counterpoise." Still, developing her grain metaphor from Matthew, if seed failed to take root in one spot, "the fowl of the air may carry it away to some more propitious clime. And I myself . . . may be that bird." Then, too, being a bird from Boston seems to have had some advantages. The following month, joking to Hedge about the doors that had been opened to her in Providence because of her association with William Ellery Channing, whose cult of female followers Hedge had in the past ridiculed, she wrote flippantly: "I too . . . in this region of *(entres nous)* as complete Philistency as can exist at Bangor am received as a *'female* whom that truly eminent divine' delighteth to honor. That ever such should be my pass-port!!"[3]

Surely Providence was no Boston. On this, certainly most Bostonians would have agreed with Fuller. ("P is not a very spiritual place," Clarke reported Channing's telling him the following year; "it is very moral—which is quite consistent with the absence of all high morality.") Still, it was not exactly a cultural waste-land, either. In fact, in some respects this bustling community of about twenty thousand, whose numbers had almost doubled since 1820, was New England's most progressive city. Certainly, for better or worse (and obviously in Fuller's view, for worse), it was its most industrial one. For the past several decades its rural roads, greenbelts, and seaport smells had been rapidly receding, as nearby cotton mills, woolen factories, and, within the city, sundry manufacturing com-panies came to dominate the landscape. It was also, even more than Boston, a heterogeneous city, containing a sizable and long-time resident black commu-nity; large numbers of factory and free-floating laborers, recently swollen by the building of canals; and, most recently, a rapidly growing influx of Irish Catholic immigrants (derisively called, perhaps even more freely than in Boston, *"Pad-dys"* by the town's class-conscious natives). Politically, like Boston, Providence was predominantly Whig. But Providence Whigs, even more than their generally pro-Irish but antiblack and agrarian-oriented Democratic counterparts, put on a contorted liberal face—aggressively pro–public education and (until the radi-cal "People's Constitution" suffragists polarized the city over the issue three years later) gingerly supportive of extending the state's restrictive suffrage to small-property males. Also competing, often contentiously, with both Whigs and Democrats was a potpourri of middle-class reform movements, ranging from temperance to abolitionism, that abounded in Providence and its sur-rounding towns and that even so staunch a procapitalist Whig newspaper as the *Providence Daily Journal* alternatively reproved and courted.[4]

But Providence's liberal air was mainly generated by its religious culture. Although orthodox influence was stronger than in Boston, it was more than bal-anced by the town's two flourishing Unitarian churches and—unlike Boston—a large and influential Quaker community. But mainly Providence was Baptist, and its Baptism—as one might expect of a town founded by Roger Williams—although evangelical and socially conservative, was also intellectually sophisti-cated. Moderately Arminian in theology, latitudinarian in religious practices, and, like Boston's Unitarians, generally well educated and well-to-do, Provid-ence's Baptists dominated, not only the city's commerce and industry, but also its education and culture, mainly through their control of Brown University, then headed by the educationally reform-minded Francis Wayland. Apart from Brown, it is true, Providence was pretty much a cultural backwater. The Frank-lin Lyceum had been founded six years before, and a new, modest-sized Ath-enaeum with four thousand volumes opened the following July. But there was very little music or art; theater, thanks to evangelical opposition, was virtually nonexistent; and, perhaps worst of all, from the point of view of a young sophis-ticate like Fuller, the city's literary character was largely a provincial version of Boston's. On the other hand, what Providence borrowed it rapidly assimilated; indeed, to some extent, faster than Boston itself. Phrenology, mesmerism, veg-etarianism, even (the *Journal*'s review to the contrary), Transcendentalism—cults that were looked upon by Boston's cultural establishment as either vulgar, dangerous, or ridiculous—found wide acceptance, as Fuller was soon to dis-cover, among the city's literary elite.[5]

1. Timothy Fuller, oil portrait by an unknown artist, 1820s.
(Courtesy of Willard P. Fuller, Jr.)

2. Margaret Crane Fuller, daguerreotype, early 1840s.
(Courtesy of Willard P. Fuller, Jr.)

3. *Fuller family, daguerreotype, ca. 1853–1855.* Standing, left to right: *Eugene Fuller and Margarett Crane Fuller.* Sitting, left to right: *Richard Fuller, Ellen Fuller Channing, and Arthur Fuller.* (Courtesy of Willard P. Fuller, Jr.)

4. An 1862 photograph of Arthur Fuller posed in his uniform of Union chaplain of the Sixteenth Regiment of Massachusetts Volunteers. (Courtesy of Willard P. Fuller, Jr.)

5. Richard Fuller, photograph taken a few years before his death in 1869. (Courtesy of Willard P. Fuller, Jr.)

6. Cambridge Common from the Seat of Caleb Gannett Esqr., *watercolor painted by D. Bell in 1809, the year before Margaret Fuller's birth. This view looking south over the Common shows Harvard College on the left, the First Parish Meetinghouse at the far center, and on the right, two buildings to the right of the Court House's cupola and barely visible behind a row of trees, the Fullers' later Brattle House.* (Courtesy of the Harvard University Archives)

7. View of Cambridge, *lithograph drawn by James Kidder, ca. 1830. This closeup view of the First Parish Meetinghouse and the Village (as the Harvard Square area was then called) shows the continuing bucolic appearance of the town in Margaret Fuller's last youthful years there.* (Courtesy of the Boston Athenaeum)

8. *The Fuller family house on Cherry Street in Cambridgeport, photograph, ca. 1924. The porches were added in the mid–nineteenth century. The three elms planted by Margaret's father were cut down in the 1890s. After devolving into tenements in the late nineteenth century, the structure became in 1902 a settlement house, which it remains today under the name of the Margaret Fuller Neighborhood House.* (Courtesy of the Cambridge Historical Commission)

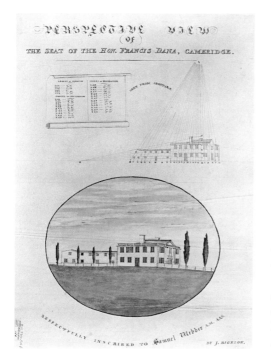

9. Perspective View of the Seat of the Hon. Francis Dana. *Drawing made in 1806 by Jacob Bigelow for his Harvard College mathematical thesis, of the Dana Hill mansion, which the Fullers owned and lived in from 1826 to 1831. The house was destroyed by a fire in 1839.* (Courtesy of the Harvard University Archives)

10. *A 1937 photograph of the Brattle house, which the Fullers occupied for their last year and a half in Cambridge. Shorn of its extensive and elaborately landscaped grounds, the house is the current home of the Cambridge Center for Adult Education.* (Courtesy of the Library of Congress)

11. *Drawing of Margaret Fuller by James Freeman Clarke, ca. 1830–1832. James Freeman Clarke, "Scrapbook of Pictures & Drawings," 1840, James Freeman Clarke Papers, Houghton Library, Harvard University.* (Courtesy of the Houghton Library, Harvard University)

12. *Drawing of James Freeman Clarke by Sarah Clarke, ca. 1838–1840. James Freeman Clarke, "Journal," 1838–1840, James Freeman Clarke Papers, Houghton Library, Harvard University.* (Courtesy of the Houghton Library, Harvard University)

13. James Freeman Clarke, photograph, early 1860s, made around the time he was serving as the general secretary of the American Unitarian Association. (Courtesy of the Unitarian Universalist Association)

14. Photograph of Frederic Henry Hedge by John A. Whipple, taken in the early 1860s, while Hedge was a professor of ecclesiastical history at Harvard Divinity School. (Courtesy of the Unitarian Universalist Association)

15. The Fullers' house in Groton, Massachusetts, photograph, 1902. The two wings were added in the 1890s. (Courtesy of the Groton Historical Society)

16. *Harriet Martineau, oil portrait by Charles Osgood, 1836, painted a few months after she met Margaret Fuller.* (Courtesy of the Essex Institute, Salem, Mass.)

17. *William Ellery Channing, oil portrait by Spiradone Gambardella, 1838.* (Courtesy of the Harvard University Art Museums)

18. *Ralph Waldo Emerson,*
daguerreotype, taken for Thomas
Carlyle in 1848, when Emerson
was lecturing in England.
(Courtesy of the Houghton
Library, Harvard University)

19. *Amos Bronson Alcott,*
daguerreotype, mid-1850s.
(Courtesy of the Louisa May
Alcott Memorial Association)

20. *The Masonic Temple on the corner of Tremont Street at Temple Place, photograph, ca. 1885. This was the site of Bronson Alcott's Temple School as well as many lectures of Ralph Waldo Emerson, Orestes Brownson, Theodore Parker, and other Transcendentalists.* (Courtesy of the Boston Public Library)

21. A. Bronson Alcott's School of Human Culture, *drawing by Francis Graeter, the Temple School's drawing master, late 1830s.* (Courtesy of the Houghton Library, Harvard University)

22. *The Greene Street School, Providence, lithograph, 1837.* (Courtesy of the Rhode Island Historical Society)

23. Caroline Sturgis Tappan, daguerreotype by Southworth and Hawes, ca. 1850, about three years after her marriage to William Aspinwall Tappan. (Courtesy of the International Museum of Photography at the George Eastman House, Rochester, N.Y.)

24. Samuel Gray Ward, salt print photograph made in 1855, five years after he assumed his father's position as the American agent for Baring Brothers. (Courtesy of the Boston Athenaeum)

25. Anna Barker Ward, oil portrait by William Morris Hunt, 1861. (Courtesy of John H. Mansfield, Mary Mansfield-Post, Charlotte Murphy, and Diana Russell; and the Department of Special Collections, the University of California, Santa Barbara Library)

26. West Street, Boston, photograph taken in the late 1860s, from the Tremont Street end, looking away from the Common. Elizabeth Peabody's bookstore and residence at Number 13, where Margaret Fuller held her Conversations, appears towards the end of the left-hand block. (Courtesy of the Bostonian Society, Old State House)

27. Elizabeth Peabody, photograph by Frederic Gutekunst, late 1850s. (Courtesy of the Schlesinger Library, Radcliffe College)

28. *William Henry Channing, photograph by Henry Ulke, ca. 1861–1864, taken around the time Channing was serving as a minister in Washington, D.C., and chaplain of the United States House of Representatives.* (Courtesy of the Unitarian Universalist Association)

29. *Theodore Parker, daguerreotype, early 1840s.* (Courtesy of the Boston Athenaeum.)

30. Margaret Fuller, early 1850s Southworth and Hawes daguerreotype copy of an unrecovered daguerreotype by John Plumbe made in July 1846, one month before she sailed for England on assignment for the New-York Tribune. *This is the only surviving photograph of Fuller.* (Courtesy of Museum of Fine Arts, Boston)

Providence's most important new progressive institution, though, was the Greene Street School itself. Actually, Hiram Fuller, the school's principal, would soon dramatically abandon the spirit of his avant-garde youth. Six years later, having sold his school and then his bookstore, he would move to New York, marry a wealthy heiress, and take over from George P. Morris and Nathaniel P. Willis their lively Cockney-conservative *New York Mirror,* which for fourteen years he would bring out as a daily newspaper, gleefully mixing partisan Whiggism, cultural gossip, and literary scandal-mongering. From this point his rough-and-tumble, genteel conservatism would take a more disastrously eccentric turn. Acting on his anti–"Black Republican" politics, as soon as the Civil War broke out, he would go to London, where he would start an anti–free suffrage, pro-Southern newspaper called (with unintended irony) *The Cosmopolitan.* Having lost virtually all his American friends and readers, he would remain in Europe, eventually working in Paris, where he would die, a forgotten freelance newspaperman.[6]

But this was in the future. At this stage of his life, the energetic Hiram Fuller was working frenetically to succeed as an innovative educational reformer. Born in Halifax, Nova Scotia, raised as an only child since the age of seven (when in one week all three of his siblings died), educated at Andover, and teaching school since he was sixteen, he had come to Providence the year before and, although only twenty-two years old, he had managed to persuade a group of influential merchants and professional men to subscribe ten thousand dollars to build him the Greene Street School. The curriculum he offered in his school was fairly standard. But his perfectionist philosophy and also some of his materials and pedagogy marked him as the disciple of Bronson Alcott he claimed himself to be. ("We must write in our journals," one student reported, "that 'our capacities are infinite—we may be, what we will be.'") Mornings usually began with Fuller reading to the assembled students a passage of Scripture followed by a parallel excerpt from Wordsworth, Coleridge, Carlyle, or some popular sentimental writer like Felicia Hemans or Martin Tupper, often followed by a "sacred" passage from Alcott's *Conversations on the Gospels.* Other notable Alcottian features that he instituted at the school were the keeping of personal journals, which he sometimes read aloud at student assemblies, and—in place of physical punishment—an array of "anti-excitement" classes and techniques intended to awaken his pupils' consciences. (One ploy he regularly tried was to announce at morning assemblies that he wanted all students who knew they were guilty of "communicating" during class to stay after school.) On the other hand, Hiram Fuller was a pretty relaxed Alcottian. Despite his pious assurance to Alcott that he was "a steadfast believer in spiritual culture," his students' journals show he had no interest in introducing Alcott's philosophically probing conversations. In place of these Fuller stressed (some even conscientious students thought overstressed) the decidedly less spiritual matters of attractive dressing and refined manners. Whenever Greene Street boys encountered their classmates in the streets—according to one student's account of one of their principal's talks on "politeness"—"Mr Fuller" requested that they not recognize them "by a broad grin" or "take off their hats like the country boys," but give "a bow" or "touch their hats gracefully." Clearly, Transcendental soul mingled with high bourgeois manners at the Greene Street School.[7]

In one respect Hiram Fuller's school did fully live up to and even surpass its original—namely, in its physical appearance. When he returned from Providence, Emerson reported to Alcott that Fuller's schoolhouse was "one of the best in the U.S." Indeed, Fuller's mentor ought to have been impressed: by all accounts, it looked as though it had been designed by a flush Alcott (as perhaps Fuller, who had gotten advice from Alcott about schoolroom design, intended it to look). The building—behind a fenced lot on the corner of Greene and Washington streets in Providence's business district—was fashioned in Greek Revival style, complete with six tall, heavy, fluted Doric columns supporting a spacious front veranda. Inside, the wide, carved front door opened to the entryway, on either side of which were the boys' and girls' dressing rooms. Once properly dressed (the boys were required to remove their shoes and put on slippers before entering), the hundred-and-fifty or so boys and girls entered through separate doors ("so they need never and do never romp or interfere," Margaret explained to her brother Arthur) into a large, orange-brown carpeted hall of white walls finished in pink and a high ceiling arched in the center. On one of these walls, prominently displayed, hung a card bearing the words "Order is Heaven's first law," the school's motto. Along the sides of the hall were sofas for visitors and assistant teachers, two recitation rooms (the primary children's rooms were in the basement), and, between the entryway doors, draped by "a neat French cloak," a piano. At the rear of the main room, on a raised platform, facing two rows each of velvet-covered black and brown desks, signifying the separately seated boys and girls, was the principal's chair and study table decorated with flowers and vases as well as (one wide-eyed female visitor noted) four "elegant cut-glass" goblets and "a handsome urn" for the students' drinking water. (Fuller merrily denied to his assembled students the local rumors that all the doorknobs were made of gold.) Behind the desk was the school's library of standard authors in a bookcase topped by a bust of Sir Walter Scott. Here and there, for inspiration, as in Alcott's school, were placed various casts and pictures, including, in place of the bust of Plato, a portrait of the eccentric, putatively Byronic, Connecticut Romantic poet James Gates Percival, and, over the piano, a large portrait of the founder himself.[8]

The pains the Greene Street School's principal took in fashioning an aesthetic environment did not go unappreciated by his new assistant. "Beautiful, and furnished with an even elegant propriety," she contentedly described the school's building in her letter to Jane Tuckerman. The school's dress code also attracted her. "Some people object to us that rather too much ambition about appearance is encouraged," she told her brother Arthur, "but if they lived there they would like the comfort of dealing with neat well dressed people as well as we do." Toward her new colleagues she contrived to be, if not quite so satisfied, at least cordial. One was the twenty-one-year-old primary school head Frances Aborn, who also taught arithmetic ("very pleasant though not remarkably handsome," one student quipped). Another was Georgianna Nias, a young, French-educated, Unitarian Englishwoman. Nias had recently separated from her British naval officer husband, and taught drawing, dancing, and French. (*"Beautiful,"* "refined," and *"kind,"* several students exulted to their families; "she has perfect manners—no one more graceful ever existed.") Fuller boarded with these women at Frances Aborn's mother's house (which she portrayed to Caroline Sturgis as clean, but small and *"dingy"*), sharing the home with three Aborn grandchildren, their parents, and Nias's three little boys and young female ward. Fortunately she liked the children, Nias's ward recalled, and she seems to have found the situation at least tolerable. One male former student thought Fuller treated her female colleagues at school "in a queenly, condescending way." ("Why, Mrs. Nias, *you* would have been worth educating," he recalled Fuller once snapped, after Nias made "a particularly bright remark.") But Fuller's letters, anyway, show little of this. "They are kindhearted but ordinary people," she described the Aborns to Caroline Sturgis, "quiet [and] unobtrusive." To Clarke she even boasted that her two colleagues "compare very favorably with those who have reputation in Boston," singling out for particular praise Mrs. Nias's "elegant" manners and "knowledge of the little arts which are known in polished society." ("So few Amern ladies had been educated with those exact and refined habits that Engh ladies are.") Regarding Hiram Fuller himself, Fuller was more ambivalent. "Mr F's is a living influence, (which can be said of few teachers)," she would later report to Clarke. But in her letter to Alcott on June 27 she gave this more measured opinion of her new principal: "Mr. Fuller is in many respects particularly suited to this business. His ready sympathy, his active eye, and pious, tender turn of thought are so adapted to all the practical part; The danger arising from that sort of education which has unfolded there is that he may not be sufficiently systematic and not observe due gradation and completeness in his plans." (She was not the only one to detect this superficiality. After he returned from Providence, Emerson recorded in his journal that Alcott's young disciple had explained to him his plans, "'that he was to keep the school 5 years—income so much; outlay so much; then he should be able to go to Europe; &c, &c.' When I repeated all this to Alcott, he expressed chagrin & contempt.") Yet, having experienced the consequences of Alcott's unbusinesslike attitudes, Fuller could at least appreciate a principal who could meet his payroll. On July 8, to Alcott's other former unpaid assistant, Elizabeth Peabody—who knew precisely what she was talking about—she wrote succinctly: "Mr. Fuller is as unlike as possible to Mr. Alcott. He has neither his poetic beauty nor his practical defects."[9]

Of course the soul of an Alcottian school ought to have been its students. Unfortunately the Greene Street's student body seemed to Fuller not very healthy. "The gulf is vast," she wrote in her journal after meeting her first classes, "wider than I could have conceived possible, between me and my pupils." One problem might have been age: instead of just "maidens," whom she had taught in Boston and had expected to teach at Greene Street, her sixty students ranged (as was typical of most academies that included girls) from eighteen-to-twenty-year-old young women down to ten-year-old boys and girls. She herself, however, put the blame for the students' "deplorable ignorance" and the "absolute burial of the best powers" squarely on their training. Indeed, teaching these students—who mostly came from well-educated Unitarian and Baptist professional and mercantile families in Providence and a few small towns in Massachusetts and Rhode Island—made her realize, she wrote in her journal, "better than before, how a man as Mr. Alcott could devote his life to renovate elementary education." It also made her appreciate anew her former principal's Socratic educational ideas. "There were details in which I thought your plan imperfect," she frankly told him in her letter of June 27:

> but it only needs to compare pupils who have been treated as many of these have with those who have been under your care to sympathize with your creed that those who would reform the world should begin with the beginning of life— Particularly do I feel the importance of your attempts to teach the uses of language and cultivate the imagination in dealing with young persons who have had no faculties exercised except the memory and the common, practical understanding. In *your* children I found an impatience of labor but a liveliness of mind, in many of *these* with well-disposed hearts, [the] mind has been absolutely torpid.

Granted there was a need—but did she think she could fill it? Her letters show that for a while she was pretty doubtful. "I . . . completed my *sacrifices* for the day," she wrote to Hedge with doubled-edged sarcasm a couple of weeks later, after one morning's teaching at "our temple." To the more enterprising Emerson she wrote a little more expansively: "There is room here, if I mistake not, for a great move in the cause of education, but whether it is I who am to help move, I cannot yet tell." Meanwhile, she announced to her Concord friend her own rationalistic version of an Alcottian program: "Activity of mind, accuracy in processes, constant looking for principles, and search after the good and beautiful, 'that's the ground I go upon' as Mr S says in Vivian Gray, and many of those who have never studied any thing but words seem much pleased with their new prospects."[10]

Eventually these breezy, bet-hedging commitments gave way to ever more confident ones. No doubt helping, whether as cause or effect, was her first "glow of returning health" since her father had died, allowing her (with Emerson's anxious encouragement) to leave off the opium she had been taking for her headaches. She also divided her sprawling Latin class into three grades. Finally she began to settle into a routine, which she described to her brother Arthur: up at four-thirty or five, reading and writing until breakfast at seven-thirty, at the school at eight-thirty (generally the principal's assembly began at nine and Fuller taught until one), then a couple hours for dinner and rest, more study or writing until teatime in the early evening, followed by a walk or visits until ten, and in bed by eleven. ("So I live very rationally.") The courses she taught that first term, in addition to Latin, were composition, elocution, and history, plus two classes in natural history and one in ethics; to this she added, the following semester, classes in French, rhetoric, and English poetry. Although she taught most of these classes only a couple of days a week, this was a considerably heavier load than the strictly history-and-literature one she had originally told friends Hiram Fuller had proposed to her. Yet, like her students' ages, it was fairly typical for academy teaching. In any case, it does not seem to have daunted her much. "My school lessons require no preparation," she assured her brother in her letter of July 5, and "are so distributed as not to fatigue me at all." Indeed, writing about her school to Elizabeth Peabody three days later, she sounded almost buoyant. "I feel so perfectly equal to all I do there, without any effort; my pupils, although miserably prepared, are very docile, their hearts are right, and I already perceive that I am producing some effect on their heads." She was particularly pleased, she told her brother, with the effect that the students' journals were having on their "power of expression," even on that of her "inferior" boys. "Last week some of theirs were read aloud to the school, though without mentioning the names of the writers. The journal of one boy who spoke of the girls as 'sweet sisters' and 'fair *as Eden's garden birds*' excited a general *smile.* We are too refined to laugh loud at the Greene St School!!" Docility and self-control—as well as imagination and head-hardening discipline—had for Fuller the teacher their charms.[11]

As teaching took up only four hours a day, this left her with (as she gloated to Peabody) "much time" to pursue her own interests. One of these was her by now well-ingrained fascination with public oratory. On August 9 she attended at the Old Town House the state Whig caucus, where she heard State Representative John Whipple and Rhode Island's most popular orator, the former Brown oratory professor and congressman Tristam Burges, speak on behalf of their party's slate of congressional candidates. Even in these years of growing popular involvement in electoral politics, it was highly unusual for a woman to attend a political convention, which is probably why she had some difficulty getting admitted. ("Mr. Farley went with me and helped me through some nonsense which lay in the way," she wrote in her journal. "I like a man who will walk with me over straws, on sticks if need be.") It was also probably why, to the socially conservative Whig Hiram Fuller—who lectured his students five days after the event "a great deal" (reported one girl) about the charms of ladies' "blushes"— her attendance was (as she wrote to Emerson that same day) "somewhat to [his] horror." Actually, her journal comments afterward showed her main interest, as usual, was not in the speakers' politics, but in their "manner." And even here, although giving them points for their oratorical tricks, she thought their "ornate" style put them a cut below "the Webster class." ("The man extending his sinewy arm over his family," she wrote of one Whipple Whiggish "faux pas," "gave . . . an absurd picture.") Still, she obviously savored her little rebellion in Providence. She told Emerson, with perhaps a touch of irony, "It is rather the best thing I have done."[12]

II

August was commencement month, and the Greene Street School marked the occasion by closing for three weeks after the eighteenth. As closing time approached, Fuller began to reconsider her situation at Providence and, in letters to Emerson, communicate her misgivings. The month before, in reply to her letter of July 3 describing her difficulties adjusting to school teaching, he had answered, "Power and Aim, the two halves of felicity seldomest meet." He had added that this lack of "work commensurate with [one's] faculty" seemed to be especially the malady of their own day, "for you cannot talk with any intelligent company without presently hearing expressions of regret & impatience whose scope affects the whole order of *good* institutions." Meanwhile, he told her, while awaiting that "revolution & regeneration" which, he said, was sure to come and "fetch us somewhat to do," there always remained "Ethics": "To feel & be heroic, is surely doing something, and is putting the capital of our being at rent in a bank that can not break, though its ostensible dividends may be far reversions. So let us deal justly walk humbly, and all the catechism." Unfortunately, as was often the case when Emerson preached his heroic-prudent message to Fuller directly, it fell on somewhat skeptical ears. "I have been in an irreligious state of mind," she answered him on August 14; "a little misanthropic and sceptical about the existence of any real communication between human beings. I bear constantly in heart that text of yours '*O my friends,* there are no friends' but to me it is a paralyzing conviction. Surely we are very unlike the Gods in 'their seats of eternal tranquility' that we need illusions so much to keep us in action." The point seemed to be that—unlike her Olympian friend who happily quoted the skeptical Montaigne—she *needed* such social "illusions," and Providence was not giving her any. She also complained—in sharp contrast to her boasts of the month before—about her shortage of time for her reading and writing. "If I cannot be differently situated," she told him flatly, "I *must* leave Providence at the end of another term." Yet—and this was still obviously the important point—she regretted nothing of even the "petty annoyances" of her job. "They have so enlarged my practical knowledge. I now begin to feel myself a citizen of the world." With these mixed feelings about her little world, she left it to visit, as she laughingly called them, her "dear *no friends,* Mr and Mrs Emerson," who had invited her to come and commune with them in Concord.[13]

Before arriving there, however, she made, as she usually did when away from Groton or Providence, numerous social calls along the way. Leaving Providence on August 19, she visited friends in Kingston, Boston, and Lowell, spent several days with her family in Groton, and from there circled back with her brother Eugene for an important event on the thirty-first in Cambridge. There, at a little after noon, in the crowded meetinghouse across from Harvard Yard, and in the company of Governor Everett, President Quincy, the faculty, and several hundred students, alumni, and distinguished guests of the college's Phi Beta Kappa Society, she heard, together with her protégées Jane Tuckerman and Caroline Sturgis, her spiritual advisor Emerson deliver his memorable oration, later titled "The American Scholar." In Providence, Emerson had addressed the torpor of the times. Here, to a far more elite audience, he called more specifically and more positively for a revolution in American intellectual culture. Directly attacking the traditional Unitarian idea of the scholar as complacent conservator of past knowledge and known truths, genteelly plying his bookish trade—an idea that had, he thought, made American intellectual life timid and decorous as well as reinforced the intellectual's social impotence—Emerson urged instead the idea of *"Man Thinking":* a scholar for whom books, practical action, human feelings—even "the common" and "the low"—would all be grist for his intellectual mill. And, as he had in Providence, he urged that at the bottom of this program lay the individual scholar's "self-trust" and disdain for the popular fashions of the moment. Indeed, it was the absence of such a faith, he thought, that explained the central social phenomenon of the times: "Young men of the fairest promise," feeling torn between careers in business, whose mere money-getting principles disgusted them, and an intellectual life that seemed merely "decent, indolent, complaisant," either turned into "drudges" or in some cases, dying of disgust, committed suicide. Instead, the young American intellectual should be taught that "he and he only knows the world," that "the world of any moment is the merest appearance," and that, therefore, "in going down into the secrets of his own mind he has descended into the secrets of all minds." With this double perspective, and its faith that "the huge world," or at least its better part, would eventually "come round to him," he declared that, not only intellectual life, but cultural life as a whole could be transformed: "A nation of men will for the first time exist, because each believes himself inspired by the Divine Soul which also inspires all men."[14]

Also hearing Emerson's message that day were Bronson Alcott, Henry Hedge, Elizabeth Hoar, and others of the orator's friends, who served to counter (in Alcott's words) "the mixed confusion, consternation, surprise, and wonder" of some who were present. What Fuller thought of this address is nowhere recorded. But its main themes ought to have been familiar enough, for they were, in practical terms, almost identical to the ones Emerson had recently been preaching in his Boston lectures and privately to her in his letters: the virtues of lonely introspection, self-reliance, and independent vocational commitment. For intellectual young people coming of age in a new and turbulent culture— where traditional vocations like the ministry were somewhat on the decline and newer, more problematically entrepreneurial and popular-minded ones like lecturing and magazine-writing were on the rise—it was a wonderfully true, complex, and heady message. Sarah Clarke, who attributed her decision to put aside her worries about "duty" and commit herself to an art career partly to Emerson's preachments to "satisfy the wants of your own soul" and follow one's vocational instincts regardless of "the prejudices of society" (as she summarized a couple of his lectures), told her brother James that winter, "His discourses are like diamonds." So they seemed—despite her grumblings about the private version of them that Emerson preached to her—to Fuller. The pungent, lyrical style, of course, captivated her. ("Mr Emerson . . . glides through a whole scale of notes by gradation," she told Clarke when he visited her in Providence the following month.) But so, too, clearly did the content. A few years later she would write to her close friend William Henry Channing, who was somewhat skeptical regarding Emerson:

> You question me as to the nature of the benefits conferred upon me by Mr. E.'s preaching. I answer, that his influence has been more beneficial to me than that of any American, and that from him I first learned what is meant by an inward life. Many other springs have since fed the stream of living waters, but he first opened the fountain. That the 'mind is its own place,' was a dead phrase to me, till he cast light upon my mind. Several of his sermons stand apart in memory, like landmarks of my spiritual history. It would take a volume to tell what this one influence did for me.[15]

Following the postprogram dinner on the commons—at which Oliver Wendell Holmes entertained with a song and Governor Everett honored his now-famous former student with a flattering toast—Fuller returned with the Emersons to Concord. There they had their usual talk, high and low. ("Margaret Fuller talking of Women, said," Emerson recorded happily in his journal, "'Who would be a goody that could be a genius?'") There the next day she also experienced something new: she attended, along with Elizabeth Hoar and Emerson's learned step-aunt Sarah Alden Ripley, her first meeting of the year-old Transcendental Club. Emerson had hinted at the change when he had invited her to Concord two weeks before. While not promising anything ("I will not certainly engage for them to break down any rules or expectations"), he had slyly added, "Who knows but the wise men in an hour more timid or more gracious may crave the aid of wise & blessed women at their session." And so, at a meeting called to discuss "the progress of Society," for the first time in American history, were women admitted to a major male intellectual society. Actually, the meeting was only one event in what Lidian Emerson, who oversaw the feeding of the seventeen participants, described as an "all-day party." On September 6, Fuller attended another meeting of the Club, this time at Clarke's mother's house in Newton, where again women attended—in addition to Fuller, this time Sarah Clarke and Elizabeth Peabody. The Transcendental Club's gender revolution, however, proved to be something of a false start. Although women would be invited and Elizabeth Peabody would attend a couple of more meetings, for its last years the Club would remain in its gender composition almost where it began—a circle of men plus Margaret Fuller.[16]

Besides integrating the Transcendental Club, Fuller also confronted while she was in Concord a more private—and contentious—gender challenge. The issue was the perennial Fuller subject of schooling. This had not been a problem as long as Margaret had been willing to serve as family tutor. But now that she had relinquished that role, things were more complicated. So, trying to balance the children's needs for secondary instruction, the family's tight budget, and her own need for a career, before she had left for Providence, Margaret and her mother had marked out a family school plan: Arthur would finish up at Leicester in the winter; Richard, while waiting his turn at school, was to stay with their mother on the farm while being tutored by a Groton schoolmaster; Lloyd (who "needs a man's control," his mother thought) was to be put under the care of "a good master" in Stoughton; and Ellen would continue for another term or so at "a good school in Boston" where she could be prepared—in case she should be, as her mother delicately put it, "under the necessity to keep school"—in both "some of the ornamental as well as solid branches." That summer, however, when Margaret's mother asked Abraham for a dispersal of funds to put the plan into effect, the wealthy, self-taught bachelor balked: the expense was needless, he told her, because the boys could go to the local school in Groton while they "earn[ed] their bread" helping her on the farm, and Ellen could simply start teaching now. Worse yet, his letter (according to Margaret's mother) was painfully "severe." Abraham brusquely taunted her for her lack of "good sense" and even had the characteristic effrontery to suggest that she was forgetting both her husband's wishes and his own right, as the children's legal guardian, to have the final say in the matter.[17]

After hesitating a couple days ("to feel calm," she told him), Margaret's mother wrote two letters—an explicit but tremulous one to Abraham, outlining why the children needed more than their "superficial" Groton schoolmaster's instruction if they were ever to have decent careers and begging him to approve the plan, and a frightened one to Margaret telling her of Abraham's taunts. Although in the past, Margaret, like her mother, had always treated her uncle with great deference in dealing with him about family financial matters, Margaret this time fired back from Emerson's house a scathing letter. "Do not," she began heatedly, "suffer the remarks of that sordid man to give you any uneasiness— Proceed to act as we agreed when I was with you. It is perfectly clear to my mind that the arrangements we then made are the right ones and I do not fear to hold myself responsible for the consequences." As for Uncle Abraham, she angrily added, "if [he] continues to annoy you in this manner," fire him. "We pay Abraham and we could as well pay another man who would confine himself to his proper post of managing the money. You must, my dear Mother," she implored, "steadily consider yourself as the guardian of the children. You must not let his vulgar insults make you waver as to giving the children advantages to which they would be well entitled if the property were only a third of what it now is." As to Abraham's taunts and veiled threats, "Do not suffer yourself to be puzzled or scared by such stuff," she said. "No Judge in the world will ever interfere with your management of the minor children unless we who are of age request it, as you are well aware we never shall." So, having bolstered her mother's legal authority (and it should be noted that conflicts between guardians and widowed mothers were not *always* decided in the latter's favor), once again she said, for the benefit of her goodhearted but scared mother, stick with the plan: fit out *all* the children for school, and do not forget Lloyd and Ellen. If necessary, she said, she would pay for Ellen herself, either by taking an extra private class or letting her have *her* share of the estate's income or even capital. In the meantime, she added, if it came to this, she would "put the affair into the hands of a lawyer: we will see if she is not to have a year's schooling from twelve to eighteen. I am not angry but I am determined. I am sure that my Father, if he could see me, would approve the view I take." In sum, she told her mother, be firm, "trust your daughter," and, above all, "pay no attention to the thoughts of your low-minded brother in law."[18]

As it turned out, she did not have to pay attention. Abraham reluctantly gave in, and by the next winter all the children except for Richard, who was held back to manage the farm for another year, continued at their private schools, paid for by money from the estate. But Margaret's intervention came with a price: when Abraham died ten years later while she was in dire financial straits in Italy, she was disgusted to discover that he had cut her mother "off without a shilling" and Margaret herself with only a tiny bequest. She was convinced that she understood the motives for this act. "My uncle . . . wished to see me fail," she complained bitterly to a friend, "because I acted against his opinion in giving my family advantages he thought, with his narrow views, useless, and defended my mother against his rude tyranny." It was a high price to pay for insisting on a perfectly ordinary male middle-class prerogative—pursuing a career while protecting the interests of the children for whom she was responsible. For Fuller the family woman, Emersonian self-reliance did not come easily.[19]

III

After her week with the Emersons, Fuller returned to Providence and resumed her teaching on September 11. Meanwhile she began to solve at least two of the problems she had complained to Emerson about the previous month. First, she stopped anguishing about whether or not to leave Providence and finally (she told Caroline Sturgis) "made up my mind to stay." Second, she discovered, if not "real communication" in Providence, at least a coterie. Actually, the Coliseum Club, which she began attending on October 18, was somewhat broader than a coterie. Organized two years before, it boasted among its forty or so members virtually every writer or literary amateur in the city and, among its guests, nearly every author who passed through. Nor was it exactly a bohemian enclave. Its members were overwhelmingly old-Providence-family Whig. Most of them were Unitarian lawyers, physicians, professors, ministers, schoolmistresses, female writers, and literary-minded matrons. As one might expect, their object was standard literary club fare—to display wit and "develope mind." The papers they gave at their biweekly meetings were likewise pretty conventional. Most of them (as they appear in their secretary's transcriptions) were on English literary or light manners-and-morals subjects, conveyed in invariably earnest, uplifting, or studiously humorous tones.[20]

Still, despite its composition and topics, the Club was not wholly a genteel affair. For one thing, its records show that members appreciated lively criticism and debate. But mainly, some of its members were interesting. The central figure was Albert G. Greene, a lawyer and later municipal court judge whose droll humor and affable manner, homespun "Yankee"-minded poems, scholarly habits, and staggering library (its twenty thousand volumes served as the early basis of the Harris Collection in American poetry at Brown) helped to set much of the tone of the circle. Other prominent men inlcuced the dilettante and poet

William J. Pabodie, a friend of Edgar Allan Poe, the German translator and Newport Unitarian minister Charles Timothy Brooks, Providence's two philanthropic Unitarian ministers Edward Brooks Hall and Frederick Augustus Farley, the conservative Whig legislator John Whipple, and—certainly the most politically radical member—Thomas W. Dorr, the later extralegal governor and principal leader of Rhode Island's ill-fated prosuffrage "People's Constitution" insurrection. Perhaps the most culturally interesting members were women, who constituted about half the Club's membership. Although most of them were the wives and daughters of prominent Whig politicians, professionals, or manufacturers, a good many were teachers like Sarah Jacobs, who would succeed Fuller at the Greene Street School, or the wives of prominent Providence reform leaders. Three of them—Lucinda Larned, Julia Curtis, and Eleanor Burrill Burges—had sons or nephews who would later join the Transcendentalists' Brook Farm or Fruitlands communities. Furthermore, four single women in the Coliseum actively promoted and popularized Transcendentalist notions and writings in their books and articles: the widow Rhoda Newcomb; Sarah Helen Whitman, a poet, critic, zealous Dorrite, and later fiancée of Edgar Allan Poe; the sentimental novelist Frances Harriet Whipple; and Ann Lynch, the later hostess of nineteenth-century New York's most famous literary salon. Indeed, these women, along with a fair number of their male colleagues, made up a circle friendlier to Transcendentalist sentiments than probably any outside of eastern Massachusetts.

One might have expected that so many culturally congenial literati would have entirely reconciled Fuller to Providence, but they did not. Her chief complaint was they were too *much* of a coterie. "Your circle at P is too narrow and you are too close together and jostle too often," she would later grumble to Sarah Helen Whitman, after Whitman relayed some unpleasant gossip about one of their members. "I used to be much annoyed while there by habits of minute scrutiny unknown in wider circles." Of course narrowness and "busy, prying" ingrowth are relative things. (Henry Adams would later say precisely the same thing about Fuller's Boston!) Also she seems to have enjoyed, at least somewhat, reading the word to these provincial aesthetes. Describing herself reading one evening later that winter "the most daring passages in Faust to a coterie of Hannah Mores," she confessed to Caroline, "I grow impatient and domineering— my liberty here will spoil my tact for the primmer timider sphere." But mainly, except for the anti-Transcendentalist Pabodie, her letters show she enjoyed the company of these Coliseumites. ("A supper, twenty gentlemen, and novels in the library!" she exulted to Greene, rubbing her hands together in contemplation of one soirée.) Besides Greene, she particularly liked and cultivated, among the men, Hall and Farley, and among the women, Whitman and (although she sometimes found her "nimbl[e]," strong-willed personality trying) Newcomb. These Coliseum friends, in turn, Whitman recalled, although a little put off by Fuller's "intellectual arrogance," were simply "dazzle[d]" by her. As well they should have been. Even apart from her own talents, she was, after all, an intimate friend and colleague of the increasingly famous Transcendentalists whom many

of them revered. Moreover, for intellectual women like Whitman and Newcomb, she was a valuable role model. "That Lady has a most extraordinary
mind," the aggressive Newcomb exclaimed admiringly to her son Charles after
hearing Fuller lecture at a Coliseum meeting. "She has been educated like a
man—but is very feminine in feelings—and so independent, that she makes
many enemies." Nor did these Coliseum members' appreciation of Fuller cease
after she left Providence. Despite their occasional spats with her, Whitman and
Newcomb remained her friends and supporters for many years, and Greene
showed *his* admiration by naming his fourth daughter Sarah Margaret Fuller
Greene. Indeed, Emerson, who frequently lectured in the city and himself had a
large following there, reported that he had heard that one return of hers after a
brief visit out of town "was a kind of ovation." This kind of homage even a
young, would-be cosmopolitan like Fuller could not easily have ignored.[21]

Besides giving Fuller her first following, the Coliseum Club and its guests gave
her her first taste of intellectual types outside the familiar Boston mold. That
October she went to hear her Coliseum colleague and the First Baptist Church's
popular young minister, William Hague. To her surprise, she liked him. She conceded in her journal that his manner of reading was as "bad, as possible." ("He
is always shouting out the emphasis on the wrong word— he is over-excited constantly.") But she appreciated the liberal Hague's lack of theological "dogma"
and loved his "unpremeditated" and earnestly "vehement" preaching style. If,
within Unitarian limits, Providence-style Baptist preaching impressed her,
Down East literary stump speaking—in the person of her quondam Portland
editor John Neal—nearly swept her off her feet. Half-prodigy, half-poseur, a garrulous literary scrapper, critic, novelist, Byronic poet, and ardent Benthamite
promoter of women's rights as well as virtually every other reform cult of the era,
Neal was a frequently invited speaker in Providence. On November 24, he gave
two talks at the Greene Street School on (for the boys) "the exercise of political
rights" and (for the girls) "the vocation of Woman in this country," which Fuller
pronounced in her journal "noble and liberal." Her appreciation of his feminism, however, did not inhibit her from having a long conversation, at a party
with Whitman, Hiram Fuller, and Greene in the latter's library later that evening, (as she described it in her journal) "upon Woman, Whigism, modern
English Poets, Shakespeare,—and, in particular, Richard the Third,—about
which we had a regular fight." Although she failed to say what were the points
in contention, she did add scrappily, "Mr. Neal does not argue quite fairly, he
uses reason while it lasts, and then, if he gets into a scrape, helps himself out by
wit, by sentiment or strings of assertions. But if I had him by myself I think I
could drive him to the wall." Still, in spite of his "exaggeration and coxcombry"
(hers was the "far more compact" mind, she decided), she was obviously taken
with this "magnetic genius" with a "lion heart" and a "sense of the ludicrous."
When he walked her home, she reported in her journal, she told him "that I liked
him very much, knew only three or four men whom I liked better—I might have
added that I knew none who was so truly a *man*." Some years later, to a mutual
friend, the literary pugilist would repay the compliment: "Remember me to her,

I pray you—as to a she-gladiator." Provincial Providence did not dim her aggressive eye for charismatic men.[22]

Fuller's meeting with Neal facilitated yet another of her acquisitions at Providence—her first direct experiences with the popular mind-cults that were beginning to be touted by reform-minded pundits as tools in the struggle to achieve self-knowledge and therefore (as one *Providence Daily Journal* writer put it) "self-improvement." At the party at Greene's—which came the week after the famous phrenology lecturer Orson Fowler came to the school to lecture and gave Fuller her first phrenological examination—Neal gave her head an elaborate reading. Actually, as Fuller's journals and letters show, she was much more interested in the newer French import of mesmerism, or (as it was also called) "animal magnetism," of which Providence, mainly because it boasted so many prominent physicians who were active promoters of the art, was then considered the American "head quarters." In September she read a couple of recently published books on the subject by its leading French exponent, Joseph Philippe François Deleuze, including Thomas Hartshorn's translation of Deleuze's *Instruction pratique sur le magnétisme animal,* published that month in Providence, which contained a large appendix of letters (from "physicians of high standing" and other professional men) reporting on the many recent "extraordinary" mesmeric cases in the city. She also went at the end of the month with James Clarke, who was in town to deliver some sermons, to see the city's most celebrated mesmeric subject, the blind somnambulist Loraina Brackett, whose "eyeless-sight" and "traveling clairvoyance" even the cautious Edward Brooks Hall, after observing them, confidently pronounced "purely a question of *fact.*" According to Clarke's account in his journal, after first being "put . . . to sleep" and incited to "involuntary action" by Dr. Capron, "she was put in communication with S.M.F. and discovered the point in her head where she was suffering from violent pain, and after some rubbing the pain was relieved." After this, Clarke had the doctor put to her a series of questions about people and objects back in Louisville. When he returned home he was deeply impressed: most of the things that "the sleeping beauty had prophesied," he excitedly wrote to Fuller, were correct! Fuller was not so enthralled with *her* mesmeric results. On October 14 she wrote to Caroline Sturgis that she was still feeling "miserably unwell" and was now better only because she had been bled. Subsequent visits did not improve things. On November 10 she wrote to Caroline, "The blind girl said my head would never be better while I read so much," to which obviously useless advice she added huffily, "She has almost entirely lost the gift of clairvoyance (if she ever possessed it,) and is good for nothing." This disappointing outcome notwithstanding, Providence's mesmerism had at least planted a seed: as intellectual interest in this "genial" practice (as Emerson would later complacently call it) continued to spread among Romantic and Transcendentalist intellectuals, so, too, would Fuller's interest in it, both as physical therapy and as paranormal experience that, like Transcendentalism, revealed powerful truths hidden deep within the individual consciousness.[23]

While Fuller was dabbling in the popular Transcendental fringes, she also showed her loyalty to the Transcendentalist center. She did not do it too soon. Already some established Unitarian ministers were beginning to telegraph friendly warnings to their younger Transcendentalist colleagues not to be too exalted in their claims for human nature, too heedless of man's dependency on God's opening of "the fountains of revelation," as one of them put it—in a word, too reducing of Christianity, as one *Christian Examiner* author wrote, "to a level with *mere naturalism.*" But it was left to the aggressive young Francis Bowen to get at the cultural heart of the matter. Bowen was later Harvard's Alford Professor of Moral Philosophy. He was a man whose whole professional career would be devoted to applying the rationalistic Lockean Common Sense philosophy that these Transcendentalists radically challenged. In a polemical article in the November issue of the *Christian Examiner,* Bowen excoriated the Transcendentalists for their arrogance, dogmatism, and exotic German borrowings. But their worst trait, Bowen charged, went deeper than these: because they vaunted so excessively subjective experience—and, just as important, went about trying to express it in impossibly obscure, "wild, and fantastical" ways— they threatened to loosen the traditional Unitarian alliance between intellectuals and men of affairs. "They have," he cried, "deepened the gulf between speculative and practical men, and by their innovations in language, they are breaking down the only bridge that spans the chasm." The implication was clear: Transcendentalism, even if it ultimately led—as Bowen was certain it would—only to social impotence, in the meantime threatened to unfit intellectually inclined young men and women for the leadership of their society, or even, perhaps, for bourgeois lives at all. Although all of this hardly amounted to the *"perfect Inquisition"* that George Ripley reported to Clarke in Louisville these sentiments were stirring up, it certainly portended a fight with high stakes.[24]

In the midst of this slowly gathering furor came Harriet Martineau's long-awaited book on America. Published in the summer and reviewed by the fall in virtually every magazine and newspaper in America, the book was the literary sensation of the year. Once again Americans anxiously peered into a European mirror, and once again most of them were very upset about what they saw. Martineau's *Society in America* was neither a ridiculing tract like those of most past English travelers, nor a profound analysis like Alexis de Tocqueville's soon-to-be-completed *Democracy in America.* The book was alternately gossipy, hectoring, fatuous, perceptive, eloquent, and entertaining. It excoriated Americans for betraying their democratic principles by, among other things, subordinating women politically, but especially by sanctioning human slavery. But what really shocked her wealthy Boston readers—who had been among her most devoted American hosts—was her broadside attack on Boston "as perhaps as aristocratic, vain, and vulgar a city, as described by its own 'first people,' as any in the world." She pointedly excepted William Ellery Channing, as well as, of course, her wealthy Boston radical abolitionist friends, whom she praised unstintingly as the city's unsung "natural aristocracy." Otherwise, she charged the city with being, for all its "superior intelligence" and "benevolent institutions," mired in "caste," "pedantry," and "Cant." Naturally this earned her, from Boston's "conventional aristocracy" (as she called its Unitarian establishment), among the most hostile reviews of the many she got in America. ("Rash," "worthless," and "rude," fumed *North American Review* editor John Gorham Palfrey.) But her book also unsettled her very unconventional Transcendentalist friends by its surprisingly vituperative attack on Alcott. Even the ordinarily mild and tolerant Sarah Clarke found it "offensive." Both a staunch moralist and, as a necessarian, a self-confessed believer in "the superior value of the discipline of circumstance to that of express teaching," Martineau was unable to see in Alcott anything more—despite her private admiration of his colleague Emerson—than a weird and dangerous example of Boston "Cant." "Large exposures might be made of the mischief this gentleman is doing to his pupils," she wrote primly, "by relaxing their bodies, pampering their imaginations, over-stimulating the consciences of some, and hardening those of others; and by his extraordinary management, offering them every inducement to falsehood and hypocrisy. His system can be beneficial to none, and must be ruinous to many." No conservative Bostonian could have written a more thoroughgoing assault on Alcott or, for that matter, Transcendentalist educational reform.[25]

Needless to say, such a book was a grave "disappointment" to Fuller. Indeed, she told Sarah Clarke, she had so little good to say about it that she had turned down a request to review it. But after Martineau sent her a signed copy and asked her how she liked it, Fuller dutifully took up her pen in November to explain why she had read the book, as she put it, with such "positive distaste." She began by discounting reviewers like Palfrey (the great majority, she assured her) who had "garbled, misrepresented, scandalously mistreated" the book. She also praised what she called Martineau's "kindly" spirit toward America, as well as her usual "high ideal standard, genuine independence," and, generally, her "vigor of mind and powers of picturesque description." But—the preliminaries out of the way—she then launched into a scathing attack on the book's "presumptuousness, irreverence, inaccuracy, hasty generalization, and ultraism," by which, she said, Martineau had destroyed her chance to gain "a lasting monument to your fame" and had done a great "injustice . . . to so important a task." Fuller was particularly distressed, she told her, by her abolitionist "ultraism." "I do not like that your book should be an abolition book," she bluntly told her. "You might have borne your testimony as decidedly as you pleased; but why leaven the whole book with it? This subject haunts us on almost every page. It is a great subject, but your book had other purposes to fulfil." Finally, after a few more shots at the book's "want of soundness, of habits of patient investigation, of completeness, of arrangement," and, most bothersome, constant "intemperance of epithet," she got to what was clearly to her the most upsetting instance, certainly of this last failing—Martineau's attack on Alcott.

> Would your heart, could you but investigate the matter, approve such overstatement, such a crude, intemperate tirade as you have been guilty of about Mr. Alcott,—a true and noble man, a philanthropist, whom a true and noble woman, also a philanthropist, should have delighted to honor; whose disinterested and res-

olute efforts, for the redemption of poor humanity, all independent and faithful
minds should sustain, since the 'broadcloth' vulgar will be sure to assail them; a philosopher, worthy of the palmy times of ancient Greece; a man whom Carlyle and
Berkeley, whom you so uphold, would delight to honor; a man whom the worldlings
of Boston hold in as much horror as the worldlings of ancient Athens did Socrates.
They smile to hear their verdict confirmed from the other side of the Atlantic, by
their censor, Harriet Martineau.

She concluded her letter (which included not one whit of her own philosophical
objections to Alcott) by expressing her fear that because of her frank criticisms,
she would lose Martineau as a friend. "I know it must be so trying," she com-
miserated a little nervously, "to fail of sympathy, at such a time, where we expect
it."[26]

In this she was certainly right. On November 28, Martineau wrote in her journal: "An immense letter from Margaret Fuller. Sad about herself, and very
severe on my book;—righteously so, but with much mistake in it. The spirit is
very noble. Do I improve in courage about learning the consequences of what I
do? I commit myself boldly, but I suffer a good deal. . . . I suffered a good deal
from her letter." Why did Fuller write such a harsh critique? Sarah Clarke, who
thought her letter was "a masterpiece of criticism, so understanding and discriminating," nonetheless also told brother James—who later wrote a more appreciative review of Martineau's book in the *Western Messenger*—that it was "the
severest thing I have seen said about her." One reason for Fuller's severity, Sarah
Clarke thought, was her honesty, and this seems at least partly right: many of
Fuller's criticisms were valid. Yet another was undoubtedly political. Like most
of her Unitarian and Transcendentalist friends, Fuller thought that Martineau's
Boston friends were too "partisan" and monomoniacal about their antislavery
politics. It was therefore obviously hard for her to identify with the ideological
rage that animated Martineau's book. Indeed, because she herself was less disaffected with—and certainly less harried by—either conventional Boston or conventional America than were Martineau and her abolitionist friends, she may
even have felt a twinge of defensive discomfort, if not distaste, at the extreme
character of Martineau's attack. Fuller was hardly, of course, an ideological
defender of conventional Boston. She was, for example—again like most of her
Unitarian and Transcendentalist friends—at least moderately sympathetic, if
not with abolitionism, at least with antislavery ideas. Two years before, she had
lavishly praised William Ellery Channing's nonabolitionist but strongly, and to
Boston conservatives, horrendously, antislavery book, *Slavery,* as a "noble" and
"refreshing . . . vote to the cause of Right." She was also plainly disgusted by the
furious conservative attacks on Martineau for her abolitionism. After the press
and local gossips first went "at her" following Martineau's announcement of her
agreement with abolitionist principles during her last winter in Boston—an act
that had horrified Elizabeth Peabody—Fuller pointedly told family and friends
that Martineau had good "reason to think ill" of Bostonians. Clearly, the fundamental source of Fuller's animus against Martineau's book was neither social
nor political, but cultural. This included, first of all, her outrage over Martineau's

personal assault on her vulnerable friend and colleague, but it also involved her shock at what obviously, she now realized, stood behind this attack: Martineau's apparent philistinism or her indifference, if not hostility, to purely cultural change. This last stance, to an incipient cultural radical like Fuller, was hardly forgiveable, despite her quavering claim in her letter that she felt they still sympathized "on several points." Finally—cultural ideology aside—the fact that the sin was committed by her revered patron and role model ("I shall not be disappointed in her," she had at the beginning of their friendship assured James Clarke), undoubtedly unleashed much of the obvious pain and anger that permeated Fuller's letter.[27]

Fuller's critique did not, at least outwardly, destroy her friendship with Martineau. Both continued to write friendly letters to each other for many years. But privately to her friends—including to some of their mutual ones—although she extolled Martineau's "vigorous eloquent" writings, she also made it clear she disliked her "credulity, exaggeration, and man deification." (This last was an allusion to Martineau's glorification of her Boston abolitionist friends in her "crack" *Westminster Review* article, "The Martyr Age of the United States.") From her side, Martineau eventually demonstrated exactly what Fuller had feared: the worm of resentment gnawed in her brain. Her ex-protégée's independence was in fact a good deal like Martineau's own "honest and frank" heedlessness of "effects," as Sarah Clarke noted. Yet she obviously saw Fuller's judgment, as Fuller saw Martineau's book, as a betrayal. In her score-settling *Autobiography,* she left a vicious attack on Fuller's "spoiled . . . pedantry and forwardness." Worse yet, at least from the point of view of the historical record—having clearly been piqued by seeing, two years before, Fuller's letter in print in her *Memoirs*— she first denied having ever gotten the letter and then, somewhat confusedly, claimed that it showed perfectly Fuller's mocking and despising of "those who, like myself" prized "objects and efforts of a higher order than her own." Fuller, of course, never read this epitaph by her former mentor, but many did then and have since. It was a sad and dishonest footnote to Fuller's honest, if hasty, assertion of her intellectual independence and Transcendentalist commitments.[28]

These commitments were also tested by another nasty imbroglio in which she became entangled that fall. The central figure this time was her former student Caroline Sturgis. Friendly with Fuller since she was thirteen, now eighteeen and living with her parents in Brookline, Caroline had recently become Fuller's closest young female protégée. In order to bring her even closer, while in Boston in September, Fuller had invited her to come and spend the winter with her in Providence. She had also spoken to Caroline's father about the plan, and he had readily agreed, or so it seemed to Fuller. But in Caroline's first letter written after Fuller returned to Providence, she said nothing about it and implied instead that she would be spending the winter in Boston. So, in her letter of reply on October 14, Fuller reminded her again of the plan and all the good reasons for it. Without having her for at least three months, as she put it, "I cannot hope to do much for you." But if she were to come for the winter, she would read with her Carlyle's *History of the French Revolution* ("fascinating"), which Fuller had read when she had stayed with Emerson, who had the only American copy, and "plenty of other good books," as well as meet some of her literary friends and "follow out a good many topicks in a more satisfactory way than you have ever yet done." After this there followed letters back and forth, with Caroline throwing up various obstacles to her coming and Fuller doggedly trying to remove them. ("I could not but laugh at your catalogue of the things you must not have—nothing striped diamonded or [above all things] *square,* that is driving me to close quarters I think.") Finally, after a few more of these obfuscating exchanges, Fuller received a letter from Caroline that caused her to explode. In it Caroline not only told her that her father had said he had never given permission for her to board with Fuller, but also evidently repeated some remarks of his about Transcendentalism that, according to Fuller (Sturgis's original letter is lost) insinuated doubts about her dependability as a matron.[29]

So here it was, finally out. William Sturgis was no reactionary boor. Skeptical of Transcendentalism and hostile to abolitionism, he nonetheless attended both groups' lectures, publicly defended their right to speak, and, in later years, earned a reputation as an eloquent defender of sailors' rights and a sympathetic lecturer on the folkways of Northwest Coast Indians, among whom he had lived for several years as a young trader. On the other hand, Captain Sturgis was both a frequent Whig state legislator and one of the wealthiest men in Boston. He was also a close friend and financial associate of the Appletons, the Lawrences, and others of Boston's rising industrial capitalists—the very "practical men" (in Francis Bowen's language) who despised abolitionists, Transcendentalists, and other social disorganizers. So it is no wonder that, regardless of what he had said to Fuller back in September, he now evidently had second thoughts—especially after Bowen's quasi-official November blast against the "midsummer madness" of Transcendentalism—about putting his daughter under the care of one of these madmen's cohorts. From her side, too, Fuller had reason to be defensive. Not only had she over the years developed friendly relations with some of the Lawrences and several other eastern Massachusetts rich families, but—more to the point—she made her living by teaching and "matronizing" adolescent girls from liberal but cautious families very much like the Sturgises. So on November 16 she sent Caroline a stinging answer, including an italics-strewn verbatim recounting of everything she claimed Caroline's father had originally told her in favor of her boarding with her. "Remembering all this distinctly," she concluded heatedly, "I cannot but feel strong indignation at the statements contained in your letter, at the levity and discourtesy with which I *seem* to be treated, and at the unnecessary trouble which has been given me." On the more substantive issue, she added:

> As to transcendentalism and the nonsense which is talked by so many about it—I do not know what is meant. For myself I should say that if it is meant that I have an active mind frequently busy with large topics I hope it is so— If it is meant that I am honored by the friendship of such men as Mr Emerson, Mr Ripley, or Mr Alcott, I hope it is so— *But* if it is meant that I cherish any opinions which interfere with domestic duties, cheerful courage and judgement in the practical affairs of life, I chal-

lenge any or all in the little world which knows me to prove such deficiency from any acts of mine since I came to woman's estate.

She closed by saying coolly that she knew that if Caroline had "dallied" with her, that it was not her fault, but if she did not come, she would not write again. "I do not wish to be needlessly agitated by exchanging another letter on this topic."[30]

As it turned out, Caroline did not come to live with Fuller that winter, although she did visit her the following week and stayed for a couple of weeks. Whether or how Caroline's father patched things up with her is not known. (Fuller herself suggested one compromise formula—that the whimsical, alienated Caroline had used "some expressions," as Fuller delicately put it, that "may have given me exaggerated notions.") But one thing at least is certain: the little spat by proxy with Caroline's father did not halt Fuller's friendship with Caroline, which continued to grow warmer and closer than ever. Nor did it interfere with Caroline's relations with the Transcendentalists, who soon became, largely through Fuller, her primary social circle. This steadfastness earned Caroline high praise from important quarters. The following month, Emerson—who had probably heard about what he would later call William Sturgis's "misbehaviour" from Fuller and Caroline when they saw him in December—actually inserted, in his Boston "Human Culture" lecture on "Heroism" that winter, which Caroline attended, this veiled reference to her: "The fair girl, who repels interference by a decided and proud choice of influences, so careless of pleasing, so wilful and lofty, inspires every beholder with somewhat of her own nobleness." Lines were being drawn in New England, and young people were beginning to choose sides. Fuller, like Emerson, was there to see that they chose rightly.[31]

IV

Despite her private cultural wars and her revived illnesses that fall, Fuller's spirits continued to be high. On November 18, "I am cheerful, steadfast," she assured her mother, who had anxiously asked about her health. "If I should never be well I yet trust to do well." Although she *was* talking to her mother (whom, unlike her friends, she always tried hard to reassure about herself), her cheerfulness seems genuine enough. For one thing she was enjoying friendly visitors. Clarke's visit (perhaps reflecting finally their mutual vocational achievements) was a particularly good one. ("Our conversations this last time were, to me," she wrote to him, "more satisfactory broken as they were than any intercourse we have had since you went to the West.") Then, after Clarke left in early October, she had Ellen with her for most of November, and, after Ellen left, Caroline Sturgis. She also had as a Providence companion Mary Channing's cousin Elizabeth Channing, who spent the winter with Frederick Farley and his wife, Jane, another Channing cousin. Also, she continued to collect local notables. On December 2, she and Caroline attended the exhibition exercises at Brown, where they were introduced to many of the faculty and, to her obvious satisfaction, Francis Wayland. "President Wayland has called on me at last," she would report almost gleefully to Caroline the following month, "charmed I presume by my assurance not appearance, mind!"[32]

As the seventh was the start of a ten-day intersession at Greene Street, on the day before, Fuller returned with Caroline to Boston. There she energetically pursued, as she usually did whenever she visited the city, a feverish social and cultural schedule. ("There were people with me all the time up to the very last minute," she later reported to Caroline Sturgis.) That first night she went to hear Emerson's opening lecture in his Masonic Temple "Human Culture" series. Afterwards she joined the speaker and Alcott, Caroline Sturgis, and others of his friends at a gathering where she gave, Alcott reported, "many interesting anecdotes" of the animal magnetism craze in Providence. Befitting her awakening interest in the arts, during the rest of week she attended a play or concert almost every night. She also continued her artistic pursuits, albeit on a reduced scale, after her return to Providence. "Ah!—then I was happy indeed," she told Caroline after describing herself lying ill on the sofa on Christmas day, reading all day and night the English Romantic musicologist William Gardiner's recently published *Music of Nature,* whose theory that music had its origins in natural and everyday human sounds Emerson had praised to her. On January 9 she even had a chance to attend at the City Hotel, much to her surprise, a hastily announced concert of the celebrated touring Alsatian-Italian diva Maria Caradori-Allan, which she enthusiastically reviewed three weeks later on the twenty-fifth for her fellow Coliseumites. ("Music, is the best language known to man," she told them, "to meet at once the wants both of sense, and soul.") Also, as in the fall, she continued to enjoy a steady trickle of visitors. Her brother Eugene, who returned with her to Providence, stayed for several days, followed in February by her mother, who stayed a month, and Jane Tuckerman, who visited her for a while in March. Nor does her local social life sound dull. "Miss Fuller is in good health, takes long walks—and even *dances*—literally, I mean," Hiram Fuller reported to Emerson. And two weeks after returning to Providence, Fuller informed Caroline merrily, "I have been out very little, three parties and one Coliseum meeting is all!"[33]

Her greatest satisfaction clearly came from her teaching. Starting that January she began a private German literature class, which she continued through the spring. Among its initial ten members (it would eventually grow to over twenty) were her stalwarts Sarah Helen Whitman and Rhoda Newcomb and another Coliseum member, Rebecca Tillinghast, the daughter of Providence's Congressman Joseph L. Tillinghast. It also included six men, among them Hiram Fuller, Albert Greene, the Reverend William Hague, and William Gammell, Brown's young professor of rhetoric. "I am a little afraid of so many grown men," she confessed to Caroline, "but I trust inspiration will be given at the time and that I shall not *seem* abashed at lecturing to so many of our natural lords and masters!!!" Finally, her Greene Street classes were steadily improving. Assuring Caroline that she was "full of my natural energy," she bragged, "I have got the school into beautiful order and Mr. F. has done his part like a man. It is very full, only one vacancy." She was particularly pleased, she told Caroline, that five or six eighteen-to-twenty-year-old girls had recently joined the school ("attracted by our renown") "for more advanced culture. This was just what I wanted," she exulted. "Add to this that my old birds seem really to appreciate the value of what is doing for them. They express a great deal of gratitude and earnestness and act upon it. I cannot but feel with a happy glow, that many minds are wakened to know the beauty of the life of thought. My own thoughts have been flowing clear and bright as amber. . . . I am *sure* I shall never regret coming into this school."[34]

Fuller's sense that her teaching at Greene Street was beginning to bear fruit was not only her perception. "She is all and even more than I expected," Hiram Fuller rejoiced to Emerson that February. Her feeling was also confirmed by the behavior of her students. Not of all of them, of course. The young boys to whom she taught Latin, although she wrote affectionately in her journal of their "sweet" and "chivalric" natures and the ease with which she was able to "govern" them, seem from later recollections of a few of them as well as reports of their female recitation mates mainly to have been overawed. "She would awe them all into a stillness by a certain imperious look and gesture impossible to describe or to resist," one of them remembered, "then as she addressed them would grow more and more eloquent, and presently to most of them incomprehensible. The dear fellows would say 'yes m'm' and 'no m'm' mostly at random, and oftenest in the wrong places, and take a long breath when dismissed to common people once more." Indeed, this former student recalled, he used to glow from her praises, but found, as he claimed other boys did, "her sarcastic condemnation" when he failed in recitations "almost unbearable." Among a few of the girls, too, Fuller's sometimes blunt, demanding style did not always go down very well. "Some of the larger girls had no lesson and a few left the class in tears," a younger student recorded in her journal after a particularly rough day of questioning by Fuller in her Latin class. "One was so overpowered with her feelings that she had a hysterical fit." Another student wrote to a friend that she thought Fuller was a highly respected, but not "beloved" teacher. Sixty-five years later, one woman still remembered with great indignation being rebuked by Fuller for naïvely writing that Pope was "not much of a poet but a good rhymer." "Preposterous," her Romantic teacher was supposed to have said when the hapless girl read her journal in class. This woman—who came from a militant abolitionist family—also recalled once refusing to recite an antiabolitionist passage in Wayland's *Moral Science* text, an act of defiance that she claimed Fuller never forgot or forgave her for.[35]

But among many, if not most, of her girls, the feeling toward Fuller was very different. Certainly this was the case with the group of older girls (alluded to in her letter to Caroline) who had joined the school that December. The leading figure was Mary Allen, the twenty-year-old niece of the Reverend Edward Brooks and Harriet Ware Hall and the daughter of the Unitarian minister Joseph Allen and his wife Lucy Ware Allen, who conducted a pedagogically liberal boarding school in Northboro, Massachusetts. A second was another twenty-year-old Northboro girl and Mary's best friend and fellow boarder at her uncle and aunt's—Anna Gale, the daughter of the wealthy, widowed Captain Cyrus

Gale, Northboro's leading citizen, and the niece of Massachusetts's former governor and current United States senator John Davis. Others included yet another Northboro friend of Mary's and Anna's, Louise Hunt, who enrolled later in the spring, and five Providence girls—Juliet Graves, Sarah Humphrey, and the three Metcalf sisters, Matilda, Evelina, and Caroline. Disarmingly earnest, sisterly, knowledge-loving, and, in this last year of their schooling, emotionally needy—this susceptible circle of Unitarian friends made up, as they liked to say, Margaret Fuller's "row" at Greene Street.[36]

This little group is also important for another reason. Like all the students at Greene Street, they kept journals, and these journals, along with their correspondence, give an excellent picture of Fuller's appeal as a teacher. "How and when did she ever learn about everybody that ever existed?" Evelina Metcalf wrote in wonderment after recounting some of Fuller's remarks in class. "I wonder if I shall know an eighth part of what she does." Mary Allen wrote to her parents after the third day of classes on December 20, "I . . . cannot find words to express my delight and wonder. It is worth a journey to P. to hear Miss Fuller talk." Ten days later Anna Gale wrote to her brother Frederick at Harvard Law School: "Miss Fuller . . . is a perfect wonder. I wish you could hear her talk a few moments. I almost stand in awe of her, she is such a literary being." But both Anna and Mary—like almost all their friends in their first letters home—also worried about the other side of their awe of Fuller's talk and erudition. "I love Miss Fuller already, but I fear her," Mary confessed in her letter to her parents. "I would not for a great deal offend her in any way. She is very satirical, and I should think might be *very severe*." Elaborating on the subject a couple of weeks later in a letter describing all her teachers at Greene Street, she wrote: "Miss Fuller is as different as you can imagine. I love her, but in a different way. I consider it a very great privilege to be under her instruction. She is very critical and sometimes cuts us up into bits. When she cuts us all in a lump, it is quite pleasant, for she is quite witty; but woe to the one whom she cuts by herself!"[37]

Mary and her friends did not have to wait very long to experience what they feared. The circumstances were these: One of their number, Juliet Graves—a reportedly reserved but (as her letters amply show) floridly sensitive girl—was one day the following month singled out by Fuller for a little satirical treatment for some "diffident" answers she gave in class. The next day, Mary, the Metcalf sisters, and others of their circle presented Fuller with a round-robin letter of protest on Juliet's behalf. The protest is lost, but Fuller, while acknowledging they were probably "more than half in jest," replied "in earnest," apologizing, not for her treatment of Julia, but for her "precarious" health and many duties that prevented her from concerning herself with their personal lives. ("I dare not be *generous* lest I should thus be unable to be *just,* dare not indulge my feelings lest I should fail to discharge my duties.") "Since I thus act by you in so miserly a spirit," she concluded,

> giving to each and all only what the letter of my obligation requires, let me take this opportunity to say that it is not because I do not value you and even (I use not the word lightly) love you. If I did not wish to *give* my love, some of my scholars would

gain it by their uniformly honorable conduct and engaging manners. And you will do me justice in believing that I generally feel much more regard than I express. And, though I cannot do for you all that another might in my place, let me assure you that, if, while under my care, or after you leave me, you should feel that I can, by any counsel or words of instruction or act of kindness, benefit you where others could not, my ear and heart will always be ready to attend to your wishes.

Give my love to J. I hope I was not too rough with her this morning. Could I but teach her more confidence and self-possession, I should be satisfied with her as much as I am now interested in her.[38]

Such a high-mindedly affectionate letter—with its thinly veiled hints of personal suffering and hidden feeling—could only have had one (no doubt intended) effect on such a sentimentally conscience-minded group: from this time on their letters and journals expressed, not just admiration, but a passionate devotion to their Miss Fuller. "Miss F. is as dear as ever," Mary Allen wrote at the end of the month to Anna Gale, who had recently withdrawn from school and returned to Northboro. "I think she is *less satirical,* than she was last term, & I love her more than words can tell. She is so funny—she makes me laugh half the time." Privately in her journal, Mary fell over herself in expressing her appreciation for the "pains" and "interest . . . out of school" their teacher showed her and her friends, a sentiment echoed in their letters by others in the group. Finally, the following fall—summing up what they all obviously felt about their heroine—another member of the group wrote to Mary Allen, now, like Anna, back in Northboro:

I cannot find words to express to you my love for dear Miss Fuller, you who know her so well can better conceive it than I describe. She is everything to me,—my teacher, my counsellor, my guide, my friend, my pillar on which I lean for support when disheartened and discouraged, and she allows me to look upon her as such. . . . I had no idea she had so much heart, but it is overflowing with affection and love.[39]

Despite such devotion—and her knack for inspiring it—Fuller clearly followed, in the classroom at least, a rigorously unindulgent regimen. Thoroughness, precision, and, above all, an initial acknowledgement (as she put it) of their "barbarous ignorance" so that (as Mary earnestly wrote) they could "feel our deficiencies" were traits Fuller's students reported her almost evangelically insisting on. She also wanted them to do something else—to think. "More thoughts" and write "suggestively" are almost refrains in her critiques of their journals. "We must *think* as well as *study,* and *talk* as well as *recite,*" Mary reported Fuller's exhorting her class. No less in Providence than in Boston were these uncommon notions—for boys *and* for girls—and in emphasizing them she merely confirmed what she had told Alcott in June about her devotion to his Socratic principles. But in her case, as she had implied in her letter, the goal was purely educational—not to reveal the Oversoul, but simply to provoke her students to internalize the material and respond to it imaginatively. To accomplish this she devised various strategies. She assigned the latest college texts, she had them write out weekly paraphrases and philosophical definitions, and she kept the lessons "*very* short" to ensure time for classroom "conversations"—all with the aim of instilling in them the idea that their studies (as Anna Gale paraphrased one of Fuller's speeches) "would lay upon our minds, like a dry husk, unless they take root sufficiently deep, to produce one little thought of our own, something entirely original." She particularly entreated her students, who as girls were excluded from giving any of the all-boy "declamations" before parents and local dignitaries, to talk in class. "We might think it a delightful thing to her to talk to so many interesting auditors, but that was not the thing," Mary reported to her parents Fuller's telling the first day's rhetoric class. "She could not teach us so, *we* must talk and let her understand our minds. She talked as fast as she could about half an hour. I never heard any one who seemed to have such a command of language."[40]

As one might infer from this last remark, however much Fuller urged her classes to talk, she nonetheless seems to have done a good deal of the talking. ("There are not more than a dozen in the class," Mary wrote happily to her parents of her ethics course, "and we have such nice times hearing Miss Fuller talk.") No doubt one reason for this was her intellectual authoritativeness: she wanted her students to reveal their minds, but once revealed, she was not shy about letting them know what she thought of their revelations. "Almost all called it a 'harmony of words,'" Mary reported her classmates answered when Fuller asked for a definition of poetry in an early rhetoric class, "which she said was very incorrect." (She also clued them in on the truth: "It clothes the thoughts of the soul in beautiful language, and by means of imagery, works upon the feelings," Mary recorded part of Fuller's lengthy definition that she gave them at the next class, "requesting us to write it in our journals.") Also Fuller's "lectures" (as this exchange showed) had a rationale to them: she had a definite Romantic point of view to get across. Sometimes she mixed it with other interests. In her Greek, Roman, and English history classes, she stressed, in high republican style, politics and culture and "the great men and teachers": the statesmen, warriors, poets, and philosophers, who, she said, "best interpret the leadings of events amid the nations." In her literature classes, though, her Romantic bias was pretty clear. In her English poetry course (which she taught in close conjunction with English and American history), although they covered the gamut from Chaucer to Bryant, her students' journals show she emphasized Shakespeare and the major Romantics. In her rhetoric class she urged her girls, in sensible Romantic fashion, to use their journals to unlearn "a stiff and formal manner of expressing oneself." She even managed to introduce in this course—while using Archbishop Richard Whately's Common Sense, argumentation-centered *Elements of Rhetoric*—a smattering of Transcendentalism! "Miss Fuller wished us to bring her some topics on which reason and understanding can be applied and a list of men of genius and talent," Evelina Metcalf wrote in her journal one day after class. And Anna Gale, after recounting somewhat skeptically Fuller's recommendation of Gardiner's "transcendentalist" *Music of Nature* (which "appears to show that there is music in everything, even in the screams of a child, or cackling of a hen"), quickly added, "I am very ignorant respecting the new subject of transcendentalism—though I should be glad to catch its spirit." If nothing else, we can at least be sure Fuller's students were some of the youngest people in America trying to grapple with Transcendentalist philosophy.[41]

It was in her ethics course—which her older girls streamed into after their rhetoric class—that Fuller seems to have gone the furthest in disseminating a Romantic intellectual line. Her students' journals show she did not do this in a sectarian way. (Her discussion, for example, of the various Christian doctrines of the Atonement, Anna Gale reported, was completely impartial.) Still, because the text she used was Wayland's moderately evangelical and enormously popular *Elements of Moral Science,* it would have been surprising if she had *not* touched on theologically sensitive subjects. And she did. In one class conversation on the issue of man's obligations to God, she explicitly dissented from Wayland's orthodox denial that God was under any moral obligation toward man. ("Since God has created us, he is under obligation to create us capable of being happy"; and besides, Anna Gale reported her as answering, "we cannot conceive of a God, without a conscience, and therefore he could not justify himself in creating a being only to be miserable.") This, of course, was pretty much the standard Unitarian position, and it seems to have gone down easily with her largely Unitarian class. ("The study I enjoy the most is . . . Moral Science," Mary Allen told her parents. "I do enjoy it exceedingly"—a sentiment that several of her friends echoed in their journals.) But Wayland's text was hardly orthodox. On the contrary, its predominant feature was its close harmonizing of revealed Christianity and the somewhat less clearly revealed moral laws of laissez-faire capitalism, evangelical benevolence, and postmillennial social progress. In challenging these last two progressivist aspects of Wayland's moralism (the surviving journals do not include any remarks about Wayland's economics), the tack she took was less Unitarian than Transcendentalist—less, that is, the view that that Wayland's perspective was insufficiently rational than that it was (as Transcendentalists often charged *Unitarianism* with being) inadequately spiritual.[42]

Occasionally her spiritualism led her into heterodox waters. On January 5, in a class on Wayland's discussion of "the defects of the system of Natural Religion," Anna Gale recorded Fuller putting in this brief on behalf of pagan spirituality:

> The ancients formed no just, pure, and sublime conceptions of a Deity, excepting Socrates, and his followers. Miss Fuller thought that no one ever had, or ever could exceed the views which he formed, and that if he had lived when Christ was upon the earth, he would have been glad to have owned him as one of his disciples. But those philosophers took no pains to disseminate their views amongst others—they thought the common people were incapable of understanding them.

Sometimes she implicitly challenged Wayland's evangelical rationalism. In one class, on the moral uses of the Scriptures, she advanced—in clear contradiction to Wayland's distinction in that day's lesson between the unenlightened and "utterly annihilated" Old Testament and the completely commanding New—

the view that the entire Bible should be understood, "in an intellectual point of view," as sublimely poetic and "symbolical." But her sharpest challenges to Wayland's moralism were her objections to its ethical worldliness. During the class discussion of divine obligation, for example, she stoically denied Wayland's cheerful evangelical assertion that the world was designed (as he put it) "in such a way as to promote our highest happiness here." ("She thought it was not, for those who were the most pure, and good were those who met with the most troubles, and afflictions, they were the most worthy to suffer.") Similarly, in another exchange, she suggested that, despite his ardent defense of revealed Christianity, Wayland's moral-government analogy (that we are to God what servants are to masters) failed to encompass the vast "difference" between us and God. In yet another discussion she rejected Wayland's bland assertion that there would never be another dispensation because it would contradict the postmillennial idea of ongoing progress. ("Miss Fuller said she did not see why there should not be another, if we ever should become so corrupt as to need one.") At one point in the discussion she even attacked Wayland's idea, widely held by evangelicals, of a millennial age—or the notion that history would one day end in, or (in its postmillennial formulation that Wayland favored) was in the process of evolving toward, a new heaven and new earth of universal peace and felicity—as a materialist fantasy:

> She thought there never would be a state of perfection in this world. If sin ceased to exist, virtue must. Some people have fixed the period for the commencement of the millenium within ten years from now, and some believe that all our heaven will be here, they cannot conceive of any thing more beautiful than some parts of this earth, and if it were not for sin it would be perfect. Miss Fuller said she would not deny but that this might be so, but she was not so fond of pitching her tent here, she was not so much attached to this world, and she liked to think of living in some higher sphere, where our minds will be more enlarged, and exalted.

Indeed, so pronounced was Fuller's antievangelicalism that in one class she criticized both missionaries that conservative evangelicals like Wayland favored ("Miss Fuller said she had no faith in missionaries, she thought that was not the way by which the heathen were to be converted") and the more radical evangelical reformers.

> Miss Fuller said she did not think, it was any one's duty to go about the streets crying, and denouncing against the sins of the people, like the ancient prophets Jeremiah and Isaiah, yet there have been people, maniacs, or those who were so far carried away by the enthusiasm of their feelings, as to consider this to be their duty.[43]

In this last remark Fuller almost sounds—but for her granting of evangelical "maniacs" their rights—like a conservative Unitarian rationalist. In fact, the world-historical view she presented to her students as an alternative to millennialist evangelicalism, as her allusion to wanting to live "in some higher sphere" would suggest, was hardly rationalist or conservative. Anna's lengthy account of the March 2 class's discussion about divine obligation and the existence of evil and suffering made this pretty clear. While evincing little hope for social perfection, Fuller nonetheless concluded her remarks, Anna reported, with her own Romantic version of an old Western progressivist faith:

> In the course of the conversation Miss Fuller remarked, that she believed the soul was progressive, though some are contented with supposing that we shall always remain in the same state. If this be true, if the soul is actually to go on progressing through the ages, and ages of eternity, why may we not suppose that in the course of that endless period of time, we may even surpass the angels, in knowledge, power, and glory, if it is possible to surpass them, and why may not this be one reason why God has created us differently.[44]

There was, moreover, at least one worldly value whose progress Fuller tried to get her students to yearn for: female culture. She could sometimes be a little cryptic about it. She seems to have taken particular pleasure in recounting mythological stories of the wild huntresses Atalanta and Daphne, who resisted all their male pursuers so that they could (in one student's words) "live in the enjoyment of 'single blessedness.'" (As Atalanta was eventually outfoxed by one of her lovers and Daphne was turned into his favorite plant, a laurel tree, by her father, the river-god to whom she prayed for escape, the moral must have seemed a bit ambiguous.) Mostly, though, her students' journals show, she proselytized straightforwardly: she read from Anna Jameson, Madame de Staël, and other "distinguished" female writers; she reported on the feats of contemporary women artists and performers; she asked her history and literature classes (in a departure from her "great men" theory) to give accounts of important women in English history; and she encouraged her students to try out some of her favorite intellectual roles. "She said it was not to be expected that women would be good Astronomers or Geologists or Metaphysicians," Evelina Metcalf wrote in her journal, recounting one of Fuller's perorations on "the great advantages" of history, "but they could and are expected to be good historians." Again, on yet another day: "She spoke upon what woman could do—said she should like to see a woman everything she might be, in intellect and character." She also confronted male prejudice—even in the lives of her literary greats. One day in a class on Milton, Anna Gale recounted:

> Miss Fuller said she once saw a beautiful picture of him. He was represented as sitting at his door, with a mild look from his blind eyes, his hair parted in front and hanging in curls, as was the fashion in those times, whilst his daughters sat near him, one reading, the other writing. But she said she did not take so much pleasure in it as she should if she did not know, that they did not understand what they were doing, for he would not allow his daughters to be instructed.

Despite her desire to fire up her young charges, Fuller at the same time seems to have avoided anything that smacked of excessive feminine flattery. Although in one class Mary Allen reported her saying "that women's writings were more delicate, more elegant, more spritely than those of the other sex," she also made it pretty clear that not all women writers were exactly of the highest caliber. Indeed, the sharpest barbs her students recorded in their journals were several aimed at popular female sentimental writers whose stock in trade was precisely a maudlin and self-flattering kind of "delicacy." Immediately following her entry on Fuller's lament over Milton, Anna reported the following withering bit of sarcasm directed at the English poet and novelist Letitia Landon:

> Miss Landon was a poetess, who caused us some amusement. Her poetry is not very valuable. It is very sentimental, being mostly about broken hearts, forlorn lovers, and those who had been disappointed in their love. One of the young ladies asked if Miss Landon's heart had been broken. Miss F. said she did not know, that if it had, it was probably mended. Some broken hearts seem to get mended again, fastened together by putty, or something, whilst others always remain broken. Miss F. said if we read her poetry we must sigh over it, or we should be much behindhand, for many ladies read it, and wept over it. It would introduce us to many ladies with swanlike necks, more ladies with swanlike necks than were in this school.[45]

How much Fuller influenced her girls in these affairs of the heart and head is hard to say. Certainly the immediate effect was palpable. "It makes me proud when I hear such things as this," Evelina Metcalf wrote in her journal after recounting Fuller's report in class later that spring about a daughter of France's King Louis Philippe making "a beautiful statue," "for it shows what our sex is capable of doing and encourages us to go on improving and doing all we can to show that we are not entirely incapable of intellectual cultivation as some think." Nor did they exactly overlook their teacher as a source of feminine pride. "Would that there were more like her in this world," Evelina wrote at the end of her last term with Fuller, the following winter. "How very different the state of society would be if one half the women that composed it had the high, exalted views of Miss Fuller." The long-term effects are less clear. Most of "Fuller's row" went on to marry and live apparently conventional lives as wives and mothers. Yet virtually all taught school for varying periods between leaving the Greene Street School and marrying. Intellectually, too, they seem to have carried on something of the school spirit. "I was much pleased with the way in which some of my girls received the lectures," Fuller would tell Emerson a couple of years later, after returning from a visit to Providence shortly after he had completed a lecture series there. "They understood at once." This judgment seems a little rash: the later letters of her row show them well within the conventional Unitarian fold. Perhaps a more accurate, if more modest, indication of the mark the Greene Street School and their favorite Miss Fuller had on the circle was left by Mary Allen. A year after withdrawing from school, Mary wrote to her fiancé that the kinds of young ladies she most admired were like those she knew as her friends at the Greene Street School. "They do not live to dress and visit, and gossip and get married. They are studious to improve themselves, to do good, to live for their higher natures." Had she read this—whether a Transcendentalist injunction or not—their teacher no doubt would have been pleased.[46]

V

At the beginning of March in 1838, Fuller moved with the Aborns from their cramped quarters into Susan Aborn's new boardinghouse, which Mary Allen described as "large" and "beautiful." Also on March 7, the Greene Street School recessed for a four-day intersession, which Fuller, stretching it out to six, filled by staying in Brookline with the Sturgises, seeing a small mob of old friends, and hearing Emerson give his "Human Culture" lecture, "The Heart," in Cambridge. She also saw Alcott, now facing the imminent collapse of his Temple School, who read to her from the latest version of his "Psyche" manuscript, now retitled, appropriately enough, "Evangele, or Apocalypse." ("The city is an offense unto me. It stinketh.")[47]

Despite these satisfying, or at least diverting, events, Fuller's letters that spring showed her, in contrast to her buoyant state in the winter, increasingly restless and dissatisfied. After receiving from Clarke that March a glowing tribute to her teaching talents ("this is a great and benign influence to exercise—this is what God has given you to work"), she responded lukewarmly. Although she was sincerely interested in and often loved "the human beings whose eyes speak the possibilities of their souls; larvae though they be at present," she nonetheless wrote emphatically, "giving my soul to such business is out of the question." As for his tribute to her personal teaching ("what I am, I owe in large degree to your influence," he had said), she warmly thanked him for it, of course. But she also told him such praises ("so often spoken to me"), while consoling, still did not change the sad reality that her life, compared with "the aims prescribed by my youthful aspirations," was hopelessly "inadequate." Other letters to friends told similar woeful tales. By May she would write to Clarke, "I . . . think that the last two months, on the whole, are the most miserable part of my existence yet." The reasons for all this downcast talk are not hard to come by. First, by the spring her headaches and other ailments returned with a vengeance. ("I have for some weeks been obliged to pass great part of my time in bed when out of school," she wrote to Clarke in May.) This in turn, as it usually did, inspired depressive thoughts. ("I die," she told Clarke. "I know not how long I shall be in dying, some years perhaps.") Also, after nine months, she was beginning to regret being separated so long from her friends (a separation required, she wrote sorely, "because the most finite considerations make it seem a duty"). But mainly she regretted what teaching in Providence was doing to the sphere of influence that *she* had hoped God had given her to work in—her writing.[48]

Sometimes her bitterness spilled over even into her usually cheerful letters to her mother. "You need not be afraid of my exerting my mind too much," she had assured her sardonically in November. "Heaven, I believe, had no will that I should accomplish any-thing great or beautiful." But Emerson, as usual, was her psychic lightning rod for these sorts of literary complaints. On the very day that Clarke had sent her his eulogy and a few days before she had left Providence for her break, she had sent to her Concord sage, then getting under way several more series of his much-talked-about "Human Culture" lectures, a communiqué confessing that she was in a "very sombre and sullen" mood. "I have shut the door for a few days and tried to do something— You have *really* been doing something! And that is why I write— I want to see you and still more to hear you. I must kindle my torch again." As for any of her new Providence friends doing any of this, she was transcendentally caustic: "I see no divine person. I myself am more divine than any I see— I think that is enough to say about them." Even the eminent Dr. Wayland, whom she had gotten to know (and who reportedly liked her), could not fill the bill. "He would never understand me, and, if I met him, it must be by those means of suppression and accommodation which I at present hate to my heart's core." (She was certainly right about Wayland, whose whole ethical philosophy, as she ought to have known from his text-book, was dedicated to suppression and accommodation.) Indeed, she grumbled to the antiaccommodationist Emerson, "I hate every-thing that is reasonable just now, 'wise limitations' and all. I have behaved much too well for some time past; it has spoiled my peace." But mainly what distressed her, she said, "is to find or fear my theory a cheat— I cannot serve two masters, and I fear all the hope of being a worldling and a literary existence also must be resigned— Isolation is necessary to me as to others. Yet I keep on 'fulfilling all my duties' as the technical phrase is except to myself."[49]

Notwithstanding these continuing confessions to her "unsympathizing, unhelpful, wise good" friend about her lack of divine friends, hallowed time, and (subtextually) "Sanctissime" himself—still, she wrote. Her main literary project, of course, remained her Goethe biography. On her last day in Boston before originally coming to Providence, she had left for John Sullivan Dwight, a recent Harvard Divinity School graduate who had been soliciting translations from Transcendentalists for his *Select Minor Poems of Goethe and Schiller* for George Ripley's European literature series, what she called the "sorry sight" of her "book of translations." Eventually Dwight selected two perfectly competent ones ("To a Golden Heart, Worn Round His Neck" and "Eagles and Doves"), which appeared in the volume the following year. Mostly, though, she worked on her biography. By the fall she had finished the last of the small library of books by Goethe's circle that her touring friends the Farrars and Sam Ward had sent her during the summer. ("I give to them all the time I have," she had told Caroline Sturgis.) Later in the spring she finally got her collection of Goethe's writings ("posthumous works and all"), allowing her to send back to Clarke his forty-volume set that she had been using. Her voluminous notes show how hard she worked. "List of what is still to be examined in Goethe's works." And, a little further on: "Vol 1st. Read the dedication once more, and all the poems, as much as possible out in the woods." And again: "Read all the first four volumes again and again." These notes, outlines, and fragmentary "plans" of chapters also show the kind of book she was trying to put together—a full-scale life based on a wide reading in European Romantic literature and dedicated to one high Romantic proposition: that (as she noted in one early sketch of Goethe's youth) "every thing in his nature was subordinated to the intellect" and thereby sublimated into his great artistic achievements.[50]

Meanwhile, her initial difficulties continued. Transcendentalist friends continued to nudge her to emphasize the ethical and religious in Goethe, but she remained adamant about sticking to her intellectual and aesthetic "point of view." "I do not go to him as a guide or friend," she told Emerson, who had asked her about Goethe's "religion or morality," "but as a great thinker, who makes me think, a wonderful artist who gratifies my tastes." She also continued to be vexed by the problem of Goethe's sexual life. "Will you, Henry," she implored Hedge in a letter a week after writing Emerson, "can you tell me all the scandal about Goethe—about his marriage and so forth? I have asked Mr Emerson and others whom I thought might know, but the little they can tell only puzzles and disturbs me." How could the liaison with Christiane Vulpius have been, she asked him, "at so decorous a court and under the eye of the Grand Duchess— I hope you will be able to give me light." She had found nothing, she added, in any of the books she had gotten from Europe, and asked him to send her immediately any information he knew about the subject. This time—despite his strong encouragement of her project and their similar approaches to German literature—she drew an even bigger blank than she had with Clarke. "I am the last person to be consulted in such matters," Hedge answered a little bluntly. "I know nothing of Goethe's liaisons, which seem to interest you so much." He suggested she ask Emerson to ask Carlyle.[51]

She had what she thought was a better idea. While in Boston in December, she had learned that the touring English critic Anna Jameson—who while in Germany had actually lived with the family of Goethe's daughter-in-law and whose subsequent sketches of German writers Fuller had thought "brilliant"— had just left the city, where she had been staying at William Ellery Channing's. It probably also did not hurt her interest that Jameson, with close friends like Elizabeth Barrett, Lady Byron, and Fuller's erstwhile mentor Harriet Martineau, was one of the best-connected female literary figures in England. So, once back in Providence, after learning from the visiting portrait painter Cephas Giovanni Thompson that he expected to see Jameson in New York before she left for England, Fuller hurriedly dashed off for Thompson a list of questions to give to her along with an impassioned letter asking for help. In its breathless eagerness and tortured self-deprecations, the letter was vintage Fuller in a pre-mentor frenzy. "You seemed to feel a natural delicacy about any new disclosures," she conceded that Channing had told her.

> But oh! if I could but see you I am persuaded that you would tell me all I wish to know— Is it quite impossible for me to see you? How I wish I was famous or could paint beautiful pictures and then you would not be willing to go without seeing me. But now—I know not how to interest you,—the miserable frigid letter within will not interest you— Yet I am worthy to know you, and be known by you, and if you could see me you would soon believe it, and now I need you so very much.

She then gave her a detailed account of her teaching schedule to explain why it would be difficult for her to come to New York, quickly adding: "You must not get an ugly picture of me because I am a schoolmistress. I have not yet acquired that 'strong mental odour' that Coleridge speaks of. I am only teaching for a little while and I want to *learn* of you." She concluded with the inevitable:

> Be so good as not to speak of my intended work—it is known only to a few persons. Precarious health, the pressure of many ties make me fearful of promising what I

will do.— I may die soon—you may never more hear my name. But the earnest
aspiration, the sympathy with greatness never dies— Es lebt im Asche—
    Respectfully

                                                        S. M. Fuller.[52]

Whatever the socially sensitive Anna Jameson thought of this crazily innocent
but heartfelt letter is not known. But she got it or, if not, she got some query from
Fuller, which she answered (the letter is lost) with some sort of rebuff. Fuller
would later give her the half-benefit of the doubt by speculating that Jameson
had probably thought her "impertinent" for considering such an ambitious project. (She said nothing about the possible indelicacy of her inquiries.) Still, she
was clearly miffed. "I did not ask Mrs Jameson for any thing except some local
particulars, and still think her conduct ungenerous," she wrote a year later huffily (and a little disingenuously) to Caroline Sturgis. But then again perhaps it was
"not so much so," she added, since, after having read Jameson's book on her
Canadian travels (which included some material about Goethe and her German
studies), "I now think her knowledge more scanty than I had supposed."
Another potential English female mentor exposed by her American book![53]
    While laboring to clear away the thickets in her Goethe research, Fuller man-
aged that winter to eke out a few critical pieces of her own. For the past year
Clarke had been urging her to resume writing for his *Western Messenger,* but she
had put him off. "It is, literally, a fact that I have had *no* time," she had answered
one of his pleas for "a good bundle" in the summer, adding, however, that she
hoped to write something for him. But write what? He suggested, as usual, that
"religious subjects would be preferred," or perhaps—trying to prod her toward
popular topics—something on animal magnetism. She scotched this last idea.
("'Tis a subject in which I take no interest at present," she told him crisply.)
Instead, after throwing out a few more highbrow cultural topics, including Emerson's Phi Beta Kappa address and Wayland's recent anti–radical reform book,
The Limitations of Human Responsibility, she finally settled on two literary articles. As with her previous *Messenger* pieces, though, she tried to give them a
culturally critical twist.[54]
    The first was a two-part essay, which Clarke published in the January and Feb-
ruary issues, on Theodor Körner, one of the writers she had earlier intended to
include in her aborted German authors series. Because of his heroic death at
twenty-two while fighting in a volunteer regiment during the anti-Napoleonic
Wars of Liberation, the young poet and dramatist was a virtual icon in Germany.
With an admiration for political heroics as high as her taste for literary melo-
drama was low, Fuller tried to do him Romantic justice. In all his writings, even
the most beautiful, she conceded, Körner failed of mastery. Partly he lacked originality and depth, but mainly, she said, his moral earnestness—or his need
"either to love or to despise"—kept him from portraying characters as complex
wholes. "Of such stuff," she wrote sternly, "are made the orator and the lyric
poet, but not the epic or dramatic poet." On the other hand, she took to task her
anti-Romantic foil Heine for calling Körner's martial verses "uncouth." On the

contrary, she said, it was precisely their unpolished artlessness that made them so suited to their primitive, un-Wordsworthian purpose. "These are such as the Welsh bards may have melodised on their rude harps, to inspirit their country-men for the conflict, or to echo back the shouts of victorious joy. Born of the moment, they draw us close to the moment, which poems like those of our pres-ent intellectual day, 'the expression of remembered emotion,' as one of our greatest poets has told us they are, can never do." Having aesthetically salvaged Körner's poetry by one of her favorite historicist Romantic maneuvers, she con-cluded by saying that above all we should be attracted to Körner "by the sim-plicity with which this generous heart and lively imagination, lent themselves without reserve" to national longings for "Freedom"—"circumstances which in themselves are poetry." Surely, she wrote, this mingling of word and deed was still eloquent, even in these times when "worthless demagogues compass their selfish ends by vaunting in every market-place, sentiments only fit for the lips of saints and martyrs." It was the old republican heroism of her "Brutus" article in new, Romantic clothing.[55]

Her second article, which she completed in February and which appeared in April, also packed a contemporary cultural punch. It was a review of *Letters from Palmyra* (later entitled *Zenobia*) by the retired Unitarian minister William Ware, an uncle of Mary Allen's and the son and younger brother of Harvard Divinity School's two Henry Wares. This recent first novel of what would soon be a popular trilogy of epistolary novels chronicled the social and political strug-gles between the early Christians and Roman authorities. Her appraisal was tem-perate. Clearly, she said—despite the claims of its "panegyrists"—the novel was neither a great work nor a great "antique"; its characters were too sketchily drawn and its "atmosphere" was wholly modern. Yet "to be imbued, thoroughly pervaded by the spirit of another era" was a very difficult task. Successful mod-ern examples in the genre were few, and Ware's novel was vastly superior to the "many tiresome almanacks of past centuries, and catalogues of old clothes" that had inundated the market in recent years. What made it superior as well as refreshing, she argued, was that although it was not sufficiently living as an aes-thetic or historical work, it had one very important quality that recommended it: "The book is full of life—the life of sincere emotion, of earnest meditation." This was particularly remarkable, she noted, because the novel was written by a minister. Here she could not resist making, in Clarke's Unitarian but Transcen-dental-minded magazine, a backhanded, Transcendental swipe at the Unitarian ministry (without specifically mentioning it by name). It was a profession, she said, "in constant danger of looking at the decorous till it forgets the lovely, of teaching the rule till it forgets the spirit, of grasping duty and quite losing beauty." Happily, Ware was made in a different mold: "In the heart of the writer the fire on the altar of beauty has not been quenched by the mists of a timid and formal morality, a morality founded rather upon the fears as to the social con-tract, than on the piety inspired by a human nature made in the likeness of a divine nature." After a few more compliments on the novel's lack of a "jargon of morality" ("even the contrast between Paganism and Christianity is not forced into over bold relief"), she concluded on a culturally high, if slightly patronizing note: "How much to say of an American book written by a busy professional man. We thank him heartily for showing what men can do under such circumstances."[56]

Like her earlier *Messenger* criticism, her forceful but somewhat ex cathedra articles received mixed reviews from her friends. After getting her *Palmyra* review from her, Clarke informed her that he liked it, but he still thought her writing style lacked condensation and point. "It is too Latinized," and in this respect, he thought, "the reverse of Mr. Emerson's." (For most people, he added diplomatically, "it would be good, but I do not like to have your thoughts weakened in the expression, and when I know how strikingly you express yourself in conversation I am disappointed when I meet the same thoughts in writing.") Also, he thought, "there is a kind of sentimentalism, shall I call it? which I always wonder at, in your elaborate articles. Perhaps this is lady-like, yet somehow it likes me not." This last remark got her attention. "I thank you for your critiques on my style," she answered, "but I want you to define more precisely what you mean by my 'sentimentalism.'" As if he needed any reminder, she added, "Sentimentality is what I most detest." In his reply, after belittling his criticisms ("the faults, if they are faults, will correct themselves"), Clarke explained himself: "By 'sentimental' I mean a predominance of feeling over thought. You express the feeling, the effect upon the eye or taste, but the cause, the idea, that which produces the effect is not so distinct and pointed." In sum, he said, "I should like to see a little more of *argument* in your style." Mr. Emerson, on the other hand— who took a considerably dimmer view of arguments in intellectual discourse than did his ministerial colleague Clarke—would the following month criticize Fuller's writing style from almost the opposite point of view. "One thing struck me"—he would write to her later after praising the "very sprightly sense & criticism & brave determination, & truth throughout" of a "portfolio" of her letters and journals that she had left with him while visiting that month—"the absence of abstract propositions. If I write too many aphorisms I think you write too few." Also, more than Clarke, Emerson—who would soon be sounding his own aphoristic blast at the Unitarian ministry—clearly found the tenor of Fuller's cultural remarks highly appealing. So, after reading her *Palmyra* review, he sent her a fan letter. "Its superior tone its discrimination & its thought make it remarkable," he told her grandly, "& indicate a golden pen apt for a higher service hereafter."[57]

Besides her *Messenger* articles, Fuller also used the Coliseum Club that spring as a cultural sounding board. The occasion was a full-dress Club debate on the subject of "progress of Society"—or, more specifically, whether there had been any. The participants followed predictable lines. John Whipple began the series on March 8 with a sneeringly rationalist attack on the whole proposition: God had determined that man would always be a mixture of good and evil, modern technology had produced horrendous evils as well as benefits, and political institutions, the key to progress, were no better now than they had been in ancient Greece and Rome. Two subsequent meetings' speakers—the family chronicler

Eliza Lyman, and Edward Hall (Lucinda Larned's paper was not recorded)—took, from the opposite side, essentially liberal Christian views: despite some residual evils in modern society, Christianity had given to the world a new benevolence that, together with the diffusion of knowledge, guaranteed social progress. Fuller, who gave her paper after Larned's, on April 19, presented a radically conservative Romantic alternative.[58]

After sympathetically summarizing Whipple's "ingenious" arguments, she turned to address one particular aspect of the question—cultural progress. She granted that there may have been in the contemporary world a greater proportion of well-informed and (although she was not entirely convinced) good men than in earlier times, but that by itself hardly constituted great intellectual progress. By contrast, the signs of cultural regression were everywhere. For one thing, the whole ethos of the age was one of "comparison, analysis and extended action," and, however valuable for the sciences, such a spirit was clearly inimical to the creative arts. Moreover, the age's "best thinkers"—the Romantic intellectuals—hardly spoke as though we were living through an era of great cultural advance. On the contrary, they rejected wholesale the vaunted signs of modern progress—utility, technology, and social solidarity—and were rushing back to mysticism, aestheticism, and a spiritually questioning individualism. Finally, the nations of even the West gave little evidence of modern cultural progress. Except for England, Germany, and France, Europe was steeped in superstition, while Greece and Italy, the cradles of Western civilization, were now virtually cultural nonentities. Nor did America look likely for the moment to salvage Western culture. "Turn to our own comfortable country even now, despite Jackson and Van Buren," she told her Whiggish audience. "Look into the mind of the N England farmer or Mechanic. He has merit, he has virtue, he is not without intellect and culture. But compare him with the ideal man and exult if you can. How large a share has *he* in your boasted bank of knowledge? And hundreds of years may elapse before the Sandwich Islander is brought up even to *his* level." As for the notion that one could look hopefully for cultural advances to come from popular education or the diffusion of knowledge, it was simply chimerical to think that these things were making the world any *spiritually* richer than in former times, and for a simple reason: these merely external reforms left untouched man's organic and spiritual nature. "Man is not a vessel into which you can pour at will your golden wine; he is like a plant, and nothing that he cannot assimilate is of value to him." Or, as she also put it, "The materials for thinking can only be valuable in proportion as the mind is trained to think"—which is why "the most refined minds" in "the most civilized countries," she said, were revolting against "the cumbrous apparatus of our education" and "sighing for the simplicity of antique development and flying from the complex influences of modern intellect to the Greek ideal."[59]

Before concluding her Romantic brief against the idea that the modern world had progressed culturally, she addressed two issues raised by Lyman (and later by Hall). The first was the notion that women's education and cultural status had advanced appreciably. She agreed the questions were now being debated

more than ever, which was good, but she doubted, she said, whether male prejudices had significantly lessened, and—more provocatively still—she ques-
tioned whether women were actually likely to gain much from being subjected
to the unphilosophical brain-stuffing schemes their putative champions in these
debates usually proposed for them. How could we think they would when we
saw the results of these schemes in, as she put it, "the sickly consciousness man-
ifest in the writings of such women as M de Stael, Mrs Jameson, Mrs Hemans
and even Miss Edgeworth." (So much for the European "women of genius"!)
On the second issue, of Christianity—which she said was the historical force
most "friends of progress" usually looked to most—she gave several reasons for
rejecting this deus ex machina. First, she said, even if Christianity were to spread
throughout the globe, as she fully expected it to do, because it satisfied so much
of man's nature, this would not guarantee to the masses necessarily any moral,
let alone intellectual improvement: "the sectarian sword will always profane the
Cross by its alliance," and, like all religions, "it will be received verbally by the
crowd, spiritually by the few." Did her rejection of Christian progress make her
world-view quietistic? Not at all, she said. Our natural sense of duty and a desire
to keep the world from regressing were sufficient motives to keep hard at work
doing our best. Did it make it make her view *"'gloomy?'"* On the contrary, it
militated only against national self-aggrandizement. "It is much more comform-
able to my ideas of Divine Justice, that all the races of man should have equal
means of improvement, each its own light and own shadow." Her disavowal of
Christian progress also militated against excessive worldliness. In an argument
that was virtually identical to the one she preached to her students in her conversation on the idea of the millennium, she said, "It seems to me a low mate-
rialistic tendency which insists on the soul's making a heaven on this earth,
merely because the scene is the only one familiar to our imagination." Finally,
she said, her nonprogressivist view was much more consistent than a progressivist one with two of mankind's greatest ethical ideas—"the great principle of compensation," which consoled us for our suffering, and "the promises of Jesus,"
which represented, not a heaven on earth, but "the final destination of the
soul."[60]

We do not know how most of Fuller's fellow Coliseumites reacted to her antiprogressivist Romantic assault. Hall, who concluded the series on May 17—
ignoring her distinction between moral and intellectual progress—expressed
amazement that she could not comprehend that "the principles of *Christian civilization,*" because of their unique spirituality, would not eventually produce
intellectual as all other kinds of progress. Some of the more Transcendentalist
types, on the other hand, were deeply impressed. "I went to the Coliseum Thursday Evg," Rhoda Newcomb wrote to her son Charles the next day, "& there
heard a long piece of 24 pages from Miss Fuller—a Capital piece—upon the
progress of Society—against its advancement—exactly my view Charley—very
ably accomplished." Actually, Fuller's view was not exactly orthodox Transcendentalism, a fact which she herself revealed a little dramatically toward the end
of her talk. "I was present a few months since at a meeting of gentlemen, who,

in intellect and literary cultivation, may vie with any in N. England," she reported. "They talked upon this subject; I was struck by the incompleteness of view in many whose opinions, I, on other topics, highly value. Out of seventeen, there were only two against progress; yet nothing forcible was said in its favor." She did not say who the two were, but the half-Platonized Emerson may have sympathized with at least some of her views. (The concept of compensation, for example, was right out of Emerson's lexicon.) But the prophetic Emerson would have certainly blanched at Fuller's more extreme elitist and pessimistic remarks; they probably would have struck him as not too different from the very "selfish" and "unpractical" sorts of Romantic ideas he thought he had left behind when he returned from Europe. Of course, Fuller was hardly consistent. In her "Modern British Poets" articles, she had touted her self-conscious Romantic heroes as "pilot-minds" of their age. Also, even in her talk, she displayed, underneath all her cultural gloom, an obviously strong desire for cultural change. "This time, like all times, is a very good one, if we but know what to do with it," Emerson had said in his Phi Beta Kappa oration. It would still be a while before Fuller would find out for herself what that was.[61]

VI

Shortly after the Coliseum Club adjourned for the summer, the Greene Street School readied itself for *its* summer recess. Fuller jumped the gun a bit by taking off the last few days of the following week to visit friends in New Bedford. The act elicited from her "row" cries of consternation. "Miss Fuller has been absent the last two days," Juliet Graves wrote forlornly to Anna Gale on May 25, "but it seems a month almost since I have seen her." By Monday the twenty-eighth she was back, but only barely. The next day the entire school went Maying at the wealthy Moses Brown's farm, where the costumed students sang a song composed by Fuller, and two days later, the day after the last of the term, in the early morning Fuller left for Boston. As Emerson had urged her to give them "the most you can give us at Concord," she brought Caroline Sturgis with her on the eighth, and they stayed the weekend, discussing, among other topics, the very issue Fuller had debated in her Coliseum paper. ("I do not accept this complaint of the morbidness of this Age of consciousness or introversion," he wrote in his journal, echoing words that he had used in his "American Scholar" oration. "This crisis or state is as natural as any state, must be foreseen & forearmed & forebalanced & undoubtedly has its own checks & *good fruit,* though S.M.F. laughs at my word.") After leaving Caroline in Concord and continuing up to Groton to visit her mother, on June 12, the day after classes reconvened, Fuller resumed her teaching. Even then she managed to extend her vacation a little by going down at the end of the week to Newport to see the anchored French battle frigate *Hercule,* which had been drawing "immense crowds." A week and a half later she wrote a long, picturesque letter to Richard, Arthur, and Lloyd, detailing her adventures on board. After describing with particular gusto the quarters of King Louis-Philippe's son François, who was the ship's rear admiral, she imagined him standing or walking on the balcony at sunset or on moonlight evenings, "while this mighty vessel is dashing through the waters leaving a broad and sparkling wake for him to watch." She added for the benefit of her no-doubt-impressed little brothers, "I thought I should much like to command such a vessel, despite all the hardships and privations of such a situation."[62]

She may have wanted to command a frigate on the seas, but for the moment she was having trouble coping with more earthbound demons. One was the "bad state" of her health, which continued to depress her. Also, the past-ninety-degree July heat worked her up "almost to a frenzy," she told Caroline Sturgis, particularly during her mile-and-a-half walk to school. "I have been obliged to sit down and cry a long while after I got there to relieve myself and repeat the process on returning home. Home! Oh Cary," she cried, "my extreme weakness has made me feel so homeless, so forlorn! at times I have felt so much the need of somebody to bring me strengthening drinks, or to bathe my head." She added, "This is the first time I have really felt so utterly incompetent to do any thing." Often since her religious experience in Cambridge, when she had felt despondent, she had turned to religious thoughts for solace, but this time she took a further step. Moved by the sudden death of Hall's wife and Mary Allen's Aunt Harriet the week before, on July 1 at Edward Hall's church she took her first Communion. Though this was undoubtedly a meaningful experience for her, a letter she wrote to a friend around this time shows her still struggling to attain the "grace" she said she had once felt. "With my mind I prize high objects as much as then," she said; "it is my heart which is cold." She added: "Sometimes I fear that the necessity of urging them on those under my care dulls my sense of their beauty. It is so hard to prevent one's feelings from evaporating in words."[63]

Fortunately for Fuller's emotional state—religious and otherwise—the Greene Street School closed on August 10 for a one-month vacation. "Tossed to and fro" in "an agonizing conflict between my duty and my nature," she wrote in her journal from Boston, "I am in a state of sickly unresisting sensitiveness such as I do not remember in myself ever before—I despise but cannot conquer it." This time she sought human solace: "I want to lean my head on some friendly bosom." The first friendly bosom that seemed to offer itself was that of young Sam Ward, whom she had corresponded with while he was in Europe. Ward had returned to Boston the previous month from New York, where he had been working in a mercantile firm since his arrival in the United States at the beginning of the year. He and Fuller agreed to meet in the gallery of the Athenaeum. Sitting down and staring at the pictures while awaiting "Raffaello" (as she liked to call him), "I sank into a soothing reverie," she afterwards wrote in her journal. "I felt, the blessed influence of the ideal world once more. I am surrounded with records of lives which were passed in embodying thought not in laboring for clothes, furniture, and houses. I breathed my proper atmosphere and preened my ruffled pinions." While Fuller was soothing her spirits, Ward arrived: "Raffaello when he came did not seem to be more disposed to observe than myself. But I had not the benefit of his exquisite taste. But perhaps there was nothing worthy of its exercise." After paying the proper aesthetic homage, to the scene and to each other, they spent the rest of the day together:

> What a drive we had that afternoon! It was one of those soft gloomy times the sun is wearied out, he is asleep; and you feel a right to rest also. Gleams of brassy light succeeded a gentle pattering shower and we sped homeward by the palest starlight. Nature seemed to sympathize with me today. She was not too bright, she was not too wild and I was with the only person who ever understood me at once in such moods.

This was not the last dreamy day Fuller would have with this artistically serious young man.[64]

On the afternoon of August 15, on her way to visit her mother in Groton, she stopped by to see her very different male friend in Concord. Although she and Emerson spent hours happily leafing through a prized portfolio of engravings of paintings that Ward had brought back with him from Europe, she remained throughout the visit, she later told Lidian, "in a state of weak sensitiveness." Some of her bitterness seeped out even before this lover of "cheerfulness and fortitude," as she teasingly called him. Her behavior seems to have startled Emerson: "Life is a pretty tragedy especially for women," he wrote in his journal the day after she left. "On comes a gay dame of manners & tone so fine & haughty that all defer to her as to a countess, & she seems the dictator of society. Sit down by her, & talk of her own life in earnest, & she is some stricken soul with care & sorrow at her vitals, & wisdom or charity cannot see any way of escape for her from remediless evils." Fuller's gloom followed her the next day to Groton. It was while she was at her mother's that, after taking a long, "beloved" walk through the wildflower-studded surrounding woods, she wrote up her childhood remembrance of her mother's flower garden that ended with her lament that unlike the flowers (and, by extension, her mother), she herself neither produced nor embodied any beauty, but instead retained only the influence "of the viewless air." Clearly the handsome Ward and his beautiful art had not done much more than religion to make her feel good about her unbeautiful life.[65]

Despite all the anguish, she reported to Jane Tuckerman, she had "excellent times" with Emerson, her mother, and "with my own soul." Also—and perhaps fortunately for her object of "finding some influence which might draw me from myself"—the rest of her vacation was on a considerably lower pitch. Retracing her steps, she traveled to Waltham, where she stayed with the witty and (in her nephew Waldo's half-admiring phrase) intellectually "very muscular" Sarah Alden Ripley. As so often when despairing about her identity, she picked herself up when she encountered an older intellectual woman who had seemed to have established hers. "I admire her," Fuller wrote enthusiastically to Jane. "So womanly, so manly, so childlike, so human! She is as unfettered as we, yet very *wise*." From Waltham, after stopping briefly in Cambridge on August 30 to attend with Emerson the annual Phi Beta Kappa exercises, she continued to Newport; by now, as it was for her well-to-do Unitarian friends, her favorite summering place. "Such cloudless sunsets," she exclaimed to Jane, "with floods of rose and amber light; such overpowering moonlight, such wood walks, such beach walks, and all with proper people." Two were certainly that: William Ellery Channing, at whose summer house she stayed, and his unsettled, but to Fuller increasingly attractive, nephew William Henry ("as noble as ever," she blithely told James Clarke). She also made two additions to her growing collection of handsome male aesthetes: Rhoda Newcomb's eighteen-year-old son, Charles King Newcomb, and the wealthy, Göttingen-trained Baltimore scion and Germanophile critic George Henry Calvert. All in all, she afterwards told Jane, it was a "halcyon" close to a summer of "great anxiety."[66]

Back in class the day after the fall term began on September 10, Fuller returned to the duties that were giving her much of this anxiety. Indeed, no sooner had she arrived, she would later tell Charles Newcomb, than she "passed into a condition as busy, as wearisome, though, surely, not as annoying, as I ever knew in Providence." That week, at the behest of various friends, she acquired three barely teen-age girls to supervise and board with her at Mrs. Aborn's while they attended the Greene Street School: William Ellery Channing's niece Lilly Gibbs and two "little friends" of Clarke's, Ellen Clark and Emma Keats, the daughters of two of Clarke's Louisville merchant friends and parishioners, L. B. Clark and George Keats, the brother of the English poet John Keats. "Matronizing" such young girls she found irksome. Ellen and Emma, though "winning," she told Clarke, were too immature to be "susceptible" to her teaching, and Lilly, though "docile and amiable" enough, she told Lilly's cousin Mary Channing, was "peculiarly callous and self-satisfied." ("I never saw a child whom it was so difficult to put to the blush.") Also, in response to the entreaties of some of her older students for religious instruction, she started a weekly private class on the Old Testament—an interesting task, she thought, but again, somewhat time-consuming.[67]

Finally, she resumed her regular testing of Providence's cultural waters. As usual, her success was mixed. In mid-October she began attending a two-month series of lectures on Shakespeare by her old Boston-Cambridge conservative Romantic acquaintance, Richard Henry Dana, Sr. The talks, which he would repeat in Boston the following winter, were the first extensive American criticism of Shakespeare from a Romantic point of view, and in her journal notes, she amply complimented his rigorously nonmoralistic, loosely Coleridgian interpretations of the dramatist's plays for being "delicately refined" and full of "exquisite taste." At the same time, she took him to task for his critical naïveté: "Mr. Dana has read no modern criticism on Shakespeare (wishing to keep his own impressions untouched) so he repeats things current since the Schlegels and fights with Dr. Johnson. . . . When he has told you what *he* likes, the pleasure of intercourse is over; for he is a man of prejudice more than of reason, and though he can make a lively *exposé* of his thoughts and feelings, he does not justify them. In a word, Mr. Dana has the charms and the defects of one whose object in life has been to preserve his individuality unprofaned." Still, on second thought, she added, perhaps his readings were "better for his abstinence," since, "as the audience generally is very ignorant, there are only six or eight of us who are likely to be wearied at times." Indeed, her biggest caveat—as it had been when she had argued with him about the value of magazines and newspapers two years before—concerned Dana's Wordsworthian cultural preciosity: "The man of genuine taste and refinement undervalues those rockets and cannon blasts which are needful to rouse the still vulgar mind to attention." She may have thought of herself as a socially skeptical Romantic, but when she saw the genuine article, she recoiled like a cultural evangelical.[68]

As her faintly bored remarks about Dana and his audience show, Fuller's feelings about Providence culture had not changed much since she had first arrived. Meanwhile, she faced a mounting accumulation of more serious problems. Her continued deteriorating health was one. ("Miss Fuller was so unwell that it seemed to be with difficulty that she could say much," one student noted in her journal in one of numerous such entries that fall.) Her sister, who visited her that November, sometimes substituted for her in her history and natural science classes, and for a while her mother contemplated renting the Groton house and moving to Providence with the boys so she could help take care of her. But by the fall they decided that would be impractical. At the same time, all was not well at the school. Whispering, tardiness, and other disciplinary problems, mainly among the boys, had begun to surface, which, from student journals, Hiram Fuller seems to have had great difficulty handling. Also, rumors had been circulating, Mary Allen reported, about "the heretical doctrines" taught at Greene Street. By the fall, plans were afoot, among a group of Calvinist and some non-Calvinist citizens, to "break up the school" by building a competing one nearby, which they would do by the spring. These problems, plus declining enrollments, would cause a discouraged Hiram Fuller in a little more than a year to close his school permanently.[69]

Long before this happened, Fuller had decided to quit the school herself. (When he learned of her leaving, Alcott predicted that this would "seal its downfall.") By the time she returned to Providence in August, she had made the decision. In her letter to Lidian Emerson the following week, she had spoken bitterly of wanting an escape from "uncongenial pursuits and the oppressive intercourse with vulgar minds." To other friends she was more specific. "I am wearied out," she told Almira Barlow on November 8. "I have gabbled and simpered, and given my mind to the public view these two years back, till there seems to be no good left in me." And on December 9, she wrote to William Channing: "I am on the point of leaving Providence, and I do so with unfeigned delight, not only because I am weary and want rest, because my mind has so long been turned outward and longs for concentration and leisure for tranquil thought, but because I have been always in a false position and my energies been consequently much repressed." One thing she thought repressed them, as she implied to Almira Barlow, was the process of teaching (in Juliet Graves's words) "minds . . . sadly uncultivated." ("She cannot exercise her brightest, highest powers, for they cannot be understood," Juliet told Mary Allen, speculating about Fuller's departure.) Also, judging by her past complaints to Emerson about her Providence colleagues, not all the "vulgar" minds that weighed her down were her students—a fact her theoretically individualist but, when it came to literary practice, surprisingly social-minded "Auricular confessor" Emerson could have told her. (Discussing the way Providence's provinciality had undermined Albert Greene's literary potential, Emerson would later remark to her that "he ought to have been surrounded by great examples.") There was one additional spur. Earlier in the summer, in his preface to the first volume of his *Specimens,* Ripley announced that a life of Goethe was "in preparation for this Work, from original documents." Surely this was something, she must have known by now, that could be produced, if at all, only if she resigned from full-time teaching at Greene Street.[70]

So, her mind made up, it only remained for her to complete her final tasks. The fall term ended on November 28, but, perhaps to give her replacement, Sarah Jacobs, more time to get ready, she stayed on for a couple of weeks after winter classes began on December 3. The last few days she gave summary lectures in her history, rhetoric, and poetry classes, which she thought were good enough (although she never did it) to "bear being worked up into popular articles." Her final day was on the nineteenth, and she dedicated it to farewells. Several of her students have left highly dramatic reports of these last meetings, recounting Fuller's impassioned defenses of her severe, sometimes "ironical" teaching style, her revelations of her dangerously bad health and vocational disappointments, and her voice-choking appeals to them to look, as she did, to "that religion which can alone support us in this sorrowing world." ("Is it wicked, dear M."—discussing one classroom scene after Fuller had left, of "our own little circle . . . talking and weeping alternately for a long time," Louise Hunt asked her former comrade Mary Allen—"if I compare ourselves to that little band of disciples after the crucifixion of their Master? Their sorrow was no doubt deeper, but could it have been *more sincere.*") But the best picture of the way Fuller saw these last classes is her heartfelt, but more sober sketch of them that she wrote in her journal. After describing her rhetoric class ("I . . . expressed my gratification that the minds of so many had opened to some notion of criticism, analysis, and a love of beauty"), her meeting with her English poetry class (where she received an "elegant" copy of her favorite Shakespeare and a ring), and her "sweet" farewell to her boys, she finally turned to her last meeting with all her older girls.

> There were about forty present.
>
> I began by telling them that I thought them now sufficiently instructed to appreciate, in some degree, the difficulties by which I had been oppressed while teaching them. I gave an account of the false impressions which were given me of the position I should there occupy. I gave them some idea of the barbarous ignorance in which I found them, appealed to their remembrance and told some facts in confirmation of these extraordinary statements. I showed how all my efforts had, necessarily, been directed to stimulate their minds, and prepare them for discipline. . . .
>
> I thanked them for the favorable opinion of my government they had so gener-

ously expressed. But though they could none of them remember instances in which I had been unjust, I remembered three, and specified the persons (all of whom were present, sobbing as if their hearts would break). I thanked them for the moral beauty of their conduct towards me, said that an appeal to conscience had never failed to be answered, and that I had the happiness of being confirmed in the belief that young persons, generally, could be governed by appeals to their higher nature.

I spoke with a clear conscience of the care which I had taken to avoid interfering with the opinions or prejudices of their parents, however opposed to my own. I had always spoken of truth—I offered as *my* view of truth and felt that I had not only in words but in heart combined tolerance and delicacy with perfect frankness.

I assured them of my true friendship, proved by my never having cajoled or caressed them into good. Every word of praise had been earned; all my influence over them was rooted in reality; I had never softened nor palliated their faults; I had appealed, not to their weakness, but to their strength; I had offered to them always, the loftiest motives, and had made every other end subordinate to that of spiritual growth. With a heartfelt blessing, I dismissed them; but none stirred, and we all sat for some moments, weeping. Then I went round the circle and bade each, separately, farewell.[71]

In these accounts of her final classroom sermons, many Fullers leap out: high-pitched, demanding, critical, affectionate, prayerful, self-dramatizing, and, above all—as she intended to be—inspiring. They also hint at her achievements while at Greene Street: she had found an audience, demonstrated her platform charisma, perfected her talents as a teacher, confirmed her commitment to female culture, and discovered at least a little of life beyond Boston. "I have learned so much," she told Channing in her farewell-to-Providence letter of December 9, "that I cannot but suppose my experience is to be of further use."[72]

CHAPTER EIGHT

Conversations
(1838–1840)

I

"Packing, paying and parties, talk and tears." Fuller thus happily described in her journal her last days in Providence. "A degree of feeling was excited at the time," she added, "which I did not expect. Presents and promises of unceasing remembrance &c abounded." Her two weeks in Boston were more of the same. "It was all tea and dinner parties, and long conversations and pictures," she informed Clarke. She did have one disappointment in Boston. She was unable to hear, on January 2, Emerson's new "Human Life" series lecture on genius because he postponed it to the following Wednesday (he wrote in his journal) "on account of my unaccountable vigils." ("His excitement in preparing his lectures is so great he cannot sleep," his Aunt Sarah Ripley wrote to his Aunt Mary Moody Emerson. "[He] lies awake all night, and night after night.") Fuller, who complained to Emerson that she "stayed in town only to hear it, and shall have no chance at another this winter," was not very sympathetic. After learning just before she left from a girl she had sent to inquire about him at the Alcotts that he had only "lost a night's rest!!" and was now "perfectly restored," she twitted him, "Imagine my indignation: lost a night's rest! as if an intellectual person ever had a night's rest; one too of that sect who are supposed to be always

> 'Lying broad awake and yet
> Remaining from the body, and apart
> In intellect, and power, and will, To hear
> Time flowing in the middle of the night
> And all things creeping to the day of doom.'

—that such an one should adjourn a lecture on Genius because he has lost a night's sleep."[1]

While chiding Emerson for his untranscendental sloth, Fuller was busily demonstrating how little capacity *she* had for it. She saw the irony herself. "For seven years," she wrote to Caroline Sturgis, "I have never been able to pass two months so much as I please and never expect it again"; and yet, since coming home on January 3, "I have been as industrious as any beaver." To be sure, she tried somewhat to enjoy "the Elysian peace" at her mother's she had told friends she had dreamed of. She turned Lilly Gibbs over to Ellen and her mother for the winter and sent off Emma Keats and Ellen Clark to a "liberal" and "refined" Boston school "of the first respectability." ("I want a softer and more genial atmosphere around me," she explained to their patron, Clarke. "The public ways of life present rough inaccessible places in plenty without bringing them so near home.") Except for a few walks and one visit to church to take Communion, she stayed mostly in her room. Meanwhile, her mother and sister mended her clothes, while she tried, by donning loose robes ("that I might lie down, whenever I have severe pain, and apply friction"), to do the same for her body. But mainly that winter she worked. She arranged all her masses of papers of the last several years. She had put her brothers and sister on notice before she arrived that she would not resume her old role of family preceptor. ("Two years incessant teaching" had made her want "an absolute respite from that occupation," she had told Richard.) Nonetheless, she dutifully gave Ellen German instruction and Richard Latin and composition lessons twice a week. She also read, of course—mostly Plato, Coleridge, and her German books, along with her usual bundles of British quarterlies, English novels, and (to "ready myself to sleep") debates in Congress. And she wrote letters—lots of them. During her first ten days back she wrote twenty and made herself, she told Caroline Sturgis, "sick from fatigue." After convalescing in bed a few days, she started in again. By February 7 she was up to thirty-six ("all long ones") and complaining to Caroline, "I write a great deal too much, and at this rate shall never get well." By the end of the month, she had written fifty letters. She had definitely returned.[2]

Despite all her labors, her letters showed her in a basically upbeat mood. In a January 7 letter to Clarke, whom she had heard successfully preach when he had visited Providence the previous month, she happily quoted to him the passage from his youthful journal that she had left with him, saying that if he ever did succeed as a minister, he would owe it all to her. "It seems I am a sybil for my friends, Cassandra only to myself." She also soon had reason for feeling at least a little sibylline about herself. After two months of further translating and revising, on February 25 she finished the last pages of her translation of Eckermann's *Gespräche mit Goethe* and sent them off to George Ripley. She completed her preface on her birthday, and four days later the four-hundred-page *Conversations with Goethe in the Last Years of His Life* was published by Hilliard Gray and Company as the fourth volume in Ripley's *Specimens of Foreign Standard Literature* series. Except for a few omissions dictated by the need to squeeze the whole into the series' format and some lapses into stilted diction, her translation was a generally close yet idiomatic and forceful rendering. Eleven years later it was paid the compliment of being plagiarized by the London drama critic John Oxenford, whose virtually identical translation remained the standard one for

the next century. Meanwhile, her book made an important contribution to
Goethe's reputation in America. Rather than supporting the image of Goethe as
a morally suspect writer who had created the tempestuous, tortured *Werther* or
the profound, but in America little-read, *Faust,* Goethe's conversations as
recorded by his reverential young secretary introduced Americans for the first
time to the Weimer poet as a keen and accessible critic overflowing with wise
reflections on art, social ethics, and the literary vocation. Fuller's Germanico-
Transcendentalist friends were ecstatic. "The translating this book," Emerson
wrote to her, "seems to be a beneficent action for which America will long thank
you. The book might be called—Short way to Goethe's character—so effectively
does it scatter all the popular nonsense about him, & show the breadth of common sense which he had in common with every majestic poet, & which enabled
him to be the interpreter between the real & the apparent worlds." The book's
small vogue was not limited to Concord. The following day Fuller reported complacently to her brother Eugene that "in Providence all the copies sold immedy,
and the people like it very much." She added that even Sam Ward's banker
father was reading it "with great devotion and likes it much. I should think if he
did, most would."[3]

Fuller's book also attracted some attention because of its preface. Pushing
aside the concerns that preoccupied most American commentators on Goethe—his personal morals and his religious opinions—she focused squarely on
the Goethe she thought mattered: the thinker and artist. In so doing she presented a brief that, although only a condensed overview, exceeded in both sensitivity and comprehensiveness anything that had yet been published on the poet
in America. She began, in the lawyerlike mode of her "Brutus" article, by tersely
reducing the objections to Goethe to four:

> He is not a Christian;
> He is not an idealist;
> He is not a Democrat;
> He is not Schiller.

But unlike most American defenders of Goethe (including most of her Transcendentalist colleagues), who tried to refute or palliate these charges, she readily
admitted them, but declared them irrelevant. Instead, adopting her favorite
Goethean maneuver, she addressed herself to the questions of what standards
the Weimar author set for himself and how, in carrying them out, he made these
negative qualities not only comprehensible but admirable. On the vexed question of Christianity, for example, she wrote: "In his love of form Goethe was a
Greek; constitutionally, and by habit of his life, averse to the worship of sorrow.
His God was rather the creative and upholding than the paternal spirit; his religion, that all his powers must be unfolded; his faith, 'that nature could not dispense with Immortality.'" On the other hand, she said, Goethe was not insensible to spiritual beauty in human character. Yet this spiritual element, she
pointed out, was not painted with any particular partiality and, more important,
was always refracted through his art: "Those who cannot draw their moral for

themselves had best leave his books alone; they require the power as life does."
In a like manner she disposed of the rest of the charges. Was he a nonidealist?
Would it have been better that "instead of looking at objects with the single aim
of ascertaining their properties, he would have examined them only to gain from
them what most favored his plans"? Was he an aristocrat? The artist or literary
man was often "thrown into this body, by his need of repose, and firm ground
to work his proper way." As to the lame criticism that he was not Schiller, neither
was Shakespeare, Milton; they were two great natures and that was good. She
then went on to define positively wherein she thought Goethe's greatness lay: As
a counterbalance "to the spirit of the age," by his preference to "the perfecting
of the few to the slight improvement of the many" and his believing

> more in man than men, effort than success, thought than action, nature than prov-
> idence. . . . As one of the finest lyric poets of modern times. . . . As the best writer of
> the German language, who availed himself of all its advantages of richness and flex-
> ibility, and added to them a degree of lightness, grace, clearness, and precision,
> beyond any other writer of his time; who has, more than any other, tended to correct
> the fantastic, cumbrous, centipede style indigenous to Germany. As a critic, on art
> and literature, not to be surpassed in independence, fairness, power of sympathy,
> and largeness of view. As almost the finest observer of his time of human nature, and
> almost as much so of external nature.

Finally—warming to the trait she had always deeply admired in Goethe—"as a
mind which has known how to reconcile individuality of character with universality of thought; a mind which, whatever its faults, ruled and relied on itself
alone; a nature which knew its law and revolved on its proper axis, unrepenting,
never bustling, always active, never stagnant, always calm."[4]

Still, despite the high place she put him in, she denied being "a blind admirer
of Goethe." Unlike Carlyle, she said, she saw important limitations in both
Goethe's character and his art, and she listed them: "His aversion to pain and
isolation of heart," the absence in his writings of any partiality to "the holy and
heroic elements," and the fragmentary character of much of his criticism. She
even detected a certain loss of "architectural vigor" in his later works. "I think
he had the artist's eye, and the artist's hand, but not the artist's love of structure."
But in the end, she dismissed these imperfections as minor compared with
Goethe's genius. Furthermore, she argued—as she had in her "Brutus" article—
with geniuses like Goethe, the danger was rarely one of uncritical adulation but
the far more frequent one of "flippant irreverence. Not all that the heavens contain is obvious to the unassisted eye of the careless spectator. Few men are great,
almost as few able to appreciate greatness." As for the question of *how* great, time
alone, she said, as Dante's and Shakespeare's reputations have shown, would
ripen "the grand historical standing point . . . from which a comprehensive view
could be taken of him." In the meantime, she added imperially, "it is safer to
take off the hat and shout *Vivat!* to the conquerer who may become a permanent
sovereign, than to throw stones and mud from the gutter." It was an eloquent
testimony, and even friends whose views of Goethe were different from hers

applauded it. Emerson, who worried more than she did about Goethe's ironic hardness and aloofness toward common humanity, told her it was "a brilliant statement—with which I have no quarrel, but great contentment & thanks instead." And Clarke—who on the other end of the spectrum admired Goethe more as a heroic moralist than anything else—told her he took back all his criticisms of her "printed style" and sang (as he put it) "my Palinodia." Her preface, he crowed, was "a masterpiece of composition, clear yet cogent, dignified yet playful, with *point* to attract attention and weighty matter to occupy the thought."[5]

Fuller seems to have wanted to keep up the momentum of her Eckermann book, because the very same afternoon she finished it, she began her next and very different project—the arrangement of the papers of another formidable male figure from her past. She found the task rather daunting. On March 4, she reported to Caroline Sturgis that although she had been at work day and night for a week and had examined more than a thousand of her father's papers, "I seem scarcely to have made an impression on the great heaps of paper." But, she granted, the work was "very interesting . . . and [it] teaches me a great deal." Indeed, she wrote that same day to Charles Newcomb that she found it "so interesting that I cannot think of anything else." "My poor father!" she exclaimed. "If I were disposed to draw a hackneyed moral, surely there never was a fitter occasion. These papers had been accumulating forty years. College journals[,] themes, law minutes, minutes of the most interesting debates in the Mass and U S legislature, a voluminous correspondence on almost all subjects." He had never in all these years, she said, had time to examine these papers himself and had just completed the building of a study to house them the day before he died. "Well as I knew my father, I know him hourly better and respect him more as I look more closely into those secrets of his life which the sudden event left open in a way he never forsaw. Were I but so just, so tender, so candid toward man so devout towards a higher power." She did not say what the "hackneyed moral" she might have drawn was. One, though, suggests itself. After retiring from politics and withdrawing to the confines of a private domestic life, her father failed—whether because of incapacity, isolation, or bad luck—to translate his public thoughts into memorable public writing. His daughter, whose withdrawal to a more private sphere had never been exactly a choice, faced a similar difficulty with *her* public thoughts. It remained to be seen how she would respond to *that* worldly Goethean challenge.[6]

II

With the sorting of her father's papers, Fuller ended her days in Groton. The previous fall, her mother, who had no need for a farm and wanted to live with Margaret, had sold their house, and in the winter she and Margaret began looking for a new one. After the Emersons had tried but failed to find them a suitable rental in Concord ("I shall be so glad of so brilliant an accession to our village as your coming would make"), they finally settled on what was then an almost equally rural and attractive location—the Boston suburb of Jamaica Plain. There, in mid-April, following a couple of "delightful" and "interesting" week-long visits, first with the Emersons and then with Dr. Channing and his family, Margaret joined the rest of the Fullers. The family had arrived on the first, and rented a "pretty" house and property called Willow Brook—named after a broad, clear, willow-lined stream nearby—to continue a suburban version of their rustic life at Groton. Richard, whom Margaret had persuaded to lighten the family financial burden by studying with a tutor at home for one more year ("Rely upon me, your faithful friend," she had told him), raised chickens, pigs, and a few cows. Their mother kept house and cultivated a large vegetable garden on their half acre. Arthur—who was preparing himself for Harvard at Sarah and Samuel Ripley's boarding school in Waltham a couple of miles away—came home on weekends to help with household chores. Meanwhile Margaret savored the aesthetic delights of the Massachusetts countryside she had learned to appreciate in Groton. A month after moving there she wrote to a friend, "I do nothing but go to the rocks to gather the wild columbines, or lie down by the gay little brooks, walk, ride, study and write a very little." Two weeks later she told Charles Newcomb: "You need not send me wildflowers, for I never saw them in such profusion as now. The columbine wreathes the foot of every rock, the wild geranium purples the lanes, and the woods are absolutely paved with violets!"[7]

Besides its bucolic setting, Jamaica Plain had another advantage for Fuller—its five-mile proximity to Boston's center allowed her to indulge her fast-growing passion for music and art. In music the opportunities remained pretty limited. She organized parties of friends to hear the German concert violinist and pianist Ludwig Rackemann. She also attended the concerts put on by the Boston Academy of Music's new instrumental music director, Henry Schmidt. But it was with art that Fuller had the most luck. Ward's large portfolio of engravings of Renaissance and Neoclassical paintings helped. Also, the previous September the Athenaeum had added to its gallery of plaster casts of antique sculptures the large Brimmer collection of art books and engravings of paintings from major French and Italian museums. Finally, on April 24, a retrospective exhibition of Washington Allston's paintings had opened at Harding's Gallery on School Street. Enormously popular, the show attracted, over its two-and-a-half-month extended run, thousands of Bostonians, who squeezed into the gallery's small rooms to gaze in hushed reverence and awe at the city's—and America's—only internationally certified Romantic artistic genius. Fuller took it all in. She had had ("at last") an interview with Allston when she had been in Boston at the end of December and had verified that he was, indeed, the genuine article. ("He is as beautiful as the towncriers have said," she had reported to Emerson. "Unfortunately, I was so fascinated, that I forgot to make myself interesting, and shall not dare to go and see him.") During the summer, every few days she went ("with great delight") to the Athenaeum or her "home" at Harding's. (Indeed, so devotedly did she go to the Allston exhibit that a rumor spread that she actually fainted while looking at a picture. "I staid there too long one day, got one of my nervous spasms in the head and was obliged to send for a physician while on a visit," she merrily told Sarah Helen Whitman. ("However, do not contradict as I think it makes me appear very interesting something like the Chevalier Mozart.") She also tried to give an accounting of what she saw. She wrote a detailed critique of the Allston show after it closed. She took voluminous notes that summer and fall on her impressions of Leonardo da Vinci, Raphael, Michaelangelo, and others of her favorite Renaissance painters. And she read—"pen in hand," Emerson recalled—"Condivi, Vasari, Benvenuto Cellini, Duppa, Fuseli, and Von Waagen." Her notes show she read many others as well.[8]

What fired her passion for art is not difficult to discern. Ward was one big influence, of course; as were, to a lesser degree, Allston's only student Sarah Clarke, Emerson, and others of their friends who were excited by the pictures they saw at the Athenaeum that year. ("Our walls were hung with prints of the Sistine frescoes," Emerson recalled; "we were all petty collectors; and prints of Correggio and Guercino took the place, for the time, of epics and philosophy.") Romanticism and Transcendentalism also contributed. The mixture of the profoundly human and deeply religious in Italian Renaissance painting beautifully confirmed, as Fuller put it in her notes, "the God in man." This idealistic perspective—combined with the fact that she lacked the actual works themselves—naturally gave to Fuller's art jottings a highly allegorical character. The interpretations of Emerson, with whom she exchanged art notes, were also allegorical, but she outdid him in her self-revealing projections. ("I cannot express the delight this figure gives me," she wrote in one of her many commentaries on Raphael's and Michaelangelo's sibyls—figures she not only identified with "female genius," but also tagged with adjectives like serenely "Roman," "passionate," divinely "apprehensive," and other descriptive phrases that come very close to those she elsewhere used to describe her own qualities as a critic.) At best, her readings were impressionistically literary: she imagined, sometimes in great detail, what this or that gesture, look, stance, or bit of drapery revealed about the characters or the scene in a painting. At worst, she found in her paintings what she and Emerson and many of their friends found in nature: a visually rich but verbally silent screen against which she could project her desire for spiritual wholeness. As she put it in her notes on Michaelangelo's allegorical figures *Day* and *Night:* "I felt the truth of Mr E.'s remark so soon as I looked at Day and felt the delight we always do in detecting correspondencies between the human form and the other forms of nature. When we feel ourselves the microcosm, the whole is known." Or, in a more religious vein: "A Christ, by Raphael, that I saw the other night, brought Christianity more home to my heart, made me more long to be like Jesus, than ever did a sermon." She added, after describing in detail Christ's sweet, pure eyes and bent-back head ("as if seeking to behold the Father") and the surrounding scene, "I can never express it; but I felt, when looking at it, the beauty of reverence, of self-sacrifice, to a degree that stripped the Apollo of his beams."[9]

On the other hand, her idealistic aspirations notwithstanding, her art notes also show that she grasped what her fellow art novitiate Emerson generally ignored or dismissed—that a good part of the power of the arts, like that of nature (whose sensuousness, by contrast, Emerson appreciated), lay in their formal physicality. Occasionally that recognition even revealed to her (as it definitely did not to the self-confessedly literary-minded and "dull eye[d]" Emerson) something of the absurdity of her whole project of extracting meaning from second-rate copies. "Alas! must I never, never see for myself and die with my sixth sense undeveloped," she cried out in her journal, in the middle of a discussion of the descriptions and critiques in Quatremère de Quincy's biographies of Raphael and Michaelangelo. But mostly, art's physicality excited her. Repeatedly in her notes she praised both the imagistic Raphael and the visionary Michaelangelo for getting beyond the Christian repression of the "sensual" and creating humanistically "sensuous" art. Sometimes their sensuousness led her to revise a little her religious aesthetics. Speaking of a Raphael painting of Jesus, she wrote, "I am not one of the lovers of sorrow, but one of these forms makes me feel the might of the Cross and forbids to reject the blood, the cup of gall and vinegar, nay even the irritating ignominious crown of thorns." When the feeling the painting aroused was grossly sexual, however, she had to struggle. ("The female breast looks made for the temple of sweet & chaste thoughts, while this," she winced—speaking of the "disgusting . . . overpowering strength in the feminine form" of Michaelangelo's Sybils of Cumea—"is so formed as to remind you of the lioness in her lair, & to suggest a word which I will never write.") At other times the works gave her permission to relax a bit. Speaking of "the great difficulty of bringing two male faces any where near each other without exciting extreme disgust," she added, "Pour moi! when people embrace on the stage I am ready to die of shame and disgust at the sight. How can they endure to get so near one another, I feel"; but not so, she said, with Raphael's Jupiter's beautiful consoling kiss and embrace of Cupid. None of this made for great criticism, but at least it did what any new aesthetic shock ought to do: it jolted her presuppositions, in this case pretty deeply rooted New England idealistic ones. She confessed in her journal that, compared to her literary judgments, her "vehement" feelings about artistic works were entirely "subjective," but she thought "with proper opportunity" she could do better. In the meantime she affirmed what Emerson would have certainly approved: "The great law is to reproduce in some way all that has seemed worthy to command our thoughts. All literature, all art, even these works of M. Angelo are nothing but notes more or less significant on that text."[10]

In addition to art, that summer Fuller's nearness to Boston also facilitated for her, in this case through its libraries and bookshops, another un–New England cultural discovery—French Romantic literature. Contemporary French authors were little read in America and, if noticed at all, were widely excoriated for their (in the words of one horrified critic) "unparalleled extravagance and immorality." (Even the sophisticated Sam Ward, who would soon come to appreciate French Romantic authors himself, had warned his sister Mary, in his letter from London advising her to take Fuller's Boston German and Italian classes, "the clearer you steer of [French] literature the better.") Despite her adolescent love of Rousseau and her extensive reading in classical and eighteenth-century

French authors, Fuller herself had never shown much interest in contemporary French Romantic writers. She had read but not liked Chateaubriand (too *"ancien regime"* and "far too French") and had read admiringly a little of Victor Hugo. Otherwise, her general impression of contemporary French Romantics, she claimed, looking back that year, was that they were—certainly compared with her Germans—sensationalistic and immature. But that summer she began gobbling up from the bookstores Pierre-Jean de Béranger, Félicité Robert de Lamennais, Alfred Vigny, and other post-Restoration liberal and radical Romantics. In July and August she signaled their arrival in her canon by writing up a series of "impressions" of *"la jeune France."* These were her first extensive writings on recent contemporary literature. She privately showed them to Emerson and other friends.[11]

The first thing she dispensed with in these semipersonal "critiques" was her earlier prejudice that French writers somehow lacked moral seriousness— always a key test for her. On the contrary, she wrote, "I . . . begin to see . . . what the bloody rain of the revolution has done to fertilize her soil, naturally too light." As writers she found them generally full of (as she said of Béranger) "wit, high sentiment, and spontaneous grace," but not great. Her single exception— and the judgment showed, as well as any she ever made, her willingness to buck cultural prejudices—was Honoré de Balzac. Although the bold-faced eroticism of Balzac's novels made them the most widely condemned of all French books, in her notes she praised him for "facing the dark side of human nature" or (as she put it a little more fastidiously) "the fearlessness with which he takes mud into his hands and dips his foot in slime." Usually she could not endure this when done, she said, "as with most Frenchmen, with an air of gay recklessness"; but Balzac did it, she assured her friends, with the "stern manliness" of a Cervantes. She went on to praise lavishly the ingeniousness and realism of Balzac's characters and plots. She even shrewdly saw the "sublime" sentiment in Balzac, noting, for example, the ironic fact that the character of Goriot in *Le Père Goriot,* "mirabile dictu," was "as much ennobled, made as poetical by abandonment to a single instinct, as others by the force of will." Still, despite her great admiration for his artistic powers, she sometimes found Balzac's vices of the instincts—so different from the more satirized or sublimated crimes of passion she was familiar with in English novels—a bit *too* much to take. At the end of her notes on *Goriot* she confessed, "This book was too much for my nerves, and would be, I suppose, for that of most people accustomed to breathe a healthier atmosphere." She also confessed finding "the skepticism as to *virtue*" in Balzac's novels disturbing. In her journal a few months later she was more blunt. Speaking of the "the French tone" of *Louis Lambert,* she muttered: "I hate the ever-recurring 'sublime,' 'immense,' *'exquis'* &c. Already to me the writings of la jeune France savor of a clique, & ennuyer almost as much as Boston society. Then," she added, Bostonianlike, "Balzac is so tedious with his physiology!"[12]

The French writer who most fascinated Fuller, though, was a figure in some ways even more notorious than Balzac—George Sand. Although Sand was condemned even in France for her series of lovers and her scathing attacks on marriage in her early romance novels, neither scandal fazed Fuller. In her critiques of Sand she ignored the gossip and praised the novels, many of which she read several times. One thing she liked, predictably enough, was their "smouldering" style ("not vehement, but intense, like Jean Jacques"). But she also lauded their message, which, she thought, was not self-indulgent or anti-social at all, but Romantically, even heroically, stoic. "This is my ideal," she excitedly wrote, speaking of Sand's *Jacques;* "the soul that, capable of the most delicate and strongest emotions, can yet look upon the world as it is, . . . and, without any vain optimism or weak hope of a peculiar lot, can, as Jacques says *accept life.* This is the true stoicism not to be insensible but superior to pain." She also admired Sand's ability not only to portray "the heroic woman," but to do so from within a woman's consciousness, an ability that, to Fuller, made Sand almost unique in literature. The novels she most admired, though, were not Sand's feminist romances, but her recent, more difficult, less popular, semi-mystical fictional works like the socialistic mystery thriller *Spiridion* and, espe-cially, the ecstatic feminine-Faustian closet drama *Les sept cordes de la lyre,* which she read right after it was published in the spring in the *Revue des deux mondes.* This was not so much because she admired them as novels. The use of "character painting" in *Spiridion* as a vehicle for political ideas seemed to her intellectually dilettantish. Nor was it exactly because of their message. It is true she *was* intrigued a little, although not convinced, by the subjectivist, aesthetics-minded humanitarianism espoused by Sand and her circle of Saint-Simonian socialist friends, which "would seem to approach the faith of some of my friends here, which has been styled Psychotheism." (She added: "The practical opti-mism is much the same as ours, except that there is more hope for the masses—soon.") But what really excited her about these novels was, not their politics, but their unabashed intellectuality. "I am astonished at her insight into the life of thought," she wrote. "She must know it through some man." She then went on darkly:

> Women, under any circumstances, can scarce do more than dip the foot in this broad and deep river; they have not strength to contend with the current. . . . It is easy for women to be heroic in action, but when it comes to interrogating God, the universe, the soul, and, above all, trying to live above their own hearts, they dart down to their nests like so many larks, and, if they cannot find them, fret like the French Corinne. Goethe's Makaria was born of the stars. Mr. Flint's Platonic old lady a *lusus naturae,* and the Dudevant has loved a philosopher.[13]

This was a harsh verdict on women (and perhaps also on herself). It was also, with its last allusion to Sand's intellectual subserviency to the socialist theorist Pierre Leroux, severe on Sand. This submissiveness was not the only weakness she found in Sand. In reading a little later her epistolary miscellany *Lettres d'un voyageur,* she was shocked to discover a broad streak of self-indulgent sentimen-tality. "Here . . . what do I see? An unfortunate woman wailing her loneliness, wailing her mistakes, writing for money! O she has genius, and a manly grasp of mind, but not a manly heart! Will there never be a being to combine a man's

mind and a woman's heart and who yet finds life too rich to weep over?—
Never?" Yet, despite the fact that Sand's derivativeness and frailty *"à la mode
du genre féminin"* ("no self-ruling Aspasia she") made her fail for Fuller as a
heroic model, the Frenchwoman's writings did reveal to her one extraordinarily
important idea—that it was possible to write in a literary genre that combined
the emotional, private, and "feminine" with the intellectual, public, and "masculine." And if Sand could do it, why not she also? "These books have made me
for the first time think," she wrote in her journal,

> I might write into such shapes what I know of human nature. I have always thought
> that I would not, that I would keep all that behind the curtain, that I would not write,
> like a woman, of love and hope and disappointment, but like a man of the world of
> intellect and action. But now I am tempted, and if I can but do well my present work
> and show that I can write like a man, and if but the wild gnomes will keep from me
> with their shackles of care for bread in all its shapes of factitious life, I think I will try
> whether I have the hand to paint, as well as the eye to see. But I cannot but feel that
> I have seen from the mouth of my damp cave, stars as fair, almost as many, as this
> person from the Flèche of the Cathedral [in *Les sept cordes de la lyre*] where she has
> ascended at such peril. But I dare boast no more, only please fate be just and send
> me an angel out of this golden cloud that comes after the pelting showers I have
> borne so long.[14]

She *would* try to so paint in a few years. But except for a few tales, the medium
she would use would not be the ethereal one of Romantic fiction, but a modified
version of her more down-to-earth—and still not forgotten—genre of "intellect
and action." ("Reading in [the French moral philosopher Simon-Théodore]
Jouffroy the chapters on Mysticism and Pantheism excited greatly my desire to
be a thinker," she wrote in the middle of one of her journal critiques of Sand. "If
I cannot be an artist, or a complete Natur surely I can be a thinker.") Even that
would require her to learn a bit more of "love and hope and disappointment."
It would also help that she would learn what some nonfictional and not always
heroic women—including herself—were capable of doing.[15]

III

A couple of months before Fuller contemplated her future, she had begun savor-
ing her summer. On June 10 she wrote to Sarah Helen Whitman: "I am as happy
as I can be. My health is much improved. I have beautiful Nature, beautiful
books, beautiful pictures, beautiful engravings, and retirement and leisure to
enjoy and use them." And, she might have added—in explaining why "I feel
myself blest now in living at harmony with myself which I never did in your
city"—beautiful people. Of course, some of her social time in Boston was taken
up by what she called her "rye bread days"—numberless visits, parties, and
excursions with siblings, cousins, aunts, uncles, acquaintances, and friends of
friends, gossiping about engagements, marriages, and careers in Boston-Cambridge's upper-middle-class Unitarian community. Yet even about this rye-
bread world ("all dull & damp without") she could sound protective, even pro-

vincial. On the eighth she reported to her brother Eugene that she had met that morning at the Allston gallery the wealthy New York Ward brood. The group included Sam Ward, the later "Wizard of Wall Street" (and no relation to Margaret's Boston Sam Ward), and his sister Julia, the future author Julia Ward Howe, later one of her followers and biographers but at this time a twenty-year-old, coquettish young socialite. "The eldest of these swains was frightfully ugly," Fuller sniffed; "both walked as if their backs were out of joint (which I take to be the present fashion) and wore their hair very long and curled at the edges, whether by the hand of Nature or Art I know not." Nor was young Julia spared any of this Bostonian social clawing. "The second Miss W. is not to be compared with Ellen for beauty, and if I could judge from the little I saw of the well known Julie she is inferior to E. in mind and as affected as she can be. I was inclined to be more worldly and low-minded than is my wont," she assured her brother, "and to murmur at the attention these wealthy damsels attracted when if poor Ellen had been there nobody would have noticed her, despite her beautiful face."[16]

But mainly Fuller's move to Jamaica Plain expedited, not regional warfare, but renewed socializing with her growing army of intimate friends. These included many of her old Boston-Cambridge friends like Eliza Farrar, Ellen Sturgis Hooper, and Sarah Clarke, as well as her exiled clergymen soul mates Hedge, Clarke, and William Henry Channing, who frequently visited the area. They also embraced her newer Transcendentalist colleagues like Emerson, Alcott, and the Ripleys; many of their friends or relations like Lidian Emerson, Elizabeth Hoar, and Sarah Alden Ripley; and less intimate, but still loyal supporters like William Ellery Channing and Elizabeth Peabody. Finally, they included Fuller's close circle of young friends and protégées: Jane Tuckerman, Mary Channing, Marianne Jackson, Anna Shaw, Anna Loring, and, most intimate of all, the attractive, cultivated trio of Anna Barker, Sam Ward, and Caroline Sturgis. This last group of young people shared certain characteristics. They were deeply absorbed in each other's psyches, intellectual aspirations, and social passions. They were strongly sympathetic to Transcendentalism and the latest trends in European Romantic music, literature, and art. They were also drawn from some of Boston's wealthiest and most prominent mercantile and professional families, many of whose older members, like the Lorings, the Shaws, and the Russells, whom Fuller was also friendly with, were active participants in the city's various reform causes. In a word, they were the young hopefuls of avant-garde Boston. Speaking of this group as a whole, but especially this last little circle, Emerson later wrote:

> She wore this circle of friends, when I first knew her, as a neckless of diamonds about her neck. They were so much to each other, that Margaret seemed to represent them all, and, to know her, was to acquire a place with them. The confidences given her were their best, and she held them to them. She was an active, inspiring companion and correspondent, and all the art, the thought, and the nobleness in New England, seemed, at that moment, related to her, and she to it. She was everywhere a welcome guest. The houses of her friends in town and country were open to her, and every

hospitable attention eagerly offered. Her arrival was a holiday, and so was her abode. She stayed a few days, often a week, more seldom a month, and all tasks that could be suspended were put aside to catch the favorable hour, in walking, riding, or boating, to talk with this joyful guest, who brought wit, anecdotes, love-stories, tragedies, oracles with her, and, with her broad web of relations to so many fine friends, seemed like the queen of some parliament of love, who carried the key to all confidences, and to whom every question had been finally referred.[17]

This is an impressive testimonial, especially in view of Emerson's own later star-crossed tenure in Fuller's "parliament of love." This is hardly to say, of course, that Fuller lacked enemies. A fair portion of ex-Federalist, old-family Boston society continued, in the words of Samuel Gray Ward, who knew that world as well as any, to "set its face against her." Also, Oliver Wendell Holmes, James Russell Lowell, and Belinda Randall are only a few of the conventional, headstrong, or sensitive Boston-Cambridge *young* people who shrank from Fuller's presence as one might from a disease. As she became in later years increasingly associated with controversial movements and ideas and lent her acerbic pen to their defense, she would acquire more such antagonists, and the legend of "Fuller, the ridiculed eccentric" would grow. Nor was the problem only other people's prejudices and foibles. Clearly, real traits in Fuller's personality continued to make her enemies. One trait that certainly earned her a fair share was her "demonical" fondness for "annihilating" people who provoked her (as she said of one exchange with the cynical William Pabodie) by their "low vanity." The sweet and saintly Elizabeth Hoar, whose admiration for Fuller's wit and intellect was almost boundless, put it as judiciously as she could: "She was, perhaps, impatient of complacency in people who thought they had claims, and stated their contrary opinion with an air. For such she had no mercy. But, though not agreeable, it was just. And so her enemies were made."[18]

Even if they were not Fuller's enemies, many were also put off by what they saw as her arrogant manner. Emelyn Story, who knew her through mutual friends like the Lorings and the Shaws—and who would later become a close friend of Fuller's in Italy—recalled that she thought of her then "as a person on intellectual stilts, with a large show of arrogance and little sweetness of temper." Even her friends were sometimes startled by her penchant for making remarkable egotistical pronouncements that showed her "full of self-esteem" (as one friend put it). "Margaret at first astonished and repelled us by a complacency that seemed the most assured since the days of Scaliger," Emerson recalled. "She spoke, in the quietest manner, of the girls she had formed, the young men who owed everything to her, the fine companions she had long ago exhausted." In one startling recollection that has become legendary in the canon of Fuller tales, Emerson later reported her one day telling Sam Ward "that she had seen all the people worth seeing in America, & was satisfied that there was no intellect comparable to her own." One can easily make, of course (as many of her friends made), allowances for these sorts of advertisements of her "rather mountainous ME" (in Emerson's phrase). Some pointed out that they were, like her pugnacity, something of a family trait. Others speculated that they were an understandable byproduct of her isolated early education or possibly her need as a woman to fight for an education and a career. Still others noted that her most outrageously egotistical statements were balanced by humbly prayerful and self-deprecating entries in her journals, and, in any case, when said aloud, were often said with an ironic smile or laugh, as if to acknowledge their outrageousness. In the most outrageously Fulleresque defense of all, Perry Miller, speaking of her reported boast to Ward, has suggested that "in the prospective of American intellectual history her observation may, in fact, be the simple truth." Still, however true or untrue, these explanations (except, perhaps, for the laugh) obviously did not by themselves make the results any more endearing. Finally—quite apart from her perceived arrogance or egotism—Fuller's everyday repartee irritated some. "The feeling she excited among good sort of people like Mary R[otch] &c," Emerson later reported—speaking of Eliza Farrar's wealthy, New Bedford Quaker-turned-Unitarian, spinster aunt, whom Fuller was very fond of—"was that she was sneering, scoffing, critical, disdainful of humble people, & of all but the intellectual."[19]

All of this said, it should also be said that there were many other sorts of "good" people who did not have these feelings about Fuller at all. Or if they did, like Emerson they ultimately dismissed them as secondary. Indeed, what seems most striking about Fuller's social life after she moved back to the Boston area is less the number of enemies she made than the literally hundreds of men and women of various sorts who were devoted—some extraordinarily so—to her as a friend. So large did this theme loom in her life that when Emerson and William Channing first conceived of the idea of publishing the *Memoirs,* they thought they would entitle it "Margaret and her Friends." What, then, one wants to know, was the specific chemistry that, despite Fuller's reputed eccentricities and arrogance, held all these friendships together?[20]

Certainly, everyone seems to have agreed, there was not any strong claim for her personal beauty. A daguerreotype (Illus. 30) taken several years later shows her small, delicate ears; her broad, rounded forehead like her mother's; and slightly bulging, dark, blue-gray eyes, in the picture almost closed as she gazes down upon an open book. It also reveals a rather heavy jaw, thin lips, and, from her father, a fairly prominent Roman nose. On the other hand, her hair, which surviving samples show was dark blonde to light brown, remained long and thick enough to be done up, as it usually was, chignon-fashion, and her friends reported that her smooth, white hands and arms, which she moved in graceful, animated ways in conversation, were attractive. Many friends thought that because of both (as one put it) "her passionate love of the beautiful" and the physical attractiveness of her sister and mother and many of her female friends, she was prone to disparage her appearance more than it deserved. ("I cannot help wearying myself of this ugly cumbrous mass of flesh," she would cry out in her journal some years later. "I hate not to be beautiful, when all around is so.") It was probably because of this self-consciousness that, despite her nearsightedness, she used her lorgnette sparingly, which Sam Ward thought gave her "a strained and distant look and awkward air." It was certainly for this reason of "womanly vanity" (as one of her friends suggested) that she habitually laced herself tightly, a practice that several believed made worse the slight curvature of her spine that

(as one wrote) "threw her head forward in an unfortunate manner." Yet, even
about this, one of her most noted characteristics, it is hard to find agreement.
Oliver Wendell Holmes described her "long and flexile neck," in a remarkable
Medusalike metaphor, as "arching and undulating in strange, sinuous movements, which one who loved her would compare to a swan, and one who loved
her not to those of the ophidian who tempted our common mother." Her friend
William Henry Channing gave a more complete and sympathetic—and certainly less masculinely hysterical—account of this and Fuller's other physical
trademarks:

> The gray eye, rich brown hair and light complexion, with the muscular and well-
> developed frame, bespoke delicacy balanced by vigor. . . . She certainly had not
> beauty; yet the high arched dome of the head, the changeful expressiveness of every
> feature, and her whole air of mingled dignity and impulse, gave her a commanding
> charm. Especially characteristic were two physical traits. The first was a contraction
> of the eyelids almost to a point,—a trick caught from near-sightedness,—and then
> a sudden dilation, till the iris seemed to emit flashes;—an effect, no doubt, depen-
> dent on her highly-magnetized condition. The second was a singular pliancy of the
> vertebrae and muscles of the neck, enabling her by a mere movement to denote each
> varying emotion; in moments of tenderness, or pensive feeling, its curves were swan-
> like in grace, but when she was scornful or indignant it contracted, and made swift
> turns like that of a bird of prey.[21]

As both Holmes's and Channing's remarks amply show, Fuller's physical
traits had a way of melting into social ones. And of these various traits, which
explain the secret of her many friendships, first and foremost, many of her
friends thought, was what Sarah Clarke called her "immense capacity for social
intercourse." Clarke may have known this side of Fuller better than anyone else,
having fled from her for several years because she feared her "too powerful
dominion," before finally succumbing to her friendly assaults. Emerson wholeheartedly agreed: "Persons were her game, specially, if marked by fortune, or
character, or success;—to such was she sent. She addressed them with a hardihood,—almost a haughty assurance,—queen-like." Once her humbled
"quarry"—to use Sarah's brother James's term—was won over, he or she seems
to have undergone a conversion experience. "When within her sphere," Sarah
Clarke later wrote—in a phrase that one can find repeated in the testimony of
almost all Fuller's close friends—"those points of her character which had at first
offended me pleased me. . . . That which at first had seemed offensive arrogance
now became a beautiful pride." Besides aggressive persistence, Fuller also clearly
won many friends by her well-honed talents as an intellectual entertainer. She
was always "full of fun," one young friend recalled. Even Emerson, who, as we
have seen, was initially put off, as he put it, by "the unprofitableness of all this
derision & joking & crackling of thorns under a pot," soon became charmed by
her conversation and, as his friends reported and his recent letters certainly
showed, increasingly sought out her friendship in part just for that. Others in
Emerson's gracious, witty, and high-minded family circle did also, even if they
felt compelled to explain themselves in rather high-minded ways. Elizabeth
Hoar, for example, who adored Fuller's talk (especially, she claimed, for its

"power of bringing out Mr. Emerson"), directly confronted the charge that Fuller's satirical style bespoke a sneering and scoffing character. In a letter about Fuller to a friend of hers after Fuller left from her visit with the Emersons in late March, she wrote:

> You would, perhaps, have an impression of levity, of want of tenderness, from her *superficial* manner. The mean hindrances of life, the mistakes, the tedium, which eat into your soul, and will take no form to you but the tragic, she takes up with her defying wit and sets them down in comic groups and they cease to be "respectabilities." You feel at first as if this included ridicule or disregard of the sufferings they bring to you; but not so. Her heart is helpfully sympathetic with all striving souls. And she has overcome so much extreme physical and mental pain, and such disappointments of external fortune, that she has a right to play as she will with these arrows of fate.[22]

Her efforts, talents, and sufferings granted, what exactly in Fuller's character made her friends want to respond as deeply as their papers show they did? The retiring and down-to-earth Sarah Clarke, who remained a steadfast, but by no means uncritical, friend, thought that the key to the influence Fuller exerted over her friends was

> her unusual truth-speaking power. She not only did not speak lies after our foolish customs, but she met you fairly. She broke her lance upon your shield. Encountering her glance, something like an electric shock was felt. Her eye pierced through your disguises. Your outworks fell before her first assault, and you were at her mercy. And then began the delight of true intercourse. Though she spoke rudely searching words, and told you startling truths, though she broke down your little shams and defenses, you felt exhilarated by the compliment of being found out, and even that she had cared to find you out. I think this was what attracted or bound us to her.

While Sarah Clarke described Fuller's hold on her friends as a sort of ravishment, others remembered it more as a result (which some thought naturally flowed from her fascination with individual character) of her extraordinary empathy. "Like a moral Paganini," her brother James, who knew this side of Fuller well, recalled, "she played always on a single string, drawing from each its peculiar music." And one man told Emerson: "No one ever came so near. Her mood applied itself to the mood of her companion, point to point, in the most limber, sinuous, vital way. . . . Ah! she applied herself to the mood of her companion, as the sponge applies itself to water." But whether it was ravishing or empathetic, all agreed she had such a hold on people, and that it allowed her to extract, even from the most reticent, "surprising confessions" and "extraordinary narratives" that made their friendship with her seem almost magical. James and Sarah's gay-spirited younger brother, Chicago merchant William Clarke, would describe to Fuller, in not atypical language, the effect of one conversation with her during her trip West a few years later: "Suddenly a tide of feeling swept away this barrier, and long pent emotions gushed forth." "She was the wedding-guest," Emerson wrote, "to whom the long-pent story must be told; and they were not less struck, on reflection, at the suddenness of the friendship which had established, in one day, new and permanent covenants. She extorted the secret of life, which cannot be told without setting heart and mind in a glow; and thus had the best of those she saw."[23]

One reason, of course, she had the best was probably that she projected a good deal of it onto them. Certainly Emerson thought so. She encouraged them to believe, he wrote, that they "lived in a superior circle," and, as a consequence, "they suppressed all their commonplace in her presence." This, of course, was an old penchant with Fuller, going back to her Cambridge days. But her letters show it was particularly strong after she moved back to Boston. This was probably due to several things—the peculiar character of some of her friendships; the greater vistas of influence Boston life opened to her; and, undoubtedly, her recent reading in contemporary French and German Romantic literature, which was permeated—much more than the older Romantic texts she had read in her youth—by variously ethereal, passion-laden, and ideologically charged cults of friendship. (In one of her critiques of Sand, she minutely compared Sand's heroines with similar figures she knew among her friends.) Whatever the cause, both her letters and later recollections show her strong propensity at this time and for the next several years for throwing a brilliant glow of psychic, social, and moral excitement around her friendships. In the section of the *Memoirs* that he edited, Emerson painted a vivid portrait of what he remembered of this (as she liked to put it) "embellishing" or "translat[ing]" of her friends, especially in their moments of "crisis," in her private conversations with them:

> With the firmest tact she led the discourse into the midst of their daily living and working, recognizing the good-will and sincerity which each man has in his aims, and treating so playfully and intellectually all the points, that one seemed to see his life *en beau,* and was flattered by beholding what he had found so tedious in its workday weeds, shining in glorious costume. Each of his friends passed before him in the new light; hope seemed to spring under his feet, and life was worth living. The auditor jumped for joy, and thirsted for unlimited draughts. What! is this the dame, who, I heard, was sneering and critical? this the blue-stocking, of whom I stood in terror and dislike? this wondrous woman, full of counsel, full of tenderness, before whom every mean thing is ashamed, and hides itself; this new Corinne, more variously gifted, wise, sportive, eloquent, who seems to have learned all languages, Heaven knows when or how,—I should think she was born to them,—magnificent, prophetic, reading my life at her will, and puzzling me with riddles like this, "Yours is an example of destiny springing from character:" and, again, "I see your destiny hovering before you, but it always escapes from you."[24]

No doubt Emerson was not Fuller's only friend to experience a mingled sense of relief and excitement at discovering Fuller pointing her lance at his destiny instead of at him. One the other hand, both the seeming dithyrambic frenzy and ironic distancing are pure Emerson. Furthermore, however often she may have struck such high-pitched tones with her friends (and they certainly may be found in some of her letters), they were not the only thing she did for them. Both her letters and theirs show that she also devoted—daily, weekly, year after year— enormous amounts of *prosaic* energy to her friends: counseling them, instructing them, and generally catering, often in tender and painstaking ways, to their various personal needs and concerns. "I always have time for my friends," she would assure Sarah Shaw, and they knew it and loved her for it. Finally, if they did glow under her influence, the glow they felt was clearly not always the frenzied one that Emerson recalled. That this was so is well illustrated by this passage from the journal she kept on a visit to Emerson's a few years later, when her friendship with him had cooled somewhat. She is discussing the intellectually bold but socially wary Henry Hedge, whose longtime friendship with Fuller was something of a puzzle to Emerson.

> This day H. Hedge passed with us, and in the afternoon I went with him to Cambridge. I did not enjoy seeing him while we were at Concord. Seeing him & S. Ward with Waldo, I understand why he should always suspect them of being mere men of the world and men of talent; they are so with him; he sits with his lovely courteous *un*confiding smile and *sees* them merely, & they are seen not known. But the moment I am alone with either it is another thing. H's manner so glassy and elaborate before[,] full of soul[,] the tones of his voice entirely different.

To see expressions, hear tones, and receive thoughts "which no one else ever saw or heard from the same parties" (as Emerson put it after recalling this incident in her *Memoirs)* was a rare trait, and Emerson, who was attuned to a different sphere, fully understood its value. "Margaret, wherever she came," he wrote in his journal while he was working on the *Memoirs,* "fused people into society, & a glowing company was the result. When I think how few persons can do that feat for the intellectual class, I feel our squalid poverty."[25]

And, one might add, she accomplished that feat not just for the avant-garde intellectual class. Looking through her and her Boston compatriots' papers, one finds these scenes—her walking along laughing and joking with Harvard's rhetoric professor, Edward T. Channing; spending the morning at the home of the University's austerely conservative Greek professor and later president, Cornelius C. Felton, leafing through German art books; learning from her old friend Lydia Maria Child that her brother Convers Francis (Henry Ware, Jr.'s, successor as Parkman Professor of Pulpit Eloquence, whose daughter Fuller instructed) regarded her as "a prime favorite of his." Nor—Emerson's observation about Fuller's "game" of hunting the rich, successful, and heroic notwithstanding—are these images restricted to the intellectual elite. "Around my path how much humble love has flowed," she wrote in her journal after spending a day with her Crane family cousin Caroline Kuhn, her brother Lloyd, and the Farrars. "These every day friends never forget my heart, never censure me, make no demands on me, load me with gifts and services & uncomplaining see me prefer my intellectual kindred. I am ungrateful, as Timon was to his servants." Nor did only her Boston friends and acquaintances feel her presence. "She could not make a journey, or go to an evening party," Emerson maintained, "without meeting a new person, who wished presently to impart his history to her." More remarkable, even nouveau-riche types who discomfited some of her old-family, cultivated friends did not always put her off. "I stand in a certain awe of the moneyed men, the manufacturers, and so on," Sarah Alden Ripley told Emerson, speaking of her Waltham neighbors, "knowing that they will have small interest in Plato, or in Biot; but I saw them approach Margaret, with perfect security, for she could give them bread that they could eat." Emerson, who later confessed to having been constantly astonished by Fuller's catholic powers of socializing, summed up his understanding of her talents this way: "Some persons are thrown off their balance when in society; others are thrown on to balance; the excitement of company, and the observation of other characters, correct their biases. Margaret always appeared to unexpected advantage in conversation with a large circle. She had more sanity than any other; whilst, in private, her vision was often through colored lenses."[26]

How did Fuller regard her social talents? Certainly she knew of and took pride in them. "My museum is so well-furnished that I grow lazy about collecting new specimens of human nature," she had ostentatiously yawned to Caroline Sturgis just before leaving Providence. A little more startlingly, Emerson later reported that she had once told him that "no man gave such invitation to her mind as to tempt her to a full expression; that she felt a power to enrich her thought with such wealth and variety of embellishment as would, no doubt, be tedious to such as she conversed with." Yet even Emerson, who fully stressed, perhaps overstressed, "the arrogant tone" of these sorts of pronouncements, also had an inkling of the pathos of such one-way social gifts—or, as he put it, her "ebullient sense of power, which she felt to be in her, which as yet had found no right channels." Fuller felt the pathos, too.[27]

This is nicely shown in a journal account she wrote of her most extensive trip that summer—her one-week stay at the beginning of August, in Bristol, Rhode Island, at the house of her Prescott classmate Mary Soley DeWolfe and her family. Mary had five years earlier married William Bradford ("Braddy") DeWolfe, the youngest son of the notoriously wealthy slavetrader, privateer, and one-time United States senator James ("Captain Jim") DeWolfe. The elder DeWolfe had recently died and had bequeathed to his favorite son and his wife "The Mount," a lavishly furnished and ornately designed three-story mansion set in a thousand acres of heavily wooded land overlooking the Bristol bay. Fuller evidently considered her ten-day stay at The Mount significant because she kept a detailed journal of it, which she sent, as she did most of her journal-critiques that summer, to Emerson.[28]

Like her previous accounts of the high society she encountered on her vacations with her wealthy summering friends, her report was pretty negative. She bristled, Unitarianlike, at some of the women's rote "crown of thorns" Episcopalian sentimentality and shuddered at the thought of "how much blood and tears all the luxury around me cost." Mostly, though, she affected a studied anthropological tone, as though she were describing the ways of primitive tribes. "The girls of this family look like Italian peasants, so large-limbed, and dark skinned with brilliant eyes and free though somewhat elephantine gait and gesture. They had with them a couple of Phila girls of the dwarfed and pallid class commonly to be met in our cities. We went out to the shore and seated ourselves on the rocks. I was down by the water's edge, and looking up at the group above, M. who sat in the midst looked like a queen, and the D'Wolf girls her Amazonian guards who had brought in these leaden girls as captives." Toward the "stagnant and animal though not what would be styled sensual" lifestyle of the DeWolfes, she cast a more indulgent look. While noting the irrelevance of "the chateau life" in democratic America, she still found Braddy's devotion to his daughters and animals and to nature appealing. ("A spontaneous character even of this grade is not without interest in this country of workies where they are so rare.") In a more personal vein, she also praised Mary's household skills, dignified manners, and quiet elegance. "Her life is almost wholly external but she is very complete and elegant in it. You are not pained, and do not wish her more," she wrote, adding her favorite Goethean definition of character, "for she is and does as nature intended." Mary also had, she happily noted, "a fine sense of the ludicrous," which Fuller found particularly amusing because "whatever she says she never lays aside her deliberate elegance of manner." ("I so seldom see any one that is not perfectly obtuse on this score and who does not suppose that these burlesque extravaganzas much show ill nature or want of sentiment that I in this way have a good deal of pleasure with her.") And indeed, some of the best touches in her journal are her recountings of their mutual "drollery." One of her best is a ludicrous account of what actually sounds like a rather harrowing experience of being chased to and fro, open parasols in hand, by one of Braddy's untamed horses behind a walled-in pasture that they had entered. In these episodes one can easily see—her moral misgivings about Mary's lifestyle apart—Fuller's frolicsome, girlish side with an equally playful and high-toned, if nonintellectual, young woman.[29]

Despite the antics and the anthropology, though, Fuller ended her social chronicle on a somewhat darkly ambiguous note. Clearly, the burden of having been, as she put it, the only "live wire" in the household began to take a toll. She wrote on the day she left: "I am not sorry to go, for in the evgs, as the circle is so narrow, and I felt a desire to make them pass pleasantly, I was obliged to make more exertion than I like. I dislike so much to be entertaining at present. I feel as if I were breaking a vow." But mostly what sobered her was an offhand comment of Mary's.

She remarked a day or two since that she thought I had "a very contented disposition." At first I was struck with admiration at myself on hearing this remark. I thought I must have surprizing power over myself to produce such an impression when I am so impatient and aspiring by nature. But, on reflection, I could see what had struck her. She sees me destitute of all she thinks valuable beauty, money, fixed station in society, unsustained, uncertain as to the future. She must look upon mine as une vie manquée, and, ignorant of my mental compensations, admire at my gay and serene manner, and talk. I see too that kindness as much as affection dictates the attentions she heaps upon me and I like her the better for it. I am willing those of her sort shd be kind to me, from those who can see farther into my nature I want, will have nothing but spontaneous love.

This is a balanced conclusion. Yet it must have been a little unsettling for her to think that, but for her "mental compensations," her life appeared to be "une vie manquée." Moreover, as it so happened, at this moment she was in the throes of demanding "sponteneous love" from several friends who *could* see farther into her nature than could Mary, and she was finding the whole experience rather distressing.[30]

IV

After a short boat ride from Bristol on the morning of the ninth, Fuller arrived in Providence to spend the night before returning the next day to Jamaica Plain. She was met on the landing by her young friend Charles Newcomb, who promptly whisked her away to a "house . . . full of people." All day they kept coming, until by the time she left to go home at three, it seemed to her, she wrote in her journal, she had seen "almost every one in P." Amid a few tears and a good deal of laughter and silliness, Providence's local literati paid their respects to their returning heroine. "They made a great joke of my avatar, said it had been placarded in the streets, and that I thought more of myself than Jackson or La Fayette, for they staid all night at least. Mrs W[hitman] got upon the floor and insisted on having a piece of lace that was torn from the bottom of my frock 'as her share' and, what amused me most of all, they brought an immensely fat baby in a go cart [Albert Greene's daughter Sarah Margaret Fuller] who, they said, was named for me."[41]

Such a rousing ovation from so loyal a throng in the provinces should have raised Fuller's spirits correspondingly. But it did not. After a similar one on the way to Bristol, she remarked laconically: "Even shallow love is grateful sometimes. One must be thankful for any thing on a journey." More generally, one would have thought that the completion of her Eckermann book, followed by (as she told Caroline Sturgis) her "first leisure summer" in nearly ten years, not to mention her jaunts to Boston galleries and her beloved, "healing" seashore, would have, if not lifted her mood, at least calmed her nerves. Instead—her June 10 boasts to Whitman about her happy condition notwithstanding—that summer she suffered repeated attacks of headaches as severe as any she had ever known. At Nahant, which she visited in mid-June with her sister, Ellen; Caroline Sturgis; and Sophia Ripley; she had headaches two of her three days there, one so "frenzied," she told Jane Tuckerman, that in the afternoon she "went to bed, and covered my eyes with wet towels." They subsided after she returned, but soon started up again, reaching their full fury for several days at The Mount. Worse yet, as soon as she returned, there descended on her, she told Jane, "a mood of sadness, nay of gloom, black as Hades, which I have vainly striven to fend off by work, by exercise, by high memories." Finally, as so often with Fuller, psychic and physical torments were compounded by a social one. Indeed, it was the biggest social crisis she had faced since her adolescence. One trigger was Caroline Sturgis.[32]

Of all of Fuller's young protégées, the twenty-year-old Caroline was the most fascinating and problematic. Her favored yet scarred family life undoubtedly contributed a good deal to both. As did her sisters, Caroline attended Boston's best private schools. Her wealthy father indulged her tastes for her cultivated, outré social and intellectual circles. With her mother she was not so lucky. The daughter of John Davis, the judge of the United States District Court for Massachusetts, Elizabeth Davis, an intelligent but brooding woman, after the death of their only son, abandoned her family for a year when Caroline was twelve and thereafter suffered lifelong periodic fits of depression and nervous breakdowns. It was during the year of her mother's absence that Fuller, already a close friend of her older sister, Ellen, had first met Caroline. Fond of styling herself in her letters "a poor orphaned child," for most of her teens and twenties, Caroline avoided as much as she could of home life (which, she said, looked to her "spectral" and felt like "a ride on a porcupine's back") and flitted about among her family's various New England woodland and seashore vacation homes and those of her older literary friends in Boston, Concord, and elsewhere. Although she was poetically talented like her sister, Ellen, her greatest talents—and certainly her personality—are best displayed in her letters. Reading these by turns dreamy, witty, whimsical, irreverent, acute, and melancholic letters, one can easily see why the "gipsy-like" Sturgis, despite her unprepossessing appearance (Higginson would later describe her as "very plain but with fine eyes"), would be attractive to literary people as disparate as Emerson and William and Henry James.[33]

Actually, Caroline had become something more than just attractive to Fuller; she had by now become her most intimate female friend. As with most of Fuller's friends, it was not at first an easy intimacy—or so it would seem from the demanding and oracular letters Fuller had written to Caroline from Groton the winter before moving to Jamaica Plain. Of course oracular pronouncements had become an aspect of her relationship with several of her young protégées during the past couple of years. ("I touched the secret of the universe, and by that touch was invested with talismanic power which has never left me, though it sometimes lies dormant for a long while," she had informed Jane Tuckerman the previous fall in her letter about her Thanksgiving day religious experience.) But all of this was fairly mild compared to the high-pitched mix of moral advice and Romantic oratory she dispensed to Caroline. Much of the first sort that winter had centered on relations between the sexes. To help give Caroline a taste of what was in store for her as a future intellectual Romantic, she had sent her a bundle of James Clarke's old letters about his youthful love affairs. (This promiscuous circulation, by modern standards, of private correspondence was something many of Fuller's friends indulged in, although none went so far—or was given as much latitude in doing so by their friends—as Fuller.) "On looking them over they seemed to me among the most valuable I possessed," Fuller wrote, in the vein of a romantic epistolary connoisseur, adding: "Perhaps some things may slightly disgust you in detail but I think when you have got through and look at it as a whole you will think it a fine picture of an intellectual friendship, and an interesting history of growth of a practical character. I think many critiques on books and pictures will interest you. And it will let you see how a large class of men feel towards women, more clearly than you could in books." She had also tried to warn her of the dangers lurking in youthful Boston social circles. In several letters Fuller had devoted particular attention to scolding her for her association with "The Brother and Sister Club," a high-spirited, dandyish, and mildly flirtatious circle of wealthy, literary-minded Harvard students and graduates and their sisters and girl friends that included, among others, the club's petted neophyte literati, James Russell Lowell and William Wetmore Story, and their future wives, Maria White and Emelyn Eldridge. Clearly these were not the sort of aspiring Transcendentalist types she was grooming Caroline for! "I think they are," she had told her squarely, "base persons with all their elements of beauty. This may not be Delphic but it has struck me so from the very first.— Now you have got out of your sublime fit, and want to try experiments don't, Dear, walk in the mud." She had been especially "repelled," she had added, by Caroline's recent letter detailing the amusement she had had, in a young Margaret Fullerish–sounding way, satirizing some Harvard undergraduates at a recent party at Maria White's: "I sympathize entirely with your keen perception of [one senior's] ridiculous points but to laugh a whole evening at vulgar nondescripts is that an employment for C. who I thought had the heroic element in her. Who was born passionately to love, to admire, and sustain Truth." She went on to assure Caroline, at best half-truthfully, that her own satirical bent "has always been forced upon me and is the accident of my existence. I would not *want* the sense of [the ridiculous] when it comes for that would show an obtusement of mental organization, but on peril of my soul I would not move an eyelash to look for it."[34]

Besides setting her straight about the proper Romantic social manners, Fuller also that winter and spring had tried to indoctrinate her in weightier matters. One was her own volcanically Romantic philosophy of life. "The mere Idealist vexes me more than the mere Realist, because he seems to me never to have lived," she had lectured Caroline in one letter. "He might as well have been a butterfly; he does not know the human element." Again: "I love the love lit dome about I cannot live without mine own particular star; but my foot is on the earth and I wish to walk over it until my wings be grown. I will use my microscope as well as my telescope." And from the microscopic to the subterranean: "I love the stern Titanic part, I love the crag, even the Drachenfels of life— I love its roaring sea that dashes against the crag," and so on through lava rushes, ghostly northern firs, trembling lizards, wounded snakes, and a couple of dozen other strange and bizarre natural forms. And, finally, on to the intellectually heroic: "For my part I shall never be happy, unless I could live like Pericles and Aspasia. I want the long arcade, the storied street, the lyre and garland. I want the Attic honey on the lip, the Greek fire in the eye. This cannot be, and we cannot be happy, but we need not, we will not be vulgar— We will live better than we do now. We will be as good as the feudal ages." Much of this, of course, was a throwback—albeit in more eerie German Romantic dress—to the heroic Romanticism of her youth, which Sturgis (Goethe and Wordsworth notwithstanding) seems to have revived in Fuller. The other weighty theme that had run through Fuller's letters to Caroline had been her insistent offering of herself up, not just as a great friend, but *the* great, even imperiously great, friend in Caroline's life. "I did not know I had repaired from you," she had written to Caroline in the spring, in answer to her complaint that Fuller had not been sufficiently confiding. "But I take my natural position always, and the more I see, the more I feel that it is regal.— Without throne, sceptre, or guards, still a queen!— I shall not, of course, think about it, but let things take their natural course." Again, less regally, but obviously still thinking about it: "Probably, no other person you know could be so much to you as I."[35]

There is nothing in Sturgis's correspondence that suggests that she resented any of this extravagant talk. Even Fuller's regal claims did not seem to bother her. And she was positively drawn to her older friend's dark, aspiring Romanticism. Fuller's recent brooding poem, "Drachenfels"—in which the poet looks down on the hidden "haunts of man" and feels a profoundly "desolate" yet strangely "proud," even liberating, sense of loneliness—"had much effect on her thoughts," she told Fuller. In a similar vein, though in a lower key, Caroline saved as a favorite of hers a stoically Romantic poem Fuller had sent to her that spring on her favorite flower, which concluded:

> Learn from the Columbine to live alone,
> To deck whatever spot the fates provide
> With graces worthy of the garden's pride,
> And to deserve each gift that was denied.[36]

But that still left one difficulty. For, beyond emotional power and intellectual influence over Caroline—and probably, too, the chance to relive her own "smouldering" youth—she also wanted affection from her. As so often with her young friends, she had strangely overbearing ways of showing it. "I was somewhat pained by your want of affection towards me while in Boston," she had written to her after arriving in Groton. "But I could not seriously think there was any danger of your ceasing to love me. There is so much in me which you do not yet know and have faculties to apprehend that you will not be able I believe, to get free of me for some years." She could also sound a little disingenuous (or perhaps self-deceiving) about her project. "I do not wish to urge myself on you as a heroic or a holy friend. I believe it is best to receive me principally through the intellect," she blandly told her, then quickly adding, "Yet love me as much as you can." Social historians tell us that the nineteenth-century notion of women's unique spirituality and "kindred" nature commonly encouraged sentimental expressions of homosocial passion among a large number of middle-class women in this period. In this sense, Fuller's demands on Caroline were not unusual. On the other hand, Fuller's letters to Caroline were hardly sisterly or sentimental, and this was the problem, as it had been in her adolescence: she had a weak voice for expressing the intimate or affectionate, much less the erotic, feelings she demanded or wanted from others. So, not surprisingly, when she demanded something of these of Caroline, the passionate but (in Henry James's phrase) "socially impulsive" girl balked. At Nahant the issue came to the surface. According to Caroline, Margaret had asked her if she loved her and (she wrote in the margin of one of Fuller's bitter letters) "I could not at once say yes." For the rest of the vacation they quarreled, and, after returning, Fuller, deeply hurt, told Caroline she wanted to end their *"intimate"* friendship. Not until the winter—after months of mutual silence punctuated by cautiously affectionate letters—did their friendship get repaired or (as Fuller put it the following year) "redeemed from 'the search after Eros.'"[37]

Fuller's allusion to the beautiful, libidinous boy Eros, who is seduced by his foster mother in the fairy tale in Novalis's *Heinrich von Ofterdingen,* might have been intended, at least unconsciously, as something more than a vague literary phrase. For the tides of emotion that swept over the beaches of Nahant were only the crest of a much larger wave for Fuller that summer. To locate the source of *that* wave, one needs to turn to another figure in Fuller's circle.

In a painting that the Romantic portraitist William Page did a couple of years later of Sam Ward—in a high-buttoned dark coat, with his dark, thick, longish hair swept to the side over a high, Fullerlike brow crowning an oval face of large, liquid eyes, sensuous nose and lips, and softly boyish yet stolid expression—he looks very much like the Puritan aristocratic aesthete depicted by his modern biographer. His highly respected father, Thomas Wren Ward, whom he was close to, was something, in a more worldly way, of a post-Puritan himself. Besides being the successful American agent for Baring Brothers, the English firm that financed most Anglo-American trade, the bookish elder Ward was also one of Boston's prime cultural leaders, serving for many years as the treasurer of both Harvard University and the Boston Athenaeum. Naturally he saw to it that his son received a first-rate schooling. Unfortunately for his father, that schooling, first at Boston Latin School, where Ward placed first in his class, and later at the progressive Round Hill School (which young Ward liked) and Harvard (which generally bored him), altogether confirmed his sense of himself (as he put it) as "a student and literary man" rather than, as the seven generations of Wards before him, a merchant. This feeling was confirmed by his frequent visits to the Athenaeum library and gallery and, after his graduation, by his year-and-a-half tour of Europe in the company of the Farrars and Harvard's professor-turned-author, George Ticknor.[38]

It was further confirmed when, after returning to the United States in early 1838, Ward renewed his friendship with Fuller, who introduced him to Emerson. Together they drew Ward into the growing circle of more or less Transcendentalist young people they were gathering around them. Although the more bizarrely religious of the band bemused him, Ward cultivated friendships, if a little warily (one of them thought because of his "fear of ridicule"), with the more literary and bohemian among them. He was especially taken with the unbohemian Emerson. His letters show that this was more because of Emerson's example as a poised and independent literary intellectual than his specific ideas. Ward's Goethean aestheticism would always keep him distant from Emerson's idealism. Nonetheless, he maintained a lifelong friendship with the Concord sage. From their side, too, Fuller and Emerson found Ward to be a valuable companion. Although barely twenty when he returned from Europe, Ward astonished many in their circle with his intellectual sophistication and commanding manner. ("His mind seems formed to subdue others to its influence—so clear, so cool, so decided & sure in his opinions," Sarah Clarke would tell Fuller a few years later; "he must always control the minds of those near him, except in the very few instances where he meets his equal.") The few fragments of his intellectual reflections that survive from these couple of years support this perception. Also, apart from Emerson, Ward was the only one of their circle to have actually viewed firsthand the major European masterpieces, and his portfolio of copies of them, which he would lend to Emerson in the fall of the following year, was an important stimulus to their circle's growing passion for painting.[39]

Most of all, Ward was drawn to Fuller, whose "literary insight & power of assimilation," he would later write, he had found "astonishing." He later claimed that Fuller had been the first person to open up to him the spiritual value of modern German and Italian literature, the most important intellectual passions of his life. But art and literature were not the only passions Ward stimulated in Fuller. She also fell in love with him, although exactly how or when is not clear. After their trip together to Trenton Falls, they mostly carried on their friendship by mail. While Ward was traveling in Europe, they wrote frequently to each other. All of this correspondence is lost, but if the one surviving and already quoted letter she wrote before he left—about her fascination with the heaving, bosomlike, "undulatory motions" of water—is any indication, whatever was personally revelatory was pretty heavily veiled. After he returned and they had their happy August meeting at the Allston gallery (even two years later she would remember being then in "the heights of bliss"), her references to him in her letters assumed an increasingly affectionate tone. In February she asked Caroline Sturgis to make a large, decorated box to hold all her letters, verses, and sketches "from my friend Raphael," which she intended to "keep . . . devoted to him while I live." "I agree with you that this is not pretty enough for him, though quite pretty enough for me," she told Caroline, urging her to line his with a softer and paler color than she had used for hers. "He is such an Ariel that he deserves to be ministered to of every creature's best."[40]

By this time, Ward was gone on a six-month pleasure and business trip through the Ohio Valley down to New Orleans. After he returned in April, they resumed their friendship on, if anything (at least so Fuller would later claim), an even more affectionate plane than before. But by June it was clear to Fuller that something was seriously wrong, a fact no doubt that caused her, out of a desire for some reassurance, to press Caroline at Nahant for a declaration of love. In July, obviously worried, she wrote to him anxiously:

> No, I do not distrust you, so lately as you have spoken the words of friendship. You would not be so irreverent as to dare tamper with a nature like mine, you could not treat so generous a person with levity.
>
> The kernel of affection is the same, no doubt, but it lies dormant in the husk. Will ever a second Spring bid it put forth leaf and flower? I can make every allowance. The bitterness of checked affections, the sickness of hope deferred, the dreariness of aspirations broken from their anchorage. I know them all, and I have borne at the same time domestic unhappiness and ruined health.
>
> I know you have many engagements. What young man of promising character

and prosperous fortunes has not one waiting his every hour? But if you are like me, you can trample upon such petty impossibilities; if you love me as I deserve to be loved, you cannot dispense with seeing me. . . .

We did not begin on the footing of rational good-will and mutual esteem, but of intimacy; and I should think, if we ceased to be intimate, we must become nothing to one another.

We knew long ago that age, position, and pursuits being so different, nothing but love bound us together, and it must not be *my* love alone that binds us. I want a friend that could realize to me what is expressed in Byron's ["Stanzas to Augusta"] —"Though the day of my destiny's over, &c" And above all the line "Though loved, thou forborest to grieve me!"[41]

Evidently, foot-trampling demands, threats, appeals, and even Byronic self-pity failed to work. In early September, in a seething letter, she exploded in desperation and anger:

You love me no more— How did you pray me to draw near to you! What words were spoken in impatience of separation! How did you promise to me, aye, and doubtless to yourself, too, of all we might be to one another.

We are near and with Spring's fairest flower I poured out my heart to you.— At an earlier period I would fain have broke the tie that bound us, for I knew myself incapable of feeling or being content to inspire an ordinary attachment. As soon as I saw a flaw I would have broke the tie. You would not— You resented, yet with what pathetic grace, any distrust on my part. *Forever, ever* are words of which you have never been, are not now afraid.

—You call me your best of friends, your dearest friend, you say that you always find yourself with me. I doubt not the depth of your attachment, doubt not that you feel my worth. But the confiding sweetness, the natural and prompt expression of attachment are gone—are they gone forever?

The rest of the letter was a point by point enumeration of all the evidence that showed, despite his protestations of respect and friendship for her, his real emotional indifference towards her. ("The confiding sweetness . . . are gone. . . . The sympathizing contemplation of the beautiful in Nature, in Art is over for us.") Still, she said, despite all this, she would not break things off. Instead, in an extraordinary conclusion, seething with both self-abnegation and presumption, she declared:

I will wait— I will not complain— I will exact nothing— I will make every allowance for the restlessness of a heart checked in its love, a mind dissatisfied with its pursuits. I will bear in mind that my presence is like to recal all you have need to forget and will try to believe that you would not be with me lest I "spoil you for your part on life's dull scene," or as you have said "call up the woman in you."

You say you love me as ever, forever. I will, if I can, rely upon your word, believing you must deem me entitled to unshrinking frankness.

You have given me the sacred name of Mother, and I will be so indulgent, as tender, as delicate (if possible) in my vigilence, as if I had borne you beneath my heart instead of in it. But Oh, it is waiting like the Mother beside the sepulchre for the resurrection, for all I loved in you is at present dead and buried, only a light from the tomb shines now and then in your eyes. But I will wait, to me the hardest of all tasks, will wait for thee whom I have loved so well. I will never wound thy faith, nor repel thy heart, never, never! Only thyself shall have power to divorce my love from its office of ministry,— not even mine own pride shall do it. So help me God, as I keep this vow, prays

ISOLA.[42]

On the surface, such mournful and elevated pleadings sound suspiciously reminiscent of Fuller's one-way romance with George Davis eight years before. (Her ever-loyal brother Richard would later disparage Ward to Margaret as "another George Davis.") Particularly when one adds to this Fuller's allusion to another love in Ward's life—along with her intimation that this was the reason for his withdrawal—the feeling of déjà vu would seem to be confirmed. But it would also be superficial. For one thing, the maternalistic Christian and German Romantic death rattles at the end of her letter suggest a relationship, if no less ethereal than that with Davis, certainly at least at a higher emotional and intellectual pitch. For another, the serious-minded, artistically inclined Ward was a more complicated and, from Fuller's point of view, considerably more susceptible figure than the flippant, worldly-wise young Davis. Furthermore—though with most of Ward's side of the correspondence lost, we cannot be certain of this—it seems highly unlikely that Fuller would have alluded, however histrionically, to pledges by Ward unless he had indeed pledged that spring or summer, however obscurely or platonically, his love *"forever, ever."* Finally, to complicate the matter still further, the young woman in this triangle was no mere acquaintance, but none other than Fuller's close and enormously admired friend Anna Barker. In order to understand the full complexity of Fuller's love tangles, it is necessary to know something about Anna.[43]

V

Even among Fuller's large collection of talented and well-to-do young female friends, Anna Barker stood out. For one thing, she was not a Bostonian. Although her parents were New Englanders, she was born and lived for twenty-one years in New York City. After this, in 1834, her father, the flamboyant and extremely wealthy, Democratic New York merchant Jacob Barker, following one of his numerous financial gyrations, moved the family to New Orleans. There Anna attended for a while an upper-class Catholic convent school. After this she continued to shuttle among her family's various town and country houses in New York and Newport. In the second place, she and her family were not Unitarians, but Quakers. Such a variety of high *and* liberal viewpoints, together with her large family's closeness, probably explain the affectionate, sensitive, spiritual-minded, and, above all, generous characteristics one finds her displaying in her diary and letters. (Her friends were charmed by her habit of giving *them* presents on her birthday.) She was reasonably well read in contemporary English, French, and German Romantic literature, which she seems to have blithely filtered through a sentimental version of her Hicksite liberal Quakerism. "That we ought to trust all and love all, and that then all would become worthy of trust and love," Sarah Clarke would state as her "sweet doctrine" at a Transcendentalist discussion the following year. But mainly she impressed others by her lively and gracious social charm and dazzling beauty. Certainly she impressed the Boston-Cambridge Unitarian and Transcendentalist friends whom she saw whenever she visited her cousin Eliza Farrar. "You should have seen [her]," Emerson would write ecstatically—and rather typically—to his probably startled Calvinistic confessor Aunt Mary after he met Anna in the fall; "a vision of grace & beauty—a natural queen—just returned from Europe, where as here she received incense every day, in all places, which she accepts with high glee & straightway forgets from her religious heart. She is the very heroine of your dreamed romance which you related to Charles & me at Elm Vale once."[44]

For Fuller, too, Anna Barker was a romantic heroine. Higginson speculated that Eliza Farrar had originally introduced Margaret to her younger cousin, who was three years younger than Margaret, with the idea of offering her as "a charming model" in the ways of young womanhood. If true, this certainly would have given Fuller one initial push toward heroine-making. They also kept up contact. After Fuller moved to Groton, in addition to vacationing together during Anna's yearly summer treks from New York, and later New Orleans, to Cambridge and Newport, they wrote to each other frequently while Anna was in Europe. Numerous references in Fuller's letters and journals during this time show how much Anna meant to her. "Have I ever told you how much I love her?" she had asked James Clarke about her "amica del cuore" a few months before her father died. "Never could fancy create a being of greater purity grace and softness. . . . If I write a novel I shall take Anna for my heroine." Over the next few years, she dedicated most of her poems, including her first serious Romantic ones like "Drachenfels" and "The Hieroglyphic Spell," to Anna as her "beloved" or (as she put it aptly in one poem) "my heart's sister and my fancy's love." William Henry Channing—who had himself been attracted to Anna and had often seen the two together during these years in Cambridge and Newport—thought that the deep attraction Anna had had for Margaret had been her allure as her unrealized alter ego:

> Susceptible in temperament, anticipating with ardent fancy the lot of a lovely and refined woman, and morbidly exaggerating her own slight personal defects, Margaret seemed to long, as it were, to transfuse with her force this nymph-like form, and to fill her to glowing with her own lyric fire. No drop of envy tainted the sisterly love, with which she sought by genial sympathy thus to live in another's experience, to be her guardian-angel, to shield her from contact with the unworthy, to rouse each generous impulse, to invigorate thought by truth incarnate in beauty, and with unfelt ministry to weave bright threads in her web of fate.[45]

Even if one discounts Channing's literary ornateness, that Margaret felt for Anna as a more beautiful, graceful self is very plausible. It is also likely that Margaret was attracted to Anna as a sexual object. Many of her references to Anna are laden with, not only ethereal passion, but homoerotic passion as well. One of her favorite gambits—in which her male friends also freely indulged—was to compare (as in one letter to her favorite sex-role exchange partner Clarke) "*my* Anna" with their young wives, fiancées, and lovers. But the best example of this sort of thing is suggested by a journal entry Fuller wrote three years later, after her passion for Anna had subsided. Recording the thoughts she had had while recently leafing through a collection of pictures of famous French men and women during and after the Revolution, she wrote:

> Nothing fixed my attention so much, as a large engraving of Me Recamier in her boudoir. I have so often thought over the intimacy between her and Me de Stael. It is so true that a woman may be in love with a woman, and a man with a man. It is so pleasant to be sure of it because it is the same love that we shall feel when we are angels when we ascend to the only fit place for the Mignons where
> Sie fragen nicht nach Mann und Weib—
> It is regulated by the same law as that of love between persons of different sexes, only it is purely intellectual and spiritual, unprofaned by any mixture of lower instincts, undisturbed by any need of consulting temporal interests, its law is the desire of the spirit to realize a whole which makes it seek in another being for what it finds not in itself. Thus the beautiful seeks the strong, and the strong the beautiful, the mute seek the eloquent &c the butterfly settles always on the dark flower. Why did Socrates love Alcibiades?— why did Korner love Schneider? how natural is the love of Wallenstein for Max, that of Me de Stael for de Recamier, mine for Anna Barker. I loved Anna for a time I think with as much passion as I was then strong enough to feel— Her face was always gleaming before me, her voice was echoing in my ear, all poetic thoughts clustered round the dear image. This love was a key which unlocked for me many a treasure which I still possess, it was the carbuncle (emblematic gem) which cast light into many of the darkest caverns of human nature.— She loved me, too, though not so much, because her nature was "less high, less grave, less large, less deep" but she loved more tenderly, less passionately. She loved me, for I well remember her suffering when she first would feel my faults and knew one part of the exquisite veil rent away, how she wished to stay apart and weep the whole day. Then again that night when she leaned on me and her eyes were such a deep violet blue, so like night, as they never were before, and we both felt such a strange mystic thrill and knew what we had never known before. Now well too can I now account for that desire which I often had to get away from her and be alone with nature, which displeased her so, for she wished to be with me all the time. . . . I thought of all this as I looked at Me Recamier and had one thought beside which has often come into my mind, but I will not write it down; it is so singular that I have often thought I would never express it in any way; I am sure no human being but myself would understand it.[46]

It is tantalizing, of course, to speculate on exactly what thought was so singular that she refused to write it down. The idea that would probably first strike many modern readers—that it was a conscious wish for a homosexual experience— seems unlikely. (She would a few years later praise unstintingly in her journal two poems of the lesbian poet Sappho, but then add, "as woman she is repulsive.") Indeed, on one level, in her musings about Anna, she may not have been expressing much that was sexual at all. Both popular boosters of women's "kindred" homosocial passions and highbrow Romantic writers of the period often had a way of seeming to promote, while actually diffusing and sublimating, sexual expressions that are hard for later franker—or cruder—generations to grasp, and certainly Fuller's proclaiming of the purely "spiritual" in homosocial love would fit into this pattern. On the other hand, Goethe's hermaphroditic Mignon and the notoriously, if virginally, voluptuous and bisexually flirtatious Madame Récamier—posed in what one de Staël biographer has called Récamier's "awe-inspiring" boudoir—definitely have a bisexual flavor that seems rather different from what one usually finds in either the sentimental female friendship literature or Anglo-American Romantic writings. Furthermore, one element in Fuller's erotic self-consciousness put her far beyond the pale of most Anglo-American friendship writings; namely, her sense, which she often expressed in these years in her journals, that the possessive emotions she felt for Anna and, to a lesser degree, other young women were those, not of a "kindred spirit," but an *opposite* one. And not just an opposite one, she suggested, but one that was defined (as she put it in a journal account that fall of one dream she had about the "feminine" Anna) by its "masculine traits." Thus, too, in this entry, the mysterious "carbuncle"—a symbol of potency she got from Novalis and which she variously associated in this passage with her love for Anna, "a key which unlocked for me many a treasure," and an "emblematic gem . . . which cast light into many of the darkest caverns of human nature"—she would later write in her journal came in two genders: "The female cast out light, the male has his within himself. Mine is the male." Some of this, no doubt, is traceable to Fuller's recent reading in German and French Romantic literature, where sex-role swapping as well as passionate displays of emotional attachment to both sexes sometimes figure prominently. But this would still beg the question of why Fuller, unlike most men *and* women of her generation, responded so passionately and personally to this literature. Clearly, her latent bisexual feelings, going back to her remembered feelings for Ellen Kilshaw and her mother, were not a mere literary affectation, but a deeply ingrained part of her emotional makeup. This would explain why, given her basically heterosexual identity as well as the conventions of her culture, these bisexual feelings often led to tense relations and sometimes serious social crises.[47]

One of the most serious of these crises was the one she had to face that summer when she had to confront the fact that the two people whom she was most passionately attracted to were in the process of revealing their own "elective affinities," not for her, but for each other. The two had first gotten acquainted after Anna, who was four years Sam's senior, having finally arrived in England in the summer of 1837, had traveled with the Farrars to Switzerland to meet Sam, who had been touring the continent. They were together for two months, and he soon fell in love with her. That love was renewed when they spent several months together during his trip in the winter of early 1839 to New Orleans and Anna came home ("most unexpectedly" he would tell his father) from Europe. He then revealed to her and a little later to his parents that he wanted to marry her, and she likewise "confessed her affection" as well as undoubtedly her attraction to him. (A few years later, Sarah Clarke would report to Fuller that when she had recently seen them, Anna quoted Sam "at every other word as before.") There was, however, one major stumbling block—money, or, as Sam would later delicately put it in a letter to his father, the requirement that he satisfy "not only her feelings but her tastes." On this they had agreed: "There was very little probability of such a connexion unless my plans of a scholar's life gave place to some lucrative profession." So, after returning to Boston in April and going to work for his father, Sam struggled with the dilemma Margaret gently alluded to in her letter of July: he disliked business and he wanted a literary career, but he also wanted Anna. Finally, after a year of sometimes difficult courtship—with Sam pledging to unite "the character of a literary man and a man of business" and Anna struggling to overcome her doubts—they married. For a few years Ward worked for his father, contributed papers on art and literature to his Transcendentalist friends' *Dial,* and for a while tried living as a gentleman farmer in the Berkshires—a sort of (in Emerson's word) "chateaux" version of the 1840s Transcendentalist effort to solve the vocational problem by combining frugality, farm work, and writing. Then, feeling guilty and dissatisfied with the life of a literary dilettante, he returned to Boston to take his father's place as the American agent for Baring Brothers. After the Civil War the Wards moved to New York, where Anna emerged as a popular socialite and Sam distinguished himself, as his father had, as a prominent patron of literature and the arts, serving for many years as a founder and trustee of the Metropolitan Museum of Art and a backer of E. L. Godkin's liberal Republican *Nation.* Like most New Englanders who had once been touched by the Transcendental virus, the Wards retained remnants of their youthful Romantic faith. In middle age Anna converted to Roman Catholicism. Sam, meanwhile, clung to his Goethean pantheism, although salting it with the seasoning of a Victorian man of the world. "Every day," he wrote in a late essay on the philosophy of dress, citing Goethe's approval of the importance of appearances, should be "more or less a *jour de fete.*" In this connection he found post-Romantic wisdom in Jean Anthelme Brillat-Savarin's curiosity, *The Physiology of Taste; or, Meditations on Transcendental Gastronomy,* which explored the influence of spiritual eating habits on work, marriage, dreams, and (that quintessentially Victorian preoccupation) getting fat.[48]

Emerson's concern, later expressed to Fuller on the eve of Ward's marriage, about the union's "consequences to the history of his genius" would seem to have been confirmed by Ward's later history. Fuller's near-panic over its personal consequences for her was not delayed so long. The first thing that had to go was the passion. The surviving fragments of Ward's letters to her in these months (which Fuller copied into a journal) show why. Although in them he affirmed his desire for "the gush of mingling souls" and "the fiery action of mind on mind," he also denounced his past wish "to cast myself into the arms of some other nature" as "womanish," lamented he was "not yet a man," confessed his "mind seeks shelter in silence," and, above all, declared (consistently, he said, with the "the modern school in literature"), "I do not love to reason over, think over, or write over past sensations. . . . The principle of action is strong within me, and I cannot endure that the beautiful in feeling should not be manifested by the high in action, rather than in that inward life which to many of the highest seems to suffice." When one sets these strong but somewhat quaking assertions of masculinity, inward reserve, and outward action against Margaret's rather fantastic appeals to him to trample underfoot all his petty engagements for her and come to her while she served as a tender, indulgent mother who had borne him "beneath my heart instead of in it" or a mother "waiting . . . beneath the sepulchre for the resurrection," one can easily see the difficulty. These were hardly the sorts of sexual ideals that "a boy just coming into life" (as he described himself to his father) on the eve of making a momentous decision about a career and a wife would have felt very comfortable hearing. It is no wonder that Fuller, who knew about Anna and Sam's romance, herself worried in her September letter that "my presence is like to recal all you need to forget" or "that you would not be with me lest I 'spoil you for your part on life's dull scene,' or as you have said 'call up the woman in you'"—she might have said, the "child" or, as she also repeatedly said in her journal and letters about him, "son."[49]

Nor, clearly, did Fuller's Romantic ideal of sublimated passion any longer allure him. In a letter he wrote to her that fall, possibly in reply to hers of September, young Ward told her that her ideas "brought home to my mind the reflection how widely apart are the points from which life is surveyed by those whose personal experience of passion has been thorough, and those in whom it has (though giving brightness to the fancy and earnestness to the thoughts) remained comparatively undeveloped." In reply to her idea of (as he put it) "a new, vast, and tumultuous class of human emotions" of the sort inspired in Jesus by his attachment to Mary, he answered even more bluntly: "*I*, too, once knew and recognized the possibility of Platonic affection. It is possible to those who have never passed the line. Before that, all the higher classes of emotion all the nobler views of life exist, but in a shape that seems sublimated and idealized to the more experienced: to those who *have* passed that line, the higher emotions and the passions are apt to be always afterward inextricably commingled." In her journal, into which she copied this letter several years later, she added the note, "so writes the sentimental man of the world and he, once my Rafaello, would now write so too."[50]

Yet Sam was also something more than a sublimated or regressive sexual object for Fuller, and his looming marriage to Anna portended for her not only sexual frustration, but also, as it would seem for others of her Transcendentalist friends, a cultural betrayal. Indeed, as so often with Fuller, the two realms were so mixed as to be almost impossible to disentangle. Once in her journal, after speaking of the appeal of a simple, active peasant girl in a song of Robert Burns's, she conceded, "In the hour of baffled effort . . . I find it in my heart to approve W's choice and envy him that he has bound himself to do & be no more." But this was a minor note. More typical was an imaginary debate she wrote out in her journal that fall, between the narrator and a "son of the Gods" who has "sold

[his] birthright" of art in order to receive in exchange "not merely the fairest, but the sweetest and holiest of earth's daughters." Defending his choice, the young man says his love is not only "exclusive and peculiar," but also comprehends the universe. To this his interlocutor replies: "But if the Intellect be repressed, the idea will never be brought out from the feeling. The amaranth wreath will in thy grasp be changed to one of roses, more fragrant, indeed, but withering with a single sun!" Three years later in a long, friendly letter to him, she was more direct, if not about Anna, at least about his career. After praising his standing so well "steadily drudging at your broker's shop, like many another son of Adam," she frankly confessed, "I had longed to see you a painter, and not a merchant." She described the "ravishment" she had felt when she had seen him spring ashore after his Italian voyage, "as light as some creature of the element, and the translation of all the beauty of many centuries." She went on to recall how "I used to gaze on you, and say to myself, this man must needs be the painter of our country, and as one in the serried ranks of his friends, I shall witness his victories over immortal beauty. . . . Many times, in imagination, have I sat in your studio, and wept over my inadequate strength to grasp the greatness of your landscapes or statues in my eye, and played some comic part among your creations which went nigh to lunacy." This was her old Cambridge dream of being swept up or away by a new male American culture hero, with a vengeance! So, she wrote, "when I learned you were to become a merchant, to sit at the dead wood of the desk, and calculate figures, I was betrayed into unbelief." Although professedly self-mocking about "these silly thoughts," she was obviously dead serious about her sense of betrayal, both personal and cultural. The language of her honorable conclusion makes this transparent: "I feel assured, both by the honor I bear your deeds, and by the respect I feel that the path you now creep in is the best."[51]

Perhaps her bitterest, albeit subconscious, expressions of feeling about the Barker–Ward marriage and the path it required him to "creep in" came two months after her letter in the form of a journal entry about a recent visit she had made at the fashionable Louisburg Square apartment that Ward's father had given the couple. Here one can clearly see, not only the resentment, but the terror of social exclusion from bourgeois life that her friends' marriage conjured up in the lower depths of her mind:

Sam was away, and I slept with Anna the first time for two years. It was exquisitely painful to feel that I loved her less than when we before were thus together in confiding sleep, and she too is now so graceful and lovely, but the secret of my life is sealed to her forever. I never speak of the inmost experience, but listen to her graceful talk. I took pleasure in sleeping on Sam's pillow and before closing my eyes solicited that visions like his might come to me but I had a frightful dream of being imprisoned in a ship at sea, the waves all dashing round, and knowing that the crew had resolved to throw me in. While in horrible suspense, many persons that I knew came on board. At first they seemed delighted to see me & wished to talk but when I let them know my danger, & intimated a hope that they might save me, with cold courtliness glided away. Oh it was horrible those averted faces and well dressed figures turning from me, from captive, with the cold wave rushing up into which I was to be thrown.[52]

In her letters that fall, she expressed nothing as irrational or terrifying as this dream: sleeping with Anna on Sam's pillow, suddenly giving way to her impotence, scornful rejection, and imminent death, tacitly agreed to by her "well dressed" friends. (One might note, parenthetically, this dream's resonance with her childhood drowning nightmares, which had been stimulated by another impossible love triangle.) But the emotions she did express that fall were turbulent enough. At the beginning of October, wrestling with her great decision, Anna arrived at Fuller's for a visit. After she left the following week, Fuller wrote to Caroline Sturgis, who had sent her a peacemaking letter while Anna was still there, that she "could not think of our relation, so filled was I so intoxicated, so uplifted by that eldest and divinest love." Although she did not mention the subject to Caroline, Margaret and Anna undoubtedly talked about Sam. After Anna left, she reported: "I was obliged to take immedy to my bed, and am not yet really well enough to be up. The nights of talk and days of agitation, the tides of feeling which have been poured upon and from my soul have been too much for my strength of body or mind." She was not so intoxicated with Anna, though, that she could not launch another attack on Caroline: "I loved you, Caroline, with truth and nobleness. . . . How this love was turned sickly, how deeply it was wounded you know not yet, you do not fully understand what you did or what passed in my mind." Undoubtedly the hapless Caroline did not![53]

Meanwhile, the wound that had intensified her demands on Caroline, Margaret tried to heal over, at least superficially. Shortly after Anna left, she received a letter from Sam (which may have been the one she excerpted in her journal) answering her doleful and accusatory letter of the previous month. In her reply she said she now "understood . . . perfectly" his recent withdrawal and by implication (although she did not mention it) his refusal to talk about his problems with Anna. "Though I might grieve that you should put me from you in your highest hour and find yourself unable to meet me on the very ground where you had taught me most to expect it, I would not complain or feel that the past had in any way bound either of us as to the present. . . . Truth and honor noble natures owe to one another, but love and confidence are free gifts or they are nothing." So, carefully sidestepping how much their past "love and confidence" had been one-way, she concluded with what before she had denied was possible: while no longer intimates, they might still be friends. "The knowledge I have of your nature has become a part of mine, the love it has excited will accompany me through eternity. My attachment was never so deep as now, it is quite unstained by pride or passion, it is sufficiently disinterested for me to be sure of it." For now, though, she urged:

Think of me no more at present. Give yourself up to the holy hour and live in the celestial ray which shines on you at present. O I could weep with joy that real life is lived. Do you not feel how I should grieve to be the ghost to cross the path of true communion in the Elysian grove. Live without me now. Do not bid yourself remember me, but should an hour come by and by when the curtain shall be dropped and the lights extinguished and you have any need of me, you will find me in my place and find me faithful to you.[54]

As this picture of her ghost hovering ambiguously around the curtain hiding "real life" suggests, Fuller's attachment to Ward was not yet quite wholly "unstained by pride or passion." But it was diffused. "I am tranquil," she assured Ward, "after the season when 'many a feeling long, too long, repressed Like autumn flowers dared blossom out at last.'" This was true: passion had finally blossomed out in her life—sisterly for Caroline, maternal for Sam, and erotic for Anna. Unfortunately, the love-objects failed to respond to or recognize the various fantasies—power-driven, sexual, and vocational—Fuller spun around them. Her "ebullient sense of power" (to borrow Emerson's phrase) had still not found its "right channels."[55]

Yet as she tranquilized her emotions that fall, she also pondered them. As had her disillusionment over George Davis eight years before, her disappointment with Ward triggered in her mind large thoughts about her life, although this time not religious but social ones. She was now nearly thirty years old. She had had numerous close relations with young single men. Some of these, like Charles Newcomb, never married, while the majority who did, like Davis, Clarke (who married that summer), and now Ward, chose more conventionally feminine mates. Fuller herself was not without insight into all of this. That fall and winter she filled her journal with reflections about her loveless state. Almost all focused on her bi-gender identity as the source of her plight. "A man's ambition with a woman's heart,—'tis an accursed lot," she wrote bitterly. But why should this be? Sometimes she thought the reason was her own deeply flawed personality. "Of a disposition that requires the most refined and most exalted tenderness, without charms to inspire it," she would write later in the spring of her beloved androgynous, incest-child Mignon in Goethe's *Wilhelm Meisters Lehrjahre.* "Poor Mignon! fear not the transition through death. No hell can have in store worse torments than thou art familiar with already." At other times she seemed to link her lack of feminine "charms" more irrationally to her "masculine traits." In a remarkable account of a couple of dreams she recorded in her journal that fall, she even symbolically associated those traits with what sound very much like male body parts. In one dream that made her think of Anna when she awoke, a giant butterfly that, having declined the "skinny finger" of a woman who had been "alluring" it, settled on her large forehead, plunged his feet into her brow, until the excruciating pain in her head forced her to wake up. In a second one—rather like the one she would later have about the well-dressed people refusing to keep her from being thrown overboard—she lay in agony with a back pain, but was passed by scornfully because her body was too heavy to lift, until she was finally comforted by a beautiful young woman who looked like Anna Barker. Finally, in a poem she wrote in her journal ("To the Face Seen in the Moon"), she wrote of seeking reassurances by looking at the moon, with "thy soft Mother's smile so pensive bright," only to add melancholily:

> But, if I steadfast gaze upon thy face
> A human secret, like my own, I trace,
> For through the woman's smile looks the male eye
> So mildly, steadfastly but mournfully.[56]

Her journal musings show she saw her "masculine traits" as not only intrinsic or metaphorically physical. Once in her journal—in one of the first overtly feminist declarations she ever recorded—she gave a perfectly rational explanation of why any woman might refuse a "feminine" role in a gendered culture that exploited woman's feminine characteristics:

> Woman is the flower, man the bee. She sighs out melodious fragrance and invites the winged laborer. He drains her cup, carries off the honey. She dies on the stalk: He returns to the hive well fed and praised as an active member of the community.

Mostly, though, insofar as she saw her single state as a product of cultural prejudices, it was not because she saw herself as Everywoman, but just the opposite. In a journal entry that was undoubtedly at least partly inspired by one of Ward's that she copied ("My mind requires in its friendships, not stimulus, but repose"), she wrote:

> I think perfectly true, (though in no gross or sneering sense) what Goethe and his [*illegible*] say that women who love and marry feel no need to write. But how can a woman of genius love and marry? A man of genius will not love her; he wants repose. She may find some object sufficient to excite her ideal for a time but love perishes as soon as it finds it has grasped the shadow for the substance. Divorce must take place for the large nature will not find one capable of continuing its consort. Nor can children of the flesh satisfy the longing of the spirit for its maternity (as with Mrs R[ipley]). Such a woman cannot long remain wed, again she is single, again must seek and strive. Social wedlock is ordinarily mere subterfuge and simulacrum: it could not check a powerful woman or a powerful man.[57]

Fate, will, or cultural construction—clearly she regarded her single state as a product of all three. Perhaps more important, though, how did she value it? In her journal that fall she wrote a poignantly frank and self-critical, yet hopeful evaluation of her situation:

> I have no home on earth, & [yet] I can think of one that would have a degree of beautiful harmony with my inward life. But driven from home to home as a Renouncer I get the picture and poetry of each. Keys of gold, silver, iron, and lead are in my casket.
>
> No one loves me.
>
> But I love many a good deal, and see some way into their eventual beauty. I am growing better, and shall by and by be a worthy object of love, one that will not any where disappoint or need forbearance.

> Meanwhile I have no fetter on me, no engagement, and as I look on others almost every other, can I fail to feel this a great privilege. I have no way tied my hands or feet. And yet the varied calls on my sympathy have been such that I hope not to be made partial, cold or ignorant by this isolation. I have no child, and the woman in me has so craved this experience that it has seemed the want of it must paralyze me. But now as I look on these lovely children of a human birth what slow and neutralizing cares they bring with them to the mother. The children of the muse come quicker with less pain and disgust, [and] rest more lightly on the bosom.

Indeed, far from completely lamenting her single state, Fuller was even beginning that fall to find in it, not just ordinary compensations, but—in line with her "woman of genius" analysis—transcendent powers. She made this clear enough in a letter she wrote that October to her old would-be beau, George Davis, with whom she had recently finally made up. ("George and I are friends again," she rejoiced to Clarke. "All the clouds of misunderstanding are rolled away.") Inspired probably (the rest of the letter is missing) by her rapprochement with Davis or her falling-out with his replacement, or both, she took a long, stern, Romantic look back on her past.

> I want words to express the singularity of all my past relations; yet let me try.
> From a very early age I have felt that I was not born to the common womanly lot. I knew I should never find a being who could keep the key of my character; that there would be none on whom I could always lean, from whom I could always learn; that I should be a pilgrim and sojourner on earth, and that the birds and foxes would be surer of a place to lay the head than I. You understand me, of course; such beings can only find their homes in hearts. All material luxuries, all the arrangements of society, are mere conveniences to them.
> This thought, all whose bearings I did not, indeed, understand, affected me sometimes with sadness, sometimes with pride. I mourned that I never should have a thorough experience of life, never know the full riches of my being; I was proud that I was to test myself in the sternest way, that I was always to return to myself, to be my own priest, pupil, parent, child, husband, and wife. All this I did not understand as I do now; but this destiny of the thinker, and (shall I dare say it?) of the poetic priestess, sibylline, dwelling in the cave, or amid the Lybian sands, lay yet enfolded in my mind. Accordingly, I did not look on any of the persons, brought into relation with me, with common womanly eyes.
> Yet, as my character is, after all, still more feminine than masculine, it would sometimes happen that I put more emotion into a state than I myself knew. I really was capable of attachment, though it never seemed so till the hour of separation. And if a connexion was torn up by the roots, the soil of my existence showed an unsightly wound, which long refused to clothe itself in verdure.[58]

Her claim to Davis that she had never looked on anyone "with common womanly eyes" was hardly true, as Davis knew full well. Like so many of the stories she told about herself, it was a personal myth. But for that reason it was also partly true and, of course, useful. Like Sophocles's Philoctetes, she was beginning to discover the strength that her "unsightly wound" made possible. It only remained for her to find the right bow and target.

VI

She did not waste any time. In the afternoon of August 26, 1839—or the week before she mailed her "You love me no more" lament to Sam Ward—Bronson Alcott rode to Jamaica Plain to consult with her about her idea of holding a series of weekly "Conversations for a circle of women in Boston." The next day she sent to Sophia Ripley a lengthy prospectus outlining her plans. Of course, even a plan as pregnant as this had its practical sides. One was money. Although with the sale of the Groton place the family's capital had increased, so had its expenses. Yearly rent for the Willow Glen house was $200. Also, that month Arthur had entered Harvard College, and Richard was soon to follow. Meanwhile, Margaret had been without an income for over six months—her longest period of unemployment since her father's death. Such facts must have confirmed her fear upon leaving the Greene Street School that, however much she wished never to teach again, circumstances might dictate otherwise. Still, if she *were* to teach, where would that be? She toyed for a while with reviving her old plan of "meddling with the West" and even contemplated moving with her family to Cincinnati, where William Channing had recently settled, and opening "an expensive establishment of which I should have the sole responsibility." But she soon scotched that idea. (If "the *East* was not at a sufficiently advanced step of culture for my plans, how then should her younger sister be!!!" she had told Channing.) But to Channing she had also hinted at another idea: "I am not without my dreams and hopes as to the education of women." These last, she had said, taking a swipe at her old utilitarian mentor, "are not at all of the Martineau class, but, though brilliant, such, I think, as you, or any spiritual thinker however sober-minded would sympathize in." She had added the half-hopeful thought that "should this prove at last my vocation," she was certain she would be entering "an occupation in which few persons of ability are at present engaged."[59]

Actually, on this point, Fuller characteristically exaggerated a little. It could be argued that it was precisely the *increases* in the number and ability of persons engaged in the field of female education in these years that made advanced plans like Fuller's even thinkable. The previous two decades had witnessed the taking-off of American women's education. Private female seminaries, such as Susan Prescott's, which Fuller attended as an adolescent, had proliferated. These schools, for the first time in the nation's history, had made mass middle-class, female secondary schooling comparable in accessibility and quality to that at most of the boys' academies and many college preparatory "grammar schools." Often the mighty evangelical churches and benevolent organizations financed these schools on the grounds that women's supposedly unique self-sacrificial virtues would gain greater influence and thus guarantee the "salvation" of an otherwise overly expansive and competitive republic.[60]

By the end of the 1830s, however, the fabric of this crusade *was* beginning to look a little frayed. In the first place, it left untouched the mushrooming numbers of working-class and immigrant girls. Even for educating middle-class females its deficiencies were becoming apparent. As even friendly critics were starting to note, except for a small number of female seminaries like Emma Willard's and Catharine Beecher's, knowledge at most of these schools was still largely conceived of as ornamental and invariably taught by rote. This weakness, in turn, was related to a fundamental contradiction in the whole female education movement. On one hand, it trumpeted the opening up of the widest possible vistas of intellectual accomplishment. On the other hand, the schools it created were intended to prepare middle-class young women for only two occupations: that of wife and mother or (mostly for single girls) teaching. For most, these occupations seem to have sufficed. But these limited activities still left a significant number of young single women who, barred from college, possessed no clear social role, and a certain number of older educated women for whom, for a variety of reasons, the roles of wife and mother were insufficient. This was particularly true of a sizable number of Boston matrons and young women who were too well-to-do to hanker after underpaid teaching positions. These women were usually liberal in their religious views and therefore not attracted to the benevolence crusades sponsored by evangelical churches that absorbed many women. Most important, they were brought up in the highly education- and culture-conscious families and circles that abounded in Unitarian Boston and, as a consequence, were taught to nourish an interest in literature and thought almost as much as in conventional domestic roles. These were precisely the sort of women who flocked to the Conversations of Margaret Fuller, who was herself partly the product of these same influences.

To understand why many of these women so enthusiastically joined Fuller's Conversations, one needs to consider a little more closely who the most prominent of them were. One group, which made up the most active core of the classes, consisted of Fuller's close friends, all ardent supporters of the Transcendentalist movement and intimates of its leading figures. These included old friends like Eliza Farrar, Almira Barlow, Ellen Sturgis Hooper, and Anna Barker, who joined the Conversations after she moved to Boston, as well as Fuller's doted-on former students Caroline Sturgis, Jane Tuckerman, Mary Ward, Marianne Jackson, and Mary Channing. A second, related category comprised a large number of still younger single women, mostly in their late teens or early twenties. Neither so intellectual nor so Transcendental-minded as Fuller's protégées, still they were high-spirited, interested in new trends, socially active in Boston literary and reform circles, and, most important, although not intimate with her, ardently devoted to Margaret Fuller. These included, in descending order of devotion: Ednah Littlehale and her friend Mary Ann Haliburton; the younger Peabody sisters Mary and Sophia (soon married, respectively, to the educational reformer Horace Mann and the struggling young writer Nathaniel Hawthorne); and (Fuller's former suspicions notwithstanding) Maria White, the humanitarian fiancée of Boston's semidelinquent, budding young poet, James Russell Lowell.[61]

A third group consisted of women married or otherwise related to men prominently associated with social reform movements. Among these were the wives of virtually all the leading Transcendentalists and many important abolitionist leaders. Many of these, like Lidian Emerson, Elizabeth Hoar, Sophia Ripley, and Sarah Clarke, were Fuller's friends, while others she knew only as passing acquaintances or through their husbands. Like Elizabeth Davis Bancroft, the witty second wife of the historian and Democratic party leader George Bancroft, Lydia Cabot Parker, the kindly, self-effacing wife of the young Transcendentalist minister Theordore Parker, and Mary Greeley, the wife of the soon-to-be *New-York Tribune* editor Horace Greeley, who would later travel to Boston to attend the Conversations, most of these women were essentially private persons. There were also several women who were activists in their own right, most notably Ann Terry Phillips, the wife of the rising young abolitionist orator and colleague of William Lloyd Garrison, Wendell Phillips; and Louisa Gilman Loring, married to Fuller's friend Ellis Gray Loring, a wealthy lawyer and also an associate of Garrison's. Finally, the classes attracted a small number of locally well-known female writers and educators, like Sarah Alden Ripley, Elizabeth Peabody, and Fuller's old friend, the abolitionist writer Lydia Maria Child.

These women—like virtually all the women who attended the meetings— shared certain general characteristics worth noting. One was their already high education. Practically all, like Fuller, had either attended one of Boston's elite private schools or been tutored by a sympathetic scholarly father or brother. Almost all were multilingual and well read in classical and modern literature. Nearly all were religious liberals, with a minority holding conventional Unitarian views and a larger number leaning toward some variety of Transcendentalism. All of this would seem to establish the group as a fairly typical Unitarian elite, which it surely was, but with a difference. Clearly, the often-repeated view that the women who attended Fuller's classes were an offshoot of Boston's "gorgeous" aristocracy (in Harriet Martineau's fatuous phrase) is seriously misleading.[62]

Most of them, to be sure, were fairly—some very—well off, although several, like the Peabody sisters and Sophia Ripley, came from eminent lineages but struggling families. Most were the wives or daughters of successful merchants or professional men, usually from old Massachusetts families with strongly pro-Whig sympathies. Yet almost none of these families were connected with Boston's new, politically conservative industrial wealth, and the few who were, like the Sturgises, generously donated to philanthropies and causes. Indeed, beyond class, status, and education, the most salient feature of the group as a whole was the strong ties many of the women had, like Fuller's friends in general, to various social reform movements. The large number of Transcendentalist and abolitionist wives and supporters has been mentioned, but other radical causes were represented, too. Anna Blake Shaw and her sister-in-law Sarah Sturgis Shaw— who would later be the object of enormous sympathy and pride in New England circles during the Civil War as the mother of the martyred colonel of the black Fifty-fourth Massachusetts Infantry, Robert Gould Shaw—were in these years active supporters of the Fourierist socialist movement. Also a Fourierist supporter and fellow class member was Anna's sister Sarah Shaw Russell, the wife of George Russell, the cofounder of William Sturgis's firm, Russell and Sturgis.

Not all of Fuller's members came bearing such radical credentials. The classes also included a fair sprinkling of considerably more conservative Unitarian women, although even some of these, when one looks closely enough, reveal curious connections. Sixty-six-year-old Eliza Morton Quincy, for example, who was the wife of Josiah Quincy, the former mayor of Boston and the current president of Harvard and like her husband a staunch, conservative Unitarian, was also the mother of the radical Garrisonian abolitionist Edmund Quincy and the grandmother of Josiah Phillips Quincy, the "wonderful and divine" six-year-old star of Alcott's excoriated Temple School conversation classes. Furthermore, even the most conservative of these women had to be willing to meet and talk, as many Unitarian women were not, with the likes of Ann Phillips or Louisa Loring. They had to be willing also to associate with a group that, as soon as it was organized, was talked about, according to Sarah Clarke, as "a kind of infidel association, as several noted transcendentalists were engaged in it." If it was a feminine elite—and it certainly was—it was also an avant-garde elite, and both these facts help explain why Fuller's women, already identified with libertarian or uplifting heterodoxies, were so well primed for her elite-minded, avant-garde proselytizing.[63]

Fuller's first class met at noon on Wednesday, November 6. The day was strategically chosen so that the women, many of whom would travel from Brookline, Cambridge, Concord, and other outlying towns, some of them from as far away as Providence and New York, could conveniently attend Emerson's winter lecture series on the "Present Age," later in the evening. The place the meetings were held was also strategic and suggestive of larger stirrings: the front parlor of Elizabeth Peabody's combination house and bookstore at 13 West Street. The function of the house was to make available to a wide audience the latest Transcendentalist and Romantic books and journals, as well as to provide a place for the elect and their friends to meet, exchange ideas, and plan their various enterprises. The bookstore itself was not officially to open until the following July, but in the meantime, Peabody shrewdly made the room available to Fuller and her potential book-buying pupils at no charge. There on the battered chairs that Peabody had collected from her countless schoolrooms over the years, in a room soon crammed with books and her sister Sophia's offered art supplies and paintings and her brother Nathaniel's homeopathic drugs, with a view overlooking the narrow cobblestone street sandwiched between the Common and the city's business district, in a neighborhood then still partly residential but increasingly known for its fashionable stores and shops, twenty-five women met for two hours to talk. For this privilege, each woman paid ten dollars for a ticket of admission to the two-hour, thirteen-week series. This was a high price; it would net Fuller a decent half-time income of almost $500 per year. This was over three times what Alcott brought in—when he brought in anything—from his conversations, and about two-thirds of what Emerson then made from an equivalent number of lectures. Despite the charge, Fuller's classes were so popular that in February she began a new series. So, every Wednesday or sometimes Thursday, at either eleven or noon, through the winter and spring for the next five years—

for as long, in fact, as she resided in the neighborhood of Boston—Fuller led two three-month series of Conversations. Each series included twenty-five to thirty-five women. The participants eventually numbered over a hundred.

What Fuller proposed to do for these women was novel. First, she intended to assert intellectual leadership. Experiments in advanced female education were not without precedent, of course. Although women were still excluded from the American Lyceum, recently the Scottish Owenite socialist Frances Wright and the abolitionist sisters Sarah and Angelina Grimké had made widely publicized, controversial platform appearances before mixed audiences of men and women. But these women spoke as ideologues rather than as intellectuals and made no special appeal to women, except, as in the case of the Grimké sisters, as potential political activists. More intellectual, or at least more "literary," was the eccentric critic Delia Bacon, who delivered somewhat histrionic lectures and "dramatic readings" on literature, art, and history before predominantly female audiences in the early 1830s. Also in these years Elizabeth Peabody began her periodic "reading parties" and "historical conferences" for young Boston women, including several who would later become members of Fuller's classes. But Bacon's lectures were more entertaining than educational, and Peabody made no large claims of advancing important philosophical principles or affecting female culture radically. Fuller proposed to do both, in substance by providing a new plan of female education.[64]

She had first outlined her rationale for her Conversations in her August 27 prospectus to Sophia Ripley. At the very least, she suggested, such meetings would be worthwhile if they only supplied a place of mutual "stimulus and cheer" for Boston's many well-educated and thinking women who, she said, despite the city's "pretensions to mental refinement," had nothing at all of this kind. Her own ambition, though, she confessed, went much further: she wanted, not merely to socialize women, but to educate them, essentially by changing their way of thinking. This she hoped to accomplish by two means. First, she wanted "to systematize thought" by reviewing its various departments and endeavoring to place them "in due relation to one another in our minds," and so "give a precision in which our sex are so deficient"; chiefly, she thought, "because they have so few inducements to test and classify what they receive." Second, she hoped to define the objects of thought, or "to ascertain what pursuits are best suited to us in our time and state of society, and how we may make the best use of our means of building up the life of thought upon the life of action." Around such goals she hoped to assemble a circle, not out of the usual feminine salon motives of "vanity or pedantry," but out of an earnest desire, as she put it, to answer "the great questions. What were we born to do? How shall we do it? which so few ever propose to themselves 'till their best years are gone by."[65]

This, then, was her idea. In the context of early American women's education, it was strikingly original. In essence, it combined traditional Enlightenment emphases on logic and empirical inquiry with the Romantic ideal, developed most recently by Emerson, of uniting thinker and doer, and applied these notions to a realm widely regarded as completely alien to them—female thought and culture. There was one major problem: how to reconcile a call for the integration of thought and action with the reality of American women's severely restricted sphere of activity. Fuller was not unmindful of this challenge. On the contrary, she saw it as arising from the heart of what was fundamentally wrong about American female education. Contemporary middle-class women, she told the first meeting of the Conversations, unlike their agrarian grandmothers, led lives that were devoted primarily to "the cultivation of the affections." They therefore had "a great deal of leisure," which, to make the best use of it, many devoted to intellectual pursuits. The problem was that this intellectuality had also produced enormous "pedantry" and "superficiality"—precisely because it was disjoined from practical activity. "Women now are taught all that men are— Is it so?" she asked.

> Or is it not that they run over superficially even *more* studies—without being really taught any thing. Thus when they come to the business of life & the application of knowledge they find that they are *inferior*—& all their studies have not given them that practical good sense & mother wisdom & wit which grew up with our grandmothers at the spinning wheel. Is not the difference between [the] education of women & that of men this— Men are called on from a very early period to *reproduce* all that they learn— First their college exercises—their political duties—the exercises of professional studies—the very first action of life in any direction—calls upon them for *reproduction* of what they have learnt— This is what is most neglected in the education of women—they learn without any attempt to reproduce— The little reproduction to which they are called seems mainly for the purposes of idle display.[66]

Still, the problem remained: how to supply this connection between productive life and intellectual learning without a drastic revision in American gender relations, especially in the economic sphere. This was exactly what Fuller would advocate several years later. Why, then, did she stop short of such an obvious conclusion from her premise in these earlier years of the Conversations? One is tempted to attribute it to her caution, and that, in turn, to the extreme novelty of the idea of economic equality at this time, even in America's incipient feminist circles. Yet such a single explanation, while undoubtedly true, overlooks the positive core of Fuller's feminism both then and later. For one thing, in both periods Fuller's central concern was with women's intellectual and spiritual character, and she saw employment largely as a means to that end. Second, for Fuller, as for Emerson and other Transcendentalists, intellectual and aesthetic work ideally was as activist and worldly as—not to mention more emotionally satisfying than—the activity of any businessman or politician. This assertion, in fact, was the basis of the Transcendentalists' whole critique of the complacently passive, derivative, and genteel (they also sometimes added "effeminate") character of the contemporary Boston-Cambridge intellectual or "scholar." The assertion also formed the basis of their appeal to young men and—although this has never been sufficiently recognized—young women, who found themselves by either choice or circumstance barred from the traditional institutional careers of their culture, whether the ministry, politics, or housewifery. It is no wonder that these young people, whether at Emerson's lectures, Fuller's classes, or later at Brook Farm, found extraordinarily attractive Transcendentalism's claim to make out of intellectual life itself an activity and a career divorced from institutions and based on the lonely creations or discoveries of the self-reliant individual. What Fuller tried to do was simply to adapt this complex of ideas—a radical revision of the popular antebellum idea of self-culture—to her group of Boston women. In effect, she offered them a way by which they might achieve privately some of the same intellectual benefits that the sphere of public activity denied to them supposedly conferred. That way, as she explained to the women that first day, was the Conversations themselves.[67]

Of course these were not "conversations" in the ordinary sense. The ideal of a conversation as a critical intellectual method derived from Plato, whose Socratic dialogues Fuller read and reread and came more than ever to admire in the months before she began her meetings. ("I have been reading Plato all the week," she would write to Emerson before one meeting, "hop[ing] to be tuned up thereby.") The Romantic Age was itself the age of the conversation, and de Staël, Coleridge, Goethe, and many other great Romantic talkers must have given Fuller further stimulus for developing intellectual conversations among her women. Finally, Transcendentalism's own great Platonic-Romantic talker Bronson Alcott not only had promulgated the idea of the conversation as a revolutionary educational tool, which Fuller had put into practice in her Greene Street classes, but more recently had begun to tout the conversation as a potentially powerful popular cultural force. For Alcott, as for many European devotees of the form, that power resided in its capacity for revealing profoundly subjective truths. If to outsiders these "conversations" sounded more like collective monologues than traditional intellectual discourse, this was precisely the point. Also American Transcendentalists like Alcott admired these kinds of conversations for specific intellectual reasons—because their spontaneity and fluidity seemed to them to mimic the deeper spiritual truths that written or "frozen" language could never capture, and because, unlike the passive medium of the popular lecture, they promoted originality and intellectual self-reliance. Personal and practical factors undoubtedly also played a part in attracting Fuller to the conversation form. These included her lack of opportunity, as a woman, to lecture; her talent for informal talk; and probably, too, the example of Alcott, who while preparing the previous fall to give up the last of his schools, had launched a series of moderately successful traveling conversations in various towns in eastern Massachusetts.[68]

Theoretical considerations were still critical to her. Indeed, as her answer to the conundrum of women's education, they were crucial. As she explained in her introductory lecture, she was not there "to *teach* any thing," but "to call . . . out the thought of others" in order, she said, to encourage the kind of intellectual reproduction and activity inside a classroom that men were able to experience outside of one. Nor did she overlook the more philosophical aspects of the problem. That winter she wrote in her journal: "The best that we receive from any thing can never be written. For it is not the positive amount of thought we have received, but the virtue that has flowed into us, and *is* now us, that is precious. If we can tell no one thought yet are higher, larger, wiser the work is done. The best part of life is too spiritual to bear recording." Five years of conversing with her women only reinforced her intuitionist views. After concluding the final series of her Conversations, she recorded in her journal an account of a recent talk she had had with Henry Ware, Jr.'s, widow, Mary Ware, who, she said, was "trying to get interested" in teaching, and the young education author, Anna Jackson Lowell:

> I talk with a Goethean moderation on this subject, which rather surprizes her & Anna Lowell who are nearer the entrance of the studio. I am really old on this subject, in near eight years experience, I have learnt as much as others would in eighty from my great talent at explanation, tact in the use of means, & immediate & invariable power over the minds of my pupils. My wish has been more & more to purify my own conscience when near them, give clear views of the aims of this life, show them where the magazines of knowledge lie, & leave the rest to themselves & the Spirit who must teach & help them to self-impulse.[69]

Such was her theory. With its emphasis on learning as private and piactical and social only in a very spiritual sense, it was both hardheaded and experimental, demanding and curiously complacent. (Certainly Fuller was sufficiently so about her own "immediate and invariable power.") At its deepest level, of course, it was mystical. It was, in short, rather like Fuller herself.

VII

Ideally, to have an adequate sense of what these Conversations were like—lacking the critical elements of voice and gesture—one would need to have verbatim transcripts. Instead, what we have are a few very inadequate, fragmentary reports. Most of those printed in Fuller's *Memoirs* in their grave sententiousness or studied spontaneity read (as at least one was probably intended to be) as contrived parodies of high Romantic talk. What remains are a couple of dozen summary reports from a much larger number that Elizabeth Peabody kept. However Peabodylike in their ponderousness, they at least summarize many of Fuller's opinions as well as briefly characterize the remarks of others. Together with later recollections, they give us a sense of what these meetings must have been like for some of the participants.[70]

Physical descriptions of Fuller, as usual, vary considerably. After returning from her second meeting the following year, young Caroline Healey wrote this fairly sober description in her journal: "She is under size, delicately formed with rather sharp features and light hair. Her head is small, but thrown almost wholly in front of the ears. Her forehead is of good height. Her nose inclines to the Roman, and her mouth is thin and ungraceful. Her eyes are small & grey. But their flash is vivid and her laugh is almost childlike. Her manners are reserved, but those of one who has seen good society." Healey said nothing about Fuller's dress, which several participants later described as "beautiful," even "sumptuous." Caroline Sturgis, on the other hand, told Emerson there was "nothing of special expense or splendor in her toilette," a view consistent with the then-young Transcendentalist follower George William Curtis's recollection that, while admiring in others beautiful dressing and ornament, Fuller herself ordinarily dressed "simply, but dowdily and never handsomely." Higginson also noted that Fuller's dress fitted with the clothes of most of the women of her circle, who generally favored "the well-kept black silk or modest alpaca of that period." In general, Emerson plausibly thought, her "'beautiful looks'" that young people came away admiring were an effect of her beautiful talk. "When she was intellectually excited, or in high animal spirits, as often happened, all deformity of features was dissolved in the power of the expression."[71]

About that power there was no controversy: virtually every commentary at the time or later included at least some paean to Fuller's wonderful speech at these Conversations. Of its numerous qualities, three were usually singled out. Some stressed, as Henry Hedge had in describing her adolescent speech, its "commanding" character, deriving from the highly precise and discriminating way she was able, as William Channing said, "to analyze, to sum up." Others by contrast later claimed that what most struck them was the perfectly natural, seemingly effortless character of her talk. "The fact was," recalled Hedge, who attended a second year's Conversation series to which men were admitted, "her speech, though finished and true as the most deliberate rhetoric of the pen, had always an air of spontaneity which made it seem the grace of the moment,—the result of some organic provision that made finished sentences as natural to her as blundering and hesitation are to most of us." But what seems to have most impressed many of the women at Fuller's Conversations were two more imaginative qualities of her speech: her stunning (in Caroline Healey Dall's words) "flow of language" and, related to this, her extraordinary capacity for associating "far divergent links, in the chain of thought." One can also see this in her writing, but there she seems to have had less control over it. Hedge thought it was because "she required the stimulus of attentive ears and answering eyes, to bring out all her power." Emerson, who attended the second year's series with Hedge, agreed. "In her writing she was prone to spin her sentences without a sure guidance, and beyond the sympathy of her reader. But in discourse, she was quick, conscious of power, in perfect tune with her company, and would pause and turn the stream with grace and adroitness."[72]

If some of these reports make her more transcendental flights sound as though they eclipsed conversation of any sort, some evidence would seem to show that they sometimes did. "Nobody else said much when she was in the Delphic mood," Charles Congdon recalled from her Providence soirées. Even Elizabeth Peabody began one report the following year with "Miss Fuller's fifth conversation was pretty much of a monologue of her own." But by all accounts this was unusual. The overwhelming recollections of participants suggest that Fuller tried hard to make her Boston meetings, as she had told Sophia Ripley she intended them to be, theaters of real intellectual interaction. Edward Everett Hale, who attended the mixed Conversation series a year and a half later, recalled of the members: "Nine tenths of them were in the mood of people paying homage. . . . But she would not and did not accept it. The skill, the tact, with which she threw back the ball of conversation, so as to start this listener or that, and the success with which she made him speak and say his best, were clear tokens of her real genius." Nor apparently did Fuller lavish her attentions only on the best and the brightest. Participants recalled she kept her famous penchant for sarcasm to a minimum; others remembered that she always "brought down, at last" her opening "exordiums . . . to a possible level for others to follow"; and still others recalled she even encouraged—and this *was* unusual for Fuller—the slow-witted. Emerson reported that all the women he interviewed "testify to her extreme candour & tenderness, to every feeblest expression of opinion from any member of her class." "Of course," one "very competent witness" told him, "it was not easy for every one to venture her remark, after an eloquent discourse and in the presence of twenty superior women, who were all inspired. But whatever she said, Margaret knew how to seize the good meaning of it with hospitality, and to make the speaker glad, and not sorry, that she had spoken." One woman later put it biblically: "In these gatherings the blind received their sight and the dumb spoke."[73]

Contemporary reports support these recollections, although they also suggest that Fuller did not find her women right away "inspired." Sarah Clarke gave this account of the first meeting the following week to her brother James: "She had about twenty-five ladies to begin with, who all and each declared they should not speak a word. Accordingly, the first day she took the conversation into her own hands and explained to them her wishes and intentions in so animating a manner that they turned about and declared that it would be base in the extreme not to be willing to do all they could, while she so generously did her part." Fuller's own view was less sanguine. She wrote to Emerson after the second meeting: "I could not make those ladies talk about Beauty. They would not ascend to principles, but kept clinging to details." Still, taking the longer view, she was at least cautiously pleased with the first results. "From the very first I took my proper place, and never had the feeling I dreaded, of display, of a paid Corinne," she boasted to a friend in one letter, although she also noted, "I am never driven home for ammunition, never put to any expense; never truly called out . . . though I feel how superficially I am treating my subject." Finally, once the talk began to flow, the reports became more positive. One Boston woman, who joined the class after the eighth meeting, exultingly wrote to a friend in New Haven that the "gifts and graces" and "high . . . earnestness" of the speakers gave to the discussions the quality of "a Platonic dialogue," while their lack of "pretension or pedantry" gave them a tone as "simple as that of children in a school class." Even Fuller, who, as usual, was her own harshest critic, wrote glowingly to a friend after the third meeting:

> My class is singularly prosperous I think. I was so fortunate as to rouse at once the tone of simple earnestness which can scarcely, when once awakened, cease to vibrate. All seem in a glow and quite as receptive as I wish. They question and exam-

ine, yet follow leadings; and thoughts (not opinions) have been trumps every time. There are about 25 members, and every one, I believe, full of interest. The first time, ten took part in the conversation; the last still more. Mrs Bancroft came out in a way that surprized me. She seems to have shaken off a wonderful number of films. She showed pure vision, sweet sincerity, and much talent. Mrs Josiah Quincy keeps us in good order and takes care yt "Xy" and "morality" are not forgotten.[74]

In trying "to make those ladies talk," Fuller had several trumps she relied on. For one thing, she had, as she suggested here, a solid core of at least ten fairly erudite friends, many of whom held, within a broadly Transcendentalist range, a variety of points of view—from Peabody's grave Coleridgian idealism and Lidian Emerson's dark Swedenborgianism, to Ellen Hooper's coolly skeptical naturalism and Caroline Sturgis's exuberant, Fullerlike Prometheanism. Furthermore, Peabody's reports show they were not at all shy about bringing these views forth. In addition, ever earnest herself, Fuller knew well how to stimulate the feeling in others. ("Thus she speaketh plainly, and what in her lies," Sarah Clarke noted after describing to her brother one Fuller appeal for participation. "And we feel that, when she so generously opens her mind to us, we ought to do no less to her.") But she also exploited a number of pedagogical devices, some of which she had used in her Providence classes. At many meetings she asked her "assistants" (as she called them) to write brief essays on the following week's topic, which she would then read or have read and have the women evaluate. As she had become convinced, since teaching at Alcott's school, that language was critical in cultivating the imagination, she often asked the women for definitions of key words like "faith" or "beauty," about which, she told them at the first meeting, "we knew words & had impressions, & vague irregular notions," but no real, systematic "thoughts." Her object, she said, was Socratic: first, to find out "how much less we knew than we thought," and second, to turn "these impressions into thoughts . . . by making a simple & clear effort for expression." When she did this in one class, one woman reported the definitions "called forth questions, comments, and illustrations, on all sides," and Peabody's reports likewise show this was often the case. By many accounts, Fuller could also be, as at the Greene Street School, a vigorous questioner. In trying thus to get her women (as she said in her letter to Sophia Ripley) "to lay aside the shelter of vague generalities, the cant of coterie criticism, and the delicate disdains of *good society*" and "see their friends undefended by rouge or candlelight," she sometimes had to confront "that sort of vanity . . . which wears the garb of modesty"—in other words, the well-worn mask of nineteenth-century feminine sentimentality. In a letter to her brother James after their sixth meeting, Sarah Clarke described one such confrontation. A lady, Clarke reported, insisted upon "her sex's privilege to judge of things by her feelings, and to care not for the intellectual view of the matter. 'I am made so,' says she, 'and I cannot help it.' 'Yes,' says Margaret, gazing full upon her, 'but who are *you*? Were you an accomplished human being, were you all that a human being is capable of becoming, you might perhaps have a right to say, "I *like* it therefore it is good"—but, if you are not all that, your judgement must be partial and unjust if it is guided by your feelings alone.'"[75]

This quintessentially Fulleresque notion of the intellectual life as a kind of moral and aesthetic imperative carried over into the subject matter of the Conversations themselves. The topic of her first series was Greek mythology. She conceded—and always regretted the fact—that she did not read Greek. Still, the sources she did use were certainly good ones—principally Homer, Plutarch, and the major Greek playwrights in translation; Roman authors like Ovid, Hesiod, and Apuleius; and myriad studies of ancient and Renaissance art. In addition, she was deeply versed in the manifold ways German Romantic writers, from Goethe to Novalis, used Greek myths as shaping forces in their art and philosophy. For theory she borrowed freely from Thomas Taylor's translations of the Neoplatonist Proclus. She also relied heavily on the historical, philological, and critical writings of German scholars like Johann Winckelmann, Arnold Heeren, and especially Friedrich Creuzer, whose massively erudite *Symbolik und Mythologie der alten Völker* she vastly preferred to the superficial, pro-Christian interpretations of Jacob Bryant.[76]

In her introductory remarks at the second meeting, she gave many obvious reasons for her choice of subject: the Greek myths were serious yet playful, objective and tangible, separated from all local subjects, and associated with all our ideas of art. But her primary intellectual interest in the myths was clearly as a vehicle for her Romantic philosophy. As she said in a Conversation the following year, summing up her point of view, the Greek mythologies should not be construed, as they usually were, "from a narrow religious point of view." (Typically, even sympathetic English and American commentators at this time viewed the Greek myths as prefigurings of Christianity.) Rather, she argued, taking a strikingly modern and anthropological view, the narratives should be seen as "symbolical of a deep . . . intellectual and aesthetic life." In her introduction she elaborated on what she thought that life was. First and foremost, she said, following her German mentors, it was psychic—the adaptation of natural sensations to human consciousness through a metaphorical way of thinking. The Greek, she noted, "was all life & energy, & personified all he beheld— He *saw* the Oreads, & Naiads & Nereids— Their forms as described by the poets—as formed by the artists—are the very lines of Nature humanized as the eye of the child humanizes the forms in the fire and in the clouds—every where seeing faces." Such a way of thinking and seeing also had, as she said in a later Conversation, important aesthetic implications: "The Greeks loved not cold abstractions. They delighted to read the spirit in the forms." Finally, the myths held, she told the women, Transcendentalist-style religious significance: "They brought heaven down to earth. They had no devil. . . . Heaven, hell, and earth were girt in one iron chain [of] productive energy."[77]

At this second meeting, according to Peabody, a number of women raised objections to this perspective. As one might expect from a Unitarian group, these seem to have been more moral or cultural than religious. At one point, for example, after Fuller had said that one could not help but sometimes be envious of the Greek's psychic powers, Eliza Quincy (in Peabody's words) "expressed wonder & some horror at the thought of *Christians* envying *Heathen Greeks.*" To this, Peabody reported, Fuller answered back in various ways. First, she said, softening somewhat the antiprogress line she had stated in Providence, that she had "no desire to go *back*" because "we had the elements of a deeper & higher civilization." Nonetheless, she argued, there were important *cultural* respects in which the Greeks *were* superior, particularly in their plastic and synthetic powers, which were progressively diminished, she thought, following Schiller and other German commentators, by modern civilization's increasing emphasis on "analysis & sentiment." Furthermore she took, like Giambattista Vico and her favorite, Johann Gottfried Herder, a spiral rather than a strictly linear view of history: civilizations rose and declined, and "the Christian was *in its infancy*— the Greek *in its maturity*." Finally, she encouraged the women again to conceive of religions anthropologically—not as frozen theological or moral codes but as historically distinct yet overlapping cultural systems. Greek art, for example, she said in another Conversation, "expressed immortality as much as Christian art, but did not throw it into the future by preëminence," to which she added, "The idealization of the human form makes a God. The fact that man can conceive and express this perfection of being, is as good a witness to immortality, as the look of aspiration in the countenance of a Magdalen." Or, as Peabody summarized Fuller's more polemical formulation that second meeting: "These fables & forms of Gods were the reverence for & idealization of the universal sentiments of religion—aspiration—intellectual action of a people whose political & aesthetic life had become immortal— We should approach it then with respect & distrust our own contempt of it."[78]

From Peabody's reports, these sorts of disputes seem to have disappeared after the second Conversation. The main reason was probably that Fuller's focus shifted from considering the myths as expressive of an entire cultural system, to considering the gods, as she put it in her introductory lecture, as "great instincts—or ideas—or facts of the internal constitution separated & personified." So, beginning with the third Conversation, she organized the classes around various gods, a sort of Transcendentalist faculty psychology: Prometheus was made the type of Pure Reason; Jupiter, of Creative Energy or Will; Minerva, Intellectual Power or Practical Reason; and so on. At her best, her typologizing, even in the second- and third-hand reports that have survived, shows her breaking free from the static interpretations this method easily lends itself to. In one Conversation, Peabody reported Fuller's contrast of Apollo as "Genius" with Bacchus as "Geniality": "[Bacchus's] whole life was triumph. Born from fire; a divine frenzy; the answer of the earth to the sun,—of the warmth of joy to the light of genius. He is beautiful, also; not severe in youthful beauty, like Apollo; but exuberant,—and liable to excess"—and so on through various Bacchus or Bacchus-like figures in Greek fables, Indian mythology, and even the Bible, that illustrated the basic Apollonian-Dionysian duality that would later be promulgated by Friedrich Nietzsche.[79]

Only in one area did some of the women have difficulty with this approach— and that one was morality. Again, the issue was not strictly theological. No one, for example (at least as Peabody reported), raised any objections to Fuller and other women's use of the term "fable" to apply to both Greek and biblical narratives. Several of the women especially blanched at Fuller's Goethean acknowledgement of the value of sin and even evil in the stories of some of these godly instincts. "Miss Fuller was asked whether with her views she could be said to believe in any *evil*—for if evil was but the condition of a necessary & desirable development—it was a good." Her reply (which, laconic as it was, would always be her view of the matter) was "that evil was *temporary*—but it was *real* while it lasted." Other women sometimes also raised sexual concerns about these instincts. A young friend of Sarah Clarke's, Lucy Goddard, Peabody reported, "said that it disturbed her that Genius was so inconstant in its loves." To this Fuller answered, Genius was a personified instinct and not a man, and that (sidestepping the question of how much it should be cultivated!) inconstancy was *its* necessary attribute: "Genius loved *beauty* in all its manifestations & forever pursued it & was always unfortunate." When Peabody, on the other hand, offered a highly abstract justification for Venus's hatred of Psyche as expressing "the essential discord between the Universal Beauty, & any human embodiment of beauty," Fuller brought the metaphor soundly back to earth: "Miss F. said yes— that might be the original idea—but it was not Raphael's—who represented Venus as *such* a pet!"[80]

This psycho-mythologizing, by all accounts, was a popular approach, and there are several likely reasons. For one, of course, it offered a good deal of room to discuss literary subjects in perennially interesting psychological ways. But it also undoubtedly served more historically specific needs. For one thing, it allowed the women who were friends, wives, or young followers of the leading Transcendentalist figures, who had not had the benefit of formal training in philosophy or theology, to discuss the movement's latest concepts in a fairly loose and accessible fashion. One Conversation that year, for example, led to a discussion (as Fuller reportedly summarized it) of "different views of inspiration,— how some had felt it was merely perception; others apprehended it as influx upon the soul from the soul-side of its being." On the other hand, for outsiders such a psycho-intellectual approach gave to what might have otherwise seemed merely literary themes an intriguing, larger philosophical significance. Finally, and perhaps most important, it also permitted, under the rubric of "spiritualizing" the myths, a good deal of psychological fantasizing. For it is clear that Fuller was not only asking these women to shed their cultural prejudices and, as she said in one Conversation, "denationalize" themselves. ("I assure you," she boasted to a friend after the third class, "there is more Greek than Bostonian spoken at the meetings.") She was also encouraging this, for the most part, rather socially restrained and vocationally circumscribed group of Boston matrons, reformers, and spirited young women to see themselves and their destinies in rather extraordinary terms. And this was true for Fuller herself. One of her favorite mythological figures was Minerva, the goddess of wisdom, whom she described in her notes for the Conversations as "a child of counsel, birth of the brain, a virgin &

a warrior"—a rather good, if unintended, history of her life. Minerva was a figure Fuller would refer to repeatedly in later years, very often with veiled reference to herself.[81]

Fuller's intellectually soundest Conversations, though, were probably not the ones on mythology, but those of the second series that she began in February, and that she repeated again the following fall, on the fine arts. She prepared the way in January by concluding her first series with several meetings on poetry. She explained what she had been doing in a letter to Sarah Helen Whitman on the twenty-first:

> I [began] . . . by dividing the universe into Poesy, Philosophy, Prose then Poesy (fol-lowing Coleridge's classification) into Poetry, Music, Painting, Sculpture, architec-ture and the histrionic art. We then took up Poetry and, after some consideration of its various forms, are taking up the poets. Shakspeare and Burns next time. This in reference to some discussion of the words satire wit and humor called up by the ques-tion given out for the last time, Whether there be any such thing as satirical poetry? I wish you would write and send me *your* definitions of poesy, poetry, wit and humor, fancy and imagination.

The key term here is "poesy," a term both she and Coleridge got from the post-Kantian philosopher Friedrich Schelling and that Fuller used as the controlling concept of all her arts Conversations. As she defined it in her journal, it was "the expression of the sublime and beautiful, whether in measured words or in the fine arts. The human mind apprehending the harmony of the universe and mak-ing new combinations by its laws." The great advantage of this concept was that it allowed Fuller to discuss all the arts in relation to one another without entirely collapsing their formal differences. The reports of the women's remarks are too meager to tell how deeply they applied this idea, but they at least show them grappling with its ambiguities.[82]

How did Fuller's fellow Bostonians regard these Conversations? The women's many Transcendentalist and liberal Unitarian friends, of course, thought well of the meetings. Yet they also had their detractors. The evidence is scanty, but one sort were clearly orthodox and conservative Unitarian types who were scandal-ized, as several of her friends reported, by the conversations' "transcendentalist" associations and their transcendence of "'common sense.'" (After hearing Emerson lecture, the twenty-three-year-old evangelical Episcopalian Julia Ward Howe would report to her sisters, "I have had hardly the least dash of Transcen-dentalism," adding, "and to-morrow [don't be shocked!] a conversation at Miss Fuller's.") A number of radical abolitionists, as Fuller would discover the fol-lowing year, were also offended by Fuller's aloofness in her classes toward the cause of antislavery. But the bulk of the Conversations' disparagers, Higginson remembered, simply found the project too "audacious" and Fuller herself full of her usual "vanity and presumption" for undertaking it. Some of this even got back to Fuller. In her journal the following winter, after recording the charges she had heard made against herself and some of the women in the classes as "affected," "artful," and "arrogant," she wrote angrily, "I wonder they can reconcile their consciences to treat us so civilly, if they think so of us."[83]

Whatever other Bostonians thought of their Conversations, however, there is no question what the participants thought of them. Fuller herself was very pleased. In her January 21 letter to Sarah Helen Whitman, she exulted, "There I have real society, which I have not before looked for out of the pale of intimacy." In later years, as her friendships expanded among them, her feelings would grow even warmer. She also thought the Conversations strengthened her understanding of her aesthetic principles. "My conversations will be of use to me in this respect," she happily noted in her journal a week after writing to Whitman. "To be less rapid, less brilliant, more searching be my aim!" Meanwhile she had gotten something more than friendship and principles; she had gotten a constituency, and her friends noted its excellent effect on her. "Certain it is," Elizabeth Peabody would write in her journal after the first month of Conversations the following winter, "that Margaret never appears, when I see her, either so brilliant and deep in thought, or so desirous to please, or so modest, or so heart-touching, as in this very party." As for the women themselves, they, too, were pleased, even ecstatic. "I never heard, read of, or imagined a conversation at all equal to this we have now heard," Emerson quoted "a lady of eminent powers, previously by no means partial to Margaret" as having reportedly said after leaving a meeting on West Street the second year. Very similar comments could be duplicated in dozens of surviving reports, which would grow, in later years, even more enthusiastic as Fuller added to her arts topics Conversations on a variety of social and ethical subjects.[84]

Perhaps more helpful, though, in understanding what these Conversations elicited from the women, other than pride and admiration, are two more ideologically introspective reports. One is a letter from a seventeen-year-old Cambridge girl, Sarah Hodges, the daughter of a Unitarian minister, and a private German student of Fuller's, to her friend Esther Mack. High-spirited, humorous, worshipful of Fuller and, like all of Fuller's young female followers, morally earnest ("Oh! Esther if *you* complain of selfishness!—my life seems all for *self*"), still, she was finding the Conversations difficult. Although she had attended the previous third-year series with an anxious desire "to live a higher life," she told Esther, she recently had come to feel profoundly dissatisfied with them. "My . . . objection to these conversations is that I sometimes feel as if I would rather not have doubts and difficulties suggested to me which I have not yet met with in my experience of life; and as if a simple faith in the words of Jesus were better than, even better without, all philosophy and reasoning or mortal men. Yet I suppose," this conservative, down-to-earth young Unitarian woman added wistfully, "the right way is to have the former firmly and by it to judge the truth of the latter." By contrast, the later feminist activist and writer Ednah Dow Littlehale Cheney, who was a year older than Sarah and who attended the same last three years of the Conversations that Sarah did, had almost the opposite feeling about their effect on her. In her autobiography she wrote: "I found myself in a new world of thought; a flood of light irradiated all that I had seen in nature, observed in life, or read in books. Whatever she spoke of revealed a hidden meaning, and everything seemed to be put into true relation. Perhaps I could best express it by saying that I was no longer the limitation of myself, but I felt the whole wealth of the universe was open to me." No doubt this sublime egotism and sense of being privy to an esoteric universe of meaning were what more than one aspiring Unitarian woman took away from Fuller's paeans to poesy.[85]

But the best perspective of Fuller's Conversations is finally historical. First, they contributed to the growth of organized American feminism. Out of these meetings would come later Boston feminist writers and intellectuals like Cheney, Caroline Healey Dall, and Julia Ward Howe. Also, prominent feminist leaders—like Elizabeth Cady Stanton and Paulina Wright Davis of New York and Lucinda Chandler of Chicago—would later look back on these Conversations as the central precedent and model for many of their clubs and organizations through which they would seek to nurture American women's intellectual autonomy and self-emancipation. Second, and perhaps more important, they initiated the growth of a countercultural tradition in American women's culture. For the kind of culture Fuller advocated in her classes was clearly not, contrary to the charges of some of her abolitionist detractors, the conventionally pedantic, ornamental sort that irritated outsiders so often found characteristic of the nineteenth-century Boston female world. Even less did it follow the narcissistic and self-flattering conventions so pervasive in many of the female magazines and popular novels of the period. Rather, for all its earnestness, it was tough-minded and self-critical. Essentially, the idea of culture that Fuller disseminated in her classes was a resurrection of the radical vision announced in the mid-1830s by Emerson and Alcott—of culture, not as a means to wealth or status, but to man as a concept-creating, symbol-making animal. These ideas of "man thinking" and mind-as-activity were radical enough in early nineteenth-century America. But to apply them, whether fancifully or methodically, to women, whose very intellectual identity and claim to cultural validation were defined by official culture as flowing precisely from their passive and therefore pure absorption of common-sense values and divine wisdom, was culturally subversive. It was for this subversiveness, just as much as for their aspirations, that Fuller's Conversations deserve to be remembered. This may not have made her into the "sibylline dwelling in the cave," but it did put her on the way to becoming antebellum America's foremost female activist of the mind.[86]

CHAPTER NINE

The Transcendentalist

(1839–1840)

I

In starting her Conversations for women, Fuller launched her career as a Transcendentalist leader. Her timing was propitious. Three years earlier, the Transcendental Club had begun as merely a private discussion club of a few Unitarian ministers anxious to introduce into their sect more spiritually vigorous modes of thought. Apart from outraged newspaper editorials about Alcott's Temple School and a few isolated alarm bells sounded by Harvard academics like Andrews Norton and Francis Bowen, there had been little indication that the scholarly articles and obscure-sounding pamphlets of the "Transcendentalists" (as they were beginning to be called) were even being noticed. But this public indifference ended dramatically with Emerson's delivery of his remarkable address to the graduating class at the Harvard Divinity School in July 1838. In this Transcendental jeremiad, Emerson joined, more radically than any of the band had ever dared, an assertion of the "intuition . . . of the laws of the soul" with a startling assault on all remnants of "historical Christianity," including Jesus' partial divinity, still adhered to by most Unitarians. Even more pointedly, he attacked the "formalist" and "spectral" preachers who relied on these traditional doctrines. The words, one should remember, were spoken, not by an upstart outsider like Alcott, but by a prominent Unitarian minister in the sect's very citadel. The address sent shock waves through the Unitarian community. "The old tyrant of the Cambridge Parnassus" (as Emerson privately called Norton) denounced it in a furious article in the *Boston Daily Advertiser* as an impious, "incoherent rhapsody." But the consternation did not come only from longtime Transcendentalist-baiters like Norton. Nathan Hale, Jr., the *Advertiser*'s editor's son, indignantly wrote to his momentarily rusticated Harvard classmate James Russell Lowell, that Dean Palfrey was "very much hurt about it" and even the moderates "are a little frightened—As for the Divinities I want to kick every one I see—I think it was actually insulting in them to choose Emerson, knowing what must come, for such an occasion, and doubly so to have it printed when they have heard the worst. I think it will ruin him however, he has gone too far."[1]

Emerson had indeed gone "far." But far from ruining him or his circle, his address helped bring to birth Transcendentalism as a public movement. It is true this had its less cheering side: it suddenly marked the Transcendentalists as outsiders and rebels. This had been for some time Alcott's status, and now it was also Emerson's; not for another thirty years would he be invited again to address a Harvard audience. Indeed, even moderate Transcendentalist Unitarian ministers were vulnerable to attack and ostracism in the Unitarian community as long as they continued to defend ideas associated with religious radicals like Emerson. But there was also a positive side. For one thing, there was no longer any question about the Transcendentalists' importance. They were now, truly, as Norton advertised them in his counterassault in August, "The New School in Literature and Religion." Characterizations of the new sect by Norton and most of his Divinity School and Boston ministerial colleagues as *"dangerous"* and "disastrous and alarming" only heightened the effect. Furthermore, the controversy strengthened the Transcendentalists' sense of their collective identity. Transcendentalists held many different theological points of view, ranging from the pantheistic Neoplatonism of Alcott and Emerson to the partly supernatural Christianity of Hedge and Clarke. Nonetheless, while continuing to debate these differences among themselves, they publicly emphasized what was to them the more important issue—the defense of the intuitive basis of religious truth. Naturally, too, this meant the defense of Emerson, whose plea for "first, soul, and second, soul, and everymore, soul" in religion they publicly embraced as essentially theirs.[2]

The Transcendentalists matched their new profile with a new public aggressiveness. At the beginning of the year, the intellectually brawny, self-taught Unitarian minister Orestes Brownson brought out the first issue of his *Boston Quarterly Review.* In it he hammered away at the "infidelity" of Unitarian anti-Transcendentalists like Norton and Bowen, while promoting his own kind of "objective" Transcendentalism and radically prodemocratic political philosophy. Other Transcendentalists took action on the cultural front. That fall, George Ripley published the first two volumes of his *Specimens of Foreign Standard Literature,* which included later that spring Fuller's *Conversations with Goethe.* With this popular series of translations by younger Transcendentalists, the circle unfurled its banner—in the face of conservative Unitarian attacks on their "diseased admiration" of these very "standard" Continental Romantic and post-Kantian texts—of a new cosmopolitanism in American literature. Finally, the following summer brought a sure sign of a party in the making—a full-blown pamphlet war between Norton and Ripley. The debate, which attracted widespread press attention throughout the North, was ostensibly about the Transcendentalists' discounting the religious value of the "evidence" of Jesus' reported miracles that rationalistic Unitarians like Norton advanced in defense of Christianity. But for Ripley, as for most Transcendentalists, behind this neg-

ative theological position and the positive counterclaim of an intuitionist religious faith, lurked a more broadly cultural premise: the Transcendentalists'
democratic yet elevated idea of the "scholar" or intellectual, which Ripley
charged their liberal-now-turned-illiberal seniors like Norton with betraying. "I
honor the learned," Ripley concluded his first pamphlet,

> when they devote their attainments to the service of society; when they cherish a
> stronger interest in the welfare of their brethren, than in the luxury of their books;
> when they bring the researches of science to the illustration of truth, the correction
> of abuses, and the aid of the sufferer; but if they do not acknowledge a higher light
> than that which comes from the printed page; if they confound the possession of
> erudition with the gift of wisdom; and above all, if they presume to interfere in the
> communion of the soul with God, and limit the universal bounty of Heaven with
> their "smoky cells," I can only utter my amazement.[3]

In addition to intellectual conflicts with conservative Unitarians, two other
factors also helped stimulate a more radical ethos among the Transcendentalists.
One was the changing social character of their circle. Although some early Transcendentalists like Alcott, Brownson, Elizabeth Peabody, and, to some extent,
Margaret Fuller herself, came out of decidedly non–Boston-Cambridge-Brah-
min backgrounds, the majority were from the center of these. By the late 1830s,
however, most of the new young men coming around the group were comparative outsiders: young Harvard graduates like Theodore Parker, the Lexington
farmer's son; or Jones Very, the oldest child of the common-law widowed wife
of a Salem sea captain; or Henry David Thoreau, the son of a Concord store-
keeper and pencil maker. Even more important, though, was the fact that an
increasing number of these young men, whatever their origins, were renouncing
the social ideals of their traditional elite. Leaving abbreviated ministerial careers
after graduation, or never starting them in the first place, they were becoming
writers, poets, artists, reformers; even, in a few cases and for a time, farmers and
day laborers. Such heterogeneity, even if somewhat artificial, was certainly a far
cry from the decorous Transcendental Club that only three years earlier had initially excluded Alcott because of his nonclerical status, and its consequences for
the history of Transcendentalism were far-reaching. Suddenly there appeared a
potential constituency for testing Emerson's oft-repeated preachment that the
freeing of individuals from institutional commitments was the key to carrying
"the spiritual principle" into new forms of literature and life. Meanwhile, if
nothing else, the circle's new recruits injected into its midst a youthful, secular,
and bohemian air it had never had before.[4]

The other radicalizing influence on the Transcendentalists was the general
ideological climate in the Northeast. Three developments heated the atmosphere. First, older and more conservative social reform movements like temperance and education were becoming, in the maelstrom of increasingly adven-
tist-minded evangelical revivalism, partly eclipsed, if not infected themselves, by
more populist and perfectionist causes. These included abolitionism, nonresis-
tance, phrenology, dietary reform, and, most recently, communitarianism.
Although in many ways very different, all these movements shared the protean

and profoundly evangelical belief that individuals needed in various ways to "come out" from a corrupt world; that if they did, they could be liberated from sin and ignorance; and if the process were repeated sufficiently, it would produce, by a sort of moral kinesis, virtually boundless social progress. Second, the economic depression that had begun two years before continued to worsen, not only bringing commercial paralysis and unprecedented suffering for America's working classes, but also emboldening further already-alienated middle-class reformers and intellectuals. Indeed, even Emerson—who heretofore had shown not a particle of social radicalism—privately rejoiced in the dissatisfaction that "such emphatic & universal calamity" brought out in him. ("Pride, and Thrift, & Expediency, who jeered and chirped and were so well pleased with themselves and made merry with the dream as they termed it of philosophy & love," he wrote gloatingly in his journal soon after the initial panic set in, "Behold they are all flat and here is the Soul erect and Unconquered still. . . . Let me begin anew. Let me teach the finite to know its Master. Let me ascend above my fate and work down upon my world.") Lastly, the depression polarized American politics. While out-of-office Whigs successfully turned the economic bad times to their advantage against Jackson's hapless successor, Martin Van Buren, in Northeastern states like New York and Massachusetts, radical "Locofoco" or "Equal Rights" Democrats gained at the expense of both Whigs and conservative Democratic party regulars. That winter Massachusetts elected its first Democratic governor, the "radical" Marcus Morton, narrowly defeating the incumbent and the darling of Massachusetts intellectual Whiggery, Edward Everett. In their joining Jeffersonian assaults on "privilege" with newer, Romantic conceptions of the divinity of the common people and the popular will, these radical Democratic politicians and the pundits who supported them gave to American politics—just as much as the middle-class reformers they to some extent competed with—a new ideological edge.[5]

Altogether, these contradictory and overlapping developments encouraged a critical, dissatisfied, and millennially expectant tone in Northern culture that would continue to grow until the Civil War. That Transcendentalists should rush in to add their own sympathetic notes to that harmony—or cacophony—of reforms should not be surprising. Transcendentalist ministers like George Ripley had absorbed the traditional Channingite Unitarian uneasiness over self-seeking materialism and its patrician corollary belief in the responsibility of "the better sort" to arouse the capacities of society's poor and downtrodden. At the same time, more culturally radical Transcendentalists like Emerson, Alcott, and Brownson had recently come to extract from the new philosophy important protodemocratic notions: the potential divinity of individual men and women; the necessity to liberate souls from spiritually confining institutions; the call to achieve an organic integration of thought and action, labor and consciousness, intellectuals and common life, were all—potentially at least—socially radical Transcendentalist ideas.[6]

Finally, by 1839, many Transcendentalists were becoming extremely hopeful about the possibilities for what some of them were beginning to call "democratic" change. That year George Ripley began reading about European and American pietistic communities, an interest that would soon join with his dissatisfaction with the social conservatism of the Unitarian church to propel him out of the ministry and into a full-time career as a communitarian socialist leader. Simultaneously, Orestes Brownson, who had been trumpeting the ideals of Saint-Simonian socialism for several years, accelerated his efforts, along with those of his friend and patron George Bancroft, now the Democratic boss of Massachusetts, to convince his fellow Transcendentalists that a new, radicalized Democratic party was the political mechanism for social regeneration. Political radicalism now began to infect the Transcendentalist movement as a whole. Former anti-Democrats like George Ripley and James Freeman Clarke privately declared their "conversion . . . to Democracy" or "loco foco[ism]." The moderately Transcendentalist *Western Messenger* began publishing articles trumpeting the British working-class Chartists, "Loco-focoism," and "the development and realization of true democratic ideas." After hearing Emerson's opening lecture in his series "The Present Age" in December—in which he had welcomed "the fruitful crop of social reforms" that favored "pure truth" and "simple equity" over "mere commodity" and "the Colleges and all monied foundations of learning or religion" that favored "tradition"—Theodore Parker excitedly wrote the moderate Transcendentalist Club member Convers Francis: "It was *democratic*-locofoco thghout, & very much in the spirit of Brownson's article on 'Democracy and Reform' in the last 'Quarterly'. . . . *Bancroft* was in ecstasies." It is true that such "democratic" enthusiasm was somewhat misleading. Neither Ripley nor Clarke, for example, was especially pro-Democratic *party,* and Emerson, who privately stigmatized the party as "vain & loud" and "wholly commercial," harbored, in addition, deep skepticism about the prospects of achieving social regeneration through *any* social or political institution. So, even more, did Alcott (who coolly wrote in his diary, "The Kingdom of truth is within, not out there, in Church or State. Vox populi vox diaboli"). But, as Parker's letter shows, these were strategic matters that club members, for now, talked about, if at all, only fleetingly. Transcendentalists like Ripley continued to sound the call for a "philosophical democracy," and Emerson continued to urge his audiences to abandon all those unequal, luxurious, and "artificial modes of life" in business, labor, diet, and even housekeeping arrangements that make a person "a slave" and thereby "disgrace the soul." For the moment at least, Transcendentalism seemed to be indeed, as Emerson styled it, a "party of the Future."[7]

How did Margaret Fuller fit into that party? One answer would have to be: philosophically at least, not very differently than she had three years earlier when she had first gotten to know Emerson and Alcott. Despite her readings in Plato, Coleridge, and, intermittently, post-Kantian philosophy, Fuller still had not found it necessary or congenial to work out anything like a systematic philosophy of the mind. On the other hand, her subjectivist aesthetics inspired by her German Romantics at least implied one. Meanwhile, her loyalty toward her own homegrown and now besieged Tiecks and Novalises remained as fierce as ever.

"The other day," she wrote in her journal that winter," while visiting a person whose highest merit, so far as I know, is to save his pennies, I was astounded by hearing him allude to some of most approved worth among us, thus: 'You know *we* consider *those men* insane.'" She filled up the rest of her paper with comparisons of the various poets, philosophers, reformers, and others of her friends among the Transcendentalists, to Jesus and Paul; and their detractors to the apostle's worldly adversaries, the Roman officials Festus and Agrippa, concluding: "'Children of this generation!'—ye Festuses and Agrippas!—ye are wiser, we grant, than 'the children of light'; yet we advise you to commend to a higher tribunal those whom much learning, or much love, has made 'mad.' For if they stay here, almost will they persuade even you!"[8]

What fired Fuller's loyalty? Certainly—as her philippic to Caroline Sturgis two years before had announced—her friendships with leading Transcendentalists had a good deal to do with it. But so, too, did her evolving religious views. Her recent Communion experiences notwithstanding, she, like all Transcendentalists, had come to embrace a largely subjective standard of religious experience. "I deem if the religious sentiment is again to be expressed from our pulpits in its healthy vigor," she told Charles King Newcomb, who had inquired that winter about her views on the current religious debates, "it must be by those who can speak unfettered by creed or covenant; each man from the inner light." And in a letter to William Henry Channing in the spring, she opined: "The reason [Christianity] has so imperfectly answered to the aspirations of its Founder is, that men have received it on external grounds. I believe that a religion, thus received, may give the life an external decorum, but will never open the fountains of holiness in the soul." But one of her most revealing Transcendentalist statements at this time was included in a lengthy letter about her religion to Channing the following fall. Grumbling that she had let herself be "cheated out of my Sunday" by going to hear the popular, conservative New York Unitarian minister Orville Dewey, she went on to explain, in true Transcendentalist fashion, her dissatisfaction with both orthodox supernaturalism and Unitarian rationalism:

> As he began by reading the first chapter of Isaiah and the fourth of John's Epistle, I made mental comments with pure delight. "Bring no more vain oblations." "Every one that loveth is born of God, and knoweth God." "We know that we dwell in Him, and He in us, because he hath given us of the Spirit." Then pealed the organ, full of solemn assurance. But straightway uprose the preacher to deny mysteries, to deny the second birth, to deny influx, and to renounce the sovereign gift of insight, for the sake of what he deemed a *"rational"* exercise of will. As he spoke I could not choose but deny him all through, and could scarce refrain from rising to expound, in the light of my own faith, the words of those wiser Jews which had been read.

She concluded this part of her letter by conceding she could see why "he looked at things as he did." There *was* once a time, in reaction to the "old religionists" who talked about grace and conversion merely "technically, without striving to enter into the idea," when it had been worthwhile to assert, as had the Unitarians, the dignity of human nature and the oneness of the infinite spirit. But now, she said, the "old dogmas" had to be reinterpreted. "I would now preach the Holy Ghost as zealously as they have been preaching Man, and faith instead of the understanding and mysticism instead &c." But why go on? she seemed to be saying. Indeed, in two final, capsule sentences on Dewey's hearers, she distilled more evangelical-Transcendentalist vitriol than perhaps any of her band ever did: "O that crowd of upturned faces with their look of unintelligent complacency. Give me tears and groans rather if there be a mixture of physical excitement and bigotry."[9]

As this last gesture makes clear enough, Fuller's primary religious interests were not strictly theological. "Rev A. Norton has been amusing his learned retirement by preparing more furniture for the booksellers shelves," she wrote in bored amusement to Emerson later in the spring. Nor was this kind of controversy to Fuller's taste. In one of the two "Chat[s] in Boston Bookstores," which she published the following summer in Brownson's *Boston Quarterly Review,* she had her alter ego Professor Partridge, while upbraiding Professor Norton for his dictatorial presumption and absurd "terror . . . of the German philosophers and theologians," nonetheless concede that it is not through these "passages-at-arms" (so preferred by New Englanders to "a creative work") "that I love to consider the world of thought." The fact is that all her writings in 1839 and 1840 that saw (in William Henry Channing's words) "the full dawn of the Transcendental movement in New England" show clearly that Fuller initially looked to Transcendentalism, not primarily, as many did, to give birth to a new theology or church, but rather to help stimulate a cultural awakening. In a long letter she wrote to Channing in the spring about the movement, she explained her position: "Since the Revolution, there has been little, in the circumstances of this country, to call out the higher sentiments. . . . The need of bringing out the physical resources of a vast extent of country, the commercial and political fever incident to our institutions, tend to fix the eyes of men on what is local and temporary, on the external advantages of their condition." The country's recent "superficial diffusion of knowledge," by depriving the multitude of "sentiments of reverence," was likely "to vulgarize rather than to raise" thought. This vulgarization "is in no way balanced by the slight literary culture common here, which is mostly English, and consists in a careless reading of publications of the day, having the same utilitarian tendency with our own proceedings." The result of all these forces was a profound cultural torpor. But now, happily, New England's increasing age and leisure had produced, she said,

> a violent reaction, in a small minority, against a mode of culture that rears such fruits. They see that political freedom does not necessarily produce liberality of mind, nor freedom in church institutions—vital religion; and, seeing that these changes cannot be wrought from without inwards, they are trying to quicken the soul, that they may work from within outwards. Disgusted with the vulgarity of a commercial aristocracy, they become radicals; disgusted with the materialistic working of "rational" religion, they become mystics. They quarrel with all that is, because it is not spiritual enough. They would, perhaps, be patient if they thought this the

mere sensuality of childhood in our nation, which it might outgrow; but they think
that they see the evil widening, deepening,—not only debasing the life, but corrupt-
ing the thought of our people, and they feel that if they know not well what should
be done, yet that the duty of every good man is to utter a protest against what is done
amiss.[10]

So it was as a badly needed cultural protest movement that the Transcendentalists received Fuller's heartiest applause. Extending that protest into politics
and reform, however, was something else again. One can find in her journals at
this time occasional denunciations of the greed and narrowness of "the men who
manage the practical interests of this great country." But this was still insufficient
to shake her loose from her inherited liberal Whiggery. After reading Governor
Morton's moderately Locofoco inaugural address calling for getting government
out of the business of promoting banks and corporations, the most she could
muster was the compliment that it was "an extremely well written paper
meseems, surely democracy *sounds* well, if no more." She was even more skeptical about the idea—increasingly talked of in Transcendentalist circles—that
their cultural awakening might help bring about a radical social transformation.
As her blast against progress in Providence had shown, she had drunk too deeply
of the German Romantics—alienated and culturally radical, but politically conservative—to be taken in by radical social visions. "Utopia," she told Channing
flatly in her long letter, "is impossible to build up. At least, my hopes for our race
on this one planet are more limited than those of most of my friends." She
added, echoing her old master Goethe, "I accept the limitations of human
nature, and believe a wise acknowledgment of them one of the best conditions
of progress."[11]

At least one of her Transcendentalist friends thought he glimpsed another
Fuller on the horizon. James Clarke, increasingly reform-minded now, wrote
that winter to his sister, Sarah, of English Romantics like Walter Savage Landor
whose self-reliance led them to admire only the great man and not the "spirit of
humanity"—a "danger," he thought, that also infected Emerson, notwithstanding "his profound respect for human nature." He added:

> S.M.F. has less theoretic respect for humanity than R.W.E.—but more natural affin-
> ity with the mass—when she gets her principles & feelings in harmony she will do
> something. Her complex & various nature draws her in many directions. Her sense
> of the beautiful & keen discriminating mind, cause her to be exclusive in her tastes
> & aristocratic in her principles. Her practical tendency takes her back to the multi-
> tude—her inborn love of fame causes that no whisper from the vast human race shall
> be indifferent to her— What a Sphynx is that girl! who shall solve her?[12]

In the future, circumstances (as Clarke here implicitly predicted) would provide some solutions. Meanwhile, in her long letter to Channing, Fuller tried, if
not to solve, at least to qualify, her seeming social conservatism. For one thing,
she said, her lack of engagement with questions of politics and reform was an
inevitable consequence of her circumscribed gender status. "My position as a
woman, and the many private duties which have filled my life, have prevented

my thinking deeply on several of the great subjects which these friends have at heart." She also made it clear to the eagerly reformist Channing that disengagement did not mean neutrality. While conceding that she found the social opinions of younger Transcendentalists often "crude," "undiscriminating," and even potentially dangerous, she yet saw in them "promise of a better wisdom than in their opponents." Here her grounds were partly idealistic: "That is the real life which is subordinated to, not merged in, the ideal; he is only wise who can bring the lowest act of his life into sympathy with its highest thought." But mainly her reasons were religious: "Their hope for man is grounded on his destiny as an immortal soul, and not as a mere comfort-loving inhabitant of earth, or as a subscriber to the social contract. . . . Man is not made for society, but society is made for man. No institution can be good which does not tend to improve the individual." Finally, she appreciated the social utility of even illusory prophecies. "Were not man ever more sanguine than facts at the moment justify, he would remain torpid, or be sunk in sensuality. It is on this ground that I sympathize with what is called the 'Transcendental party,' and that I feel their aim to be the true one. They acknowledge in the nature of man an arbiter for his deeds,—a standard transcending sense and time,—and are, in my view, the true utilitarians." Although in later years she would articulate more ambitious social visions, this pragmatic test would never be very far from her mind.[13]

II

Despite these only-moderate sympathies with the Transcendentalist contagion, Fuller was a welcome figure at Club discussions. On September 16, at Convers Francis's house in Watertown, she attended what was her second meeting since first being introduced to the group two years before. It was on the subject (appropriately enough, given the circle's growing notoriety) of "Esoteric and Exoteric doctrine." The remaining final seven meetings over the following year, which Fuller would attend except for two, would likewise encompass themes that were more broadly cultural and reform-minded than in previous years—from "the Inspiration of the Prophet and bard, the nature of Poetry, and the causes of the sterility of Poetic Inspiration in our age and country," to "the doctrine of Reform" and "the organization of a new church." Records of the character and tone of the discussions are scanty. Friendly outsiders who occasionally attended these or similar Transcendentalist gatherings later reported on what seemed to them their exasperatingly Delphic quality. "There was a constrained, but very amiable silence," George William Curtis recalled of one meeting at a later, short-lived, partial reincarnation of the Club, "which had the impertinence of a tacit inquiry, seeming to ask, 'Who will now proceed to say the finest thing that has ever been said?'" In a word, it was Fuller's kind of club, and the principals, by all accounts, treated her accordingly. William Henry Channing, who attended the meeting that day, which was also his first, later wrote:

It was a pleasing surprise to see how this friend of earlier days was acknowledged as a peer of the realm, in this new world of thought. Men,—her superiors in years, fame and social position,—treated her more with the frankness due from equal to equal, than the half-condescending deference with which scholars are wont to adapt themselves to women. . . . It was evident that they prized her verdict, respected her criticism, feared her rebuke, and looked to her as an umpire. Very observable was it, also, how, in sidetalks with her, they became confidential, seemed to glow and brighten into their best mood; and poured out in full measure what they but scantily hinted in the circle at large.[14]

Channing, who attended a couple of more meetings when he was in town the following year, has also left an evocative portrait of Fuller's typical speaking manner at these gatherings. Although in his usual purple prose, it has—as one might expect from someone who was himself a powerful extemporaneous public speaker—a strong ring of professional credibility. "Near-sighted and habitually using an eye-glass," he recalled, "she rapidly scanned the forms and faces." Then,

when her turn came, by a graceful transition she resumed the subject where preceding speakers had left it, and, briefly summing up their results, proceeded to unfold her own view. Her opening was deliberate, like the progress of some massive force gathering its momentum; but as she felt her way, and moving in a congenial element, the sweep of her speech became grand. The style of her eloquence was sententious, free from prettiness, direct, vigorous, charged with vitality. Articulateness, just emphasis and varied accent, brought out most delicate shades and brilliant points of meaning, while a rhythmical collocation of words gave a finished form to every thought. She was affluent in historic illustration and literary allusion, as well as in novel hints. She knew how to concentrate into racy phrases the essential truth gathered from wide research, and distilled with patient toil; and by skilful treatment she could make green again the wastes of commonplace. Her statements, however rapid, showed breadth of comprehension, ready memory, impartial judgment, nice analysis of differences, power of penetrating through surfaces to realities, fixed regard to central laws and habitual communion with the Life of life. Critics, indeed, might have been tempted to sneer at a certain oracular grandiloquence, that bore away her soberness in moments of elation; though even the most captious must presently have smiled at the humor of her descriptive touches, her dextrous exposure of folly and pretension, the swift stroke of her bright wit, her shrewd discernment, promptitude, and presence of mind.[15]

While Fuller's public favor with the Transcendentalists was growing, so, too, were her personal relations among them. Their letters and journals that summer, fall, and winter show her constantly consulting, visiting, and socializing with the leading Transcendentalists and their families and friends. Toward most of the older figures in the circle, Fuller's feelings, like her attitudes toward the movement, remained mixed: increasing confidence vied with continuing skepticism. This was true of her old friends George Ripley and his learned wife Sophia. The "timidity" (as she wrote in her journal) of George's early *Christian Examiner* articles on German authors had in the past bothered her. Also, George's personal reticence and Sophia's (as Fuller termed it) "factitious" manner beneath her burning intellectual and reform zeal seem to have kept intimacy pretty much at bay. ("I can talk with him endlessly though not deeply, with her I can go only a step though she loves me and I her, she seldom misunderstands me, he often.") Still, she appreciated their steady support for her writing and classes. She also admired George's erudition and growing enthusiasm for social reform, although she harbored doubts about his abilities as an ideological leader. Sophia, she told William Channing, "usually goes higher and sees clearer than he does."[16]

One old Transcendentalist friendship that definitely improved with social contact was that with Alcott. Of course Alcott's continuing high opinion of her helped. "I think her the most brilliant talker of the day," he wrote in his diary after spending the afternoon with her during her short spring intersession at the end of her first year at Greene Street. And again, after some "fine talk on high topics" when she stopped in Boston after leaving the school in December, he gloated: "Miss Fuller is the most remarkable person of her sex, now extant, amongst us. . . . Her erudition is wide, her intellect is robust, her insight sharp and deep." He was also persistent. "I am sorry you missed Mr Alcott who still gropes after & explores the irreconcileable light of your star," Emerson wrote to her in August. "It is plain he cannot let you rest until he know whether this undeniable lustre be planetary or solar, kindred or alien." In November they exchanged journals—a solemn sign of Transcendentalist friendship-making— and by the following June he blithely informed her, she said, that they "looked at things in the same way" and "had only a veil of words between us." Of course this was not true, and Fuller knew it. Indeed, as if to confirm the fact, she enclosed with her letter a copy of her 1837 journal, which contained her critique of the excessive idealism of his reform "mission." By this time, however, she had come to take the chastened but just view of Alcott that Emerson had finally come around to from the opposite direction—that although a bad writer and too much obsessed with his image as a social redeemer, Alcott was a great teacher, an endearing intellectual companion, and a man of often acute spiritual insight. "With me alone," she wrote to Emerson the following spring after one visit with him, "he is never the Messiah but one beautiful individuality and faithful soul. Then he seems really high and not merely a person of high pretensions."[17]

Not all of Fuller's friendships benefited from familiarity. One that did not was that with Elizabeth Peabody. To a large extent this was inevitable. Peabody was more a Romantic Channingite than a Transcendentalist radical: deeply devoted to education as a kind of cultural religion; anxious to avoid any sign of "Egotheism" in the circle's philosophy; fully accepting the notion that woman's primary place was as a custodian of culture in the family and school; and boundlessly hopeful, Unitarian-style, about social progress and her countless causes and charities. She was, if hardly the naïve, disheveled, "shop-worn" do-gooder caricatured by Henry James in the character of Miss Birdseye in *The Bostonians,* certainly the prime representative of the fervently "genteel" side of the Transcendentalist circle. But it seems to have been less Peabody's intellectual gentility that annoyed Fuller than her personal style; particularly her fuzzy writing, her social tactlessness, and, above all, her tendency to "idolize" (in Fuller's term) persons in her orbit. "There is so much in you," Fuller would several years later bluntly tell her, after listing several of these faults, "that is hostile to my wishes, as to character, and especially as to the character of a woman." One need not be a depth psychologist to detect behind Fuller's hostility, besides her stoic, self-poised ideal of womanhood, a need perhaps to distance herself from an older woman whose career as a teacher, magazine writer, and intellectual entrepreneur, despite their obvious differences, superficially resembled Fuller's own. But for either ideological or psychological reasons, the repugnance was there. Was there cruelty in this? Peabody's worshiped mentor William Ellery Channing thought there was. "Miss Fuller," Emerson reported his once saying to her at Channing's house, "when I consider that you are all that Miss P[eabody] wished to be, and that you despise her, and that she loves and honors you, I think her place in Heaven must be very high." Neither Fuller's moderate scorn, however—which Peabody knew about and accepted—nor Peabody's worries about Fuller's egoism prevented the two women from cooperating in friendly ways in joint Transcendentalist ventures. Nor, typically, did these negative feelings inhibit this generous, learned, tireless *"Boswell"* of the Transcendentalists in her unflagging boosting of Fuller's career and reputation. Paradoxically—whether out of extraordinary sympathy or self-deception—the impractical Peabody provided Fuller with perhaps her most practical friendship in the Transcendentalist circle.[18]

If Fuller was dubious about some of the older Transcendentalists, she was even more so about their main rising star. He was the West Roxbury Unitarian minister, Theodore Parker, just her age, whom she had first met the year after his graduation from Harvard Divinity School three years before. The eleventh and youngest child of a hardworking small farmer, Parker was a voracious, self-taught polymath who had worked his way through Harvard and would soon take over from Ripley the role of the movement's chief theological pugilist. Unfortunately for Fuller, some of this belligerence carried over to his relations with her. "Miss Fuller is a critic, not a creator, not a seer, I think," he wrote in his journal after one intellectual argument he had with her in July. "Certainly she is a prodigious woman, though she puts herself upon her genius rather too much. She has nothing to do with God out of her. She is not a good analyst, not a philosopher." Again, more testily, the following September: "Miss Fuller gives way too often to petty jealousies, contemptible lust of power, & falling into freaks of passion." Caroline Healey Dall, who as a young girl adored them both, thought that the reason Parker "hates Margaret" was that in their imperiousness "they resemble each other." This is plausible, although his "genius for depreciation" (as one of his friends called it) went considerably beyond the "scoffing" he complained about in Fuller. Also, their *differences* undoubtedly contributed not a little to their unfriendliness. Parker's democratic instincts were visceral, and his aesthetic understanding was as weak as his theological knowledge was monumental. Not surprisingly, he took great offense at the "transcendental nonsense" about "the 'absence of art' in America" that Fuller "twaddle[d] forth." Their gender attitudes hardly mixed well. Although later a strong supporter of women's rights, in his personal friendships with women, of which he had many, he frequently avowed an exclusive preference for "affection," "beauty," and "subtlety" in women ("in striking contrast to my own direct and blunt modes of mental operation") as against, he pointedly emphasized in his journal, "the Macedonian-phalanx march of good Miss [Fuller]."[19]

From her side, Fuller was less than enthralled with Parker. "Mr P. seems a calm and accurate thinker," she wrote in her journal that winter, but definitely not "masterly." She also disliked his negative and "polemical" intellectual style. (It was better, she thought, to "pour . . . in upon the world the tide of truth.") On the other hand, if there was a serious animus between the two, Fuller's papers show that it was wholly on Parker's side. "He was in a fine glow," she wrote to William Channing after hearing Parker's fiercely Transcendentalist sermon "Idolatry"; "*you* would have said he looked *manly*. I quite loved him." Furthermore, from Parker's papers it is clear that, despite his hostility toward Fuller, her talents were not entirely lost on him, either. After one convivial party at Fuller's house in September, he paid Fuller the compliment of associating her with one of the great Romantic cultural heroines of their circle: "Miss Fuller resembles *Mme de Stael* more than any woman I know." Indeed, considering the differences between the two, it seems a triumph of sorts that Fuller was one of only two women (the other was the sentimental Felicia Hemans!) whose writings this compulsive bibliophile and self-confessed belittler of the literary "efforts of women" thought worthy enough to "adorn my book-shelves."[20]

In addition to mingling with Transcendentalist leaders that year, Fuller also mixed with some of their younger, more alienated, aesthetic-minded followers. She was the friendliest with the more searching of these, like the two artistically talented, frustrated, itinerant Unitarian ministers John Sullivan Dwight and Christopher Pearse Cranch, and the reclusive, introspective young Charles King Newcomb, who Fuller cultivated as an ethereal protégé. With the most anointed—and most notorious—of this type, on the other hand, Fuller was the wariest. He was Jones Very, a brilliant Harvard graduate who had twice won the Bowdoin Prize. Very had been dismissed the previous fall from his position as Greek tutor and committed for a month to Charlestown's McLean asylum for the insane, following, on the heels of his religious conversion, decidedly un-Harvard classroom pronouncements about his revelations from God. Deeply impressed, Emerson had pressed on Fuller at the beginning of the year some of Very's poems and criticism, which Very had given him, as one persecuted mystic to another. Fuller was not so impressed. She failed to see entirely the "inspired & prophetical side" to Very that Emerson had touted to her. "His state is imperfect," she wrote in her journal after one conversation with him that winter, during which he spoke with her about his new "will-less existence" as a latter-day Christ. "He thought himself a Son, he should therefore abide as Calenus in the desert and let the ravens bring him food. But he sometimes uses his human will and understanding and so falsifies his thought." Mocking the "sing song" sonnet form that Very used in his poetry, she sneered, "See the leaf, the ripple, none of your sing song in his style (God's!)." Still, she told Emerson, after criticizing Very's mystically Christian interpretation of *Hamlet* that Emerson had lent her as "rather probed at an inquiring distance than grasped," she added, "I am . . . greatly interested in Mr Very. He seems worthy to be well known." Also, she was at least sufficiently taken with Very's poetry—or what it symbolized culturally—to have her "Professor Partridge" praise Very's recently published *Essays and Poems* in a *Boston Quarterly Review* "Chat" that winter for having, despite its "unfinished" and "homely" style, "an elasticity of spirit, a genuine flow of thought, and an unsought nobleness and purity almost unknown amid the self-seeking, factitious sentiment, and weak movement of our overtaught, and over-ambitious literature, if, indeed, we can say we have one."[21]

Much more than Very, Fuller was taken with another, considerably more worldly, alienated young poet around the Transcendentalist circle that year. He was her future brother-in-law, the younger William Ellery Channing. His mother had died when he was five. His father, Walter Channing, was the dean of the Harvard Medical School, and his uncles included, besides his famous namesake, Washington Allston and the college's eminent rhetoric professor, Edward T. Channing. Rejecting his inheritance, the restless Channing had dropped out of Harvard after two months. He spent the next five years studiously reading ("which [Emerson wrote] he took the greatest pains to conceal"), worrying his father, and writing poetry, which Sam Ward and Caroline Sturgis, his closest friends, circulated among their circle. Fuller had first met Channing at a party at his Uncle William Ellery's two years before. Her account was indicative of things to come from this hot-and-cold, hypersensitive young man: "I concluded from what M[ary Channing] had said that he came to see *me;* however after looking at me for a while between his fingers he fairly turned his back upon me and began talking in a whisper to Wm. When I got up to go away he jumped up and walked home with me, John, our man, maintaining his post on the other side!" She heard more of his praises sung by Sturgis and Ward and saw him a little that summer before he went off to become, for a while, a farmer in Illinois. More important, as she read more of his unconventional poetry, she became—as Emerson had with Very—deeply impressed. "The dignity of Ellery's aspiration astounds me," she wrote in her journal that winter. "It makes my own seem low and external. . . . Ellery's view is as spiritual as Mr Alcott's [and] he has a far finer sense of beauty without priggishness or cant. Truly the life of soul is all to him." Indeed, so impressed was she with Channing's poetry, his studied indifference to acclaim, and his casual brusqueness and dark humor—which she seems to have taken for sincerity—that she could sound positively distressed about her own ambitious intellectual identity. "As I read Ellery, my past life seems a poor excuse for not living, my so called culture a collection of shreds and patches to hide the mind's nakedness— Cannot I begin really to live and think now." Soon enough, Fuller would have reason to think more critically of what she would later call Channing's noble "goblin-gleam," but for now she evidently wanted a little of the Transcendentalist-bohemian virus herself.[22]

While her encounters with one Transcendentalist Channing nephew that fall and winter were forcing Fuller to question her life's project, her talks with an older, more aspiring one were helping confirm her in it. She had known William Henry Channing ever since her Cambridge days, although they had not been close. "I wonder why you and M. Fuller have never come nearer to each other," his best Divinity School friend Clarke had mused shortly after their graduation. "Is it that you feel her defects to be similar to your own, & she not being on the right way would exercise a bad influence on the growth of your mind?" Channing himself recalled having been repelled by her "scathing satire" and "imperious . . . air." But whatever their origins, these ugly "mists," he claimed, eventually "melted away." In his conversion Channing's own personality undoubtedly helped. He was tall and elegant, with black hair and dark complexion and deeply set, brilliant eyes, high cheekbones, and finely chiseled features that would dramatically complement the fervid bursts of allegorically charged eloquence that later made him one of the reform movements' most electric platform speakers. In fact, this discursively erudite, captivating, enthusiastic, and perennially erratic and impractical favorite orphaned nephew of Dr. Channing could not have been more perfectly constituted to fill the role of Transcendentalist soul mate left vacant by the now married and psychologically settled James Clarke. Recent developments in Channing's life also encouraged the friendship. For the past several years he had been searching for a way of putting his yearning for social regeneration to work. In this search he had wandered, much to the consternation of his family and the worry of his friends, from Boston, to Cincinnati, to Rome, to a working-class church in New York, and finally in 1838, by now married and with an infant daughter, back to Cincinnati, where the following May he was ordained as the minister of the First Unitarian Church. It was that summer, Channing later recalled, when he was in Boston getting ready to move his family to Cincinnati, that he and Fuller for the first time became intellectually close. That they did so just when they were both straining to launch their respective careers as Transcendentalist reformers undoubtedly added an extra bit of intensity.[23]

One can see this clearly enough in their letters that fall and winter. A few days after their last meeting in early November, Fuller wrote in farewell: "I wish I could hear you speak at the same time with Waldo, for it would be beautiful to me to see my two friends thus brought near to one another upon a common platform." Consistent with this platform-consciousness, as she and her earlier westering friend Clarke had, they also sent each other plaintively commiserating letters about their mutual frustrations over their limited horizons. "I confess to you I am restless, and not energetic enough to make for myself the sphere I crave," Channing wrote to her later that winter from Cincinnati. After getting a similarly confessing but also consoling letter on the same theme from Fuller, Channing answered with his own words of gratitude and encouragement: "I have felt all along that I was the one to be aided in our intercourse. And I feel, too, though you may be slow to credit it, that I have been. For sincerely, I do think you have done more to unfold my buried nature than any friend. . . . You shall write nobler books than ever George Sand could conceive."[24]

The two frustrated writer-reformers also had their differences. The most important intellectual one was their differing views of American culture. Ideologically radical (he had already criticized Emerson in Brownson's *Boston Quarterly Review* for not being sufficiently warm toward "the great social idea of our era"), while personally genteel, Channing felt acutely uncomfortable, he later recalled, with Fuller's "gratuitous . . . hypercriticism" of the "new demi-gods in literature, art and fashion." Who these "demi-gods" were or what her criticisms were he did not say, although one can get an inkling from his later description of an argument they had had one evening at Newport the previous summer about American literature—"she contrasting its boyish crudity, half boastful, half timid, with the tempered, manly equipose of thorough-bred European writers, and I asserting that in its mingled practicality and aspiration might be read bright auguries." One sharp remark of hers that winter, about the much-touted, newly published Boston Brahmin authors William Hickling Prescott and Richard Henry Dana, Jr., finally provoked Channing to a "remonstrance," which in turn brought forth from Fuller this spirited defense of her critical stance:

> If a horror of the mania for *little great men* so prevalent in this country, if aversion to the sentimental exaggerations to which so many are prone, if a feeling that most people praise as well as blame too readily and that overpraise desecrates the lips and makes the breath unworthy to blow the coal of devotion[,] if rejection of the P's and D's from a sense that the priestess must reserve her paeans for Apollo, if untiring effort to form my mind to justice, to keep my judgment calm and revere only the superlatively good that my "praise might *be* praise," if this, C. be to offend, then have I offended.
>
> O my friend we have gone apart far, but sometime thou shalt know me. Meanwhile, do not put the cross above the Sun. Thou thyself didst own it, all the good that I have done is by calling every nature for its highest.
>
> I will admit I want gentleness, but not tenderness, nor noble faith.[25]

In this last move, of course, Fuller shifted the issue from the cultural to the personal. Their correpondence shows that Channing readily accepted the gambit. Indeed, contrary to his claim in the *Memoirs* that after that summer his earlier reservations about Fuller all but vanished, her quotations from his letters accusing her of "over-great impetuosity," "determined exaggeration," "arrogance," and other like "damning" charges over the next several years clearly show they did not. It does seem, however, from the very few of Channing's letters that have survived, that ultimately he did come to fully accept the notion that her "Egoism" was, as she always insisted, neither self-indulgent nor mean, but bespoke (as he put in the *Memoirs*) "a stoical grandeur that commands respect." Certainly *he* respected it; mainly, it would seem, because he recognized that her egoism evinced a capacity to "make all who were in concert with her feel the miracle of existence" that *his* more abstract impetuosity sorely lacked. "My social nature is defective," the ideologically social Channing confessed to her that winter. "Joyfully would I take a few lessons from you in the art of aiding others to find their own souls." But Channing had a couple of his own arguments to bring forward. One was to try to bring her around to the idea—as he would try to do for others of his individualistic Transcendentalist friends—that her personalistic "noble faith" ought to be applied to the reconstruction of society. Their argument over *that* proposal would emerge the following year and go on for many more. Meanwhile, despite Fuller's literary "hypercriticism," Channing clearly knew how to play upon one string of cultural hope of *hers*. In his account of their argument about "boyish" American literature, he wrote that at one point, "betrayed by sympathy, she laid bare her secret hope of what Woman might be and do, as an author, in our Republic. The sketch was an outline only, and dashed off with a few swift strokes, but therein appeared her own portrait, and we were strangers no more."[26]

III

Channing was not the only Transcendentalist that fall of 1839 to press Fuller for lessons in the arts of private socializing. Urgent requests also came from the one Transcendentalist who from the beginning of their acquaintance had always meant the most to Fuller. And the fact that they came from her "dear *no friend*" Emerson—whose skepticism about the "porcupine impossibility of contact with men" had been something of a refrain in his letters to her—spoke volumes about the rising social temperature in Transcendentalist circles at this time. Only the previous fall, in thanking her for a package of some of her friends' correspondence that she had sent him, he had told her: "We are armed all over with these subtle antagonisms which as soon as we meet begin to play, & translate all poetry into stale prose! It seems to me that almost all people *descend* somewhat into society." Of course, physical proximity made socializing easier. In late March, on her way to occupy her new house in Jamaica Plain, Fuller had stopped for a week at the Emersons', a stay that inaugurated a pattern of regular visits of a week or more every few months, which would continue for as long as she lived in or near Boston. Emerson later left a very appreciative recollection of those visits:

> She had so many tasks of her own, that she was a very easy guest to entertain, as she could be left to herself, day after day, without apology. According to our usual habit, we seldom met in the forenoon. After dinner, we read something together, or walked, or rode. In the evening, she came to the library, and many and many a conversation was there held, whose details, if they could be preserved, would justify all encomiums. They interested me in every manner;—talent, memory, wit, stern introspection, poetic play, religion, the finest personal feeling, the aspects of the future, each followed each in full activity, and left me, I remember, enriched and sometimes astonished by the gifts of my guest. Her topics were numerous, but the cardinal points of poetry, love, and religion, were never far off. She was a student of art, and, though untravelled, knew, much better than most persons who had been abroad, the conventional reputation of each of the masters. She was familiar with all the field of elegant criticism in literature. Among the problems of the day, these two attracted her chiefly, Mythology and Demonology; then, also, French Socialism, especially as it concerned woman; the whole prolific family of reforms, and, of course, the genius and career of each remarkable person.[27]

In Fuller's papers of the past couple of years, one can easily find equally appreciative remarks about Emerson. "He is to me even nobler than he was," she had told James Clarke after seeing Emerson during her March intersession the previous year; "wise, steadfast, delicate, one who will neither disappoint my judgement nor wound my taste." Emerson's mask of dignified sangfroid in the face of recent public and private vilification raised his image in her mind ever higher. (In fact, he was inwardly agitated and defiant about the uproar he had caused.) "You know how they have been baying at Mr Emerson," she had written Clarke shortly after Emerson's Divinity School address, "'tis a pity you could not see how calmly he smiles down, on the sleuth-hounds of— public opinion." And, more glowing yet, in her journal after her visit with Emerson that August: "Twenty four hours with my friend, R.W.E.— What pride to be his friend! I felt myself unworthy when I compared my view of his position with his own, so high, so calm." It is true she also added: "Beam alway thus, though bright particular star— I would not have thee nearer. I like to look up,— but my foot is on the earth, and the earth thou dost not know, maugre all thy boasted powers of vision.

Oh thou art blind
With thy deep seeing eyes."

But this dark foreshadowing of things to come was an exception. Virtually everything she wrote about Emerson that year and the next breathed of her deep appreciation of his "serene and elevated nature" and, mingled in her mind with it, his rising public stature as a cultural hero-critic. "Mr Emerson is lecturing well," she wrote later that winter to Hedge, after attending Emerson's first "Present Age" lecture. "His introductory was noble. He makes statements much nearer completeness than ever before; this all the audience feel."[28]

Turning to their friendship as reflected in their correspondence, one finds it to have been up to this point pretty much what snatches of their letters have shown—mutually very interested, appreciative, helpful, entertaining (even, on Fuller's part at least, teasingly so), but still, except for her teaching and writing complaints, more congenial than deeply personal. Much of it, of course, was literary. She sent him packages of her essays, journals, sketches, and other literary "experiments." She continued to lend him her Goethe and other German books. She fired off critical opinions on the latest British books and quarterly articles that caught her eye. From his side, he continued to press on her *his* favorite authors, particularly Plato and Coleridge, but also saltier Renaissance favorites like Bacon and Ben Jonson. He kept her supplied with free tickets to his lectures and, in response to her eager requests, the latest intelligence on the English literary scene from his correspondence with Carlyle and other British writers. Most of all, he continued to feed her encouraging words about her writing. As he had when he had answered her vocational complaints while she was at Providence, he couched much of his literary advice in Transcendentalist terms. In response to her suggestion in the spring that she was thinking about writing an "experiment Chapter" of her life of Goethe, he had written: "On our beginnings seems somehow our self possession to depend a good deal, as happens so often in music. A great undertaking we allow ourselves to magnify, until it daunts & chills us and the child kills its own father. So let us say; self possession is all; our author, our hero, shall follow as he may. I know that not possibly can you write

a bad book a dull page, if you only indulge yourself and take up your work somewhat proudly, if the same friend bestows her thoughts on Goethe who plays now
at the game of conversation & now writes a journal rich gay perceptive & never
dull." Warming to his theme, he had urged even a little literary mayhem. "It
seems too so very high a compliment to pay to any man, to make him our
avowed subject, that the soul inclines to remunerate itself by a double self trust,
by loftier and gayer sallies of joy & adventure, yes & I think by some wicked
twitting & whipping the good hero himself, as often as occasion is, by way of
certifying ourselves that he still keeps his place there & we ours here, and that we
have not abated a jot of our supremacy over all the passengers through nature.
They must all be passengers whosoever and howsoever they be, & *I* the inmate
and landlord, though I were the youngest & least of the race. On these conditions,
no subject is dangerous: all subjects are equivalent."[29]

This was useful (if tough) advice on self-reliance. However apt, this sort of talk
did have a rather hortatory character for a personal letter, and this seems to have
bothered her a little. "S. M. F. writes me," Emerson recorded in his journal later
in the fall, "that she waits for the Lectures seeing well after much intercourse that
the best of me is there." (She was right on one level: he would later cheerfully
mine a number of his letters to her, as he did his journals, for essays.) She may
have also found the burden placed on her a little awesome, as she had coyly
hinted to him in her reply. "I am at present . . . walking through Creation in a
way you would nowise approve. The flowers peep, the Stars wink, the books
gaze, the men and women bow and curtsey to me, but nothing nor nobody
speaks to me, nor do I speak." Still, her letters and journals show she deeply
appreciated Emerson's literary advice and encouragement ("I pray you always
to encourage me whenever you can") and also tried, at least in part, to follow
it.[30]

Her letters that fall *do* show a new assertiveness toward Emerson, but in an
area that was only partly literary. Some of it was inspired by her recent discovery
of French social Romantic literature, which she urged on a skeptical Emerson
even more aggressively than she had Goethe and the German Romantics. "I am
sorry you read the wrong Sands first," she wrote to him on November 24,
"though in André there is a vein of the best in the two others is seen her worst.
Mauprat is at the shop now, it is worth your reading, but not your buying and
they let them out by the week. I shall get for you Les Sept Cordes de la Lyre, if
ever it is in my power." Meanwhile, along with Sand, she tried out on him something more literally social romantic: under the rubric of literary experimenting,
she attempted to draw him into her complex web of intimate friendships. In her
letter to him on the twenty-fourth, on the heels of a "concluding headach of a
three weeks course"—that had begun, not accidentally, immediately after the
denouement of her romantic friendship with Ward—she wrote instructively but
also excitedly:

> I send you the canto in the poem of Caroline which I half promised. I have had many
> doubts about it, but finally I see so much beauty here that I cannot be willing not to
> share it with you, especially as I cannot hope to share it with any other person. I have

given her last letter of the winter that you may better appreciate the flux and reflux of mind. Next to this read the two passages in my journal where I have turned the leaf, they were read by her and to the conversations which sprung from them several passages in her letter refer. To make the whole complete you should see a letter of mine upon the wind; but neither C. or I has that now.

And so on, through Fuller's "Drachenfels" poem, which had influenced Sturgis ("it is to that she refers about the dragon voice!"), her "poetical journal" ("even the translns bear some reference to Anna, W. and myself"), and other assorted papers from her "grove of private life, into which you might step aside to refresh yourself from the broad highway of philosophy." She concluded by telling him how long he could keep the papers, that she had judiciously "taken out some leaves," and that she was not going to tell Caroline she had shown him her papers "till by and by when all is as past to her as to me."[31]

Of course this mingling of writing and friendship in rebound from a romantic disappointment was not new with Fuller. She had tried a version of it with her story "Lost and Won." What was new and surprising was that this time, socially anyway, she succeeded: the man of Olympus was seduced. Just why he was is rather a mystery, especially in view of the very explicit lecture on the "perpetual disappointment" inherent in all social relations that he had delivered to her the previous fall when she had sent him a package of others of her young friends' letters. Actually, as with most important things, Emerson was of two minds about what he called his "churl's mask." In the very journal passage in which, in answer to Fuller's ironic remark about his lectures' containing the best of him, he reminded himself of the rich psychic and intellectual compensations of his "solitude [with] the impersonal God," he also freely conceded "the ludicrousness of the plight." ("Most of the persons whom I see in my own house I see across a gulf.") Nonetheless, however much solitude and engagement were balanced in his consciousness, the weight of preference was clearly with the former. So the question remains: what tipped the balance the other way? Certainly one factor was his increasing fascination with Fuller's little circle of attractive young Transcendentalist fellow travelers. ("So lovely, so fortunate, &," he sighed in his journal after finally meeting Anna Barker at a party at Fuller's on October 4, "so remote from my own experience.") Possibly also tempting him in headier ways was the same thing that had no doubt partly tempted Fuller—their recent reading in George Sand, Bettina von Arnim, and other European Romantic authors whose writings teemed with accounts of romantic friendships among the European literati. But as it was Fuller herself who first introduced all these personal and literary gems to him and constantly kept them polished and gleaming before his eyes, the major credit for his partial conversion to a transcendentalism of the heart must be given to her.[32]

That it was, however, at least in the beginning, only partial is clear from his journals. On October 21, he reported on an overnight visit the night before from Alcott and Fuller (five days after her "farewell" letter to Ward): "Cold as I am, they are almost dear. . . . And then to my private ear a chronicle of sweet romance, of love & nobleness which have inspired the beautiful & brave. What is good to make me happy is not however good to make me write. Life too near paralyses Art. Long these things refuse to be recorded except in the invisible colors of Memory." What is striking is that after this initial Wordsworthian hesitancy ("we wish to be very sure our diamonds are not Brazil Topazes," he had told her on October 1), none of this reticence or ambivalence was reflected in his letters to Fuller. On the contrary, after the crucial meeting of the twentieth, Emerson seemed, if anything, *anxious* to pass what he called "the only formidable test that was applied to Goethe's genius"; one that, he pointedly told her, *that* genius failed. (He was referring to Bettina von Arnim's largely spurious reworking of her correspondence with Goethe, *Goethes Briefwechsel mit einem Kinde,* the recent English translation of which had become a rage in the Transcendentalist circle that summer and fall.) "He is too discreet and cowardly to be great and mainly does not make one adequate confession of the transcendent superiority of this woman's aims and affections in the presence of which all his Art must have struck sail." And so he adopted all of Fuller's extravagantly fanciful nomenclature in referring to Anna Barker ("your Recamier") and her other young friends, even once—in referring to Ward as "The Prince-of-the-Purple-Island"—outdoing *her.* More melodramatically, on November 27 he answered her letter and package of romantic disclosures with this extraordinary bit of gratitude and self-forgetfulness:

My dear friend,
    You are as good—it may be better than ever—to your poor hermit. He will come yet to know the world through your eyes. The pacquet came safe & afforded me a rich hour last eve. on my return from a dubious society. I plunge with eagerness into this pleasant element of affection with its haps & harms. It seems to me swimming in an Iris where I am rudely knocked ever & anon by a ray of fiercer red, or even dazzled into momentary blindness by a casual beam of white light. The weal & wo is all Poetic—I float all the time—nor once grazed our old orb. How fine these letters are! I do not know whether they contented or discontented me most. They make me a little impatient of my honourable prison—my quarantine of temperament wherefrom I deal courteously with all comers, but through cold water,— and while I get a true shrift of their wit, do now think I get never an earnest word from them. I should like once in my life to be pommelled black & blue with sincere words. That is the discontent—But all the while it seems to me that superlatives must be bought by many positives—for one eagle there go ten dollars—and that these raptures of fire & frost which so effectually cleanse pedantry out of conversation & make the speech salt & biting, would cost me the days of wellbeing which are now so cheap to me, yet so valued—I like no deep stakes—I am a coward at gambling—I will bask in the common sun a while longer; especially that this middle measure offers,—good friends who will recite their adventures in this field of fate. I will at least pay the price of frankness & you shall command such narratives in turn as a life so seqestered by temperament affords.[33]

In brief, what he was asking was nothing less than to be emotionally "pommelled black and blue," but miraculously with no scars, and all in the service of making his speech and writing "salt and biting." This was a tall order, which it would have taken a genius of a taller or at least very different sort from Emerson's to keep from breaking down into its mutually repellent parts. That Emerson at this time, despite his professed cowardice at social gambling, was willing to risk such a breakdown and its attendant "haps and harms" is absolutely clear from his correspondence with Fuller that winter. On December 12, he wrote to her from Concord, so differently from his admonition about diamonds and topazes on October 1:

> Forget, I pray you, the conversation at Mr Adams's [the Boston house of his old friend and financial advisor Abel Adams], for I do not wish to dissect a real rose or a friend. I am wise & whole this morning, and think sympathy better than criticism & will entertain a new relation at least as highly & poetically as it is offered. So forget what I said, for some words offended my own ear whilst I spoke them & became treasonous presently when you told me more of W. I have higher surer methods in my mind now—I will leave meddling and trust to great Magic. It may be of little import what becomes of our personal webs, but we will be equal to an Idea so divine as Friendship.

Two weeks later, on December 23—or the day after he wrote his sentimental letter to his Aunt Mary about Anna Barker as "the very heroine of your dreamed romance"—he wrote to her again:

> I have read through a second time today the entire contents of the brown paper parcel and startled my mother & my wife when I went into the dining room with the declaration that I wished to live a little while with people who love & hate, who have Muses & Furies, and in a twelvemonth I should write tragedies & romance. I heartily thank you for the pacquet, which is fragrant with fine affection & sentiment. You are brave, and in your relation to your friends shall be always honoured and long hereafter thanked.[34]

"Always honoured and long hereafter thanked"—it must have sounded to Fuller a little like a memorial tribute, hardly what she could have hoped her encouragement of Emerson's social recklessness in relation to her might have brought forth. What she hoped for, she kept hidden in the privacy of her journal. After hearing Emerson's "Present Age" lecture on religion at the Masonic Temple the following month, she wrote—at almost the very moment Emerson was thanking in *his* journal "the great God [who] gave to me" this circle of friends ("my relation to them is so pure that we hold by simple affinity; & the Genius of my life being thus social the same affinity will exert its energy on whosoever is as noble as these men & women, wherever I may be")—this harsh portrayal of Emerson as a friend:

> Mr E. scarce knows the instincts. And uses them rather for rejection than reception where he uses them at all.
> In friendship with RWE, I cannot hope to feel that I am his or he mine. He has nothing peculiar, nothing sacred for his friend. He is not to his friend a climate, an atmosphere, neither is his friend a being organized especially for him, born for his star. He speaks of a deed, of a thought to any commoner as much as to his peer. His creed is, Show thyself, let them take as much as they can. Thus are lost all the sweet gradations of affinity, the pleasures of tact.— A noble trust, a faith in the corre-

spondencies of nature is the basis of this conduct but it is not regulated by demoniacal tact! (What an expression this.) His friendship is only strong inference and he weighs and balances, buys and sells you and himself all the time. I love to keep the flower shut till my breeze and then open its blushful bloom to the friend alone. He too would wait, but in a different way. He would wait till esteem was challenged. I till the chain of affinity vibrated.[35]

This was a trenchant Romantic critique. Certainly it was Romantic in appealing to "gradations of affinity," "sacred" intimacy, and, above all, the idea of the "demoniacal" or instinctual that preoccupied Goethe and many German Romantics, and that Emerson, largely through her, was also intrigued with at this time. Her critique was also insightful in exposing the very non-Romantic, severely Platonic stoicism that *was* the dominant thrust of much of Emerson's character and social thought. In this instance, this highly self-conscious thinker deceived himself about the "simple affinity" by which he held his friends. But Fuller's blast was not just a philosophical critique; it was also a personal revelation of love, and on that score, in the conclusion of her entry, she blamed herself as much as Emerson.

Why cannot I enter in sincerest depths with this friend whom I so esteem, love and among the living whom I personally know alone revere. I know not. I am doomed to play with the hour when my soul is most penetrated. Tonight 22d Jany when I was so proud of his austere simplicity and boundless truth, when I turned from little and compromising men to repose in his calm self reliance as on the heart of the Eternal the moment I met him face to face I could not choose but jest. It is strange in me, surely no mortal is more sincere or of a more presumptuous fearlessness, but I cannot endure being seen at my devotions. I have always said I like to pray in an oratory. O for the full utterancy of the heart of love. It should not weary— I would make it so eloquent, if I dared but speak at all!

She did not mention one additional caveat—that her perhaps unintended pun on "oratory," which she had once obscurely used in a letter to Emerson two years before in Providence to describe what he meant to her, bespoke a fundamental confusion about what in fact she did want from this Platonic orator. But what she did not speak, she dreamt. The following May, after returning from a visit to Providence a month after the end of a series of lectures that Emerson had given in the city, she gave Caroline Sturgis a report of what she had heard of Emerson's triumph, along with her own possessive reaction to some of the gossip. ("I amused myself with destroying two or three gnats which were trying to make themselves of consequence by buzzing about the lion, but I can't say I performed the office Sybilline thus put upon me in a very pious spirit.") Still, after saying that "all this idle talk" at least led her later to have a "divine dream" about Emerson, she then described it:

I thought I was with him on the rocks near a castellated place on the sea shore. I was dying and had that transparent spiritual feeling that I do after I have been in great pain, as if separated from the body and yet with memory enough of its angelic mood. We talked on every subject, and instead of that perpetual wall which is always grieving me now, the talk led on and on like [the manuscript breaks off at this point].[36]

None of these dreams of love and death (which she so often associated with love's absence) was communicated to Emerson. The closest she came that winter and spring was her reply on December 26, in answer to his provocative letter three days before:

> If you could look into my mind just now, you would send far from you those who love and hate. I am on the Drachenfels, and cannot get off; it is one of my naughtiest moods. Last Sunday, I wrote a long letter, describing it in prose and verse, and I had twenty minds to send it you as a literary curiosity; then I thought, this might destroy relations, and I might not be able to be calm and chip marble with you any more, if I talked to you in magnetism and music; so I sealed and sent it in the due direction.[37]

What she was saying, then, considering her feelings, was simple and rather sensible: in order to keep his friendship, she would decline to become for him one of his supposedly coveted "people who love and hate." But there was also an implicit subtext: if he continued to press her—and even, possibly, if he did not—he might very well get what he asked for. This was the sort of ambiguity that neither friendships nor the coteries that nourished them could stand for very long without some sort of crisis, either self-destructive or creative. It remained to be seen which Fuller would choose to provoke.

IV

"Were we near I should have a vast deal to tell you," she wrote to Henry Hedge a few days after writing her tantalizingly cautionary note to Emerson, "but my life is rather a subject for a metaphysical romance than a gazette." It was not just wariness, however, that probably caused her to pause in her "search after Eros." She was ill and under a doctor's care for almost the entire winter of 1839–1840, making her feel (she told Charles Newcomb) "restless and languid" and, as she did not say, in a less than socially heroic mood. She was also very busy. She had had with her since November Charles's younger sister Charlotte, along with her former Louisville charges, Emma Keats and Ellen Clark. Emma especially, she happily reported to Clarke, was "much more reasonable in social relations" and "in earnest about her own mind." ("I can do for her now as much as is ever worth while for one person to do for another.") Her mother boarded the girls, for which Margaret paid her, while she instructed them. She told Hedge she did not like the "domestic care" involved in having "three young ladies . . . to be carved into roses 'with flowers and foliage overwrought.'" But she assured Clarke that she and Emma were "good friends." In fact, she would wear and use for many years the seal ring with an engraving of a lamb and the inscription "feed my lambs" that Emma had given her the year before.[38]

Most of her time, of course, was taken by her Wednesday morning Conversations. After Emerson's "Present Age" lectures ended on February 12, she took the evenings to give for a couple of months, at the house of William Channing's mother, Susan Higginson Channing, a series of weekly classes for a small circle of women drawn from the larger body, on Goethe's writings on aesthetics and the fine arts. Her notes show she treated not only Goethe's ideas, but also, at least in a fragmentary way, German Romantic theories of representation, as well as the general problem of critical standards. Her tone seems to have been, as usual in her classes, both serious and light. ("Read also some descriptions of pictures, and was led to give an account of Makaria and her connexion with the solar system!") She "took pleasure" in all her classes, she told Almira Barlow, but she also worried, as she told Hedge, that they "break . . . up my time a good deal." To Charles Newcomb she was more downcast: she was deathly tired of being "always ill, always interrupted" and having, despite all her intellectual activity, "little outward token." The "outward token" she meant, of course, was her writing. In fact, she was writing that winter more than she ever had in her life. This time, however, she was doing it—and undoubtedly, hence, her anxiety on the subject—for a new journal that she and many of her Transcendentalist colleagues hoped would change the course of American literature.[39]

It had been nearly five years since Hedge and Ripley had abandoned their idea of publishing a "journal of spiritual philosophy." If anything, the idea was now more timely than ever. Despite the explosion of magazine publishing during the past two decades—not to mention the continued public cries for a great, new, independent American literature—even non-Transcendentalist literary intellectuals were finding the American periodical scene depressingly frustrating. "It is intolerable," the struggling short-story author Nathaniel Hawthorne wrote at the beginning of the year to his rising Brahmin poet friend Henry Wadsworth Longfellow, who was considering starting a literary journal, "that there should not be a single belles-lettres journal in New-England." For Transcendentalists, who looked for belles-lettres and a good deal more, the picture naturally was much worse. The nation's premier highbrow literary-intellectual journal, Boston's *North American Review,* remained pretty much what it had been since its inception—up-to-date and judicious, but to Fuller and her friends, also ponderous and prolix, a pale imitation, as they saw it, of the British reviews on which it was modeled. ("When I read the North American Review," Emerson wrote in his journal, "I seem to hear the snore of the muses.") In fact, under the editorship of the cautious, anti-Transcendentalist Divinity School dean, John Gorham Palfrey, the *North American* had abandoned, not only much of its former friendliness to European Romantic currents, but also much of its literary critical acumen as well. At the other extreme, the periodicals that benefited the most from the recent explosion of magazine publishing activity—the fast-proliferating women's magazines—published mostly banal and sentimentally didactic stories and essays. During the past decade, a number of higher quality, general-interest monthly magazines had begun to appear, that, unlike the quarterly reviews, devoted a good deal of space to original belles-lettres. But except for one or two short-lived and now defunct experiments, like the Buckinghams' *New-England Magazine* and its successor, Park Benjamin's *American Monthly Magazine,* that Fuller had contributed to, these monthlies were published in Philadelphia and New York and relied on writers, like Hawthorne and Longfellow, with already established reputations. Furthermore, they were mostly either, like the New York *Knickerbocker,* hostile to outré intellectual tendencies like Transcendentalism, or, like the Philadelphia *Graham's,* uninterested in serious philosophy or criticism. The single exception, the recently founded *United States Magazine and Democratic Review,* which successfully mixed original stories, criticism, and democratic political writing, was regarded by most Transcendentalists as hopelessly tainted by its status as a Democratic party organ. Indeed, in this instance Bronson Alcott could have been speaking for the group as a whole when, earlier in May, at a Transcendental Club discussion of the state of American periodicals, he pronounced them all—with the single exception of William Lloyd Garrison's radical abolitionist *Liberator*—"destitute of life, freshness, independence."[40]

Meanwhile, some Transcendentalists, while they were collectively venting their unhappiness over the absence of a satisfactory intellectual magazine, were also privately beginning to revive talk about bringing out one of their own. One obvious goad was the resignation that spring of the *Christian Examiner*'s half-sympathetic, tolerant coeditor James Walker, thus ensuring, in the atmosphere of Unitarian reaction after Emerson's Divinity School address, the closing to the Transcendentalist ministers of what had been their primary organ. Another incentive undoubtedly was the Transcendentalists' perception (in Sarah Clarke's words) that "hundreds of girls and boys who are dissatisfied with the existing state of things in the planet" were clamoring for an organ to which they could look for guidance. Yet a third catalyst was the appearance that year of a transatlantic prototype—the English *Monthly Magazine,* edited by the energetic, Gothic-Romantic poet and magazine writer John A. Heraud. The magazine of this "loquacious scribacious little man" (as Carlyle called him in a letter to Emerson) freely mixed popularizations of post-Kantian philosophy, esoteric mystical commentary, literary effusions, and idealistic calls for child-centered education and communitarian socialism. Alcott, who for the past couple of years had been receiving fan mail from several of its education-reform contributors praising him as their inspiration, was, not surprisingly, most taken with the journal. ("Many of the articles seem on reading like passages from my own thought.") But even more sober-minded Transcendentalists like Ripley, who were unconnected with (as Alcott called them) "our English brethren," told Alcott they wished they could bring out "a journal of like character among ourselves."[41]

Their first movement in bringing this prolonged wishing to fruition came when the Transcendental Club met at the Boston minister Cyrus Bartol's house on September 18 and discussed for the first time "the subject of a Journal designed as the organ of views more in accordance with the Soul." Alcott, Hedge, and Fuller, members' journals show, all heartily endorsed the idea, and Emerson, who did not attend the meeting, afterwards strongly seconded the plan. No definite action was taken at the meeting, but by the spring the group would agree on one important issue—to accept Alcott's proposal to call the new journal *The Dial.* He had given the name to a collection of his "Scriptures" or thoughts that he had culled from his diary and his manuscript "Psyche," because it was an apt symbol, he thought, of the soul's "circuits through nature and man." The sundial marked "the motions of thy sun," he would explain later, a little more rigorously, in the *Dial,* just as the natural soul followed and thereby embodied the progress of the spirit. This heavily Neoplatonic symbolism was probably accepted—or understood—only by a few, but the vaguer, Romantic associations of light, nature, and progress made it a popular choice in Transcendentalist circles. "I think it excellent," James Clarke would write Fuller later that spring from Louisville, "significant of those who believe in the progress of time and who watch it, not in the bustle of a city, but amid the flowers and leafiness of a garden walk."[42]

Finding a name was fairly easy. Other decisions required more finesse. One concerned jurisdictional relations with the other recently established, ostensibly Transcendentalist, journals. In the case of James Freeman Clarke's *Western Messenger,* there was no real problem. Although it attracted as contributors many of the leading eastern Massachusetts Transcendentalists, and had recently become a strong, if moderate, defender of embattled Transcendentalism as well as other controversial Eastern reform movements, the *Messenger*'s orientation was still in the main more broadly Unitarian and literarily middlebrow than philosophically Transcendentalist or aesthetically experimental. "I do not undervalue your pet, but its whole character is popular," Fuller had told Clarke earlier in the year in explaining her reluctance to publish her verses in the *Messenger.* "I would use for it such a poet as Milne rather than Tennyson and Bryant rather than R.W.E." In any case, even apart from their friendly, if lukewarm, feelings about it, the *Messenger* was obviously too far from the center of Transcendentalist ferment for the future *Dial*ers to regard it as anything other than secondary to their own more cosmopolitan venture.[43]

Orestes Brownson's *Boston Quarterly Review* presented more difficulties. Brownson had established himself as a prolific and highly visible champion of Transcendentalist philosophy; he had founded his review, in part, in order to attack freely the movement's conservative Unitarian opponents; he published it in the heart of the movement's storm center; and he covered in its pages a wide range of philosophical, religious, and literary issues. When he learned of the proposed new Transcendentalist magazine, he made its sponsors a generous offer—that they abandon their plan and write instead for his magazine, and he would promise to publish their contributions even if he disagreed with them, as long as they were signed. But the Transcendentalism that Brownson preached in his journal was very distinctive. It was oriented toward a radicalized Democratic party in politics, an idealistic Christianity in social ethics, and a "scientific" or "Absolute" Transcendentalism in philosophy. A still greater difficulty was Brownson himself. Polemical, something of a loner (he had stopped going to Transcendental Club meetings after the first year), and openly hostile to the personalism, pantheism, and cultural elitism he found in Emerson and Alcott, he looked to them like something less than an ideally tolerant colleague. ("Brownson never will stop & listen," Emerson wrote in his journal; "neither in conversation but what is more, not in solitude.") Not surprisingly, then, when Brownson called on Alcott on October 19 to offer his proposal, Alcott wrote afterward in his journal: "No good could come from such seeming union; it would provoke opposition rather." So, the next morning he rode with Fuller to Concord to convince his two colleagues of the necessity of having "an organ of our own, wherein we can have entire freedom: in which the purest thoughts and tastes may be represented." Emerson and Fuller readily agreed. (They had seen one of Fuller's "Boston Bookstore" dialogues defaced with slightly absurd footnote attacks on the antiprogressivist cultural opinions of her fictional Professor Partridge.) The *Dial* had survived its first friendly take-over bid.[44]

The more difficult question, however, remained: if not Brownson as editor, then who? Alcott had been the earliest and most persistent advocate of publishing "a free Journal for the soul." In addition—trying to snatch victory from defeat—ever since the collapse of his educational career, Alcott had been more anxious than anyone in the group to establish himself as a cultural reformer. But he does not seem to have been considered. Probably he was ruled out by his friend Emerson, who had been struggling with Alcott's "monotone" prose for years, by his inattention to "literary duty" (as Alcott put it). The natural choice, for reasons of public recognition alone, thought Parker (and no doubt others), was Emerson. But although he wholeheartedly supported the idea of a journal for all the "fine" young people he saw coming around the circle "who would write a few numbers of such book, who write nowhere else," Emerson still absolutely refused to be editor. Possibly his skepticism about whether the journal would ever "reach the day" may have been a factor. He expressed this doubt to his brother William, but to Fuller and his colleagues he emphasized his prior commitments to his upcoming "Present Age" lecture series and his first book of essays. Others ruled themselves out for similar reasons. Hedge, who Parker had thought might serve with Fuller as a coeditor under Emerson, was obviously too far from Boston to be of much help. As an alternative, Emerson suggested Ripley, who had been an active proponent of the project. But Ripley, who was still in charge of the *Specimens of Foreign Literature* series and was just then engrossed in seeing through the press the first of his pamphlet replies to Andrews Norton, also declined. So they were at an impasse. "I believe we all feel much alike in regard to this Journal," Emerson wrote Fuller; "we all wish it to be, but do not wish to be in any way personally responsible for it." All, that is, but the newest and youngest of the Club's inner circle. In fact, after Emerson, Fuller seems to have been almost everyone's second choice. Even the unfriendly Parker wrote in his journal the day after the Club meeting, "Emerson Miss Fuller & Hedge alone are competent to the work." Emerson himself was more blunt: it had to be either Ripley or herself, he told her in a letter four days before their October 20 meeting, or there would not be a journal.[45]

In many ways Fuller was the ideal choice for the post. Among her colleagues she was the most well read in foreign Romantic literature and belles-lettres. More important, she was also the most intellectually engaged and sophisticated about problems of literary form. It is true she was comparatively deficient in theology and philosophy, but even this had at least the advantage of making it unlikely she would impose a narrow philosophical standard on the journal (a big worry of Alcott's with Brownson). Furthermore, she had two qualities indispensable for an editor of a new intellectual journal. One was her widely acknowledged talent as a conversationalist and social mediator. The other was her superior experience and shrewdness in publishing in magazines beyond the usual Unitarian fold. (On September 24, she wrote to Peabody, who had published in the newly minted *Democratic Review* and had suggested that Fuller try it: "Are they good pay [for I have heard the contrary]—? Will they pay me *unasked?* or torture all my lady like feelings as almost all other persons have with whom I have been concerned.") Finally, she had one additional important credential: she obviously wanted the job. The day after she wrote Peabody—and only a week after the Club met on the eighteenth—she wrote in her journal: "It is now proposed that I should conduct a magazine which would afford me space and occasion for every thing I may wish to do." She did worry, if only momentarily, about the undertaking's "tax" on her "health and spirits." But between a tax and all she wished to do, the decision could not have been very difficult. During her visit on October 20, she agreed to accept the editorship.[46]

So, although "with sleepy eye & flagging spirits," Emerson recorded in his journal the next morning after Fuller and Alcott left, the "good tidings" of the "new literary plans," which he cheerfully, if a little skeptically, announced to the vacationing Elizabeth Hoar two weeks later: "Margaret Fuller is to edit the long predicted Journal—if we die not before the sight—George Ripley having promised to undertake all the business part of it for her. She even meditates a number as soon as April, though she prefers to wait until Autumn, which looks like a century in such affairs." Alcott, on the other hand—who, as usual, had no such temporal worries—was ecstatic. "She has," he wrote in his journal the day after the meeting, "a deeper insight into character than any of her contemporaries, and will enrich our literature."[47]

<h1 style="text-align:center">V</h1>

For the moment Emerson's skepticism was a more accurate guide to Transcendentalist realities than Alcott's enthusiasm. "Immersed in preparations" (she told Clarke) for her upcoming Conversations, Fuller waited over two months before taking the first steps to put together the first issue. Meanwhile—and more ominously—she began to express in her journal as well as to friends grave doubts about herself as a writer. This was not new, of course. She had done this before when she had first tried her hand at writing at Groton. Nor had her comments since that time been exactly self-congratulatory, especially about her imaginative writing. "I am ashamed when I think there is scarce a line of *poetry* in them," she had written to Caroline Sturgis only the previous February in a letter giving Sturgis permission to read her poems. "All 'rhetorical and impassioned' as Goethe said of Me de Stael." But now the public warning buzzer had sounded, and the anguish and self-contempt she poured out in her letters and journals seem, if anything, even more palpable than they had been at Groton. "When I look at my papers," she confessed bleakly to Emerson, "I feel as if I had never had a thought that was worthy the attention of any but myself." And in her journal, this time not about her ideas ("I have all the great thoughts," she boasted sardonically), but about her process: "How can I ever write with this impatience of detail. The first suggestion of a thought delights— to follow it out wearies and weakens me. And now today reading Shelley's Defense of Poetry do I not see how he loved to write!" Indeed, so frustrated were her thoughts about her literary incapacity that winter and early spring, that in one anguished entry, she described it—as she sometimes had in the past her other psychic frustrations— as something almost physical:

> Often, too often do I wish to die. My spirit sinks and my whole heart grieves: My day is poor of thought and deed, my body is a burden not an instrument. I have few thoughts, too much feeling, O that I should live to write this. I feel within myself an immense power, but I cannot bring it out. I stand a barren vine stock from which no grape will swell though the richest vine is slumbering in its root.[48]

The feminine bodily images in this passage might suggest that one source of her sense of "barrenness" was her unconscious fear of, or protest against, her core gender identity. This is plausible, but also, without more of her conscious associations with her imagery, highly speculative. A more fruitful or, at any rate, better supported, line of inquiry would be to ask, what did *she* think was the cause of her "barrenness?" From her journals and letters in these months, it is clear she thought the main cause was her audience. Sometimes she could sound, as in a letter to a friend, almost defiant about it. "What a vulgarity there seems in this writing for the multitude! We know not yet, have not made ourselves known to a single soul, and shall we address those still more unknown? Shall we multiply our connections, and thus make them still more superficial?" And in a letter to Elizabeth Hoar, explaining why she could not reveal to her "thought[s] I might have told you," she announced, "I could not bear to be eloquent and poetical. It seems all mockery thus to play the artist with life, and dip the brush in one's own heart's blood. One would fain be no more an artist, or a philosopher, or a lover, or a critic, but a soul ever rushing forth in tides of genial life, or retiring evermore into precious crystals, too pure to be lonely." Most of her remarks in these months about what she called the problem of "the hearer," though, were less Romantically "squeamish" (as James Clarke called her reluctance to publish in his *Western Messenger*) than self-deprecating: she knew the fundamental problem lay, not just in writing for an audience, but with herself— in particular with her inability to *imagine* a sympathetic or congenial audience. "I am musical," she confessed in her journal, echoing the worry she had expressed six years before about her talents at conversation. "I need the sympathetic eye, the presence of other beings to call out the tide of mine. Yet how long has this influence been inadequate. Now much do I need to work for an ideal presence, if I could be stimulated to aught worthy of me." She added, with a sigh: "I admit it, leider, I seem to be only a poor improvisatrice. And the minstrel days are passed—one must be a band or nothing."[49]

Of course this paralyzing uncertainty about an audience—and, by extension, a self-sustaining public identity—was a common ailment of many of her Transcendentalist friends. Partly it stemmed from the inevitable difficulty they had, like other Romantic writers, in fulfilling Romanticism's heroic demand—to express simultaneously the profoundest truths of the self and the largest instincts of mankind. "Genius seems to me excusable in taking the public for a confidant," she had told Clarke the previous winter, justifying on classic high Romantic grounds her refusal to print her merely "personal" verses in his *Messenger*. "Genius is universal and can appeal to the common heart of man." Romantic theory further insisted that one accomplish this feat by oneself, and also pronounced that one either did this or was a failure. As Fuller put it, aptly summing up both sides of the formula, "one must be a band or nothing." It is easy to see how high Romanticism produced a fair amount of high anxiety in its literary adherents.[50]

The Transcendentalists' nervousness also stemmed from the peculiar conditions of their American cultural inheritance. They were largely bereft of the established ministerial or Revolutionary subcultures of their eighteenth-century forefathers; at the same time, they were brought up to feel keenly the responsibility to create an American culture to match their splendid inherited American polity. Not surprisingly, many Transcendentalists, like other American Romantics, often betrayed, behind their Adamic bravado, a good deal of literary nervousness. Fuller, whose doubly challenging American republican and European Romantic inheritances were both deeply rooted, felt this nervousness with unusual depth and pathos. Nor did she feel she could get much consolation from the Emersonian Romantic maneuver of evading the problem of cultural connection by expanding the self to include the culture. Emerson's "theory at least that there is no need of adaptation and gradation," she told Clarke in her letter, "is entirely opposed to mine." The cultural cul-de-sac this left her in, she described movingly in a letter later in the spring soliciting writings for the *Dial* from her equally anxious and aspiring soul mate William Channing:

> I have myself a great deal written but as I read it over scarce a word seems pertinent to the place or time. When I meet people I can adapt myself to them, but when I write, it is into another world, not a better one perhaps, but one with very dissimilar habits of thought up to this where I am domesticated. How much those of us who have been much formed by the European mind have to unlearn and lay aside, if we would act here. I would fain do something worthily that belonged to the country where I was born, but most times I fear it may not be. . . .
>
> My dear friend, you speak of your sense of "unemployed force."— I feel the same. I never, never in life have had the happy feeling of really doing any thing. I can only console myself for these semblances of actions by seeing that others seem to be in some degree aided by them. But Oh! really to feel the glow of action, without its weariness, what heaven it must be! I cannot think, can you, that all men in all ages have suffered thus from an unattained Ideal. The race must have been worn out ere now by such corrosion.[51]

Here she expressed her solidarity with her generation of cultural pioneers. But there was one important difference between Fuller and most of her literary colleagues that made her feel especially domesticated in an alien sphere: she was not entirely like "all men" because she was a woman. Nor was this for Fuller an abstract social issue. It was a thoroughly psychic and even literary question: as a woman she felt, on some level, alien to *all* public roles and therefore all traditional public literary forms. As she explained in her letter to a friend later in the spring:

> For all the tides of life that flow within me, I am dumb and ineffectual, when it comes to casting my thought into a form. No old one suits me. If I could invent one, it seems to me the pleasure of creation would make it possible for me to write. What shall I do, dear friend? I want force to be either a genius or a character. One should be either private or public. I love best to be a woman; but womanhood is at present too straitly-bounded to give me scope. At hours, I live truly as a woman; at others, I should stifle; as, on the other hand, I should palsy, when I would play the artist.

In sum, then, if Fuller felt anxious over the American Romantic writers' project (in Harold Bloom's phrase) "to 'complete' their fathers," her anxiety—and therefore her "palsy"—was doubled by the ambivalence she felt over whether or not, as a woman, she could "play" the role of a public artist of any sort. Indeed, given her "straitly-bounded" sense of her womanhood, it is hardly surprising that when she tried hardest to play the artist, she felt, not only that she was "dumb and ineffectual," but that—in the gendered physical associations of her journal entry—her very body itself seemed "a burden, not an instrument."[52]

Over and above her ambivalences, her desire "to feel the glow of action" finally determined, if not how she felt, at least what she did. That fall and winter she culled her unpublished papers for possible articles. She wrote drafts of several of her early *Dial* sketches and critical essays. She also drew up a list of topics for future pieces. These ranged from essays on William Ellery Channing's place in American history, Alexis de Tocqueville on democracy, and Rousseau in America ("I would fain do my very best here"), to "Essays on the advantages of sickness" and a series of "character short stories" based on accounts of love affairs told to her by her friends. Although almost absurdly eclectic as well as mostly never to be realized ("The poem is written, all but the verses," she joked), if nothing else her plans at least show her grappling with ways to connect the private and public and the American and European sides of her divided literary consciousness. Meanwhile, she played with ideas of possible experimental literary forms she thought might fit her "improvisatrice" sensibility. "There is something very propitious to good writing in the form of dialogue. The regular build of an Essay (maugre the unpretending name) is dangerous. It tempts to round the piece into a whole by filling up the gaps between the thoughts with—words—words—words."[53]

By the spring, the process of writing and receiving criticism seems to have at least partly quieted her more extreme self-doubts. "I accept all these persons say of my writing with certain limitations," she wrote sensibly in her journal in early April. "The advice or opinions of friends are only useful to one who has steadfastness enough to use them in his own way. They may modify but must never alter the line of action to which nature impels you." This was good Emersonian advice; if not in the prophetic, certainly at least in the pragmatic vein. And, her secret doubts about Emerson as a friend notwithstanding, as she practiced her writing, it was clearly Emerson she listened to. On April 15, he sent her a letter with some criticisms but also with strong praise of their "serene . . . tone" and readability. "I am charmed with Mr E's letter recd yesterday," she wrote two days later in her journal. "I think he avoids falsehood and flattery with more sweetness and at the same time with as much clearness and decision as any one I have ever known or known of. — O might I be as modest and as pious without obliterating any feature of my character of which presumptuous self trust is at present so leading a feature." Emerson himself could not have asked for a more ambiguously self-reliant reaction than this![54]

Emerson's response, along with others she got, was also useful for another reason: it inspired her to write out later that day her most considered judgment of the literary prospects she thought her editorship opened for her. Grumbling and still nervous, she began: "Every body finds fault with me just now, some in one way, some in another — With regard to this new journal not only shall I be exposed to make enemies on every side, but be stripped for a time of the reputation I have enjoyed for talents and knowledge. We are in a sad position Raphael & I as others, poor authors whose works have been talked of too much while yet in the port-folio; the public when it has a fair oppory to judge them is disappointed just in proportion to the vivacity of its prestige. It had nursed its fancy with promises of what these works should be and is very angry that they do not realize its hopes." She then zeroed in on her greatest worry—that the gap between her conversational talents and her writing abilities would make her seem, not just disappointing, but somehow fraudulent. Again, as in her winter meditations on her public-private ambivalences, she connected this problem of form to her position as a woman. This time, though, rather than seeing her problem as insoluble, she asserted, however tremulously, a cautious hope for future achievement:

> Then a woman of tact and brilliancy like me has an undue advantage in conversation with men. They are astonished at our instincts. They do not see where we got our knowledge and while they tramp on in their clumsy way we wheel and fly and dare hither and thither and seize with ready eye all the weak points (like Saladin in the desert). It is quite another thing when we come to write, and without suggestion from another mind to declare the positive amount of thought that is in us. Because we seemed to know all they think we can tell all — and finding we can tell so little lose faith in their first opinion of us *which natheless was true.*
>
> Then these gentlemen are surprized that I write no better because I talk so well. But I have served a long apprenticeship to the one, none to the other. I will write well yet, but never I think so well as I talk for then I feel inspired and the means are pleasant; my voice excites me, my pen never.
>
> I shall by no means be discouraged, nor take what they say for gospel, but try to sift from it all the truth & use it. I feel within myself the strength to dispense with all illusions and I will manifest it. I will stand ready and rejoice in the severest probations![55]

VI

While preparing herself for the coming probationary battles, Fuller also had the no-less-formidable task of preparing her young and equally unseasoned troops for the job of introducing (as Emerson put it to her) the "new Age" in American literature. This was no easy assignment for her. Her few remarks on American writing in her published writings had been almost unrelievedly disdainful. Even more awkward for a cultural organizer, her current views of American literary prospects were also dim. That very winter she wrote up notes for a lengthy, somber essay on America's cultural prospects. The paper never appeared in print, but in her notes for it she argued that the "superficiality," "sentimentality," and "hack verbiage from which books and articles without end" were manufactured showed, rather than the dawn of a new literary age, "many signs of the late days of a lower Empire." More moderate statements of her literary pessimism had already not only earned her reproofs from her social reform-minded colleagues like Brownson and Channing, but had also put her at odds even with more culturally radical, but no less modernist, Transcendentalists like Emerson. Yet she, too, as Channing recalled (and as her journals confirm) had by this time come to nourish her own American literary fantasy. If this was not the phantasm of America's "boyish" literature her young colleagues hoped for (in Channing's recollected disparaging phrase of hers about American literature), then at least it was vaguely connected to "what Woman might be and do, as an author, in our Republic."[56]

Through what means did Fuller think either "the Woman" or the "boy" could become American authors? The answer she soon came to was: through the same form that both were necessarily forced to adopt—"private" writings. Indeed, if there was one magnetic element in Transcendentalism that drew Fuller to the movement, beyond its oft-touted compensatory idea of an autonomous "inward life," it was the notion preached to her by Emerson, in letters and on the platform, that the private writings of "common," "low," "lonely and obscure," aspiring souls, could be, like conversations, as valuable as, or—because of their naturalness and sincerity—even superior to, the artificial and pretentious achievements of the "public" culture. She did not come to this idea easily, however. In one entry that winter she wrote out a lengthy and balanced debate with herself over the propriety (the year before she had told Clarke the practice would make her feel "profaned") of "this writing private thoughts for printing." But finally she came to accept the idea, and not, perhaps, surprisingly. What better solution could there be, after all, both to her own problem of literary womanhood and to the difficult task of creating, if not an American literature, at least a major literary journal out of the writings of mostly unknown young men and women? Indeed, in one discussion of the issue in her journal that winter, she posed the question in almost combative terms. Her target was the rising star of George Ticknor's successor as Smith Professor of French and Spanish at Harvard—Henry Wadsworth Longfellow, whose technically deft but decorously sentimental poetry would soon make him the most popular American poet of the nineteenth century. That December he had published his first, much-praised collection of poetry, *Voices of the Night,* which she mercilessly seized upon as a foil for her avant-garde project:

> I suppose Mr Longfellow would think me assuming, as he seems to me, for neither can much cultured I vindicate my right to speak and not repeat. But this reflection will not prevent my lip from curling at this air of superiority in one who disturbs the public with performances as worthless. Reading to day a few lines of his I thought with perfect refreshment of such lives as C[aroline]'s & E[llen] S[turgis] and W[ard]'s so private and so true, where each line written is really the record of a thought or a feeling. Even lines manquées like D[ana]'s are better, for if no fruit ripened, at least there was a real blossom born of the tree and not one of taffeta gummed on for counterfeit.

She concluded with one last sustained blast at the works of her journal's antitype:

> Longfellow's poems—
>   a melancholy monument of the evils of culture for the sake of being cultivated, not of growing. Imageless imagery as where the "lids of Fancy's sleepless eyes" are made "the gates to Paradise"— book words, that convey nothing to the fancy of the Amer[ica]n reader.— Parade of trans[lation]s from various languages, well enough to do as an exercise, but collected in a book, chaff that mocks at hunger![57]

Tearing down new idols was one thing, of course; finding gods to put in their place, quite another. By the first of the year she was beginning to take stock. Besides Emerson, who promised to write for every issue for a year, she expected Ripley to contribute regularly. She also looked hopefully to the younger members of the Transcendentalist circle; particularly Dwight, but also Parker. ("He cannot be the leader of my journal in the Heavy stern line, but his learning and just way of thinking will make him a very valuable aid.") For poetry she looked to Ellen Hooper, Sam Ward, and especially her Promethean protégée Caroline Sturgis. (In Sturgis's poems, she wrote grandly in her journal, "I see a higher faith, a higher inspiration, than has breathed from lives for a long time back. They mourn not over the blight of external disaster, the rebuff of the world, or the crash of affections; but for nobleness unachieved, high faculties left inert, & the circle of beauty broken, which we feel we ought to reunite. Such thoughts seem to announce a flux of waters which may one day pile up Miltonic peaks on the shore.") Finally, on New Year's Day, as Ripley (she said) "was too busy fighting the battles of Spinoza and other infidels," she dashed off urgent pleas for aid from her clerical friends in the hinterlands, Clarke, Channing, and Hedge. From each she tried to collect on a past dream. To Clarke she wrote a buoyant letter reminding him of his "old prophecy . . . about 'the joint forces of our *Maga* scattering all chaff before the wind,'" and asking him for "some vigorous work from your hand." To Channing she wrote bluntly, "I want to know what part you propose to take in the grand symphony and I pray you to answer me directly for we must proceed to tune the instruments"; adding, in a postscript, a reminder of *his* past high talk: "At Newport you prophecied a new literature; shall it dawn on 1840." For Hedge, the magazine ideal's original mover, she sounded (after pointedly informing him they depended on him "for the first No. and for solid bullion too") the most "millennial" of all: "My friend, I really hope you will make this the occasion for assailing the public ear with such a succession of melodies that all the stones will advance to form a city of refuge for the just." More personally, she added: "I think with the greatest pleasure of working in company with you. But what will it be? will you give us poems or philosophy or criticism, and how much, for we are planning our first No. by the yard."[58]

Despite her lofty pleas and personal appeals, the results of her first canvassing were not encouraging. Clarke, who was mired in a half-dozen projects while trying to keep the nearly moribund *Western Messenger* afloat and preparing to return to the East with his pregnant wife, wrote to his sister Sarah over a month later that she should tell Fuller he wished her success, but only vaguely promised to "try to write some thing for it." Channing, who had seemed to Fuller (as she had reminded him) "so really in earnest" and had even boasted of having articles "ready written," delayed writing her for nearly two months and, when he did, offered her only future installments of a yet-unwritten "religious novelette" entitled (appropriately enough) "Ernest the Seeker." He also frankly told her that for now he intended to concentrate on his writing for the *Messenger,* which he would soon take over, and that in her "grand concert" he expected to be "a listener only." But the really discouraging word came from Hedge. It was also a response that gave her her first taste of the difficulties involved in bringing out a literary-cum-sectarian journal.[59]

In retrospect, Hedge's response should not have been altogether surprising. In spite of his reputation for being the "Moses" of the Transcendentalists, Hedge was coming to occupy an increasingly precarious position in their radicalized circles. He remained as committed as ever to post-Kantian intuitive philosophy as well as, privately at least, as contemptuous as ever of the "rigid, cautious, circumspect" ministers and academics who dominated Boston-Cambridge Unitarianism. But he also disliked the Transcendentalists' recent turn toward what he called "popular" preaching, and even more, the "open and avowed dissent" from any kind of biblical supernaturalism by Transcendentalists like Emerson and Parker. This could only promote, he would soon complain to his moderate friend Convers Francis, "a vast amount of skepticism in the world." The dissatisfaction in his moderate-to-conservative Bangor church over *his* Transcendentalist views (some of his parishioners would soon try to get him dismissed because of them) clearly also added to his nervousness. So he began to backpedal, starting with his answer to Fuller on January 16. "You frighten me with your sudden announcement," he began anxiously. Rather, though, than revealing any of the intellectual misgivings that lay behind his consternation, he listed, somewhat lamely—considering to whom he was writing—his poor health, low income, four children, and other personal circumstances as reasons preventing him from expending "any extra effort" on "our joint concern." Still, after recalling somewhat bitterly that the idea of a Transcendentalist magazine had originally been his and worrying a bit about his "selfishness," he promised her that he would try to write a series of discourses either on metaphysics or on Christianity and modern philosophy. He warned her, however, "You must let me be anonymous & say *'We,'* adding, disingenuously: "I wish you would all do so. The slight mystery attending an anonymous publication gives it interest which it is hardly worth while to sacrifice for the Quarterish downrightness of signatures & first persons singular." He also implored her to exercise vigorously "a sharp censorship of the pieces submitted for publication," in order, he said, to ensure that all articles be "not only good but significant." He ended by assuring her "my whole heart is with you, & . . . all I have of intellectual energy & of literary resource is at your command."[60]

Such cryptic avowals of diffidence and heartfelt pledges were obviously a little too cryptic for Fuller. So, after pushing ahead the publication date to July, she wrote to him on March 10, begging, "Henry, I adjure you, in the name of all the Genii, Muses, Pegasus, Apollo, Pollio, Apollyon, ('and must I mention'—) to send me something good for this journal before the 1st May." Dismissing all his excuses ("I also am a father," she reminded him), she told him frankly, "All mortals, my friend, are slack and bare; they wait to see whether Hotspur wins, before they levy aid for as good a plan as ever was laid." Fuller's innocent allusion to *Henry IV*'s fiery, impetuous Sir Henry Percy and his treacherous co-conspirator Glendower must have made Hedge smile nervously. In any case, if not the allusion, *something* in the letter smoked him out. Two weeks later he finally revealed the real issue: identifying himself publicly with Transcendentalists like Emerson and Alcott, he said, would make him "stand forth as an atheist in disguise," and this he simply could not do. Indeed, he implied, because of these public impressions, perhaps the whole idea of a Transcendental journal should be abandoned.[61]

This was no small blow. Hedge's criticisms of Alcott were one thing; Fuller knew of them and had already once before kept him from publishing them. Even his concern for his professional career and livelihood was understandable. But his sudden disowning of the whole enterprise must have been unsettling for Fuller, to say the least. Abandoned by her one-time mentor, she immediately wrote for advice to her new mentor, then lecturing in Providence. From his lecture room, where he was given her letter and enclosure, Emerson answered her reassuringly and defiantly. "If the outer wall gives way, we must retire into the citadel. I do not wish any colleagues whom I do not love, and though the Journal we have all regarded as something gay & not something solemn, yet were I responsible, I would rather trust for its wit & its verses to the eight or nine persons in whose affections I have a sure place, than to eighty or ninety celebrated contributors." Indeed, Emerson added, "I am very sorry for Henry Hedge. It is a sad letter for his biography: he will grieve his heart out by & by & perhaps very soon, that he ever wrote it." As for Hedge's view of the magazine, "it is quite worthless. The poor old public stand just where they always did,—garrulous orthodox conservative whilst you say nothing; silent the instant you speak; and perfectly & universally convertible the moment the right word comes."[62]

These were brave and consoling words. How true they were remained to be seen. Meanwhile, Emerson's prediction was at least partly right; if Hedge did not repent his letter (or, as Emerson also predicted, "beg it of you . . . & beg you to forget it"), he did contribute for the second issue his one and only article, "The Art of Life, the Scholar's Calling." In it he argued, predictably, that the intellectual, devoted solely to "self-culture," "must be a radical in speculation" but "by taste averse, by calling exempt, from the practical movements around him." Unfortunately, such social aloofness earned him only scorn from younger Transcendentalists like Theodore Parker. ("A man of unstable water," Parker snorted to Hedge's friend Francis. "You put your finger on him, and he ain't there.") Fuller and Emerson, in contrast to the pugnacious Parker, continued to speak affectionately and admiringly of Hedge's "free wit," learning, and literary sophistication (as he did, even more, of theirs) until the end of their lives. Yet they also realized that an ideological breach had opened. Emerson, perhaps because Hedge's view was uncomfortably close to his own, was particularly sharp. After hearing Hedge's Phi Beta Kappa address, "Conservatism and Reform," the following year, he sneeringly characterized in his journal its posture of ideological neutrality as "the profoundness of superficiality[,] the most universal & triumphant seeming." Fuller—whose friendship with Hedge was older and whose appreciation of his intellectual talents greater—was more generous. "Idealism is with him only a matter of taste; he is a man of the world and a scholar but neither poet nor philosopher," she told William Channing after hearing the oration of the future Harvard professor and American Unitarian Association president. "And Waldo said he never saw the root of every thing cut away with such sweetness nor any thing to surpass the easy elegance with which he poised himself in the air after taking away all possible foot hold."[63]

By the time Fuller wrote this, she was firmly placed on her own idealistic platform. But at this moment she was beginning to feel a little "poised in the air" herself. First of all Hedge's withdrawal underlined the nagging question of the *Dial*'s intellectual leadership. She hoped to get from Emerson, she told Channing on March 22, "good literary criticisms, but his best thoughts," she feared, "must, I suppose take the form of lectures for the present." But if not Emerson or Hedge or any of their young ministerial colleagues, whom could Fuller rely on to supply the "Heavy stern line" of religious and philosophical articles for their magazine? Nor was this issue of leadership—and therefore, by extension, definition and purpose—only Fuller's worry. On March 28, Emerson wrote to his mother from Providence: "You must know I am reckoned here a Transcendentalist, and what that beast is, all persons in Providence have a great appetite to know: So I am carried duly from house to house, and all the young persons ask me, when the Lecture is coming upon the Great Subject?" Indeed, he added, all his lectures "seem . . . to be regarded as mere screens & subterfuges while this dread Transcendentalism is still kept back." After he returned the following week, he wrote in his journal more seriously: "At Providence . . . the young men & several good women freely expressed to me their wish for more light, their sympathy in whatever promised a better life. They inquired about the new Journal of next July. I was compelled to tell them that the aims of that paper were rather literary than psychological or religious. But the inquiry & the tone of these inquirers showed plainly what one may easily see in Boston & Cambridge & the villages also—that what men want is a Religion."[64]

Transcendentalist religion may have been what young people wanted, but Fuller, even more than Emerson, knew this was not likely to be what they would get from the *Dial*. Even back in January she had told Clarke that their journal would be "literary rather than Theological." Still, in her letters to friends and potential correspondents, she valiantly tried to put this fact in its most Transcendental light. "There are no party measures to be carried, no particular standard to be set up," she told Channing in her March 22 letter. Rather, therefore, than trying to "aim at leading public opinion," the *Dial,* she said, would aim at two more individualistic though no less "high" goals: "to afford an avenue for what of free and calm thought might be originated among us" and to "stimulat[e] . . . each man to think for himself, to think more deeply and more nobly by letting them see how some minds are kept alive by a wise self-trust."[65]

However modest, even these aims, Fuller well knew, would not be easy to achieve. For, in addition to the absence of a ready-made "Religion," Fuller had by this time a more fundamental question to worry about: where *were* all those obscure voices anxious to emit their "free and calm" thoughts? In her March 10 letter to Hedge, in which she had pleaded with him to "write, my friend, write," she had ended half-jokingly, "I could make a number myself with the help Mr. E. will give, but the Public, I trow, is too astute a donkey not to look sad at *that.*" By the twenty-second, even before she got Hedge's reply, she was in a more somber mood. "I am not sanguine as to the amount of talent which will be brought to bear on this publication," she told Channing after outlining her objectives. "I find all concerned rather indifferent, and see no promise for the present. I am sure we cannot show high culture, and I doubt about vigorous thought."[66]

Fortunately, as Fuller's spirits sank, her heretofore skeptical colleague Emerson's began to rise. Increasingly excited by all the literary young people that he and Fuller were attracting around them, he tried to spur Fuller on. "I tell you," he wrote in his March 30 letter, after listing many of them, "if these persons added unto You, would promise me their assistance I should think I had the best club that ever made a journal." And, while cautioning her that his book still "is necessarily primary with me," he now offered, in contrast to his stated "abhorrence" in the winter of contributing anything more than "honest labor of some sort" for a year, to "write as many pages as you wish." He also doubled his efforts to help get out the first issue. He already, in February, after trying and failing to get his own publisher, Little and Brown, to bring out the *Dial* on acceptable terms, had gotten the Boston firm of Weeks, Jordan and Company, which had previously published many pamphlets by the Transcendentalists, to agree to publish the *Dial*. But mainly he used his contacts and influence to collect contributions. He got from his young protégé Henry Thoreau an "Elegy" and, later in the spring, an essay on Perseus. He eagerly gave her "two excellent little poems" he received from Christopher Cranch. All winter and spring he pursued the maddeningly elusive Ellery Channing, begging to allow him to select for the *Dial* some of his poems that his friend Ward had given him. ("I feel my dear Sir, that the pleasure I take in this poetry fully authorizes me to make this request. My quarrel with our poets is that they are secondary & mimetic but you may thank the god for intuition & experience").[67]

Of course, responsibility for design, arrangement, and scheduling continued to rest with Fuller. "What is your purpose or wish in regard to contributions?" Emerson asked on April 15. "Are they to be anonymous, or initialed, or blazoned? What is the size of the book? Mr A. asks how much you want, & is large in his measures." She did get some help in copyediting from Ripley. (Claiming to be "ignorant and careless in these details," she told William Channing on the nineteenth, "You may be sure Mr R. will be miserable if there is a comma amiss, and he is to be the corrective as I the [*illegible*] element in this organization.") But for selecting and editing, the bulk of the help she got was, again, from Emerson. Although he complained about it to his brother William, to Fuller he seems to have been entirely receptive to assignments, and she, for her part, was eager to give them to him. ("Caroline Sturgis [Fuller wrote on the twelfth] has given that we should have the poems, and they will be sent you that you may choose ethically or lyrically?") Sometimes the two traded advice. "I read through [Thoreau's "Perseus"] this morning," he wrote in a letter accompanying one package of manuscripts, "& foresee that it may give you some hesitations. There is too much manner in it—as much as in Richter—& too little method, in any common sense of that word—Yet it has always a spiritual meaning even when the literal does not hold: & has so much brilliancy & life in it that in our bold bible for The Young America, I think it ought to find a place." The piece eventually went through several more revisions until, after much "blotting & sandpaper," Emerson finally pronounced it—and Fuller agreed—"excellent."[68]

Even in more delicate matters they were usually in agreement. Alcott was a case in point. Emerson, significantly, failed even to mention Alcott in his March 30 list of potential contributors on whom he thought they should rely. Yet it had been Alcott, more than any other older Transcendentalist, who had hungered the most for a friendly periodical for his writings. Privately, he was already worrying that the new journal "will consult the temper and be awed by the bearing of existing things," and thus only partially satisfy "the hope of the hopeful, and feed the hunger of the starving amongst us." Hungry but still hopeful himself, he eagerly sent to Emerson his "Orphic Sayings"—a series of oracular "Apothegms" intended to express the "essence" of his mind without "insignificant detail." Unfortunately, for Emerson, who had already pained Alcott by severely criticizing his earlier writing, it was the absence of detail that was the significant thing. On May 8 he wrote to Fuller: "One grave thing I have to say, this, namely, that you will not like Alcott's papers; that I do not like them; that Mr Ripley will not; & yet I think, on the whole, they ought to be printed pretty much as they stand, with his name in full." The reason, he thought, was that "those who know him will have his voice in their ear whilst they read, & the sayings will have a majestical sound." He concluded generously: "Some things are very good: for the most part, they are open to the same fault as his former papers, of being cold vague generalities. Yet if people are properly acquainted with the prophet himself,—& his name is getting fast into the stellar regions,—these will have a certain fitting Zoroastrian style." Fuller agreed. After "a (to me) very pleasant visit" with him the following week, she wrote to Emerson: "I think his 'Sayings' are quite grand, though ofttimes too grandiloquent. I thought he bore my strictures with great sweetness for they must have seemed petty to him."[69]

In addition to sharing the collecting and editing burden with Fuller in the last few months before publication, Emerson often made suggestions for the magazine generally. When he requested that she print something, she usually obliged. Other suggestions she followed or not depending on her inclination. One important matter the two discussed together extensively was the *Dial*'s introduction. In late April she sent him a draft of an introductory essay she had written. The draft has not survived, but one can get at least an inkling of its belligerent character from Emerson's critique of it that he sent her on the twenty-first. After saying that it was "written with talent & strength," he went on: "This paper addresses the public; and explains, it refers to the contemporary criticism; it forestals objection; it bows, though a little haughtily, to all the company; it is not quite confirmed in its own purpose." He particularly objected to the essay's defensive tone. "I do not like the early preparations for defence & anticipation of enemies in the sentence about—'this disclaimer may be forgotten' &c. &c. Simply say, 'We do not think alike' &c but leave out this canny bit of American caution. Don't cry before you are hurt." But more fundamentally, he asked, why did they even need "a formal Introduction?" Why make promises that obviate the doing? ("Every good doctrine, sentence, verse, which we shall promulgate, is the best doing, & the best trumpet.") Why make comparisons that only invite bickering? ("The world is wide enough for sense & nonsense too.") Indeed, he asked, why insist so much on this particular journal at all? "This form of our writing, this Journal, may not continue to please us, but our thought & endeavor we know will continue to please us, & to exist. I would not therefore insist much on this enterprize but solely on the Universal aims." Finally, he revealed to Fuller that extraordinary confidence about audience that either lay behind or flowed from his Olympian gestures of radical self-trust: "With the old drowsy Public which the magazines address, I think we have nothing to do;—as little with the journals & critics of the day. If we knew any other Journal, certainly we should not write this. This Journal has a public of its own; its own *Thou* as well as *I;* a new-born class long already standing waiting for this voice & wondering at its delay. They stand before their doors in the highway on tiptoe looking down the road for your coming."[70]

To these "hard words" Fuller replied on the twenty-fifth: "It is no wish of mine to have an introduction or to write it, and all that you say on that score had occurred to me, but Mr Ripley and the publishers both thought it very desirable." Still, she promised to show Ripley what he had written, adding, editorlike: "Those parts you thought too fierce, he thought not sufficiently so. I know not whether I can find the golden mean between you. What you have written pleases me greatly." Indeed it did: the next day she asked *him* to write "a prologue." This he immediately did, although not without some grumbling about having "learned not to send a capricious offer another time." Even a week after writing one of the most buoyant sendoffs in American literature, he was still grumbling. "I hope ere this [he wrote on May 8] you have digested your chagrin concerning the Introduction I send you Nay have fairly got Mr Ripley at work to try his hand in drafting a Declaration of Independence. When he has tried, suppose we apply to Dr Channing—indeed I would send the requisition all round the Table to every member, & then print the Dial without any, & publish the Rejected Introductions in a volume."[71]

Still, introduction or not, news of Transcendentalism and its impending magazine was beginning, if faultily, to attract public attention. When Emerson had lectured in Providence in March, he had been told of one man, he reported to his mother, who, when asked what Transcendentalism was, had "in good earnest defined it as 'Operations on the Teeth.'" The newspapers did little better with the journal. On April 4, Horace Greeley's *New-Yorker* announced that Weeks, Jordan and Company would soon publish a new "theological and literary magazine" under "the Editorial direction of Ralph Waldo Emerson and associates." The corrected notice that appeared in the *New-Yorker* and the *New York Evening Post* the following week was only slightly improved: after misstating the title of the new "Transcendental Magazine" as *The Harbinger,* it listed the editors as Emerson and "Miss Sophia Margaret Fuller." Fortunately for the reputation of the elect, on May 4, Weeks, Jordan issued a prospectus for "THE DIAL: A Magazine for Literature, Philosophy, and Religion," which tried to set the movement and its journal on a surer foundation. The circular, probably written by Ripley, began by affirming that "the purpose of this work is to furnish a medium for the freest expression of thought on the questions which interest earnest minds in every community." It also insisted that the magazine's aim was to discuss "principles" rather than to promote "measures," adding that it would examine sympathetically the ideas of "the leading movements of the present day," while maintaining "an independent position with regard to them." It even conceded that its contributors were united by little "but the love of intellectual freedom and the hope of social progress" based on faith in "Divine Providence" and "the living soul." The *Dial,* it declared, "will endeavor to promote the constant evolution of truth, not the petrifaction of opinion." Still, after promising that as both a "Magazine" and a "Review" its contents would offer "something both for those who read for instruction, and those who search for amusement," the circular revealed the journal's unmistakable Transcendentalist goals:

> In literature, it will strive to exercise a just and catholic criticism, and to recognize every sincere production of genius; in philosophy, it will attempt the reconciliation of the universal instincts of humanity with the largest conclusions of reason; and in religion, it will reverently seek to discover the presence of God in nature, in history, and in the soul of man.

In sum, the prospectus loftily concluded, "The DIAL, as its title indicates, will endeavor to occupy a station on which the light may fall; which is open to the rising sun; and from which it may correctly report the progress of the hour and the day."[72]

Meanwhile, news of the *Dial*'s coming birth was circulating in Boston and to points beyond. Andrews Norton was so agitated by the thought of a "Transcendental Review" spreading its "great evil . . . throughout our community" that on April 22 he pled unsuccessfully with John Gorham Palfrey to have the *North American Review* print a statement "giving a blow to Transcendentalism, from which," he growled, "it would not recover to work any essential mischief among us." At the other end of the local liberal spectrum, four days later Alcott wrote proudly to his friends of the advent of the new magazine, through which "we of the sublunary world are to be informed of the time of day in the transcendental regions." In a more earthly vein that week, Emerson informed Carlyle that "my friend Margaret Fuller's Journal . . . will give you a better knowledge of our young people than any you have had." Privately, Emerson was, if saltier and more literary, no less expectant than Alcott: "Our American letters are, we confess," he wrote in his journal a month later, "in the optative mood; but whoso knows these seething brains, these admirable radical projects, these talkers who talk the sun & moon away will believe that this generation cannot pass away without leaving its mark."[73]

While Emerson was thinking of history, Fuller was worrying about copy. As the final hours ticked away, she was also growing nervous about all those "newborn" souls who were supposedly "stand[ing] . . . on tiptoe looking down the road" for the Transcendentalists' coming. "There are only thirty names on the Boston subscription list to the 'Dial,'" she wrote with alarm to Emerson on May 31. He wrote back reassuringly: "I think the fact of thirty names on the subscription paper of no import whatever. The people who will buy this book will not put their names to a paper which is read with curious eyes to know who is of 'These men.' I know the book will sell in a short time." She continued to fret. A week later, irked that in order to reach the 136 pages promised in the prospectus she would have to leave out, for this issue, Emerson's long essay on modern literature and add several poems by herself and Sarah Clarke, she wrote him a worried letter about the issue's quality. To this he responded with a gentle tap and a final call to literary faith:

> I shall grieve if you are not content with what is printed. Can we not explode in this enterprize of ours all the established rules of Grub Street or Washington Street? leave out all the ballast or Balaam and omit to count pages? One hundred thirty six pages! Our readers, who, I take it, are the sincere & the sensible, will not ask, Are there 110 or 150 pages? but Is there one page? Every dull sentence vulgarizes the book and when we have inserted our gems from the papers of love & friendship we shall feel that we have wronged our angels by thrusting them into unfit company. But you do not mean that this number is not good. It is & shall be.[74]

Fuller was not so sure. But then, at this point she was still more the editor than the prophet. In her letter of April 19, she described for William Channing what she thought her role would be. "I do not expect to be of much use except to urge on the laggards, scold the lukewarm, and act Helen Mac Gregor to those who love compromise, by doing my little best to sink them in the waters of Oblivion!!" A righteous censor for her outlaw clan—surely she could be that. Whether either she or her band had, when it came down to it, anything more creative to offer was something else again. She reflected on these things in her letter to Channing:

> Things go on pretty well, but I dare say people will be disappointed, for they seem to be looking for the gospel of transcendentalism. It may prove as your Jouffroy says it is with the French ministry; the public wants something positive, and finding such and such persons excellent at fault finding raises them to be the rulers, when lo! they have no noble and full Yea, to match their shrill and bold Nay, and are hurled down again— Mr Emerson knows best what he wants but he has already said it in various ways.— Yet I deem the experiment is well worth trying; hearts beat so high, they must be full of something, and here is a way to breathe it out quite freely.— It is for dear New England that I wanted this review; for myself, if I had wished to write a few pages now and then, I had ways and means of disposing of them. But in truth I have not much to say, for since I have had leisure to look at myself I find that, so far from being a great original genius, I have not yet learned to think to any depth, and that the utmost I have done in life has been to form my character to a certain consistency, cultivate my tastes, and learn to tell the truth with a little better grace than I did at first. For this the world will not care much, so I shall only hazard a few critical remarks, or an unpretending chalk sketch now and then, till I have learned to do something.[75]

These were somewhat grim thoughts for a prebattle meditation, as hers invariably were whenever she conjured up her "genius" phantom. Yet she knew that the impending *Dial* was a turning point—both for her circle of "love & friendship" and for herself. Since childhood she had dreamed of becoming a public personage. For nearly the past decade, she had yearned for a career as a professional author. Meanwhile she had been honing her skills as a literary critic and, along the way, accumulating—notwithstanding her self-deprecating claim to Channing—a bundle of unpublished papers. These, given her refusal to have her writing "mutilated, or . . . dictated to suit the public taste," were likely to remain unpublished without a journal like the *Dial*. Finally, within the year, she had come to embrace the Transcendentalist movement because she saw it in an opportunity to revolutionize American cultural taste. Certainly hearts *did* beat high in her "dear New England"—and hers among them. "Mediocrity is obscurity," her father had told her exactly twenty years to the week before. She now had a chance to test both sides of that republican equation.[76]

Abbreviations

The following abbreviations are used in the notes.

Sources

"AJ36"   Joel Myerson, "Bronson Alcott's 'Journal for 1836,'" *Studies in the American Renaissance, 1978,* ed. Joel Myerson (Boston: Twayne, 1978), 17–104.

"AJ37-1" Larry A. Carlson, "Bronson Alcott's 'Journal for 1837' (Part One)," *Studies in the American Renaissance, 1981,* ed. Joel Myerson (Boston: Twayne, 1981), 27–132.

"AJ37-2" Larry A. Carlson, "Bronson Alcott's 'Journal for 1837' (Part Two)," *Studies in the American Renaissance, 1982,* ed. Joel Myerson (Boston: Twayne, 1982), 53–167.

AL   *The Letters of A. Bronson Alcott,* ed. Richard L. Herrnstadt (Ames: Iowa State University Press, 1969).

"AS40"   Joel Myerson, "Bronson Alcott's 'Scripture for 1840,'" *ESQ: A Journal of the American Renaissance,* v. 20 (4th Quarter 1974), 236–59.

CL   *The Letters of James Freeman Clarke to Margaret Fuller,* ed. John Wesley Thomas (Hamburg: Cram, de Gruyter, 1957).

"CLS"   Sarah Clarke, "Letters of a Sister," proof sheets, Houghton Library, Harvard University.

"CJ33"   Robert D. Habich, "James Freeman Clarke's 1833 Letter-journal for Margaret Fuller," *ESQ: A Journal of the American Renaissance,* v. 27 (1st Quarter 1981), 47–56.

CU-SB   University of California, Santa Barbara Library, Department of Special Collections.

ChL   *Lydia Maria Child: Selected Letters, 1817–1880,* ed. Milton Meltzer and Patricia G. Holland (Amherst: Univ. of Mass. Press, 1982).

CtY   Yale University, Beinecke Library.

DM   Caroline W. Healey [Dall], *Margaret and Her Friends; or, Ten Conversa-tions with Margaret Fuller upon the Mythology of the Greeks and Its Expres-sion in Art* (1895; Boston: Roberts Brothers, 1897).

ECC   *The Correspondence of Emerson and Carlyle,* ed. Joseph Slater (New York: Columbia University Press, 1964).

EEL   *The Early Lectures of Ralph Waldo Emerson,* ed. Robert E. Spiller, Stephen E. Whicher, and Wallace E. Williams, 3 vols. (Cambridge: Belknap Press of Harvard University Press, 1959–1972).

ECW   *The Collected Works of Ralph Waldo Emerson,* ed. Alfred E. Ferguson et al., 4 vols. to date (Cambridge: Harvard University Press, 1971–).

EJ   *The Journals and Miscellaneous Notebooks of Ralph Waldo Emerson,* ed. William H. Gilman et al., 16 vols. (Cambridge: Harvard University Press, 1960–1982).

EL   *The Letters of Ralph Waldo Emerson,* Vols. I–VI, ed. Ralph L. Rusk, Vols. VII–VIII, ed. Eleanor M. Tilton, 8 vols. to date (New York: Columbia University Press, 1939; 1990–).

ESL   *The Selected Letters of Lidian Jackson Emerson,* ed. Dolores Bird Carpenter (Columbia: University of Missouri Press, 1987).

EW   *The Complete Works of Ralph Waldo Emerson* [Centenary Edition], ed. Edward Waldo Emerson, 12 vols. (Boston: Houghton, Mifflin, 1903–1904).

FC   Richard F. Fuller, *Chaplain Fuller: Being a Life Sketch of a New England Clergyman and Army Chaplain* (Boston: Walker, Wise, 1863).

"FJ39"   Robert N. Hudspeth, "Margaret Fuller's 1839 Journal: Trip to Bristol," *Harvard Library Bulletin,* 27 (October 1979), 445–70.

"FJ42-1"   Joel Myerson, "Margaret Fuller's 1842 Journal: At Concord with the Emersons," *Harvard Library Bulletin,* 21 (July 1973), 320–40.

"FJ42-2"   Robert D. Habich, "Margaret Fuller's Journal for October 1842," *Harvard Library Bulletin,* 33 (Summer 1985), 280–91.

"FJ44-1"   Martha L. Berg and Alice de V. Perry, eds., "'The Impulses of Human Nature': Margaret Fuller's Journal from June through October 1844," *Proceedings of the Massachusetts Historical Society,* v. 102, 1990 (Boston, 1991), 38–126.

"FJ44-2"   "Fragments of Margaret Fuller's Journal," 1844–1845, Fruitlands Museums, Harvard, Massachusetts.

FL   *The Letters of Margaret Fuller,* ed. Robert N. Hudspeth, 5 vols. to date (Ithaca: Cornell University Press, 1983–).

FMW   Fuller Manuscripts and Works, Houghton Library, Harvard University.

FP   Margaret Fuller Papers, Massachusetts Historical Society.

FPL   S. Margaret Fuller, *Papers on Literature and Art* (New York: Wiley and Putnam, 1846).

FR   Richard F. Fuller, *Recollections of Richard F. Fuller* (Boston: privately printed, 1936).

"FS"   Margaret Fuller, "Scrapbook," 1838–1844, Perry-Clarke Collection, Massachusetts Historical Society.

FSL   S. M. Fuller, *Summer on the Lakes, in 1843* (Boston: Charles C. Little and James Brown, 1844).

FW   S. Margaret Fuller, *Woman in the Nineteenth Century* (New York: Greeley & McElrath, 1845).

HO   Thomas Wentworth Higginson, *Margaret Fuller Ossoli* (Boston: Houghton, Mifflin, 1884).

HW   *The Centenary Edition of the Works of Nathaniel Hawthorne*, ed. William Charvat et al., 20 vols. to date (Columbus: Ohio State University Press, 1962–).

MB   Boston Public Library, Department of Rare Books and Manuscripts.

MCR-S   Radcliffe College, Schlesinger Library.

MH   Harvard University, Houghton Library.

MH-AH   Harvard Divinity School, Andover-Harvard Theological Library.

MHarF   Fruitlands Museums, Harvard, Massachusetts.

MHi   Massachusetts Historical Society.

MT   Perry Miller, ed., *The Transcendentalists: An Anthology* (Cambridge: Harvard University Press, 1950).

MWA   American Antiquarian Society.

MaHi   Maine Historical Society.

OAH   Margaret Fuller Ossoli, *At Home and Abroad; or, Things and Thoughts in America and Europe,* ed. Arthur B. Fuller (Boston: Crosby, Nichols, 1856).

OA   Margaret Fuller Ossoli, *Art, Literature, and the Drama,* ed. Arthur B. Fuller (Boston: Brown, Taggard and Chase, 1860).

OC   Margaret Fuller Ossoli Collection, Boston Public Library.

OL   Margaret Fuller Ossoli, *Life Without and Life Within; or, Reviews, Narratives, Essays, and Poems,* ed. Arthur B. Fuller (Boston: Brown, Taggard and Chase, 1860).

OM   *Memoirs of Margaret Fuller Ossoli,* ed. R. W. Emerson, W. H. Channing, and J. F. Clarke, 2 vols. (1852; Boston: Brown, Taggard and Chase, 1860).

"ON"   "Notebook Margaret Fuller Ossoli," [1851], in *The Journals and Miscellaneous Notebooks of Ralph Waldo Emerson,* Vol. XI, 455–509, ed. A. W. Plumstead, William H. Gilman, and Ruth H. Bennett (Cambridge: Harvard University Press, 1975).

OW   Margaret Fuller Ossoli, *Woman in the Nineteenth Century, and Kindred Papers Relating to the Sphere, Condition and Duties, of Woman,* ed. Arthur B. Fuller (Boston: John P. Jewett, 1855).

PL   *Letters of Elizabeth Palmer Peabody: American Renaissance Woman,* ed. Bruce A. Ronda (Middletown, Conn.: Wesleyan University Press, 1984).

RPB   Brown University Library, John Hay Library.

| *SAR* | *Studies in the American Renaissance,* ed. Joel Myerson (Boston: Twayne, 1977–1982; Charlottesville: University Press of Virginia, 1983–). |
| ScU | University of South Carolina, Thomas Cooper Library. |

People

AB (ABW)	Anna Barker (Ward)
ABA	Amos Bronson Alcott
ABF	Arthur Buckminster Fuller
AG (AGB)	Amelia Greenwood (Bartlett)
AGG	Albert Gorton Greene
AP (APB)	Almira Penniman (Barlow)
CKN	Charles King Newcomb
CPC	Christopher Pearse Cranch
CS (CST)	Caroline Sturgis (Tappan)
EF	Eugene Fuller
EH	Elizabeth Hoar
EK	Ellen Kilshaw
EKF	Ellen Kilshaw Fuller
EPP	Elizabeth Palmer Peabody
ER (ERC)	Elizabeth Randall (Cumming)
ERF	Eliza Rotch Farrar
FHH	Frederic Henry Hedge
GR	George Ripley
GTD	George T. Davis
HM	Harriet Martineau
JFC	James Freeman Clarke
JN	James Nathan
JSD	John Sullivan Dwight
JT (JTK)	Jane Tuckerman (King)
LF	James Lloyd Fuller
LJE	Lidian Jackson Emerson
LMC	Lydia Maria Child
MCF	Margarett Crane Fuller
MF	Margaret Fuller
RFF	Richard Frederick Fuller
RN	Rhoda Newcomb
RWE	Ralph Waldo Emerson
SC	Sarah Clarke
SGW	Samuel Gray Ward

SHW	Sarah Helen Whitman
SP	Susan Prescott (Wright)
SR	Sophia Ripley
TF	Timothy Fuller
TP	Theodore Parker
WEC2	William Ellery Channing II
WHC	William Henry Channing
WHF	William Henry Fuller

Notes

In these notes I have given full citations to all quoted material. I have also indicated some secondary works that have provided me with major sources of information or influenced my interpretations in substantial ways.

The copies of Fuller's letters and journal entries in the *Memoirs of Margaret Fuller Ossoli* present special problems. The censorship and rewriting of these fragments by the editors, especially her most effusively friendly ones, Channing and Clarke, have made them clearly corrupt sources. For this reason I have consistently used, in place of a *Memoirs* Fuller text, an original Fuller manuscript, a Hudspeth edition letter, or, as a last resort, a copy in the Fuller Manuscripts and Works. Unfortunately, as some *Memoirs* Fuller texts survive in no other form, I have decided—as Hudspeth has—to use them. My main reason is that *not* to utilize these copies, which on the whole are more accurate than not, would be a more serious distortion of the historical record than to utilize them. Also, by exploiting internal and external evidence, I have often been able to mitigate at least one of their weaknesses—their frequent lack of dates and (in the case of letters) identified recipients.

My editorial apparatus is as follows. In the text I have reproduced quotations as they appear in the sources cited, including their spelling and punctuation. Exceptions are slips of the pen, typographical errors, and obliterated but contextually obvious letters and punctuation marks, which I have silently corrected. I have also not reproduced editors' additions, authors' insertion marks, or (except occasionally and where I identify them as such) authors' cancellations. Unrecovered but likely words, punctuation marks or letters occasionally required for clarity, and all other inserted material I have placed in brackets. In the notes I have placed within brackets and an asterisk likely dates and recipients for *Memoirs* copies of letters and journal entries. I have also used brackets and an asterisk for date and recipient identifications that differ from those assigned in published editions. I have employed brackets without an asterisk for dates and recipients I have assigned for unpublished manuscripts. Brackets without an asterisk for published works are those used by the editors. Occasionally I have spliced together several sources for a single quoted passage. Where this is the case I have cited all the sources in the note.

Preface

1. By the early 1980s, a small but growing number of excellent studies began to appear that collectively presented a new intellectual agenda for American women's history. Three outstanding books on the early period that particularly influenced me in my work on Fuller were Ann Douglas, *The Feminization of American Culture* (New York, 1977); Linda K. Kerber, *Women of the Republic: Intellect and Ideology in Revolutionary America* (Chapel Hill, 1980); and Mary Kelley, *Private Woman, Public Stage: Literary Domesticity in Nineteenth-Century America* (New York, 1984). A similarly influential book that appeared at this time that sought to integrate women's history and (in this case) the great traditions of Western politics was Jean Bethke Elshtain, *Public Man, Private Woman: Women in Social and Political Thought* (Princeton, 1981). For three recent vigorous (if ideologically very different) defenses of the relevance of Western high culture for an understanding of women and gender consciousness, see Deirdre David, *Intellectual Women and Victorian Patriarchy: Harriet Martineau, Elizabeth Barrett Browning, George Eliot* (Ithaca, 1987); Camille Paglia, *Sexual Personae: Art and Decadence from Nefertiti to Emily Dickinson* (New Haven, 1990); and Elizabeth Fox-Genovese, "The Claims of a Common Culture, Or, Whose Autobiography?" in her *Feminism without Illusions: A Critique of Individualism* (Chapel Hill, 1991), chap. 7.

2. Because the *Memoirs of Margaret Fuller Ossoli* is both a memoir and a posthumous collection of extracts from Fuller's journals and letters, depending on the context, I refer to it as either "the" or "her" *Memoirs.* For comprehensive listings of writings on Fuller, see Joel Myerson, *Margaret Fuller: An Annotated Secondary Bibliography* (New York, 1977); and idem, "Supplement to *Margaret Fuller: An Annotated Secondary Bibliography*," *SAR, 1984,* 331–85. The only modern book-length studies to treat Fuller seriously as a thinker and historical figure have been, not biographies, but anthologies: Perry Miller, ed., *Margaret Fuller, American Romantic: A Selection from Her Writings and Correspondence* (Garden City, N.Y., 1963); and Bell Gale Chevigny, *The Woman and the Myth: Margaret Fuller's Life and Writings* (Old Westbury, N.Y., 1976). While my own interpretation of Fuller's life and thought diverges in some important respects from theirs, I have found both of them very valuable.

3. [Ca. Jan.–Mar. 1839], JFC Papers, MH ("Sphynx"); May 7, 1852, *ECC, 478 ("eat").*

4. The cultural concepts of "private" and "public" are much contested in modern sociological theory. For a recent astutely historical critique of this literature as applied to the history of women, see Mary P. Ryan, *Women in Public: Between Banners and Ballots, 1825–1880* (Baltimore, 1990), 3–18.

5. To Walter Whitman, July 21, 1855, *EL*, VIII, 446 ("foreground").

6. Quoted in *OM,* I, 64 ("seeking"). In constructing my life of Fuller, I have been instructed by many fine recent studies of the problem of writing women's lives, but two deserve particular mention for their suggestiveness: Carolyn G. Heilbrun, *Writing a Woman's Life* (New York, 1988); and Wendy Lesser, *His Other Half: Men Looking at Women through Art* (Cambridge, Mass., 1991).

Chapter One

1. To WHC, Apr. 19, 1840, *FL*, II, 131 ("dear New England").

2. "Mythology" Journal, [ca. 1842], FMW, Box 1 ("poetry"); Arthur Buckminster Fuller, with additions by Edith Davenport Fuller, *Historical Notices of Thomas Fuller and His Descendants, with a Genealogy of the Fuller Family, 1638–1902* (Cambridge, Mass.,

1902), 3 ("tour of observation"); quoted in Thomas Wentworth Higginson, *Old Cambridge* (New York, 1899), 3 ("soul-ravishing"); quoted in Fuller, *Historical Notices,* 5 ("But surely God").

3. J. F. Fuller, *A Brief Sketch of Thomas Fuller and His Descendants with Historical Notes* (Appleton, Wis., 1896), 6, 8 ("Lieut. Fuller").

4. Anna Buckminster Williams to Sarah Williams Fuller, Nov. 24, 1782, FMW, I, 31 ("needed the rod"); Will of Abraham Williams, Mar. 14, 1781, ibid., 33 ("cheapest sort"); Fuller, *Historical Notices,* 8 ("vigorous understanding"); TF to MCF, Feb. 3, 1820, FMW, III, 106 ("deserves").

5. Clifford K. Shipton, s.v. "Timothy Fuller," *Sibley's Harvard Graduates,* 16 vols. (Cambridge, Mass., 1873–1885; 1933–1972), XIV, 601 ("dissimulation"); "Thanksgiving Sermon," Chilmark, Nov. 26, 1778, FMW, I, 28a ("Slaughter and Blood"); Timothy Fuller to ?, Jan. 31, 1776, ibid., 24 ("Bantering"); Fuller, *Historical Notices,* 6 ("girdeth on"). The most complete material on Fuller and his dismissal is in FMW, I. See also Fuller, *Historical Notices,* 6–7, 21–22; William Bentley, *The Diary of William Bentley, D.D.,* 4 vols. (Salem, Mass., 1905–14), III, 172; Francis Everett Blake, *History of the Town of Princeton,* 2 vols. (Princeton, Mass., 1915), I, 135–37, 146–57, 322–26, II, 106–7; and Shipton, "Timothy Fuller," 601–5.

6. *Remarks on that Part of the Strictures on the Rev. Mr. Thacher's Pamphlet, which Relates to the Controversy between Mr. Fuller and the People of Princeton* (Boston, 1784), 18 ("office for life"); Fuller, *Historical Notices,* 7 ("crushing"); n.d., FMW, I, 1 ("Stigma"). The FMW "General Index," 24, incorrectly identifies the author of this document as Abraham Williams. Cf. Timothy Fuller's obliquely antislavery, sectionalist attack on the disparity in representation and taxation between North and South, recorded in Jonathan Elliot, ed., *The Debates in the Several Conventions on the Adoption of the Federal Constitution,* 5 vols. (Philadelphia, 1876), II, 44.

7. Oct. 13, [1792], "Diary Kept by Elizabeth Fuller," Blake, *History of Princeton,* I, 319 ("sixteen"). Sarah Fuller gave birth to eleven children, but one girl died in childhood.

8. *HO,* 11 ("'forty Fullers'"); statement of Charles G. Loring, quoted in "Obituary Notice," *Monthly Law Reporter,* New Series, 5 (Oct. 1852), 356 ("raillery"). The best source for the Fuller brothers is FMW, but useful details may also be found in Fuller, *Historical Notices,* 16–17, 21–22; "Obituary Notice," 354–60; Henry H. Fuller, s.v. "Henry Holton Fuller," *Memorial Biographies of the New England Historic Genealogical Society,* 9 vols. (Boston, 1880–1908), I, 410–22; Nathaniel Paine, s.v. "Elisha Fuller," ibid., II, 353–57; and *FR,* 82–86.

9. MCF to TF, Jan. 11, 1824, FMW, VIII, 95 ("volubility"); to RFF, [Mar. 7, 1846], *FL,* IV, 194 ("slippery customer"); Jan. 18, 1824, FMW, VII, 98 ("selfish"); MCF to TF, Jan. 11, 1824, FMW, 95 ("unpropitious[ly]"); to MCF, Jan. 3, 18[20], FMW, III, 77 *("the world");* Jan. 21, 1834, FMW, VII, 180 ("wealthy Cit"); to MCF, Sept. 5, 1837, *FL,* I, 301 ("vulgar"); Abraham W. Fuller to Sarah Williams Fuller, Nov. 4, 1808, FMW, I, 76 ("prudent"); ABF to EF, Apr. 11, 1847, FMW, XIII, 138 ("excitement").

10. To Richard F. Fuller, Jan. 27, 1841, FMW, VIII, 94 ("refresh the body"); "Diary of Timothy Fuller," July 15, 1801, FMW, II, 2 ("rabble"). The best sources for the life of Timothy Fuller are his diary and letters in FMW. A number of Fuller's published writings may also be found in FMW. Edith Davenport Fuller has compiled selections from his college diary in her "Excerpts from the Diary of Timothy Fuller, Jr., an Undergraduate in Harvard College, 1798–1801," *Cambridge Historical Society Publications,* v. 11 (Cambridge, Mass., 1920), 33–53.

11. Sept. 21, 1797, FMW, II, 66 ("very easy"); to MCF, Feb. 3, 1820, FMW, III, 106

("indelicate"). The correspondence of Timothy Fuller and his Harvard friends in FMW shows their attraction to radical Enlightenment authors. For discussions of similar intellectual interests in undergraduate circles at this time, see Samuel Eliot Morison, *Three Centuries of Harvard, 1636–1936* (Cambridge, Mass., 1936), 184–85; and Henry F. May, *The Enlightenment in America* (New York, 1976), 234–35.

12. *An Oration,* [Feb. 22, 1799], 14–15, FMW, I, 47 ("monsters"); "Aut Caesar, aut nullus," Nov. 7, 1800, FMW, Box B ("contemptible mortal"). The classic discussion of republican ideology is J. G. A. Pocock, *The Machiavellian Moment: Florentine Political Thought and the Atlantic Republican Tradition* (Princeton, 1975). Significantly, perhaps, "Aut Caesar" was one of Fuller's few themes that did not receive the usual double-mark, a result that he noted in his diary with some disgust: "My theme I consider, as the best I ever wrote." "Diary of Timothy Fuller," Nov. 9, 1800, FMW, II, 2.

13. "Diary of Timothy Fuller," Oct. 13, 1800, FMW, II, 2 ("indignation"); Dec. 1, 1800, ibid. ("oppressive laws"); Nov. 26, 1800, ibid. ("Admirable legislators"); Dec. 11, 1800, ibid. ("ungracefully received"); Jan. 21, 1801, ibid., 79 ("precisely my wish"). For post-Revolutionary youth psychology and student rebellions in this period, see Steven J. Novak, *The Rights of Youth: American Colleges and Student Revolt, 1798–1815* (Cambridge, Mass., 1977). Morison, *Three Centuries of Harvard,* 174–84, briefly discusses student rebellions at Harvard in the 1790s. In interpreting Fuller's speeches as partial reflections of post-Revolutionary familial ideology, I have also found valuable Jay Fliegelman, *Prodigals and Pilgrims: The American Revolution Against Patriarchal Authority, 1750–1800* (Cambridge, England, 1982).

14. "Diary of Timothy Fuller," Nov. 15, 1804, FMW, II, 6 ("petty arts"); Samuel Ripley to Ezra Ripley, Nov. 10, 1805, printed in James B. Thayer, *Rev. Samuel Ripley of Waltham* (Cambridge, Mass., 1897), 17 ("man-brute"); Jan. 21, 1801, FMW, I, 79 ("boldness"); TF to Lemuel Shaw, Mar. 7, 1822, Lemuel Shaw Papers, MHi ("visionary"); TF to MCF, Apr. 12, 1824, FMW, IV, 154 ("*frank* conversations"). For the ideology and politics of Adams Federalism, see Manning J. Dauer, *The Adams Federalists* (Baltimore, 1963). For Massachusetts Republicans, see Paul Goodman, *The Democratic-Republicans of Massachusetts: Politics in a Young Republic* (Cambridge, Mass., 1964); and Ronald P. Formisano, *The Transformation of Political Culture: Massachusetts Parties, 1790s–1840s* (New York, 1983), chaps. 3–7.

15. Jan. 3, 18[20], FMW, III, 77 ("Laborers"); Mar. 28, 1820, ibid., 154 ("rational religion"); *The Election of President of the United States, Considered* (Boston, 1823), 18 *("brothel");* Feb. 2, 1819, *The Annals of the Congress of the United States, The Fifteenth Congress—Second Session, November 16, 1818, to March 3, 1819* (Washington, D.C., 1855), 986 ("sanguinary"); "Diary of Timothy Fuller," Dec. 1828, FMW, II, 15 ("stupifying"); *An Oration, Delivered at Faneuil Hall,* 6 ("disciplined"). The best study of enlightened ideals in America is May, *Enlightenment in America.* The literature on republicanism is large and still growing, but a good recent introduction is Joyce Appleby, ed., "Republicanism in the History and Historiography of the United States," Special Issue of *American Quarterly,* 37 (Fall 1985), 461–598. Paul Goodman has a fine—and, for Timothy Fuller, quite apposite—discussion of Antimasonry and old republican ideology in his *Towards a Christian Republic: Antimasonry and the Great Transition in New England, 1826–1836* (New York, 1988), chap. 2. For Massachusetts Antimasonry, see also Formisano, *Transformation of Political Culture,* chap. 9.

16. "Diary of Timothy Fuller," Oct. 9, 1803, FMW, II, 5 ("God will not reward"); *FR,* 23 ("Washington Bible"); to MCF, Mar. 5, 1820, FMW, III, 134 ("falling together"); to MCF, Feb. 13, 1821, ibid., 117 ("camppreachers"); Dec. 31, 1820, ibid., 209 ("mendi-

cants"). Conrad Wright, "Institutional Reconstruction in the Unitarian Controversy," in Conrad Edick Wright, ed., *American Unitarianism, 1805–1865* (Boston, 1989), 20–26, includes a good, succinct discussion of early Unitarian views on religious establishment in Massachusetts.

17. "Diary of Timothy Fuller," Jan. 10, 1805, FMW, II, 6 ("scientific reading"); Jan. 27, 1821, FMW, IV, 14 ("negligence"); Apr. 28, 1824, ibid., 162 ("fig for me"); to MCF, Apr. 18, 1824, ibid., 157 ("intellectual laziness"); to MCF, Feb. 13, 1821, FMW, III, 117 *("sneer[ing]"); Apr. 18, 1824, FMW, IV, 157 ("duodecimo"); "Diary of Timothy Fuller," Apr. 18, 1824, FMW, II, 13 ("disinclination"). For a good recent study of the lawyer as man of letters in the early Republic, see Robert A. Ferguson, *Law and Letters in American Culture* (Cambridge, Mass., 1984).

18. "Diary of Timothy Fuller," Aug. 28, 1798, FMW, II, 1 ("respectable characters"); to MCF, Apr. 10, 1824, FMW, IV, 153 ("coarse & harsh"); Mar. 5, 1818, FMW, III, 53 ("just retribution"); "Diary of Timothy Fuller," July 21, 1801, FMW, II, 2 ("This behavior").

19. "Whether familiarity with females be beneficial to Students," n.d., FMW, Box B ("ornaments"); "Diary of Timothy Fuller," Mar. 6, 1802, FMW, II, 3 (*"delicious* hour[s]"); Nov. 21, 1801, ibid. *("through the lips!");* Feb. 15, 1802, ibid. (*"plurality* of loves"); May 10, 1802, ibid. ("malignant feelings"); May 11, 1802, ibid. ("cautioned them").

20. Feb. 25, 1824, FMW, IV, 131 ("first to separate"); Nov. 27, 1820, FMW, III, 192 ("ladies"); "Diary of Timothy Fuller," Aug. 5, 1800, FMW, II, 2 ("improper"); Aug. 7, 1802, ibid., 4 ("man of sense").

21. "Diary of Timothy Fuller," Dec. 2, 1802, FMW, II, 5 ("melted in tenderness"); to Sarah Williams Fuller, July 26, 1807, FMW, I, 81 ("censures"); TF to MCF, Feb. 15, 1824, FMW, IV, 126 ("accidental walks").

22. RFF, "Memorial of Mrs. Margaret Fuller," *OM,* I, 373 ("crude views"); to WHC, [Dec. 14, 1845], *OM,* I, 173–74 ("primitive piety"). There are a few useful facts on the life of Margarett Crane Fuller in RFF, "Memorial of Mrs. Margaret Fuller," 373–86, but the best source is the large collection of her letters in FMW. Facts on the Cranes and the town of Canton may be found in Daniel T. Huntoon, *History of the Town of Canton* (Cambridge, Mass., 1893).

23. RFF, "Memorial of Mrs. Margaret Fuller," 374 ("gayety"); to ABW, Dec. 23, 1843, *FL,* III, 166 ("good fortune"); RFF, "Memorial of Mrs. Margaret Fuller," 376 ("ferrul[ing]").

24. MCF to TF, Feb. 12, 1818, FMW, VI, 16 ("pretty Girls"); Anna D. Gale, "School Journal," Feb. 6, 1838, Gale Family Papers, MWA ("so young"); *HO,* 18 ("'timid-friendly'"); MCF to TF, Dec. 1, 1820, FMW, VI, 95 (too *"dignified").*

25. To MCF, Dec. 17, 1819, FMW, III, 34 (*"too* frugal"); Apr. 28, 1820, ibid., 174 ("equip"); Mar. 7, 1820, ibid., 136 (*"beauty* and *shape"*); Jan. 4, 1821, FMW, IV, 2 ("polite and rational"); "Diary of Timothy Fuller," Jan. 23, 1813, FMW, II, 8 ("by my side"); TF to MCF, Feb. 13, 1823, FMW, IV, 74 ("easy talent"); to MCF, Apr. 24, 1820, FMW, III, 172 ("banishment"); Feb. 25, 1823, FMW, IV, 80 ("how much *inferior"*); Feb. 7, 1818, FMW, III, 31 ("foolish capers"); Feb. 6, 1824, FMW, IV, 121 ("lover's appointment"); Feb. 9, 1821, ibid., 20 ("egregious vanity").

26. Jan. 27, 1823, FMW, VII, 66 ("dear presence"); Jan. 17, 1818, FMW, VI, 58 ("ambition"); Jan. 21, 1825, FMW, VII, 155 *("Fame");* Jan. 2, 1823, ibid., 57 *("family picture[s]");* Dec. 22, 1822, ibid., 52 *("dialogue[s]");* Jan. 12, 1818, FMW, VI, 5 ("run up stairs"); Jan. 28, 1819, ibid., 66 ("seeing you"). For two influential discussions of the rise

of the companionate marital ideal, see Lawrence Stone, *The Family, Sex and Marriage in England, 1500–1800* (New York, 1977), chap. 8; and Carl N. Degler, *At Odds: Women and the Family in America from the Revolution to the Present* (New York, 1980), chaps. 1–2. For a sensitive recent portrayal of the role of private sentiment in upper-class marriages in a Southern state in this period, see Jan Lewis, *The Pursuit of Happiness: Family and Values in Jefferson's Virginia* (Cambridge, England, 1983), chap. 5.

27. Dec. 31, 1821, FMW, VIII, 185 ("beings placed under us"); to MF, Apr. 20, 1841, ibid., 205 *("picturesque");* Dec. 23, 1818, FMW, VI, 41 ("cultivate my mind"); Feb. 15, 1819, ibid., 75 ("Lady F."); Dec. 26, 1818, ibid., 42 ("corner").

28. To TF, Feb. 19, 1819, FMW, VI, 78 ("indulges herself"); to TF, Feb. 23, 1824, FMW, VII, 113 ("'Pilot'").

29. To TF, Dec. 10, 1822, FMW, VII, 47 ("unprofitable"); to MF, Mar. 6, 1825, FMW, VIII, 198 *("first Cause");* to RFF, Feb. 25, 1838, ibid., 92 ("pillow"); May 5, 1841, ibid., 97 ("infidel like Hume"); to TF, Feb. 26, 1824, FMW, VII, 124 ("sectarian[s]"); Feb. 17, 1822, ibid., 12 ("enthusiasts"); Feb. 4, 1822, ibid., 7 ("fool").

30. Jan. 21, 1819, FMW, VI, 61 ("pride"); to ABF, Aug. 13, 1848, FMW, VIII, 24 ("lie passive"); to TF, Dec. 12, 1824, FMW, VII, 137 ("carefull dearest").

31. To MF, Sept. 13, 1824, FMW, VIII, 41 ("grieved for"); ERF to MF, July 25, [1843], FMW, XVII ("gentle spirit"); MCF to MF, Mar. 6, 1825, FMW, VIII, 198 ("nursing talents"); to RFF, July 9, 1848, FMW XVII, 25 ("agreeable companions"); RFF, "Memorial of Mrs. Margaret Fuller," 380 ("faults of others"); Jan. 20, 1824, FMW, VII, 99 ("*my* work"); quoted in MF, letter, n.d., *OM,* II, 123 ("flowers"); MF, letter, n.d., *OM,* II, 122 ("domesticated"). For the garden as the "consecrated terrain of the feminine sensibility" for mid–nineteenth-century popular American writers, see Douglas, *Feminization of American Culture,* 369–70, n104.

32. Nov. 15, 1820, FMW, VI, 88 ("constant care"); Dec. 31, 1823, FMW, VII, 90 ("not allowed"); to MCF, Feb. 25, 1824, FMW, IV, 131 ("doctrines of our parlor"); Jan. 20, 1824, FMW, VII, 99 ("instability of affection"). The classic study of the contradictory consequences of women's sense of their separate sphere in this period is Nancy F. Cott, *The Bonds of Womanhood: "Woman's Sphere" in New England, 1780–1835* (New Haven, 1977). For a recent cogent critique of the "separate spheres" concept in women's historiography, see Linda K. Kerber, "Separate Spheres, Female Worlds, Woman's Place: The Rhetoric of Women's History," *Journal of American History,* 75 (June 1988), 9–39.

33. Mar. 3, 1818, FMW, III, 52 *("speak out");* to TF, Jan. 26, 1818, FMW, VI, 9 *("enlarg[ing]");* Jan. 6, 1825, FMW, VII, 149 ("handsome ladies"); Jan. 12, 1818, FMW, VI, 5 ("fashionable Belles"); Jan. 21, 1819, ibid., 62 ("polite young man").

34. TF to MCF, Mar. 6, 1820, FMW, III, 135 ("orthographical inadvertances"); Jan. 5, 1823, FMW, VII, 58 ("*encouraging* epistle"); MCF to TF, Mar. 8, 1822, ibid., 19 ("high Mightiness"); Feb. 5, 1824, ibid., 105 ("literary member").

35. June 5, 1824, FMW, VIII, 187 (*"debating* the subject"); Jan. 26, 1819, FMW, VI, 64 ("look upon you").

36. MCF to TF, Jan. 10, 1823, FMW, VII, 60 ("promised land"); TF to MCF, Nov. 22, 1820, FMW, III, 189 ("posterity").

Chapter Two

1. Valuable guides to early nineteenth-century Cambridge's topography and architecture are the Cambridge Historical Commission's *Survey of Architectural History in Cambridge,* 5 vols. (Cambridge, Mass., 1965–1977), and *East Cambridge,* revised edition

by Susan E. Maycock (Cambridge, Mass., 1988); and Bainbridge Bunting, completed and edited by Margaret Henderson Floyd, *Harvard: An Architectural History* (Cambridge, Mass., 1985).

2. Thomas Wentworth Higginson, "Life in Cambridge Town," in Arthur Gilman, ed., *The Cambridge of Eighteen Hundred and Ninety-Six* (Cambridge, Mass., 1896), 40 ("picked class"). Although quaintly cloying, the best brief sources for social life in Cambridge in these years are James Russell Lowell, "Cambridge Thirty Years Ago," in *The Writings of James Russell Lowell,* 10 vols. (Boston, 1890), I, 74–92; Higginson, "Life in Cambridge Town"; idem, *Old Cambridge* (New York, 1899), chap. 1; and Charles Eliot Norton, "Reminiscences of Old Cambridge," *Cambridge Historical Society Publications,* v. 1 (Cambridge, Mass., 1906), 11–23. Valuable reminiscences of Cambridge society and culture may also be found scattered through the memoirs and biographies of the legion of prominent nineteenth-century intellectual and literary figures who grew up, went to school, or taught there. For a more critical contemporary view of antebellum Cambridge, see Harriet Martineau, *A Retrospect of Western Travel,* 3 vols. (London: Saunders and Otley, 1838), III, 25–55. For the town's institutional developments, see Lucius R. Paige, *History of Cambridge, Massachusetts, 1630–1877* (Boston, 1877); D. Hamilton Hurd, ed., *History of Middlesex County, Massachusetts,* 3 vols. (Philadelphia, 1890), I, 1–238; and Henry C. Binford, *The First Suburbs: Residential Communities on the Boston Periphery, 1815–1860* (Chicago, 1985). Three recent comparative studies of Boston elites in these years that shed much light on Boston-Cambridge social values are E. Digby Baltzell, *Puritan Boston and Quaker Philadelphia: Two Protestant Ethics and the Spirit of Class Authority and Leadership* (New York, 1979), chaps. 13–18; Frederic Cople Jaher, *The Urban Establishment: Upper Strata in Boston, New York, Charleston, Chicago, and Los Angeles* (Urbana, Ill., 1982), chap. 2; and William H. Pease and Jane H. Pease, *The Web of Progress: Private Values and Public Styles in Boston and Charleston, 1828–1843* (New York, 1985). Although somewhat one-sided, Ronald Story, *The Forging of an Aristocracy: Harvard & the Boston Upper Class, 1800–1870* (Middletown, Conn., 1980) is also useful.

3. Norton, "Reminiscences," 13 ("everybody's tradition").

4. Higginson, *Cheerful Yesterdays* (Boston, 1899), 3 ("No child"); quoted in Caroline Ticknor, *Dr. Holmes's Boston* (Boston, 1915), 9 ("Know old Cambridge?").

5. Statement of MF, quoted in Sarah Clarke to MF, May 14, 1847, FMW, X, 38 ("narrowness"); "Diary of Timothy Fuller," Sept. 13, 1803, FMW, II, 5 ("introduce business"); Lowell, "Cambridge," 70 ("struck by malaria"). For Cambridgeport, in addition to the works cited in note 2, see S. S. Simpson, *Two Hundred Years Ago; or, A Brief History of Cambridgeport and East Cambridge* (Boston, 1859).

6. *FR,* 8 ("unsavory"); MCF to MF, Jan. 3, 1825, FMW, VIII, 195 ("strong hold"); journal, [ca. Aug. 1838], FMW, IX, 264 ("very ugly"); to RFF, Aug. 5, 1842, *FL,* III, 81 ("merely gentle").

7. "Attempt by Margaret (Crane) Fuller to recall Margaret Fuller's childhood," [1850], FMW, VIII, 183 ("more of my thoughts"); to EF, Feb. 20, 1818, FMW, II, 51 ("your waggon"); Feb. 4, 1820, FMW, III, 107 ("dangers"); Mar. 6, 1820, ibid., 135 *("fair chance");* Feb. 19, 1819, FMW, VI, 78 ("good natured"); "Attempt by Margaret (Crane) Fuller to recall Margaret Fuller's childhood," [1850], FMW, 183 ("buoyant spirits"). For early American attitudes toward breast-feeding, see Catherine M. Scholten, *Childbearing in America: 1650–1850* (New York, 1985), 62, 71–73.

8. Jan. 16, 1814, FMW, II, 5 ("unusually forward"); "sketch of youth," *OM,* I, 13–14 ("coming home"); "sketch of youth," *OM,* I, 14 ("vast difference"). Because I consider Margaret Fuller's autobiographical sketch partly questionable, my use of it here and else-

where in this chapter deserves some explanation. Most of Fuller's biographers have treated this unfinished fragment as a literal rendering of her childhood. This is obviously wrong. The chronology is often mixed up, scenes seem to be partly fabricated, and her childhood consciousness is sometimes obviously distorted. Indeed, much of the sketch, which the *Memoirs* editor James Freeman Clarke rightly calls an "introductory chapter to an auto-biographical romance" (*OM*, I, 11), is perhaps better seen less as an autobiography than as a psychological and literary document of her adulthood. Yet Fuller clearly intended the sketch to be, at least on some level, an "autobiographic chapter" (RWE to MF, Nov. 5, 1843, *EL*, III, 222), and many of the facts it records are supported by her letters and jour-nals. Also, like other semiautobiographical pieces she composed, the sketch, if carefully used, is a potentially revealing symbolic guide or association to repressed childhood feel-ings that more socially conscious material such as letters do not reveal. At the same time, these latter documents are crucial in revealing equally important childhood thoughts and circumstances that Fuller overlooked or suppressed in her later recollections. In dealing with these problems of retrojection and association, I have been guided by both the tone of her remembrances—for example, how "literary" or "adult" they sound—and the degree to which they are supported or contradicted by the contemporary evidence in her and her family's letters and journals. Finally, her sketch, although painfully self-pitying, is also—like many of her self-probings—psychologically acute, and where her insights seem persuasive, I have sometimes drawn on them.

For guides to the biographical use of autobiographical sources, I have found useful Gor-don Allport, *The Use of Personal Documents in Psychological Science* (New York, 1942); Roy Pascal, *Design and Truth in Autobiography* (Cambridge, Mass., 1960); Sigmund Freud, "A Childhood Recollection from Dichtung und Warheit," in *Standard Edition of the Complete Works of Sigmund Freud*, XVII (London, 1955), 145–58; Emma N. Plank, "Memories of Early Childhood in Autobiographies," *Psychoanalytic Study of the Child*, v. 8 (1953), 381–93; and Erik Erikson, "On the Nature of Psycho-Historical Evidence: In Search of Gandhi," *Daedalus*, 97 (Summer 1968), 695–730. Recent sensible suggestions for the historical use of psychological evidence may be found in Peter Gay, *Freud for His-torians* (New York, 1985); and Geoffrey Cocks and Travis L. Crosby, eds., *Psycho/His-tory: Readings in the Method of Psychology, Psychoanalysis, and History* (New Haven, 1987).

9. Mar. 18, 1820, FMW, III, 144 ("much greater proficiency"); Edward Everett Hale, *A New England Boyhood* (1893; New York, 1927), 17 ("low type"); to ABF, Apr. 3, 1841, FMW, VIII ("great[ly]"); TF to MCF, Apr. 9, 1820, FMW, III, 162 ("literary pursuits"); *FW*, 27 ("companion"); "sketch of youth," *OM*, I, 14 ("heir"); Feb. 10, 1820, FMW, III, 113 ("effeminate & idle life"). Cf. Margaret Fuller's generally similar speculations about her father's motives in teaching her in *OM*, I, 14, 42. For Locke's thoughts on home instruction, see his *Thoughts on Education* in *The Educational Writings of John Locke*, ed. James L. Axtell (London, 1968), 148, 164–65. I have found considerable evidence of home tutoring of young children among Boston-Cambridge's intellectual Unitarian fam-ilies in the first quarter of the nineteenth century. I have also found that of Margaret Full-er's male and female friends who were tutored at home, most were taught at least in advanced subjects either by their father or by an older brother. Carl Kaestle and Maris A. Vinovskis (*Education and Social Change in Nineteenth-Century Massachusetts* [Cam-bridge, England, 1980], 48–49, 56–57) discuss the lingering practice of early home instruction in antebellum Massachusetts. For evidence indicating the prevalence of father-centered child-rearing advice in colonial America, see Philip J. Greven, ed., *Child-Rearing Concepts, 1628–1861: Historical Sources* (Itasca, Ill., 1973), 42–45, 72–73; and

John Demos, *Past, Present, and Personal: The Family and the Life Course in American History* (New York, 1986), chap. 3. For the decline of that tradition and the rise of the "moral mother" ideal—variously republican, evangelical, and Romantic—see Linda K. Kerber, *Women of the Republic: Intellect & Ideology in Revolutionary America* (Chapel Hill, 1980), chap. 9; Ruth H. Bloch, "American Feminine Ideals in Transition: The Rise of the Moral Mother, 1785–1815," *Feminist Studies,* 4 (June 1978), 101–28; and Anne L. Kuhn, *The Mother's Role in Childhood Education: New England Concepts, 1830–1860* (New Haven 1947).

10. Jan. 1802, FMW II, 4 ("disgusting"); Jan. 22, 1820, FMW, III, 94 ("very sensible"); to EK, Feb. 16, 1835, TF, "Letter Book," FMW, Box 3 ("My notions"). Mason Wade made the claim—which has been frequently repeated in subsequent writings on Fuller—that Timothy Fuller "had hoped that his first child would be a son" and he therefore only raised Margaret as one because he had none until his third child (*Margaret Fuller: Whetstone of Genius* [New York, 1940]). There is no evidence for these assertions. On the contrary, as these quotations show, it was at least in part *because* Margaret was a girl that he was so vitally interested in her education. For arguments and efforts in favor of improving female education after the Revolution, see Janet Wilson James, *Changing Ideas about Women in the United States, 1776–1825* (1954; New York, 1984), chap. 4; Mary Beth Norton, *Liberty's Daughters: The Revolutionary Experience of American Women, 1750–1800* (Boston, 1980), chap. 9; and Kerber, *Women of the Republic,* chap. 7. An excellent discussion of the contributions of Enlightenment and republican ideological changes to the transformation of notions about female status and intellect in the early Republic may be found in Ruth H. Bloch, "The Gendered Meanings of Virtue in Revolutionary America," *Signs: Journal of Women in Culture and Society,* 13 (Autumn 1987), 37–58.

11. "Attempt by Margaret (Crane) Fuller to recall Margaret Fuller's childhood," [1850], FMW, VIII, 183 ("her superior intelligence"); Apr. 16, 1814, FMW, III, 7 ("learns to read"); Jan. 1, 1815, FMW, II, 8 ("any common book"); to EK, Feb. 16, 1835, TF, "Letter Book," FMW, Box 3 *("children's books").*

12. Journal, [ca. early Mar. 1834], FMW, Box A ("attacks of delirium"); "sketch of youth," *OM,* I, 16 ("dripped with blood"); FHH, quoted in Thomas Wentworth Higginson, Notes, [188–?], OC, 22 ("habit of the time"); *HO,* 22 ("same way"); quoted in Thomas Wentworth Higginson, Notes, [188–?], OC, 22 ("half the body"). Margaret Fuller discusses her father's obsession with "the premature development of [her] mental powers" and indicates her agreement with the contrary "warnings of physiologists" of her day in journal, [ca. early Mar. 1834], FMW, Box A; and "sketch of youth," *OM,* I, 14–15. For contemporaries' recollections of the predilection for "precocious teaching" in Boston-Cambridge Unitarian professional circles in this period, see Higginson, *Old Cambridge,* 25–26; idem, *Cheerful Yesterdays,* 13–16; and Hale, *New England Boyhood,* 20–21. For the popular, Romantic-influenced reaction against "intellectual precocity" in the medical and educational literature of the 1830s and 1840s, see Kuhn, *Mother's Role,* chap. 5; Kaestle and Vinovskis, *Education and Social Change,* chap. 3; and Joseph F. Kett, *Rites of Passage: Adolescence in America, 1790 to the Present* (New York, 1977), 133–43. Morison, *Three Centuries of Harvard,* 183–84, discusses trends in Harvard's entering-age requirements.

13. "Sketch of youth," *OM,* I, 12, 14–15 ("feelings . . . on me"). Of course, several of Margaret Fuller's symptoms, especially sleepwalking and hallucinations, are classic symptoms of hysteria, which, in Freudian literature, are often linked to father fixations. In the same vein, some of the dream symbols that she recalled from her nightmares, including detached eyes pressing on her and twigs and rocks that "streamed blood on me" (ibid.)

could be interpreted, in Freudian parlance, as phallic symbols. But lacking extensive associations on Fuller's part that would link the symbols to the father object, the connection remains only an abstract speculation. For an extensive analysis of a case of hysteria and its relation to a father fixation in an adolescent girl, see Sigmund Freud, *Fragment of an Analysis of a Case of Hysteria* (1905), in *Standard Edition,* VII (London, 1961), 3–122.

14. "Sketch of youth," *OM,* I, 15 ("nervous affections"); n.d., quoted in *OM,* I, 228 ("self-tormentor"); n.d., "ON," 485 ("when I am ill"); MF, journal, [ca. early Mar. 1834], FMW, Box A ("morbid sensibility"); "sketch of youth," *OM,* I, 16 ("glooms and terrors").

15. FMW, V, 1 ("with diligence"); ibid., 2 ("quite trifling employment").

16. TF to MCF, Dec. 29, 1819, FMW, V, 3 *("good sense");* Jan. 20, 1818, ibid., 2 ("bear pain"); Dec. 29, 1819, ibid., 3 ("plain & easy"); Jan. 4, 1818, ibid., 1 ("trace my route"); Jan. 25, 1820, ibid., 5 ("easily excel me"). Perry Miller's statement—although more bombastic than most—echoes a commonly found view of Timothy Fuller's child-rearing practices: "In a manner typical of that time in New England, [Margaret's] father, Timothy Fuller, dominated the family with a tyrannical masculinity that he thought was affection, but that actually amounted to what must be called persecution, or even sadism." Miller, *Margaret Fuller,* x. Margaret Fuller's brother Richard gives a portrait of Timothy Fuller as an affectionate but rationalistically authoritative father in *FR,* 9–23, which may be usefully compared with Margaret Fuller's recollections in her "sketch of youth." For evidence of differing evangelical and liberal Protestant concepts of child-rearing in the eighteenth and early nineteenth centuries, see Greven, ed., *Child-Rearing Concepts;* and idem, *The Protestant Temperament: Patterns of Child Rearing, Religious Experience, and the Self in Early America* (New York, 1977). Most discussions of child-rearing ideas in the postcolonial period have slighted early Enlightenment and republican currents in favor of later "Romantic" influences in the antebellum period. Two exceptions that I have found helpful are Daniel Calhoun, *The Intelligence of a People* (Princeton, 1973), chap. 3; and Peter Gragg Slater, *Children in the New England Mind: In Death and in Life* (Hamden, Conn., 1977), chap. 4. A valuable portrait of English republican Enlightenment views of childhood may be found in Isaac Kramnick, *Republicanism and Bourgeois Radicalism: Political Ideology in Late Eighteenth-Century England and America* (Ithaca, 1990), chap. 4. Two older but still useful studies of child-rearing ideas in antebellum America are Robert Sunley, "Early Nineteenth-Century American Literature on Child Rearing," in Margaret Mead and Martha Wolfenstein, eds., *Childhood in Contemporary Cultures* (Chicago, 1955), chap. 9; and Bernard Wishy, *The Child and the Republic: The Dawn of Modern American Child Nurture* (Philadelphia, 1968). See also Degler, *At Odds,* chaps. 4–5.

17. "Sketch of youth," *OM,* I, 17 ("must not speak"); to ABF, Dec. 15, 1836, FMW, VIII, 15 *("order");* "Attempt by Margaret (Crane) Fuller to recall Margaret Fuller's childhood," [1850], ibid., 183 ("extreme accuracy"); Dec. 30, 1823, FMW, IV, 101 *("double portion");* Feb. 22, 1820, FMW, V, 5 ("carelessness").

18. Dec. 29, 1819, FMW, V, 3 *("without any date");* Jan. 25, 1820, ibid., 5 ("proper sentiments"); to EK, Apr. 19, 1818, FMW, II, 24 *("precocious* daughter"); to MCF, Dec. 24, 1819, FMW, III, 70 ("well written"); Feb. 9, 1820, ibid., 112 ("quite entertaining"); Feb. 22, 1820, FMW, V, 5 ("so many corrections"); Jan. 18, 1818, FMW, III, 21 ("This kiss"); Dec. 11, 1820, ibid., 199 ("My remonstrances").

19. Mar. 5, 1818, FMW, VI, 26 ("shed tears"); Jan. 30, 1819, ibid., 68 ("eye brightened"); Jan. 12, 1818, ibid., 5 ("all you write of her"); Jan. 13, 1818, *FL,* I, 81 ("Valpy's Chronology"); Feb. 24, 1818, ibid., 82 ("not write"); Mar. 5, 1818, ibid., 83 ("disappointed").

20. Dec. 16, 1818, *FL,* I, 84 ("spies"); Jan. 8, 1819, ibid., 86 ("your maxim").

21. "Sketch of youth," *OM,* I, 17–18 ("His influence"); journal, [ca. Fall 1839], FMW, Box A ("masculine"). For a cogent discussion of the problem of "true" and "false" selves by the psychoanalyst who has made the subject an important center of his work, see D. W. Winnicott, "Ego Distortion in Terms of True and False Self," in his *The Maturational Processes and the Facilitating Environment* (London, 1965), 140–52. A related line of argument is developed by another important "self-psychoanalyst" in Heinz Kohut, *The Analysis of the Self: A Systematic Approach to the Psychoanalytic Treatment of Narcissistic Personality Disorders* (New York, 1971); and idem, "A Note on Female Sexuality," in his *The Search for the Self: Selected Writings of Heinz Kohut, 1950–1978,* 2 vols. (New York, 1978), II, 783–92.

22. MF, "Lillo," [ca. early 1840s], FMW, Box A ("Martinet"); journal, 1844, quoted in *HO,* 31 ("incedo regina"); to RFF, May 12, 1842, *FL,* III, 64 ("power of attention"); Jan. 6, [1842], ibid., 33 ("no 'Word-Hero'"); *FW,* 27–28 ("self-dependence").

23. To WHC, Oct. 28, 1840, *FL,* II, 175–76 ("ideal Father"); to JN, July 22, 1845, *FL,* IV, 137 ("childishly").

24. Dec. 17, 1820, FMW, VI, 102 ("*tender* mother"); Oct. 9, 1824, FMW, VIII, 191 ("Almost all children").

25. [1810], FMW, VI, 1 ("mind like yours"); Dec. 28, 1823, FMW, IV, 100 ("absent"); Nov. 25, 1820, FMW, VI, 92 ("'hard for me'"); Feb. 15, 1819, ibid., 74 ("my neglect"); Feb. 17, 1818, ibid., 18 ("any sin"); Feb. 26, 1818, FMW, III, 48 ("when I get home"); Dec. 19, 1820, FMW, VI, 103 ("uncommon *child*"); Apr. 5, 1820, FMW, III, 159 ("quite a stranger").

26. Apr. 17, 1820, *FL,* I, 99 ("As I promised"); Dec. 2, 1821, ibid., 114 ("not as interesting to you"); Dec. 9, 1821, *FL,* I, 115 ("his secretary").

27. [Ca. Aug. 1838], FMW, IX, 264 ("loved to gaze").

28. [Ca. May 1833], FMW, Box 4 ("mother's death"); journal, [ca. early 1840s], FMW, Box A ("girlish"). For Margaret Fuller's other autobiographically allusive fictional sketch, in which the protagonist appears as a boy, see "Lillo," [ca. early 1840s], FMW, Box A. For an account of one of her mother-death dreams a few days after she accepted Horace Greeley's offer to move to New York and write for the *Tribune,* see her journal entry, Sept. 25, 1844, "FJ44-1," 119. In my understanding of Margaret Fuller's childhood psychology—and particularly her relationship with her mother—I have been influenced by the large and often brilliant recent literature in feminist-oriented psychoanalysis. Among the studies I have found most helpful are Juliet Mitchell, *Psychoanalysis and Feminism: Freud, Reich, Laing and Women* (New York, 1974); Dorothy Dinnerstein, *The Mermaid and the Minotaur: Sexual Arrangements and Human Malaise* (New York, 1976); Nancy Chodorow, *The Reproduction of Mothering: Psychoanalysis and the Sociology of Gender* (Berkeley, 1978); and Jessica Benjamin, *The Bonds of Love: Psychoanalysis and the Problem of Domination* (New York, 1988). Classic texts and insightful critiques of them are conveniently collected in Jean Strouse, ed., *Women and Analysis: Dialogues on Psychoanalytic Views of Femininity* (1974; Boston, 1985). For good, recent collections by, respectively, a contemporary psychoanalytic theorist and two groups of literary scholars, see Janine Chasseguet-Smirgel, ed., *Female Sexuality* (Ann Arbor, 1970); Shirley Nelson Garner, Claire Kahane, and Madelon Sprengnether, eds., *The (M)other Tongue: Essays on Feminist Psychoanalytic Interpretation* (Ithaca, 1985); and Richard Feldstein and Judith Roof, eds., *Feminism and Psychoanalysis* (Ithaca, 1989).

29. Feb. 7, 1847, FMW, VIII, 216 ("more to you"); "Attempt by Margaret (Crane) Fuller to recall Margaret Fuller's childhood," ibid., 183 ("constant exercise"); journal, [ca. 1834], FMW, Box A ("fault"); to WHC, Dec. 17, 1849, *FL,* V, 300 ("genuinely"); n.d.,

OM, II, 121–22 ("grateful"); to WEC2, [Oct. 3, 1841], *FL,* II, 239 ("lay nun"); RFF, "Memorial of Mrs. Margaret Fuller," 376 ("our ideal sentiment").

30. [Ca. May 1833], FMW, Box 4 ("divine direction"); MF to JN, [July] 22, 1845, *FL,* IV, 137 ("gentleness"); MF to JFC, Aug. 14, 1845, FP ("genero[sity]"); journal, [ca. Aug. 1838], FMW, IX, 264 ("viewless air").

31. To MCF, [ca. Nov. 1819], FMW, II, 40 ("mild virtues"); TF to MCF, Dec. 31, 1819, FMW, III, 75 ("national prejudices"); TF to MCF, Feb. 25, 1820, ibid., 126 ("accomplishments"); to MCF, July 20, 1818, FMW, II, 25 ("what my dear Margaret is"). Apart from Margaret Fuller's letters and recollections, all that is known of Ellen Kilshaw is contained in her correspondence and the references to her in FMW.

32. To MCF, Jan. 3, [1820], FMW, III, 77 ("little friend Sarah Margaret"); to MCF, Oct. 27, 1818, FMW, II, 26 ("men . . . to ladies"); June 22, 1819, ibid., 37 ("politics"); Nov. 15, 1820, ibid., 55 ("Shall I confess").

33. "Sketch of youth," *OM,* I, 33 ("intoxicat[ed]"); to TF, Jan. 16, 1820, *FL,* I, 94 ("misfortunes"); TF to MCF, Feb. 21, 1824, FMW, IV, 129 ("poor Ellen"); EK to MCF, July 24, 1819, FMW, II, 38 ("mortification"). Fuller's language in her autobiographical sketch clearly reflected her adult preoccupation with the idea of female friendship. But the connection also worked the other way: her unconventional attraction to that ritual was at least partly rooted in her past experiences, of which her friendship with Ellen Kilshaw was one.

34. MCF to TF, Dec. 27, 1822, FMW, VII, 54 ("wink[ed] at"); MCF to TF, Dec. 18, 1822, ibid., 50 ("saucy"); MCF to TF, Jan. 15, 1821, FMW, VI, 115 ("ultra Republican principles"); MCF to TF, Jan. 2, 1823, FMW, VII, 57 *("slave").*

35. Feb. 4, 1821, FMW, VI, 124 *("rock steadily");* Apr. 17, 1820, *FL,* I, 99 ("punish him"); Mar. 29, 1822, ibid., 121 ("stupid child"). The best sources for the lives of Margaret's older brothers are FMW and *FL.*

36. Oct. 1, 1823, FMW, II, 11 ("reluctant"); to MCF, Jan. 6, 1824, FMW, IV, 106 ("unsatisfactory"); Dec. 11, 1819, FMW, III, 60 ("noise"); Dec. 21, 1822, FMW, IV, 47 ("by no means"); TF to MCF, Jan. 9, 1818, FMW, III, 19 ("pretty"); Dec. 28, 1823, FMW, IV, 100 (*"commend* him").

37. To RFF, Aug. 11, 1842, *FL,* III, 86 ("indulgent"); Joseph Palmer, obituary notice, *Boston Daily Advertiser,* quoted in Fuller, *Historical Notices,* 12 ("softening of the brain"); to JFC, Aug. 17, 1833, FP ("no ambition"); [May 15, 1844], OC, 99 ("poor brother"); MF to RFF, Aug. 11, 1842, *FL,* III, 86 ("nurture").

38. For reminiscences of the Port School, see Simpson, *Two Hundred Years Ago,* 105–6; Oliver Wendell Holmes, "Remarks made at a meeting of the Massachusetts Historical Society, September, 1865," *Proceedings of the Massachusetts Historical Society,* v. 8, 1864–1865 (Boston, 1866), 456–57; and idem, "Cinders from the Ashes," in *The Writings of Oliver Wendell Holmes,* 14 vols. (Cambridge, Mass., 1891–1892), VIII, 240–43.

39. Dec. 25, 1819, *FL,* I, 91 ("corrections"); Holmes, "Cinders from the Ashes," 242–43 ("'smart'"). For the extensive use of physical punishment by teachers at Boston Latin in this period, see Pauline Holmes, *A Tercentenary History of the Boston Public Latin School, 1635–1935* (Cambridge, Mass., 1935), 82–86.

40. Feb. 3, 1820, *FL,* I, 96 ("Virgil"); Holmes, "Cinders from the Ashes," 241 ("revelation"); [ca. 1820], *FL,* I, 92 ("victim"); ibid., 101–2 ("poor Mary").

41. "Sketch of youth," *OM,* I, 18–22 ("rock").

42. Dec. 8, 1822, FMW, VII, 46 ("neglect"); to JFC, Feb. 1, 1835, FP ("Greek history"); *DM,* 162 ("naked"). On the classical reading of revolutionary and early republican intellectuals, see May, *Enlightenment in America,* 292.

43. Dec. 25, 1819, *FL*, I, 91 ("intelligent sensible book").

44. Jan. 16, 1820, *FL*, I, 94–95 ("I am not romantic").

45. Jan. 27, 1820, FMW, III, 99 ("What whim"); Jan. 25, 1820, FMW, V, 5 (*"higher* order").

46. Mar. 11, 1822, FMW, VII, 21 ("ridiculous"); Apr. 13, 1820, FMW, V, 6 ("true taste"). Useful information about the debate over novels and novel reading in the early Republic may be found in Herbert Ross Brown, *The Sentimental Novel in America, 1789–1860* (New York, 1940). For the critical and philosophical background of the controversy, see William Charvat, *The Origins of American Critical Thought, 1810–1835* (Philadelphia, 1936), chap. 7; and Terence Martin, *The Instructed Vision: Scottish Common Sense Philosophy and the Origins of American Fiction* (Bloomington, Ind., 1961). For a recent challenging view of early American novel-reading that emphasizes gender conflict, see Cathy N. Davidson, *Revolution and the Word: The Rise of the Novel in America* (New York, 1986), chaps. 3–4, 6. Linda Kerber includes a balanced and perceptive discussion of the subject in her *Women of the Republic*, 237–46. See also James, *Changing Ideas*, chap. 5.

47. Feb. 22, 1820, FMW, V, 5 *("any stile");* to TF, Mar. 20, 1820, *FL*, I, 98 ("delighted me"); "Diary of Timothy Fuller," Mar. 27, 1820, FMW, III, 153 ("stile"); "sketch of youth," *OM*, I, 14 ("Queen Anne's man"); Abraham W. Fuller to Sarah Williams Fuller, June 13, 1820, FMW, V, 76 ("modern novels"); journal, [ca. Nov. 1835], FMW, Box A ("sallies").

48. "Sketch of youth," *OM*, I, 25, 30–31 ("Smollett"). For the increasing censorship of selections of literature for children after 1820, see Ruth Miller Elson, *Guardians of Tradition: American Schoolbooks of the Nineteenth Century* (Lincoln, Nebr., 1964), 235–37.

49. "Sketch of youth," *OM*, I, 22, 25, 30–32 ("wide invention").

50. Jan. 5, 1820, FMW, III, 79 ("needle work"); TF to MCF, Mar. 12, 1820, ibid., 139 ("pretty girls"); TF to MCF, Mar. 16, 1820, ibid., 142 ("eyes"); Jan. 12, 1820, ibid., 86 ("Greek"); Jan. 22, 1820, ibid., 94 *("solid books");* Apr. 13, 1820, FMW, V, 6 ("mediocrity"); Dec. 3, 1820, ibid., 7 (*"All* accomplishments").

51. Nov. 20, 1819, *FL*, I, 88 ("queen"); Dec. 17, 1820, FMW, VI, 102 *("desponding");* ibid., enclosure ("SORROW"); [ca. Winter 1820–1821], FMW, IX, 9 ("Love your enemies").

52. Feb. 22, 1821, FMW, IV, 27 ("dreamed"); Nov. 23, 1820, FMW, VI, 91 ("weary of it"); Dec. 24, 1820, ibid., 105 ("no progress"); quoted in Jan. 9, 1821, ibid., 112 ("my beautiful box"); Jan. 15, 1821, *FL*, I, 109 ("witty"); Nov. 22, 1820, ibid., 104 ("bad pen"); Jan. 5, 1821, ibid., 107 ("wishes").

53. Dec. 3, 1820, FMW, V, 7 ("better you write"); to MCF, Nov. 11, 1820, FMW, III, 183 ("whip"); to MCF, Feb. 22, 1820, ibid., 125 ("harangue[s]"); to MCF, Feb. 26, 1820, ibid., 129 ("maniack"); Nov. 22, 1820, *FL*, I, 104 ("very keen"); Dec. 4, 1820, ibid., 105–6 ("mischivous").

54. Dec. 11, 1820, FMW, III, 199 ("'silly'"); TF to MF, Nov. 13, 1824, FMW, V, 37 ("red hot shot"); Dec. 15, 1819, FMW, III, 62 ("forgot"); MCF to TF, Jan. 9, 1821, FMW, VI, 112 ("thousand castles"); TF to MCF, Apr. 7, 1820, FMW, III, 160 ("flattering"); TF to MCF, Dec. 25, 1820, ibid., 206 ("commendations").

55. To TF, Jan. 20, 1821, FMW, VI, 117 *("well bred");* Jan. 5, 1821, *FL*, I, 108 ("two cents"); Jan. 20, 1821, FMW, VI, 117 (*"wisely* observed"); Jan. 27, 1821, FMW, IV, 14 ("preferable"); Jan. 14, 1821, ibid., 7 ("musick"). For a reminiscence of Mrs. McKeige's school, see Ellen Tucker Emerson, *The Life of Lidian Jackson Emerson*, ed. Dolores Bird Carpenter (Boston, 1980), 26–29.

Chapter Three

1. Quoted in Edward H. Hall, "Reminiscences of Dr. John Park," *Proceedings of the American Antiquarian Society,* v. 7 (Worcester, Mass., 1892), 87 ("I do use medals"); quoted in ibid., 89 ("rhapsodical intimations"). There is no comprehensive modern treatment of the antebellum private secondary school movement. But valuable overviews may be found in Lawrence A. Cremin, *American Education: The National Experience, 1783–1876* (New York, 1981); Barbara Miller Solomon, *In the Company of Educated Women: A History of Women and Higher Education in America* (New Haven, 1985), chap. 2; and Keith Melder, "Mask of Oppression: The Female Seminary Movement in the United States," *New York History,* 55 (July 1974), 261–79. For information, see also Thomas Woody, *A History of Women's Education in the United States,* 2 vols. (1929; New York, 1966), I, 329–459; Harriet W. Marr, *The New England Academies Founded Before 1826* (New York, 1959); and Theodore R. Sizer, ed., *The Age of Academies* (New York, 1964). The best source for the opinions and personality of John Park is his Journal, 5 vols., MB. For Park and his school, see Justin Winsor, ed., *The Memorial History of Boston,* 4 vols. (Boston, 1881), IV, 343–44; and Hall, "Reminiscences," 69–93.

2. To TF, Dec. 22, 1822, *FL,* I, 122 ("kind and sweet"); Dec. 19, 1822, FMW, VII, 51 ("expatiate upon"); Jan. 25, 1821, *FL,* I, 110–11 ("fatiguing"); ibid., 113–14 ("not cried once").

3. To TF, Jan. 5, 1821, *FL,* I, 107 ("acquaintance"); *FL,* I, 115–16 ("sermon"); ibid., 118 ("thirteen times").

4. *FL,* I, 117 ("all sisters").

5. To TF, Mar. 11, 1822, FMW, VII, 21 ("trundle bed"); MCF to TF, Feb. 24, 1822, ibid., 14 ("tears"); MCF to TF, Mar. 11, 1822, ibid., 21 ("domestick regulations").

6. Quoted in "ON," 482 ("wonderful child"); *OM,* II, 5 ("prodigy"); statement, *OM,* I, 92–93 ("country girl").

7. *FL,* I, 119 ("splendour"); Mar. 22, 1822, ibid., 120 ("hoarse"); to TF, Mar. 20, 1822, FMW, VII, 25 ("highly endowed").

8. FMW, VII, 36 ("*not* well"); Apr. 21, 1822, ibid., 38 ("restore her health"); to TF, Mar. 11, 1822, ibid., 21 ("vexatious").

9. MF to TF, Dec. 22, 1822, *FL,* I, 121 ("address"); quoted in MCF to TF, Dec. 22, 1822, FMW, VII, 52 ("'more than she could remember'").

10. *FL,* I, 122 ("disappointed"); ibid., 124 ("weak").

11. TF to MF, Mar. 3, 1822, FMW, V, 10 *("useful books");* MF to TF, Dec. 22, 1822, *FL,* I, 121 ("regret"); Dec. 15, 1822, FMW, V, 11 ("soon part").

12. June 12, 1824, FMW, V, 22 ("kept assunder"); MCF to TF, Feb. 26, 1824, FMW, VII, 124 ("genteel"); TF to MCF, Dec. 22, 1823, FMW, IV, 97 ("galas"); to TF, Nov. 20, 1820, FMW, VI, 90 *("patrician").* For some later contemporary claims—sharply disputed by Frederic Henry Hedge—that the Fullers were socially ostracized in Cambridge, see Thomas Wentworth Higginson, Notes, [188–?], OC, 22.

13. Dec. 22, 1822, *FL,* I, 122 ("expense"); Jan. 12, 1823, ibid., 125 ("rude"); quoted in Thomas Wentworth Higginson, Notes, [188–?], OC, 22 ("offence"); Jan. 22, 1823, FMW, IV, 63 ("promised account"); TF to MCF, Jan. 28, 1823, ibid., 66 ("pleasant"); to TF, Jan. 30, 1823, *FL,* I, 127 ("agreeable"); MCF to TF, Jan. 31, 1823, FMW, VII, 68 ("disappointed"); MCF to TF, Jan. 19, 1823, ibid., 63 ("relieved"); TF to MCF, Jan. 26, 1823, FMW, IV, 65 *("well over").*

14. Quoted in Thomas Wentworth Higginson, Notes, [188–?], OC, 22 ("older set"); Jan. 30, 1823, *FL,* I, 127 ("cotillon party").

15. To Sarah W. Fuller, Nov. 1, 1820, *FL,* I, 103 ("tall girl"); quoted in *OM,* I, 91

("robust"); TF to MCF, Mar. 2, 1824, FMW, IV, 134 ("eruption"); journal, [ca. early Mar. 1834], FMW, Box A ("bright and ugly"); quoted in Thomas Wentworth Higginson, Notes, [188–?], OC, 22 ("amazed"); Jan. 9, 1821, FMW, VI, 112 ("flattering"). For age-mixing in this period, see John Demos, "The Rise and Fall of Adolescence," in his *Past, Present, and Personal,* 100–101. For European travelers' perceptions of American young people's "presumptuousness," see William Bridges, "Family Patterns and Social Values in America, 1825–75," *American Quarterly,* 17 (Spring 1965), 5–6.

16. Quoted in *OM,* I, 92 ("unpopular"); Dec. 15, 1822, FMW, VII, 49 ("Lady"); to MCF, Dec. 21, 1822, FMW, IV, 47 ("with the ferule"); Jan. 12, 1823, *FL,* I, 126 ("modish"); Jan. 19, 1823, FMW, V, 12 ("Your account").

17. Mar. 24, 1824, FMW, VII, 121 ("too independent"); to MCF, Jan. 10, 1821, FMW, IV, 5 ("dancing"); ibid. ("no *small* child"); Dec. 14, 1823, ibid., 93 ("cheapen her value"); Feb. 14, 1824, ibid., 125 ("too discreet").

18. *HO,* 28–29 ("father decided"). From Higginson's notes that he wrote when he was researching his biography of Margaret Fuller, it would seem that his main source for his assertion about her father's social domination was Hedge. "Father wd. constantly interfere 'Sarah Margaret, do not &c &c.'" Notes, [188–?], OC.

19. MCF to TF, Apr. 1, 1822, FMW, VII, 30 *("respectablilty"); *MCF to MF, Dec. 31, 1821, FMW, VIII, 185 ("deportment").

20. MCF to TF, Feb. 16, 1823, FMW, VII, 74 *("mournful"); *Jan. 20, 1824, ibid., 99 ("opinionative"); Dec. 29, 1823, ibid., 89 ("repulsive"); Mar. 1, 1822, FMW, VIII, 186 ("father's *views*").

21. "Adolescence and Youth in Nineteenth-Century America," *Journal of Interdisciplinary History,* 2 (Autumn 1971), 296 ("sexual maturity"). For the conventional prescriptive literature about women in the antebellum period, see Barbara Welter, "The Cult of True Womanhood: 1820–1860," reprinted in her *Dimity Convictions: The American Woman in the Nineteenth Century* (Athens, Ohio, 1976), 21–41. Tocqueville's comments on American girlhood may be found in his *Democracy in America,* ed. Phillips Bradley, 2 vols. (New York, 1945), II, 201–3. The best discussion of adolescence in this period is Kett, *Rites of Passage,* chaps. 1–5. See also the author's "Adolescence and Youth," 283–98, and the suggestive analysis in Demos, *Past, Present, and Personal,* 99–104. There is no comprehensive study of nineteenth-century American girlhood, but see the useful essay by Barbara Welter, "Coming of Age in America: The Girl in the Nineteenth Century," in her *Dimity Convictions,* 3–20.

22. Jan. 19, 1824, FMW, IV, 112 ("four *daughters*"); Jan. 30, 1820, FMW, III, 102 ("elopement").

23. Sept. 30, 1803, FMW, II, 5 ("docility"); Feb. 21, 1821, ibid., 10 (*"nice* delicacy").

24. To MCF, Dec. 8, 1823, FMW, IV, 90 ("Greek?"); Jan. 22, 1822, FMW, V, 9 ("manners"); Feb. 2, 1824, FMW, IV, 119 ("musick"); Dec. 22, 1823, ibid., 97 *("employments"); *Dec. 12, 1823, ibid., 92 *("neatness").*

25. Joel Myerson, "Caroline Dall's Reminiscences of Margaret Fuller," *Harvard Library Bulletin,* 22 (Oct. 1974), 421 ("training").

26. *FL,* I, 130 ("progress").

27. Reprinted in Samuel Abbott Green, *Groton Historical Series* (Groton, Mass., 1893), v. 3, no. 9, p. 405 ("Orthography"). Information on Susan Prescott and her school is scanty, but see Green, *Groton Historical Series,* v. 1, no. 1, p. 5; no. 5, pp. 8–11; and no. 6, p. 26. For background on antebellum female seminaries and male academies, see the works cited in note 1 of this chapter. In developing my notion of private academies and seminaries as quasi-custodial institutions enveloped in a semiagrarian, familial, and

bureaucratic ideology, I have been influenced by David J. Rothman's *The Discovery of the Asylum: Social Order and Disorder in the New Republic* (Boston, 1971).

28. *Columbian Centinel* (Boston), Apr. 10, 1824, reprinted in Green, *Groton Historical Series*, v. 3, no. 9, p. 405 ("manners").

29. FMW, V, 13 ("rather incline"); FMW, IV, 134 ("painful thing"); ibid., VII, 118 ("least encouragement"). For the "Great Rebellion of 1823," see Samuel Eliot Morison, *Three Centuries of Harvard*, 230–31; and Bernard Bailyn, "Why Kirkland Failed," in Bernard Bailyn et al., *Glimpses of the Harvard Past* (Cambridge, Mass., 1986), 27–29.

30. Apr. 10, 1824, FMW, VII, 130 *("cruel"):* FMW, V, 13 ("feminine discipline").

31. *FL,* I, 132–33 ("very much prefer").

32. *FL,* I, 135 ("not see you"); Apr. 5, 1824, FMW, II, 13 ("assuring her"); FMW, V, 15 ("country lady").

33. FMW, VII, 130 ("affectionate letter"); *FL,* I, 136–37 ("heart at ease"); FMW, V, 16 ("go 'among strangers'").

34. *FL,* I, 138–39 ("contented"); n.d., *OM,* I, 132 ("memory").

35. FMW, V, 18 ("cheerful tone"); June 1, 1824, ibid., 19 ("tell me").

36. June 5, 1824, FMW, VIII, 187 ("father omitted"); Oct. 9, 1824, ibid., 191 ("excellent advice"); Sept. 13, 1824, ibid., 189 ("certain individual"); Sept. 26, 1824, ibid., 190 ("Divine truths").

37. June 7, 1824, FMW, V, 20 ("news").

38. TF to MF, Dec. 22, 1824, FMW, V, 39 ("entertaining"); June 21, 1824, ibid., 23 ("charitable feelings"); Oct. 8, 1824, ibid., 33 ("measured").

39. Dec. 20, 1824, *FL,* I, 144 ("pleasure"); Jan. 31, 1825, ibid., 147 ("Stoical tone"); Jan. 5, 1825, ibid., 146 ("beloved study"); Jan. 13, 1825, FMW, V, 42 (*"instrument* of study").

40. FMW, VII, 162 ("playful"); FMW, V, 44 *("slovenliness"); FL,* I, 148–49 (*"men* of *business").*

41. To MCF, Apr. 12, 1824, FMW, IV, 154 ("indispensable"); May 25, 1824, FMW, V, 18 ("advisor . . . *friend");* July 7, 1824, ibid., 26 ("deficiencies"); Sept. 29, 1824, *FL,* I, 143 ("gold"); Jan. 5, 1825, ibid., 146 ("adopted daughter"); TF to MCF, Apr. 12, 1824, FMW, IV, 154 ("impression"); to MF, June 26, 1824, FMW, V, 25 ("flattering"); quoted in Green, *Groton Historical Series,* v. 1, no. 1, p. 7 ("inspired").

42. *FSL,* 83 ("too early stimulated"). For Margaret Fuller's suggestion that the Mariana character was at least partly autobiographical, see July 25, 1844, "FJ44-1," 87; and *FL,* 198–99.

43. *FSL,* 83, 85, 92–93 ("ruled masterly").

44. "Manhood of Goethe," n.d., FMW, Box A ("absolute sway"); Caroline H. Dall to Thomas Wentworth Higginson, May 12, 1884, OC, 211 ("childish error"); Jan. 1830, *FL,* I, 160 ("painful recollections"). For Margaret's mother's remembrance of Margaret's childhood acting, see JFC, "Journal of the Understanding," Oct. 10, 1832, JFC Papers, MH.

45. To MCF, Apr. 12, 1824, FMW, IV, 154 ("modest"); to MF, Feb. 12, 1824, FMW, V, 14 *("utmost aid");* Dec. 3, 1824, FMW, VII, 135 ("lonely"); Dec. 22, 1824, FMW, V, 39 ("remain at home").

Chapter Four

1. For Harvard in these years, in addition to the sources cited in Chap. 2, note 2, see Andrew P. Peabody, *Harvard Reminiscences* (Boston, 1888); Morison, *Three Centuries of Harvard,* chaps. 9–10; and Bailyn, "Why Kirkland Failed," 19–44.

2. For a discussion of the international character of post-Napoleonic European literary life, see Heinrich von Treitschke, *History of Germany in the Nineteenth Century,* 7 vols. (New York and London, 1915–1919), II, chap. 3. For heightened confidence in American literary prospects after 1815, see Benjamin T. Spencer, *The Quest for Nationality: An American Literary Campaign* (Syracuse, N.Y., 1957), chaps. 2–3; and Robert E. Spiller, ed., *The American Literary Revolution, 1783–1837* (New York, 1967).

3. Carl Bode, *The American Lyceum: Town Meeting of the Mind* (New York, 1956) is the standard study of that movement, but it can be usefully supplemented by the incisive analysis in Donald M. Scott, "The Popular Lecture and the Creation of a Public in Mid-Nineteenth-Century America," *Journal of American History,* 66 (Mar. 1980), 791–809. The best analysis of Boston-Cambridge's literary culture may be found in Lawrence Buell's *New England Literary Culture: From Revolution through Renaissance* (Cambridge, England, 1986), chaps. 2–4. Although impressionistic and sentimental, Van Wyck Brooks's *The Flowering of New England* (New York, 1936), chaps. 1–6, is still valuable for Boston-Cambridge culture. More critical is Martin Green, *The Problem of Boston: Some Readings in Cultural History* (New York, 1966), chaps. 1–4. Also illuminating is a series of essays by Lewis P. Simpson: "'The Intercommunity of the Learned': Boston and Cambridge in 1800," *New England Quarterly,* 23 (Dec. 1950), 491–503; "Joseph Stevens Buckminster: The Rise of the New England Clerisy," in Simpson's *The Man of Letters in New England and the South: Essays on the History of the Literary Vocation in America* (Baton Rouge, 1973), 3–31; and "The Tudor Brothers: Boston Ice and Boston Letters," in ibid., 32–61. The most complete study of the Göttingen scholars is Orie William Long, *Literary Pioneers: Early American Explorers of European Culture* (Cambridge, Mass., 1935). But for a recent astute reconsideration of their experience, see Lilian Handlin, "Harvard and Göttingen, 1815," *Proceedings of the Massachusetts Historical Society,* v. 95, 1983 (Boston, 1984), 67–87.

4. *Three Centuries of Harvard,* 244 ("palmy days"); "Unitarian Christianity: Discourse at the Ordination of the Rev. Jared Sparks, Baltimore, 1819," in *The Works of William E. Channing, D.D.,* 6 vols. (Boston, 1849), III, 87 ("gloomy"); "Likeness to God: Discourse at the Ordination of the Rev. F. A. Farley, Providence, R.I., 1828," in ibid., 228 ("likeness"). The authoritative study of antebellum Boston-Cambridge's established Unitarian intellectual leadership is Daniel Walker Howe, *The Unitarian Conscience: Harvard Moral Philosophy, 1805–1861* (Cambridge, Mass., 1970). For a recent excellent discussion of Unitarian literary aspirations, see Lawrence Buell, "The Literary Significance of the Unitarian Movement," in Wright, *American Unitarianism,* 163–79. Valuable material on the socioeconomic character of the Unitarian denomination in Massachusetts may be found in Richard E. Sykes, "Massachusetts Unitarianism and Social Change: A Religious Social System in Transition" (Ph.D. diss., University of Minnesota, 1966).

5. "Unitarian Christianity," 96 ("judiciousness").

6. *FL,* I, 150 ("glory"); *FL,* I, 151–52 ("distinction"). For American reaction to Lafayette's tour, see Fred Somkin, *Unquiet Eagle: Memory and Desire in the Idea of American Freedom, 1815–1860* (Ithaca, 1967), 131–74.

7. To GTD, Dec. 17, 1842, *FL,* III, 105 *("arrogance");* Nov. 6, 1843, ibid., 156 ("Hamlet"); to CS, July 24, [1840], *FL,* II, 154 ("powerful eye"); Nov. 6, 1843, *FL,* III, 156 ("ardent"); MF to Albert H. Tracy, Sept. 26, 1843, ibid., 150 ("dear child").

8. Journal, 1844, quoted in *HO,* 31 ("admire"); to SP, July 11, 1825, *FL,* I, 151 ("characteristics"); quoted in *HO,* 306 ("peculiarity"); LMC to Francis Shaw, [Oct. 1846], *ChL,* 231 ("forget *herself* ").

9. Aug. 21, 1830, *FL,* I, 168 ("domestick groupe").

10. May 14, 1826, *FL,* I, 154 ("assemblage"); quoted in Thomas Wentworth Higgin-

son, Notes, [188–?], OC, 22 ("national gov't"); Mar. 5, 1826, *FL*, I, 152–53 ("Duke Nicholas"); Jan. 3, 1828, ibid., 155 ("Sir William Temple").

11. FMW, Box A ("'Possunt'"). At the bottom of this theme she later wrote: "Theme corrected by father: the only one I have kept; it shows very plainly what our mental relation was."

12. MF to JFC, Oct. 25, 1830, FP ("beautiful"); n.d., *OM*, I, 110 ("double existence"); "Lillo," FMW, Box A ("French period"); to JFC, [Oct. 11, 1831], FP ("my pleasure"); Jan. 10, 1827, *FL*, I, 154 ("Italian poets"); JFC, *OM*, I, 112 ("familiar"); Peabody, *Harvard Reminiscences*, 48 ("voluntary").

13. To AG, n.d., MH ("sad"); to AG, Mar. 30, [1830], *FL*, I, 164 ("tragick"); journal, Sept. 1839, FMW, Box A ("prophet[ic]" and "sat at [his] feet"); MF to JFC, Aug. 14, 1845, FP ("fire"); May 14, 1826, *FL*, I, 154 ("brilliant De Stael"). An overview of American Romantic tastes may be found in G. Harrison Orians, "The Rise of Romanticism, 1805–1855," in Harry Hayden Clark, ed., *Transitions in American Literary History* (1954; New York, 1967). For a recent cogent discussion of the origins and nature of antebellum Romantic preferences, see Henry F. May, "After the Enlightenment: A Prospectus," in his *The Divided Heart: Essays on Protestantism and the Enlightenment in America* (New York, 1991), chap. 8.

14. To JFC, [Oct. 29, 1830], FP ("console"); to [?], [Winter] 1830–1831, *FL*, I, 173 ("imbecile"); to [?], Dec. 17, 1829, ibid., 156–57 ("credulity"); Mar. 5, 1826, ibid., 153 ("How delighted"). The literature on European Romanticism is, of course, enormous. Robert F. Gleckner and Gerald E. Enscoe, eds., *Romanticism: Points of View*, Second Edition (Englewood Cliffs, N.J., 1970) is a good introduction to contending interpretations. Two classic studies of the emergence of early European Romanticism are Ernst Cassirer, *The Philosophy of the Enlightenment* (1932; Princeton, 1951); and Walter Jackson Bate, *From Classic to Romantic: Premises of Taste in Eighteenth-Century England* (Cambridge, Mass., 1946). The best recent study of the movement as a whole remains M. H. Abrams's powerful *Natural Supernaturalism: Tradition and Revolution in Romantic Literature* (New York, 1971).

15. Jan. 3, 1828, *FL*, I, 155 ("aching wish").

16. Quoted in *FR*, 8 ("Soap Works"); Fuller, *FC*, 17 ("prosperous"); TF to MCF, July 26, 1828, FMW, IV, 167 ("*home-house*"); to GTD, Dec. 17, 1842, *FL*, III, 105 ("love to look").

17. TF to MCF, May 21, 1820, FMW, III, 180 ("skirmishes"); TF to MCF, Dec. 23, 1819, ibid., 69 ("exile"); "Remarks on the Nomination of Edwd Everett, for Representative to Congress, & the Pamphlet in his favor," Oct. 25, 1824, FMW, I, 97 *("Federalists")*; to MF, Sept. 26, 1824, FMW, V, 31 ("discipline"); *HO*, 27, 29 ("elaborate affairs").

18. Statement, *OM*, I, 91 ("painfully conscious"); MCF to TF, Jan. 15, 1824, FMW, VII, 97 ("*uncommon* beauty"); May 15, 1824, FMW, V, 17 ("extraordinary beauty"); statement, *OM*, I, 92 ("positive plainness"); MF to JFC, June 2, 1835, FP ("delightful").

19. Quoted in *HO*, 25 ("come into school"); to Thomas Wentworth Higginson, Jan. 9, 1884, OC, 248 ("stranger").

20. Jan. 10, 1827, *FL*, I, 154 ("natural person"); [after Oct. 1827?], *ChL*, 10 ("raciness").

21. *HO*, 35 ("mother's feet"); to GTD, Jan. 23, 1830, Caroline Wells Healey Dall Papers, MCR-S ("'geniuses'"). For documents that reveal something of the character of these Cambridge women, see "Mrs. Stephen Higginson's letter-diary for Oct. 22, 1827–Mar. 20, 1828," *Cambridge Historical Society Publications*, v. 2 (Cambridge, Mass., 1907), 20–32; and *Letters of Ann Storrow to Jared Sparks*, ed. Frances Branshaw Blanshard, *Smith College Studies in History*, v. 4 (Northampton, Mass., 1921).

22. The best source for Eliza Farrar's life is her *Recollections of Seventy Years* (Boston, 1866). For a useful brief sketch, see Elizabeth Bancroft Schlesinger, "Two Early Harvard Wives: Eliza Farrar and Eliza Follen," *New England Quarterly,* 38 (June 1965), 147–67. Details of Farrar's life and family background may also be found in John M. Bullard, *The Rotches* (New Bedford, Mass., 1947), 112–23, 126–30, 140–50, and 287–351.

23. RWE, *OM,* I, 299 ("promise"); *HO,* 36 ("mould her"); *The Young Lady's Friend* (1836; New York, 1870), 41, 130, 257–58 ("express vocation"). For a fine discussion of antebellum manners manuals, see Karen Halttunen, *Confidence Men and Painted Women: A Study of Middle-Class Culture in America, 1830–1870* (New Haven, 1982).

24. ERF to MCF, Sept. 3, 1850, FMW, XVII, 37 ("lessons"); Mar. 17, 1836, *FL,* I, 246 ("harsh"); to MCF, Mar. 24, [1851], FMW, XVII, 35 ("never go to bed"); "Lillo, " [early 1840s], FMW, Box A ("elected a Mother").

25. July 20, 1840, "CLS" ("dogmati[c]"); RWE, *OM,* I, 203 ("sneering"); journal, [ca. early 1833], FMW, Box A ("prudish girls"); JFC, *OM,* I, 104 ("half-voluptuous"); to APB, Mar. 9, 1834, *FL,* I, 199 ("laughter-loving"); MF to GTD, Dec. 19, 1829, Caroline Wells Healey Dall Papers, MCR-S ("in-dwelling"); MF, journal, [ca. early Mar. 1834], FMW, Box A ("morbid"); MF to JFC, [Aug. 24, 1832], FP ("Wordsworthian"); JFC, *OM,* I, 104 ("harmonious"); to JFC, Nov. 13, 1834, FP ("'Mother was before her'"); quoted in JFC, "Journal of the Understanding," May 16, 1832, p. 134, JFC Papers, MH ("perfectly idle").

26. To APB, Mar. 9, 1834, *FL,* I, 199 ("blue-stocking"); Higginson, *Cheerful Yesterdays,* 18 ("musical queen").

27. To WHC, [Aug. 29, 1841], *FL,* II, 227 ("haughty"); to TF, Feb. 22, 1824, *FL,* I, 135 ("Germanicus"). Accounts of Hedge's early life may be found in Orie W. Long, *Frederic Henry Hedge: A Cosmopolitan Scholar* (Portland, Me., 1940); Charles Wesley Grady, "A Conservative Transcendentalist: The Early Years (1805–1835) of Frederic Henry Hedge," *SAR, 1983,* 57–87; and Bryan F. Le Beau, *Frederic Henry Hedge, Nineteenth Century American Transcendentalist: Intellectually Radical, Ecclesiastically Conservative* (Allison Park, Pa., 1985).

28. Helen Davis to JFC, Sept. 25–29, [1833], JFC Papers, MH ("gracious[ness]"); "ON," 498 ("no chance"); June 14, 1835, *CL,* 97 ("plaything"); *OM,* II, 6 ("sprightliness"); quoted in *OM,* I, 280 ("raved"); WHC, *OM,* II, 6 ("scathing"); EPP to ?, n.d., "ON," 482 ("laughing"); statement, *OM,* I, 95 ("Her conversation").

29. Statement, *OM,* I, 95–96 ("masculine mind"); *OM,* I, 96, 107 ("interior capability"); to JFC, [Oct. 11, 1831], FP ("poetiz[ing]"); *OM,* I, 64–65, 96–97 ("balloon").

30. Statement, *OM,* I, 94 ("never so happy"); n.d., MH ("former state"); Mar. 30, [1830], *FL,* I, 164 ("Byronized"); Nov. 19, 1830, *FL,* I, 171 ("Simplicetta"). For excellent interpretations of the culture of female friendships in antebellum America, see Carroll Smith-Rosenberg, "The Female World of Love and Ritual: Relations Between Women in Nineteenth-Century America," in her *Disorderly Conduct: Visions of Gender in Victorian America* (New York, 1985), 53–76, 305–13; and Cott, *Bonds of Womanhood,* chap. 5.

31. Nov. 19, 1830, *FL,* I, 172 ("Sentiment"); Jan. 5, 1835, ibid., 217 ("weakly souls").

32. MF to FHH, July 4, 1833, *FL,* I, 190 ("ladylike"); Apr. 23, 1833, in Robert D. Habich, "James Freeman Clarke's 1833 Letter-journal for Margaret Fuller," *ESQ, 27* (1st Quarter 1981), 49 ("sentimentalities"); Apr. 25 [24], 1833, in ibid., 50 ("pride"); JFC, "Journal of Myself," [early 1832], Perry-Clarke Collection, MHi ("noble sentiment").

33. *OM,* I, 87 ("premature"); quoted in Francis M. Thompson, *History of Greenfield, shire town of Franklin County, Massachusetts,* 3 vols. (Greenfield, Mass., 1904–1931), II, 1,172 ("best conversationalist"); "Autobiography," chap. 4, p. 6, JFC Papers, MH *("let-*

ting himself go"); OM, I, 104 ("contempt"); Jan. 26, 1834, "CLS" ("college frolics"); Dec. 6, 18[35], FP ("herd").

34. Quoted in MF to JFC, Jan. 1, 1840, FP ("fit to eat"); MF to JFC, July 27, 1833, FP ("new impression"); [ca. Jan. 1830]*, *FL,* I, 158–59 ("feeble natures"); quoted in MF to GTD, Jan. 23, 1830, Caroline Wells Healey Dall Papers, MCR-S ("temporarily"); Jan. 23, 1830, ibid. ("not *dis*believe").

35. Quoted in MF to AB, [Feb. 1838], Ward Papers, MH ("Some *equal bosom*"); GTD quoted in MF to JFC, [Jan. 26, 1832], FP ("hero"); Nov. 26, 1833, FP ("giddy"); Dec. 29, 1829, Caroline Wells Healey Dall Papers, MCR-S ("resemblance"); Dec. 19, 1829, ibid. ("come to me"); [ca. Oct. 1839]*, *OM,* I, 100 ("conjugal"); n.d., MB ("sweet thoughts"); "Journal of Myself," Sept. 14, 1831, Perry-Clarke Collection, MHi ("Designs").

36. "Autobiography," chap. 4, p. 12, JFC Papers, MH ("Coleridge showed me"). The best biography of Clarke is Arthur S. Bolster, Jr., *James Freeman Clarke: Disciple to Advancing Truth* (Boston, 1954). Also useful are James Freeman Clarke, *Autobiography, Diary and Correspondence,* ed. Edward Everett Hale (Boston, 1891); and John Wesley Thomas, *James Freeman Clarke: Apostle of German Culture to America* (Boston, 1949).

37. [Early Mar. 1830]*, *CL,* 9 ("Cousin Mine"). This letter is misdated in *CL. OM,* I, 66 ("views of life"); [Mar. 27, 1830], FP ("sad process"); Apr. 11, 1830, *CL,* 15 ("approaching happiness")

38. "Studies towards the life of a business woman. Being conversations with Mrs. R. P. Clarke in the winter of 1884–5, by Caroline H. Dall," 3 vols., I, 22–23, JFC Papers, MH *("'Poor James!'");* quoted in MF to JFC, May 1, 1830, FP ("Elizabeth affair"); quoted in Apr. 11, 1830, *CL,* 15 ("lofty metaphysics").

39. Apr. 11, 1830, *CL,* 12 ("confiding"); MF to JFC, May 7, 1830, FP ("fancies"); Apr. 11, 1830, *CL,* 13 ("electrify my stupor"); FP, and *OM,* I, 69–70 ("person of Genius").

40. MF to JFC, May 7, 1830, FP *("roused");* [Oct. 11, 1831], FP ("Expliquez moi"); Apr. 11, 1830, *CL,* 13 ("unsocial").

41. Nov. 1830, *CL,* 17, 19–21 ("Dreamland"); [Oct. 29, 1830], FP ("strange secrets"); Nov. 2, 1830, FP ("detached scenes"); [Oct. 29, 1830], FP ("horrid dream").

42. MF to JFC, Nov. 2, 1830, FP ("confidence[s]"); [Oct. 28, 1830], FP ("attach-ment"); [postdated] Nov. 1830, *CL,* 26 ("give up Love"); "Book of Extracts and Synop-ses," Mar. 16, 1830, Perry-Clarke Collection, MHi ("'to you I owe it'").

43. [Postdated] 1830, *CL,* 9 ("fair Elschen"); MF to JFC, Aug. 14, 1845, FP ("sober suited"); to [GTD, ca. Oct. 1839]*, *OM,* I, 100 ("strictly fraternal"); to CS, Jan. 27, 1839, *FL,* II, 43 ("morbid"); Jan. 18, 1831, FP ("unsuited"); "Journal of Myself," Jan. 2, 1833, Perry-Clarke Collection, MHi ("reality").

44. *FL,* I, 174 ("dearest friend"); [ca. Feb. 1831]*, *OM,* I, 79 ("not answered"); [ca. Feb. 1831]*, ibid. ("closely scanned").

45. Quoted in "Journal of the Understanding," May 9, 1832, JFC Papers, MH ("con-fided"); Dec. 16, [1830], *CL,* 28 ("mannerless dog"); "Journal of Myself," Apr. 28, 1832, Perry-Clarke Collection, MHi ("different to him"); "Journal of the Understanding," May 9, 1832, JFC Papers, MH ("respect him"); JFC, "Journal of Myself," Apr. 28, 1832, Perry-Clarke Collection, MHi ("vanity"); JFC, "Journal of the Understanding," May 9, 1832, JFC Papers, MH ("great man").

46. "Journal of Myself," [ca. Apr.] 1832, Perry-Clarke Collection, MHi *("suspicious");* JFC, "Journal of the Understanding," May 9, 1832, JFC Papers, MH ("confessional[s]"); [ca. May–June 1833]*, *CL,* 36 ("give yourself up").

47. Quoted in JFC, "Journal of the Understanding," May 9, 1832, JFC Papers, MH ("some other girl"); [Jan. 26, 1832], FP ("*must* burn it"); RFF to MF, Feb. 4, 1845, FMW,

XVII, 17 ("nobleness"); Sept. 8, 1834, *CL,* 79 ("independent"); [Jan. 26, 1832], FP ("lose a friend").

48. [Ca. early 1833], FMW, Box A ("lonely"); Jan. 4, 1834, FP ("memento mori").

49. Journal, [ca. early Mar. 1834], FMW, Box A ("craved sleep").

50. To MCF, Feb. 3, 1850, FMW, XVII, 37 ("inner life"); to JT, Oct. 21, 1838, *FL,* I, 347 ("treble weight"); [ca. 1840]*, *OM,* I, 139–41 ("Thanksgiving day").

51. *OM,* I, 84 ("'parting of the ways'"); [JFC, journal, ca. 1832]*, quoted in ibid., 110 ("lectured me"); "Journal of the Understanding," Nov. 9, 1832, JFC Papers, MH ("Margaret's philosophy").

52. "Autobiography," chap. 4, p. 31, JFC Papers, MH ("another world"); *OM,* I, 114 ("wild bugle-call"). The definitive study of the transmission of German thought and literature to America is Henry A. Pochmann, *German Culture in America: Philosophical and Literary Influences, 1600–1900* (Madison, 1957). Less complete, but still useful for information on the impact of German literature in Boston-Cambridge Unitarian circles, is Stanley M. Vogel, *German Literary Influences on the American Transcendentalists* (New Haven, 1955).

53. *OM,* I, 114 ("with ease"); JFC, "Journal of the Understanding," May 9, 1832, JFC Papers, MH ("only a tasteful mind"); MF to JFC, [Aug. 24, 1832], FP ("German journal[s]").

54. JFC, "Journal of the Understanding," May 9, 1832, JFC Papers, MH ("proud reserve"); May 16, 1832, ibid. ("soft"); Dec. 11, 1832, ibid. ("mental inferiority"); May 9, 1832, ibid. ("exert myself").

55. "Journal of the Understanding," May 9, 1832, JFC Papers, MH ("pride . . . of knowledge"); Sept. 12, 1831, "Journal of People and Things," ibid. ("ends in nothing").

56. Dec. 15, 1834, *CL,* 86 ("Carlyle philosophy"); May 16, 1832, "Journal of the Understanding," JFC Papers, MH ("nothing to do").

57. "Journal of the Understanding," Oct. 10, 1832, JFC Papers, MH ("infinite pathos"); July 4, 1832, ibid. ("too long deferred"); Mar. 6, 1833, ibid. ("moved me"); Oct. 10, 1832, ibid. ("said nothing").

58. *Education in Massachusetts: Early Legislation and History* (Boston, 1869), 31 ("special vocation"); *CL,* 35 ("author"). For the status of female teachers in these years, see Richard M. Bernard and Maris A. Vinovskis, "The Female School Teacher in Ante-Bellum Massachusetts," *Journal of Social History,* 10 (Spring 1977), 332–45; and Cremin, *American Education: The National Experience,* 388–99. For pioneering studies of the rise of the professional author in America, see William Charvat, *The Profession of Authorship in America, 1800–1870: The Papers of William Charvat* (Columbus, Ohio, 1968), chaps. 2–3. The most comprehensive study of the literary careers of antebellum women authors is Kelley, *Private Woman, Public Stage.*

59. [Ca. Oct. or Nov. 1832], FP ("write books"); MF, journal, [ca. Mar. 1834], FMW, Box A ("action").

60. *FR,* 26 ("disgusted"); Apr. 9, 1820, FMW, III, 162 ("literary pursuits"); Jan. 29, 1820, ibid., 101 *("first blow");* Feb. 22, 1825, FMW, VII, 168 ("literary cabinet").

61. [Ca. Apr. 22, 1833], FP ("Very sad"); Aug. 7, 1832, FP ("live alone").

Chapter Five

1. *FL,* I, 180 ("bitter tears").

2. For Groton at this time, see Caleb Butler, *History of the Town of Groton* (Boston, 1848); and Samuel Abbott Green, *An Historical Sketch of Groton, Massachusetts, 1655–1890* (Groton, Mass., 1894).

3. *FC*, 19 ("hardening process"). For a good discussion of the contrasting, postrepublican appeal of rural living for wealthy Federalist and Whig Bostonians in these years, see Tamara Plakins Thornton, *Cultivating Gentlemen: The Meaning of Country Life among the Boston Elite, 1785–1860* (New Haven, 1989).

4. Mar. 15, 1822, FMW, VII, 23 ("retire"); to JFC, Nov. 13, 1834, FP ("sordid tasks"); *FR*, 17 ("maxims"); to TF, Oct. 14, 1833, FMW, VII, 177 ("engaged").

5. Apr. 15, 1833, FMW, VII, 175 ("homesick"); journal, [ca. Oct. 1835], FMW, Works, III, 383 ("secretly wondered"); *FR*, 35 ("Margaret's Grove"); [ca. Oct. 1835], FMW, Works, III, 385 ("where you please").

6. *FR*, 19 ("threw ourselves"); to Abraham W. Fuller, Jan. 26, 1836, FMW, VIII, 4 ("dog"); Aug. 17, 1833, FP ("inanition").

7. *FC*, 21, 45 ("at once").

8. July 4, 1833, *FL*, I, 189 (*"sigh* at least"); MF to JFC, Oct. 7, 1833, FP ("soirées"); Oct. 25, 1833, "CLS" ("swimmingly"); June 2, 1835, FP (*"dear* Sarah").

9. MF to JFC, Aug. 17, 1833, FP ("learned"); July 4, 1833, *FL*, I, 190 ("more agreeable"); to RFF, Aug. 11, 1842, *FL*, III, 85 ("tamely smiling"); [June 30? 1833], *FL*, I, 185–86 (*"sweet* wind!"); July 27, 1833, FP ("solitude").

10. [Ca. May 1833], FMW, Box 4 ("stately unfurnished house").

11. [Ca. May 1833], FMW, Works, III, 349 ("Heaven's discipline"); [July 4, 1833], FMW, Box A ("occupations").

12. *FL*, I, 196 ("so ignorant"); Feb. 7, 1834, FP ("je vaux rien").

13. MF to [JFC, ca. May 1833], CtY ("Recd payment"); *OM*, I, 231 ("rate like Gibbon's"); Feb. 1, 1835, *FL*, I, 220 ("gallop of the age").

14. [Ca. June 17? 1833], FP *("stirs"); FMW*, Box A *("affections"); June 3, [1833], FP ("heart").

15. [Ca. 1833–34], FMW, Box A ("does not thrill"); June 3, [1833], FP ("easily fathomed"); journal, Mar. 8, [1834], FMW, Box A ("modern"); [July 1?, 1833], *FL*, I, 187 ("Too rambling"); July 4, 1833, ibid., 189 ("sighing sort").

16. Journal, FMW, Box 4 ("loved to expand"); MF to JFC, [Aug. 24, 1832], FP ("Novalis journal"); journal, FMW, Box 4 ("mysticism"). Oskar Walzel, *German Romanticism* (New York, 1932) is a standard but still valuable study. For a recent analysis of the literary and aesthetic theories of the German Romantics, see Marshall Brown, *The Shape of German Romanticism* (Ithaca, 1979).

17. July 4, 1834, *FL*, I, 189 ("to anybody"); JFC, "Journal of the Understanding," Nov. 1, 1832, JFC Papers, MH ("Epicurean"); quoted in *OM*, I, 64 ("seeking"); Sept. 9, 1833, *CL*, 60 ("darkness visible"); Oct. 25, 1833, *FL*, I, 196 ("What fault"); [ca. 1834], FMW, Box A ("prosaic"). On the condemnation of Goethe in American journals, see Pochmann, *German Culture in America,* 329–31, 678–80; and Vogel, *German Literary Influences,* 13–14.

18. Aug. 7, 1832, FP ("immense superiority"); Aug. 30, 1833, FP ("live as he did"); [postdated] 1832, *CL*, 36 ("volcanic"); Aug. 17, 1833, FP ("guide me"); to APB, Oct. 6, 1833, *FL*, I, 210 ("Master"); [ca. 1835?], OC, 117 ("light of the age").

19. MF to GTD, Jan. 23, 1830, Caroline Wells Healey Dall Papers, MCR-S ("new metaphysics"); "Journal of Myself," Feb. 20, 1833, Perry-Clarke Collection, MHi ("Germans demonstrate"); [May 7], 1833, "CJ33," 53 ("all-comprehending idea"); MF to JFC, [ca. late May 1833], FP ("metaphysical philosophy").

20. MF to GTD, Jan. 23, 1830, Caroline Wells Healey Dall Papers, MCR-S ("home for theories"); Mar. 8, 1834, FMW, Box A ("religious study"); Nov. 30, 1834, *FL*, I, 213 ("evidences"); MF to JFC, [Feb. 1, 1835], FP ("foreign tongue"); to MF, Feb. 20, 1835,

MH-AH *("antidogmatical");* Mary W. Allen, letter, [1838], quoted in Harriet Hall Johnson, "Margaret Fuller as Known by Her Scholars," *Christian Register,* 89 (Apr. 21, 1910), 428 ("closet full"); to MF, Nov. 17, 1834, MH-AH ("internal spirit"); FHH to MF, Feb. 20, 1835, MH-AH ("spiritualist"); Dec. 10, [1834], MH-AH ("fable").

21. Feb. 1, 1835, *FL,* I, 223 ("shallow"); journal, [ca. Spring 1834], FMW, Box 4 ("saw not"); Feb. 1, 1835, *FL,* I, 223 ("skepticism"); journal, [ca. Spring 1834], FMW, Box 4 ("longing").

22. Journal, [ca. Spring 1834], FMW, Box 4 ("modern"); Mar. 6, 1835, *FL,* I, 226 ("new world"); Oct. 22, 1833, JFC Papers, MH ("regenerate").

23. Journal, [ca. early Mar. 1834], FMW, Box A ("Education first"); journal, Mar. 13, 1834, ibid. ("particy interesting"); [ca. early Mar. 1834], ibid. ("abuse"); Mar. 13, 1834, ibid. ("pagan").

24. Mar. 13, 1834, FMW, Box A *("genuine man");* n.d., *OM,* I, 149 ("American History!").

25. *FL,* I, 201 ("fatiguing charge"); [ca. early Mar. 1834], FMW, Box A ("forcing"); Oct. 17, 1833, *FL,* I, 194 ("Only eleven").

26. *FC,* 47 ("expatiate"); *FR,* 30 ("incite us"); *FC,* 48 ("inexpressibly").

27. *FC,* 48 ("bright responses"); ibid., 49 ("Turkey in Asia"); FMW, Box A ("Reading journal"); *FL,* I, 199–200 ("much runs out"); Mar. 20, 1834, ibid., 201–2 ("alienated"); journal, FMW, Box 4 ("small things").

28. "Coleridge's Literary Character," *Christian Examiner,* 14 (Mar. 1833), 125–26 ("metaphysics"); journal, Mar. 8, 1834, FMW, Box A ("*re*action"); July 4, 1833, *FL,* I, 189 *("write").*

29. Quoted in JFC, "Journal of Myself," May 24, 1832, Perry-Clarke Collection, MHi ("rational preaching"); Aug. 12, 1833, *CL,* 56–57 ("make myself over"); Sept. 9, 1833, *CL,* 59 ("minds of *culture*"); Aug. 12, 1833, *CL,* 57 ("cucumber parings"). For two good, contrasting books on the young Unitarian Westerners, see Elizabeth R. McKinsey, *The Western Experiment: New England Transcendentalists in the Ohio Valley* (Cambridge, Mass., 1973); and Robert D. Habich, *Transcendentalism and the* Western Messenger: *A History of the Magazine and Its Contributors, 1835–1841* (Rutherford, N.J., 1985).

30. Dec. 24, 1833, FP ("whetstone").

31. Oct. 25, 1833, "CLS" ("excellent plan").

32. Nov. 26, 1833, FP ("teaching"); FP ("schoolmistress plan"); *CL,* 73 ("wild country"). For good accounts of the antebellum campaign for female teachers in the West, see Kathryn Kish Sklar, *Catharine Beecher: A Study in Domesticity* (New Haven, 1973) chaps. 8, 12; and Polly Welts Kaufman, *Women Teachers on the Frontier* (New Haven, 1984).

33. FP ("information"); Mar. 20, 1834, *FL,* I, 201, and *OM,* I, 150 ("*only* grown-up daughter").

34. *CL,* 74 ("Two months!"); *CL,* 77 ("Bengal tiger").

35. June 4, 1834, *FL,* I, 203–4 ("regret").

36. Nov. 13, 1834, FP ("ci-devant intimates"); to JFC, Sept. 28, 1834, *FL,* I, 207 ("beautiful glen"); to APB, Jan. 5, 1835, ibid., 217 ("foolish talk"); Oct. 6, 1834, ibid., 209 ("so happy!").

37. Sept. 23, 1834, "CLS" ("given her up"); *CL,* 78–80 ("same being").

38. *FL,* I, 206–7 ("good hope"); MF to JFC, Jan. 4, 1834, FP ("unimaginative"); Mar. 29, 1835, FP ("'*mind*' only"); Sept. 8, 1834, *CL,* 79 ("active business"); Apr. 17, 1834, FP ("self-complacency"); Oct. 7, 1833, FP ("less happy").

39. MF to APB, Oct. 6, 1834, *FL,* I, 209–10 ("wandering about").

40. FP ("needlework"); [Feb. 1, 1835], FP ("Earning *money*").

41. [Ca. May 1833], CtY ("'capital'"); Dec. 5, [1834], FMW, Box A ("eight years older"); MF, journal, Mar. 13, 1834, ibid. ("vast plans"); May 2, [1834], ibid. ("cannot write").

42. May 2, [1834], FMW, Box A ("lamentations"); journal, May 1833, FMW, Box 4 ("too early"); [ca. late May 1833], FP ("Conversation").

43. Journal, May 2, [1834], FMW, Box A ("there's a woman"); journal, [ca. 1834], ibid. ("shallow"); to APB, Mar. 9, 1834, *FL*, I, 200 ("cloyed"); Mar. 1, 1834, FMW, Box A ("all women"). She went on in her March 1, 1834, journal entry to dispute the notion that feelings of suffering always blight literary talents, but the examples she gave, Tasso and Byron, were both male authors. For various illuminating interpretations of antebellum female authors' ideas of their craft, see Douglas, *Feminization of American Culture*, chaps. 2–3; Kelley, *Private Woman, Public Stage;* and Nina Baym, *Woman's Fiction: A Guide to Novels by and about Women in America, 1820–1870* (Ithaca, 1978).

44. For a good discussion of Bancroft's career at this time, see Lilian Handlin, *George Bancroft: The Intellectual as Democrat* (New York, 1984), chaps. 5–6.

45. *Boston Daily Advertiser and Patriot*, 42 (Nov. 27, 1834), 2 ("J.").

46. "Brutus," *Boston Daily Advertiser and Patriot*, 42 (Dec. 4, 1834), 2 ("H."); to FHH, Mar. 6, 1835, *FL*, I, 226 ("big wig").

47. FMW, Works, V, 693 ("Motto"); Feb. 1, 1835, *FL*, I, 223 ("mental solitude"); FMW, Box A ("How would it be"); Feb. 1, 1835, *FL*, I, 221 ("fuss"); FP ("if I were a man").

48. MH-AH ("spiritual philosophy"); *FL*, I, 225–26 ("merely 'Germanico'").

49. Dec. 19, 1833, *CL*, 69 ("lisped"); Dec. 15, 1834, *CL*, 87 ("no axioms"); to MF, [ca. Jan. 1834]*, *CL*, 72 ("Transcendental Philosophy"); William H. Venable, *Beginnings of Literary Culture in the Ohio Valley* (Cincinnati, 1891), 72 ("eastern messenger"); Feb. 20, 1835, *CL*, 88 ("first rate"); Apr. 12, 1835, *CL*, 91 ("Don't be afraid"). The best study of the *Western Messenger* is Habich, *Transcendentalism and the* Western Messenger.

50. Feb. 7, 1834, FP ("use of Metaphysics"); Apr. 28, 1835, FP ("'all no how'"); [ca. June 1833], FP ("New-England public").

51. Review of George Crabbe, *The Life of the Rev. George Crabbe*, and William Roberts, *Memoirs of the Life and Correspondence of Mrs. Hannah More*, Western Messenger, 1 (June 1835), 22–23, 25–26 ("stern pictorial").

52. To FHH, Nov. 30, 1834, *FL*, I, 214 ("abused"); "The Pilgrims of the Rhine," *Western Messenger*, 1 (Aug. 1835), 101, 103–5 ("immoral"); to ABA, May 18, 1837, *FL*, I, 274 *("overestimate[d]")*.

53. "Philip Van Artevelde," *Western Messenger* 1 (December 1835), 400–401 ("Classical").

54. Ibid., 401–3, 405–6 ("classical school").

55. Dec. 6, 18[35], FP ("blunders"); Winter, 1835–36, "CLS" *("Foreign Quarterly");* Ephraim Peabody to JFC, June 29, 1835, quoted in Habich, *Transcendentalism and the* Western Messenger, 66 ("undignified"); Apr. 6, [1835], FP ("criticisms"); *CL*, 94–95 ("nothing of books").

56. Mar. 29, 1835, FP ("*main* object"); Apr. 6, [1835], FP ("epithets"); FP *("money");* May 12, 1835, *CL*, 94 ("reading public"); June 24, 1835, *CL*, 98 ("conversational").

57. MF to JFC, June 2, 1835, FP ("divine"); *FL*, I, 230 ("extacy").

58. MF to TF and MCF, Aug. 13, 1835, *FL*, I, 232–33 ("hot"); [ca. July 27, 1835]*, "ON," 484 ("Mr Ward"); Aug. 13, 1835, *FL*, I, 233 ("kindness").

59. Aug. 13, 1835, *FL*, I, 232 ("pleasure"). Although it needs to be used with caution,

the indispensable guide to Martineau's life and character is *Harriet Martineau's Autobiography,* ed. Maria Weston Chapman (3 vols. [London, 1877]). For her American tour, see Martineau, *Retrospect of Western Travel.* Two good, contrasting biographies are R. K. Webb, *Harriet Martineau: A Radical Victorian* (New York, 1960); and Valerie Kossew Pichanick, *Harriet Martineau: The Woman and Her Work, 1802–76* (Ann Arbor, 1980).

60. June 14, 1835, *CL*, 96 ("fascinating").

61. June 27, 1835, FP ("starvation"); [ca. Aug.–Sept. 1835], FMW, Works, III, 369 ("heart beat"); June 27, 1835, FP ("no name"); [ca. Aug.–Sept. 1835], FMW, Works, III, 369 ("received me"); *Martineau's Autobiography,* II, 72 ("intolerable girl").

62. [Ca. Sept. 1835], FMW, Works, III, 371–75 ("intellectual guide"); MF to JFC, Jan. 29, 1836, FP ("happy hours").

63. Jan. 30, 1836, *FL*, I, 243 ("literary society").

64. *New England Galaxy,* Aug. 8, 1835 ("Lost and Won").

65. To MF, Sept. 9, 1833, *CL*, 60 ("coquette").

66. *CL*, 103–4 ("tremendous").

67. *CL*, 104–5 ("not as you suppose").

68. [Ca. Fall–Winter 1835–1836], FMW, Works, III, 377 ("days and nights"); *FC*, 31 ("typhus fever"); [ca. Oct. 1835], FMW, Works, III, 379 ("willing to go"); Feb. 1, 1836, *FL*, I, 243 ("Death"); [ca. Oct. 1835], FMW, Works, III, 377–79 ("My father").

69. To RFF, Aug. 11, 1842, *FL*, III, 85 ("over anxious"); *FR*, 21 ("obliged to lie down"); *FC*, 32 ("Asiatic cholera").

Chapter Six

1. Feb. 1, 1836, *FL*, I, 244 ("fatherless"); June 2, 1835, ibid., 230 ("twenty two miles"); MF to RFF, Aug. 11, 1842, *FL*, III, 85 ("destroyed"); to Abraham W. Fuller, Mar. 26, 1838, *FL*, I, 330 ("if I live"); to Albert H. Tracy, Sept. 26, 1843, *FL*, III, 150 ("dying"); to EH, Mar. 20, 1842, ibid., 55 ("death"); May 13, 1837, FP ("recover"); May 13, 1838, FP ("father died").

2. FP ("fill the place"); Jan. 7, 1836, *CL*, 112 ("impulse"); to JN, Sept. 30, 1845, *FL*, IV, 163 ("hand").

3. *HO*, 54 ("end of her days"); FMW, Works, III, 383 ("father's image"); *OM*, I, 157 ("selfishness"); [Feb. 17, 1836], FMW, Box A, *FL*, I, 246, and *OM*, I, 157 ("sustains me").

4. For Timothy Fuller's estate, in addition to references scattered throughout FMW, *FL*, and probate records, see Abraham W. Fuller to MF, May 1836, quoted in F. B. Sanborn, *Recollections of Seventy Years,* 2 vols. (Boston, 1909), II, 406–7; *FC*, 36–37; and *FR*, 27–28.

5. Enclosure to EF to MF, Feb. 14, 1841, FMW, VIII, 205 ("leaned"); RFF, "Memorial of Mrs. Margaret Fuller," 378 ("appalled"); [Feb. 17, 1836], *FL*, I, 246 ("spirit of a *man*").

6. *FL*, I, 237 ("hated"). For a good discussion of the use of judicial discretion to expand the legal rights of widowed and divorced mothers, see Michael Grossberg, *Governing the Hearth: Law and the Family in Nineteenth-Century America* (Chapel Hill, 1985), chap. 7.

7. *FL*, I, 237 ("desire to learn"); MF to Abraham W. Fuller, Nov. 17, 1835, ibid., 239 ("Father's history"); Nov. 6, 1835, ibid., 237 ("ignorant").

8. Mar. 3, 1846, *FL*, IV, 192 ("no scheme of pleasure"); to RWE, Dec. [4?], 1842, *FL*, III, 103 ("defect"); Feb. 1, 1836, Caroline Wells Healey Dall Papers, MCR-S ("profitable"); to EF, Jan. 30, 1836, *FL*, I, 243 ("best literary society"); Feb. 1, 1836, Caroline

Wells Healey Dall Papers, MCR-S ("many prospects"); Mar. 3, 1846, *FL*, IV, 192 ("ready to use"); Feb. 1, 1836, Caroline Wells Healey Dall Papers, MCR-S ("we women").

9. *OM*, I, 158 ("New-year"); Jan. 30, 1836, *FL*, I, 243 ("few thousand dollars"); Jan. 29, 1836, FP ("temporal existence"); Feb. 1, 1836, Caroline Wells Healey Dall Papers, MCR-S ("pretty trial"); Winter, 1835–1836, "CLS" ("interval"); "Lines written in Mar. 1836, by Margaret," FMW, Works, I, 75–81 ("'Not comfortless!'"). With some changes, this poem was printed by Clarke without her knowledge—and much to her displeasure when she discovered it—as "Jesus, the Comforter," in the *Western Messenger,* 4 (Sept. 1837), 20–21.

10. *FL*, I, 247 ("go with you"); quoted in F. B. Sanborn, *Recollections,* II, 406 ("means"); Aug. 11, 1842, *FL*, III, 86 *("some one"); FL*, I, 254 ("Circumstances").

11. Mar. 3, 1846, *FL*, IV, 192 ("communion"); MF to CS, Oct. 22, 1840, *FL*, II, 168 ("wretched girl"); Oct. 11, 1835, FP ("poor youth"); Apr. 19, 1836, FP ("farmer's daughter"); Jan. 24, 1839, *FL*, II, 38 ("too selfish").

12. May 23, 1836, *FL*, I, 254 ("heart-broken"); Apr. 17, 1836, ibid., 247 ("correspond with you"); [Feb. 17, 1836], ibid., 246 ("continue with us"); *OM*, I, 162–63 ("There they sit"); MF to EH, Mar. 20, 1842, *FL*, III, 55 ("tension of nerves").

13. Feb. 1, 1836, *FL*, I, 244 ("fortitude"); *FR*, 25, 27 ("family councils").

14. To Abraham W. Fuller, Jan. 14, 1836, FMW, VIII, 3 ("imperious"); *FR*, 37 ("hate Groton!").

15. *FC*, 38–39 ("presumption").

16. To ABF, Sept. 8, 1836, FMW, VIII, 13 ("indolence"); to RFF, Feb. 25, 1838, ibid., 92 ("knowledge"); to ABF, Sept. 8, 1836, ibid., 13 ("selfishness"); to RFF, Jan. 21, 1838, ibid., 91 ("burdens"); to ABF, Dec. 14, 1838, ibid., 19 ("first cause"); to RFF, Jan. 27, 1841, ibid., 94 ("blessed father"); to RFF, July 29, 1843, *FL*, III, 132 ("manly spirit"); June 3, 1840, *FL*, II, 144 ("unnatural mother").

17. N.d., quoted in *EJ*, XI, 440 ("Fullerism unbalanced"); to MF, June 30, 1844, FMW, XV, 9 ("slowness of mind"); ABF to RFF, Sept. 17, 1847, FMW, XIII, 31 ("'voices'"); ibid., Box A ("soliloquies"); Feb. 1, [ca. 1840], ibid. ("lecture"); to RFF, [Aug. 31, 1845], *FL*, IV, 158 ("*poor* Lloyd").

18. *FR*, 41 ("Madonna-like beauty"); July 27, 1841, FMW, XIV, 6 ("superior persons"); Apr. 21, 1836, FMW, IX, 40 *("will not"); Aug. 26, [1836], *FL*, I, 258 ("'calico frock'").

19. Fuller, *FR*, 33, 57 ("disgust"); Dec. 31, 1837, *FL*, I, 319–20 ("confinement").

20. To MF, May 22, 1842, FMW, XV, 27 ("family honor"); *FR*, 72, 95 ("distrust"); ABF to RFF, Aug. 9, 1848, FMW, XIII, 44 ("jocular"); quoted in *FC*, 303 ("Captain"). The best source on the later lives of the Fuller children is FMW. But also useful are *FC*; *FR*; and (for Ellen) Frederick T. McGill, Jr., *Channing of Concord: A Life of William Ellery Channing II* (New Brunswick, N.J., 1967).

21. To RFF, Aug. 11, 1842, *FL*, III, 86 ("robust"); May 30, 1841, FMW, XVII, 5 ("your example"); Nov. 22, 1843, FMW, XIII, 18 ("mentor"); n.d., *OM*, II, 125 ("guardianship").

22. *OM*, I, 164 ("'intense' times"); [ca. early 1836]*, ibid., 169 ("reading"); [ca. early 1836]*, ibid., 130 ("mistake!").

23. *Western Messenger,* 1 (Jan. 1836), 489 ("Thoughts on Sunday Morning"); journal, [ca. early Mar. 1834], FMW, Box A ("wading"); Apr. 20, 1836, *FL*, I, 249–50 ("gazers").

24. To RFF, Aug. 11, 1842, *FL*, III, 86 ("stricter method"); *FL*, I, 246 ("examining myself"); Mar. 14, [1836], FP ("really thinking").

25. MF to JFC, Dec. 6, 18[35], FP ("Life of Goethe"); Apr. 28, 1835, FP ("more

insight"); MF to JFC, Dec. 6, 18[35], FP ("ripe"); Jan. 7, 1836, *CL*, 113 ("greatness and littleness"); FP ("re-educated myself").

26. FP ("metaphysics").

27. [Ca. early 1836]*, *FL*, I, 198 ("our Goethe"); *FL*, I, 254 ("easy to say"); Jan. 7, 1836, *CL*, 113 ("religious book"); Apr. 19, 1836, FP ("Carlyle view"); [ca. early 1836]*, *FL*, I, 198 ("Eclectic"); "Heyne's and Carlyle's Opinion of Goethe," FMW, Works, I, 505 ("heathen god"). For a brief, balanced discussion of Carlyle's understanding of Goethe, see Charles Frederick Harrold, *Carlyle and German Thought, 1819–1834* (New Haven, 1934), 68–72.

28. MF to JFC, Apr. 19, 1836, FP ("troubled"); Mar. 28, 1836, *CL*, 117 ("leaned close upon Pantheism"); May 4, 1836, *CL*, 119 ("Goethe's license"); FP ("go to Europe"); Mar. 14, [1836], FP ("not shrink back").

29. *FL*, I, 254 ("my pen"); Nov. 30, 1834, ibid., 214 ("vulgar magazine"); quoted in "Margaret Fuller," Boston newspaper, Aug. [25, 1883], OC, 10 ("press"); [ca. early 1836]*, *OM*, I, 168 ("my soul").

30. April 19, 1836, FP ("West"); Apr. 28, 1835, FP ("avail me"); [ca. early 1836]*, *OM*, I, 168 ("sneer"); to Mary Peabody, May 15, [1836], *PL*, 166 ("desirous"). For a sketch of the *American Monthly Magazine*, see Frank Luther Mott, *A History of American Magazines, 1741–1850* (New York, 1930), 344–45, 602–3, 618–21.

31. *American Monthly Magazine*, 7 (June 1836), 572, 575–76, 578–79 ("precocity"). Higginson called Fuller's Mackintosh essay "one of the very best critical essays yet written in America" (*HO*, 288). But his explanation for her success—that Mackintosh's temperament "was wholly alien from hers"—was uncharacteristically undiscerning.

32. *American Monthly Magazine*, 8 (July 1836), 2–3, 5, 7, 13 ("internal improvements"). For an example of a standard conservative anti-Romantic view of Heine's book, see the review that month in the *North American*. In it the author deplored Heine's moral character and political and theological opinions, but nonetheless applauded his critique of Romanticism (43 [July 1836], 163–66).

33. Quoted in "Margaret Fuller," OC, 10 ("splendid"); *American Monthly Magazine*, 8 (Sept. 1836), 235 ("bold"); ibid. (Oct. 1836), 320–21 ("mind-emotions"). For the reception of the British Romantic poets in America at this time, see Charvat, *Origins of American Critical Thought*. Classic studies of German Romantic literary philosophy are Arthur O. Lovejoy, "The Meaning of 'Romantic' in Early German Romanticism," and "Schiller and the Genesis of German Romanticism," in his *Essays in the History of Ideas* (Baltimore, 1948), 185–227. For a cogent analysis of German Romantic critical theory, see René Wellek, *A History of Modern Criticism: 1750–1950*, Vol. I, *The Later Eighteenth Century* (New Haven, 1955), chaps. 9–11, and Vol. II, *The Romantic Age* (New Haven, 1955), chaps. 1–3. Also valuable is Jochen Schulte-Sasse, "The Concept of Literary Criticism in German Romanticism, 1795–1810," in Peter Uwe Hohendahl, ed., *A History of German Literary Criticism, 1730–1980* (Lincoln, Neb., 1988), 99–177. For a judicious estimate of the limited appeal of German Romantic literary theories at this time, see Hanna-Beate Schilling, "The Role of the Brothers Schlegel in American Literary Criticism as Found in Selected Periodicals, 1812–1833: A Critical Bibliography," *American Literature*, 43 (January 1972), 563–79.

34. *American Monthly Magazine*, 8 (Sept. 1836), 242–43, 247, 249 ("uneasy").

35. *American Monthly Magazine*, 8 (Oct. 1836), 321, 322, 325–29 ("erudite").

36. Commonplace Book, [ca. 1836–1837], Tappan Papers, MH ("any depth"); JFC to MF, July 29, 1836, *CL*, 121 ("delight[ed]").

37. Quoted in Oct. 6, 1836, *EJ*, V, 218 ("little beyond"). For an excellent guide to the

enormous literature on New England Transcendentalism, see Joel Myerson, ed., *The Transcendentalists: A Review of Research and Criticism* (New York, 1984). Also very useful are the editions of the Transcendentalists' papers that have been published in Myerson's annual, *Studies in the American Renaissance.* We still lack a modern comprehensive history of the movement. The closest substitute is Perry Miller's hyperbolic but brilliant anthology (*MT*). Joel Myerson, *The New England Transcendentalists and the* Dial (Rutherford, N.J., 1980), Part II, is an invaluable guide to the lives of the Transcendentalists. Octavius Brooks Frothingham, *Transcendentalism in New England: A History* (New York, 1876) is still useful for the philosophical background of the movement. For a good corrective to some aspects of Miller's treatment of Transcendentalist religion, see William R. Hutchison, *The Transcendentalist Ministers: Church Reform in the New England Renaissance* (New Haven, 1959). The most complete study of the literary thought of the Transcendentalists is Lawrence Buell, *Literary Transcendentalism: Style and Vision in the American Renaissance* (Ithaca, 1973). For a partial but still suggestive investigation of the social origins and character of Transcendentalism, see Anne C. Rose, *Transcendentalism as a Social Movement, 1830–1850* (New Haven, 1981). In lieu of a modern history, the best sources for New England Transcendentalism remain the voluminous writings and papers of its adherents, on which I have relied heavily in this and subsequent chapters.

38. *MT*, 8 ("religious demonstration"). Abrams's *Natural Supernaturalism* is excellent on the religious vision of European Romanticism.

39. Feb. 10, 1834, JFC Papers, MH ("skepticism").

40. Nov. 8, 1833, JFC Papers, MH ("Cambridge drone"); Apr. 30, 1838, ibid. ("effeminate"); to JFC, Apr. 27, 1835, "CLS" ("supernal coterie"); Clarence L. F. Gohdes, *The Periodicals of American Transcendentalism* (Durham, N.C., 1931), 10 ("'getting religion'"). For an unsurpassed evocation of the cultural origins of New England Transcendentalism, see "Historic Notes of Life and Letters in New England," in *EW*, X, 323–70.

41. Quoted in James Elliot Cabot, *A Memoir of Ralph Waldo Emerson,* 2 vols. (Boston, 1887), I, 244 ("protest"); May 30, 1837, *EJ*, V, 338 ("Hedge's Club"); JFC, journal, Oct. 9, 1836, Perry-Clarke Collection, MHi ("Like-Minded").

42. Miller, *MT*, xi ("Annus Mirabilis"); [ca. Nov. 1835], FMW, Box A ("their thoughts?"); Feb. 1, 1835, *FL*, I, 220 ("your Unitarianism"); [Nov. 1835], FMW, Box A ("Xty").

43. [Nov. 1835], FMW, Box A ("right ground"); "Historic Notes," 329 ("knives").

44. *Partial Portraits* (1888; Ann Arbor, 1970), 30 ("certain chords"). The large body of writings on Emerson has been growing ever larger, especially in the last decade. The standard biographies are Ralph L. Rusk, *The Life of Ralph Waldo Emerson* (New York, 1949); and Gay Wilson Allen, *Waldo Emerson: A Biography* (New York, 1981). The best introduction to his thought is still Stephen E. Whicher, *Freedom and Fate: An Inner Life of Ralph Waldo Emerson* (Philadelphia, 1953). Two studies that are valuable in placing Emerson in historical context are Joel Porte, *Representative Man: Ralph Waldo Emerson in His Time* (New York, 1979); and Maurice Gonnaud, *An Uneasy Solitude: Individual and Society in the Work of Ralph Waldo Emerson* (Princeton, 1987). Other recent books that are also helpful in contextualizing Emerson are David Robinson, *Apostle of Culture: Emerson as Preacher and Lecturer* (Philadelphia, 1982); Evelyn Barish, *Emerson: The Roots of Prophecy* (Princeton, 1989); and Mary Kupiec Cayton, *Emerson's Emergence: Self and Society in the Transformation of New England, 1800–1845* (Chapel Hill, 1989). For a good sampling of recent criticism, see Harold Bloom, ed., *Ralph Waldo Emerson*

(New York, 1985). *EL*, *EJ*, and the ongoing *ECW* remain the indispensable sources for Emerson's life and thought. The best published source for Lidian Emerson is *ESL*.

45. Sept. 8, 1833, quoted in Cabot, *Memoir of Emerson*, I, 201 ("selfish"); *ECW*, I, 7, 41–42, 44–45 ("sepulchres").

46. Feb. 5, 1835, *EL*, I, 436 ("sober joy"); Feb. 20, 1835, MH-AH ("original"); Feb. 28, 1835, "CLS" ("soaring Transcendentalist").

47. Oct. 6, 1834, *FL*, I, 210 ("clergyman"); Feb. 1, 1835, ibid., 224 ("sensation"); Nov. 9, 1834, *FL*, I, 211 ("many tears"); [ca. early 1833], FMW, Box A ("favorite Mr Emerson"); Jan. 17, 1835, MH-AH ("glow"); Apr. 17, 1834, FP *("applause");* [ca. Nov. 1835], FMW, Box A ("proof"); June 27, 1835, FP ("acquaintance").

48. JFC to RWE, Jan. 18, 1835, JFC Papers, MH ("beautiful"); *OM*, I, 201 ("genius"); quoted in Rusk, *Life of Emerson*, 234 ("prejudice"); [late July 1836], *ESL*, 49 ("sound").

49. *OM*, I, 202–3 ("still remember").

50. *EJ*, V, 186 ("worst guest"); July 31, 1836, ibid., 187 ("wise man"); Aug. 6, 1836, ibid. ("face").

51. *EL*, II, 32 ("extraordinary person"); [late July 1836], *ESL*, 49 ("We like her"); *EJ*, V, 190 ("egotism"); Nov. 15, 1836, *EL*, II, 46–47 ("Miss Fuller's gifts").

52. *EL*, II, 37 ("ride up"); *FL*, I, 260–62 ("dear friend"); *EL*, II, 38 ("make myself amends"); to William Emerson, Oct. 23, 1836, ibid., 42 ("prisoner"); to MF, Sept. 20, 1836, ibid., 37 ("poppy").

53. May 23, 1836, *FL*, I, 254 ("suffering mother"); Apr. 28, 1835, FP ("other means"); May 23, 1836, *FL*, I, 254 ("teach"); July 29, 1836, *CL*, 121 ("money-making"); Oct. 1836, FMW, IX, 41 ("classes"); May 13, 1837, FP ("20 pages"); to MF, Oct. 20, 1836, *EL*, II, 41 ("great pleasure").

54. May 13, 1837, FP ("Very interesting"); Apr. 28, 1835, FP ("magnetic power"); Ward Papers, MHi ("coming to Boston").

55. MCF to MF, Feb. [7], 1847, FMW, VIII, 217 ("sensitive"); 1837, *FL*, I, 263 ("must suffer"); to Mary [Channing]*, Oct. 7, 1838, ibid., 344–45 ("too severe").

56. *Society in America*, 3 vols. (London, 1837), III, 30 ("valuable persons"); "Introductory Remarks," *Boston Quarterly Review*, Jan. 1838, *MT*, 182 ("city of 'notions'"). Pease and Pease's *Web of Progress* presents a good portrait of Boston's new expansion and diversity in the 1830s. For a discussion of the reaction of Unitarian elites to these changes, see Rose, *Transcendentalism as a Social Movement*, chap. 1.

57. Apr. 11, 1837, *FL*, I, 269 ("boldest peep").

58. [Samuel Gray Ward], *Ward Family Papers: Collected and Written by Samuel Gray Ward* (Boston, 1900), 103 ("unpopular"); "Memoranda of interviews, conversations and public discourses," Jan. 13, [1837], FMW, Box 3 ("dispassionate"); to JFC, May 13, 1837, FP ("delightful hours"); GR to MF, Apr. 6, [1837], Emerson Family Papers, MH ("great friends"); "Memoranda," [Jan. 1, 1837], FMW, Box 3 ("settling any-thing"); Dec. 19, 1836, ibid. ("Aspasia").

59. JFC, journal, Perry-Clarke Collection, MHi *("storms"); OM*, I, 176 ("came away"); [journal, ca. Dec. 1836], *OM*, I, 175–76 ("us feminine people"); [Dec.] 1836, "Memoranda," FMW, Box 3 ("undervalue Dr Channing"); Dec. 5, 1836, ibid. ("man of expediency"). Arthur W. Brown, *Always Young for Liberty: A Biography of William Ellery Channing* (Syracuse, 1956); and Madeline Hook Rice, *Federal Street Pastor: The Life of William Ellery Channing* (New York, 1961) are the best modern biographies. For two recent sympathetic treatments of, respectively, Channing's theology and his politics, see Conrad Wright, "The Rediscovery of Channing," in his *The Liberal Christians* (Bos-

ton, 1970), 22–28; and Andrew Delbanco, *William Ellery Channing: An Essay on the Liberal Spirit in America* (Cambridge, Mass., 1981).

60. The standard biographies are Odell Shepard, *Pedlar's Progress: The Life of Bronson Alcott* (Boston, 1937); and Frederick C. Dahlstrand, *Amos Bronson Alcott: An Intellectual Biography* (Rutherford, N.J., 1982). Dorothy McCuskey, *Bronson Alcott, Teacher* (New York, 1940) is a still-useful study of Alcott's educational theories and career. Although the parallel struck me before I read his book, the Alcott–savage comparison is also made by Allen in his *Waldo Emerson*, 254.

61. [Ca. Winter–Spring 1837], "Conversations with Pupils," FMW, Works, II, 907 ("emblematic").

62. *FL*, I, 256 ("experiment"); May 13, 1837, FP ("fatiguing"); "Conversations with Pupils," [ca. Winter–Spring 1837], FMW, Works, II, 935, 953, 987 ("imagination"); May 13, 1837, FP ("valuable thoughts").

63. "Diary for 1838," Mar. 1838, [Week 11], 174, Alcott Papers, MH ("good society"); "AJ37-1," 48 ("Miss Fuller"); [Mar. 26–Apr. 1], 1837, ibid., 93 ("generous views").

64. Sept. 1, 1836, *FL*, I, 260 ("horror"); "Memoranda," FMW, Box 3 ("distrust"); to ABA, June 1840, *FL*, II, 143 ("impression"); Emerson Family Papers, MH, and *OM*, I, 172 ("O for the safe and natural way").

65. Quoted in [Joseph T. Buckingham], "Alcott's Conversations on the Gospel," *Boston Courier*, 12 (Mar. 29, 1837) ("one third absurd"); postscript to "A Parent," "To Fathers and Mothers," ibid. (Mar. 30, 1837) ("indecent").

66. Rose, *Transcendentalism as a Social Movement*, 80–83, includes a good, brief discussion of the social aspects of the furor over Alcott's book.

67. To ABA, Aug. 7, 1836, *PL*, 181 ("physiological"); *Christian Register*, 16 (Apr. 29, 1837), 66 ("LYNCHING"); to ABA, Mar. 24, 1837, *EL*, II, 61 ("miserable"); *FL*, I, 265 ("'cut up'").

68. May 23, 1837, MH-AH ("right"). Actually, Walker later wrote a fairly balanced review of Alcott's book and system for the *Examiner*'s November issue. See "Alcott's Conversation on the Gospels," *Christian Examiner*, 5 (Nov. 1837), 252–61.

69. Apr. 6, 1837, *FL*, I, 266 ("haberdasher's prentice"); MF to JFC, May 13, 1837, FP ("forlorn"); Apr. 6, 1837, *FL*, I, 266 ("'confirmed invalid'"); May 13, 1837, FP ("bad head"); July 26, 1837, *CL*, 125 ("How glad").

70. To MF, Apr. 24?, 1837, *EL*, II, 71 ("very valuable"); to MF, Apr. 19, 1837, ibid., 70 ("inestimable"); Apr. 26, 1837, *EJ*, V, 306 ("ghastly hard"); *OM*, I, 204 ("pleasure").

71. *EL*, II, 76–77 ("the great man"); June 28, 1838, ibid., 143 *("Thus far");* [July? 1838?], *FL*, I, 337 ("mental furniture"); "Memoranda," Dec. 5, 1836, FMW, Box 3 ("salt"); [July? 1838?], *FL*, I, 337 ("Truth".)

72. May 30, 1837, *FL*, I, 277 ("familiarity"); ibid., 268 ("ungracious").

73. Apr. 24?, 1837, *EL*, 71 ("No"); May 2, 1837, *FL*, I, 272 ("excitement"); *EJ*, V, 308 ("Vivian Gray"); May 4, 1837, ibid., 319 ("against my will"); May 5, 1837, *EL*, II, 74 ("Woman wise!"); May 19, 1837, ibid., 76 ("good to me").

74. *FL*, I, 274 ("thank you"); May 2, 1837, ibid., 272 ("vegetate"); June 18, 1837, ibid., 285 ("receptive state"); May 13, 1837, FP ("Life of Goethe"); Apr. 10, 1837, *EL*, II, 65 ("mercenary value"); to [?], [Summer 1837], *FL*, I, 280 ("very advantageous terms").

75. [June 24–29], 1836, "AJ36," 61 ("disciple"); to JFC, May 13, 1837, FP ("department"); to EPP, May 26, 1837, *FL*, I, 276 ("literature"); "Diary for 1838," Mar. 1838, [Week 11], 175, Alcott Papers, MH ("ample"); quoted in "Margaret Fuller," Boston newspaper, Aug. [25, 1883], OC, 10 ("How much"); to [?], [Summer 1837], *FL*, I, 280 ("immediate independence").

76. *FR,* 31 ("Father's 'praise'"); May 30, 1837, *EL,* II, 77 ("Seeing the stage stop"); June 6, 1837, *FL,* I, 283 ("Anaxagoras").

Chapter Seven

1. *FL,* I, 283 ("dear Concord"); Apr. 19, 1837, *EL,* II, 70 ("waft benedictions"); June 6, 1837, *FL,* I, 283 ("genial preachment"); "Address on Education," *EEL,* II, 197–99, 202 ("desperate conservatism").

2. *FL,* I, 284 ("noble appeal"); *Providence Daily Journal,* June 17, 1837 *("wonderment");* June 27, 1837, *FL,* I, 286 ("stony soil").

3. June 16, 1837, *FL,* I, 284 ("country"); June 27, 1837, ibid., 286 ("money getting"); July 12, 1837, ibid., 292 ("Philistency").

4. Journal, Dec. 3, 1838, Perry-Clarke Collection, MHi ("spiritual place"); quoted in Anna D. Gale, "School Journal," Feb. 21, 1838, Gale Family Papers, MWA *("Paddys").* The *Providence Daily Journal* is the best source for antebellum Providence Whiggery. John S. Gilkeson, Jr., in *Middle-Class Providence, 1820–1940* (Princeton, 1986), chaps. 1–2, helpfully discusses the class-conscious dimension of antebellum Providence's reform culture. Patrick T. Conley, *Democracy in Decline: Rhode Island's Constitutional Development, 1776–1841* (Providence, 1977) is instructive on Providence politics. Relevant details about Providence in these years may also be found in William R. Staples, *Annals of the Town of Providence* (Providence, 1843); Richard M. Bayles, ed., *History of Providence County, Rhode Island,* 2 vols., I (New York, 1891); Walter C. Bronson, *The History of Brown University, 1764–1914* (Providence, 1914); Thomas Williams Bicknell, *The History of the State of Rhode Island and Providence Plantations,* 6 vols. (New York, 1920); and Charles C. Carroll, *Rhode Island: Three Centuries of Democracy,* 4 vols. (New York, 1932).

5. For evidence of the widespread appeal of avant-garde and reform movements in the Providence area, see Charles R. Crowe, "Transcendentalism and 'The Newness' in Rhode Island," *Rhode Island History,* 14 (Apr. 1955), 33–46.

6. Hiram Fuller, *Grand Transformation Scenes in the United States; or, Glimpses of Home After Thirteen Years Abroad* (New York, 1875), 298 ("Black Republican"). The most extensive discussion of Hiram Fuller's New York publishing career appears in Perry Miller, *The Raven and the Whale: The War of Words and Wits in the Era of Poe and Melville* (New York, 1956). Facts on Fuller's later years can be gleaned from his books. See especially *North and South* (London, 1863); and *Grand Transformation Scenes.*

7. Mary W. Allen to Anna D. Gale, [Mar. 30, 1838], Gale Family Papers, MWA ("'capacities'"); Hiram Fuller to ABA, June 17, 1836, MH ("sacred"); MF, journal, [late Dec. 1838], OC, 89 ("anti-excitement"); Jan. 8–14, 1837, "AJ37-1," 42 ("believer"); Anna D. Gale, "School Journal," Jan. 31, 1838, Gale Family Papers, MWA ("politeness"). For useful sketches of the Greene Street School, see Henry L. Greene, "The Greene-St. School, of Providence, and Its Teachers," *Publications of the Rhode Island Historical Society,* New Series, 6 (Jan. 1899), 199–219; Judith Strong Albert, "Transition in Transcendental Education: The Schools of Bronson Alcott and Hiram Fuller," *Educational Studies,* 11 (Fall 1980), 209–19; idem, "Margaret Fuller's Row at the Greene Street School: Early Female Education in Providence, 1837–1839," *Rhode Island History,* 42 (May 1983), 43–55; idem, "Transcendental School Journals in Nineteenth Century America," *Journal of Psychohistory,* 9 (Summer 1981), 105–26; and Laraine R. Fergenson, "Margaret Fuller in the Classroom: The Providence Period," *SAR, 1987,* 131–

42. But the best sources for Hiram Fuller and his school are the letters and journals of Fuller's Greene Street students, several of the latter of which have been published in *SAR*.

8. June 11–17, 1837, "AJ37-2," 92 ("one of the best"); July 5, 1837, *FL*, I, 290 ("never romp"); quoted in Greene, "Greene-St. School," 202 ("Order"); to ABF, July 5, 1837, *FL*, I, 290 ("French cloak"); quoted in July 3, 1837, Laraine R. Fergenson, "Margaret Fuller as a Teacher in Providence: The School Journal of Ann Brown," *SAR, 1991,* 67 ("cut-glass"); to ABF, July 5, 1837, *FL*, I, 290 ("urn").

9. June 16, 1837, *FL*, I, 284 ("propriety"); July 5, 1837, ibid., 290 ("appearance"); Anna D. Gale to Frederick W. Gale, Dec. 30, 1837, Gale Family Papers, MWA ("not remarkably handsome"); Louise Hunt to Anna D. Gale, Feb. 16, 1838, Gale Family Papers, MWA (*"Beautiful"*); Greene, "Greene-St. School," 211 ("refined"); Anna D. Gale, "School Journal," Feb. 14, 1838, Gale Family Papers, MWA (*"kind"*); Anna D. Gale to Frederick W. Gale, Dec. 30, 1837, Gale Family Papers, MWA ("manners"); Nov. 2, 1837, *FL*, I, 311 *("dingy");* quoted in Greene, "Greene-St. School," 210–11 ("queenly"); Nov. 2, 1837, *FL*, I, 311 ("ordinary people"); Mar. 18, 1838, FP ("very favorably"); Oct. 1, 1[837], FP ("little arts"); Mar. 18, 1838, FP ("living influence"); *FL*, I, 287 ("suited to this business"); Nov. 6, 1837, *EJ*, V, 419 ("chagrin"); *FL*, I, 291 ("defects"). In his *Recollections of a Busy Life* ([New York, 1868], 173), Horace Greeley claimed that Fuller was never paid her salary. But both Fuller's successor, Sarah S. Jacobs, and Fuller's colleague Frances Aborn White—both of whom were in a position to know— strongly denied this to Higginson. "I am sure she did receive *all* her salary regularly," White assured him. Frances M. White to Thomas Wentworth Higginson, 188–?, OC, 267. See also *HO*, 80.

10. [Ca. June 1837]*, *OM*, I, 177 ("gulf is vast"); MF to EPP, May 26, 1837, *FL*, I, 276 ("maidens"); [ca. June 1837]*, journal, *OM*, 177 ("ignorance"); *FL*, I, 287 ("compare pupils"); July 12, 1837, ibid., 292 *("sacrifices");* July 3, 1837, ibid., 288 ("cause of education").

11. MF to EPP, July 8, 1837, quoted in *HO*, 81 ("returning health"); July 5, 1837, *FL*, I, 291 ("very rationally"); ibid., 289–90 ("no preparation"); July 8, 1837, ibid., 292 ("perfectly equal"); July 5, 1837, ibid., 289 ("power of expression"). For Fuller's later hint to her students that Hiram Fuller had given her "false impressions . . . of the position" she was to have occupied at the school, see her farewell speech to her students, recorded in her journal, [late Dec. 1838], OC, 89.

12. July 8, 1837, *FL*, I, 292 ("much time"); [Aug. 1837], OC, 87 ("some nonsense"); Aug. [14]*, 1837, Fergenson, "School Journal of Ann Brown," 69 ("blushes"); Aug. 14, 1837, *FL*, I, 295 ("horror"); [Aug. 1837], OC, 87 ("manner"); [Aug. 1837], *OM*, I, 180 ("ornate"); [Aug. 1837], OC, 87 ("Webster class"); Aug. 14, 1837, *FL*, 295 ("best thing"). For the absence of women at political rallies and conventions before the 1840s, see Ryan, *Women in Public,* 132–41.

13. July 18, 1837, *EL*, 88 ("Power"); *FL*, I, 294–95 ("irreligious").

14. *ECW*, I, 53, 63, 67, 69–70 *("Man Thinking").*

15. Quoted in Rusk, *Life of Emerson,* 263 ("mixed confusion"); to JFC, Aug. 20, 1838, "CLS" ("duty"); Dec. 16, 1837, ibid. ("prejudices"); JFC, journal, [Oct. 1837], Perry-Clarke Collection, MHi ("glides"); [ca. early 1840s]*, *OM*, I, 194–95 ("Mr. E.'s preaching").

16. Oct. 20, 1837, *EJ*, V, 407 ("goody"); Aug. 17, 1837, *EL*, II, 95 ("rules"); MF, essay, Apr. 19, 1838, in Tess Hoffmann, "Miss Fuller Among the Literary Lions: Two Essays Read at 'The Coliseum' in 1838," *SAR, 1988,* 45 ("progress of Society"); to Lucy Jackson Brown, Sept. 2, 1837, *ESL*, 59 ("all-day party"). Sarah Alden Ripley and Sophia Ripley

would also attend one more Transcendental Club meeting each. For a convenient listing of Club attendants and topics, see Joel Myerson, "A Calendar of Transcendental Club Meetings," *American Literature,* 44 (May 1972), 197-207.

17. MCF to Abraham W. Fuller, Aug. 28, 1837, FMW, VIII, 8 ("man's control"); to Abraham W. Fuller, Feb. 3, 1836, ibid., 5 ("keep school"); MCF to Abraham W. Fuller, Sept. 3, 1837, ibid., 9 ("bread").

18. Sept. 3, 1837, FMW, VIII, 9 ("to feel calm"); Sept. 5, 1837, *FL,* I, 300-302 ("sordid man").

19. MCF to MF, May 27, 1847, FMW, VIII, 217 ("shilling"); to Mary Rotch, May 29, 1848, *FL,* V, 71 ("see me fail").

20. Oct. 14, 1837, *FL,* I, 303 ("stay"); "The Book's own Introduction," The Coliseum, 2 vols., I, 4, RPB ("develope mind"). For an impressionistic, but useful, discussion of the Coliseum Club and its members, see Charles R. Crowe, "Transcendentalism and the Providence Literati," *Rhode Island History,* 14 (July 1955), 65-78. The best primary sources are the papers of Newcomb, Greene, and other Club members, deposited at RPB.

21. Jan. 21, 1840, *FL,* II, 119 ("Your circle"); MF to CKN, Oct. 2, 1841, ibid., 237 ("prying"); [Feb. 14? 1838], *FL,* I, 325 ("daring passages"); [ca. 1838], ibid., 321 ("A supper"); MF to EF, June 8, 1839, *FL,* II, 72 ("nimbl[e]"); "Evenings with the Author of 'Old Grimes,'" *Providence Daily Journal,* Mar. 27, 1868 ("arrogance"); Apr. 20, 1838, CKN Papers, RPB ("That Lady"); *OM,* I, 320 ("ovation").

22. Oct. 1837, OC, 88, and [Oct. 1837], *OM,* I, 184 ("bad"); [late Nov. 1837], OC, 88, and [late Nov. 1837]*, *OM,* I, 181 ("fight"); to Elizabeth Oakes Smith, Mar. 11, 1846, MaHi ("she-gladiator"). For a revealing self-portrait of the man, see John Neal, *Wandering Recollections of a Somewhat Busy Life* (Boston, 1869). Benjamin Lease, *That Wild Fellow John Neal and the American Literary Revolution* (Chicago, 1972) is a good critical study.

23. "The Magnetizer," *Providence Daily Journal,* June 20, 1837 ("self-improvement"); JFC, journal, [Oct., 1837], Perry-Clarke Collection, MHi ("head quarters"); *Practical Instruction in Animal Magnetism,* rev. ed. (New York, 1843), 217 ("high standing"); ibid., 230 ("extraordinary"); to T. C. Hartshorn, Dec. 1, 1837, Deleuze, *Practical Instruction,* 300 ("question of *fact*"); [Oct. 1837], Perry-Clarke Collection, MHi ("put . . . to sleep"); Nov. 20, 1837, *CL,* 127 ("sleeping beauty"); *FL,* I, 303 ("unwell"); ibid. 313 ("good for nothing"); "Historic Notes," *EW,* X, 337 ("genial"). For a useful overview of nineteenth-century American mesmerism, see Robert C. Fuller, *Mesmerism and the American Cure of Souls* (Philadelphia, 1982). Allan Angoff, "Hypnotism in the United States of America," in Eric J. Dingwall, ed., *Abnormal Hypnotic Phenomena: A Survey of Nineteenth-Century Cases,* 4 vols. (New York, 1968), Vol. IV, includes (7-16) a discussion of mesmerist activity in Providence.

24. Orville Dewey, quoted in *MT,* 158 ("revelation"); Martin Luther Hurlbut, "Furness's *Remarks on the Gospels,*" *Christian Examiner,* 22 (Mar. 1837), 122 *("naturalism");* "Locke and the Transcendentalists," ibid., 23 (Nov. 1837), 184, 193 ("gulf"); Mar. 29, 1837, JFC Papers, MH *("Inquisition").*

25. *Society in America,* III, 30-32 ("aristocratic"); "Miss Martineau's *Society in America,*" *North American Review,* 45 (Oct. 1837), 424 ("worthless"); to JFC, July 19, 1837, "CLS" ("offensive"); *Society in America,* III, 174-75 ("mischief").

26. *FL,* I, 307-10 ("disappointment").

27. *Martineau's Autobiography,* III, 201 ("immense letter"); Jan. 21, 1838, "CLS" ("masterpiece"); Dec. 16, 1837, ibid. ("severest thing"); Anne Warren Weston to Debora Weston, Oct. 21, 1836, Weston Papers, MB ("partisan"); [ca. Winter 1835-1836]*, *OM,*

I, 129–30 ("cause of Right"); to EF, [Dec. 13, 1835], *FL,* I, 240 ("at her"); to EKF, Apr. 21, 1836, ibid., 251 ("think ill"); ibid., 310 ("on several points"); Jan. 29, 1836, FP ("not be disappointed").

28. To CS, Feb. 7, [1839], *FL,* II, 48 ("man deification"); to JFC, Jan. 21, 1838, "CLS" ("honest and frank"); MF to EKF, Apr. 21, 1836, *FL,* I, 251 ("effects"); *Martineau's Autobiography,* II, 73 ("pedantry and forwardness").

29. *FL,* I, 303–4 ("do much for you"); to [?], Sept. 2, [1837], ibid., 300 ("fascinating"); Nov. 2, 1837, ibid., 311 ("catalogue").

30. "Locke and the Transcendentalists," 171 ("midsummer madness"); *FL,* I, 314–15 ("strong indignation"). For a useful sketch of William Sturgis, see Charles G. Loring, "Memoir of the Hon. William Sturgis," *Proceedings of the Massachusetts Historical Society,* v.7, 1863–1864 (Boston, 1864), 420–73.

31. *FL,* I, 315 ("exaggerated notions"); "ON," 505 ("misbehaviour"); *EEL,* II, 336 ("fair girl"). Not surprisingly, both Fuller and Sturgis took a great interest in this lecture. See *FL,* I, 328, 338.

32. *FL,* I, 316 ("cheerful"); Oct. 21, 1837, FP ("Our conversations"); Jan. 3, 1838, *FL,* I, 323 ("Wayland").

33. Jan. 3, 1838, *FL,* I, 322 ("people"); [Dec. 3–9, 1837], "AJ37-2," 136 ("anecdotes"); Jan. 3, 1838, *FL,* I, 322 ("happy"); "Some remarks upon Madame Caradori," in Hoffmann, "Two Essays," 42 ("Music"); Feb. 10, 1838, Emerson Family Papers, MH *("dances");* Jan. 3, 1838, *FL,* I, 323 ("three parties").

34. Jan. 3, 1838, *FL,* I, 322–23 ("afraid").

35. Feb. 10, 1838, Emerson Family Papers, MH ("more than I expected"); Dec. 1838, OC, 89 ("sweet"); quoted in Greene, "Greene-St. School," 210–11 ("awe them"); May 16, 1838, Fergenson, "School Journal of Ann Brown," 89 ("hysterical fit"); Adeline Brown to Mary W. Allen, Oct. 28, 1838, Allen-Johnson Family Papers, MWA ("beloved"); quoted in Marble, "Margaret Fuller as Teacher," 343 ("Preposterous").

36. Dec. 12, 1838, Frank Shuffelton, "Margaret Fuller at the Greene Street School: The Journal of Evelina Metcalf," *SAR, 1985,* 38 ("row").

37. Dec. 12, 1838, Shuffelton, "Journal of Evelina Metcalf," 39 ("How and when"); quoted in Johnson, "Her Scholars," 427 ("worth a journey"); Dec. 30, 1837, Gale Family Papers, MWA ("awe of her"); Jan. 1, 1838, quoted in Johnson, "Her Scholars," 427 ("cuts us up").

38. Johnson, "Her Scholars," 428 ("diffident"); quoted in ibid. ("half in jest").

39. [Mar. 30, 1838], Gale Family Papers, MWA *("less satirical");* "Greene St. Journal No. 2," quoted in Judith Strong Albert, "Margaret Fuller and Mary Ware Allen: 'In Youth an Insatiate Student'—A Certain Kind of Friendship," *Thoreau Quarterly Journal,* 12 (July 1980), 14 ("pains"); Oct. 28, 1838, quoted in Johnson, "Her Scholars," 428 ("my pillar").

40. [Late Dec. 1838], OC, 89 ("barbarous ignorance"); to Anna D. Gale, June 15, 1838, Gale Family Papers ("our deficiencies"); Aug. 2, 1837, Fergenson, "School Journal of Ann Brown," 68 ("more thoughts"); Mary Ware Allen, "Greene St. School Journal No. 3," quoted in Strong, "Margaret Fuller and Mary Ware Allen," 17 ("suggestively"); Jan. 18, 1838, quoted in Johnson, "Her Scholars," 427 ("must *think*"); Sept. 24, 1838, Fergenson, "School Journal of Ann Brown," 102 ("conversations"); "School Journal," Jan. 5, 1838, Gale Family Papers, MWA ("dry husk"); Dec. 20, 1837, quoted in Johnson, "Her Scholars," 427 ("*we* must talk").

41. Jan. 18, 1838, quoted in Johnson, "Her Scholars," 427 ("hearing Miss Fuller talk"); "Greene Street Journal," Jan. 12, 1838, I, 45, quoted in Albert, "Transcendental

School Journals," 111 ("'thoughts of the soul'"); MF, journal, [late Dec. 1838], OC, 89 ("lectures"); Evelina Metcalf, journal, Apr. 26, 1838, ScU ("great men"); to ABF, Dec. 20, 1840, *FL*, II, 196 ("best interpret"); Mary Ware Allen, "Greene Street School Journal," II, 11, quoted in Albert, "Transcendental School Journals," 116 ("stiff"); May 2, 1838, ScU ("reason and understanding"); "School Journal," Jan. 5, 1838, Gale Family Papers, MWA ("transcendentalism").

42. Anna D. Gale, "School Journal," Mar. 2, 1838, Gale Family Papers, MWA ("created us"); Jan. 18, 1838, quoted in Johnson, "Her Scholars," 427 ("enjoy"). For a recent vigorously pursued argument emphasizing the worldliness of Wayland's kind of evangelicalism, see James Turner, *Without God, Without Creed: The Origins of Unbelief in America* (Baltimore, 1985), chap. 3.

43. "School Journal," Jan. 5, 1838, Gale Family Papers, MWA ("ancients"); *The Elements of Moral Science,* ed. Joseph L. Blau (Cambridge, Mass., 1963), 133 ("annihilated"); Anna D. Gale, "School Journal," Feb. 2, 1838, Gale Family Papers, MWA ("symbolical"); *Elements of Moral Science,* 146 ("happiness"); Anna D. Gale, "School Journal," Mar. 2, 1838, Gale Family Papers, MWA ("worthy"); Feb. 9, 1838, ibid. ("difference"); Jan. 19, 1838, ibid. ("corrupt"); Feb. 2, 1838, ibid. ("maniacs").

44. "School Journal," Mar. 2, 1838, Gale Family Papers, MWA ("soul was progressive").

45. Sept. 25, 1838, Fergenson, "School Journal of Ann Brown," 102 ("'single blessedness'"); "Greene Street School Journal No. 2," 55, quoted in Albert, "Margaret Fuller and Mary Ware Allen," 13 ("distinguished"); Dec. 18, 1838, Shuffelton, "Journal of Evelina Metcalf," 42 ("historians"); Mary Ware Allen, "Greene Street School Journal No. 1," 77, quoted in Albert, "Margaret Fuller and Mary Ware Allen," 13 ("everything"); "School Journal," Jan. 12, 1838, Gale Family Papers, MWA ("beautiful picture"); "Greene Street School Journal No. 2," 55, quoted in Albert, "Margaret Fuller and Mary Ware Allen," 13 ("women's writings"); "School Journal," Jan. 12, 1838, Gale Family Papers, MWA ("Landon").

46. May 7, 1838, ScU ("makes me proud"); Dec. 12, 1838, Shuffelton, "Journal of Evelina Metcalf," 39 ("more like her"); May 31, 1840, *FL*, II, 135 ("They understood"); to Joshua J. Johnson, Nov. 8, 1839, Allen-Johnson Family Papers, MWA ("higher natures").

47. To Anna D. Gale, June 15, 1838, Gale Family Papers, MWA ("large"); ABA, "Diary for 1838," Mar. 1838, [Week 11], 173, Alcott Papers, MH ("Evangele"); "Psyche an Evangele; in Four Books," 1838, 104, Alcott Papers, MH ("stinketh").

48. Mar. 1, 1838, *CL*, 129 ("given you"); Mar. 18, 1838, FP ("out of the question"); May 13, 1838, FP ("miserable"); Mar. 18, 1838, FP ("I die").

49. Nov. 18, 1837, *FL*, I, 316 ("need not be afraid"); Mar. 1, 1838, ibid., 327 ("sombre").

50. MF to RWE, Mar. 1, 1838, *FL*, I, 327–28 ("Sanctissime"); to JSD, May 31, 1838, ibid., 281 ("sorry sight"); *Select Minor Poems, Translated from the German of Goethe and Schiller* (Boston, 1839), 31, 104–5 ("To a Golden Heart"); Aug. 16, 1837, *FL*, I, 297 ("all the time I have"); MF to JFC, May 13, 1838, FP ("posthumous works and all"); notes, [ca. Oct. 1837], FMW, Box A ("List").

51. July 3, 1837, *FL*, I, 288 ("go to him"); July 12, 1837, ibid., 292–93 ("scandal"); Aug. 2, 1837, MH-AH ("know nothing").

52. MF to JFC, June 2, 1835, FP ("brilliant"); Dec. 22, 1837, *FL*, I, 318 ("could but see you").

53. To CS, Mar. 4, 1839, *FL*, II, 60 ("impertinent").

54. Oct. 21, 1[837], FP ("*no* time"); July 26, 1837, *CL*, 126 ("good bundle"); May 13, 1838, FP ("no interest").

55. "Karl Theodor Korner," *Western Messenger,* 4 (Jan. 1838), 309 ("Of such stuff"); ibid. (Feb. 1838), 374 ("uncouth"); ibid. (Jan. 1838), 311 ("worthless demagogues").

56. "Letters from Palmyra," *Western Messenger,* 5 (Apr. 1838), 25–29 ("panegyrists").

57. Mar. 29, 1838, *CL*, 130 ("Latinized"); May 13, 1838, FP ("Sentimentality"); May 21, 1838, *CL*, 132 ("argument"); June 28, 1838, *EL*, II, 142 ("aphorisms"); May 24, 1838, ibid., 135 ("golden pen").

58. MF, Apr. 19, 1838, essay, in Hoffmann, "Two Essays," 45 ("progress of Society").

59. Ibid., 45–46, 48 ("ingenious").

60. Ibid., 48–50 ("sickly consciousness").

61. "Progress—Opinions—Assertions—Religions—& cetera," Coliseum, II, RPB *("Christian civilization");* Apr. 20, 1838, CKN Papers, RPB ("my view"); Hoffmann, "Two Essays," 51 ("meeting of gentlemen"); *ECW*, II, 66–67 ("This time").

62. Gale Family Papers, MWA ("absent"); May 4, 1838, *EL*, II, 129 ("give us"); June 13, 1838, *EJ*, VII, 16 ("this complaint"); Mary W. Allen to Anna D. Gale, June 15, 1838, Gale Family Papers, MWA ("immense crowds"); June 28, 1838, *FL*, I, 334–35 ("command").

63. MF to Thesta Dana, May 30, 1838, *FL*, I, 333 ("bad state"); July [24?], 1838, ibid., 338 ("frenzy"); [ca. summer 1838]*, *OM*, I, 196 ("cold").

64. [Ca. Aug. 1838], OC, 122 ("to and fro").

65. [Aug. 19, 1838], *FL*, I, 340 ("sensitiveness"); to RWE, Mar. 1, 1838, ibid., 327 ("cheerfulness"); Aug. 17, 1838, *EJ*, VII, 48 ("tragedy"); [ca. Aug. 1838], FMW, IX, 38 ("viewless air").

66. Sept. 21, 1838, *FL*, I, 341 ("excellent times"); *EJ*, IX, 147 ("very muscular"); Sept. 21, 1838, *FL*, I, 341–42 ("very *wise*"); Sept. 21, 1838, *FL*, I, 342 ("proper people"); Sept. 15, 1838, FP ("noble"); Sept. 21, 1838, *FL*, I, 341 ("halcyon"); to Elizabeth S. Calvert, Nov. 16, 1838, ibid., 352 ("anxiety").

67. Mar. 4, 1839, *FL*, II, 56 ("wearisome"); MF to JFC, Sept. 15, 1838, FP ("little friends"); MF to EPP, May 26, 1837, *FL*, I, 275 ("Matronizing"); Jan. 8, 1839, FP ("winning"); Sept. 15, 1838, FP ("susceptible"); Oct. 7, 1838, *FL*, I, 344 ("blush").

68. [Ca. Oct.–Nov. 1838], OC, 85, and *OM*, I, 185–86 ("delicately refined"). For a thoughtful discussion of Dana's lectures, see Doreen M. Hunter, *Richard Henry Dana, Sr.* (Boston, 1987), 114–26.

69. Oct. 25, 1838, Fergenson, "School Journal of Ann Brown," 106 ("so unwell"); [Apr. 1838], Allen-Johnson Family Papers, MWA ("heretical doctrines").

70. "Diary for 1838," Dec. 1838, [Week 52], 500, Alcott Papers, MH ("downfall"); [Aug. 19, 1838], *FL*, I, 341 ("uncongenial pursuits"); ibid., 351 ("gabbled"); ibid., 353–54 ("leaving Providence"); [Oct. 1838], Allen-Johnson Family Papers, MWA ("sadly uncultivated"); May 4, 1838, *EL*, II, 129 ("Auricular confessor"); Mar. 30, 1840, ibid., 269 ("great examples"); "Editor's Preface," *Specimens of Foreign Standard Literature,* I (Boston, 1838) ("original documents").

71. Journal, [late Dec. 1838], OC, 89 ("popular articles"); [Louise Hunt]*, Dec. 22, 1838, quoted in Johnson, "Her Scholars," 429 ("wicked"); [late Dec. 1838], OC, 89, and *OM*, I, 179–80 ("forty present").

72. *FL*, I, 354 ("further use").

Chapter Eight

1. [Ca. late Dec. 1838], OC, 89 ("Packing"); Jan. 7, 1839, FP ("parties"); Jan. 1, 1839, *EJ*, VII, 163 ("vigils"); Jan. 1, 1839, quoted in James B. Thayer, *Rev. Samuel Ripley of Waltham* (Cambridge, Mass., 1897), 46 ("excitement"); Jan. 7, 1839, *FL*, II, 32 ("night's rest!!").

2. Mar. 4, 1839, *FL*, II, 58 ("beaver"); Dec. 9, 1838, *FL*, I, 354 ("Elysian peace"); MF to JFC, Sept. 15, 1838, FP ("liberal"); Jan. 8, 1839, FP ("more genial atmosphere"); to CS, Mar. 4, 1839, *FL*, II, 58 ("friction"); Oct. 30 [27?], 1838, *FL*, I, 349–50 ("respite"); to CS, Mar. 4, 1839, *FL*, II, 59 ("sleep"); Feb. 7, [1839], ibid., 48 ("long ones").

3. Jan. 7, 1839, FP ("Cassandra"); June 7, 1839, *EL*, II, 201–3 ("translating this book"); June 8, 1839, *FL*, II, 73 ("sold immedy"). Emma Gertrude Jaeck, "John Oxenford as Translator," *Journal of English and Germanic Philology*, 13 (Apr. 1914), 214–37, convincingly demonstrates Oxenford's plagiarisms. For recent criticisms of the Oxenford translation, see J. P. Eckermann, *Conversations with Goethe*, ed. Hans Kohn, trans. Gisela C. O'Brien (New York, 1964), xiv–xvi; and *Goethe: Conversations and Encounters*, ed. and trans. David Luke and Robert Pick (London, 1966), 23–25.

4. *Conversations with Goethe in the Last Years of His Life, Translated from the German of Eckermann* (Boston, 1839), xii–xxiii ("not a Christian").

5. Ibid. ("blind admirer"); June 7, 1839, *EL*, II, 203 ("brilliant statement"); Oct. 8, 1839, *CL*, 137 ("masterpiece").

6. *FL*, II, 59 ("heaps of paper"); ibid., 56–57 ("My poor father!").

7. Feb. 7, 1839, *EL*, II, 181 ("accession"); to EF, Mar. 31, 1839, *FL*, II, 62 ("delightful"); to CKN, Apr. 18, 1839, ibid., 64 ("interesting"); Oct. 30 [27?], 1838, *FL*, I, 349 ("rely upon me"); May 13, 1839, *FL*, II, 66 ("columbines"); May 29, 1839, ibid., 68 ("wildflowers").

8. Jan. 7, 1839, *FL*, II, 32 ("towncriers"); to CKN, May 29, 1839, ibid., 68 ("home"); Jan. 10, 1839, ibid., 75 ("nervous spasms"); *OM*, I, 266 ("pen in hand"). For an informative account of the Allston show, see Elizabeth Garrity Ellis, "The 'Intellectual and Moral Made Visible': The 1839 Washington Allston Exhibition and Unitarian Taste in Boston," *Prospects: An Annual of American Cultural Studies*, v. 10, ed. Jack Salzman (New York, 1985), 39–75.

9. *OM*, I, 266–67 ("petty collectors"); journal, [ca. Summer–Fall 1839], OC, 111 ("God in man"); journal, [ca. Sept. 1839], FMW, Box A ("delight"); journal, [Aug. 1838], FMW, IX, 38 ("female genius"); journal, [ca. Sept. 1839], FMW, Box A ("Roman"); journal, Sept. 20, [1839], ibid. ("correspondencies"); journal, [ca. Aug. 1838], *OM*, I, 191 ("A Christ"). For a valuable discussion of Transcendentalist ideas about art, see Neil Harris, *The Artist in American Society: The Formative Years, 1790–1860* (1966; Chicago, 1982), chap. 7.

10. RWE to SGW, Oct. 27, 1839, *EL*, VII, 358 ("dull eye[d]"); [ca. 1839], FMW, Box 3 ("sixth sense"); MF, journal, [ca. Aug.–Sept. 1839], Emerson Family Papers, MH ("sensual"); journal, [Sept. 1839], FMW, Box A ("Cross"); MF, journal, [ca. Aug.–Sept. 1839], Emerson Family Papers, MH ("disgusting"); journal, [Sept. 1839], FMW, Box A ("male faces"); [ca. 1839], ibid. ("subjective").

11. "Dramas of Victor Hugo," *American Quarterly Review*, 19 (Mar. 1836), 167 ("immorality"); to Mary G. Ward, Nov. 8, 1836, Ward Papers, MHi ("steer"); journal, [ca. Aug. 1839], FMW, Box A *("ancien regime")*. For surveys of American opinion of contemporary French literature, see Howard Mumford Jones, *America and French Cul-*

ture, 1750–1848 (Chapel Hill, 1927); and Henry Blumenthal, *American and French Culture, 1800–1900: Interchanges in Art, Science, Literature, and Society* (Baton Rouge, 1975).

12. RWE to MF, Sept. 9, 1839, *EL*, II, 223 ("critiques"); journal, [ca. Aug. 1839], FMW, Box A ("revolution"); journal, [ca. Aug. 1839]*, *OM*, I, 258 ("wit"); journal [ca. Aug. 1839], FMW, Box A ("slime"); [ca. Winter 1839–1840], "FS," 157 ("physiology!").

13. Journal, [ca. Aug. 1839], FMW, Box A ("smouldering"); journal, [ca. Summer 1839]*, FMW, Works, III, 297–99 *("accept life");* letter, [ca. Aug. 1839], *OM*, I, 245–47 ("character painting"). For Sand's reputation in America and England, see Howard Mumford Jones, "American Comment on George Sand," *American Literature,* 3 (Jan. 1932), 389–407, and Patricia Thomson, *George Sand and the Victorians* (New York, 1977).

14. Journal, [ca. Aug. 1839], FMW, Box A ("unfortunate woman"); journal, [ca. Summer 1839]*, FMW, Works, III, 303–5 ("These books").

15. [Ca. Aug. 1839], FMW, Box A ("thinker").

16. June 10, 1839, *FL*, II, 75–76 ("happy"); journal, [ca. 1840–1842], OC, 116 ("rye bread days"); June 8, 1839, *FL*, II, 72 ("swains").

17. *OM*, I, 213 ("neckless of diamonds").

18. [Ward], *Ward Family Papers,* 102 ("against her"); to RWE, May 31, 1840, *FL*, II, 135 ("annihilating"); n.d., quoted in *HO*, 119 ("no mercy").

19. "The Private Marriage," [1851–1852], OC, 178 ("intellectual stilts"); George William Curtis to [Daniel Ricketson], Apr. 23, 1856, George William Curtis Papers, MH ("self-esteem"); *OM*, I, 234 ("complacency"); "ON," 498 ("no intellect comparable"); *OM*, I, 236 ("mountainous ME"); Miller, *Margaret Fuller,* x ("simple truth"); "ON," 500 ("sneering"). Emerson himself could not seem to be able to make up his mind about Fuller's social arrogance. After citing Mary Rotch's opinion, he wrote in the notebook he compiled for use in composing the *Memoirs:* "It is a superficial judgment. Her journals are thoroughly religious, tearful, tragic in their tenderness & compunction at shortcomings, and the tone of conversation was only the pastime & necessity of her talent." "ON," 500–501. But when he came to write on the subject in the *Memoirs,* he gave, if not precisely a contradictory, certainly a differently emphasized, estimate: "In conversation, Margaret seldom, except as a special grace, admitted others upon an equal ground with herself. She was exceedingly tender, when she pleased to be, and most cherishing in her influence; but to elicit this tenderness, it was necessary to submit first to her personally. . . . Her instinct was not humility,—that was always an afterthought." *OM*, I, 237.

20. "ON," 258 ("Margaret and her Friends"). The theme of friendship dominates the *Memoirs,* too much so. See especially *OM*, I, 72–111, 201–19, 280–91, 311–16; II, 39–71. Channing wrote in his section: "She was, indeed, The Friend. This was her vocation." *OM*, II, 40. Sometimes this thematic domination is pernicious. See, for example, Emerson's use of the theme to reduce, if not quite dismiss, Fuller's professional ambitions in *OM*, I, 321–24.

21. Statement of FHH, *OM*, I, 93 ("love of the beautiful"); May 1844, "ON," 498 ("mass of flesh"); [Ward], *Ward Family Papers,* 103 ("distant look"); Caroline Healey Dall to Thomas Wentworth Higginson, May 29, 1908, FMW, Box A ("womanly vanity"); George William Curtis to [Daniel Ricketson], Apr. 23, 1856, George William Curtis Papers, MH ("head forward"); "Cinders from the Ashes," 242 ("flexile neck"); *OM*, II, 35–36 ("gray eye").

22. N.d., quoted in *HO*, 118 ("dominion"); *HO*, 117 ("immense capacity"); *OM*, I, 213 ("her game"); ibid., 75 ("quarry"); to EH, n.d., FMW, X, 42 ("beautiful pride");

George William Curtis to [Daniel Ricketson], Apr. 23, 1856, George William Curtis Papers, MH ("full of fun"); "ON," 500 ("crackling of thorns"); to Mrs. Hannah L. Chappell, Apr. 3, 1839, in Elizabeth Maxfield-Miller, "Elizabeth of Concord: Selected Letters of Elizabeth Sherman Hoar (1814–1878) to the Emersons, Family, and the Emerson Circle (Part Two)," *SAR, 1985,* 152 ("levity").

23. Quoted in *HO,* 117 ("truth-speaking power"); *OM,* I, 97 ("moral Paganini"); quoted in ibid., 312 ("so near"); *OM,* I, 214 ("confessions"); ibid., 312 ("narrative"); Sept. 20, 1843, FMW, X, 5 ("tide of feeling"); *OM,* I, 214 ("wedding-guest").

24. *OM,* I, 214 ("superior circle"); to WHC, Dec. 17, 1849, *FL,* V, 300 ("embellishing"); n.d., *OM,* I, 207 ("translat[ing]"); to Albert H. Tracy, Nov. 6, 1843, *FL,* III, 156 ("crisis"); *OM,* I, 215 ("life en beau").

25. Oct. 26, 1845, *FL,* IV, 165 ("time"); [Sept. 17], 1842, "FJ42-1," 336 ("Hedge"); *OM,* I, 313 ("no one else"); Oct. 27, 1851, *EJ,* XI, 449 ("fused people").

26. LMC to MF, Aug. 23, 1844, FMW, XVI, 43 ("prime favorite"); [ca. 1840–1842], OC, 116 ("humble love"); *OM,* I, 286 ("new person"); quoted in ibid., 216 ("moneyed men"); *OM,* I, 216 ("balance").

27. Oct. 1838, *FL,* I, 343 ("museum"); quoted in *OM,* I, 236 ("no man"); *OM,* I, 236–37 ("arrogant tone").

28. For facts on the DeWolfe family, see M. A. DeWolfe Howe, *Bristol, Rhode Island: A Town Biography* (Cambridge, Mass., 1930); and George Howe, *Mount Hope: A New England Chronicle* (New York, 1959).

29. [Aug. 9]*, 1839, "FJ39," 467 ("crown of thorns"); Aug. 2, 1839, ibid. ("blood and tears"); [Aug. 6]*, 1839, ibid. ("Amazonian guards"); [Aug. 10]*, 1839, ibid., 467–68 ("stagnant"); [Aug. 6]*, 1839, ibid., 463–64 ("ludicrous").

30. [Aug. 10]*, 1839, "FJ39," 467 ("not sorry to go"); [Aug. 6]*, 1839, ibid., 464–65 ("'contented disposition'").

31. [Aug. 10]*, 1839, "FJ39," 469 ("full of people").

32. July 31, 1839, "FJ39," 456 ("shallow love"); July 11, 1839, *FL,* II, 82 ("leisure summer"); to EH, Aug. 17, 1839, ibid., 84 ("healing"); June [ca. 21?], 1839, ibid., 77 ("frenzied"); Aug. 1839, ibid., 82 ("sadness").

33. Apr. 6, 1842, "The Letters of Caroline Sturgis to Margaret Fuller," *SAR, 1988,* 223 ("orphaned child"); CS to MF, [ca. Oct. 1, 1837], FMW, X, 28 ("porcupine's back"); Thomas Wentworth Higginson to George Willis Cooke, n.d., quoted in George Willis Cooke, *An Historical and Biographical Introduction to Accompany* The Dial, 2 vols. (1902; New York, 1961), II, 60 ("gipsy-like"); to Franklin B. Sanborn, Aug. 10, 1875, MHarF ("fine eyes"). The best portrait of Caroline Sturgis is that gleaned from her letters, most of which to MF have been published in Dedmond, "Letters of Caroline Sturgis." George Santayana includes an interesting recollection of the later Sturgis family, whom he was related to, in his *Persons and Places: The Background of My Life* (New York, 1944), chap. 4.

34. Oct. 21, 1838, *FL,* I, 347 ("talismanic power"); Jan. 10, 1839, *FL,* II, 35 ("disgust you"); Jan. 27, 1839, ibid., 41 ("base persons"). For "The Brother and Sister Club," see Martin Duberman, *James Russell Lowell* (1966; Boston, 1968), 42–44.

35. Jan. 27, 1839, *FL,* II, 40–41 ("mere Idealist); Apr. 17, [1838], *FL,* I, 352 ("queen"); Mar. 4, 1839, *FL,* II, 60 ("no other person").

36. "Drachenfels," [1836], OC, 145 ("haunts"); to RWE, Nov. 24, 1839, *FL,* II 98 ("effect"); MF to CS, May 19, 1839, Tappan Papers, MH ("Columbine").

37. To CS, Jan. 10, 1839, *FL,* II, 34 ("smouldering"); Feb. 7, [1839], ibid., 47 ("through the intellect"); *Notes of a Son and Brother* (New York, 1914), 213 ("impul-

sive"); to CS, Oct. 7, 1839, *FL*, II, 94 ("say yes"); [June 28? 1839], ibid., 79 *("intimate");* [1840?], ibid., 107 ("'Eros'"). Smith-Rosenberg, "Female World of Love and Ritual," is the classic study of homosocial passion in the lives of nineteenth-century middle-class American women.

38. To Thomas W. Ward, Dec. 2, 1843, Ward Papers, MHi ("literary man"). The best picture of Ward is provided in his letters, collections of which are in the Ward Papers at MH and MHi, and the Ward-Perkins Papers at CU-SB. Ward's *Ward Family Papers* contains valuable reminiscences. David Baldwin, "Puritan Aristocrat in the Age of Emerson: A Study of Samuel Gray Ward" (Ph.D. diss., University of Pennsylvania, 1961), is a useful biographical study. Also informative are idem, "The Emerson-Ward Friendship: Ideals and Realities," in *SAR, 1984;* and Eleanor M. Tilton, "The True Romance of Anna Hazard Barker and Samuel Gray Ward," in *SAR, 1987,* 53–72.

39. WEC2 quoted in MF, "Memoranda," Jan. 13, [1837], FMW, Box 3 ("ridicule"); [ca. Apr. 1847], FMW, X, 38 ("subdue others"). Some of Ward's reflections were copied by Fuller into her journal, [ca. Fall 1839], FMW, Box A.

40. To James Elliot Cabot, Aug. 11, 1882, CU-SB ("literary insight"); to RWE, [Apr. 25], 1840, *FL*, II, 133 ("bliss"); Feb. [21?], 1839, ibid., 49 ("Raphael").

41. *FL*, II, 80–81 ("not distrust you").

42. First days of Sept. 1839, *FL*, II, 90–91 ("love me no more").

43. To MF, Feb. 4, 1845, FMW, XVII, 17 ("another George Davis").

44. To JFC, Dec. 6, 1840, "CLS" ("trust all"); Dec. 22, 1839, *EL*, II, 244 ("natural queen"). Anna Barker's papers are in the Ward Papers at MH and MHi, and the Ward-Perkins Papers at CU-SB. Baldwin, "Puritan Aristocrat," and Tilton, "True Romance," provide useful sketches of Barker. For Jacob Barker, see his *Incidents in the Life of Jacob Barker, of New Orleans, Louisiana* (Washington, D.C., 1855).

45. *HO*, 36 ("model"); Apr. 28, 1835, FP ("love her"); "To the Same/ In answer to the letter of January 6th, 1836," [ca. Jan. 1836], OC, 145 ("fancy's love"); *OM*, II, 8 ("fill her").

46. MF to JFC, Jan. 1, 1840, FP (*"my* Anna"); [Oct. 1842], "FJ42-2," 286-87 ("Recamier").

47. [Aug.] 6, 1844, "FJ44-1," 110 ("repulsive"); J. Christopher Herold, *Mistress to an Age: A Life of Madame de Staël* (Indianapolis, 1958), 288 ("awe-inspiring"); [ca. Fall 1839], FMW, Box A ("masculine traits"); [June 27], 1844, "FJ44-1," 64 ("male"). An indication that at least part of Fuller's expressions of homosocial passion were considered innocent and culturally acceptable is the fact that Emerson, Channing, and Clarke—who otherwise in her *Memoirs* suppress any hint of sexual boldness on Fuller's part—printed this journal passage, only censoring Barker's name and toning down the language a little. *OM*, I, 283–84. Smith-Rosenberg, "Female World of Love and Ritual," is excellent on the semi-erotic dimension of late eighteenth- and nineteenth-century female friendship literature. See also Nancy F. Cott, "Passionlessness: An Interpretation of Victorian Sexual Ideology, 1790–1850," *Signs: Women in Culture and Society,* 4 (Winter 1978), 219–36. But for a cogent revisionist interpretation that emphasizes the passionate, companionate character of nineteenth-century middle-class American women's private heterosexual expressions, see Karen Lystra, *Searching the Heart: Women, Men, and Romantic Love in Nineteenth-Century America* (New York, 1989). Lillian Faderman, *Surpassing the Love of Men: Romantic Friendship and Love Between Women from the Renaissance to the Present* (New York, 1980), is a valuable survey of female homosexual and homosocial themes in modern Western literature. For a good, brief discussion of heterosexual role reversals in Friedrich Schlegel's novel *Lucinde*—a key German Romantic text with which

Fuller was quite familiar—see Ursula Vogel, "Humboldt and the Romantics: Neither *Hausfrau* nor *Citoyenne*—the Idea of Self-Reliant Femininity in German Romanticism," in Ellen Kennedy and Susan Mendus, eds., *Women in Western Political Philosophy* (Brighton, England, 1987), 115–17.

48. [Oct. 1842], "FJ42-2," 287 ("elective affinities"); Mar. 4, 1839, Ward Papers, MHi ("unexpectedly"); SGW to Thomas W. Ward, May 1, 1840, ibid. ("affection"); May 14, 1847, FMW, X, 38 ("every other word"); Dec. 2, 1843, Ward Papers, MHi ("tastes"); to CS, ca. Feb.? 1845, *EL*, III, 279 ("chateaux"); manuscript, n.d., quoted in Baldwin, "Emerson-Ward Friendship," 308 *("jour de fete")*. For a sober account of the Barker-Ward courtship, quite unfriendly to Fuller, see Tilton, "True Romance."

49. Aug. 29, 1840, *EL*, II, 327 ("his genius"); [ca. Fall 1839], FMW, Box A ("womanish"); May 1, 1840, Ward Papers, MHi ("boy"); to RWE, Nov. 1841, *FL*, II, 249 ("son").

50. Quoted in July [5], 1844, "FJ44-1," 77 ("Platonic affection").

51. [Ca. Winter 1839–1840], "FS," 164 ("W's choice); [ca. Fall 1839], FMW, Box A ("son of the Gods"); Aug. 21, 1842, *FL*, III, 88–90 ("broker's shop").

52. [Oct. 30], 1842, "FJ42-2," 290 ("Sam was away").

53. Oct. 7, 1839, *FL*, II, 93 ("intoxicated").

54. Oct. 15, 1839, *FL*, II, 95–96 ("understood . . . perfectly").

55. Ibid., 96 ("tranquil").

56. [Ca. Winter 1839–1840], "FS," 173 ("man's ambition"); Mar. 23, 1840, "ON," 497 ("Poor Mignon!"); [ca. Fall 1839], FMW, Box A ("skinny finger"); [ca. Fall 1839], "FS," 149 ("male eye").

57. [Ca. Fall 1839], FMW, Box A ("bee"); quoted in ibid. ("repose"); [ca. Fall 1839], FMW, Box A ("woman of genius").

58. [Ca. Fall 1839], OC, 120 ("no home"); Jan. 1, 1840, FP ("friends again"); *OM*, I, 98–99 ("past relations").

59. ABA, "Diary for 1839 from July to December," Aug. 26, 1839, 175, Alcott Papers, MH ("Conversations"); Dec. 9, 1838, *FL*, I, 354–55 ("education of women").

60. For the antebellum female seminary movement, see the works cited in chap. 3, note 1. Good treatments of early nineteenth-century women's education may be found in Cott, *Bonds of Womanhood,* chap. 3; Kerber, *Women of the Republic,* chap. 7; and Solomon, *In the Company of Educated Women,* chaps. 1–3; Sklar, *Catharine Beecher;* Anne Firor Scott, "What, Then, Is the American: This New Woman?" *Journal of American History,* 65 (December 1978), 679–703; and idem, "The Ever Widening Circle: The Diffusion of Feminist Values from the Troy Female Seminary, 1822–1872," *History of Education Quarterly,* 19 (Spring 1979), 3–27.

61. For a discussion of the social and ideological character of Fuller's Conversation classes, see my "Margaret Fuller as Cultural Reformer: The Conversations in Boston," *American Quarterly,* 39 (Winter 1987), 509–28.

62. *Harriet Martineau's Autobiography,* II, 71 ("gorgeous"). Higginson (*HO,* 121–29) demolished Martineau's myth, but it continues to crop up. See, for example, Mason Wade, *Margaret Fuller: Whetstone of Genius* (New York, 1940), 74–75.

63. *EJ*, V, 175 ("wonderful"); to JFC, Nov. 17, 1839, "CLS" ("infidel association").

64. See, for the Grimkés' tours, Gerda Lerner, *The Grimké Sisters from South Carolina: Pioneers for Woman's Rights and Abolition* (1967; New York, 1971), 146–204, 226–28; for Wright's lectures, Celia Morris Eckhardt, *Fanny Wright: Rebel in America* (Cambridge, Mass., 1984), 171–224; for Bacon's meetings, Vivian C. Hopkins, *Prodigal Puritan: A Life of Delia Bacon* (Cambridge, Mass., 1959), 49–57, 66–70; and for Peabody's

classes, Josephine Elizabeth Roberts, "A New England Family: Elizabeth Palmer Peabody, 1804–1894, Mary Tyler Peabody (Mrs. Horace Mann), 1806–1887, Sophia Amelia Peabody (Mrs. Nathaniel Hawthorne), 1809–1871" (Ph.D. diss., Western Reserve University, 1937).

65. *FL*, II, 86–87 ("stimulus").

66. EPP, "Journal of Margaret Fuller's Conversation Classes," [ca. Nov. 1839], EPP Papers, MWA, and *OM*, I, 329 ("*more* studies"). For a discussion of the inquiry method in Enlightenment thought, see Peter Gay, *The Enlightenment: An Interpretation,* Vol. II, *The Science of Freedom* (New York, 1969), chap. 3. Classic Romantic texts arguing for the organic integration of thought and action in education and culture are Schiller's *Über die ästhetische Erziehung des Menschen* (1795), Goethe's *Wilhelm Meisters Lehrjahre* (1795–1796), and Emerson's "American Scholar" (1837), all of which Fuller knew well. Remarks on this theme are also scattered through Eckermann's *Conversations with Goethe.* For antebellum anti-intellectual notions of female culture, see Barbara Welter, "The Cult of True Womanhood, 1820–1860," and "Anti-Intellectualism and the American Women, 1800–1860," in her *Dimity Convictions,* 21–41, 71–82, 204–11, 218–20. But for a somewhat different view, cf. Susan P. Conrad, *Perish the Thought: Intellectual Women in Romantic America, 1830–1860* (New York, 1976).

67. JFC to RWE, Apr. 30, 1838, JFC Papers, MH ("effeminate"). A thorough study of the relation between vocation and ideology among the Transcendentalists and their male *and* female followers is much needed. On Emerson, see the fine discussions in Henry Nash Smith, "Emerson's Problem of Vocation—A Note on 'The American Scholar,'" *New England Quarterly,* 12 (March 1939), 52–67; Lewis P. Simpson, "Emerson's Early Thought: Institutionalism and Alienation," in his *Man of Letters,* 62–84; Robinson, *Apostle of Culture;* and, most recently, Cayton, *Emerson's Emergence.* The vocational question is central to Elizabeth R. McKinsey's argument in *Western Experiment.* It also permeates Ann Douglas's *Feminization of American Culture,* although Douglas subsumes most Transcendentalists under her category of Northeastern liberal ministers and women. David Brion Davis, ed., *Antebellum American Culture: An Interpretive Anthology* (Lexington, Mass., 1979), 1–83, provides a good introduction to the idea of self-culture and other popular notions of vocation in the antebellum period. For valuable discussions of various strategies by which some antebellum women outside Fuller's circle sought or were urged to seek intellectual self-culture despite restricted vocational opportunities, see Lee Virginia Chambers-Schiller, *Liberty, a Better Husband: Single Women in America— The Generations of 1780–1840* (New Haven, 1984), 77–126; and Jane Roland Martin, *Reclaiming a Conversation: The Ideal of the Educated Woman* (New Haven, 1985), 103–38.

68. Dec. 26, 1839, *FL*, II, 104 ("tuned up"). "Never since the Renaissance," writes H. G. Schenk, "had intellectuals conversed with each other so much for the purpose not of exhibiting their *esprit* nor of pursuing truth by rational argument and counter-argument, but of inspiring each other in the never-ending art of revealing truth." *The Mind of the European Romantics: An Essay in Cultural History* (1966; New York, 1969), 161. One influential contemporary discussion of the Romantic form of conversation Fuller was familiar with was in de Staël's *Germany,* 3 vols. (London, 1813), I, 101–22. See also William Hazlitt, "On the Conversation of Authors," *Selected Essays of William Hazlitt,* ed. Geoffrey Keynes (London, 1934), 446–74. For a cogent discussion of the art of conversation among American Transcendentalists, see Buell, *Literary Transcendentalism,* 77–101. Lewis Perry, "'We Have Had Conversation in the World': The Abolitionists and Spontaneity," *Canadian Review of American Studies,* 6 (Spring 1975), 3–26, is an inter-

esting consideration of the influence of one aspect of Romantic conversation on antebellum social reform. Alcott has much to say about the theory of conversations in his journals. For useful discussions, see Shepard, *Pedlar's Progress,* 174–79, 226–46; and Dahlstrand, *Amos Bronson Alcott,* 123–27, 216–19.

69. EPP, "Journal of Margaret Fuller's Conversation Classes," [ca. Nov. 1839], EPP Papers, MWA ("*teach* anything"); "FS," 168 ("The best"); [July] 25, 1844, "FJ44-1," 94 ("self-impulse").

70. Besides Peabody's summaries, the only other extensive report of Fuller's Conversations is Caroline Healey Dall's *(DM)* on the classes Fuller gave for men and women in the spring of 1841.

71. Journal, Mar. 8, 1841, Joel Myerson, "Caroline Dall's Reminiscences of Margaret Fuller," *Harvard Library Bulletin,* 22 (Oct. 1974), 422 ("under size"); quoted in *OM*, I, 332, 336 ("beautiful"); *OM*, I, 337 ("toilette"); to [Daniel Ricketson], Apr. 23, 1856, George William Curtis Papers, MH ("dowdily"); *HO*, 127 ("alpaca"); *OM*, I, 337 ("'beautiful looks'").

72. *OM*, I, 95 ("commanding"); quoted in Edith D. Fuller, "Margaret Fuller," 12, FMW, Box B ("analyze"); *OM*, I, 95 ("her speech"); Sept. 18, 1846, in Myerson, "Dall's Reminiscences," 426 ("flow of language"); statement, *OM*, I, 94–95 ("answering eyes"); *OM*, I, 337 ("spin her sentences").

73. *Reminiscences,* 118_ ("Delphic mood"); *OM*, I, 340 ("monologue"); statement, Clarke, *Autobiography,* 142–43 ("homage"); quoted in *OM*, I, 336 ("exordiums"); "ON," 501 ("tenderness"); quoted in *OM*, I, 336–37 ("inspired"); quoted in Edith D. Fuller, "[Paper] Read at State Normal College, Albany, N.Y., Feb. 1900," FMW, Box B ("dumb spoke").

74. Nov. 17, 1839, "CLS" ("not speak a word"); Nov. 1839, *FL*, II, 97 ("ladies talk"); [ca. Autumn? 1839?], ibid. ("paid Corinne"); quoted in *OM*, I, 333 ("Platonic dialogue"); Nov. 25, 1839, *FL*, II, 101, and "ON," 476 ("prosperous").

75. Dec. 14, 1839, "CLS" ("speaketh plainly"); statement of Edward Everett Hale, in Clarke, *Autobiography,* 142 ("assistants"); EPP, "Journal of Margaret Fuller's Conversation Classes," [ca. Nov. 1839], EPP Papers, MWA ("knew words"); quoted in *OM*, I, 333 ("on all sides"); Aug. 27, 1839, *FL*, II, 87–88 ("garb of modesty"); Dec. 14, 1839, "CLS" ("her sex's privilege").

76. Indications of some of the sources Fuller used in her mythology Conversations may be found in *DM*. For a good overview of Fuller's views on mythology, see Robert D. Richardson, Jr., "Margaret Fuller and Myth," *Prospects: An Annual of American Cultural Studies,* v. 4, ed. Jack Salzman (New York, 1979), 168–84.

77. EPP, report, [ca. Nov. 1840]*, *OM*, I, 342 ("aesthetic life"); EPP, "Journal of Margaret Fuller's Conversation Classes," [ca. Dec. 1839], EPP Papers, MWA ("personified"); "Genesis of the Greek Gods," Feb. 20, 1841, FMW, Box A ("cold abstractions").

78. EPP, "Journal of Margaret Fuller's Conversation Classes," [ca. Dec. 1839], EPP Papers, MWA ("horror"); EPP, report, [ca. Nov. 1840]*, *OM*, I, 345 ("immortality"); EPP, "Journal of Margaret Fuller's Conversation Classes," [ca. Dec. 1839], EPP Papers, MWA ("contempt"). Peabody was not the only Transcendentalist to be annoyed with these conversative Unitarian objectors. "Would you believe it," Sarah Clarke wrote indignantly to her brother James four days later, "on this first opening of the subject the conversation once or twice came into a comparison of the religious privileges of the Greeks and our own. Margaret exerted herself very much to keep it off that track, seeing it would lead to endless theological discussions, and I hope she has put a stop to it." Nov. 17, 1839, "CLS."

Pertinent remarks on aspects of German Romantic ideas of Greek culture and mythology may be found scattered through volumes 1 and 2 of Wellek, *History of Modern Criticism.* For classic discussions of various Romantic "spiral" views of history and culture, see Lovejoy, *Essays,* 166–227; and Abrams, *Natural Supernaturalism,* 141–324.

79. EPP, "Journal of Margaret Fuller's Conversation Classes," [ca. Dec. 1839], EPP Papers, MWA ("instincts"); report, [ca. Dec.–Jan. 1839–1840]*, *OM,* I, 333 ("Born from fire").

80. EPP, "Journal of Margaret Fuller's Conversation Classes," [ca. Dec. 1839], EPP Papers, MWA ("fable").

81. EPP, report, [ca. Nov. 1840]*, *OM,* I, 342 ("inspiration"); *DM,* 55 ("spiritualizing"); *DM,* 28 ("denationalize"); Nov. 25, 1839, *FL,* II, 102 ("more Greek"); "Genesis of the Greek Gods," [ca. 1839–1840], FMW, Works, V, 453 ("child of counsel"). For a recent popular version of this kind of feminine psycho-mythologizing, see Jean Shinoda Bolen, *Goddesses in Everywoman* (San Francisco, 1984).

82. *FL,* II, 118–19 ("dividing the universe"); [ca. Fall 1839], FMW, Box A ("harmony").

83. Nov. 17, 1839, "CLS" ("transcendentalist"); CPC to JSD, Apr. 14, 1840, quoted in F. DeWolfe Miller, "Christopher Pearse Cranch: New England Transcendentalist" (Ph.D. diss., University of Virginia, 1942), 97 ("'common sense'"); 1842, quoted in Laura E. Richards and Maud Howe Elliott, *Julia Ward Howe,* 2 vols. (Boston, 1916), I, 71–72 ("shocked!"); *HO,* 109 ("audacious"); Dec. 10, 1840, OC, 90 ("arrogant").

84. *FL,* II, 118 ("real society"); Jan. 28, [1840], Margaret Fuller Ossoli Notebook, Emerson Family Papers, MH ("My conversations"); report, [ca. Dec. 1840]*, *OM,* I, 340 ("this very party"); quoted in *OM,* I, 338 ("I never heard").

85. Dec. 16, 1842, FMW, X, 155 ("all for *self*"); *Reminiscences of Ednah Dow Cheney* (Boston, 1902), 205–6 ("hidden meaning").

86. On the narcissistic character of antebellum popular women's literary culture, see Douglas, *Feminization of American Culture.* But for recent and more sympathetic revisionist interpretations of some of this literature along various lines, cf. Baym, *Woman's Fiction;* Kelley, *Private Women, Public Stage;* and Jane Tompkins, *Sensational Designs: The Cultural Work of American Fiction, 1790–1860* (New York, 1985), 122–85.

Chapter Nine

1. "The Divinity School Address," *ECW,* I, 77, 82, 85 ("intuition"); Sept. 5, 1838, *EJ,* VII, 63 ("tyrant"); "The New School in Literature and Religion," *MT,* 195 ("rhapsody"); July 24, 1838, James Russell Lowell Papers, MH ("ruin him").

2. To JFC, July 8, 1838, "CLS" *("dangerous");* "New School," *MT,* 193, 195 ("disastrous"). For contrasting interpretations of the degree and character of the Unitarian–Transcendentalist conflict at this time, see *MT,* 157–246; Hutchison, *Transcendentalist Ministers,* chap. 3; Charles Crowe, *George Ripley: Transcendentalist and Utopian Socialist* (Athens, Ga., 1967), chap. 5; and Rose, *Transcendentalism as a Social Movement,* chap. 3. My own view is that although Miller may have exaggerated some of the differences between the two camps, as well as overlooked important divisions within them, he was right in arguing for a fundamental and overriding split in Unitarian ranks at this time over the Transcendentalist challenge.

3. Bowen, "Locke and Transcendentalists," 175 ("diseased admiration"); *The Latest Form of Infidelity Examined* (Boston, 1839), *MT,* 220 ("the learned").

4. "The Transcendentalist," in *ECW,* I, 204 ("spiritual principle"). There is as yet no

study of the social composition of the Transcendentalist circle or of their followers. My generalizations are based on my reading in the Transcendentalists' papers and standard biographies. The backgrounds of the Transcendentalist leaders make an interesting comparison with those of the leading figures in the other major antebellum Boston avant-garde elite—the also predominantly Unitarian, but more old-family, upper-class "Boston Clique" of Garrisonian abolitionists. See Lawrence J. Friedman, *Gregarious Saints: Self and Community in American Abolitionism, 1830–1870* (Cambridge, Mass., 1982), chap. 2.

5. May 21, 1837, *EJ*, V, 331–32 ("calamity"). There is still no satisfactory in-depth study of antebellum reform. A standard survey is Alice Felt Tyler, *Freedom's Ferment: Phases of American Social History from the Colonial Period to the Outbreak of the Civil War* (1944; New York, 1962); and a useful overview is Ronald G. Walters, *American Reformers, 1815–1860* (New York, 1978). For a recent suggestive interpretation, see Lewis Perry, *Childhood, Marriage, and Reform: Henry Clarke Wright, 1797–1870* (Chicago, 1980). John Higham, *From Boundlessness to Consolidation: The Transformation of American Culture, 1848–1860* (Ann Arbor, 1969) is an insightful and pertinent essay on antebellum culture and ideology. The best introductions to the evangelical background are Perry Miller, *The Life of the Mind in America from the Revolution to the Civil War* (New York, 1965), chaps. 1–3; Nathan O. Hatch, *The Democratization of American Christianity* (New Haven, 1989); and Richard Rabinowitz, *The Spiritual Self in Everyday Life: The Transformation of Personal Religious Experience in Nineteenth-Century New England* (Boston, 1989). For good discussions of the philosophy of "come-outerism," see Whitney R. Cross, *The Burned-Over District: The Social and Intellectual History of Enthusiastic Religion in Western New York, 1800–1850* (Ithaca, 1950); and Lewis Perry, *Radical Abolitionism: Anarchy and the Government of God in Antislavery Thought* (Ithaca, 1973), chap. 4. For an overstated but still useful discussion of the radicalizing effect of the depression on American literary intellectuals, see William Charvat, "American Romanticism and the Depression of 1837," *Science and Society*, 2 (Spring 1938), 67–82. Varying interpretations of the "radical" or Locofoco Democrats may be found in Arthur M. Schlesinger, Jr., *The Age of Jackson* (Boston, 1945), chaps. 12–24; John Ashworth, *'Agrarians' and 'Aristocrats': Party Political Ideology in the United States, 1837–1846* (London, 1983); Formisano, *Transformation of Political Culture*, chap. 12; and Sean Wilentz, *Chants Democratic: New York City the and Rise of the American Working Class, 1788–1850* (New York, 1984).

6. There is no comprehensive study of the social thought of the Transcendentalists, but for recent valuable analyses of some of its aspects, see Taylor Stoehr, *Nay-Saying in Concord: Emerson, Alcott, and Thoreau* (Hamden, Conn., 1979); Rose, *Transcendentalism as a Social Movement;* and David S. Reynolds, *Beneath the American Renaissance: The Subversive Imagination in the Age of Emerson and Melville* (New York, 1988), chap. 3. In contrast with these books, which emphasize in varying degrees the distinctiveness of Transcendentalist reform thought, two older influential studies (John William Ward, *Andrew Jackson: Symbol for an Age* [New York, 1955], chap. 4; and Stanley M. Elkins, *Slavery: A Problem in American Institutional and Intellectual Life* [1959; Chicago, 1976], chap. 4) stress the affinities between Transcendentalism and, respectively, Jacksonian democracy and abolitionism. A third school of interpretation sees social Transcendentalism as distinctive, but also apolitical, or even conservative. The best statements of this point of view are Schlesinger, *Age of Jackson,* chap. 29; and Duane E. Smith, "Romanticism in America: The Transcendentalists," *Review of Politics,* 35 (July 1973), 302–25. For a recent provocative interpretation of Emerson's Transcendentalist social

criticism as radically "populist," see Christopher Lasch, *The True and Only Heaven: Progress and Its Critics* (New York, 1991), 243–79.

7. Orestes A. Brownson to George Bancroft, Nov. 10, 1837, quoted in Thomas A. Ryan, *Orestes A. Brownson: A Definitive Biography* (Huntington, Ind., 1976), 122 ("conversion"); Nov. 20, 1837, *CL*, 127 ("loco foco[ism]"); James Handasyd Perkins in the *Western Messenger,* 7 (Aug. 1839), 221, quoted in Habich, *Transcendentalism and the* Western Messenger, 131 ("Loco-focoism"); CPC to JFC, Feb. 16, 1839, in Leonora Cranch Scott, *The Life and Letters of Christopher Pearse Cranch* (Boston, 1917), 44 ("true democratic ideas"); "The Present Age," *EEL*, III, 196–97 ("fruitful crop"); Dec. 6, 1839, MB ("ecstacies"). Parker added, "One grave, Whig-looking gentlemen heard Emerson the other night & said he could only account for his delivering such a lecture on the supposition that he wished to get a place in the Custom House under George Bancroft." Sept. 23, 1836, *EJ*, V, 203 ("loud"); "Diary for 1839 from July to December," Oct. 18, 1839, 319, Alcott Papers, MH ("vox diaboli"); George Bancroft, *Globe,* Mar. 9, 1838, quoted in Crowe, *George Ripley,* 133 ("philosophical democracy"); "The Present Age," *EEL*, III, 261 ("artificial"); to JFC, Jan. 12, 1840, "CLS" ("slave"); "The Present Age," *EEL*, III, 187, 267 ("disgrace"). Of course, already radically reform-minded Transcendentalists like Brownson and William Henry Channing had recently begun to note in print that Emerson's individualism made him lukewarm toward collective ideas of reform, but in 1839 this was still a muted issue.

8. [Ca. Winter 1839–1840]*, *OM*, II, 15, 18 *("those men").*

9. Feb. 24, 1840, *FL*, II, 123 ("inner light"); [ca. Spring]* 1840, ibid., 110 ("holiness"); Oct. 25, 1840, ibid., 172–73 ("O that crowd").

10. Apr. 12, 1840, *FL*, II, 129 ("furniture"); "Chat in Boston Bookstores.—No. II," *Boston Quarterly Review,* 3 (July 1840), 327–28 ("terror"); *OM*, II, 12 ("full dawn"); [ca. Spring]* 1840, *FL*, II, 108–9 ("Since the Revolution").

11. [Ca. Winter 1839–1840], "FS," 159 ("men who manage"); [ca. Winter 1839–1840], "FS," 160 (*"sounds* well"); [ca. Spring]* 1840, *FL*, II, 109 ("Utopia").

12. [Ca. Jan.–Mar. 1839], JFC Papers, MH ("theoretic respect").

13. [Ca. Spring]* 1840, *FL*, II, 109–10 ("position as a woman").

14. ABA, "Diary for 1839 from July to December," Sept. 16, 1839, 242, Alcott Papers, MH ("Esoteric"); "Emerson," [H. Theodore Tuckerman], ed., *Homes of American Authors* (New York, 1853), 251 ("finest thing"); *OM*, II, 18–19 ("pleasing surprise").

15. *OM*, II, 19–21 ("Near-sighted").

16. [Nov. 1835], FMW, Box A ("timidity"); Oct. 28, 1840, *FL*, II, 174 ("factitious"). The best biography of George Ripley is Crowe, *George Ripley.* There is no comprehensive treatment of Sophia Ripley; the best source is her letters, some of which are in FMW.

17. "Diary for 1838," Mar. 1838, [Week 11], 173, Alcott Papers, MH ("brilliant talker"); Dec. 1838, [Week 52], ibid., 499–500 ("remarkable person"); Aug. 16, 1839, *EL*, II, 216 ("gropes"); to ABA, June 1840, *FL*, II, 143 ("veil of words"); [ca. Winter early 1837], Emerson Family Papers, MH ("mission"); May 31, 1840, *FL*, II, 135 ("Messiah"). Cf. Emerson's almost identically judicious views of Alcott in his May 1 and 2, 1839, letter to Fuller (*EL*, II, 198). Fuller's increasingly favorable view of Alcott's abilities and ideas was probably also nurtured by her own experience as a teacher and conversation leader. See *FL*, I, 287.

18. EPP, "Egotheism, the Atheism of Today" (1858), reprinted in Peabody's *Last Evening with Allston and Other Papers* (Boston, 1886), 246 ("Egotheism"); *The Bostonians* (London, 1886), in Henry James, *Novels, 1881–1886,* ed. William T. Stafford (New York, 1985), 824 ("shop-worn"); Dec. 26, 1844, *FL*, III, *253–54* ("idolize"); July 19, 1850, *EJ*, XI, 259 ("despise her"); TP, "Journal," [ca. Aug. 2, 1839], I, 187, MH-AH *("Boswell").*

In lieu of a satisfactory biography yet to be written, the best introduction to Peabody is the fine collection *PL*. Also useful are two dissertations: Roberts, "A New England Family"; and Hersha Sue Fisher, "The Education of Elizabeth Palmer Peabody" (Ph.D. diss., Harvard University, 1980).

19. [Ca. July 25, 1839], "Journal," I, 182, MH-AH ("her genius"); [ca. Sept. 1–2, 1840], ibid., 446 ("jealousies"); journal, Aug. 7, 1859, Myerson, "Caroline Dall's Reminiscences," 419–20 ("hates Margaret"); TP, June 17, 1839, journal, quoted in Sanborn, *Recollections,* II, 546 ("scoffing"); to GR, Oct. 29, 1859, John Weiss, *Life and Correspondence of Theodore Parker,* 2 vols. (New York, 1864), II, 377 ("transcendental nonsense"); quoted in Henry Steele Commager, *Theodore Parker* (Boston, 1936), 180 ("affection"); journal, quoted in Weiss, *Life of Parker,* I, 290 ("beauty"). The best modern biography of Parker is still Commager's *Theodore Parker,* but it can be usefully supplemented by three older studies: Weiss, *Life of Parker;* Octavius Brooks Frothingham, *Theodore Parker: A Biography* (Boston, 1874); and John White Chadwick, *Theodore Parker: Preacher and Reformer* (Boston, 1901).

20. [Ca. Winter 1839–1840], "FS," 162 ("Mr P."); to Mary Rotch, Feb. 5, 1843, *FL,* III, 120 ("polemical"); [Apr. 5, 1841], *FL,* II, 206 ("loved him"); Sept. 19, 1839, "Journal," I, 233, MH-AH *("Mme de Stael");* journal, quoted in Weiss, *Life of Parker,* I, 290 ("my book-shelves").

21. Mar. 8, 1839, *EL,* II, 191 ("inspired"); [ca. Winter 1839–1840], "FS," 156 ("imperfect"); journal, [ca. Fall 1839], FMW, Box A ("sing song"); Mar. 4, 1839, *FL,* II, 53 ("worthy"); "Chat in Boston Bookstores.—No. I," *Boston Quarterly Review,* 3 (Jan. 1840), 132 ("unfinished"). For good biographical treatments of Very, see William Irving Bartlett, *Jones Very: Emerson's "Brave Saint"* (Durham, N.C., 1942); and Edwin Gittleman, *Jones Very: The Effective Years, 1833–1840* (New York, 1967).

22. *OM,* I, 210 ("conceal"); "Memoranda," Jan. 13, 1837, FMW, Box 3 ("fingers"); [ca. Winter 1839–1940], "FS," 161–62 ("Ellery's aspiration"); Aug. 1, 1844, "FJ44-1," 107 ("goblin-gleam"). McGill, Jr., *Channing of Concord,* is a useful biography, but Robert N. Hudspeth's critical study, *Ellery Channing* (New York, 1973), also includes important biographical material, as does Francis B. Dedmond's "The Selected Letters of William Ellery Channing the Younger (Part One)," *SAR, 1989,* 115–218; and "The Selected Letters of William Ellery Channing the Younger (Part Two)," *SAR, 1990,* 159–241.

23. Oct. 22, 1833, JFC Papers, MH ("similar"); *OM,* II, 6–7 ("scathing satire"). The only full-length biography of Channing is Octavius Brooks Frothingham, *Memoir of William Henry Channing* (Boston, 1886). For a good brief portrait, see Thomas Wentworth Higginson, "William Henry Channing," in Samuel A. Eliot, ed., *Heralds of a Liberal Faith,* 3 vols. (Boston, 1910), III, 59–66.

24. [Ca. early Nov. 1839]*, *FL,* II, 31 ("two friends"); Feb. 25, 1840, quoted in Frothingham, *Memoir of Channing,* 168 ("restless"); [Winter 1839]*, ibid., 181 ("nobler books").

25. Quoted in *MT,* 187 ("social idea"); *OM,* II, 23 ("hypercriticism"); ibid., 7, 23 ("boyish crudity"); [ca. Winter 1839–1840]*, "FS," 166–67 *("little great men").*

26. Quoted in [ca. early 1840s]*, *OM,* II, 65, 110–11 ("impetuosity"); [Aug. 28], 1842, "FJ42-1," 329 ("damning"); statement of WHC, *OM,* II, 112–13 ("Egoism"); Feb. 25, 1840, quoted in Frothingham, *Memoir of Channing,* 168 ("defective"); *OM,* II, 7–8 ("Woman").

27. Aug. 14, 1837, *FL,* I, 295 ("dear *no friend*"); Nov. 14, 1839, *EJ,* VII, 301 ("porcupine impossibility"); Oct. 12, 1838, *EL,* II, 168 *("descend"); OM,* I, 217–18 ("easy guest").

28. Mar. 18, 1838, FP ("even nobler"); Sept. 15, 1838, FP ("baying"); [ca. Aug.

1838], FMW, IX, 264 ("Twenty four hours"); to CKN, Apr. 18, 1839, *FL*, II, 64 ("serene"); ibid., 114 ("lecturing well").

29. May 1, 1839, *EL*, II, 197–98 ("whipping").

30. Nov. 14, 1839, *EJ*, VII, 301 ("best of me"); June 3, 1839, *FL*, II, 68 ("Creation").

31. *FL*, II, 99 ("wrong Sands").

32. To MF, Oct. 12, 1838, *EL*, II, 168 ("disappointment"); Nov. 14, 1839, *EJ*, VII, 301 ("churl's mask"); Oct. 7, 1839, ibid., 259 ("lovely").

33. *EJ*, VII, 273 ("Cold as I am"); *EL*, II, 226 ("Brazil Topazes"); July? 31? 1839?, ibid., 210 ("formidable test"); June 18, 1839, ibid., 205 ("your Recamier"); to EH, Nov. 4, 1839, ibid., 230 ("Prince-of-the-Purple-Island"); ibid., 238–40 ("your poor hermit").

34. *EL*, II, 242 ("Forget"); ibid., 245 ("love & hate").

35. [Jan. 22, 1840], Emerson Family Papers, MH ("instincts").

36. Ibid. ("Why cannot I enter"); Mar. 1, 1838, *FL*, I, 327 ("oratory"); May 26, 1840, MB ("on and on").

37. *FL*, II, 104 ("naughtiest moods").

38. Jan. 1, 1840, *FL*, II, 113 ("metaphysical romance"); to CS, [1840?], ibid., 105 ("Eros"); Feb. 24, 1840, ibid., 123 ("languid"); Jan. 1, 1840, FP ("more reasonable"); Jan. 1, 1840, *FL*, II, 114 ("carved into roses"); Jan. 1, 1840, FP ("good friends"); to JFC, Sept. 15, 1838, FP ("feed my lambs").

39. [Ca. Mar. 1840], FMW, Box A ("solar system!"); July 1840, *FL*, II, 145 ("took pleasure"); Jan. 1, 1840, ibid., 114 ("time"); Feb. 24, 1840, ibid., 123 ("little outward token").

40. FHH to MF, Feb. 20, 1835, MH-AH ("spiritual philosophy"); Jan. 12, 1839, *HW*, XV, 288 ("intolerable"); June 13, 1838, *EJ*, VII, 18 ("snore of the muses"); "Diary for 1838," May 8, 1839, 745, Alcott Papers, MH ("destitute"). The best discussion of the genesis of the Transcendentalists' magazine is in Myerson, *New England Transcendentalists,* chaps. 1–2. Mott, *History of American Magazines,* Parts II–III, is a still very useful guide to the antebellum periodical scene.

41. [Ca. Fall 1838], "CLS" ("hundreds"); *ECC*, 264 ("loquacious scribacious"); "Diary for 1839 from July to December," Nov. 30, 1839, 444, Alcott Papers, MH ("my own thoughts"); Nov. 1, 1839, ibid., 375 ("English brethren"); Sept. 28, 1839, ibid., 264 ("like character").

42. ABA, "Diary for 1839 from July to December," Sept. 18, 1839, 249, Alcott Papers, MH ("Journal"); Feb. 1840, "AS40," 242 ("Scriptures"); "Orphic Sayings," *Dial,* I (July 1840), 85 ("motions"); May 24, 1840, *CL*, 138 ("excellent"). For a succinct elucidation of the Neoplatonic significance of Alcott's trope of the sundial, see Barbara Carson, "Proclus' Sunflower and *The Dial," English Language Notes,* 9 (Mar. 1974), 200–202.

43. Jan. 8, 1839, FP ("your pet"). That fall, when Fuller was thinking of writing a series of essays on the state of the fine arts in America, she wrote in her journal that she thought of proposing it to the *Messenger,* but that it "in no way seems a fit receptacle. It seems scarcely right to put them there merely for the sake of seeing them in print." [Ca. Fall 1839], FMW, Box 1. For the Eastern Transcendentalists' attitudes toward the *Messenger,* see Habich, *Transcendentalism and the* Western Messenger, 92–93, 113–14, 161, 164. Joel Myerson suggests that the apparent success of the *Messenger,* if anything, spurred the Easterners in their enterprise by giving them the false idea that their journal "could easily succeed in Boston, the center of the Transcendental movement." Myerson, *New England Transcendentalists and the* Dial, 36.

44. Orestes A. Brownson, "Cousin's *Philosophy," Christian Examiner,* 21 (Sept. 1836), 41 ("scientific"); Oct. 26, 1842, *EJ*, VIII, 305 ("never will stop"); "Diary for 1839

from July to December," Oct. 19, 1839, 320, Alcott Papers, MH ("No good"). The best biography of Brownson remains Arthur M. Schlesinger, Jr., *Orestes A. Brownson: A Pilgrim's Progress* (Boston, 1939), but Thomas R. Ryan's sprawling *Orestes A. Brownson* includes many useful details.

45. "Diary for 1839 from July to December," Sept. 28, 1839, 264, Alcott Papers, MH ("Journal for the soul"); Oct. 21, 1839, ibid., 322 ("literary duty"); to William Emerson, Sept. 26, 1839, *EL*, II, 225 ("nowhere else"); Dec. 12, 1839, ibid., 243 ("personally responsible"); Sept. 19, 1839, "Journal," I, 233, MH-AH ("competent").

46. *FL*, II, 91–92 ("good pay"); FMW, Box 1 ("every thing").

47. *EJ*, VII, 273 ("new literary plans"); Nov. 4, 1839, *EL*, II, 231 ("predicted Journal"); "Diary for 1839 from July to December," Oct. 21, 1839, 322, Alcott Papers, MH ("enrich our literature").

48. Oct. 15, 1839, FP ("Immersed"); Feb. [21?], 1839, *FL*, II, 49 ("ashamed"); Apr. 1840, ibid., 127 ("my papers"); Apr. 24, 1840, FMW, Box A ("all the great thoughts").

49. [Ca. Spring 1840]*, *OM*, I, 296 ("vulgarity"); May 15[?]*, 1839, *FL*, II, 66 ("play the artist"); [ca. Fall]1839, FMW, Box A ("the hearer"); Jan. 8, 1839, FP ("squeamish"); [Winter 1839–1840], "FS," 160, 164 ("improvisatrice"). For a good discussion of the concept of core gender identity, see Robert J. Stoller, "Facts and Fancies: An Examination of Freud's Concept of Bisexuality," in Strouse, *Women and Analysis,* 343–64.

50. Jan. 8, 1839, FP ("Genius"). For a provocative analysis of Emerson and other American Romantic writers' conflation of self and America, see Sacvan Bercovitch, *The Puritan Origins of the American Self* (New Haven, 1975), chap. 5. Buell's *Literary Transcendentalism* includes several cogent discussions of the literary self-image of the Transcendentalists. See especially chaps. 1–2, 10–12. A study of the generational character of antebellum intellectual culture awaits its historian. But for a beginning, at least for political culture, see George B. Forgie, *Patricide in the House Divided: A Psychological Interpretation of Lincoln and His Age* (New York, 1979).

51. Mar. 22, 1840, *FL*, II, 125–26 ("scarce a word").

52. [Ca. Spring 1840]*, *OM*, I, 297 ("private or public"); *The Anxiety of Influence* (New York, 1973), 68 ("'complete' their fathers"). In *The Madwoman in the Attic: The Woman Writer and the Nineteenth-Century Literary Imagination* (New Haven, 1979), Sandra M. Gilbert and Susan Gubar present a feminist revision of Bloom's quasi-Freudian theory of patrilineal literary inheritance. Although their concerns, like Bloom's, are more purely psycholiterary than mine here, I have found their arguments about women writers' "anxiety of authorship" very helpful in stimulating my thinking about Fuller's struggles to formulate a public literary identity. (See especially chap. 2.) For two important contrasting studies of the responses of predominantly non-Romantic antebellum women writers to this problem of private and public authorial identities, see Douglas, *Feminization of American Culture;* and Kelley, *Private Woman, Public Stage.*

53. [Fall 1839]*, Journal "1840," FMW, Box 1 ("my very best"); Apr. 24, 1840, ibid., Box A ("dialogue").

54. Journal "1840," FMW, Box 1 ("advice"); *EL*, II, 281 ("serene . . . tone"); Journal "1840," FMW, Box 1 ("Mr E's letter").

55. Journal "1840," FMW, Box 1 ("finds fault").

56. Dec. 12, 1839, *EL*, II, 243 ("new Age"); Journal "1840," FMW, Box 1 ("hack verbiage"); *OM*, II, 7–8 ("boyish").

57. "The American Scholar," *ECW*, I, 67 ("common"); "The Editors to the Reader," *Dial,* I (July 1840), 2 ("lonely and obscure"); Jan. 8, 1839, FP ("profaned"); "FS," 169–71 ("Mr Longfellow").

58. [Ca. Winter 1839–1840], "FS," 163 ("Heavy stern line"); [ca. 1839–1840], "ON," 488 ("higher faith"); to WHC, Jan. 1, 1840, *FL*, II, 111 ("busy fighting"); FP ("old prophecy"); *FL*, II, 111 ("symphony"); to JFC, Jan. 1, 1840, FP ("millennial"); *FL*, II, 113 ("bullion").

59. Feb. 8, 1840, JFC Papers, MH ("some thing"); Jan. 1, 1840, *FL*, II, 111 ("in earnest"); Feb. 25, 1840, quoted in Frothingham, *Memoir of Channing*, 167–68 ("listener only").

60. Mary Moody Emerson to FHH, Dec. 20, 1838, quoted in Le Beau, *Hedge*, 168 ("Moses"); FHH to Convers Francis, Feb. 14, 1843, Washburn Collection, MHi ("rigid"); FHH to MF, Nov. 17, 1834, MH-AH ("popular"); FHH to Convers Francis, Feb. 14, 1843, Washburn Collection, MHi ("dissent"); FMW, XVI, 23 ("You frighten me"). For varying interpretations of Hedge's connections with Transcendentalism, see Le Beau, *Hedge;* Joel Myerson, "Frederic Henry Hedge and the Failure of Transcendentalism," *Harvard Library Bulletin*, 23 (Oct. 1975), 396–410; and Doreen Hunter, "Frederic Henry Hedge, What Say You?" *American Quarterly*, 32 (Summer 1980), 186–201.

61. *FL*, II, 124 ("I adjure you"); Mar. 24, 1840, quoted in Myerson, "Frederic Henry Hedge," 404 ("atheist").

62. Mar. 30, 1840, *EL*, II, 270–71 ("worthless").

63. To MF, Mar. 30, 1840, *EL*, II, 271 ("beg it of you"); *Dial*, 1 (Oct. 1840), 181 ("self-culture"); Mar. 1848, MB ("unstable water"); to MF, Mar. 30, 1840, *EL*, II, 270 ("free wit"); Aug. 27, 1841, *EJ*, VIII, 31 ("superficiality"); [Aug. 29, 1841], *FL*, II, 227 ("matter of taste").

64. *FL*, II, 126 ("literary criticisms"); *EL*, II, 266 ("Great Subject"); Apr. 7, 1840, *EJ*, VII, 341–42 ("Religion").

65. Jan. 1, 1840, FP ("literary"); *FL*, II, 126 ("no party measures").

66. *FL*, II, 125 ("donkey"); ibid., 126 ("not sanguine").

67. *EL*, II, 271 ("best club"); to MF, Dec. 12, 1839, ibid., 243 ("abhorrence"); to MF, Nov. 14, 1839, ibid., 234 ("Elegy"); to MF, Mar. 3, 1840, ibid., 258 ("little poems"); Jan. 30, 1840, ibid., 253 ("thank the god").

68. *EL*, II, 282 ("your purpose"); *FL*, II, 130 ("ignorant"); ibid., 128 ("ethically"); Apr. 21? and 23?, 1840, *EL*, II, 287 ("hesitations"); to MF, Apr. 15, 1840, ibid., 281 ("blotting"); to MF, Apr.? 27?, 1840, ibid., 293 ("excellent").

69. Apr. 1840, "AS40," 244 ("the starving"); to MF, Apr. 8, 1840, *EL*, II, 276 ("Apothegms"); ibid., 294 ("grave thing"); May 31, 1840, *FL*, II, 135 ("grand").

70. *EL*, II, 285–86 ("This paper").

71. To MF, Apr. 24, 1840, *EL*, II, 290 ("hard words"); *FL*, II, 232 ("too fierce"); to MF, Apr.? 27?, 1840, *EL*, II, 292 ("capricious offer"); ibid., 294 ("Rejected Introductions").

72. To Ruth Haskins Emerson, Mar. 28, 1840, *EL*, II, 266 ("'Operations on the Teeth'"); quoted in Myerson, *New England Transcendentalists*, 44 ("literary magazine"); "Diary for 1840," May 1840, 79 ("DIAL").

73. Palfrey Papers MH ("blow"); ABA to Hannah Robie, Apr. 26, 1840, quoted in Myerson, *New England Transcendentalists*, 44 ("sublunary world"); Apr. 21, 1840, *ECC*, 269 ("Margaret Fuller's Journal"); June 1, 1840, *EJ*, VII, 364 ("optative mood").

74. *FL*, II, 136 ("thirty names"); June 7, 1840, *EL*, II, 304 ("no import"); June 21, 1840, ibid., 305–6 ("rules of Grub Street").

75. *FL*, II, 130–31 ("Helen Mac Gregor").

76. [To EPP, ca. early 1836]*, *OM*, I, 168 ("mutilated"); Apr. 13, 1820, FMW, V, 6 ("Mediocrity").

Index

Cross-references preceded by a Roman numeral, I through V, are to the subsections under the entry *Fuller, Margaret.*

abolitionism, American 208, 222–23, 224–25, 291–92, 304, 309
Aborn, Frances, 210
Aborn, Susan, 211, 236, 248
Adams, Abel, 328
Adams, John, 10, 133, 134
Adams, John Quincy, 11, 13, 14, 21, 22, 78, 93
Adams, Henry, 219
Adams, Louisa Catherine Johnson (Mrs. John Quincy), 21, 69
adolescent friendship, in early Republic, 99
Aesop's Fables, 31
Alcott, Amos Bronson, 206, 209, 210, 211, 215, 249
    controversy over, 198–200, 206, 209
    and *Dial,* 332, 334, 335, 346
    early life and personality of, 195, 209, 386 n60
    philosophy and outlook of, 182, 195–96, 237, 296, 308, 310, 311, 333
    on MF, 197, 202, 317, 335
    MF's appraisals of: appreciative, 205, 212, 231, 199–200, 223–24, 317, 402 n17; critical, 197–98, 201–2, 320
    MF's relations with, 203, 228, 263, 290, 317, 326
    works: *Conversations with Children on the Gospels,* 198; "Orphic Sayings," 346–47; "Psyche," 195, 237, 333
    See also Temple School

Allen, Joseph, 229
Allen, Lucy Ware, 229
Allen, Mary Ware, 229, 230, 231, 232, 235, 236–37, 241
Alexander I, Tsar of Russia, 89
Alfieri, Vittorio, 57, 90, 150, 190
Alison, Archibald, 57
Allston, Harriet, 73
Allston, Washington, 85, 91, 257–58
American literature, 85
American Monthly Magazine (Boston), 142
American Monthly Magazine (New York), 175, 180, 331
American Quarterly Review, 118
Anti-Masonic party, 11, 144
Apuleius, 301
Ariosto, Ludovico, 90, 190
Arnim, Bettina von, 326
    work: *Goethes Briefwechsel mit einem Kinde,* 327
Austen, Jane, 90

Bachi, Pietro, 84–85, 190
Bacon, Delia, 294
Bacon, Francis, 324
    work: *Essays,* 62
Balzac, Honoré de, *Le Père Goriot; Louis Lambert,* 260
Bancroft, Elizabeth Davis, 292, 300
Bancroft, George, 57, 72, 84, 98, 105, 124, 145, 292, 311

Bancroft, George (*continued*)
    works: "The Influence of Slavery on the
        Political Revolutions in Rome," 144;
        History of the United States, 144
Baptism, in Providence, 208, 220
Barker, Anna Hazard, 291, 327, 328
    life and personality of, 98, 155, 279–80
    marriage and later life of, 282–83
    MF's visits with, 124, 140, 142, 152, 280
        286
    MF's friendship with, 263, 326
    MF's passion for, 280–82, 285–86, 287,
        396 n47
    See also Ward, Samuel Gray
Barker, Jacob, 152
Barlow, Almira Penniman, 46, 97, 98, 102,
    124, 180, 291
Barlow, David Hatch, 97, 124
Barrett, Elizabeth. *See* Browning, Elizabeth
    Barrett
Bartlett, Amelia Greenwood. *See*
    Greenwood, Amelia
Baxter, Richard, *The Saint's Everlasting
    Rest,* 16
Beck, Charles, 84
Beecher, Catharine, 291
Belcher, Deborah Fuller ("Debby," aunt), 69
Benjamin, Park, 175
Bentham, Jeremy, 188
Béranger, Pierre-Jean de, 260
Berni, Francesco, 90
Biddle, Nicholas, 87
biographies of MF, x, 15, 31, 33, 358 n2, 364
    n8, 365 n10
    *See also Memoirs of Margaret Fuller
        Ossoli* (Emerson, Channing, and
        Clarke)
Blair, Hugh, 57
    work: *Lectures on Rhetoric and Belles
        Lettres,* 75
Bloom, Harold, 338
Bokum, Hermann, 190
Boston Academy of Music, 257
Boston Athenaeum, 85, 89, 115, 190, 246,
    257
Boston Courier, 198
Boston Centinel, 186
Boston Columbian Centinel, 71
Boston Daily Advertiser, 57, 145, 197, 199,
    307
Boston English Classical School, 57, 71, 72,
    74
Boston Lyceum for Young Ladies, 56
    character of, 57–58

MF at, 58, 59–63, 64, 65, 67, 70, 80
    See also Park, John
Boston, Mass.
    culture of, 85–86, 192–93, 222–23
    MF in society of, xi, 59, 60–61, 63, 73,
        191–94, 207, 226, 264–65, 269–70,
        273–74; *see also* I. friendships
    See also Cambridge, Mass.; Unitarianism,
        American
Boston Quarterly Review, 308, 321
Bowen, Francis, 222, 307, 308
Bowring, Sir John, 188
Brackett, Loraina, 221
Brillat-Savarin, Jean Anthelme, *The
        Physiology of Taste; or, Meditations
        on Transcendental Gastronomy,* 283
Brook Farm, 97, 219, 296
Brooks, Charles Timothy, 219
"The Brother and Sister Club," 273–74
Brown, Charles Brockden, 90
Brown, Moses, 245
Brown, Thomas, 89
Brown University, 208, 227–28
Browning, Elizabeth Barrett, 239
Brownson, Orestes A., 87, 182, 192, 308,
    310, 311, 335
    MF's dealings with, 183, 333–34, 340
Brutus, Marcus Junius, 90, 144–45
Bryant, William Cullen, 91, 177, 232, 333
Buckingham, Edwin, 175, 331
Buckingham, Joseph T., 175, 198–99, 331
Burgis, Eleanor Burrill, 219
Burgis, Tristam, 213
Buckminster, Joseph Stevens, 4
Bulwer-Lytton. *See* Lytton, Edward George
    Bulwer-
Burns, Robert, 284
Byron, Anne Isabella Milbanke, Lady, 239
Byron, George Gordon, Lord, 86, 119, 154
    MF influenced by, 106
    MF's view of, 91, 101, 103, 127, 150, 178
    works: *Manfred,* 177; "Stanzas to
        Augusta," 278

Caesar, Gaius Julius, 9, 47, 133, 135, 144
    work: *Commentaries on the Gallic War,*
        54
Calhoun, John C., 11
Calvert, George Henry, 248
Cambridge, Mass.
    culture of, 24–26
    MF in society of, 63–66, 73, 85, 94–95,
        96–97, 120, 124, 264–65, 269–70; *see
        also* I. friendships

See also Boston, Mass.; Harvard College; Unitarianism, American
Cambridgeport, Mass., 26–27
Cambridge Port Private Grammar School (Port School), 63
  MF at, 45–46, 56, 87
Canton, Mass., 16
Capron, Dr., 221
Caradori-Allan, Maria, 228
Carlyle, Thomas, 117, 129, 147, 174, 175, 177, 185, 193, 209, 324, 332
  MF influenced by, xi, 115, 116
  on MF, x
  MF's dissent from, 173, 255
  works: *History of the French Revolution,* 202, 225; *Sartor Resartus,* 181
Cellini, Benvenuto, 258
Cervantes, Miguel de, 51–52
Chandler, Lucinda, 306
Channing, Edward, T., 84, 269
Channing, Elizabeth, 227
Channing, Ellen Fuller. *See* Fuller, Ellen Kilshaw
Channing, Mary, 191, 193, 227, 248, 263, 291, 320
Channing, Susan Cleveland, 58, 60
Channing, Susan Higginson, 95
Channing, Walter, 320
Channing, William Ellery, 58, 95, 98, 191, 195, 207–8, 222, 239, 321
  outlook of, 86, 115, 194
  on MF, 318
  MF's view of, 194–95, 207, 338
  MF's relations with, 140, 152, 194, 207, 248, 263
  work: *Slavery,* 224
Channing, William Ellery, II, 170, 345–46
  MF's view of, 320
Channing, Wiliam Henry, 95, 265, 313, 341, 342
  life and outlook of, 98, 106, 320–21, 340
  on MF, 321–22, 322–23
  MF's view of, 248, 321
  recollections of MF by, 60, 99, 266, 280, 298, 315–16
  work: "Ernest the Seeker," 342
Charles XII, King of Sweden, 35
Chateaubriand, Vicomte François-René de, 260
Chaucer, Geoffrey, 232
Cheney, Ednah Dow Littlehale, 291, 305–6
Child, Lydia Maria, 118, 292
  on MF, 88

MF's friendship with, 94–95
  work: *The Oasis,* 146
child-rearing, antebellum
  in America, 27, 29, 31, 33, 68
  in Boston-Cambridge, 29–30, 31, 364 n9
children, antebellum, social forwardness of, 64–65, 68
Christian Examiner, 136, 146, 147, 175, 182, 199, 222, 316, 332
Christian Register, 199
Cicero, Marcus Tullius, 45, 47, 57, 71, 75, 145
Clark, Ellen, 248, 253, 330
Clark, L. B., 248
Clarke, James Freeman, xii, 110–11, 112, 124, 130, 153, 157, 182, 186, 187, 207, 277
  and *Dial,* 341, 342
  advice of, to MF: literary, 151–52, 173, 240, 242, 256, 336; social, 111; vocational, 138–39
  inferiority to MF, feelings of, 116, 139
  life and outlook of, 98, 104–5, 137, 147–48, 149, 199, 221, 224, 308, 311, 321
  on MF, x, 109, 114, 133, 314, 321
  MF influenced by, 105
  MF's view of, 273
  MF's differences with, 107–8, 127–28, 129–30, 147–48, 173–74, 239
  MF's friendship with, 105–9, 116–17, 118, 263, 273, 281
  MF's German studies with, 115–16
  MF's influence on, 109, 237, 253
  MF's quarrel with, 140–42
  mutual encouragement of MF and, 106–7, 109, 116, 118, 137, 172, 201, 237
  recollections of MF by, 90–91, 100, 102, 266, 267
  vocational situations, differences in, between MF and, 117–18, 139, 141–42
Clarke, Rebecca Hull, 104–5, 106, 124
Clarke, Samuel, 104
Clarke, Sarah, 164, 182, 186, 215, 216, 223, 258, 276–77, 280, 283, 292, 293, 332, 349
  on MF, 102–3, 151, 224, 266, 267, 299, 300
  MF's friendship with, 125, 141, 157, 263
Clarke, William H., 267
Clay, Henry, 11
Cogswell, Joseph G., 57, 84, 105
Colburn, Warren, 75

Coleridge, Samuel Taylor, 91, 106, 108, 115, 144, 171, 180, 185, 209, 239, 253, 296, 304, 311, 324
    MF's view of, 150, 177, 178, 179
    works: *Aides to Reflection,* 105; "Dejection: An Ode," 179
Coliseum Club
    character of, 218–19
    MF in debate on progress at, 242–45
    MF's relations with members of, 219–21, 228, 337–38
Colman, George, the younger, *Blue Beard,* 59
Colman, Mrs., 56
Combe, George, 144
Common Sense philosophy, 8, 57, 89, 222
Condivi, Ascanio, 258
Congdon, Charles T., 298
Constantine (Pavlovich), Grand Duke of Russia, 89
Conversations, 330, 335
    ideological significance of, 295–96, 303–4, 306, 307, 399 n78
    membership characteristics of, 291–93, 300
    MF's personal motives for, 290, 296
    MF's qualities as leader of: speech, 298–99; pedagogy, 300
    MF's view of, 299–300, 305
    subjects of, 301–4, 305, 399 n78
    success of, 293–94, 304–6
    theory of, 294–97
Cooper, James Fenimore, 85, 118
    The Pilot, 19
Cosmopolitan, 209
Cousin, Victor, 180
Crabbe, George, 148
Craigie, Andrew, 93
Cranch, Christopher Pearse, 319, 345
Crane, Abigail ("Abba," aunt), 16, 20, 33, 35, 43, 58
Crane, Elizabeth Crane ("Betsey," aunt), 16
Crane, Elizabeth Jones Weiser (grandmother), 16, 58, 136
Crane, Henry (great-grandfather), 16
Crane, Peter (grandfather), 16, 18, 58
Crane, Peter, Jr. (uncle), 16
Creuzer, Friedrich, *Symbolik und Mythologie der alten Völker,* 301
Cumming, Elizabeth Randall. *See* Randall, Elizabeth
Curtis, George William, 298, 315
Curtis, Julia, 219

Dall, Caroline Healey, 82, 306
    on MF, 70, 297, 298, 318
Dana family (Cambridge, Mass.), 25, 63
Dana family (Groton, Mass.), 125
Dana, Francis, 93
Dana, Martha, 80, 121
Dana, Richard Henry, Jr., 87, 322
Dana, Richard Henry, Sr., 85, 91, 177
    MF's view of, 194, 248–49, 341
Dana, Samuel, 80, 121
Dana, Susan, 193
Dante Alighieri, 90, 203, 255
    work: *Divina Commedia,* 190
Davis, George T., 106, 109, 115, 116, 156, 157
    personality and outlook of, 98, 102–4, 105, 149
    on MF, 104, 180
    MF's attraction to, 102–3, 104
    MF's falling-out with, 105, 109–12, 114, 140–41, 279, 287, 289
Davis, Helen, 98, 99, 125, 126, 157
Davis, John (judge), 273
Davis, John (senator), 230
Davis, Margaret, 98, 125
Davis, Mrs. Wendell, 156
Davis, Paulina Wright, 306
Deleuze, Joseph Philippe François, *Instruction pratique sur le magnétisme animal,* 221
deism, 103–4
Democrats, 11, 208, 310, 311, 314, 332
Demosthenes, 90
depression, American (1837–1843), 310
Dewey, Orville, 187
DeWolfe, James, 270
DeWolfe, Mary Soley, 80, 98, 270, 271
DeWolfe, William Bradford, 270, 271
Dial, 283
    MF as organizer of, xii, 335, 341–48
    MF chosen as editor of, 334–35
    MF's view of, 345, 349–50
    MF's writings for, 338
    origins of, 147–48, 331–34, 404 n43
    reputation of, 348–49
    See also Emerson, Ralph Waldo; magazines, antebellum
Dickinson, Edwards, 45, 56
Disraeli, Benjamin, 90, 149
    work: *Vivian Grey,* 107, 203, 212
Dix, Dorothea, 118
Doddridge, Philip, 16
Dorr, Thomas W., 219

Duppa, Richard, 258
Dwight, John Sullivan, 238, 319, 341
  work: *Select Minor Poems of Goethe and
    Schiller,* 238

Eckermann, Johann Peter, *Gespräche mit
    Goethe* (MF's translation of), 204,
    253–54
Edgeworth, Maria, 55, 91, 244
  work: *The Parent's Assistant,* 30
Edinburgh Review, 115, 127
education, of boys, antebellum, 29, 30, 45,
    57–58, 89
Eichhorn, Johann Gottfried, 132
Eldridge, Emelyn. *See* Story, Emelyn
    Eldridge
Eliot, William Greenleaf, 98, 99, 124, 137
Elliot, Mary, 46
Elliott, Stephen, 64
Embargo, of Thomas Jefferson
    Administration, 8, 27
Emerson, Charles Chauncy, 184, 185, 186,
    280
Emerson, Edward Bliss, 73, 184, 185, 186
Emerson, Ellen Louisa Tucker, 184
Emerson family, 169
Emerson, Frederick, 197
Emerson, George B., 57, 71, 72, 118
Emerson, Lidian Jackson, 187, 216, 256,
    292, 300, 328
  on MF, 188–89
  personality and outlook of, 185–86
Emerson, Mary Moody, 184, 186
Emerson, Ralph Waldo, xi, 3, 73, 170, 196,
    199, 210, 211, 221, 223, 227, 273,
    280, 283, 293, 317, 320
  advice of, to MF: literary, 242, 250, 324–
    25, 339; medical, 212; solicited by
    MF, 237–38, 270, 336; vocational,
    214, 215
  appreciation of MF by, 188–89, 203, 205,
    216, 256
  books and papers exchanged between MF
    and, 201, 258–59, 260, 324, 325–26
  and *Dial:* attitude toward, 332, 334, 335,
    343, 345, 347, 349; assistance to, 341,
    345–48
  influence of, 185, 186, 215, 276, 295–96,
    304
  life and personality of, 184–86
  MF encouraged by, 190, 242, 254, 256, 339
  MF influenced by, 215–16, 294, 340
  MF's admiration for, 202, 207, 215, 321,
    323–24, 329, 350
  MF's attendance at lectures of, 206–7,
    214–15, 216, 228, 237, 324, 325
  MF's criticisms of, 269, 324, 325, 328–29
  MF's differences with, 201–2, 238–39,
    245, 256, 258–59, 314, 319, 337, 340
  MF's early interest in, 186–87
  MF's first meeting with, 187–89
  MF's growing intimacy with, 323–30
  MF's influence on: literary, 201, 203, 325;
    social, 203, 323; 325–28
  MF's private feelings of love for, 329–30
  MF's visits with, 187–90, 202–3, 205, 216,
    218, 225–26, 245, 247, 323, 326,
    334–35
  philosophy and outlook of, 147, 182, 185,
    195, 202, 308, 333, 310, 311, 342,
    343–44
  recollections of MF by, 258, 263–64, 265,
    266, 267–68, 269, 270, 298, 299
  works: "Address on Education," 206–7;
    "The American Scholar," 214–15,
    245; "The Divinity School Address,"
    307–8, 324, 332; "The Editors to the
    Reader," 347–48; "The Heart," 237;
    "Heroism," 227; "Introductory,"
    311, 324; *Nature,* 185, 186, 203;
    "Thoughts on Modern Literature,"
    349
Emerson, Ruth Haskins, 186, 328
Emerson, Waldo, 203
Emerson, William, 185
Enfield, William, *Institutes of Natural
    Philosophy, Theoretical and
    Experimental,* 78
Enlightenment, 9, 18, 29, 30, 33, 89
Epictetus, 89
European literature instruction, in America,
    91, 191
evangelical Protestantism, 12, 33, 87, 182,
    234, 309–10
Everett, Edward, 84, 85, 86, 93, 105, 144,
    216, 310
  MF's view of, 59, 195
Everett family, 63, 124

Farley, Frederick A., 206, 213, 219, 227
Farley, Jane, 227
Farrar, Eliza Rotch, 112–13, 124, 135, 153,
    187, 291
  life and outlook of, 95–96

Farrar, Eliza Rotch (*continued*)
  MF's friendship with, 96, 97, 263
  work: *The Young Lady's Friend,* 96–97
Farrar, John, 95–96, 97
Farrars (John and Eliza Rotch), 63, 99, 140,
    142, 152, 155, 238, 269, 276
Fay, Harriet, 46, 64, 73, 74
Fay, Samuel P. P., 46, 66
Federalists, 8, 10, 11, 12–13, 85, 86, 93
Felton, Cornelius C., 124, 269
feminism, American, 295, 306
Fénelon, François de Salignac de la Mothe,
    57
Ferguson, Adam, 31
Fichte, Johann Gottlieb, 173
Fielding, Henry, 5, 51, 52
Follen, Charles, 84, 85, 115, 116, 147
Foreign Quarterly Review, 115, 151
Fourierist socialist movement, American,
    292
Fowler, Orson, 221
Francis, Convers, 269, 315, 342
Francis, Lydia Maria. *See* Child, Lydia
    Maria
Fraser's Magazine, 174–75
Frederick II, King of Prussia, 89
Freeman, James, 105, 106, 161
Frisbie family, 63
Frost, John, 63, 65
Frothingham, Nathaniel L., 59, 61
Fruitlands, 219
Fuller, Abraham Williams (uncle), 7–8, 43,
    51
  MF's clash with, over siblings' schooling,
    216–18
  MF's dealings with, 59, 61, 66, 72, 163,
    165
Fuller, Arthur Buckminster (brother), 67, 82,
    168, 216, 249, 257, 290
  life and personality of, 43, 121, 122–24,
    165, 167, 170
  MF's advice to, 140, 169–70
  MF's influence on, 170–71
  MF's instruction of, 135
Fuller brothers (uncles), 7, 63; *see also*
    specific uncles
Fuller, Edward (brother), birth and death of,
    43
Fuller, Ellen Kilshaw (sister), 21, 58, 82, 187,
    217, 227, 249, 253, 263
  life and personality of, 43, 123, 168, 170
  MF's advice to, 168–69
  MF's instruction of, 135, 253
Fuller, Elisha (uncle), 33, 43, 54, 63, 64, 75

Fuller, Elizabeth (aunt), 6, 33, 43
Fuller, Elizabeth Tidd (ancestor), 4
Fuller, Eugene (brother), 43, 58, 61, 63, 82,
    94, 162, 228
  life and personality of, 44–45, 123
  MF's tutoring of, 45, 88
  MF's view of, 45
Fuller family
  relatives of, and MF, 43, 262–63
  servants of, 11, 18, 43, 123–24
  style of, and MF's personality, 55–56, 88
  Unitarianism of, 20, 28, 48, 112
  See also Fuller, Margarett Crane; Fuller,
    Timothy; *specific relatives*
Fuller, Henry Holton (uncle), 7, 33, 42, 43,
    56, 59, 63, 64, 170, 190
Fuller, Hiram, 206, 220, 221, 249
  career and outlook of, 204, 209–10, 211,
    213
  on MF, 228, 229
  MF hired by, 204–5
  MF's view of, 211
  See also Greene Street School
Fuller, James Lloyd (brother), 43, 88–89,
    122, 170, 216, 217, 269
  mental problems of, 168
  MF's instruction of, 35
  MF's view of, 168
Fuller, Julia Adelaide (sister), death of, 28,
    32

FULLER, MARGARET

I PERSONALITY AND TRAITS
  action, zeal for, 134, 142, 146, 163
  affection, craving for, in childhood, 35–36,
    37, 39, 44
  ambition, 47–48, 54, 87, 106–7, 114, 126,
    164
    See also III. ambition
  appearance, 65, 93–94, 265–66, 271, 297–
    98, 316
  arrogance, 37, 46, 97, 127, 211, 264–65,
    321, 322, 394 n19
  boldness, 196, 245–46, 260–61
  competitiveness, 46, 58, 61, 193–94, 262–
    63
  conversational powers, 99–100, 151, 174,
    267, 298–99, 339
  dancing, 59, 66, 67, 73, 228
  domestic labors, 43–44, 63, 82–83, 88–89,
    121, 164–65
    See also Groton, Mass.; II. teaching
  dreams, 31, 40–41, 108, 125–26, 282,
    285–86, 287, 329

See also I. psychological problems; II. dreams; II. irrationalism

educational frustrations, 89, 92, 127
See also education, antebellum, of boys; women, antebellum

egotism, 88, 191, 194, 264–65, 273, 274–75, 297, 322, 339

eloquence as speaker, 268, 298, 316, 317

enemies, 46, 99, 264–65, 273–74

erudition, 90–91, 115–16, 127, 268

family head, 162–63, 166–67, 171, 205, 216–18, 290
See also I. siblings, MF's moral training of

father figures, 37, 113, 187

fictional identities, 37, 53, 80–82, 97, 258, 303–4, 313, 320, 334

friendships
  and gender, 100–102, 111
  and Romantic literature, 99, 101–2, 105–7, 268, 273–75, 279, 282, 326, 329
  MF's friends' characteristics in, 46–47, 97–99, 263–64.
  MF's qualities as friend in, 99–100, 263–64, 265, 266–69, 394 n20
  MF's view of, 237, 253, 269, 270, 271, 272
  See also adolescent friendship, in early Republic; women, antebellum; I. passions; II. friendship; II. gender relations; *specific friends*

fun, 28, 56, 266, 271

gender identity, problems of, xii, 36, 39–40, 41, 42–43, 47, 70, 82, 100, 261–62, 282, 287–88, 289
  See also II. women; III. gender identity, as writer

gender status, problems of, 87, 146, 162, 163, 194, 288, 314–15
  See also women, antebellum; I. vocational frustrations; II. feminism; II. women

guilt, 81–82, 158, 161, 164

health problems, 32, 157–58, 160–61, 166, 200, 203, 212, 237, 246, 249, 253, 257–58, 267, 272

homes, 27, 92–93, 119–20, 121–22, 256–57

humor, 99, 101, 202, 203, 231, 266–67, 271, 274

income: inheritance, 162, 165, 190; publishing, 254, 335; teaching, 142, 190, 191, 200, 211, 293–94

industriousness, 253, 256

intellectual, identity as, x–xi, xii, 113–14, 126, 134, 261–62, 289, 303–4, 306
  See also II. intellectual, role of

magnetism, personal, 100, 267–70, 322

mentor, desire for, 117, 130, 155, 186, 225, 237–38, 239–40

as mentor, for girls, 191–92
  See also Greene Street School; *specific girls*

money needs, 138, 139, 151, 166, 175, 190, 196, 204, 216, 218, 271, 290, 335

mother figures, 42–43, 80, 82, 95–97, 247

name, 46–47, 49

passions, 109–12, 114, 158, 275–76, 277–79, 280–82, 287
  See also I. friendships; I. sexuality; II. gender relations; II. sexuality

perfectionism, 52, 100, 322

precocity, intellectual, 30–32, 38, 51–52, 62, 65
  See also II. precocity, intellectual

presumption, social, 109, 274–75

psychological problems: in childhood, 31–32, 365–66 n13; depression, 32, 53–54, 158, 160–61, 166, 194, 237, 246, 247, 272
  See also I. dreams

reading habits, 32, 89, 92, 115, 127, 204

rebelliousness, in early adolescence, 65–66, 67, 78–80

righteousness, 109, 111–12, 199–200, 217–18, 223–24, 226–27

sarcasm, 55–56, 61, 65, 78, 97, 99, 229, 230, 231, 236, 265, 299, 321

self-criticisms: intellectual, 117, 127, 172, 175–76, 237, 253; moral, 126, 194, 238, 339
  See also III. self-appraisals

sexuality, 31–32, 39–40, 42, 108, 114, 221, 281–82, 287, 396 n47
  See also I. gender identity, problems of; I. passions; II. gender relations; II. sexuality

siblings, MF's moral training of, 139–40, 167–71
  See also Groton, Mass.; II. teaching; *specific siblings*

studiousness, 35, 54, 62, 71, 87, 92, 126, 127, 130, 171

support for others, 109, 116, 121, 136–37, 146, 165–66, 268–69

Fuller, Margaret (*continued*)
   travel, 119, 135, 138, 146, 152–53, 155, 163–165, 166, 270–72
      See also Groton, Mass.; Providence, R.I.
   unmarried state, 88, 118, 271, 288–89
      See also II. gender relations
   vocational frustrations, 117–19, 139, 163, 165, 166
      See also I. gender status, problems of; II. teaching; II. women; III. publishing

II INTELLECTUAL AND CULTURAL ATTI-
   TUDES AND PREOCCUPATIONS
   American culture, ix–x, 133–34, 138, 139, 149–50, 225, 243, 337
      See also II. American literature
   American literature, 90, 241–42, 322, 340
   antislavery, 146, 223–25, 270, 304
   art, 246–47, 257–59, 262, 272, 284–85, 304
   Bible, 34, 48, 75, 132, 143, 164, 233–34, 248
      See also II. Christianity; II. religion; II. Unitarianism, American
   Boston-Cambridge culture, 26, 85, 101, 120, 200
      See also Boston, Mass.; Cambridge, Mass.
   Christianity, 48, 103–4, 112–13, 131–34, 164, 244, 246, 253, 311
      See also II. Bible; II. religion; II. Transcendentalism, American; II. Unitarianism, American
   drama, 35, 49, 59, 80, 81–82, 127, 150, 228
   dreams, 107–8
      See also I. dreams; II. irrationalism
   English literature, 51, 90
      See also II. Romantic literature
   fatalism, 91–92, 113
   feminism, 235, 243–44, 288, 295–96
      See also I. gender status, problems of; II. women
   fiction, 48–49, 50–51, 55, 56, 90, 102, 142–43, 149, 156, 262
   French literature, 51, 63, 87, 90–91
      See also II. Romantic literature
   friendship, 104, 111–12, 277–79, 328–29, 368 n33
      See also women, antebellum; I. friendships; I. passions; II. gender relations
   gender relations, 273–74, 288

genius, 87, 106–7, 288, 337, 338, 350
German literature, 115–16, 128–31, 176–77, 255
   See also German literature, in America; II. Romantic literature
Greek literature, 33, 47, 48, 53, 54, 63, 87, 89
Greco-Roman mythology, 48, 235, 301–4
heroism, 42, 47–48, 90, 111, 241, 274, 284–85
history, 33, 35, 51, 61, 127, 133–34
intellectual, role of, xi, 134, 301, 306
   See also I. intellectual, identity as
irrationalism, 32, 127, 129, 171–72, 173, 221
   See also I. dreams; II. dreams
Italian literature, 63, 87, 90–91
Kantian philosophy, German post-, 131, 147–48, 173, 180, 183, 311
Latin literature, 31, 33, 34, 45, 47–48, 54, 61, 63, 89–90
literary criticism, 48–49, 52, 62, 78, 149–50, 322
music, 35, 49, 53, 54, 56, 63, 87, 228, 257
nature, 91, 125, 257, 262
New England culture, 3, 148, 313–14
middle-class values, New England, 140, 165, 259, 260, 262–63, 270–71
oratory, 55, 59, 146, 213
philosophy, 62, 75, 87, 89, 95
   See also II. Kantian philosophy, German post-
poetry, 107, 129–30, 179
politics, 89, 134, 195, 213, 243, 253, 314
precocity, intellectual, 31, 52, 135, 176
   See also I. precocity, intellectual
primitivism, 92, 243, 274
religion, 103–4, 112–14, 126, 233–34, 244, 270, 273
   See also II. Bible; II. Christianity; II. Transcendentalism, American; II. Unitarianism, American
republicanism, x, xii, 13, 47–48, 145, 241
Romantic aesthetic theory: and the arts, 228, 232–33, 258, 304, 331; and literary criticism, 149–50, 177–80, 232, 254–55; and writing, 171–72, 336–37
Romanticism, xi, xii, 91–92, 103, 106–7, 108, 114–15, 127–28, 129, 183, 243–45, 248–49
   See also Romanticism; Transcendentalism, American; II. religion; II. Romantic aesthetic

theory; II. Romantic literature; II.
Transcendentalism, American
Romantic literature
English, 91, 127–28, 171
French, 91, 259–62, 325–26
German, x, 116, 128–31, 171, 177, 183,
301, 302, 311, 314
See also Romantic aesthetic theory;
Romanticism; I. friendships; II.
Romanticism
satire, 46–47, 49, 274, 313
sentimentalism, 42, 49, 51, 100, 101–2,
236, 242, 270, 275–76, 300
sexuality, 149, 173–74, 239, 259, 260,
281–82, 284
See also I. sexuality
society, 136, 154, 182–83, 234, 243–44,
302, 314–15, 323
Stoicism, 90, 104, 126, 275, 322
studies
in adolescence, 87, 89–92
in childhood, 30–31, 33, 34, 35, 47–48,
51–52, 53, 54, 62, 63
See also Boston Lyceum for Young
Ladies; Cambridge Port Private
Grammar School; Groton, Mass.;
Miss Prescott's Young Ladies' Seminary
teaching
attitude toward, 118, 190, 200–201
plans for, in West, 138–39, 190, 290
in private lessons, 191, 330
in private literature classes, 190–91,
330–31
of siblings, 44, 45, 63, 82, 88
See also Green Street School; Groton,
Mass.; Providence, R.I.; Temple
School; women, antebellum
Transcendentalism, American, ix, xi–xii,
147–48, 182–84, 226–27, 232–35,
236, 241–42, 244–45, 311–15, 337,
340, 350
See also Coliseum Club; Conversations;
Dial; Greene Street School;
Romanticism; Transcendental Club;
Transcendentalism, American; II.
Kantian philosophy, German post-;
II. religion; II. Romantic aesthetic
theory; II. Romanticism
Unitarianism, American, x, 112–13, 124,
183, 241–42, 311–12
See also Fuller family; Unitarianism,
American; Transcendentalism,
American; II. Christianity; II.
Transcendentalism, American

women
culture of, ix, xi, 235, 243–44
education of, x, 290
as intellectuals, xii, 127, 194, 261–62,
288
status of, 87, 323
as writers, 119, 144, 235–36, 244, 323,
340, 380 n43
See also Conversations; Greene Street
School; women, antebellum; I. gender
status, problems of; II. feminism; III.
gender identity, as writer

III WRITING TRAITS AND ATTITUDES
ambition, 142–43, 262, 335, 350
See also I. ambition
criticisms of others, 151, 180, 242, 298
gender identity, as writer, 51, 97, 262, 336,
337–38, 339, 405 n52
See also I. gender identity, problems of;
II. women
letters, 34–36, 54–55, 253, 273–74, 325–
26
method, 337, 338
plans, 49, 143, 172, 175, 180
publishing, 138, 174–75, 335, 340
See also magazines, antebellum
self-appraisals, 117, 118–19, 143–44, 151,
174, 237–38, 335–39, 350
See also I. self-criticisms
unpublished papers, 128, 143, 258–59,
260–62, 270, 338, 350
vocation, 118–19, 136, 142, 174–75, 190,
238, 240
See also II. women

IV PUBLISHED WORKS
Woman in the Nineteenth Century, 37
"Brutus," 144–46, 241, 254, 255
"Chat in Boston Bookstores.—No. I," 320
"Chat in Boston Bookstores.—No. II,"
313, 334
*Conversations with Goethe in the Last
Years of His Life, Translated from the
German of Eckermann,* 204, 253–56,
272, 308
"Eagles and Doves" (translation from
Goethe), 238
"Jesus, the Comforter," 164, 382 n9
"Karl Theodore Korner," 240–41
"Letters from Palmyra," 241–42
"The Life of Sir James Mackintosh," 175–
76, 383 n31
"Lost and Won: A Tale of Modern Days
and Good Society," 155–57

Fuller, Margaret (*continued*)
  "Modern British Poets," 177–80, 183, 245
  "On Sunday Morning When Prevented by
    a Snow-Storm from Going to
    Church," 171
  "Philip Van Artevelde," 149–50, 151
  "The Pilgrims of the Rhine," 149, 150–51,
    156
  "Present State of German Literature,"
    176–77
  Review of George Crabbe, *The Life of the
    Rev. George Crabbe,* and William
    Roberts, *Memoirs of the Life and
    Correspondence of Mrs. Hannah
    More,* 148–49, 151
  "To a Golden Heart, Worn Round His
    Neck," (translation from Goethe), 238

V UNPUBLISHED AND POSTHUMOUSLY PUB-
    LISHED MATERIAL
  "Columbine," 275
  "Drachenfels," 275, 280, 326
  "The Hieroglyphic Spell," 280
  "Progress of Society," 243–45
  "sketch of youth," 28, 32, 36, 37, 363–64
    n8, 368 n33
  "Some remarks upon Madame Caradori,"
    228
  Torquato Tasso by Johann Wolfgang von
    Goethe (translation), 128, 138, 187
  "To the Face Seen in the Moon," 287–88

Fuller, Margarett Crane (mother), 7, 28, 41,
    43, 64, 67, 216, 217, 218, 245
  gender consciousness of, 21–22
  on Groton farm, 122, 123–24, 136, 139,
    167; *see also* Groton, Mass.
  intellectual outlook of, 18–20, 21, 60
  life and personality of, 16, 17, 20–21
  marriage of, 15, 16, 17–18, 21–23
  MF influenced by, 15, 21, 23, 40–41, 161
  MF's rearing by: in MF's childhood, 23,
    27, 33, 37–38, 48, 56, 60, 61, 63; in
    MF's adolescence, 65–67, 70, 72–73,
    74, 76–77, 80, 82–83; *see also* child
    rearing
  MF's relationship with, 35, 37–41, 82–83,
    139, 192, 203, 227, 237, 247, 249,
    253, 282
  as widowed mother, 162–63, 167
Fuller, Richard Frederick (brother), 22, 43,
    67, 82, 94, 119, 157, 158, 162, 168,
    216, 249, 279, 290
  life and personality of, 122–24, 165–66,
    167, 169, 170

  MF's advice to, 140, 169, 257
  MF's influence on, 170–71, 205
  MF's instruction of, 135
Fuller, Sarah ("Sally," aunt), 43, 59, 60, 65,
    66, 72
Fuller, Sarah Williams (grandmother), 4–5,
    59, 61, 65
Fuller, Thomas (ancestor), 3–4
Fuller, Timothy (father), 7, 41, 43, 64
  death of, 158–59; MF's reaction to, 160–
    61, 164, 256
  estate of, 161–62, 163, 165
  on Groton farm, 122–23, 124, 134, 139;
    see also Groton, Mass.
  at Harvard College, 8–10
  intellectual outlook of, 8–9, 11–13, 21, 51
  literary advice, to MF, 49–51, 56, 78, 144–
    45
  literary ambitions of, 119, 122
  marriage of. *See* Fuller, Margarett Crane
  MF influenced by, 13, 23, 32, 36–37, 47–
    48, 52, 119, 134, 140, 167–68, 184,
    205, 217, 350
  MF's argument with, over schools, 72–76
  MF's rearing by: in MF's childhood, xi,
    23, 27–28, 29–32, 33–36, 48, 53, 56,
    62–63, 365 n10, 366 n16; in MF's
    adolescence, 65–70, 75–76, 77–78,
    80, 82–83, 94; *see also* child rearing;
    women, antebellum
  MF's relationship with, 35–37, 48–49, 54–
    56, 78–80, 113, 114, 139, 158
  personality of, 8, 13–15
  politics and political career of, 7, 10–11,
    32–33, 63, 93, 119, 134, 144
  women, views of, 14–15, 16–17, 21–22,
    53, 68–69
Fuller, Timothy (grandfather), 4, 5–6
Fuller, William Henry (brother), 33, 43, 58,
    82, 162
  life and personality of, 44, 123
  MF's tutoring of, 44, 88
Furness, William Henry, 153
Fuseli, Henry, 258

Gale, Anna D., 229–30, 231, 232, 233–35
Gale, Cyrus, 229–30
Gammell, William, 228
Gannett, Ezra Stiles, 54
Gannett family, 63
Gannett, Mrs. Thomas Brattle, 21
Gannett, Thomas Brattle, 21, 48, 54
Gardiner, William, *Music of Nature,* 228,
    232–33
Garrison, William Lloyd, 292, 332

German literature, in America, 115, 116
Gibbon, Edward, 127, 145
Gibbs, Lilly, 248, 253
Gill, Moses, 6
Goddard, Lucy, 303
Godkin, Edwin Lawrence, 283
Godwin, William, 9, 90, 168
    work: *Mandeville,* 107
Goethe, Christiane (née Vulpius), 174, 239
Goethe, Johann Wolfgang von, xii, 101, 116,
        124, 134, 136, 148, 150, 177, 186,
        190, 195, 274, 296, 301, 327, 331,
        335
    MF's projected biography of 172–74, 204,
        238–40, 250, 324–25
    MF's view of: admiring, 117, 130–31,
        238–39, 254–55, 271, 297; critical,
        255; sympathetic, 129–30, 256;
        troubled, 130, 173–74, 239
    reputation of, in America, 129, 254
    works: *Die Italienische Reise,* 130; *Faust,*
        177, 190, 219, 254; *Wilhelm Meisters
        Lehrjahre,* 130, 201, 261, 287
Goldsmith, Oliver
    works: *The Deserted Village,* 34, 49, 50;
        The Traveller, 50; *The Vicar of
        Wakefield,* 51
Gore, Catherine, 144
Graham's Magazine, 332
Graves, Juliet, 230, 245, 249–50
Greeley, Horace, 292, 348
Greeley, Mary, 292
Greene, Albert G., 218, 219, 220, 228
Greene, Sarah Margaret Fuller, 220, 272
Greene Street School, 204, 300
    character of, 209–12, 249
    MF's view of, 210–12
    MF's teaching at: courses, 212–13, 232–
        36; feelings about, 212–13, 228–29,
        237–38, 239, 246, 249–50; pedagogy,
        212, 231–32; private Bible class, 248;
        reputation, 229; Transcendentalist
        philosophy, promotion of, 232–35,
        236; women's culture, promotion of,
        235–36
    MF's circle of students at: devotion of, to
        MF, 231, 250; on MF as a teacher,
        229–31; MF's attention to, 230–31,
        250–51; MF's influence on, 228–29,
        236
    MF's resignation from, 249–51, 290
    value of MF's experience at, 251
    See also Fuller, Hiram; Providence, R.I.
Greenwood, Amelia, 46, 97, 98, 100, 142
Greenwood, Francis William Pitt, 46

Greenwood, William Pitt, 46
Grimké, Angelina, 294
Grimké, Sarah M., 294
Groton Athenaeum, 122, 127
Groton, Mass.
    character of, 121–22
    Fuller farm at: family labors at, 123–24,
        166–67; family views of, 122–23;
        MF's view of, 123, 125–26
    MF's sewing at, 124, 136, 142
    MF's studies at, 127–34
    MF's teaching of siblings at, 134–36, 139,
        142, 167, 253
    MF's travels away from, 124–25, 139–40,
        142
    MF's view of, 125
Gustavus II Adolphus, king of Sweden, 143

Hague, William, 220, 228
Hale, Edward Everett, 298–99
Hale, Elizabeth, 80
Hale, Nathan, Jr., 307–8
Haliburton, Mary Ann, 291
Hall, Edward Brooks, 219, 221, 229, 243,
        244, 246
Hall, Harriet Ware, 229, 246
Hartshorn, Thomas, translation of
        *Instruction pratique sur le
        magnétisme animal* (Deleuze), 221
Harvard College, 24–25, 31, 45, 72
    and Cambridge culture, 25–26, 84–85,
        105
Harvard Divinity School, 307–8
Hawthorne, Nathaniel, 172, 175, 332
    work: *The Blithedale Romance,* 97
Hawthorne, Sophia Peabody, 291
Healey, Caroline. *See* Dall, Caroline Healey
Hedge family, 63
Hedge, Frederic Henry, 31, 95, 124, 186,
        187, 215, 263, 332
    Dial, disowned by, 341, 342–44
    intellectual advice of, to MF, 115, 132
    life and outlook of, 98, 136, 139, 146, 147,
        180, 182, 308, 331, 342, 344
    MF influenced by, 115
    MF's differences with, 136, 147, 199–200,
        239
    MF's view of, 98, 269, 344
    mutual encouragement of MF and, 136,
        172
    recollections of MF by, 60–61, 64, 65, 89,
        93–94, 99–100, 298
    Transcendentalists on, 342, 343–44
    work: "The Art of Life, the Scholar's
        Calling," 344

Hedge, Levi, 31, 64, 98
 work: *Elements of Logick,* 75
Hedge, Mary Kneeland (Mrs. Levi), 95
Heeren, Arnold, 301
Heine, Heinrich, 240–41
 work: *Die Romantische Schule,* 177, 383
   n32
Helvétius, Claude-Adrien, 9, 89
Hemans, Felicia, 86, 209, 244, 319
Heraud, John A., 332
Herder, Johann Gottfried, 302
Hesiod, 301
Higginson family, 25, 63
Higginson, Louisa Storrow, 95
Higginson, Thomas Wentworth, 8, 17, 25,
   140, 273, 298
 reports to: about MF, 89, 94, 95, 96, 161;
   about MF's family, 7, 66–67, 88,
   93
 works: *Cheerful Yesterdays,* 26; *Margaret
   Fuller Ossoli,* x; *Old Cambridge,*
   31
Hillard, George S., 98
Hilliard, Francis, 64
Hilliard Gray and Company, 253
Hoar, Elizabeth, 186, 215, 216, 264, 266–67,
   292
Hodges, Sarah, 305
Holmes, Abiel, 25, 45, 65
Holmes family, 63
Holmes, John, 87
Holmes, Oliver Wendell, 26, 45, 87, 98, 216,
   264
 on MF, 46, 266
 MF's view of, 193–94
Home, Henry, Lord Kames, *Elements of
   Criticism,* 78
Homer, 301
Hooper, Ellen Sturgis, 98, 156, 191, 201,
   263, 273, 291, 300, 341
Hooper, Robert William, 201
Horace, 26, 47, 57
Howe, Julia Ward, 263, 291, 304, 306
Hugo, Victor, 260
 work: *The Hunchback of Notre Dame,*
   142–43
Hume, David, 31
 work: *History of Great Britain,* 19
Humphrey, Sarah, 230
Hunt, Louise, 230, 250
Hutchinson, Anne, 4

Irving, Washington, 118
 works: *Bracebridge Hall,* 62; *The Sketch
   Book,* 85

Jackson, Andrew, 11, 21, 78, 87, 153, 195,
   243, 272, 310
Jackson, Charles, 191
Jackson, Charles, Jr., 201
Jackson, Marianne, 191, 192, 263, 291
Jackson, Patrick Tracy, 191
Jacobi, Friedrich Heinrich, 173
Jacobs, Sarah, 219, 250
Jahn, Johann, 132
James, Henry, 184, 273, 275
 work: *The Bostonians,* 317
James, William, 273
Jameson, Anna, 144, 235, 239–40, 244
 work: *Winter Studies and Summer
   Rambles in Canada,* 240
Jean Paul (Johann Paul Friedrich Richter),
   116, 128, 171, 346
 works: *Flegeljahre,* 171; *Titan,* 171, 190
Jefferson, Thomas, 10, 86, 133–34
Jesus, 20, 48, 86, 112, 195, 284, 308, 312
Johnson, Samuel, 50, 248
Joinville, François, Duc de, 245–46
Jonson, Ben, 324
Jouffroy, Simon-Théodore, 262, 350

Kant, Immanuel, 105, 173, 180
Keats, Emma, 248, 253, 330
Keats, George, 248
Keats, John, 178, 248
Kelly, Noah, 165
Kilshaw, Ellen, 74
 life of, 41, 43, 53
 MF's friendship with, 41–43, 47, 49, 82,
   282, 368 n33
 on MF, 41, 42
Kimball, Miss, 46
Kirkland family, 63
Kirkland, John T., 45, 84
Kittredge, Charles B., 135
Klopstock, Friedrich Gottlob, 143
Klopstock, Meta, 143
Kneeland, Abner, 199
Knickerbocker Magazine, 175, 332
Körner, Theodor, 116, 240–41, 281
Kuhn, Caroline (cousin), 269

Lafayette, Marquis de, 87, 272
Lamennais, Félicité-Robert, 260
Landon, Latitia Elizabeth, 236
Lane Seminary, 146
Larned, Lucinda, 219, 243
Lawrence, Amos, 80
Lawrence family, 125
Leicester Academy, 14, 30, 45
Leonardo da Vinci, 258

Leonidas, 90
Leroux, Pierre, 261
Lesage, Alain-René, *Gil Blas,* 102
Lespinasse, Julie-Jeanne-Élénore de, 90
Lessing, Gotthold Ephraim, 128, 190
Liberator, 332
Ligne, Charles-Joseph de, 89
Little, Charles C., and James Brown
    publishers, 345
Littlehale, Ednah Dow. *See* Cheney, Ednah
    Dow Littlehale
Livy, 47
Locke, John, 29, 89, 95, 222
Longfellow, Henry Wadsworth, 190–91,
    331, 340–41
Loring, Anna, 263
Loring, Ellis Gray, 292
Loring family, 263, 264
Loring, Louisa Gilman, 292, 293
Lothrop, Samuel Kirkland, 45
Louis XVIII, King of France, 19
Louis-Philippe, King of the French, 245
Lowell, Anna Cabot Jackson, 297
Lowell family, 25, 63
Lowell, Francis Cabot, 191
Lowell, James Russell, 26, 27, 31, 264, 274
Lowell, Maria White, 274, 291
Lyceum, American, 7, 85, 294
Lyman, Eliza, 242–43
Lynch, Ann, 219
Lytton, Edward George Bulwer-, 90, 151,
    155, 156
  works: *The Last Days of Pompeii,* 149;
    Pelham, 149

McKean, Susanna Sarah, 78
McKeige, Elizabeth, 56
Mackintosh, Sir James, 175–76
magazines, antebellum, 175, 331–32
Mann, Horace, 7
Mann, Mary Peabody, 291
Manzoni, Alessandro, 150
Mariana (character), 80–82
marital ideal, antebellum, 18
Marsh, James, 147
Martineau, Harriet, 192, 239, 292
  as advisor to MF, 164, 172, 186
  American tour of, 153–54, 224
  on MF, 154, 187, 225
  MF's view of, 154–55, 225, 290
  MF's falling out with, 222–25
  works: *Illustrations of Political Economy,*
    153; "The Martyr Age of the United
    States," 225; *Society in America,*
    222–23

Mary Mother of Jesus, 284
Melville, Herman, 172
Memoirs of Margaret Fuller Ossoli
    (Emerson, Channing, and Clarke), x,
    187, 265, 268, 269, 297, 322, 392 n20
mesmerism, 208, 221, 228
Metcalf, Caroline, 230
Metcalf, Evelina, 230, 232, 235, 236
Metcalf, Matilda, 230
Metternich, Wenzel Lothar, Fürst von, 202
Michelangelo Buonarroti, 258, 259
Miller, Perry, 180–81, 182, 265
Milnes, Richard Monckton, 333
Milton, John, 51, 89, 127, 196, 235, 236,
    255
  work: *Paradise Lost,* 50, 75
Mirabeau, Comte de, 202
Miranda (character), 37
Missouri Compromise, 10, 11
Miss Prescott's Young Ladies' Seminary, 73,
    74
  character of, 71–72
  MF at, 75, 78, 80–83, 121–22
  See also Prescott, Susan
Molière, 51–52, 57
Monroe, James, 10, 11
Montaigne, Michel Eyquem de, 214
Monthly Magazine, 332
Moore, John, *Zeluco,* 48, 49, 50
Moore, Thomas, *Letters and Journals of
    Lord Byron, with Notices of His Life,*
    101
More, Hannah, 148–49
Morison, Samuel Eliot, 86
Morris, George P., 209
Morton, Marcus, 310
Mother Goose's Melodies, 31
Mozart, Wolfgang Amadeus, 258

Napoleon Bonaparte, 19, 85, 90, 133, 202
Nation, 283
Neal, John, 155, 220–21
Nietzsche, Friedrich, 302
Newcomb, Charles King, 248, 272, 319
Newcomb, Charlotte, 330
Newcomb, Rhoda Mardenbrough, 219, 220,
    228, 244
New England culture, antebellum, 85–86
New England Galaxy, 155
New-England Magazine, 175, 331
New Monthly Magazine, 136
Newton, Sir Isaac, *Philosophiae naturalis
    principia mathematica,* 76
New-Yorker, 348
New York Evening Post, 348

New York Mirror, 209
Nias, Georgianna, 210–11
Nicholas I, Tsar of Russia, 89
North American Review, 86, 118, 139, 144, 175, 177, 223, 331
Norton, Andrews, 86, 115, 124, 148, 167, 198, 307, 308–9, 349
    MF's view of, 313
Norton family, 63, 140
Norton, Jane, 167
Novalis (Friedrich von Hardenberg), 116, 282, 301, 311
    MF's view of, 128–29, 130, 131, 148, 173
    works: *Heinrich von Ofterdingen,* 129, 276; *Die Lehrlinge zu Sais,* 129
novel reading, in the early Republic, 50, 51

Olney, Martha Crane, 47
Otis family, 63
Ovid, 48, 301
Oxenford, John, 253–54

Pabodie, William J., 218–19, 264
Page, William, 276
Paley, William, *Natural Theology,* 62
Palfrey, John Gorham, 124, 175, 177, 223, 331
Park, John, 56, 57–58, 60, 61, 63
    See also Boston Lyceum for Young Ladies
Parker, Lydia Cabot, 292
Parker, Theodore, 292
    life and outlook of, 309, 311, 318, 342, 344
    on MF, 318–19, 334
    MF's relations with, 318–19
    MF's view of, 319, 341
Parkman, George, 95
Parks, Dana, 59
Parsons, Anna Q. T., 94
Partridge, Professor (character), 313, 320, 334
Payne, John Howard, *Clari; or, The Maid of Milan,* 79
Peabody, Elizabeth Palmer
    life and outlook of, 118, 129, 168, 195, 196, 197, 199, 204, 216, 224, 294, 300, 309, 317
    MF's relations with, 175, 187, 189, 263, 317–18, 292, 293, 318
    MF's view of, 317–18
    recollections of MF by, 60, 99, 177
    reports on MF's Conversations by, 297, 298, 301, 302, 303, 305
Peabody, Ephraim, 151
Peabody, Mary. *See* Mann, Mary Peabody

Peabody, Sophia. *See* Hawthorne, Sophia Peabody
Peck, Mrs. William D., 95
Peirce, Benjamin, 98
Penniman, Almira. *See* Barlow, Almira Penniman
Percival, James Gates, 210
Perkins, George, 87
Petrarch, 90, 190
Philip II, King of Spain, 35
Phillips, Ann Terry, 292, 293
Phillips, Jonathan, 193
Phillips, Wendell, 292
phrenology, 208, 221
Piccolomini, Max, 281
Plato, 128, 133, 180, 195, 253, 296, 311, 324
Plutarch, 301
    work: *Parallel Lives,* 47, 145
Poe, Edgar Allan, 219
Poliziano, Angelo (Politian), 90
Pompey, 133
Pope, Alexander, 229
Prescott, James, 71
Prescott, Mary Oliver, 71
Prescott, Susan, 71, 73, 80
    MF's attachment to, 75, 78, 80, 82
    MF's literary correspondence with, 87, 88, 89, 91, 92
    See also Miss Prescott's Young Ladies' Seminary
Prescott, William Hickling, 322
Priestley, Joseph, 9
Proclus, 301
Providence Daily Journal, 207, 221
Providence, R.I.
    character of, 207–8
    MF's cultural activities at, 213, 227–28, 248–49
    MF's feelings about being in, 214, 218, 237–38, 246, 249–50, 252
    MF's German literature classes at, 228–29
    MF's travels away from, 214, 218, 228, 237, 245–46, 246–48
    MF's view of, 207, 213, 248–49
    MF's visitors in, 221, 227, 228, 249, 253
    See also Coliseum Club; Greene Street School
psychoanalysis, 32, 108, 363–64 n8, 365–66 n13, 366 n21, 367 n28, 405 n49
Pulci, Luigi, 90
Puritanism, New England, 12, 13, 15–16, 19, 21, 23, 24, 25, 33, 193

Quincy, Edmund, 293
Quincy, Eliza Morton, 293, 300, 301

Quincy, Josiah, III, 31, 87, 293
Quincy, Josiah, IV, 31
Quincy, Josiah Phillips, 293
Quincy, Quatremère de, 259

Racine, Jean, 89
The Rambler, 50
Ramsay, David, *Life of Washington,* 51
Randall, Belinda, 99, 124, 264
Randall, Elizabeth, 46, 97–98, 99, 106, 109,
    124, 125–26
Randall, John, 46
Randolph, John, 55
Raphael, 258
Récamier, Jeanne-François, Mme. de, 281,
    282
Redman, Thomas, 46
reform, antebellum, 192–93, 208, 309–10
    See also abolitionism, antebellum;
    women, antebellum
republicanism, American, 9, 21
Republicans, 10, 11, 13, 16
Retz, Cardinal de, 89
Revue de deux mondes, 261
Richardson, Samuel, 90
    work: *Clarissa,* 104
Ripley, George, 73, 194
    career and outlook of, 115, 147, 182, 222,
        308–9, 310, 311, 318
    and *Dial,* 332, 334, 335, 341, 346, 347–48
    MF's friendship with, 183, 193, 263, 316–
        17
    MF's view of, 316–17
    work: *Specimens of Foreign Standard
        Literature,* 204, 250, 253, 308
Ripley, Samuel, 257
Ripley, Sarah Alden Bradford, 186, 216,
    252, 257, 292
    on MF, 269–70
    MF's view of, 247
Ripley, Sophia, 292, 332
    MF's friendship with, 193, 263, 316–17
    MF's view of, 316–17
Robespierre, Maximilien de, 9
Robinson, Charles, 125, 127, 132, 189
Roland, Marie-Jeanne Phlipon, Mme., 127
Romanticism, 85, 86, 105, 115
    See also Transcendentalism, American; II.
        Romanticism; II. Romantic
        literature; II. Transcendentalism,
        American
Ross, Mrs., *Hesitation; or, To Marry, or Not
    to Marry?,* 48–49
Ross, Sir John, *Narrative of a Second
    Voyage of Discovery,* 183

Rotch, Mary, 265
Round Hill School, 57
Rousseau, Jean-Jacques, 32, 105, 259, 261
    MF influenced by, 91, 103, 106, 338
    work: *Les Confessions,* 91–92
Roy, Rammohun, *The Precepts of Jesus,* 92
Rowson, Susanna, 155
Rush, Benjamin, 29
Russell family, 263
Russell, Harriet, 110, 111, 140, 156, 157
Russell, Sarah Shaw, 292

Saint-Simonians, 183, 261, 311
Sales, Francis, 190
Sallust, 57
Saltonstall family, 63
Sand, George, 326
    MF's view of, 260–62
    works: *Jacques,* 261; *Lettres d'un
        voyageur,* 261–62; *Les sept cordes de
        la lyre,* 261, 262, 325; *Mauprat,* 325;
        Spiridion, 261
Sappho, 281
Schelling, Friedrich Wilhelm Joseph, 304
Schiller, Friedrich, 116, 130, 150, 178, 190,
    302
    MF's view of, 128, 254, 255
    work: *Wallenstein,* 92
Schlegel, August Wilhelm, 128, 177, 178,
    248
Schlegel, Friedrich, 177, 178, 248
    work: *Lucinde,* 128
Schmidt, Henry, 257
Scott, Sir Walter, 86, 210
    MF's view of, 51, 55, 91, 107, 178
    works: *Guy Mannering,* 42; *The Pirate,* 19
Second Great Awakening. *See* evangelical
    Protestantism
Sedgwick, Catharine Maria, 118
Shakespeare, William, 51–52, 191, 195, 232,
    248, 250, 255
    works: *Hamlet,* 319, *Henry IV,* 343;
        Richard III, 220; *Romeo and Juliet,*
        51
Shaw, Anna, 263
Shaw, Anna Blake, 292
Shaw family, 263, 264
Shaw, Robert Gould, 292
Shaw, Sarah Sturgis, 292
Shelley, Percy Bysshe, 86–87
    MF's view of, 91, 100, 117, 127, 178–79
    MF influenced by, 119
    work: *The Defence of Poetry,* 336
Shepard, Thomas, 4
Sheridan, Richard Brinsley, *The Rivals,* 82

Smith, Adam, *Wealth of Nations,* 62
Smollett, Tobias George, 51, 52
Socrates, 195, 233, 281
Soley, John, 80
Soley, Mary. *See* DeWolfe, Mary Soley
Sophocles, 289
Sotheby, William, *Oberon,* 51
Southey, Robert, 179
The Spectator, 50, 51
Spinoza, Benedict de, 341
Staël, Anne-Louise-Germaine Necker, Mme.
    de, 89, 95, 235, 296, 319, 335
  MF's view of, 91, 172, 244, 281. 282
  works: *Considerations on the French
    Revolution,* 19; *Corinne,* 261; *De
    l'Allemagne,* 115, 177
Stanisbury, Mr., 55
Stanton, Elizabeth Cady, 306
Stearns, William, 45
Stearns, William G., 64
Storrow, Ann Gillam, 95
Story, Emelyn Eldridge, 264
Story family, 63
Story, Joseph, 84, 98
Story, William Wetmore, 274
Sturgis, Caroline, 298
  life and personality of, 191, 272–73, 300,
    320, 346
  MF as social and intellectual advisor of,
    207, 227, 245, 273–75, 291, 325–26
  MF's early friendship with, 225–27, 228,
    263
  MF's view of, 192, 341
  MF's quarrel with, 275–76, 277, 286, 287
Sturgis, Elizabeth Davis, 273
Sturgis, Ellen. *See* Hooper, Ellen Sturgis
Sturgis, William, 191, 225–27, 292
Sumner, Charles, 98
Swedenborgianism, 129
Swedenborg, Emanuel, 180

Tacitus, Cornelius, 47, 71
Tasso, Torquato, 57, 90, 91, 190
Taylor, Henry, *Philip Van Artevelde,* 149–50
Taylor, Thomas, 301
Temple School, 293, 300, 307
  character of, 195–97
  MF's teaching at, 196–97, 200, 204
  demise of, 200, 205, 237
  See also Alcott, Amos Bronson
Temple, Sir William, 89
Tennyson, Alfred, Lord, 333
Thackeray, William Makepeace, 102
Thompson, Cephas Giovanni, 239

Thoreau, Henry David, 170, 309
  works: "Sympathy," 345; "Aulus Persius
    Flaccus," 345, 346
Thorndike, Sarah Dana, 193
Ticknor, George, 84, 86, 91, 105, 276
Tieck, Ludwig, 116, 128, 190, 311
  work: *Geschichte des Herrn William
    Lovell,* 112
Tillinghast, Joseph L., 228
Tillinghast, Rebecca, 228
Tocqueville, Alexis de, 68
  work: *Democracy in America,* 222, 338
Todd, William C., 70
Tracy, Albert H., 88
Transcendental Club, 182, 189, 307, 309,
  332, 333
  MF's attendance at meetings of, 216,
    244–45, 315–16, 332, 335, 388–89
    n16
Transcendentalism, American
  movement of: ix, 276, 277, 348; activities,
    147–48, 182; controversy over, 222;
    origins, 180–82; radicalization of,
    307–11, 344–45, 400 n2, 400–401 n4,
    401–2 n6, n7; in West, 137, 147–48
  philosophy of, 136, 139, 180–81, 184, 196,
    221, 337
  See also Coliseum Club; Conversations;
    Dial; Greene Street School; Temple
    School; Transcendental Club;
    Unitarianism, American; II. Kantian
    philosophy, German post-; II.
    Transcendentalism, American;
    specific Transcendentalists
Tuckerman, Jane, 191, 228, 263, 291
Tupper, Martin, 209

Unitarianism, American
  in Boston-Cambridge, 25, 86–87, 103,
    115, 192, 193, 196, 222–23
  and child-rearing, 31, 68, 364 n9
  at Harvard College, 11–12
  in Massachusetts, 12, 16, 122, 125
  theology of, 112, 113
  See also Boston, Mass.; Cambridge, Mass.;
    Conversations; Fuller family; Fuller,
    Margarett Crane; Fuller, Timothy;
    Harvard College; Transcendentalism,
    American; II. Transcendentalism,
    American; II. Unitarianism,
    American
*United States Magazine and Democratic
  Review,* 332

Valpy, Richard, *Poetical Chronology of Ancient and English History,* 35
Van Buren, Martin, 195, 243, 310
Vasari, Giorgio, 258
Velleius Paterculus, Gaius, 145
Very, Jones, 309
  MF's view of, 319–20
  work: *Essays and Poems,* 320
Vico, Giambattista, 302
Vigny, Alfred de, 260
Virgil, 26, 31, 37, 45, 47, 48, 57, 135
Voltaire, 57, 90
Vose, Mary, 46, 55

Waagen, Gustav Friedrich, 258
Waldo, Daniel, 55
Walker, James, 200, 332
Wallenstein, Albrecht von, 281
War of 1812, 27
Ward, Anna Barker. *See* Barker, Anna Hazard
Ward, Julia. *See* Howe, Julia Ward
Ward, Mary, 191, 291
Ward, Samuel, 263
Ward, Samuel Gray, 259, 269, 320, 341, 345
  life and outlook of, 155, 276–77, 282–84
  on MF, 191, 264–65, 277
  MF influenced by, 257, 258, 276–77
  MF's attraction to, 246–47, 277
  MF's expression of love for, 277–79, 287
  MF's friendship with, 152–53, 263
  MF's reaction to courtship and marriage of, 283–89, 325
  MF's view of, 284–85, 339, 341
  See also Barker, Anna Hazard
Ward, Thomas Wren, 254, 276, 283
Ware, Elizabeth, 74
Ware family (elder), 63, 99
Ware, Henry, Jr., 124, 241, 269
Ware, Henry, Sr., 74, 241
Ware, Mary Lovell Pickard, 297
Ware, William, *Letters from Palmyra* (later entitled *Zenobia*), 241–42
Warren, Mercy Otis, *History of the Rise, Progress, and Termination of the American Revolution,* 51
Washington, George, 9
Watts, Isaac, 16
Wayland, Francis, 208, 227–28, 238
  works: *The Limitations of Human Responsibility,* 240; *The Elements of Moral Science,* 229, 233–34
Webster, Daniel, 11, 87, 193, 213

Webster family, 63
Webster, Grace Fletcher (Mrs. Daniel), 13
Webster, Harriet F. Hickling (Mrs. John White), 95
Webster, John White, 95
Weeks, Jordan and Company, 345, 348
Western Messenger, 147–48, 150, 182, 199, 224, 311, 342
  MF's view of, 151, 175, 240, 333, 336, 337, 404 n43
Weston, Nathan, 101
Whately, Richard, *Elements of Rhetoric,* 232
Whigs, 11, 86, 122, 208, 213, 310, 311
Whipple, Frances Harriet, 219
Whipple, John, 213, 219, 242, 243
White, Maria. *See* Lowell, Maria White
Whitman, Sarah Helen, 219, 220, 228, 272
Whitman, Walt, xi
Whittier, Elizabeth (cousin), 59
Whittier family, 58–59, 60, 61
Whittier, Martha Anne (cousin), 116
Whittier, Martha Fuller (aunt), 58, 60, 61, 65–66
Whittier, Simeon C. (uncle), 58, 59
Wieland, Christoph Martin, 51
Willard, Emma, 291
  Journal and Letters from France and Great Britain, 144
Williams, Abraham (great-grandfather), 4–5
Williams, Anna Buckminster (great-grandmother), 4–5
Williams, Roger, 208
Williams, Susan Ann Buckminster (cousin), 59, 60
Willis, Nathaniel Parker, 142, 155, 209
Winckelmann, Johann Joachim, 128, 301
Wollstonecraft, Mary, *A Vindication of the Rights of Woman,* 30
women, antebellum
  culture of, xi, 21, 68
  education of: in America, 29, 57, 71–72, 89, 290–91, 294; in Boston-Cambridge, 29–30
  friendships of, 100, 275, 281–82
  history of, ix, 358 n1
  vocational status of: as teachers, 118, 290; as writers, 118
Wordsworth, William, 177, 209, 274
  American opinion of, 177
  MF's view of, 91, 127–28, 177, 178, 179, 183
Wright, Frances, 294
Wright, John, 71
Wright, Susan Prescott. *See* Prescott, Susan